Dr. & Mrs. J. R. Beeke

W9-BNZ-173

12th EDITION

MISSION HANDBOOK:

NORTH AMERICAN PROTESTANT MINISTRIES OVERSEAS

12th EDITION

MISSION HANDBOOK:

NORTH AMERICAN PROTESTANT MINISTRIES OVERSEAS

1979

Prepared and edited by

MISSIONS ADVANCED RESEARCH AND COMMUNICATION CENTER

Samuel Wilson, Editor

MARC

919 West Huntington Drive, Monrovia, California 91016

A Ministry of World Vision International

This Twelfth Edition of the **Mission Handbook: North American Protestant Ministries Overseas** is the successor to a series originally started by the Missionary Research Library which was formerly part of the Division of Overseas Ministries of the National Council of the Churches of Christ. The Seventh, Eighth and Ninth Editions were sponsored by the Missionary Research Library with the actual compilation done by the Missions Advanced Research and Communication Center (MARC), a division of World Vision International.

The Twelfth Edition was produced in its entirety by MARC.

Library of Congress Number 76-55223

ISBN 0-912552-34-4

Printed in the United States of America

Foreword

The Twelfth Edition of the **Mission Handbook: North American Protestant Ministries Overseas** is the fifth edition to be issued by the Missions Advanced Research and Communication Center (MARC). During these 12 years there have been significant changes in the makeup and direction of the North American Protestant mission force. As you read the description of many of the agencies listed in this directory, you will see a growing emphasis on commmunity development and other dimensions of social involvement with the people to whom North Americans are attempting to minister. You will also notice a rising number of specialized agencies who are attempting to challenge North Americans to a greater involvement with the Two-Thirds World which is so different from North America.

The story of North American missions is still breathtaking. There are many American corporations whose individual gross income far exceeds the combined income of all North American overseas agencies. Many of them have a staff that far exceeds the size of the North American Protestant mission force. However, none can point to the "return on investment" that is demonstrated by the Spirit-filled demonstration of God's power by what must be considered a small handful of men and women.

And yet we sense that the situation is changing dramatically. As North Americans have become conscious that the United States and Canada is not the **real** world, and as North American Christians have been moved to meet the spiritual and social needs of that other world, large numbers of younger men and women are responding to the need.

In May of 1979, Dr. Samuel Wilson was appointed Director of MARC. One of his responsibilities was the editorship of the **Mission Handbook**. I commend both Dr. Wilson and the **Mission Handbook** to you.

Edward R. Dayton
Monrovia, California
October 1980

Table of Contents

Abbreviations

A	Approximate	EFMA	Evangelical Foreign Missions Association
Admin.	Administrative or Administrator	EMCM	Encyclopedia of Modern Christian Missions
Agncy	Agency		
Anthro.	Anthropology		
Apdo.	Apartado	Episc.	Episcopal
Apt.	Apartment	Evang.	Evangelical, Evangelism, Evangelistic
Apos.	Apostolic		
Assoc.	Associate or Association	Exec.	Executive
		Fdr.	Founder
Asst.	Assistant	Fed.	Federal
Ave.	Avenue	Fell.	Fellowship
Bapt.	Baptist	Fld.	Field
Bd.	Board	For.	Foreign
Bib.	Bible	FOM	Fellowship of Missions
Blvd.	Boulevard	Found.	Foundation
Brit.	British	Gen.	General
CCC-CWC	Canadian Council of Churches, Commission Exec. on World Concern	Govt.	Government
		Hist.	History
		IFMA	Interdenominational Foreign Mission Association
Ch(s)	Church(es)		
Chm.	Chairman		
Chr.(s)	Christian	Ind.	Independent
Cncl.	Council	Inc.	Incorporated
Comm.	Committee, Commission	Intl.	International
Conf.	Conference	Is.	Island, Islands
Coord.	Coordinator	LCWE	Lausanne Committee for World Evangelization
C.P.	Caixa Postal		
Ctr.	Center		
Dem.	Democratic	MARC	Missions Advanced Research and Communications Center
Dept.	Department		
Dir.	Director		
Div.	Division	Mag.	Magazine
DOM-NCCCUSA	Division of Overseas Ministries, National Council of Christ Churches of Christ in the U.S.A.	Mgr.	Manager
		Min.	Ministries or Minister
		Miss.	Missiology
		Mo.	Monthly
		Msn.	Mission
Dr.	Doctor	Msns.	Missions
E	Estimate	Msny.	Missionary
E.	East	Msnys.	Missionaries
Ed.	Education	Mtg.	Meeting

N.	North		Rte.	Route
NA	Not Available		R.R.	Rural Route
N.A.	North American		S.	South
NAPMOD	North American		Sec.	Secretary
	Protestant Ministries		Sem.	Seminary
	Overseas Directory		Soc.	Society
Natl.	National		Social.	Socialist
NCCCUSA	National Council of		Supt.	Superintendent
	Churches of Christ		S.T.	Short Term
	in the U.S.A.		Ste.	Suite
No.	Number		Svc.	Service
NR	Not Reported		TAM-	The Associated Missions
O'seas	Overseas		ICCC	International Council
P.	People's			of Christian Churches
Phil.	Philosophy		T	Total
Pl.	Place		TEE	Theological Education
Port.	Portuguese			by Extension
P.O.	Post Office		Terr.	Territory
Prac.	Practical or		Theol.	Theology or Theological
	Practice(s)		Tr.	Trust
Pres.	President		Treas.	Treasurer
Presb.	Presbyterian		U.S.	United States
Princ.	Principles		U.S.A.	of America
Prof.	Professor		V.	Vice
Prog.	Program		W.	West
Qtr.	Quarterly		WCC	World Council of
Rd.	Road			Churches
Rel.	Religious or		Wk.	Weekly
	Religions		Wld.	World

STATE ABBREVIATIONS

Alaska	AK		New Jersey	NJ
Alabama	AL		New Mexico	NM
Arizona	AZ		New York	NY
Arkansas	AR		North Carolina	NC
California	CA		North Dakota	ND
Canal Zone	CZ		Ohio	OH
Colorado	CO		Oklahoma	OK
Connecticut	CT		Oregon	OR
Delaware	DE		Pennsylvania	PA
District of Columbia	DC		Puerto Rico	PR
Florida	FL		Rhode Island	RI
Georgia	GA		South Carolina	SC
Hawaii	HI		South Dakota	SD
Idaho	ID		Tennessee	TN
Illinois	IL		Texas	TX
Indiana	IN		Utah	UT
Iowa	IA		Vermont	VT
Kansas	KS		Virginia	VA
Kentucky	KY		Virgin Islands	VI
Louisiana	LA		Washington	WA
Maine	ME		West Virginia	WV
Maryland	MD		Wisconsin	WI
Massachusetts	MA		Wyoming	WY
Michigan	MI			
Minnesota	MN		**CANADA**	
Mississippi	MS			
Missouri	MO		Alberta	AT
Montana	MT		British Columbia	BC
Nebraska	NE		Manitoba	MN
Nevada	NV		New Brunswick	NB
New Hampshire	NH		Newfoundland	NF

Northwest Territory	NW	Yukon	YK
Nova Scotia	NS		
Ontario	ON	**PACIFIC ISLANDS**	
Prince Edward Is	PE		
Province of Quebec	PQ	Guam	GU
Saskatchewan	SK		

ABBREVIATIONS UTILIZED IN COUNTRIES OF SERVICE LISTING

British Virgin Is.	British Virgin Islands
C. America - general	Central America - general
Central African Rep.	Central African Republic
China, People's Rep.	People's Republic of China
Germany, Dem. Rep.	German Democratic Republic
Germany, Fed. Rep.	Federal Republic of Germany
Korea, Dem. P. Rep.	Democratic People's Republic of Korea
Korea, Rep. of	Republic of Korea
Lao, Peoples Dem. R.	Democratic People's Republic of Lao
Latin America - gen.	Latin America - general
Pacific Trust Terr.	Pacific Trust Territory
U.S. Virgin Is.	United States Virgin Islands
U.S.S.R.	Union of Soviet Socialist Republics
Vietnam, Soc. Rep.	Socialist Republic of Vietnam

Introduction

This present volume, **Mission Handbook: North American Protestant Ministries Overseas,** is the Twelfth Edition in a series published since 1953. The purpose of this book is to provide in a single volume a convenient reference to descriptive and statistical data on all North American Protestant overseas ministries or related agencies with overseas operations, plus analytical and interpretive material that will help give a better understanding of the dynamics of mission resources based in North America.

The series began in 1953 as a mimeographed report for interested mission executives; this book has become a standard reference work for lay and professional churchmen of all denominations and traditions. Improvements in format, expansion of content, and the use (since 1968) of electronic data processing equipment for handling of the information are indicative of the increasing utility of this book throughout the Church.

The intention of this book is to include any North American individual or agency which is attempting within the context of Protestantism to minister outside of the 50 United States and Canada. This is a complicated task because what is commonly known as "missions" is a very complex system. Where does one stop? Who should **not** be included? For example, most of the giving for the work of the Protestant ministries overseas comes through local churches. Should they not be included? What about associated agencies with which Protestant agencies may be working overseas? What do we say of the multitude of services that have come into being to support the overseas efforts, most of whose work centers within the United States and Canada?

We have rather arbitrarily excluded local churches because this kind of information is very well covered in such publications as **The Yearbook of American and Canadian Churches** (see Bibliography). In addition to many agencies who send personnel overseas, we have also included many service and support agencies whose work is primarily in North America. We hope that their inclusion will give the reader or researcher a more complete overview.

Many efforts are surfacing where work here in the States has meaning for foreign mission, yet "significant resources in personnel or funds" are not spent overseas. Successful cross-cultural mission to foreign students studying in the U.S. will have impact on the planting of the Church worldwide, yet not all could be listed per se in this directory.

In order to round out the picture, we have included some information on the work of Roman Catholic agencies from North America as well as some brief statistics on other non-Protestant groups such as the Latter-Day Saints and the Jehovah's Witnesses, all of which have major overseas work. Certain other sects are pervasive, but even impressionistic data are difficult to come by and of doubtful worth.

Why a directory of **North American** ministries? Why not a directory of **all** agencies operating between the six continents? Again, the answer is not simple. But as will be seen, North America continues to be the major missions force in the world. Its very complexity demands a directory or guidebook which will permit those involved in it to understand it better. The exclusion of non-North American countries is a matter of expediency and should be only viewed as such. MARC is supporting research in the Two-Thirds World which will be published to complement the North American Directory.

The information about agencies and fields of service in the directory sections was obtained from questionnaires which were mailed in late 1979 to all known North American Protestant overseas agencies. The questionnaire used to gather this information is included in the **Appendices** and consists of four parts, covering the agency description, missionary staff, fields of service and people groups, and financial information.

An attempt was made to include every appropriate agency with overseas involvement. Names and addresses were obtained not only from previous directories, but from MARC files (which are continuously updated) and from various publications of other agencies.

About 900 questionnaires were mailed to potential respondents. If no reply was received after three requests to a particular organization, an analysis was made from available data, usually agency publications. In many cases, follow-up telephone calls were made in an effort to obtain information, and a final mailgram was sent.

If, at the time of publication, not all of the information on an agency was available, "NR" (Not Reported) has been printed in the place where the information would normally appear. Where "NR" has been indicated for financial information, this should be understood as meaning that the information was not reported at the time of printing, not necessarily that the agency was unwilling or unable to provide the data. Some organizations had not completed their 1979 financial audits at the time the questionnaires were returned and either were unable to supply current information or gave the latest available figures. In a few cases where agencies specifically stated that the information was not available, "NA" is reported. In most cases, financial information can be obtained on request from the organization.

In order to expedite the compilation of totals, in some cases where the financial data from the agency was not available, it was estimated by MARC. In such cases a footnote appears below the description. The reader should note that this is the best estimate and could easily be off by as much as 100 percent. In some few cases, the number is the agency's estimate, and an appropriate note is given.

In a few instances, agencies are listed which are actually subordinate to a larger mission agency. These subsidiary agencies are included when they appear to provide a distinct ministry or general service which is available **to other organizations** as well as to the parent body. The inclusion of MARC (a division of World Vision International) is a good example.

Where an agency has changed its name because of mergers, where it has gone out of existence, or where it is sometimes known by another name or acronym, a cross-reference has been added in the directory section to help the reader identify the agency.

The material in this **Handbook** represents, within the stated limitations, the replies as given by the missionary organizations themselves to the questionnaires sent to them. Questionnaires designed to collect mission statistics pass through many offices and therefore through many skilled and unskilled hands. The consequence is that they are subject to wide degrees of reliability. There are inevitable problems of interpretation, both on the part of the agencies in replying to the questionnaire and on the part of MARC in using those replies.

MARC has attempted to alleviate this by keeping questionnaire changes from edition to edition to a minimum. Unfortunately, even a minor change in wording lends itself to a whole set of new interpretations. The upshot is that conclusions and interpretations must be viewed as the "state of the art" and be in the form of orders of magnitude. One such instance is the error made by a number of agencies in reporting data on fields of service. These sometimes included a count of national personnel. We regret that as a consequence, counts and distribution of overseas North Americans are affected. Therefore, it should be borne in mind that this study is a report of replies and cannot in the nature of things be considered a reporting of precise comparisons, especially with regard to financial information. The work of each agency is briefly summarized, based upon its reply. If, in the interests of brevity, this summary fails to properly describe the agency or its services, then the fault must lie with us, and we apologize for such inaccuracies.

Effort has been made to avoid duplication of statistics where an agency channels its funds and/or personnel through another organization, but we may not have been aware of all such instances.

Sending Missionaries Versus Reaching People

The present edition of the **Mission Handbook** follows the tradition of its predecessors in giving information about the number of overseas staff in the countries in which they are working. However, where some editions of previous directories have put emphasis on the number of institutions and the type of work being carried out in each country, the Twelfth Edition makes a first attempt at relating mission agencies to people groups, and specifically unreached people groups. This small change in emphasis marks a major shift in missiological thinking which hopefully will be reflected in future editions.

The Ninth Edition, published in 1970, indicated that the editors subscribe to the "six continent" view of missions. In other words, we recognize that every continent contains people who are potential subjects of evangelization by Christians living on other continents. Mission is multidirectional. The United States and Canada also need evangelization. The United States and Canada have much to learn from churches on other continents and in other countries. The six continent view of missions was an important step in North American missiological thinking. It signaled the end to an era of mission activity that was moved forward by the engine of colonialism. It recognized that Christ's Church indeed

3

had become universal in the sense that there were Christians to be found in most of the countries of the world.

This understanding was further recognized by the change of the name in 1968 from **A Directory of Foreign Mission Agencies** to **North American Protestant Ministries Overseas**.

However, during the 1970s the desire of the Western Church to recognize the existence of national churches throughout the world was tempered by a growing understanding of the immensity of the uncompleted task of world evangelization. While it was true that the majority of the countries and the majority of the nation-states of the world had an established church within their borders, the assumption that this national church had the desire and the capability to complete the evangelization of the peoples within its borders came more and more in question. It became evident that there existed groups of people within major countries of the world who were so different in both their language and culture that it would require cross-cultural evangelists (missionaries) to reach them with the gospel. Members of the national church within that country might not require a passport to reach them physically, but they would need the same skill, experience and spiritual determination as those who came from "overseas."

Missionary researchers estimate that over half the world's population, over two billion people, are to be found in such culturally isolated groups. In other words, over half of the world's population is only going to hear the good news of salvation in Christ from cross-cultural missionaries, be they from Western or non-Western countries or from within their own country.

Missionary thinkers of the early 20th century were right in assuming that once a church had been established within a group, the responsibility for evangelizing the balance of that group should rest with that church. By its very nature the Church is missionary. One of the major marks of the **Christian** Church is its desire to share its faith with others. But these missiologists did not go far enough in their thinking: they failed to recognize the cultural barriers which existed within these developing nations. Unlike most Western nations, which have a uniformity of language and an immense communication and transportation system that creates a degree of cultural uniformity, these countries remained with their hundreds and thousands of diverse cultural groups. (It has only been in recent years that North Americans have begun to realize that although the majority of their citizens may share a reasonably common culture, there are indeed hundreds of such people groups within the United States and Canada.)

The missiological theory about the expansion of the Church was correct, but the geographical definition of the object of mission was wrong. We now understand that a much more useful way of thinking about the world is to think of it in terms of people groups. A people group has been defined by the Lausanne Committee for World Evangelization (LCWE): "A people is a significantly large sociological grouping of individuals who perceive themselves to have a common affinity for one another. This common affinity can be based on language, religion, ethnicity, residence, occupation, class or caste, situation, or combination of these."[1] LCWE has followed the thinking of earlier missiologists by also assuming that when a church within a particular group reaches a certain size, it has the capability of completing evangelization within itself. In terms of evangelization by the other churches outside of it, it has been "reached."

Following sociological theory, LCWE defined a **reached** group (not evangelized, but no longer dependent on cross-cultural workers) as one that was more than 20 percent Christian.[2] An "unreached" group was, then, one that was "less than 20 percent practicing Christian." In terms of overall numbers about two billion people of the world who are non-Christians have no Christians among them. Such groups have been described as "hidden peoples." Another billion non-Christians could be described as "initially," "partially" or "possibly" reached, but theoretically could still need assistance from churches outside their culture group.

Further missiological research indicates that probably no more than 10 percent of all missionaries from any country are attempting to reach the two billion people that are within these hidden groups. The other 90 percent of those who have left their own culture to serve Christ in another culture are either involved in nurturing existing churches or serving those churches. Such men and women will continue to be needed. The present edition of the **Mission Handbook** describes hundreds of agencies whose primary task is nurture and service. However, in addition to sending missionaries to nurture and to serve, there is a vast need to send more missionaries to **reach people**. It is for this reason that the current edition of the **Mission Handbook** attempts to identify **the number** of unreached people groups that a given agency is endeavoring to reach in a particular country. It is anticipated that future editions will identify specific people groups to which efforts of evangelization are being directed.

Meanwhile a parallel effort is being carried out by MARC in cooperation with the Lausanne Committee for World Evangelization in identifying and listing unreached people groups in an **Unreached Peoples** directory. This annual directory, which is published by the David C. Cook Company, first appeared in 1979. **Unreached Peoples '79** described over 600 unreached people groups. **Unreached Peoples '80** focused particularly on Muslim unreached peoples groups. Over 1,200 were listed. **Unreached Peoples '81** emphasizes people groups in Asia. Nearly 3,000 groups are listed. Each of these directories contains expanded descriptions of 70 to 90 people groups, and each directory has a cumulative index which permits the researcher to refer to previous editions for expanded descriptions.

Information for the **Unreached Peoples** directory is compiled in a computerized Unreached Peoples File which is maintained at MARC. For further information you are encouraged to write to us. A tearout postcard is bound at the back of this volume to facilitate reporting of people groups. Complete questionnaires are available from MARC.

How the Data Is Arranged and Why

Basic information that was gathered was information about **agencies**. The major exceptions are the Christian Churches/Churches of Christ and the Brethren Assemblies, both of whom send missionaries directly from local churches. Here it was necessary to construct a **fictitious agency** in order to handle the information. The first arrangement of the data then was **alphabetically by name of the agency**.

Analysis by ecclesiastical tradition or by specific functions, such as radio broadcasting, literature work and medical assistance, is valuable and of interest. Therefore, a **series of indices** was arranged to do this.

A major section lists **all the countries of the world alphabetically** and indicates the **North American** Protestant agencies and
the number of their personnel working within them. This country
listing, while valuable, can be very misleading because it does
not give an indication of many other non-North American agencies
that may be working in the same country.

Most of the overseas personnel listed as belonging to agencies
within the directory receive some kind of training prior to their
overseas experience. The primary source for such training is the
Christian colleges and seminaries within the United States. For
maximum utility, data on schools and professors of mission should
be updated annually. These sections have been dropped from this
edition in the hope of seeing an annual volume published separately.

Cautions

Statistics relating to missionary endeavors suffer from the same
problems that pertain to statistics in general and religious statistics in particular: namely, they may be unavailable, not comparable, undefined or incomplete. When using any of the data in
this **Handbook,** this caution should be kept in mind, and a careful
study made to determine the completeness and applicability of the
specific data which is being used. This is particularly true when
making comparisons over a period of time, since completeness and
definitions of the data may vary from one survey to another.

We cannot overemphasize this point. All of the information within
this directory needs to be placed in its proper context. It is
dangerous to draw conclusions about a particular agency or a particular country without gathering additional information that is
beyond the scope of this **Handbook.**

The Authors

David M. Stowe, who gives us his assessment of the mission scene,
is Executive Vice President of the United Church Board for World
Ministries. Dr. Stowe brings a seasoned perspective to commentary
on the trends as an active author, past professor and field missionary.

John E. Kyle, Missions Director of Inter-Varsity Christian Fellowship, writes on recruiting informed by his present responsibilities which include directing the now biennial Urbana Missions
Conference, and his experience as Coordinator of International Af-
fairs for the Wycliffe Bible Translators and Coordinator of Mission to the World of the Presbyterian Church in America.

Credits

This **Handbook** is the result of the efforts of many individuals and
organizations. Special thanks go first to those persons in each
agency who took their time to complete the questionnaires which
made this survey possible. The executive officers of the various
associations of mission agencies have been most helpful in providing both information and counsel. MARC staff people who have
contributed to the production of this book include Joan Collins,
Steve Crosby, Kim Finn, Vicki Hubbard, Gloria Luna and John
Pentecost. No one knows as they do the arduous details and the
endless hassles necessary to the production of such a resource.
Special thanks are in order for the entire Word Processing staff.

Corrections

Readers having more correct information on any portion of this
book are encouraged to make this information available for future
editions. Postcards for this purpose are bound in the back of the
present volume. Comments and corrections should be addressed to
MARC, 919 West Huntington Drive, Monrovia, California 91016.

Footnotes

1.   See **That Everyone May Hear** by Edward R. Dayton (Monrovia:
     MARC), 1979. For an extended discussion of a people approach
     to cross-cultural evangelism, see Edward R. Dayton and
     David A. Fraser, **Planning Strategies For World Evangeliza-
     tion** (Grand Rapids: Eerdmans), 1980.

2.   Ibid.

Mission in the '80s

An Assessment of the Future
by David M. Stowe

In 1968 the first comprehensive **Directory of North American Protestant Ministries Overseas** made possible an analysis of trends in mission which I tried to analyze and sum up in an article, "Changing Patterns of Missionary Service in Today's World" (published in the **Occasional Bulletin** of the Missionary Research Library, Volume XX, No. 1, January 1969; reprinted in **Practical Anthropology**, Volume 17, No. 3, May-June 1970). The statistical directory of the Roman Catholic Mission Secretariat, **U.S. Catholics Overseas 1968**, just off the press, furnished comparable data on what was to become in the 1970s an increasingly collaborative, or at least cooperative, mission enterprise. Now at the beginning of the 1980s what do we see happening to the trends discerned for the decade just past? And where are we heading?

In 1968 the data suggested that:

1. "The traditional missionary-sending system is stronger than ever," and

2. "The foreign missionary force is at an all-time high and still growing."

That is still true in 1980, but subject to the proviso of a third 1968 generalization:

"The center of gravity of Protestant missionary-sending is shifting constantly away from the 'ecumenical' agencies toward conservative and fundamentalist ones."

In 1960 the latter took the lead over National Council of Churches-related mission boards, and that trend has now persisted for 20 years.

Moreover, in 1968 it seemed "just possible that we stand at an extraordinary juncture in time where data just off the press . . . are already far out of date." I surmised that the statistical curves might soon "show a significant, perhaps a sudden, turn downward." That was indeed the experience of the 1970s for the Council-related boards. Personnel of many of them declined, and income stringencies, coupled with inflation, significantly reduced capacity to fund denominational and cooperative mission programs.

As the '80s begin, however, there are signs of a recovery suffi-
cient to maintain strength and perhaps surpass inflation. For the
intricate network of mission collaborations which account for so
much of the conciliar effort, European funds, particularly from
tax-supported churches in Germany, have made up the losses from
North America, just as more than a generation earlier the North
Americans had taken up the slack left by the declining relative
strength of British and German missions.

A major problem in 1968 was that of missionary "image." In the
liberal churches there was wide questioning of religious proselyt-
ism as a significant, or even valid, enterprise. Those questions
continued through the '70s, but there came also a renewed interest
in theology and religious life, coupled with an interest in other
world religions and a sense that we live in a worldwide spiritual
community of seekers. Evangelism in a "holistic" form, including
deeds of mercy and social justice as well as words of faith, is
"in."

Two other 1968 problems, the role of foreign missionaries and
their relationships with an indigenous church and its ecumenical
involvements, got dramatic visibility and became positively abra-
sive in the "missionary moratorium" debates of the 1970s.   Today
those fierce arguments have simmered down. They were really about
colonialism, and colonialism has no defenders today (even though
some practitioners may remain). It is agreed that primary responsibility for mission in each place rests with the local or nearby
Christian communities, but that missionary partnership in persons
and funds can be immensely helpful if local partners set the terms
of reference. Secular cries about an economic "neocolonialism" of
the former imperial countries are to some extent paralleled by
concern about domination of mission by Western funding power. Yet
few there are to throw out the baby of mission aid with the bath-
water of missionary relationships. A "Self-Reliance Fund" of the
Philippines United Church which has relied heavily on endowments
from missionary agencies illustrates the kind of **modus vivendi**
that missionary partners will find even when uneasy about economic
disparities.

The 1968 article reflected a persistent hope that nonprofessional
missionaries, laymen and -women pursuing their secular vocations
overseas with a Christian intention, would play an increasing
role. But the diaspora of Western Christians in business, education and other enterprises abroad has declined as secular enterprises, like churches, have become increasingly indigenized. And
the missionary intentionality of lay persons from the conciliar
churches has proved very hard to focus and implement.

At one point, however, the anonymous lay missionary may play a
critical role in the 1980s, due to a reopened missionary opportunity totally unexpected in 1968. The revolution in China following the death of Mao and the dethronement of his left-wing fol-
lowers has created a variety of opportunities for mission lay persons with competencies desired by the Chinese. They must be alert
to the constraints and sensitivities of an officially atheistic
society and willing to work quietly and patiently to express
Christian witness through the teaching of English, assisting educational excellence and exchange, or in various business enterprises. The study and interpretation of China, and the fostering
of friendship and relationships through travel to and from China,
also have important missionary dimensions.

What else lies ahead? The 1980s and 1990s will certainly turn out
to be quite different from our expectations. Long-range planning

of mission priorities and programs will become less inviting--and
less popular than in past or present grand strategizing for the
Christian conquest of the world. A missionary style of respon-
siveness, flexibility and openness will prove most effective,
testing fresh adventures and experiments in new modes and areas of
work. Effective mission will usually take the form of response to
opportunity--often spelled N-E-E-D--especially as identified by
local Christians. This venturing and responsive style will place
heavy emphasis on relationships, widening and stimulating partnerships. Heavy funding and staffing focused on traditional denominational programs will diminish for several reasons: financial
and personnel capability will decline, overseas churches will be
uneasy with the dominance implicit in large unilateral subsidy,
and mission agencies will wish to experience a wider range of
partnerships with Christians of many cultures and traditions.
More resources will go into "missions in reverse," the enabling of
missionary personnel and even programs of African, Latin American,
and Asian churches for service in Europe and North America.

There will be increasing emphasis on what might be called "partnership in depth," which means getting below the organizational
and institutional level, right down to an active involvement with
the people themselves. For example, health care was formerly
thought of as an affair of professionals who cured the sick or
gave inoculations to defend against illness. Ordinary people were
seen as consumers of what the professionals had to offer. But ordinary people will increasingly be seen, not as consumers of
health care but as primary agents of health. They must help themselves to health and take responsibility for the general level of
sanitation and hygiene, for basic nutrition and essential inocu-
lations--all the things that are most important. The specialists,
doctors, nurses, clinics and hospitals then become auxiliary rather than primary. Their role is to enable and support the people
and their own health workers, chosen out of the community and supported by the community, in creating an environment of health in
the total community.

In the same way, mission in theological education is moving toward
a deeper and wider kind of partnership. We have discerned that
the Church is seldom deficient in natural leadership resources.
Elders and deacons, women and youth, ordinary believers often
carry full responsibility for their congregations. These local
leaders will increasingly be encouraged and enabled to pursue theological studies on a part-time basis in their own localities and
at their own academic levels--sometimes quite low, sometimes high.
The seminary will come to the student, on his or her terms.
Leadership formation and selection will be fostered at the local
level. Theological reflection will be carried on right within the
ongoing life of congregations, which become the primary focus of
theological education.

This kind of shift, from mission partnerships which emphasize the
specialized and professional or technical competence of the foreign missionary to a much more self-reliant and participatory
style, will characterize nearly all fields of work. In agricultural missions, for example, indigenous peasant organizations and
cooperatives will utilize missionary resources to foster their own
self-determined aims, which will include better farming practices
but also changes in the infrastructure and context of rural
life--land holding, credit, marketing and access to other resources. Development projects of many kinds will take the same
route.

This trend toward full participation and self-determination reflects what might well be called a pervasive "radicalization" of

11

the context for mission in the 1980s. All over the world peoples formerly caught in traditional patterns of inequality, dependence and exploitation have caught a vision of their human right to a significant say about the conditions of their life and a fair share of the resources which make life more secure and comfortable. As the decade begins, successful revolutions have established new populist regimes in Zimbabwe and Nicaragua. They forecast a domino effect of such changes across Latin America and elsewhere in Africa. The vast unsettlement accompanying the ouster of the Shah of Iran and continuing unrest throughout the Middle East is mirrored in many Asian societies having repressive and exploitative regimes. Missionary effort will have to deal constantly with pre-revolutionary and revolutionary situations. This will have many implications, not all of them very clear, for the target groups with whom mission works, for the kinds of programs emphasized, for emphases in the gospel preached. A key theme in the world missions assembly of the World Council of Churches in Melbourne, 1980, picked up Jesus' statement of his own commission: "The Lord has anointed me to preach good news to the poor"; such preaching, in word and action, will be a prerequisite for relevance.

Churches which historically have had a large component of social action in their mission programs will continue to express this concern, partly in traditional ways such as education at all levels, but particularly in adult basic education and in the community-based medical and agricultural programs described above. But new forms and magnitudes of social impact, especially on behalf of the poor and oppressed, will be sought. During the 1970s, churches mounted a significant effort to minimize the social injury of international business and to maximize its benefits to Third World communities, with some missionary organizations taking the lead. Endowments accumulated by historic boards give an entree to shareholder meetings and executive suites which is being utilized effectively.

Missionaries will feel more and more responsibility to inform their home churches about problems of human rights, economic justice or social abuse in host societies, fostering the mobilization of North American and world opinion. That this may make the missionary or the traveling missionary administrator a dubious guest in the eyes of host governments is part of the price to be paid for missionary involvement in the 1980s. Just as mission agencies fought--and fight--to avoid involvement or identification with the CIA or other power systems of their own nations, so they will have to avoid becoming integrated into unjust systems in their host countries or complacent about them. The missionary has always lived in a very uneasy borderland between differing cultures and national interests, and the uneasiness may well increase.

Power struggles for global justice may involve mission organizations at the intergovernmental level. Some have helped establish, for example, a forum where Third World governments can develop strategies for securing fair access to the developing technology of satellite communication. Without such an effort the nations with highly developed communications technology would monopolize frequencies and facilities which developing nations desperately need for education and communication, with their own people and among themselves. Rights of access for noncommerical and nonmilitary programming are at issue, with very real consequences for moral and religious teaching. With the growing importance of international allocation of other resources as well as electronic frequencies, the international missionary concern and vision of Christians will be increasingly stretched.

12

This does not mean that the agenda of mission, even for more liberal Protestant and Roman Catholic groups, will simply swing from spiritual to socio-political concern. While "evangelical" missions are being drawn into wider social concern, the ecumenical agencies and orders are participating in a rediscovery of the centrality of faith and the importance of personal religious experience which is occurring in North American churches. The evangelistic intention in a broad range of social ministries may well increase, as well as a fresh focus on equipping and empowering indigenous church leadership and on church growth. In other words, a more balanced mix of religious and social relevance will probably occur along the whole spectrum of missions.

Essential to a renewed evangelistic intention will be a sensitivity to the actual religious pluralism of our world and to the increasing self-consciousness and self-confidence, even aggressiveness, which characterizes Islam, Buddhism and perhaps other faiths. Even less than before will missionaries be able to imagine that they are going out into a spiritual vacuum of either no religion or transparently "false religion." Except in remaining pockets of animism among undeveloped and isolated tribal peoples, most of the host peoples for North American missions will either be Christians already, perhaps of a persuasion other than the mission, or adherents of another faith confident of their own spiritual traditions. Among the Christians, mission should offer the help needed for revival, renewal, strengthening and stimulation. Among the non-Christians, the stance will have to be respectful, the style dialogical, the quest for a truth to be commonly perceived genuine.

That quest for ways of stating Christian faith and asserting the lordship of Christ which will be persuasive for those of other faiths--including the ideologies of non-faith or of secular success--will involve theological energy. In just what way does one believe in Father, Son and Holy Spirit in a Muslim context or a Buddhist or Hindu one? How does one confess and practice that Jesus Christ is Lord in a setting where Koran, Bodhisattva, Muhammad or Krishna is the primal religious symbol? What is the **meaning** of Christian belief and confession in such settings? Such questions suggest that the missionary enterprise is positioned precisely at the most important theological focus of the 1980s and beyond. The explication, communication and practical expression of Christian faith will take place both where the world's poor, mostly in what are still "mission fields," and the world's living faiths are encountered by Christians seeking to fulfill the Great Commission. Which means that in and with a heightening social concern and relevance, missions will have to express an equally heightened and sharpened theological and spiritual concern.

The encounter and interaction of the faith communities will be cooperative as well as, in the best and most constructive sense, competitive. That combination is difficult to achieve, but real caring for people and real engagement in dialogue both demand it. Experience in the 1970s with the World Conference on Religion and Peace suggests ways in which those committed to missionary outreach--and not only Christians but those of other faiths as well--may join forces in behalf of overriding human needs for peace or succor of war-torn populations. Part of that process involves clarifying the deepest authentic commitments and values of the various religious traditions, sharpening these in their similarities (and their differences) and proceeding to do together all that can be done without threatening the essential convictions of the several traditions. In such a process there is of course the danger of watering down and disguising essential convictions, a simulation of sharing and commonness which could be debilitating and ultimately self-defeating. But all missionary work is risky. The interreligious frontier is an intellectual and spiritual hardship post of another sort than that of the pioneers who faced cannibals. But hardship is no reason for refusing the assignment.

Finally, what about the role of the missionary herself or himself? For a long time the conciliar agencies have stressed national leadership development, indigenizing of mission and devolution of power, all of which tended to reduce the importance of the foreign missionary. A large proportion of the available funds were invested in programs which did not necessarily involve many foreign personnel--social services, relief and development, literature, literacy, translation, communication, many kinds of interchurch aid. By comparison, more conservative missions tended to focus on the sending of missionaries, defining mission largely in terms of the work of such foreign personnel. But evangelical groups are increasingly involved in service programming so that North American agencies are more and more alike in the balance between persons and program.

Conciliar missions have a substantial problem in finding well-qualified persons with a genuine sense of missionary calling. North Americans now have a style of frequent shifts in career direction and experience. There are plenty of persons who, if assured of a reasonably easy reentry into their home cultures and career ladders, are quite ready for a limited commitment overseas. Many can make a useful contribution in a year, or two or three. But they cannot in that timetable learn an exotic language and culture and develop the connections and the skills to do many of the most fundamental tasks of mission.

Some renewal of the concept of the "career missionary" is needed to balance the trend toward a wide variety of short-term assignments. With contemporary lifestyles and expectations, envisagement of such long-term, even lifetime, commitments is not easy. To some extent natural selection may operate among missionaries so as to deposit less able persons, more easily content with a comfortable niche of mediocrity, in permanent assignments overseas, while those more imaginative, able, and ambitious for wider spheres of service may tend to return to the "mainstream" of their home societies. Nevertheless, the need continues for long-term investment by at least a limited number of the ablest Christians of the 1980s in in-depth relationships overseas. Mission agencies will be conceiving and testing a variety of arrangements to make that kind and quality of missionary commitment more frequent.

Recruitment in the 1980s
by John E. Kyle

Throughout the history of the Church the recruitment of Christian missionaries has always been of strategic importance. Barnabas was a careful strategist. After laying out his plans, "then Barnabas went to Tarsus to get Paul. When he found him, he brought him back to Antioch; and both of them stayed there for a full year, teaching the many new converts" (Acts 11:25-26).

There has never been a time in the history of world missions when the recruitment of new overseas personnel was so strategic to reaching the unreached peoples of our earth for Jesus Christ as it is today.

There was a leveling off in the number of overseas missionaries recruited in North America during the 1960s and 1970s. There is, however, a new stirring abroad. Interest in world missions has been evidenced in the 1970s by the continued growth in numbers of student delegates attending the Urbana Student Missions Convention sponsored by Inter-Varsity Christian Fellowship. At Urbana '79 some 16,500 delegates were in attendance, with about 8,000 of them making written decisions expressing a desire to explore and pray about seeking God's will for their lives in the area of service in world missions. Of these, 2,000 indicated that steps would be taken toward going overseas with a mission agency. As this convention rang down the decade of the 1970s in North America, there were over 7,000 young European students meeting in a similar missions convention in Lausanne, Switzerland. The 1980s began with over 23,000 young people in North America and Europe being exposed to the cause of world missions.

The movement among Christian collegians in North America toward an interest in world missions has encouraged the sponsors of the Urbana Convention to compress future conventions to a two-year cycle. These alone might result in 10,000 decisions to attempt to go overseas during the 1980s.

Most knowledgeable people feel that the boards will be able to handle an increased number of candidates. Some observers have questioned whether the existing mission sending agencies can absorb a large number of missionary candidates whatever the source of their recruitment.

In April 1979 leaders of over twenty prominent mission sending agencies met for a Consultation on College Students and World Missions. In preparations for the Consultation these leaders were requested to share their recruitment goals for the next five-year period. All of those agencies had projected extensive growth of personnel. It was apparent that some of these major agencies expect to expand their overseas ministry during the 1980s extensively. While some have predicted that we are in the sunset of world missions, others feel that we are at a pivotal point and may actually be at the sunrise of world missions.

We are told there remain over 3 billion people on earth who have not accepted Jesus Christ as their Savior, so the task ahead is great. One missiologist has pointed out that world missions during the past hundred years has been immensely successful, which encourages mission strategists to think bigger today. The recently emerged concept of the unreached or hidden peoples, and the research under way revealing the location of these 3 billion people geographically and linguistically, has helped agencies begin to set goals as they focus on people groups.

Coupled with these facts is the work of MARC and the publication yearly of **Unreached Peoples**. There is also the inception of the U.S. Center for World Mission where the challenge to frontier missions has greatly exposed Christians to the fact that there are definable goals. Evangelical Foreign Missions Association (EFMA) leaders in Kansas City in the fall of 1979 began to plan the number of people groups each agency could reach out to in the 1980s.

The blocs of tribal, Muslim, Hindu and Chinese peoples that are unreached has struck the imagination of young Christians. It has also set the stage for the development of new strategies by mission agencies to reach these blocs of people.

The Lausanne Consultation on World Evangelization held in Lausanne, Switzerland, in 1974 focused on evangelism in a meaningful manner in a worldwide context and formed the Lausanne Committee for World Evangelization. This has given continuing encouragement to Christians in nations all around the world in the task of evangelization. The Consultation on World Evangelization at Pattaya, Thailand, in June 1980 explored how evangelization could be further encouraged at the grass-roots level within the nations of the world. Even the most casual evangelical observer realizes that God is moving in a new way. Christians from many different nations anticipate a fresh and vigorous effort to evangelize our world.

An international missionary task force may well be raised up in the 1980s as the Third World missionary-sending agencies combine forces with Western World sending agencies to develop international teams. In the midst of this emerging international movement, there could be the melding in of self-supporting missionaries to form a tremendous body of well-trained laborers that will see the task of reaching our world for Christ well on the way in the decade of the 1980s.

Some thoughtful missiologists have suggested that we are entering a new era of world missions. All of the events already mentioned could indicate that this is true. All of these facts should be considered in the face of continued world tensions: the emergence of a new China into the world scene; the breaking down of time-honored diplomatic customs, evidenced by the hostages held in Iran and simultaneously in Colombia; the aggressiveness of the U.S.S.R. in the nation of Afghanistan; the great hosts of refugees continuing to mount around the world; the oil shortages affecting the whole world, accompanied by nations in a turmoil because of economic pressures of inflation and recession which could develop into depression. And in the midst of all these upheavals is the freeing up of gold and silver to stagger the imagination of investors worldwide. Our world is in a turmoil as never before in the face of possible atomic holocaust. Therefore people in all nations are being prepared to question their very existence in a new manner, setting the stage for a new, energetic and productive period of cross-cultural evangelism.

Many are asking the question: **Will we continue to be able to field missionaries from North America**? Some feel that the decade of the 1980s will be decisive in establishing beachheads of ministry for Christ among the hidden or unreached peoples in a new era of frontier/mobile missions. There is no question that Christians in North America have the needed resources of dedicated Christians and financial capability.

Churches across North America are becoming very knowledgeable concerning world missions as they assist growing numbers of other churches through the ministry of the Association of Church Missions Committees. There are at least 250,000 committed Christian students on secular and Christian college campuses, forming a great reservoir of potential missionaries.

In light of all that has already been shared, the question needs to be raised: **Where do we go from here in the 1980s in reference to recruiting a vast host of new missionaries? What will recruitment look like as to methods, resources and results?** It is possible for us to see a new group of over 8,000 missionaries recruited and on the field by 1985.

Undoubtedly the Christian campuses, comprising Bible colleges and Christian liberal arts institutions, will continue to provide a multitude of missionaries. A new dimension will be explored as the recruitment is widened to over 2,000 secular college campuses. This will be a new and enlarging target for recruitment in the 1980s. Such groups as Navigators, Campus Crusade for Christ, Inter-Varsity Christian Fellowship and others form a network made up of students who have been trained in evangelism and discipleship, the very qualifications that make up a good church planting missionary.

More mission agencies will see the potential of students on secular campuses when they evaluate the type of person needed to reach Muslims around the world. Such students will have witnessed to fellow students in a secular setting, earned a degree in a major that will be saleable and could keep them in an overseas assignment if necessary and, in the case of engineers, trained as problem-solvers and not slot-fitters.

One agency made a survey of 650 students on three seminary campuses to which they had a response indicating that 44% of those planning on serving overseas received undergraduate training in secular schools. One wonders how many did not make it to the seminary! Many mission agencies will gear up to recruit heavily on the secular campuses as well as Christian campuses.

The follow-up of the Urbana Conventions, called **Urbana Onward**, will continue to function throughout the 1980s, opening the way to a great number of students from secular campuses that were hitherto unreachable for missionary service.

Some mission agencies, in light of the high cost of living overseas, are looking at new sacrificial programs for groups of young missionaries who are willing to live on a bare minimum salary as modeled by the Peace Corps. These programs will undoubtedly be made up of teams and will serve from two- to four-year terms. The Agape Movement may be setting a new pattern in this regard. Some larger boards will be discussing the matter of cutting back the lifestyle of long-term missionaries at the missionary's request in order to stretch finances. All of this will appeal to young, idealistic recruits.

Mission agencies will begin to research afresh their biblical and educational requirements as they receive more candidates from secular campuses where students have been involved in active Christian nurture groups such as Navs, CCC, IVCF and others. A new flexibility will be shown by progressive sending agencies that keep updating their candidate department.

Mission agencies will realize when recruiting on the secular campuses that these Christian students are being taught in a humanistic setting. They will be asking many questions, such as "Who are these mission agency people?" Some will have been raised in churches that may have a missions tradition, but only a few. Many of them will have become Christians while in college.

Many students will be willing to go overseas to serve as missionaries but need to be told how to move on out. The Christian students will not need another challenge to commitment but will need vital information as to where they might serve as overseas missionaries with the training they are obtaining or already have.

Many of these students will be facing heavy educational debts and need to be given counsel as to how they can set up a plan to eliminate such debts and still get to the mission field, while receiving additional training if needed in the meantime.

Teams of skilled mission agency recruiters will be traveling to secular campuses working in cooperation with one another to effectively penetrate. Key missionary personnel home on furlough will be seconded to groups like IVCF to work among students on Christian and secular campuses.

The 1980s will reveal an immense effort on the part of the mission sending agencies in recruitment of needed personnel to fill present and future openings on the fields overseas. This recruiting will be done among a generation of Christian students who will be aggressively and seriously seeking the ways and means to get involved in such service for Christ.

Undoubtedly the greatest need will be for a great band of prayer warriors to be raised up with North Americans joining Third World Christians in praying the Lord of the harvest that He will send forth laborers into His harvest.

Analysis of the Survey

Introduction

The questionnaire that was used to gather the information which is the subject of this analysis is reproduced in the **Appendices**. As has been previously emphasized, compilation and analysis of mission statistics is a very tenuous business. In order to give the reader an understanding of the basic data that were used in making the analysis that follows, a **Basic Data Table** is provided on the following pages. The reader should be immediately warned not to be misled by the seeming accuracy of the numbers. In many cases they **are** accurate. For example, the number of agencies listed in the book (714) is (hopefully) accurate! However, the total number of North American overseas personnel reported (53,494) is the sum of all of the questionnaires returned plus some estimates. The actual number may be somewhat different.

The calculations included in the **Basic Data Table** may not be immediately obvious to the reader. Where the numbers have been derived from other numbers or sources, the method of compilation is described in the text.

Basic Data Table

NORTH AMERICAN OVERSEAS PERSONNEL	<u>1975</u>	<u>1979</u>
Combined Overseas Personnel		
Total Person/Year Equivalent	34,901	44,442
Total Reported	35,458	53,243
Total Including Estimated	37,677	53,494
Without Short-Termers	31,186	35,861
Single Men	903	1,108
Single Women	4,653	4,683
Married Men	11,702	11,813
Married Women	11,375	11,370
Canadian Overseas Personnel		
Person/Year Equivalent	1,214	1,887
Including All Short-Termers	1,252	1,925
Without Short-Termers	1,146	1,650
U.S. Overseas Personnel		
Person/Year Equivalent	33,687	42,304
Including All Short-Termers	35,698	51,569
Without Short-Termers	30,040	34,211
World Protestant Overseas Force (Estimate)	55,000E	81,500E
North American Catholics Overseas	11,903	9,958
U.S. Catholics Overseas	7,100	5,870
Canadian Catholics Overseas	4,803	4,088
World Catholic Missions Force (Estimate)	125,000E	138,000E
North American Latter-Day Saints (All)	20,000	30,300
North American Jehovah's Witnesses	100	100E
New N. American Personnel (during report period)	4,476	10,044
New Canadian Personnel	84	343
New U.S. Personnel	4,392	9,701
Agencies Reporting New Personnel	295	270
Canadian Agencies Reporting New Personnel	15	24
U.S. Agencies Reporting New Personnel	280	246
Retired Personnel	4,366	3,546
Canadian Retired Personnel	157	187
U.S. Retired Personnel	4,209	3,365
Agencies Reporting Retired	282	164
Canadian Agencies Reporting Retired	16	20
U.S. Agencies Reporting Retired	266	144
Candidates for Overseas Ministry	2,297	3,119
Canadian Candidates	74	244
U.S. Candidates	2,223	2,875
Agencies Reporting Candidates	294	203
Canadian Agencies Reporting Candidates	15	15
U.S. Agencies Reporting Candidates	279	188
Expatriates Reported Serving with		
North American Agencies	4,099	7,034
Canadian Agencies	268	1,126
U.S. Agencies	3,831	5,908
North American Agencies Reporting Expatriates	256	173
Canadian Agencies Reporting Expatriates	13	15
U.S. Agencies Reporting Expatriates	243	158
North American Home Staff	10,687	9,215
Canadian Home Staff	NR	1,957
U.S. Home Staff	NR	7,258
Agencies Reporting Number of Home Staff	389	501

Short-Termers	1975	1979
Total Number of Short-Term Personnel Reported	5,764	17,633
Percentage of Total Overseas	16%	33%
Number Serving Overseas at Any One Time (Est.)	3,715E	8,581E
Percentage of Total Person/Year Equivalent	11%	19%
Agencies Reporting Short-Term Personnel	199	256
Agencies with Primarily Short-Term Personnel	19	45
Personnel in Agencies Primarily Short-Term	2,276	9,068
Percentage of Agencies with Short-Term Program	32%	36%
Largest Number in One Agency	1,000	5,000
Agencies Having 100 or More	12	22
Average Length of Service	24 mo.	19 mo.

Distribution of Overseas Personnel

Countries and Areas with Overseas North American Personnel or Involvement	182	192
Countries and Areas with Canadian Personnel or Involvement	77	87
Countries and Areas with U.S. Personnel or Involvement	182	192

Overseas Agencies

Listed in This Edition	620	714
Who Reported in This Edition	604	663
Canadian Agencies Reported	41	69
U.S. Agencies Reported	579	645
Reduced by Mergers	7	4
Founded Since 1975	33	47
Founded Prior to Survey Not Previously Reported	41	96
Personnel Reported in These Agencies	983	1,112
Listed for the Last Time in this Edition	16	18
Listed in Previous Edition But Dropped	32	35
Reporting Overseas Personnel	465	430
Maximum of Overseas Personnel in One Agency	2,693	2,906
Median of Overseas Personnel in One Agency	27	14
Average of Overseas Personnel in One Agency	75	103
No. of Agencies with 1,000 Personnel or More	5	4
No. of Agencies with 500 to 1,000 Personnel	8	16
No. of Agencies with less than 100 Personnel		589
Agencies with No Current Information		33

Finances	1975	1979
Estimated Income for All North American Agencies	$ 655,659,955	$ 1,148,169,321
Reported Income	$ 633,671,455	$ 1,139,568,107
Estimated Additions	$ 21,977,500	$ 8,601,214
Canadian Total Income	$ 23,028,017	$ 49,807,612
Canadian Reported Income		$ 48,400,112
Canadian Estimated Income		$ 1,407,500
U.S. Total Income	$ 632,620,938	$ 1,098,361,709
U.S. Reported Income		$ 1,091,167,995
U.S. Estimated Income		$ 7,193,714

Mission Associations	1975	1979
Number of Personnel Reported		
DOM	5,582	4,817
EFMA	7,968	9,797
IFMA	6,236	6,575
Unaffiliated	17,164	32,305
Income in Millions of Dollars		
DOM	137.4	146.1
EFMA	150.4	284.5
IFMA	70.6	97.9
Unaffiliated	297.2	619.7

Types of Ministries

	1975	1979
Percent Overseas Force Involved in Establishing Churches	28%	29.5%
Church Support	25%	38.6%
Other Ministries	47%	31.8%

Reference

	1975	1979
North American Protestant Church Membership	50,582,278	56,913,027
Canadian	2,338,195	2,219,127
U.S.	48,244,083	54,693,900
North American Population	235,400,000E	246,500,000E
Canadian Population	22,600,000E	24,000,000E
U.S. Population	212,800,000E	222,500,000E
North American Protestant Church Income (1979)	$ 5,504,000,000	$ 7,811,949,684
Canadian Protestant Church Income	$ 226,000,000	$ 357,633,159
U.S. Protestant Church Income	$ 5,278,000,000	$ 7,454,316,525

Overseas Personnel

Introduction

Since the early 1800s, the Protestant churches of North America have felt a responsibility to send their representatives to other lands and peoples. Describing this missionary dynamic is a challenging task because the desired information has not always been available or complete. Mission agencies come and go, change their names, merge, or shift their ministries, and it is difficult to make an accurate assessment of the total movement. The reader must be continually cautioned that the analysis presented in the following pages is based upon available, and not always complete, data and approximately represents the state of the North American Protestant overseas mission effort at the end of 1979 and the beginning of 1980 through the traditional sending channel of agencies.

Who Are Overseas Personnel?

There was a time in the history of the missionary movement when it was well understood that a "missionary" was someone who was making a lifetime career of serving another people, usually outside the borders of his or her own country. Such a definition is no longer accurate. The concept of missionary career is taking its place alongside other career concepts such as engineering, medicine, or law. It is a phenomenon of present North American society that individuals move in and out of such careers with a surprising degree of ease. Many men and women embarking upon a career in overseas ministry do so in full expectation that at some point in their life they will change careers or return to their home country.

As was noted in the Tenth and Eleventh Editions, the total overseas community includes a growing number of "short-term" personnel. Here again we have a term that defies definition. For example, young people serving in another country for periods as short as a few weeks or a month are reported by some agencies. There are obviously thousands of men and women who serve longer short-term periods ranging from one to six years. Some agencies include short-term personnel in their totals; most do not.

In order to establish a consistent base line, we have assumed that **all** short-termers should be included in the grand total. This represents the total number of Protestant North Americans who have served any time overseas during 1979. Where we have known that the short-term program was less than 12 months, totals have been factored and a person/year equivalent total has been derived as a separate entry in the Basic Data table to describe how many individuals may be serving as "overseas personnel" at any one time during the year.

Overseas Staff

Protestant contribution to the world missionary force is estimated at 80,000-85,000, of which 60-65 percent come from North America (U.S. and Canada).

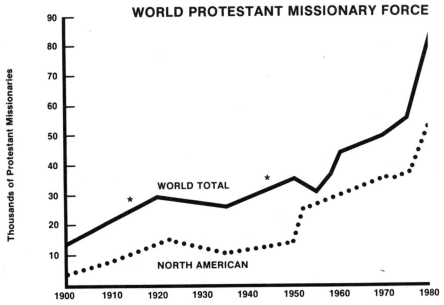

WORLD PROTESTANT MISSIONARY FORCE

*Period of World War; data unavailable

The number of Protestant missionaries has increaced since 1900 and, after 1920 the increase was due largely to more being sent from North America. Wars and economic declines reduced overseas staffs temporarily, and the graph is not necessarily valid for the periods of the world wars. After 1950 the majority of the overseas missionary staff was from North America.

The current survey of North American Protestant agencies with overseas ministries revealed 53,494 persons serving overseas during 1979. The agencies work in 192 countries and regions outside North America. Of this total 51,569 were reported to come from the United States and 1,925 from Canada. About 45 percent of the overseas staff were men, while 55 percent were women. Single women outnumbered single men in the approximate ratio of four to one.

The adjusted total for 1975 was reported in the Eleventh Edition as 36,950. To compare figures accurately, 1975 totals must again be adjusted to allow for agencies who were sending personnel in earlier years but which, for some reason, were not reported in previous surveys. (See list on page 48.) For computation purposes it was assumed that 837 of 962 personnel reported were serving in 1975. The adjusted figures for 1979 indicate that the size of the overseas missionary force far exceeds any previous peak. The increase in Canadian missionaries is especially significant, up to 1,925 from 1,252 in 1975, an increase of 55 percent.

And how has the number of overseas personnel fared as related to church membership? The U.S. mission force has continued to increase after 1969, whereas church membership reversed a decreasing trend only in 1974. The Canadian missions force as a percentage of church membership has increased steadily since 1965, when statistics were available.

From another perspective, the total number of overseas personnel, which had only kept up approximately with the percent of population increase in the U.S., has now surpassed the approximately 2.3% population increase between 1976 and 1979. The increase in missionaries is equivalent to a yearly growth of 9.7%. Even if one chose to view the surge in short-term personnel as a passing fad or quirk, the career missionary total has averaged better than a 3.5% yearly increase.

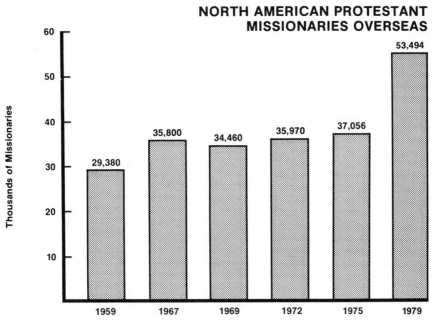

NORTH AMERICAN PROTESTANT MISSIONARIES OVERSEAS

Adjusted totals to allow for non-reporting agencies in prior years and for those agencies that have usually reported short term personnel.

Short-Term Personnel

It should be noted here that the trend which was first identified in 1970 continues: the percentage of the total overseas force made up of short-term personnel continues to grow. Of the 36,950 personnel reported overseas in the Eleventh Edition in 1975, 5,764 were reported as short-termers. This represented 15.6 percent of the total force. Of the 53,494 in 1979, 17,633 are reported as short-termers. This now represents 33.0% of the total force. In 1979, 256 agencies reported having short-term personnel, as compared to 199 in 1975. This essentially means that "career" personnel no longer are being replaced by "limited term" personnel, but themselves have entered a new expansion phase.

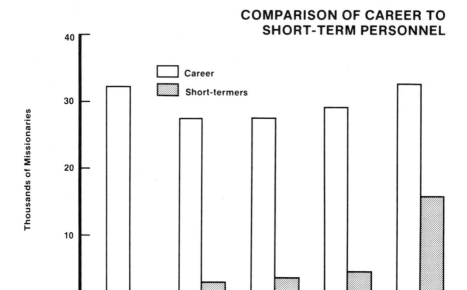

COMPARISON OF CAREER TO SHORT-TERM PERSONNEL

Career

Short-termers

Thousands of Missionaries

1967 1969 1972 1975 1979

Non-North American Personnel

Question #29 of the survey questionnaire sought the number of non-North American people serving with each agency as "overseas" personnel, i.e., serving outside their home country. This question attempted to determine the extent of internationalization of the predominantly North American-based missionary force. It was anticipated that more and more agencies are sending and supporting missionaries, not only from North America but from other nations as well, and these should be seen as full-fledged cross-cultural representatives of the gospel. These persons are distinct from what are often termed "nationals," referring to citizens of another country who are associated with a foreign mission in some capacity but who remain in their home country and whose numbers run into the tens of thousands. From the replies, it is not clear that all those responding understood this distinction; therefore, the precise totals are suspect. These statistics are included in the totals for missionary force and are not used in any other calculations in this analysis. However, the general size of the response and the comparative increase over the number reported in 1975 may be taken as indicative of such internationalization of the missionary force.

A total of 173 agencies reported 7,034 non-North American personnel serving in other countries. This compares with 256 agencies reporting 4,099 non-North American personnel in other countries in 1975.

New Personnel

Of the agencies responding, 270 agencies reported a total of 10,044 new personnel for the four-year period 1975/1979, or an average of 2,511 per year, or almost five percent of the total force. This is about the same percentage that has been reported in previous years. When compared to the growth in personnel, either this was under reported, or "casuality rates" are less than in previous reporting periods.

A total of 203 agencies reported having 3,121 missionary candidates waiting for overseas assignment, which would indicate that the number of new personnel reported may increase further in the near future.

Spouses

Is a wife or husband who accompanies her or his spouse to be considered as a missionary or overseas personnel? Some agencies commission both husband and wife; other agencies do not count the wives of missionaries as part of their staff because they consider that the primary task of the wife is that of maintaining the home and raising children.

When married women were reported by an agency, they were included in the total staff figures. However, it is very difficult to estimate how many wives who are listed as overseas personnel are actually working primarily in a support function of homemaking. Some insight can be gained by a study conducted in Brazil in the late 1960s. A survey of the Protestant missionaries in Brazil revealed that over 40 percent of the missionary wives were "engaged practically full-time in homemaking." (Missionary Information Bureau, **Occasional Paper** #10, May 1967, Sao Paulo, Brazil.)

If we assumed that 40 percent of the 11,370 married women reported in the North American mission total should not be considered as active overseas personnel, the total force would be reduced to 48,946. The latter figure is particularly significant when attempting to draw comparisons between Protestants and Catholics or between Protestants and Latter-Day Saints, neither of whom count spouses, for obvious reasons.

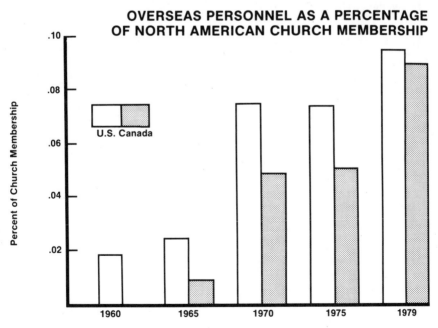

OVERSEAS PERSONNEL AS A PERCENTAGE OF NORTH AMERICAN CHURCH MEMBERSHIP

Personnel on Furlough

The number of overseas personnel actually overseas at any one time is not constant and is less than the total shown because of those on furlough. The traditional missionary "term of service" has been four to five years followed by a one-year return to the home country. Many agencies are now shortening this period and compensating by shortening furlough time proportionally. More missionaries may be on furlough at any one time than was true in the past. Previous surveys have indicated that about 20 percent of the total missionary force is on furlough at any one time.

Non-Protestant Personnel

Although this **Handbook** primarily describes the missionary activity of Protestant agencies, it may be helpful to readers to be aware of other religious missionary movements emanating from North America. This broader picture will hopefully provide a context for seeing North American religious missionary influence on the world and the comparisons with Protestant agencies and efforts may be instructive. Four major non-Protestant bodies are covered here: Roman Catholic, Orthodox, Latter-Day Saints (Mormon) and Jehovah's Witnesses.

One of the characteristics of the Mormons and the Jehovah's Witnesses is their vigorous proselytizing. Door-to-door visitation, extensive literature distribution, and large numbers of members mobilized are features of the missionary efforts of these agencies. One not surprising result of these efforts has been the substantial growth that some groups have experienced, both in converts from Roman Catholicism and historical Protestantism and from those with no allegiance to any church. Protestant missions working in the same areas with these groups would do well to take note of their effectiveness in winning others to their beliefs.

Roman Catholic

In the 50-year period from 1918 to 1968, the number of U.S. Catholic missionaries serving outside the 48 contiguous states grew from a handful to over 9,600. In the past 12 years, however, this number has declined steadily to approximately 6,393 (as of 1980) according to data of the U.S. Catholic Mission Council. These U.S. Catholic missionaries are active in 110 mission fields with 523 of them in Alaska, Hawaii and Canada. Of the 5,870 overseas personnel (serving outside the 50 States and Canada), 37 percent of these serve in only six countries: the Philippines, Peru, Brazil, Japan, Puerto Rico and Bolivia. About 47 percent are found in Latin Amercia, with Asia having the second largest number (26 percent), followed by Africa (15 percent), Oceania (12 percent) and a handful in other parts of North America, in Europe and in the Middle East.

U.S. Catholic mission societies follow the Protestant pattern of size. Although there are over 300 U.S. Catholic mission sending agencies, 12 of them account for 43 percent of the personnel. Many others have only a small handful serving abroad. Of the total of U.S. Catholic missionaries serving abroad, 3 percent are diocesan priests, 46 percent are religious priests, one percent are religious brothers, 44 percent are religious sisters, .8 percent are seminarians and 3 percent are lay persons. Of the total number of U.S. Catholic religious order priests, approximately 10 percent are serving abroad as missionaries.

Canadian Catholic missionaries serving abroad numbered 4,088 in the 1979 statistics published by the Mission Department of the Canadian Religious Conference. Of these about 36 percent were in Africa, 40 percent in Latin America, 18 percent in Asia and 4 percent in Oceania. Twenty-five percent were religious priests, 17 percent brothers and 52 percent sisters. Another 927 were serving in Canada in "home missions." In proportion to their numerical strength, the Roman Catholics of Canada sent more than three times as many missionaries to other nations as did the Catholics in the United States.

In terms of world totals, North American Catholic missionaries represent a significantly smaller percentage of all Catholic missionaries than North American Protestant missionaries represent of all Protestant missionaries. Whereas about 70 percent of the world Protestant missionary force comes from North America, about 7 percent of the Catholic missionary personnel come from this continent.

Orthodox Churches

Of the three traditional branches of Christianity, the Orthodox Church is the smallest but, in some senses, the oldest. The Orthodox churches are subdivided into three major groupings: Eastern (Chalcedonian), Oriental (non-Chalcedonian), and Assyrian (Nestorian). The Orthodox Church is composed of self-governing and mutually independent national churches throughout the world.

There are more than a dozen such church bodies in North America with a total constituency of approximately 4.1 million people. Of these, 3.7 million live in the United States. From a missionary-sending perspective, the Orthodox churches in North America are essentially self-governing and responsible for the missionary activity within its territory. For that reason, very few missionaries are sent from North America to other countries. For example, Greek Orthodox missionaries in Africa are under the jurisdiction of the Patriarchate of Alexandria, Egypt, while responsibility for Greek Orthodox activity in the Western hemisphere falls to the Greek Orthodox Archdiocese of North and South America. Some regions, however, are of general concern to the entire Church. There is one example: the Orthodox Church in America, the second largest Orthodox body in North America, has "home" missionaries in Alaska and western Canada. Much of the missionary activity of the larger Orthodox churches from North America consists of providing financial assistance, literature and making scholarships available to students from other countries who wish to prepare for the ministry. Cross-cultural and international missionary activity by Orthodox churches from this continent to date is still limited, and no comprehensive mission statistics are available. The formation of missions departments at church headquarters and the teaching of mission courses in the seminaries and theological schools are taking place and suggest a growing interest in this aspect of ministry.

Latter-Day Saints (Mormons)

Of the four bodies of Latter-Day Saints listed in the **1979 Yearbook of American and Canadian Churches,** the Church of Jesus Christ of Latter-Day Saints headquartered in Utah is the largest, with 2.1 million members reported in North America and over 3.6 million worldwide. The Mormon Church, as it is also known, has increased its membership by approximately 50 percent in the decade 1965 to 1975. Many of its members serve short terms as missionaries, either in North America or overseas. It is a common practice for each Mormon man to serve a two-year term before moving on to a secular career. The result is that there are approximately 30,300 LDS missionaries, most of whom come from North America, serving worldwide in approximately 75 different countries. As a consequence, whereas in 1951 only 8.1 percent of the total membership resided outside the United States, the percentage approached 25 by 1978, with most rapid growth in Latin America and Asia.

Jehovah's Witnesses

The Jehovah's Witnesses are known for their extensive activity in visitation and literature distribution. Their yearbook reports approximately 581,054 members in North America and approximately two million worldwide in over 205 countries. All members are considered ministers, and because of this, the actual number of persons being sent cross-culturally is relatively small. In any one year, according to the headquarters office, about 100 are estimated to go from North America to other countries.

Although the Jehovah's Witness missionary efforts from North America are thus seen as smaller in size than the Protestant contribution, they are growing at a more rapid rate than the size of the Protestant constituency. Since the influence of a missionary force is dependent not only upon the numbers but upon the commitment and degree of activity of its individual members, it should be noted that some of the non-Protestant groups have had an impact in some areas that far exceeds what might be expected from the size of the staff.

Short-Term Personnel

Short-Term Defined

What is a "short-termer?" Some years ago the question could be answered easily by saying that a short-termer was a missionary who was not planning to make overseas ministries his or her career. However, in recent years this definition has become fuzzy at both ends. On the one hand the concept of a missionary career is changing dramatically. At one time almost all missionaries thought of themselves and their calling as for a lifetime; now many missionaries plan in advance to discontinue or interrupt their missionary career sometime during their lifetime. Others take up a missionary career for eight or ten years in mid-life. Some mission agencies have recognized this trend and are commissioning missionaries for only one term of service at a time, often with a special name for this category.

On the other hand, more and more North American young people are spending a few days to a week or one to two months in some form of overseas experience. Many agencies report these **short** short-termers along with others of longer term.

When short-termers represented only a minor percentage of the total mission force, none of this made very much difference, but as can be seen by the graph on page 26, the percentage of short-termers to the total force is rising dramatically. In 1979, 256 agencies reported 17,633 persons who were serving in some form of short-term service. This represents 33 percent of the total of 53,494 individuals who are estimated to have served overseas during 1979.

Length of Service

In order to get a better understanding of the numerical impact of short-termers, agencies were asked to indicate the maximum length of service for them. Of the 256 agencies reporting short-termers, the average maximum length of service was 19 months, the maximum length of service was 72 months and the minimum length of service was one week. Obviously an agency whose maximum length of service is less than 12 months should not be viewed as having the mission force equivalent to an agency whose service is always 12 months or more. To put it another way, the number of people serving overseas at any one time is not equal to the total number of people who have served during the course of the year. Therefore, we have included in the Basic Data table a calculation which is the person/year equivalent of the 17,633 short-termers; they represent 8,581 person/years for comparison purposes. Thirty-nine agencies indicated that they had maximum length of service of less than 12 months. These thirty-nine agencies reported 13,620 short-termers.

31

When this 13,620 was modified to take into account the length of service, it was determined that they were equivalent to 4,568 full-time personnel. Therefore, to arrive at the **average** number of short-term personnel serving overseas in one year, we subtracted from the total number of short-termers reported (17,633) the number of short-termers serving less than 12 months (13,620) and added the full-time equivalent number (4,568). The average total of short-term missionaries serving overseas at any one time is therefore 8,581.

The graph on page 25 uses totals that have been modified to make all short-termers part of the total. U.S. agencies reported 17,358 short-termers, Canadian agencies only 275.

FIFTEEN AGENCIES WITH LARGEST NUMBER OF NORTH AMERICAN SHORT-TERMERS

Agency	Number of Short-Termers Reported	Number of Months Maximum Service	Equivalent Number of Full-Time	Full-Time Total Overseas
Youth With A Mission	5,000	1,000 @ 1 yr. 4,000 @ 4 mos.	2,333	1,200
Southern Baptist Convention	2,867	124 @ 1 yr. 2,743 @ 3 mos.	809	2,906
Teen Missions International, Inc.	1,800	270 @ 9 mos. 1,530 @ 3 mos.	585	19
United Methodist Church, United Methodist Comm. on Relief	985	3 weeks	57	650
World Evangelization Foundation	605	2 weeks	23	0
Wycliffe Bible Translators International, Inc.	466	60 months	466	1,781
Vacation Samaritans	325	2 months	54	20
Missions Outreach, Inc.	294	1 month	25	0
Men For Missions International	243	3 months	61	0
Operation Mobilization	200	12 months	200	295
Evangelical Alliance Mission (TEAM)	197	86 @ 24 mos. 34 @ 11 mos. 77 @ 4 mos.	136	905
Assemblies of God	170	24 months	170	1,214
United Methodist Church, World Div. of the Board Of Global Min.	166	12 months	166	938
Youth Enterprises, Inc.	150	6 months	75	6
Conservative Baptist Foreign Mission Society	114	24 months	114	501

AGENCIES PRIMARILY USING SHORT-TERMERS

Agency	Number of Full-Timers	Number Short-Termers	Maximum Length Service	Percent Short-Termers
World Evangelism Foundation	0	605	2 wks.	100%
Missions Outreach	0	294	3 mos.	100%
Men for Missions, Int.	0	243	3 mos.	100%
International Gospel League	0	100	6 mos.	100%
Wycliffe Associates	0	79	6 mos.	100%
Laos, Inc.	0	55	NR	100%
Christian Service Corps	0	53	24 mos.	100%
World Medical Mission	0	30	3 mos.	100%
Team Ventures International	0	28	24 mos.	100%
Jews for Jesus	0	25	24 mos.	100%
Totonac Bible Center	0	19	6 mos.	100%
Faith Christian Fellowship	0	17	2 mos.	100%
Young Life	0	14	NR	100%
Air Crusade	0	5	1 mo.	100%
Jewish Voice Broadcast	0	5	6 mos.	100%
U.S. Center for World Mission	0	5	12 mos.	100%
World Missionary Press	0	5	NR	100%
United Board for Christian Higher Education in Asia	0	4	NR	100%
Food for the Hungry/Canada	0	3	12 mos.	100%
Macedonian Service Foundation	0	3	12 mos.	100%
Missionary Air Transport	0	3	NR	100%
Teen Missions	19	1,800	9 mos.	99%
World Hope Foundation	2	100	3 mos.	98%
Evangelism Center	1	70	6 mos.	98%
Border Missions	4	100	7 mos.	96%
Youth Enterprises, Inc.	6	150	6 mos.	96%
CAM International Practical Missionary Training	4	69	3 mos.	95%
MAP International	4	66	6 mos.	94%
Vacation Samaritans	20	325	2 mos.	94%
Morris Cerullo World Evangelism	10	100	NR	91%
Open Doors with Brother Andrew	16	100	1 mo.	86%
American Missionary Fellowship	4	21	24 mos.	84%
Christ's Mission	4	19	30 mos.	83%
World Relief Corporation	3	14	24 mos.	82%
Youth With A Mission	887	5,000	12 mos.	81%
Self-Help Foundation	1	4	6 mos.	80%
Food for the Hungry	18	52	24 mos.	75%
Mission to Europe's Millions	13	40	3 mos.	75%
Christian Worldwide Evangelical Mission of Canada	4	12	NR	75%
OC Ministries	73	207	3 mos.	74%
Missionary Dentist	7	20	6 mos.	74%
Brethren in Christ Mission	34	80	36 mos.	70%

Agencies With Short-Termers

The number of agencies using short-termers increased from 126 in the 1973 report to 199 in the 1976 report and to 256 in 1979. Forty-three agencies reported that 8,818 personnel are primarily involved as short-termers. The agencies with the largest number of short-termers and those primarily using short-termers are shown in the preceding tables.

Use of Short-Termers by Associations

The number and percent of short-termers in the three major mission associations are shown in the following table.

SHORT-TERM PERSONNEL BY ASSOCIATION

Association	Total Personnel	Short-Term	Percent of Total
DOM	4,817	1,354	28%
EFMA	9,797	1,530	16%
IFMA	6,575	624	10%

Forecast of the Future

Agencies were asked to forecast their future use of short-termers; 259 agencies answered this question. Of these, only ten, or less than four percent, indicated any plans for decreasing their numbers of short-termers; 101, or 37 percent, indicated that they would have no change; 116, or 43 percent, indicated that they would increase some; 41, or 16 percent, indicated that they would increase greatly. These general patterns were followed by both U.S. and Canadian agencies.

Distribution of Personnel

By Continent

The distribution of missionaries by continent of service reflects
little change since 1975 (see table below). The reader must be
warned of error introduced into these data by the agencies which
included national personnel in the count by country. Agencies
reporting areas of service located 34,760 individuals by
countries, 65 percent of the total force. Latin America continues
to receive the most Protestant missionaries from North America
with about 33 percent of the overseas missionary force. This
compares with 35.5 percent in 1975, 34 percent in 1972, and with
about 32 percent in 1969. The percentage of missionaries serving
in Asia (including the Middle East) has increased from 26.8
percent in 1975 to 30.6 percent in 1979. The size of the missionary force in Africa has decreased significantly from approximately 26 percent in 1975 to 22 percent in 1979. This compares to
27 percent in 1972 and 29 percent in 1969. Europe, the second most
populous continent, has again gained slightly with about 10
percent of the overseas missionary force compared with eight
percent in 1975 and six percent in 1972. Oceania still attracts
approximately four percent of the overseas missionaries compared
to three percent in 1972. Europe and Asia have both increased
their percentage of missionaries, somewhat at the expense of
Africa. The reader is again cautioned that these statistics are
based upon only those data which specify the area of service of
the missionary force. Therefore, the changes indicated may be
more or less significant depending upon the number of agencies
which did not report the specific areas of service and the number
of missionaries involved. For comparison, the table below
provides data for the distribution of mission personnel by
continent. The second table gives the basis for an additional
comparison with US Roman Catholic missionaries.

COMPARATIVE DISTRIBUTIONS OF MISSION PERSONNEL

North American Protestant Personnel
(Number and Percent Reported)

	1972		1975		1979	
Africa	7,671	(27%)	7,768	(26.2%)	7,695	(22.2%)
Asia (Middle East)	8,700	(30%)	7,952	(26.8%)	10,628	(30.6%)
Europe (and USSR)	1,871	(6%)	2,308	(7.8%)	3,525	(10.1%)
Latin America	9,592	(34%)	10,536	(35.5%)	11,535	(33.2%)
Oceania	860	(3%)	1,109	(3.7%)	1,377	(4.0%)
TOTAL*	28,694	(100%)	29,673	(100.0%)	34,760	(100.0%)

(*) Total for which area of service was reported.

NORTH AMERICAN ROMAN CATHOLIC PERSONNEL LOCATION BY COUNTRY OF ORIGIN (NUMBER AND PERCENT)

	US		Canada		North American	
Africa	923	(15.1%)	1,499	(36.7%)	2,422	(23.7%)
Asia	1,627	(26.7%)	768	(18.8%)	2,395	(23.6%)
Europe	37	(0.6%)	NR		37	(0.1%)
Latin America	2,793	(45.6%)	1,656	(40.6%)	4,449	(43.6%)
Oceania	743	(12.1%)	165	(4.0%)	908	(8.9%)
Totals	6,123		4,088		10,211	

Major Receiving Nations

In 1979 North American Protestant agencies reported activity in 192 different countries and areas of the world. Brazil once again ranked first in the number of total missionaries with 1,995 reported, slightly lower than the 2,170 reported in 1975. Brazil has ranked first since 1967. Japan again ranked second with 1,855 missionaries, up from the 1,644 reported in 1975 but not quite as high as the total of 1,931 reported in 1972. Mexico dropped to fourth place even though the number of missionaries increased to 1,611. The Philippines now ranked third with 1,775 missionaries reported in 1979, up from 1,181 in 1975, a 50% increase in 4 years.

Other nations with greater than 50% increase include Comoro, Cyprus, Finland, Gambia Grenada, Guam, Macao, Luxembourg, Namibia, New Caledonia, Panama, Poland, Reunion, Sri Lanka, Sudan and United Arab Emirates.

Nations which have personnel reported for the first time include Andorra, British Virgin Islands, Burma, Canary Islands, Marshall Islands and Seychelles.

NATIONS WITH THE MOST PROTESTANT PERSONNEL FROM NORTH AMERICA

Nation	1972	Rank	1975	Rank	1979	Rank	Pct. Change
Brazil	2,130	1st	2,170	1st	1,995	1st	-8%
Japan	1,931	2nd	1,655	2nd	1,855	2nd	+13%
Philippines	1,187	5th	1,181	4th	1,775	3rd	+50%
Mexico	1,310	3rd	1,232	3rd	1,611	4th	+31%
India	1,247	4th	817	7th	1,433	5th	+75%
Indonesia	756	8th	858	6th	1,363	6th	+59%
Kenya	645	10th	926	5th	1,307	7th	+41%
Colombia	746	9th	780	10th	1,043	8th	+34%
Ecuador	554	14th	670	11th	816	9th	+22%
Papua New Guinea	571	12th	593	14th	790	10th	+33%
Zaire	1,052	6th	817	8th	715	11th	-12%
Nigeria	1,032	7th	802	9th	715	12th	-11%
Taiwan (Rep. of China)	567	13th	596	12th	691	13th	+16%
France	372	24th	416	22nd	652	14th	+57%
Thailand	398	18th	430	20th	637	15th	+48%
Germany (West)	391	22nd	445	19th	616	16th	+38%
Bolivia	511	16th	536	16th	597	17th	+11%
Venezuela	395	21st	457	18th	596	18th	+30%
South Africa	528	15th	595	13th	588	19th	-1%

Nation	1972	Rank	1975	Rank	1979	Rank	Pct. Change
Korea (South)	474	17th	470	17th	572	20th	+22%
Peru	630	11th	579	15th	548	21st	-5%
United Kingdom	139	---	170	---	540	22nd	+218%
Guatemala	333	24th	399	25th	478	23rd	+20%
Haiti	306	25th	325	26th	467	24th	+44%
Argentina	398	19th	399	24th	398	25th	0%
Zambia	375	23rd	427	21st	382	26th	-10%
Liberia	398	20th	406	23rd	366	27th	-10%

Over the years, Protestant missionaries have entered almost every region and nation in the world, but political and sociological changes continue to close some areas. Nations which experienced more than a 50% decrease in missionary personnel include Afghanistan, Algeria, Belize, Ehtiopia, Fiji, Iran, Laos, Lebanon, Mozambique, Trinidad and Tobago, and Zimbabwe. This picture might be significantly altered if accurate data were available and could be published for paraprofessional or "tent-making" missionaries.

COUNTRIES/AREAS WITH NO REPORTED
OVERSEAS PERSONNEL

Continent	Country/Area	Population (Most recent estimate)
Africa	British Indian Ocean Territory	2,000
	Djibouti	400,000
	Equatorial Guinea	400,000
	Mauritania	1,600,000
	Sao Tome & Principe	100,000
	St. Helena	5,147
	Western Sahara	135,000
Asia	Bhutan	1,300,000
	Brunei	200,000
	China (Peoples Republic of)	975,000,000
	East Timor	800,000
	Gaza	400,000
	Iraq	13,200,000
	Korea (North)	17,900,000
	Maldives	1,700,000
	Qatar	200,000
	Syria	8,600,000
Europe	Albania	2,700,000
	Bulgaria	8,900,000
	Channel Islands	133,000
	Faeroe Islands	41,000
	Germany (Democratic Republic) (East)	16,700,000
	Gibraltar	33,000
	Isle of Man	60,496
	Malta	300,000
	San Marino	20,638
	Vatican City (Holy See)	1,000
Latin America	Falkland Islands	2,000
	Turks and Caicos Islands	

It is important to compare not only the number of missionaries within nations but also to relate that number to the total population and the number of people groups which have been identified. Even though Brazil is ranked first in terms of number of missionaries reported, there are far fewer missionaries per thousand people than in Kenya, which has one missionary per 12,265 people. Information on people groups is limited to that provided by missionaries, nationals, and agencies as evidenced by obvious omissions in number of people groups reported. For example, only 11 people groups have been indentified in Bangladesh which has 90,600,000 people among whom 240 missionaries minister whereas in Tanzania, 263 missionaries minister among 18,600,000 people and 103 people groups.

Nation	North American Protestant Personnel	Total Population	People per Missionary	# People Groups in Unreached Peoples Data File
AFRICA:				
Kenya	1,307	15,900,000	12,165	23
Nigeria	715	77,100,000	107,832	268
Zaire	715	29,300,000	40,979	99
South Africa	588	28,400,000	48,299	4
Zambia	382	5,800,000	15,183	30
Liberia	366	1,900,000	26,811	19
Ivory Coast	265	8,000,000	30,189	54
Tanzania	263	18,600,000	70,722	103
Ghana	230	11,700,000	50,869	52
ASIA:				
Japan	1,855	116,800,000	62,965	8
Philippines	1,775	47,700,000	26,973	115
India	1,433	676,200,000	471,877	257
Indonesia	1,362	144,300,000	105,947	288
Taiwan (Rep. China)	691	17,800,000	25,760	11
Thailand	637	47,300,000	74,254	34
Korea (South)	572	38,200,000	66,783	6
Hong Kong	362	4,800,000	13,259	6
Pakistan	314	86,500,000	275,478	20
Bangladesh	240	90,600,000	377,500	11
EUROPE:				
France	652	53,600,000	82,208	5
Germany (West)	616	61,100,000	99,188	4
United Kingdom	504	55,800,000	110,714	4
Spain	346	37,800,000	109,249	1
Italy	248	57,200,000	230,645	0
Belgium	226	9,900,000	43,805	2
Austria	220	7,500,000	34,091	2
Netherlands	124	14,100,000	113,710	4
Portugal	109	9,900,000	90,826	0
LATIN AMERICA:				
Brazil	1,995	122,000,000	61,307	80
Mexico	1,611	68,200,000	42,334	106
Colombia	1,043	26,700,000	25,599	49
Ecuador	816	8,000,000	9,804	6
Bolivia	597	5,300,000	8,878	16
Venezuela	596	13,900,000	23,322	16
Peru	548	17,600,000	32,117	34
Guatemala	478	7,000,000	14,644	21
Haiti	467	5,800,000	12,420	0
Argentina	398	27,100,000	68,090	5

Nation	North American Protestant Personnel	Total Population	People per Missionary	# People Groups in Unreached Peoples Data File
MIDDLE EAST:				
Israel	207	3,900,000	18,841	8
Lebanon	88	3,200,000	36,364	1
Jordan	87	3,200,000	36,782	1
Turkey	66	45,500,000	689,394	6
Iran	57	39,500,000	675,438	40
Cyprus	42	600,000	14,286	0
United Arab Emirates	42	800,000	19,048	2
Yemen (North)	25	5,600,000	224,000	3

POPULATION AND NORTH AMERICAN PROTESTANT PERSONNEL STATISTICS BY COUNTRY

Country Name	Population (1979/80 Estimate)	North American Protestant Missionaries 1975	North American Protestant Missionaries 1979	Number People Groups Reported by Agencies
Afghanistan	15,900,000	8	3	1
Africa-general	475,000,000	0	6	0
Albania	2,700,000	0	0	0
Algeria	19,000,000	21	8	2
American Samoa	31,000	8	4	0
Andorra	31,000	0	1	0
Angola	6,700,000	30	22	5
Anguilla	6,000	NA	2	0
Antigua	75,000	11	8	0
Argentina	27,100,000	399	398	14
Asia-general	2,563,000,000	NA	39	13
Australia	14,600,000	240	268	26
Austria	4,500,000	165	220	8
Bahamas	200,000	101	96	1
Bahrain	400,000	6	8	0
Bangladesh	90,000,000	161	240	30
Barbados	300,000	19	22	1
Belgium	9,900,000	158	226	0

Country Name	Population (1979/80 Estimate)	North American Protestant Missionaries 1975	1979	Number People Groups Reported by Agencies
Belize	162,000	119	50	0
Benin	3,600,000	54	67	9
Bermuda	60,000	12	7	0
Bhutan	1,300,000	0	0	0
Bolivia	5,300,000	536	597	24
Bophuthatswana	1,000,000	NA	76	0
Botswana	800,000	86	90	10
Brazil	122,000,000	2,170	1,995	101
British Virgin Is.	13,000	0	5	0
Bulgaria	8,900,000	0	0	0
Burma	34,400,000	0	13	20
Burundi	4,500,000	95	78	49
Cameroon	8,500,000	178	184	73
Canary Islands	1,170,000	0	7	0
Cape Verde	300,000	6	4	0
Caribbean-general	30,000,000	NA	82	1
Cayman Islands	12,000	6	10	0
Central African Rep.	2,200,000	143	167	2
C. America-general	91,000,000	NA	0	0
Chad	4,500,000	67	82	19
Chile	11,300,000	287	318	3
China, People's Rep.	975,000,000	1	0	0
Colombia	26,700,000	780	1,043	68
Comoro	300,000	3	9	0
Congo	1,600,000	6	5	2
Costa Rica	2,200,000	280	260	1
Cuba	10,000,000	3	2	1
Cyprus	600,000	9	42	0
Czechoslovakia	15,400,000	0	2	1

Country Name	Population (1979/80 Estimate)	North American Protestant Missionaries 1975	1979	Number People Groups Reported by Agencies
Denmark	5,100,000	13	10	1
Djibouti	400,000	0	0	3
Dominica	100,000	15	15	0
Dominican Republic	5,400,000	131	178	3
Ecuador	8,000,000	670	816	97
Egypt	42,100,000	48	70	2
El Salvador	4,800,000	54	92	1
Ethiopia	32,600,000	519	123	10
Europe-general	484,000,000	NA	17	1
Fiji	600,000	62	30	0
Finland	4,800,000	4	43	1
France	53,600,000	416	652	19
French Guiana	66,000	2	2	0
French Polynesia	155,000	0	6	0
Gabon	600,000	33	42	0
Gambia	600,000	4	16	3
Germany, Dem. Rep.	16,700,000	0	0	0
Germany, Fed. Rep.	61,100,000	445	616	14
Ghana	11,700,000	198	230	53
Gibraltar	33,000	0	0	0
Gilbert Islands	63,000	2	2	0
Greece	9,600,000	42	65	2
Grenada	100,000	10	33	1
Guadeloupe	300,000	23	18	1
Guam	120,000	44	108	1
Guatemala	7,000,000	399	478	51
Guinea	5,000,000	14	11	0
Guinea-Bissau	600,000	8	8	2
Guyana	900,000	28	24	2

Country Name	Population (1979/80 Estimate)	North American Protestant Missionaries 1975	North American Protestant Missionaries 1979	Number People Groups Reported by Agencies
Haiti	5,800,000	325	467	8
Honduras	3,800,000	301	362	4
Hong-Kong	4,800,000	363	362	27
Hungary	10,800,000	0	2	1
Iceland	200,000	2	1	1
India	676,200,000	871	1,433	223
Indonesia	144,300,000	858	1,362	194
Iran	38,500,000	102	57	5
Ireland	3,300,000	55	89	0
Israel	3,900,000	186	207	34
Italy	57,200,000	190	248	7
Ivory Coast	8,000,000	211	265	48
Jamaica	2,200,000	180	121	0
Japan	116,800,000	1,644	1,855	32
Jordan	3,200,000	50	87	3
Kampuchea	6,000,000	6	5	11
Kenya	15,900,000	926	1,307	75
Korea, Dem. P. Rep.	17,900,000	4	0	0
Korea, Rep. of	38,200,000	470	572	7
Kuwait	1,300,000	3	5	0
Lao, People's Dem. R	3,700,000	11	4	11
Latin America-gen.	239,000,000	NA	7	0
Lebanon	3,200,000	164	88	3
Lesotho	1,300,000	28	51	7
Liberia	1,900,000	406	366	56
Libya	3,000,000	2	2	0
Luxembourg	400,000	5	12	0
Macao	300,000	1	10	1
Madagascar	8,700,000	67	50	3

Country Name	Population (1979/80 Estimate)	North American Protestant Missionaries 1975	1979	Number People Groups Reported by Agencies
Malawi	6,100,000	109	140	1
Malaysia	14,000,000	123	223	3
Mali	6,600,000	98	105	6
Malta	300,000	3	0	0
Marshall Is.	25,000	0	4	0
Martinique	300,000	10	15	0
Mauritania	1,600,000	0	0	0
Mauritius	900,000	5	8	3
Mexico	68,200,000	1,232	1,611	207
Micronesia	120,000	NA	2	0
Middle East-general	98,000,000	NA	88	4
Monaco	25,000	25	40	0
Montserrat	13,000	1	2	0
Morocco	21,000,000	59	41	3
Mozambique	10,300,000	61	11	1
Namibia	1,000,000	8	15	2
Nepal	14,000,000	111	113	15
Netherlands	14,100,000	151	124	6
Netherlands Antilles	300,000	106	112	1
New Caledonia	123,000	2	4	0
New Zealand	3,200,000	82	67	0
Nicaragua	2,600,000	114	102	4
Niger	5,500,000	136	123	10
Nigeria	77,100,000	802	715	84
Norway	4,100,000	26	23	1
Oceania-general	23,000,000	NA	5	0
Oman	900,000	12	12	0
Pacific Trust Terr.	111,000	42	44	3

Country Name	Population (1979/80 Estimate)	North American Protestant Missionaries 1975	North American Protestant Missionaries 1979	Number People Groups Reported by Agencies
Pakistan	86,500,000	220	314	22
Panama	35,500,000	3	204	14
Papua New Guinea	3,200,000	593	790	164
Paraguay	3,300,000	322	206	3
Peru	17,600,000	579	548	57
Philippines	47,700,000	1,159	1,775	172
Pitcairn Islands	70	NA	2	0
Poland	35,500,000	10	20	2
Portugal	9,900,000	53	109	5
Puerto Rico	3,500,000	266	274	0
Reunion	500,000	2	4	3
Romania	22,300,000	0	1	1
Rwanda	5,100,000	39	44	2
Samoa	200,000	11	8	0
Saudi Arabia	8,200,000	4	3	0
Senegal	5,700,000	71	143	9
Seychelles	100,000	0	6	0
Sierra Leone	3,500,000	144	137	83
Singapore	2,400,000	140	179	1
Solomon Is.	200,000	NA	18	12
Somalia	3,600,000	12	0	0
South Africa	28,400,000	595	588	30
Spain	37,800,000	228	346	20
Sri Lanka	14,800,000	34	67	10
St. Kitts-Nevis	52,000	2	2	0
St. Lucia	100,000	13	29	1
St. Vincent	98,000	6	19	1
Sudan	18,700,000	47	136	19
Surinam	400,000	75	79	23

Country Name	Population (1979/80 Estimate)	North American Protestant Missionaries 1975	1979	Number People Groups Reported by Agencies
Swaziland	600,000	149	217	6
Sweden	8,300,000	34	55	1
Switzerland	6,300,000	79	70	2
Syria	8,600,000	0	0	0
Taiwan Rep of China	17,800,000	596	691	26
Tanzania	18,600,000	307	263	4
Thailand	47,300,000	428	637	24
Togo	2,500,000	51	79	7
Tonga	90,100	2	5	0
Transkei	2,900,000	NA	12	6
Trinidad and Tobago	1,200,000	122	66	4
Tunisia	6,500,000	15	13	1
Turkey	45,500,000	52	66	5
Turks and Caicos Is.	6,000	0	0	0
U.S. Virgin Is.	107,000	29	46	0
Uganda	13,700,000	28	44	1
United Arab Emirates	800,000	20	42	4
United Kingdom	55,800,000	170	504	11
Upper Volta	6,900,000	81	132	13
Uruguay	2,900,000	119	116	2
USSR	266,000,000	4	3	0
Vanuatu	109,000	NA	4	0
Venezuela	13,900,000	457	596	3
Viet Nam, Soc. Rep.	53,300,000	67	1	11
Yemen Arab Republic	5,600,000	18	25	1
Yugoslavia	22,400,000	0	26	2
Zaire	29,300,000	817	715	25
Zambia	5,800,000	427	382	3
Zimbabwe	7,400,000	533	276	30

TOTAL NUMBER MISSIONARIES REPORTED BY LOCATION: 34,764

Overseas Agencies

Agency Types

A basic distinction in types of mission agencies can be made between those which send personnel overseas and those which do not
(often categorized as "specialized service"). This is not a hard-
and-fast distinction since some service agencies have persons on
overseas assignment, but it is one way of distinguishing types of
mission agencies. A glance through the **Directory of Agencies** will
also suggest the many types of organizations and the varied ways
that missionaries are sent and supported. To say that a person is
a "missionary" with a certain agency reveals little until the
agency is better described. Some agencies concentrate their efforts geographically or functionally; others are widely diversi-
fied. There are independent missionaries who have no affiliation
with any organization. Some agencies are little more than groups
of people who have loosely banded together to carry out a particular ministry. Still others have formalized organizations with
constitutions, by-laws, a statement of faith and a board of di-
rectors. Some have developed large organizational structures and
support staffs, while others are little more than an individual
ministry.

In listing missionary agencies, a major area in which data is
lacking relates to independent missionaries associated with groups
such as the Brethren Assemblies ("Plymouth Brethren") and the
Churches of Christ, who go as individuals or are sent from local
congregations. Centralized statistics are not generally available
and must be determined from prayer lists and calendars and from
service bureaus. Directory listings for groups such as these are
produced by MARC in standard form for convenience and do not represent actual agencies. In addition, there are some independent
missionaries who are totally unaffiliated with any agency, though
they may be responsible to local congregations, who are therefore
not shown in any way in these statistics for this **Handbook**. Their
numbers are estimated to be relatively few.

Total Agencies

Survey questionnaires were sent to about 900 agencies in North
America. Some of the responses were discarded because the agency
had no related work outside of North America. Where no survey response was received, other sources (including agency publications
and telephone contacts) were used to obtain information. Thirty-
two agencies listed in the Eleventh Edition were dropped for lack
of data. The resulting total of agencies listed probably represents over 95 percent of the existing North American Protestant
agencies having overseas ministries. Of these, 645 have U.S. offices while 69 report a Canadian address. Agencies whose head-

quarters address is not in North America are listed in the **Indices to Agencies** as international organizations.

This total compares with 584 agencies listed in the Tenth Edition (of which 570 had information entries) and 620 from the Eleventh. In the research for the current edition, 96 agencies were located which had been in existence in earlier years but, for one reason or another, had not been previously reported. Of these, 21 are Canadian agencies listed for the first time as separate entities. In previous editions the information for these agencies was included in data reported for related U.S. organizations. The number of new agencies listed for the first time for which information has never been reported is actually 75. 73 agencies, listed in the Eleventh Edition, have merged or have changed their names. No data is shown for 18 entries, but the listings are included because they were shown in the Eleventh Edition and the present entry indicates the last known status of the agency. This "final" listing permits the researcher to follow an agency through several editions of this book without encountering an unexplained "disappearance." Of the listings with data, 33 do not have current information, i.e., the data had to be taken from sources other than the questionnaire or other current source. This leaves 663 agencies listed with current information. These agencies still represent the overwhelming bulk of the personnel, funds and effort of the North American Protestant overseas endeavor.

New Agencies

Based upon replies received, 47 agencies have come into existence since the Eleventh Edition. Most of these are small specialized service agencies. In historical perspective, from 1890 until 1940, missionary agencies were founded at a rate of 25 to 50 per decade. The real impetus to establishing Protestant missionary organizations from North America came after World War II with over 125 being formed during the 1950s. The rate of founding per decade slowed very slightly as more than 110 agencies were established in the 1960s. The increase in agencies founded (123) in the '70s approached the peak figure (127) of the 1950s.

During the '70s, 67 agencies apparently ceased operations. The accompanying table shows the number of agencies founded per decade in this century (based on those agencies which have currently and previously reported a date of founding).

NUMBER OF AGENCIES FOUNDED PER DECADE

Decade of Founding	# Agencies Founded
1970 - 1979	123
1960 - 1969	112
1950 - 1959	127
1940 - 1949	88
1930 - 1939	50
1920 - 1929	45
1910 - 1919	29
1900 - 1909	26
1890 - 1899	27
1880 - 1889	22
Pre 1880	45

AGENCIES NEW TO TWELFTH EDITION, FOUNDED PRIOR TO 1976

Agency Name	Date Begun	Career	Short-Term	Total Income
ACTS International	1972	1	0	230,000
Air Crusade, Inc.	1958	0	5	54,413
American Missionary Fellowship	1817	4	21	2,675,000
Arthur Bradford Evangelistic Association	1968	0	0	78,000
Association of Free Lutheran Congregations	1962	9	4	218,880
Bible Alliance Mission, Inc.	1975	1	0	99,410
Bible Club Movement of Canada	1944	2	0	326,344
Bible Research International	1974	NR	0	10,000
Bibles for the Nations	1974	0	NR	NA
Border Missions	1950	4	100	88,000
Chinese Overseas Christian Mission, Inc.	0	0	0	NR
Christ's Mission	1883	4	19	243,000
Christian Broadcasting Network	1960	15	0	56,500,000
Christian Business Men's Committee International (Canada)	1973	NR	0	NR
Christian Life Missions	1956	0	0	15,624
Christian Literature Crusade (Ontario) Inc.	1941	4	0	34,215
Christian Literature International	1967	0	0	NR
Christian Nationals' Evangelism Commission, Inc. (Canada)	1943	4	0	312,417
Christian Transportation	1930	0	0	73,000
Christian World Publishers, Inc.	1974	2	1	55,700
Compassion of Canada	1964	0	0	1,360,228
Compassion Relief and Development, Inc.	1972	12	2	682,469
Crusade Evangelism International	1960	0	0	522,000
Emmanuel International	1975	24	22	508,353
Episcopal Church Missionary Community	1974	0	0	30,000
Erhlin Christian Polio Evangelical Alliance Mission of Canada, Inc.	1890	100	7	1,089,767
Evangelical Leadership International	1975	0	0	NR
Evangelical Missions Council of Good News	1974	0	0	50,000
Evangelical Scripture Mission	1923	0	0	44,200
Evangelical Tract Distributors (Canada)	1935	0	0	500,000
Fellowship of Artists For Cultural Evangelism (FACE)	1973	0	0	16,500
Foundation For His Ministry - Orphanage Committee	1967	26	12	192,219

Agency Name	Date Begun	Career	Short-Term	Total Income
Globe Missionary Evangelism	1973	44	30	383,630
Gospel Crusade World Wide Mission Outreach	1953	13	4	200,000
Gospel Outreach	1971	34	0	3,000,000
Harvest Fields Missionary and Evangelistic Association, Inc.	1949	11	0	NA
Harvesters International Mission, Inc.	0	0	0	NA
Heritage Village Church and Missionary Fellowship, Inc.	1973	0	0	51,000,000
Houses of Refuge, Int'l. Orphanages Assn., Inc.	1968	12	2	50,000
India National Inland Mission	1964	0	0	180,000
Inter-Varsity Christian Fellowship of Canada	1929	0	0	1,740,000
International Bible Translators	1972	0	0	NR
International Board of Jewish Missions, Inc.	1940	30	0	660,000
International Christian Leprosy Mission, Inc. (Canada)	1943	0	0	13,070
International Christian Mission	1940	0	0	NA
International Church Relief Fund, Inc.	1975	0	0	629,785
International Messianic Outreach	1974	NR	0	91,000
International Missionary Advance	1975	2	0	70,000
International Needs-USA	1975	0	0	300,000
International Prison Ministry	1970	0	1	NA
Japan Evangelistic Association, Inc.	1959	4	0	98,000
Japan Evangelistic Band (Canada)	1903	3	0	4,780
Jewish Voice Broadcast	1967	NR	5	NR
Jews For Jesus	1973	0	25	2,435,000
Leprosy Relief, Canada, Inc.	1961	0	0	1,511,640
Liebenzell Mission of Canada	1966	NR	0	18,500
Ling A. Juane Ministries, Inc.	1975	2	0	25,00
Logos Translators	1971	2	NR	28,000
Lutheran Frontier Missions	1972	11	0	150,000
Mailbox Club, The	1965	0	2	107,155
Mexican Christian Mission, Inc.	1956	3	0	150,000
Mission Aviation Fellowship of Canada	1972	12	1	300,000
Mission Possible Foundation, Inc.	1974	2	0	137,000

Agency Name	Date Begun	Career	Short-Term	Total Income
Mission Renewal Team, Inc.	1974	0	0	7,545
Mission to Japan, Inc.	1950	2	0	44,000
Missionary Leasing Company	1948	0	0	1,950
Movimiento Misionero Mundial, Inc.	1964	300	0	80,000
Navigators of Canada International, The	1968	3	1	467,196
New Tribes Mission of Canada	1968	148	2	821,888
Open Bible Ministries, Inc.	1971	3	0	30,000
Open Door Missionary Fellowship, Inc.	1952	NR	1	NR
Operation Mobilization Canada	1957	56	25	255,000
Overcomer Press, Inc.	1963	0	0	24,000
Overseas Missionary Fellowship	1865	96	11	684,004
Paul Carlson Medical Program, Inc.	1966	13	3	201,381
Pioneer Bible Translators	1974	14	0	28,983
Project Partner with Christ, Inc.	1968	8	NR	597,510
Protestant Reformed Churches in America	1926	NR	2	40,000
REAP International	1973	0	0	175,000
Release the World for Christ	1966	NR	NR	100,000
Samaritan's Purse	1969	1	NR	390,000
Society of Central Asian News (SCAN)	1974	0	0	500
South Pacific Evangelical Fellowship	1951	5	0	50,004
Sudanese Missionary Fellowship	1969	2	0	18,108
Tele-Missions International, Inc.	1954	5	0	126,702
Underground Christian Missions, Inc.	1973	0	0	NR
Vacation Samaritans	1967	20	325	200,000
Voice of Calvary	1960	0	0	555,040
Western Tract Mission	1941	0	0	158,693
World Mission Information Bank	1973	0	0	NR
World Mission Prayer League Canada	1969	12	0	61,245
World Neighbors, Inc.	1951	14	6	2,000,000
World Vision, Incorporated	1950	NR	NR	46,681,140
Worldwide Discipleship Association, Inc.	1974	0	0	640,000
Youth for Christ (Canada)	1971	12	0	7,000,000

GRAND TOTAL OF MISSIONARIES
FROM ALL AGENCIES PREVIOUSLY OVERLOOKED: 1,112
GRAND TOTAL OF SHORT-TERMERS OVERLOOKED: 639

AGENCIES FOUNDED SINCE 1975

Agency Name	Date Begun	Career	Short-Term	Total Income
African Bible Colleges, Inc.	1976	6	1	172,710
African Mission Services, Inc.	1979	0	0	50,000
Alberto Mottesi Evangelistic Association, Inc.	1977	0	0	NA
All Peoples Baptist Mission	1980	10	0	107,000
Calcutta Mission of Mercy	1977	1	0	845,000
Children of India Foundation	1977	0	0	31,168
Chinese World Mission Center	1979	0	0	65,000
Christian and Missionary Alliance in Canada	1980	110	NR	2,420,000
Christian INFO	1979	0	0	16,795
Christian Translation Ministries	1977	0	0	16,476
Correll Missionary Ministries	1978	0	0	31,336
Evangel Bible Translators	1976	9	3	199,000
Evangelical Friends Mission	1978	4	0	74,370
Evangelism Resources	1976	2	0	49,387
Faith Christian Fellowship World Outreach	1978	0	17	750,000
Faith Ministries	1979	0	0	NR
Frontier Ministries International	1979	2	NR	22,000
Gospel Outreach to India, Inc.	1976	0	0	6,151
Haggai Community	1977	0	0	1,300
Helps International Ministries, Inc.	1976	0	0	46,303
Institute of Chinese Studies	1977	0	0	4,389
International Everlasting Gospel Mission, Inc.	1978	2	0	20,000
International Fellowship of Christians	1978	3	NR	66,000
Jesus Evangelism	1976	0	0	10,000
Latin America Assistance	1976	1	NR	22,000
Life For Latins, Inc.	1977	2	0	39,000
Living Waters	1979	0	0	NA
Luis Palau Evangelistic Team, Inc.	1978	5	0	1,150,000
Lutherans For World Evangelization	1979	0	0	300
Middle East Media	1976	6	0	35,636
Mission SOS	1976	5	0	110,000
Mission Training and Resource Center	1979	0	0	250,000

Agency Name	Date Begun	Career	Short-Term	Total Income
Missionary Auto-Truck Service	1978	0	0	NR
Missionary Communications, Inc.	1979	0	0	18,818
Missions Outreach, Inc.	1976	0	294	335,658
Outreach International	1977	2	0	56,321
Petra International, Inc.	1977	8	0	15,000
Project Partner, Inc.	1976	0	NR	NR
REACH, Incorporated	1976	3	1	NR
Samuel Zwemer Institute	1979	0	0	39,718
Team Ventures International	1979	0	28	191,280
Technical Support Mission	1979	2	1	50,000
Today's Mission Incorporated	1980	0	0	169,200
United States Center for World Mission	1976	0	5	850,000
W. Shabaz Associates, Inc.	1977	0	0	NR
World Hope Foundation	1976	2	100	150,000
World Medical Mission	1977	0	30	116,000

GRAND TOTAL OF MISSIONARIES
FROM ALL AGENCIES NEW IN REPORT PERIOD: 185
GRAND TOTAL OF SHORT-TERMERS: 480

The increasing complexity of the modern world has encouraged spe-
cialization among organizations, including mission agencies. The
demands of broadcasting, literature production, language analysis
and transportation (to name only a few) have brought into being
agencies that have a specialized ministry in such areas.

Founding Date

Of the existing overseas agencies, 29 report being founded prior
to 1860, the oldest being the New York Bible Society founded in
1809.   The first overseas sending agency still in existence was
founded in 1810, what is now the United Church Board for World
Ministries of the United Church of Christ. Of the 451 **sending**
agencies who also reported a date of founding, 65 percent have
been founded since 1940; 34 percent have been founded since 1960.
Nearly half of the total missionary force belongs to missions that
have been founded since 1921.

Although there were specialized agencies, such as New York Bible
Society, which were founded prior to 1900, only 8 such **existing**
agencies show founding dates before 1900.

Although not a complete historical record, the figures below show
the existing number of sending and non-sending agencies founded in
20 year intervals. The fact that there is an increase in the number of non-sending agencies accompanied by a proportionate decrease in sending agencies may reflect the growing complexity of
the overseas missions task.   For example, of the new agencies
founded since 1975, nearly 60 percent have no career personnel
overseas.

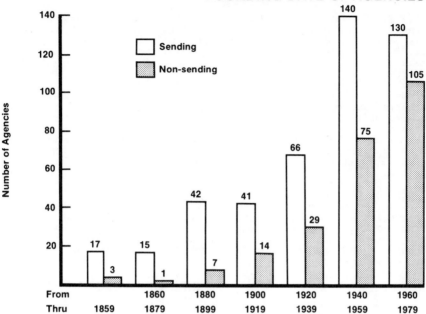

FOUNDING DATE OF AGENCIES

Number of Agencies

- ☐ Sending
- ▨ Non-sending

From		1860	1880	1900	1920	1940	1960
Thru	1859	1879	1899	1919	1939	1959	1979

Sending: 17, 15, 42, 41, 66, 140, 130
Non-sending: 3, 1, 7, 14, 29, 75, 105

451 Sending Agencies Reporting Founding Date
234 Non-sending Agencies Reporting Founding Date
TOTAL   685 agencies report founding date
TOTAL   29 agencies do not report founding date

The statistics reported for agency personnel in this book reflect the number of persons ("missionaries") serving overseas. However, this number does not represent the total staff of any one agency. Most agencies are usually larger in numbers of people employed because of additional persons who are classified as serving in the "home" office, serving as home missionaries (in the U.S. or Canada), persons under appointment who have not yet received their assignments or full support, and non-North American personnel who may be serving with the agency. For example, the Navigators are listed as having 145 overseas personnel. However, they report more than 1,548 full-time international staff members. Many of these are involved in ministries within North America, and 41 candidates who are ready to assume responsibilities overseas. Over 555 other staff members are non-North Americans, most of whom are nationals serving within their own countries. The statistics for staff members working strictly in North America's ministries, candidates and non-North America staff are not included in overseas personnel total. Wycliffe Bible Translators is a large international agency which reports 2,447 personnel, of whom approximately 27 percent are not from North America and therefore not included in this **Handbook's** statistics.

The total number of home staff reported by all agencies in North America was 7,034.

Agency Size

This year's survey shows that the bulk of existing missions continues to be comprised of many small agencies. Of the agencies listed in this directory, 457 reported that they had any overseas staff. Of these, 430 reported a specific number of career overseas personnel, 263, or 61 percent, listing from 1 to 25 people overseas. Only 18 percent of these agencies had more than 100 people overseas. These percentages, when compared with the previous survey, indicate very little change in the distribution of agencies according to size. There appears to be a trend toward a few agencies having larger numbers of missionaries. Supporting this trend the top ten agencies in numbers of any overseas personnel account for 23,472 people or 44 percent of the total missionary force reported. In the Eleventh Edition the top ten agencies represented 35 percent of the total missionary force reported.

Fifty percent of all personnel are in only 15 agencies. The ten largest agencies in reported income account for $462.78 million or 33 percent of the total income reported. This does not vary at all from the 33 percent of the total income reported for the top ten in the Eleventh Edition, though the total income has more than doubled. Only 25 agencies accounted for 50 percent of the reported income.

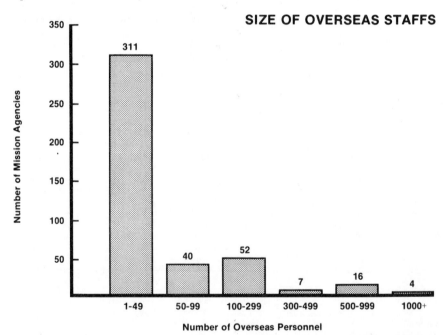

The difference in ranking by personnel and by income in the tables that follow is caused by the presence of several large service missions with large income but small overseas staff. The lists show the largest agencies by numbers of overseas personnel and by reported income for overseas ministries.

TWENTY-FIVE LARGEST AGENCIES IN REPORTED OVERSEAS PERSONNEL

Agency	1972	1975	1979	Additional Short-Term Personnel 1979
Southern Baptist Convention, Foreign Mission Board	2,507	2,667	2,906	2,866
Wycliffe Bible Translators International, Inc.	2,200	2,693	1,781	466
New Tribes Mission	701	864	1,385	30
Assemblies of God, Division of Foreign Missions	967	1,091	1,214	170
General Conference of Seventh-Day Adventists	1,546	1,360	996	111
United Methodist Church World Division Board Global Min.	951	788	938	166
Evangelical Alliance Mission, The (TEAM)	992	892	905	197
Youth With A Mission	1,009	1,190	887	5,000
Christian and Missionary Alliance	803	790	809	9
Christian Churches/Churches of Christ	1,623	1,296	699	NR
United Methodist Church Commission on Relief	100	133	650	985
Baptist Bible Fellowship International	379	458	630	0
Baptist Mid-Missions	511	905	608	14
Baptist International Mission, Inc.	334	471	596	0
Sudan Interior Mission, Inc.	818	699	590	28
Brethren Assemblies	538	547	554	0
Africa Inland Mission	514	491	511	65
Association of Baptists for World Evangelism, Inc.	351	337	502	18
Conservative Baptist Foreign Mission Society	491	485	501	114
Campus Crusade For Christ, International (Overseas Dept.)	114	217	500	77
Church of the Nazarene, General Board Dept. of World Msns.	495	462	484	70
Mennonite Central Committee	454	433	431	0
Gospel Missionary Union	288	406	389	17
United Presbyterian Church in the USA Program Agency	604	438	359	20
American Lutheran Church Division for World Missions	393	318	329	18

TWENTY-FIVE LARGEST AGENCIES IN REPORTED INCOME
(IN MILLIONS OF DOLLARS)

Agency	1973	1975	1979
Southern Baptist Convention, Foreign Mission Board	35.4	46.8	62.4
General Conference of Seventh-day Adventists	29.1	25.0	60.0
Church World Service Division of DOM-NCCCUSA	10.6	23.5T	41.2
Christian Churches/ Churches of Christ	NR	NR	40.0
World Vision International	7.4	7.9	34.8
Assemblies of God, Division of Foreign Missions	12.4	20.9	29.9
World Vision, Incorporated	NL	NL	29.0
Wycliffe Bible Translators International, Inc.	10.7T	16.9T	19.9
United Methodist Church World Division of the Board of Global Ministries	20.4	15.4	18.8
Gideons International	2.6	6.0	15.0
Church of the Nazarene, General Board Department of World Missions	5.0	11.0	15.0
Christian and Missionary Alliance	5.6	7.4	13.3
Campus Crusade for Christ, International (Overseas Department)	2.0	5.7	12.5
United Methodist Church United Methodist Committee on Relief	3.0	7.5	12.1
Compasion International, Inc.	1.6	3.0	11.1
Sudan Interior Mission, Inc.	5.0	8.5	11.1
Evangelical Alliance Mission (TEAM)	5.9	8.1	10.9
Evangelism Center, Inc.	1.8T	4.2	10.8
World Literature Crusade	2.0	9.2T	9.8
United Church Board for World Ministries	4.4	6.3	9.5
Lutheran World Relief, Inc.	2.4	4.5T	9.4
Conservative Baptist Foreign Mission Society	3.8	2.0	9.1
American Baptist Churches in the U.S.A., International Ministries	4.2T	4.6	8.1
American Bible Society	4.1	5.6	8.0
Mennonite Central Committee	1.9	4.9	7.8

T - Total Income for all Ministries

Changes in the size of the overseas staff for any given agency are often the result of one or more specific factors. Reductions may either be forced by a reduced income to the agency or may be a voluntary or planned effort to "lower the profile" on North American personnel while giving more ministry responsibility to indigenous Christians. Increases in overseas staff reported by other agencies are usually the result of expanded ministries and the openings of new fields of service, often themselves the result of increased income.

Average agency size can sometimes be a helpful statistic. Utilizing data only from the 430 agencies that reported a specific number of career overseas personnel, the mean (arithmetic average) size of the overseas staff of sending agencies is 83 people, or seven fewer than was previously reported in the Eleventh Edition. The median (midpoint) average staff is 14 people, down 7 people from that reported in the Eleventh Edition. In other words, of the 430 agencies reporting overseas staff, half (215) had 14 or fewer personnel. The large differences in the means and medians is the result of many agencies with small staffs and a few agencies with very large staffs.

Agencies No Longer Reported

33 agencies were listed for the last time in the Eleventh Edition and do not appear in the Twelfth. They are listed for the convenience of the researcher.

Agency	Reason No Longer Listed
Arabic Radio Mission, Inc.	No longer exists
Associated Gospel Churches	No overseas ministries
Association for the Final Advance of Scripture Translation (FAST)	No data since 1973
Bible Conferences and Mission, Inc.	No overseas ministries
Central Africa Broadcasting Co., Inc.	No overseas ministries
China Graduate School of Theology	No longer has operations in U.S.
Christian Outreach	No overseas ministries
Christian Reformed Church, Board of Home Missions	No data since 1973
Co-Laborers Do Brazil	No longer based in N. America
Evangelical Committee on Latin America	No longer exists
Evangelical Fellowship of Canada, Foreign Mission Commission	No overseas ministries
Evangelical International Schools, Inc.	No new information
Fellowship Foundation	Ministries no longer applicable
Fellowship of World Christians	No longer exists
Filipino Assemblies of the First Born, Inc.	No longer exists
Go Tell Communications, International	No longer based in N. America
Independent Bible Baptist Mission	No longer exists
Interlink	Ministries no longer applicable
Foundation for Theological Education in Southeast Asia	Not a mission agency
Israel's Hope, Inc.	No overseas ministries
Japan Rural Evangelism Fellowship	No data since 1973
Mission Possible of Albion, Inc.	No longer exists
Mission to Asia	No longer exists
Partnership in Mission	No longer exists
Lutheran Council in the U.S.A., Division of Mission and Ministry	No longer based in N. America

Agency	Reason No Longer Listed
Messianic Jewish Alliance of America	No longer exists
Missionary Literature Foundation	No data since 1973
Missionary Orientation Center	No data since 1973
Protestant Episcopal Church, Order of St. Helena	Not a mission agency
Southern Baptist Convention Baptist Home Mission Board	No overseas agencies
World Bible Translation Center	No longer exists
World Military Missions Crusade	No data since 1973
World Missionary Christian's Fellowship	No data since 1973
World-Wide Missionary, Inc.	No longer based in N. America
United Communications Mission, Inc.	No data since 1973

Analysis of Mission Finance

The agency listings in this **Handbook** report the income given to each agency or board from all sources. The amount of this income that was used for "overseas expenditures" is also indicated. However, these two figures can be very misleading, and those concerned with good stewardship may wish to obtain more detailed data before making an evaluation of an agency's situation or performance based upon these numbers.

Types of Agency Income

Agencies receive two types of funds, restricted and unrestricted. The restricted funds are those which are given for a specific purpose. This purpose may have been suggested by the agency, as in the case of an appeal for a particular need. Or they may have been restricted by the donor, for instance in bequest for an endowment.

Unrestricted funds are those which the agency can allocate with complete discretion. It is important to note, therefore, that because of this distinction, an agency may not have complete freedom to allocate all its resources. Too, it may necessitate the accumulation of reserves for projects that have been initiated but are not yet completed, or have been approved but are not yet started.

How the Funds Are Used

Every agency is involved in three basic operations. The first is the acquisition of resources for the ministry. The second is the conversion of those resources for the purpose of the ministry. The third is the carrying out of the ministry itself.

During recent years the cost of acquiring funds for the ministry (fund raising) has been a cause of considerable discussion by the press, consumer advocate groups and government agencies. As a consequence, most agencies are now moving to a reporting system which discriminates between the cost of fund raising and the cost of administration. Following our data collection the new Evangelical Council for Financial Accountability was formed. A list of its founding members shows 25 agencies listed in this directory.

The cost of fund raising varies tremendously and many times is a function of the type of ministry in which the agency is involved. For example, those involved in raising funds for hospitals within the United States feel that 30 to 35 percent of the amount received is a reasonable cost for fund raising. Interestingly, many consumer action groups consider this same figure as being reasonable for **their** fund raising. Most Christian agencies feel that somewhere between 15 and 25 percent is reasonable. However, circumstances have an impact on the cost of fund raising. One of the lower-cost methods of fund raising is the use of direct mail, by which the individual is asked to respond to a need presented to him in a general mailing. Individuals are more likely to respond to more emotional appeals, such as relief for earthquake victims, than they might be for the support of a program of evangelism or a Christian research program. In general, the more emotional the appeal of the need that is being met, the lower will be the cost of fund raising.

The second major expense that faces the agency is that of administration or operation. It costs money just to "stay in business." The salaries of executives, accountants, public relations personnel, etc., are all needed and are a very real expense. Unfortunately, there has not been any open discussion on what is a reasonable administrative expense. Suffice it to say that before a ministry can be carried out on a continuous basis, there must be a cost of fund raising and there must be an ongoing cost of administration.

Finally we come to the dollars that are actually spent on the ministry. But here again we need to be cautious. For instance, in the agency listing in this directory is the heading "For Overseas Ministries." The intention of this question was to ascertain the amount of funds that were sent overseas. But this is **not** the total cost of "ministry." To give an example, suppose a tractor is to be purchased and sent to an agricultural program. The funds for the tractor will actually be expended within North America. The amount spent "for overseas ministries" may involve only the delivery. But it becomes even more complicated than that. More and more thoughtful administrators are realizing that it is **effectiveness** of how money is used rather than the amount of money that is important. To send a missionary couple as evangelists in a pioneer situation and to give them only their own personal living allowance would be less-than-effective expenditure of funds. To their living support must be added the additional cost of carrying out the work on the field. If the so-called "work funds" are not provided, then what appeared to be a very low-cost operation may also be a very ineffective one.

In making any analysis of agency income and expenditures, we need to take into account the type and location of the ministry being carried on. The cost of living in urban areas normally far exceeds that of rural areas. Thus the cost of an urban ministry in many countries may be two to six times greater than the cost of a rural ministry.

Problems of Reporting

There are a number of problems in reporting income which should be recognized. Different agencies have different fiscal years. Thus, year-to-year comparisons are not always valid. Totals calculated before 1979 do not take into account such variations.

Some agencies, such as Campus Crusade for Christ or the Billy Graham Evangelistic Association, have overseas ministries which are a small portion of their total income. Many such agencies do not keep separate accounts for income raised specifically for use overseas and income raised for use within North America. Therefore, most of these agencies can only give approximate numbers.

Some agencies include in their income only those funds which are specifically designated for overseas. However, they may have other sources of income which they do not report and no accounting has been made of the differences.

Finally, some agencies make it a practice not to publish their income. This is not necessarily because they have something to hide. More often it has been a result of seeing their published figures distorted. Where an agency was either unable or unwilling to report its 1979 income, an attempt was made to estimate the agency's income. Whenever this has been done, a note to that effect appears after the listing in the directory.

Conclusions reached in this **Handbook** related to financial totals must be seen as suggesting order of magnitude rather than as being precise, **and direct comparisons may be invalid between agencies** unless the reporting bases in the ministries are comparable.

Totals

North American Protestant ministering agencies **reported** a 1979 total income from North America for overseas ministries of $1,139.6 million. The total does not include the value of "gifts-in-kind" (donated goods, products and materials), most of which were sent overseas. To this reported figure were added $8.6 million of estimated income. The resulting overall total income for 1979 was $1,148.2 million. While the growth to over one billion dollars in total income is highly significant, even more significant is that the apparent three year growth of 75 percent indicates real growth of 13.7 percent when corrected for inflation by reference to 1967 dollars Canadian agencies reported a combined total income of $49.8 million while U.S. agencies reported $1,098.4 million.

The estimates were made by referring to the number of reported missionaries and multiplying by an estimated annual income per missionary or per couple. This income was variable depending upon the nature of the agency. For non-sending agencies conservative estimates were based on data from previous directories, information from other publications, and knowledge of the nature of the ministries involved. Where it was felt that such an estimate would be misleading, none was made. Thus the estimated total should be a conservative figure.

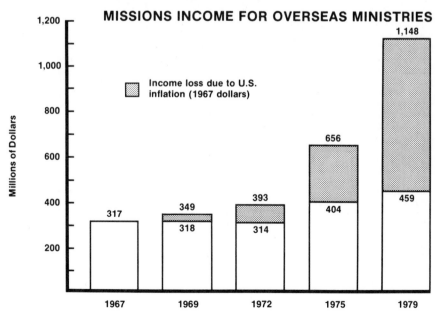

MISSIONS INCOME FOR OVERSEAS MINISTRIES

Millions of Dollars

Income loss due to U.S. inflation (1967 dollars)

1,200 — 1,148

1967: 317
1969: 349 / 318
1972: 393 / 314
1975: 656 / 404
1979: 1,148 / 459

When missions income is compared to church income within the
United States, a more positive picture appears. The graph below
shows the North American missions income as percentage of North
American church income. These two numbers are not necessarily related since a great deal of the mission income is collected outside of normal church channels, but the comparison does indicate
the interest of the North American population in supporting overseas ministries.

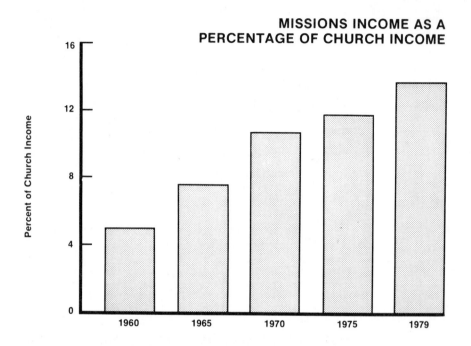

**MISSIONS INCOME AS A
PERCENTAGE OF CHURCH INCOME**

On the other side of the income coin is the change in the buying
power of the dollar in overseas markets. This has been exempli-
fied by a considerable rise in the cost of living in many foreign
countries. Although the mix of ministries makes individual comparisons invalid, the total average expenditure per missionary
gives some indication of the rapidly rising cost of carrying out
ministries overseas. The 1972 total income of $393 million sup-
ported 35,970 overseas missionary personnel along with their accompanying programs, for an average of $10,926 per person. In
1975 a total of $656 million supported 37,056 overseas personnel
and their accompanying programs for an average of $17,703 per per-
son. In 1979 a total of 1,148.2 million supported 53,494 for an
average of $21,464 per person.

Of the 599 agencies which reported income for overseas ministries,
the range of income was from $85.00 to $71 million. The average
income in 1979 was $1.9 million while the median was $250,000. In
other words, half of the reporting mission agencies showed income
for overseas ministries for 1979 of $250,000 or less. These av-
erages compare with the 1975 average of $1.2 million and a median
of $125,000, and the 1972 average of $1.2 million and a median of
$158,000.

Retirement Programs

A total of 164 agencies answered Question #25 as to whether they
had a retirement program. They reported a combined total of 3,546
missionaries supported under retirement programs. Not reported in
this directory are the large number of retirement facilities that
are operated by the larger agencies.

Support Patterns

Overseas personnel receive their personal support in a wide variety of patterns. Most of the major agencies which are related to
denominations undertake the provision for missionary salaries and
the missionary is only indirectly involved in how or from where
those (their) funds are derived. At the other end of the scale are
missionaries who are completely responsible for raising their own
support. In some agencies one of the first tasks of a missionary
is to make known his support needs to friends or churches and his
ability to accept his assignment is dependent upon whether such
support is raised.

Question #40 asks the question "Are your overseas personnel primarily responsible for raising their own personal support funds?"
Of the 455 agencies responding to this question, 401, or 88 percent, indicated that the individuals were responsible for raising
their own support.

Personnel support is only part of the total amount of funding
needed, however. In addition, funds are needed to support projects which are being implemented, such as evangelism, agriculture,
or community development.

The variations between countries and associations are shown in the
table below.

SUPPORT PATTERNS

	Number of Agencies Reporting	Number of Agencies with Personnel Raising Own Support
U.S.	408	357
EFMA	73	60
IFMA	35	34
DOM	19	11
Unaffiliated	284	249
Other	6	3
Canada	47	44
EFMA	4	3
IFMA	9	9
Unaffiliated	33	31
Other	1	1

Types of Ministries

Distribution of Personnel by Purpose

It is possible to categorize the many different ministries that are carried out by North Americans overseas into three broad categories which relate to their purpose. First are those who go as "pioneer" missionaries, to plant or establish new churches among unreached or hidden peoples for whom no culturally appropriate congregation exists at any reasonable social distance. Second are those who go to support the work of existing national churches. Third are those who carry out a host of other ministries. Question #30 asked the agency to estimate the number of its overseas personnel involved in establishing new churches (including evangelism), nurturing and developing existing churches or serving in other types of ministries. The results of responses to this question are shown in the table below.

DISTRIBUTION OF PERSONNEL BY PURPOSE

Agencies Involved	Planting Churches	Nurturing Churches	Other
All agencies	30%	39%	32%
Canada	19%	37%	44%
United States	30%	39%	31%
Nonassociated	33%	42%	24%
Division of Overseas Ministries	12%	30%	58%
Evangelical Foreign Missions Association	25%	34%	41%
Interdenominational Foreign Mission Association	28%	34%	38%

Thus we see that approximately 30 percent of all overseas personnel are considered to be involved in attempting to communicate the gospel to non-Christians, another 40 percent are involved in supporting existing churches, while the remainder are involved in a wide variety of other ministries. When one considers the large number of support systems that are required to undergird a church planting missionary, the number of those actually involved in evangelism can be considered high. (The number may be biased considerably by the way spouses were counted; see page 26.)

The wide variation in the number of those establishing churches between the Division of Overseas Ministries of the National Council of Churches (12 percent) and the Interdenominational Foreign Mission Association (28 percent) is not surprising since those associated with DOM are denominational agencies, and since the IFMA includes no denominational agencies (while EFMA does). Still, some differential might have been expected between the EFMA and the IFMA.

64

Functional Ministries

During his time in India, William Carey, the "father" of the modern Protestant missions movement, superintended an indigo factory, translated Scripture, did itinerant evangelism, and gave instruction in Indian languages. Since then missionaries overseas have found themselves engaged in a wide variety of tasks. Indeed, it is important to see that the work of a missionary is varied and not necessarily limited to establishing new churches or "preaching the gospel." The important contribution made by those in enabling ministries cannot be overemphasized. Through the effort of such service missionaries, the efforts of others involved in direct evangelism are made more effective and efficient. In some countries, overt proclamation of the Christian message is forbidden by law-and Christian workers can work only at ministries such as medicine or technical assistance, serving as "silent" witnesses to their faith.

The survey questionnaire listed 53 functions which agencies could indicate as their primary task or tasks officially adopted by the agency and to which they commit substantial resources; 693 agencies responded, with 146, or 21 percent, indicating more than five functional ministries. In the 693 responses, the minimum functional ministries indicated was one. The ten most frequently listed functional ministries comprised approximately 49.6 percent of the total responses received, whereas 51.5 percent of the responses were distributed among the other 44 functional ministries.

FUNCTIONAL ACTIVITIES REPORTED

Functional Ministry	Number of Agencies	Percent 1976	Percent 1979
Church Planting/Establishing	254	6.9	7.7
Evangelism, Personal and Small Group	211	7.6	6.4
Evangelism Mass	190	4.4	5.8
Literature Distribution	185	5.5	5.6
Education, General Christian	162	4.4	5.0
Medicine, Dental and Public Health	138	4.8	4.2
Broadcasting	130	4.4	4.0
Education Theological	125	4.4	3.8
Nurture or Support of National Churches	111	3.3	3.4
Support of Nationals	103	NA	3.2

Grouping the functional ministries in broader generic classifications, the responses received indicate a predominance of organizations involved in education, evangelism, literature, church growth, and service and support, in that order. These data indicate the significance which mission agencies attach to support functions and their effect in indirect evangelism.

Included in the **Indices to Agencies**, the mission agencies are listed by primary task. This listing is not exclusive, in that each agency is listed under each task reported in the agency questionnaire, resulting in multiple listings of agencies. The reader is referred to that section for specific listings.

GENERAL ACTIVITIES REPORTED

General Activity	Number of Agencies	Percent 1976	Percent 1979
Education	612	19	18.7
Evangelism	480	15	14.7
Literature	446	13	13.6
Humanitarian	311	12	9.6
Development	120	NA	3.7
Aid/Relief	101	NA	3.1
Childcare/Adoption	90	NA	2.8
Church Related Function	287	8	8.8
Service and/or Support	261	9	8.0
Media	223	6	6.8
Support of Nationals	216	7	6.6
Medical	156	5	4.8

The **Index to Agencies** lists agencies by function and the reader is encouraged to see for himself how different agencies are involved. Also the agency description given in the alphabetical directory will provide further data.

AGENCIES LISTED BY PRIMARY TASK

Adoption Programs

Bethany Home, Inc.
Holt International
    Children's Services, Inc.
Houses of Refuge, Intl.
    Orphanages Assn. Inc.
Mustard Seed, Inc., The
Victory Mission of the
    Americas

Agricultural Assistance

Advent Christian Gen. Conf.
    of America
Africa Inter-Mennonite
    Mission, Inc.
African Methodist Episcopal
    Church, Inc. Dept. of
    Msns.
African Methodist Episcopal
    Zion Ch., Dept. of Oseas.
    Msns.
Agricultural Missions, Inc.
American Committee for
    KEEP, Inc.
American Lutheran Ch., Div.
    For Wld. Msn.
Baptist Haiti Mission, Inc.
Bethany Home, Inc.
California Yearly Meeting
    of Friends Church, Bd. of
    Msns.
Canadian Baptist Overseas
    Mission Board
Christian Church (Disciples
    of Christ) Div. of Oseas.
    Min.
Christian Pilots
    Association, Inc.
Christian Reformed World
    Relief Committee
CODEL (Coordination in
    Development, Inc.)
Compassion Relief and
    Development, Inc.
Conservative Mennonite
    Board of Missions and
    Charities
FARMS International, Inc.
Food For The Hungry
    International
Food for the Hungry/Canada
Friends of Indonesia
    Fellowship, Inc.
Frontier Ministries
    International
General Conference
    Mennonite Church, Comm.
    on Oseas. Msn.
Good Shepherd Agricultural
    Mission, Inc.
India Christian Mission,

Inc.
International Church Relief
    Fund, Inc.
Kansas Yearly Meeting of
    Friends Africa Gospel
    Mission
Lutheran World Relief,
    Incorporated
Mennonite Central Committee
Mennonite Economic
    Development Associates
Moravian Church in America,
    Bd. of Wld. Msn.
National Baptist
    Convention, U.S.A., Inc.
    For. Msn. Bd.
Oriental Missionary
    Crusade, Inc.
Paul Carlson Medical
    Program, Inc.
Presbyterian Church in the
    U.S.A., Div. of Intl.
    Msn.
Red Sea Mission Team, Inc.,
    U.S.A. Council
Self Help Foundation
United Methodist Church
    Comm. on Relief
United Methodist Ch. Wld.
    Div. of the Bd. of Global
    Min.
Voice of Calvary
Wider Ministries Commission
World Ministries Commission
World Mission Prayer League
    Canada
World Neighbors, Inc.
World Relief Corporation
World Vision of Canada

Aid and/or Relief

Action International
    Ministries
Afghan Border Crusade
African Methodist Episcopal
    Zion Ch., Dept. of Oseas.
    Msns.
American European
    Fellowship Chrn. Oneness
    Evang., Inc.
American Friends Service
    Committee
American Mc All Association
Anchor Bay Evangelistic
    Association
Armenian Missionary
    Association of America,
    Inc.
Baptist Haiti Mission, Inc.
Bible Holiness Movement
Billy Graham Evangelistic
    Association

AGENCIES LISTED BY PRIMARY TASK

Border Missions
Calcutta Mission of Mercy
Children's Haven
  International, Inc.
Christ For The Nations,
  Inc.
Christian Aid Mission
Christian Blind Mission
  International (CBM Intl.)
Christian Life Missions
Christian Medical Society
Christian Pilots
  Association, Inc.
Church of the Nazarene,
  Gen. Bd. Dept. of Wld.
  Msns.
Church World Service
  Division of DOM-NCCCUSA
Compassion International,
  Inc.
Compassion of Canada
Compassion Relief and
  Development, Inc.
Conservative Mennonite
  Board of Missions and
  Charities
Correll Missionary
  Ministries
Defenders of the Christian
  Faith Movement, Inc.
Eastern Mennonite Board of
  Missions and Charities
Emmanuel International
Evangelism Center, Inc.
Evangelism to Communist
  Lands
FARMS International, Inc.
Fellowship of Evangelical
  Baptist Chrs. in Canada
Food For The Hungry
  International
Food for the Hungry/Canada
Friends For Missions, Inc.
Friends of Israel Gospel
  Ministry, Inc.
Friendship Ministry
  International
Global Concern, Inc.
Handclasp International
  Inc.
Heritage Village Church and
  Missionary Fellowship,
  Inc.
Hermano Pablo, Inc.
Holy Land Christian Mission
Houses of Refuge, Intl.
  Orphanages Assn. Inc.
International Church Relief
  Fund, Inc.
International Needs-USA
Jesus to the Communist
  World, Inc.
Leprosy Relief, Canada,

Inc.
Life messengers, Inc.
Lutheran World Federation,
  U.S.A. National Committee
Lutheran World Relief,
  Incorporated
MAP International (Medical
  Assistance Programs)
Mennonite Central Committee
Moravian Church in America,
  Bd. of Wld. Msn.
Mustard Seed, Inc., The
Natl. Assn. of
  Congregational Chr. Chs.
  of the U.S.A.
North American Baptist Gen.
  Msny. Soc., Inc.
Outreach, Inc.
Pan American Missions, Inc.
Project Partner with
  Christ, Inc.
Project Partner, Inc.
Providence Mission Homes,
  Inc.
Reformed Church in America
  General Program Council
Refugee Children, Inc.
Romanian Missionary Society
Samaritan's Purse
Samaritan's Purse
Southern Baptist
  Convention, Foreign
  Mission Board
Teen Missions
  International, Inc.
Tele-Missions
  International, Inc.
Trans World Missions
Underground Christian
  Missions, Inc.
United Church Board For
  World Ministries
United Methodist Church
  Comm. on Relief
Virginia Mennonite Board of
  Missions and Charities
Wings of Mercy Missions
  Inc.
World Concern/Crista
  International
World Gospel Crusades
World Hope Foundation
World Mission in Church and
  Society
World Mission Prayer League
  Canada
World Missionary
  Evangelism, Inc.
World Opportunities
  International
World Relief Corporation
World Vision International
World Vision of Canada

AGENCIES LISTED BY PRIMARY TASK

World Vision, Incorporated
Youth With A Mission

Aviation

Africa Inland Mission
Air Crusade, Inc.
America's Keswick, Inc.
Association of Baptists For
World Evangelism, Inc.
Baptist Mid-Missions
Baptist Missionary
Association of America
Christian Pilots
Association, Inc.
Christian Reformed Board
For World Missions
Evangelical Bible Mission,
Inc.
Evangelical Methodist
Church World Missions
Jungle Aviation and Radio
Service, Inc. (JAARS)
Men For Missions
International
Mission Aviation Fellowship
Mission Aviation Fellowship
of Canada
Missionary Air Transport,
Inc.
Missionary Flights
International
New Tribes Mission
Primitive Methodist Church
in the USA, Intl. Msn.
Bd.
Project Partner, Inc.
Regions Beyond Missionary
Union (Canada)
South America Mission, Inc.
Wycliffe Bible Translators
International, Inc.

Bible Correspondence Courses

New Life League

Bible Distribution

Action International
Ministries
Afghan Border Crusade
All Peoples Baptist Mission
America's Keswick, Inc.
American Bible Society
American European
Fellowship Chrn. Oneness
Evang., Inc.
Baptist Haiti Mission, Inc.
Baptist Missionary
Association of America
Bible Alliance Mission,
Inc.

Bible Literature
International
Bible Missionary Church,
World Missions Department
Bibles for the Nations
Bibles For The World, Inc.
Canadian Bible Society
Central Yearly Meeting of
Friends Missionary
Committee
Christian Church of North
America, Msns. Dept.
Christian Literature
Crusade (Ontario) Inc.
Christian Literature
International
Christian Pilots
Association, Inc.
Christian Salvage Mission,
Inc.
Christian Union General
Mission Board
Church of God General
Conference Mission
Department
Church of the Lutheran
Brethren of America, Brd.
of Wrld. Ms
Church of the Nazarene,
Gen. Bd. Dept. of Wld.
Msns.
Congregational Holiness
Church Foreign Mission
Dept.
Correll Missionary
Ministries
Defenders of the Christian
Faith Movement, Inc.
Evangel Bible Translators
Evangelical Scripture
Mission
Evangelism Center, Inc.
Evangelism to Communist
Lands
Evangelization Society of
the Pittsburgh Bible
Institute
Free Gospel Church, Inc.
Friends For Missions, Inc.
Friendship Ministry
International
Full Gospel Grace
Fellowship
Gideons International
Global Outreach Mission
Great Commission Crusades,
Inc.
Heritage Village Church and
Missionary Fellowship,
Inc.
India Evangelical Mission,
Inc.
India National Inland

Mission
International Prison
  Ministry
Jesus to the Communist
  World, Inc.
John Milton Society for the
  Blind
Living Bibles International
Messengers of the New
  Covenant, Inc.
Ministry of Mission
  Services
Mission Mailbag, Inc.
Mission Possible
  Foundation, Inc.
Mission to Europe's
  Millions, Inc.
Missionary Dentist, Inc.
Missionary Evangelistic
  Fellowship, Inc.
Natl. Assn. of
  Congregational Chr. Chs.
  of the U.S.A.
New York International
  Bible Society
Next Towns Crusade, Inc.
Norma Lam Ministries
Open Doors With Brother
  Andrew
Outreach International
Outreach, Inc.
Pan American Missions, Inc.
Pentecostal Church of God,
  World Missions Department
Pocket Testament League,
  Inc.
Prison Mission Assn., Inc.
Regular Baptists of Canada,
  Women's Missionary
  Society
Romanian Missionary Society
Scripture Gift Mission
  (Canada), Inc.
Slavic Gospel Association
Southern European Mission,
  Inc.
Spanish Evangelical
  Literature Fellowship,
  Inc.
Spanish-World Gospel
  Mission, Inc.
Sundanese Missionary
  Fellowship
Tele-Missions
  International, Inc.
Things to Come Mission,
  Inc.
Trans World Missions
Trinitarian Bible Society,
  Canada
Ukrainian Evangelical
  Alliance of North America
Undenominational Church of

the Lord
Underground Christian
  Missions, Inc.
World Gospel Crusades
World Home Bible League
World Literature Crusade
World Missions, Inc.
Youth With A Mission

Bible Memorization

Bible Club Movement of
  Canada
Bible Club Movement, Inc.
Bible Memory Association
  International
Free Gospel Church, Inc.
High School Evangelism
  Fellowship, Inc.
Maranatha Baptist Mission,
  Inc.
Missions Outreach, Inc.
Navigators, The
Trinitarian Bible Society,
  Canada

Bible Publication

Evangelism to Communist
  Lands
New York International
  Bible Society

Bible Reading

Scripture Union, U.S.A.

Bible School Literature E

Message of Life, Inc.

Bible Teaching

Friends of Israel Gospel
  Ministry, Inc.

Book Production, Writing and Publishing

Anis Shorrosh Evangelistic
  Association

Book Supply Service

Fellowship of Faith For
  Muslims

Broadcasting, Radio and TV

ACTS International
Adib Eden Evangelistic
  Missionary Society, Inc.
Africa Evangelical

Fellowship (Canada)
Africa Inland Mission
(Canada)
Africa Inter-Mennonite
Mission, Inc.
African Bible Colleges,
Inc.
African Enterprise
Alberto Mottesi
Evangelistic Association,
Inc.
All Peoples Baptist Mission
American Association for
Jewish Evangelism
American Board of Missions
to the Jews, Inc.
American European Bethel
Mission, Inc.
AMG International
(Advancing the Ministries
of the Gospel)
Andes Evangelical Mission
Back to the Bible
Missionary Agency
Bethany Missionary
Association
Bible Alliance Mission,
Inc.
Bible Christian Union, Inc.
Billy Graham Evangelistic
Association
BMMF International/Canada
Brazil Gospel Fellowship
Mission
California Yearly Meeting
of Friends Church, Bd. of
Msns.
Calvary Evangelistic
Mission, Inc./WIVV Msny.
Radio Station
CAM International
Campus Crusade for Christ,
International (Overseas
Dept.)
Canadian Bible Society
Child Evangelism
Fellowship, Inc.
Chinese for Christ, Inc.
Chinese Gospel Crusade,
Inc.
Chinese Overseas Christian
Mission, Inc.
Christ For The Philippines,
Inc.
Christian and Missionary
Alliance
Christian Baptist Ch. of
God Assn. Wld. for Christ
Msns.
Christian Broadcasting
Network
Chrn. Echoes Natl.
Ministry, Inc. (Chrn.

Crusade)
Chr. Homes Children, Inc.
Harold Martin Evang.
Assn., Inc.
Christian Information
Service, Inc.
Christians In Action
Church of the Lutheran
Brethren of America, Brd.
of Wrld. Ms
Congregational Holiness
Church Foreign Mission
Dept.
Correll Missionary
Ministries
Defenders of the Christian
Faith Movement, Inc.
Eastern European Mission
Elim Fellowship, Inc.
Evangelical Alliance
Mission of Canada, Inc.
Evangelical Mennonite
Conference Board of
Missions
Evangelism Center, Inc.
Evangelism to Communist
Lands
Evangelistic Faith Mission,
Inc.
Faith Center Global
Ministries
Far East Broadcasting
Company, Inc.
Franconia Mennonite
Conference Mission
Commission
Full Gospel Grace
Fellowship
Fuller Evangelistic
Association
Global Concern, Inc.
Global Outreach Mission
Go-Ye Fellowship
Gospel Association for the
Blind, Inc.
Gospel Mission of South
America
Gospel Missionary Union
Grace Mission, Inc.
Grand Old Gospel
Fellowship, Inc.
Heritage Village Church and
Missionary Fellowship,
Inc.
Hermano Pablo, Inc.
International Board of
Jewish Missions, Inc.
International Evangelism
Crusades, Inc.
International Films, Inc.
International Lutheran
Laymen's League
Jewish Voice Broadcast

Kansas Yearly Meeting of
Friends Africa Gospel
Mission
Latin America Mission, Inc.
Lester Sumrall Evangelistic
Association
Life For Latins, Inc.
Ling A. Juane Ministries,
Inc.
Living Waters
Luis Palau Evangelistic
Team, Inc.
Lutheran Church in
America-Div. for Wrld.
Msn. and Ecumenism
Lutheran Church-Missouri
Synod
Media Ministries Division,
Mennonite Bd. of Msns.
Mexican Border Missions
Mexican Mission Ministries,
Inc.
Mission Mailbag, Inc.
Mission to Japan, Inc.
Missionary Gospel
Fellowship, Inc.
Narramore Christian
Foundation
National Religious
Broadcasters
New Life International
New Life League
New Tribes Mission
Norma Lam Ministries
North Africa Mission
OMS International, Inc.
Open Bible Standard
Missions, Inc.
Overseas Missionary
Fellowship
Overseas Radio and
Television, Inc.
Pacific Broadcasting
Association, Inc.
Pan American Missionary
Society, Inc.
Pentecostal Free Will
Baptist Church, Inc.
Pilgrim Fellowship, Inc.,
The
Pillar of Fire Missions
Prison Mission Assn., Inc.
Romanian Missionary Society
Russia for Christ, Inc.
Slavic Gospel Association
South American Crusades,
Inc.
Southern Baptist
Convention, Foreign
Mission Board
Spanish Evangelical
Literature Fellowship,
Inc.

Spanish-World Gospel
Mission, Inc.
Sudan Interior Mission,
Inc.
Sundanese Missionary
Fellowship
Tele-Missions
International, Inc.
Things to Come Mission,
Inc.
Totonac Bible Center, Inc.
Trans World Missions
Trans World Radio
United Fundamentalist
Church
Virginia Mennonite Board of
Missions and Charities
Voice of China and Asia
Missionary Society, Inc.
Wings of Healing
Wisconsin Evangelical
Lutheran Synod, Bd. for
Wld. Msns.
Word of Life Fellowship
World Hope Foundation
World Literature Crusade
World Missionary
Evangelism, Inc.
World Missions, Inc.
World Outreach
World Radio Missionary
Fellowship, Inc.
World Vision of Canada
Worldteam
Youth For Christ/U.S.A.

Camping

Grand Old Gospel
Fellowship, Inc.
Inter-Varsity Christian
Fellowship of Canada
Society for Europe's
Evangelization (S.E.E.)
Tokyo Evangelistic Center
Trans World Missions

Camps and Conferences

Japan Evangelical Mission

Cassette Ministry

Mennonite Mission Bd. of
Pacific Coast Conf.
(Mexico Bd.)

Christian Communication

Christian Catholic Church
United Methodist Ch. Wld.
Div. of the Bd. of Global
Min.

AGENCIES LISTED BY PRIMARY TASK

Christian Family Life
Education

Bookmates International,
Incorporated

Church Construction or
Financing

American Committee for
KEEP, Inc.
Apostolic Church in Canada,
The
Baptist Bible Fellowship
International
Baptist Faith Missions
Baptist Haiti Mission, Inc.
California Yearly Meeting
of Friends Church, Bd. of
Msns.
Christ For The Nations,
Inc.
Christian and Missionary
Alliance in Canada
Christian Pilots
Association, Inc.
Church of God World
Missions
Church of the United
Brethren in Christ, Brd.
of Msns.
Church of the United
Brethren in Christ, Brd.
of Msns.
Congregational Holiness
Church Foreign Mission
Dept.
Evangelical Leadership
International
Evangelization Society of
the Pittsburgh Bible
Institute
Free Gospel Church, Inc.
Full Gospel Evangelistic
Association
Global Concern, Inc.
Harvest Fields Missionary
and Evangelistic Assn.,
Inc.
Helps International
Ministries, Inc.
Mexican Border Missions
Natl. Baptist Convention of
Amer., For. Msn. Bd.
Next Towns Crusade, Inc.
North American Baptist Gen.
Msny. Soc., Inc.
Oriental Missionary
Crusade, Inc.
Pentecostal Church of God,
World Missions Department
Pentecostal Free Will
Baptist Church, Inc.

Pentecostal Holiness
Church-World Missions
Department
Project Partner with
Christ, Inc.
R.E.A.P.
Regions Beyond Missionary
Union (Canada)
Teen Missions
International, Inc.
Vacation Samaritans

Church Extension

United Methodist Ch. Wld.
Div. of the Bd. of Global
Min.

Church Planting/Establishing

Afghan Border Crusade
Africa Evangelical
Fellowship
Africa Evangelical
Fellowship (Canada)
Africa Inland Mission
Africa Inland Mission
(Canada)
Africa Inter-Mennonite
Mission, Inc.
Afro-American Missionary
Crusade, Inc.
Air Crusade, Inc.
All Peoples Baptist Mission
Allegheny Wesleyan
Methodist Missions
American Advent Mission
Society
American Baptist
Association, Missionary
Committee
American Baptist Churches
in the U.S.A., Intl. Min.
American Committee for
KEEP, Inc.
American Missionary
Fellowship
Anchor Bay Evangelistic
Association
Andes Evangelical Mission
Anglican Orthodox Church
Apostolic Christian Church
(Nazarene), Apos. Chr.
Ch. Found.
Apostolic Church in Canada,
The
Apostolic Church of
Pentecost of
Canada-Missionary Dept.
Apostolic Faith Mission of
Portland, Oregon
Assemblies of God, Div. of
Foreign Mnsn.

AGENCIES LISTED BY PRIMARY TASK

Associate Reformed Presb.
Ch., Wld. Witness
Association of Baptists For
World Evangelism, Inc.
Association of Free
Lutheran Congregations
Baptist Bible Fellowship
International
Baptist Faith Missions
Baptist General Conference
Board of World Missions
Baptist Haiti Mission, Inc.
Baptist International
Missions, Inc.
Baptist Mid-Missions
Baptist Missionary
Association of America
Baptist World Mission
Berean Mission, Inc.
Bethany Fellowship Msns.
(Div. of Bethany
Fellowship, Inc.)
Bethel Foreign Mission
Foundation
Bethel Pentecostal Temple,
Inc.
Bethesda Mission, Inc.
Bible Christian Union, Inc.
Bible Holiness Movement
Bible Presbyterian Church,
Ind. Brd. For Presby.
For. Msns.
Bible Protestant Missions,
Inc.
Bible Translations On Tape,
Inc.
Bibles For The World, Inc.
Border Missions
Brazil Gospel Fellowship
Mission
Brethren Church, Missionary
Board of The Brethren
Church
Brethren in Christ Missions
Calcutta Mission of Mercy
California Yearly Meeting
of Friends Church, Bd. of
Msns.
CAM International
Canadian Baptist Overseas
Mission Board
Carver Foreign Missions,
Inc.
Central Yearly Meeting of
Friends Missionary
Committee
Chinese Christian Mission
Christ's Mission
Christian Aid Mission
Christian and Missionary
Alliance
Christian and Missionary
Alliance in Canada

Christian Baptist Ch. of
God Assn. Wld. for Christ
Msns.
Christian Canadian Mission
to Overseas Students
Christian Catholic Church
Christian Church of North
America, Msns. Dept.
Christian Missionary
Fellowship
Christian Nationals'
Evangelism Commission,
Inc. (CNEC)
Christian Nationals'
Evangelism Commission,
Inc. (Canada)
Christian Reformed Board
For World Missions
Christian Union General
Mission Board
Christians In Action
Church of God (Anderson,
Indiana) Msny. Brd.
Church of God (Holiness)
For. Msn. Brd.
Church of God (Seventh
Day), Gen. Conf., Msns.
Abroad
Church of God at Baden,
I.H.P.
Church of God General
Conference Mission
Department
Church of God in Christ,
Mennonite Gen. Msn. Bd.,
Inc.
Church of God of Prophecy,
World Mission Committee
Church of God of the
Apostolic Faith, Inc.
Church of God World
Missions
Church of God, USA
Headquarters
Church of the Lutheran
Brethren of America, Brd.
of Wrld. Ms
Church of the Nazarene,
Gen. Bd. Dept. of Wld.
Msns.
Church of the United
Brethren in Christ, Brd.
of Msns.
Churches of Christ in
Christian Union: Foreign
Msny. Dept.
Churches of God, General
Conference Comm. on Wrld.
Msns.
Congregational Holiness
Church Foreign Mission
Dept.
Conservative Baptist

AGENCIES LISTED BY PRIMARY TASK

Association of America
Conservative Baptist
  Foreign Mission Society
Conservative Mennonite
  Board of Missions and
  Charities
Cumberland Presbyterian
  Church, Board of Missions
Defenders of the Christian
  Faith Movement, Inc.
Eastern Mennonite Board of
  Missions and Charities
Elim Fellowship, Inc.
European Evangelistic
  Society
Evangelical Alliance
  Mission (TEAM)
Evangelical Alliance
  Mission of Canada, Inc.
Evangelical Baptist
  Missions, Inc.
Evangelical Bible Mission,
  Inc.
Evangelical Congregational
  Church Division of
  Missions
Evangelical Covenant Church
  of America, Bd. of Wld.
  Msn.
Evangelical Free Ch. of
  America, Bd. of Oseas.
  Msn.
Evangelical Friends Church,
  Eastern Region, Fr. For.
  Msnry.
Evangelical Friends Mission
Evangelical Mennonite
  Brethren Commission on
  Mission
Evangelical Mennonite
  Church, Comm. on Oseas.
  Msns.
Evangelical Mennonite
  Conference Board of
  Missions
Evangelical Methodist
  Church Bible Methodist
  Missions
Evangelical Methodist
  Church World Missions
Evangelical Scripture
  Mission
Evangelistic Faith Mission,
  Inc.
Evangelization Society of
  the Pittsburgh Bible
  Institute
Faith Christian Fellowship
  World Outreach
Far Eastern Gospel Crusade
Fellowship of Evangelical
  Baptist Chrs. in Canada
Fellowship of Grace

Brethren Church, For.
  Msny. Soc.
Fellowship of Independent
  Missions
Franconia Mennonite
  Conference Mission
  Commission
Free Gospel Church, Inc.
Friends of Indonesia
  Fellowship, Inc.
Frontier Ministries
  International
Full Gospel Grace
  Fellowship
Fuller Evangelistic
  Association
General Baptist Foreign
  Mission Society, Inc.
General Conference
  Mennonite Church, Comm.
  on Oseas. Msn.
Glad Tidings Missionary
  Society, Inc.
Global Outreach Mission
Go-Ye Fellowship
Gospel Crusade World Wide
  Mission Outreach
Gospel Mission of South
  America
Gospel Missionary Union
Gospel Outreach
Gospel Outreach to India,
  Inc.
Great Commission Crusades,
  Inc.
Greater Europe Mission
Harvest Fields Missionary
  and Evangelistic Assn.,
  Inc.
Independent Assemblies of
  God, International
Independent Faith Mission,
  Inc.
Independent Gospel Missions
India Evangelical Mission,
  Inc.
India National Inland
  Mission
International Christian
  Fellowship
Intl. Church of the
  Foursquare Gospel--Dept.
  of Msns. Intl.
International Crusades,
  Inc.
International Everlasting
  Gospel Mission, Inc.
International Missions,
  Inc.
Intl Pentecostal Ch. of
  Christ, Global Msns.
  Dept.
International Students,

75

Inc.
Japan Evangelical Mission
Japan Evangelistic
Association, Inc.
Korea International
Mission, Inc.
Language Institute For
Evangelism (LIFE)
Lester Sumrall Evangelistic
Association
Liberty Corner Mission
Liebenzell Mission of
Canada
Liebenzell Mission of
U.S.A., Inc.
Life For Latins, Inc.
Luis Palau Evangelistic
Team, Inc.
Lutheran Church in
America-Div. for Wrld.
Msn. and Ecumenism
Lutheran Church-Missouri
Synod
Lutheran Frontier Missions
Mahon Mission
Maranatha Baptist Mission,
Inc.
Mennonite Board of Missions
Mennonite Brethren
Missions/Services
Mennonite Mission Bd. of
Pacific Coast Conf.
(Mexico Bd.)
Metropolitan Church
Association
Mexican Border Missions
Mexican Christian Mission,
Inc.
Mexican Mission Ministries,
Inc.
Mexican Missions, Inc.
Middle East Christian
Outreach--USA Council
Mission Mailbag, Inc.
Mission SOS
Mission to Europe's
Millions, Inc.
Mission to the World
Missionary Air Transport,
Inc.
Missionary Church, Div. of
Overseas Ministries
Missionary Electronics,
Inc.
Missionary Evangelistic
Fellowship, Inc.
Missionary Gospel
Fellowship, Inc.
Missionary Revival Crusade
Missions of Baja
Movimiento Misionero
Mundial, Inc.
Natl. Assn. of

Congregational Chr. Chs.
of the U.S.A.
National Association of
Free Will Baptists, Bd.
of For. Msns
National Baptist
Convention, U.S.A., Inc.
For. Msn. Bd.
New Testament Missionary
Union
New Tribes Mission
Next Towns Crusade, Inc.
North Africa Mission
North American Baptist Gen.
Msny. Soc., Inc.
Northwest Yearly Meeting of
Friends Ch., Dept. of
Msns.
O.C. Ministries, Inc.
Open Bible Ministries, Inc.
Open Bible Standard
Missions, Inc.
Operation Mobilization -
Canada
Oriental Missionary
Crusade, Inc.
Orthodox Presbyterian
Church Committee on
Foreign Missions
Overseas Missionary
Fellowship
Overseas Missionary
Fellowship
Pan American Missionary
Society, Inc.
Pentecostal Assemblies of
Canada, Oseas. Msns.
Dept.
Pentecostal Church of God,
World Missions Department
Pentecostal Free Will
Baptist Church, Inc.
Pentecostal Holiness
Church-World Missions
Department
Pioneer Bible Translators
Presbyterian Church in
Canada, Board of World
Mission
Presbyterian Church in the
U.S.A., Div. of Intl.
Msn.
Primitive Methodist Church
in the USA, Intl. Msn.
Bd.
Protestant Reformed
Churches in America
Ramabai Mukti Mission
(American Council of)
Red Sea Mission Team, Inc.,
U.S.A. Council
Reformed Presbyterian Ch.
of N. America, Bd. of

AGENCIES LISTED BY PRIMARY TASK

For. Msns.
Regions Beyond Missionary
Union (Canada)
Regions Beyond Missionary
Union (U.S.A.)
Rural Gospel and Medical
Missions of India, Inc.
Salvation Army, Canada and
Bermuda
Schwenkfelder Church in the
USA and For. Bd. of Msns.
Seventh Day Baptist
Missionary Society
Slavic Gospel Association
Society for Europe's
Evangelization (S.E.E.)
South America Mission, Inc.
South Pacific Evangelical
Fellowship
Southern Baptist
Convention, Foreign
Mission Board
Southern European Mission,
Inc.
Sundanese Missionary
Fellowship
Tainan Evangelical Mission
Team Ventures International
Things to Come Mission,
Inc.
Tokyo Evangelistic Center
Totonac Bible Center, Inc.
Unevangelized Fields
Mission
United Indian Missions,
Inc.
United Missionary
Fellowship
United Pentecostal Church
Intl. For. Msns. Div.
United Presbyterian Church
in the USA Program Agency
United World Mission,
Incorporated
Victory Mission of the
Americas
Virginia Mennonite Board of
Missions and Charities
WEFMinistries, Inc.
Wesleyan Church Gen. Dept.
of Wld. Msns.
World Baptist Fellowship
Mission Agency
International
World Gospel Mission
World Literature Crusade
World Mission in Church and
Society
World Mission Prayer League
World Missions Fellowship
World Missions, Inc.
World Opportunities
International

World Presbyterian
Missions, Inc.
World-Wide Missions
International
Worldteam
Worldwide Discipleship
Association, Inc.
Worldwide Evangelization
Crusade
Worldwide Fellowship with
Jesus Christ Mission

Citizen Lobbies

Bread for the World

Communications

Amateur Radio Missionary
Service (ARMS)
Missionary Communications,
Inc.

Community Development

African Methodist Episcopal
Zion Ch., Dept. of Oseas.
Msns.
Agricultural Missions, Inc.
American Committee for
KEEP, Inc.
American Friends Service
Committee
BMMF/International (U.S.A.)
Children's Haven
International, Inc.
Christian Church (Disciples
of Christ) Div. of Oseas.
Min.
Christian Evangelical
Mission of Indonesia
Christian Reformed World
Relief Committee
Church of the Lutheran
Brethren of America, Brd.
of Wrld. Ms
Churches of God, General
Conference Comm. on Wrld.
Msns.
Compassion International,
Inc.
Compassion of Canada
Compassion Relief and
Development, Inc.
Conservative Mennonite
Board of Missions and
Charities
Daystar Communications,
Inc.
Eastern Mennonite Board of
Missions and Charities
Emmanuel International
Evangelical Mennonite

AGENCIES LISTED BY PRIMARY TASK

Church, Comm. on Oseas.
Msns.
Evangelical Mennonite
Conference Board of
Missions
Food for the Hungry/Canada
Good Shepherd Agricultural
Mission, Inc.
Houses of Refuge, Intl.
Orphanages Assn. Inc.
Jubilee, Inc.
MAP International (Medical
Assistance Programs)
Maranatha Baptist Mission,
Inc.
Mennonite Brethren
Missions/Services
Mennonite Central Committee
Mennonite Economic
Development Associates
Missionary Church, Div. of
Overseas Ministries
Moravian Church in America,
Bd. of Wld. Msn.
Paul Carlson Medical
Program, Inc.
Salvation Army, Canada and
Bermuda
Self Help Foundation
Sudan Interior Mission,
Inc.
Totonac Bible Center, Inc.
United Methodist Church
Comm. on Relief
United Methodist Ch. Wld.
Div. of the Bd. of Global
Min.
United Presbyterian Church
in the USA Program Agency
Voice of Calvary
World Concern/Crista
International
World Ministries Commission
World Relief Corporation
World Vision International
World Vision of Canada
World Vision, Incorporated
Worldteam

Computer/Data Process Services

Christian Services
Fellowship, Inc.
Intercristo
International Bible
Translators
Jungle Aviation and Radio
Service, Inc. (JAARS)
Missions Advanced Research
and Communication Center
(MARC)
World Vision of Canada

Correspondence Courses

Action International
Ministries
African Bible Colleges,
Inc.
Air Crusade, Inc.
American Messianic
Fellowship
Apostolic Church in Canada,
The
Asian Outreach
Back to the Bible
Missionary Agency
Berean Mission, Inc.
Bible Club Movement of
Canada
Bible Club Movement, Inc.
Bible Research
International
Brazil Gospel Fellowship
Mission
Calvary Evangelistic
Mission, Inc./WIVV Msny.
Radio Station
Child Evangelism
Fellowship, Inc.
Christ For The Philippines,
Inc.
Christian Union General
Mission Board
Church of God General
Conference Mission
Department
Churches of Christ in
Christian Union: Foreign
Msny. Dept.
Evangelical Alliance
Mission of Canada, Inc.
Evangelical Scripture
Mission
Evangelization Society of
the Pittsburgh Bible
Institute
Franconia Mennonite
Conference Mission
Commission
Global Outreach Mission
Go-Ye Fellowship
Gospel Mission of South
America
Heritage Village Church and
Missionary Fellowship,
Inc.
India Evangelical Mission,
Inc.
International Christian
Fellowship
International Institute,
Inc.
International Lutheran
Laymen's League
Latin America Assistance

78

AGENCIES LISTED BY PRIMARY TASK

Lord's Way Inn Ministries, Inc.
Lutheran Church-Missouri Synod
Mailbox Club, The
Media Ministries Division, Mennonite Bd. of Msns.
Mennonite Mission Bd. of Pacific Coast Conf. (Mexico Bd.)
Messengers of the New Covenant, Inc.
Mexican Mission Ministries, Inc.
North Africa Mission
Open Air Campaigners (USA)
Open Bible Standard Missions, Inc.
Overseas Missionary Fellowship
Pacific Broadcasting Association, Inc.
Prison Mission Assn., Inc.
Regular Baptists of Canada, Women's Missionary Society
Source of Light Ministries, Intl.
South Pacific Evangelical Fellowship
Spanish-World Gospel Mission, Inc.
Sundanese Missionary Fellowship
Trans World Missions
Trans World Radio
United Presbyterian Center for Mission Studies
World Gospel Crusades
World Literature Crusade
World Outreach
World Radio Missionary Fellowship, Inc.
Youth Enterprises, Inc.

Counseling

Luis Palau Evangelistic Team, Inc.
Youth For Christ/U.S.A.

Counseling of Prospective Missionary Candidates

United Presbyterian Center for Mission Studies

Developing Ethnic Art Researchers

Fellowship of Artists For Cultrual Evangelism (FACE)

Development of Human Resources

Action International Ministries
American Baptist Churches in the U.S.A., Intl. Min.
American Mc All Association
Christian Information Service, Inc.
Christian Medical Society
Christian Mission for the Deaf
Church World Service Division of DOM-NCCCUSA
CODEL (Coordination in Development, Inc.)
Compassion Relief and Development, Inc.
FARMS International, Inc.
Food for the Hungry/Canada
Gospel Missionary Union
Haggai Community
Japan-North American Commission on Cooperative Mission
Lutheran World Relief, Incorporated
Maranatha Baptist Mission, Inc.
Men For Missions International
Ministry of Mission Services
Moravian Church in America, Bd. of Wld. Msn.
Overseas Radio and Television, Inc.
REACH, Incorporated
Self Help Foundation
Southern Baptist Convention, Foreign Mission Board
United Church Board For World Ministries
World Concern/Crista International
World Ministries Commission
World Mission in Church and Society

Discipleship

Christian Amateur Radio Fellowship
Greater Mexican Missions
International Crusades, Inc.
Navigators, The

Drug Rehabilitation

Missionary Revival Crusade

AGENCIES LISTED BY PRIMARY TASK

Education in Health and Community Development

MAP International (Medical Assistance Programs)

Education, Extension

Afro-American Missionary Crusade, Inc.
Association of Free Lutheran Congregations
Bible Alliance Mission, Inc.
BMMF International/Canada
California Yearly Meeting of Friends Church, Bd. of Msns.
Church of the Lutheran Brethren of America, Brd. of Wrld. Ms
FARMS International, Inc.
Intl. Church of the Foursquare Gospel--Dept. of Msns. Intl.
International Films, Inc.
Liebenzell Mission of Canada
Pentecostal Free Will Baptist Church, Inc.
Regions Beyond Missionary Union (Canada)
Self Help Foundation

Education, General Christian

African Bible Colleges, Inc.
African Methodist Episcopal Church, Inc. Dept. of Msns.
African Methodist Episcopal Zion Ch., Dept. of Oseas. Msns.
Allegheny Wesleyan Methodist Missions
American Board for the Syrian Orphanage
American Board of International Missions
American Missionary Fellowship
Anchor Bay Evangelistic Association
Anglican Orthodox Church
Anis Shorrosh Evangelistic Association
Apostolic Christian Mission Fund
Apostolic Church of Pentecost of Canada-Missionary Dept.
Armenian Missionary

Association of America, Inc.
Associate Reformed Presb. Ch., Wld. Witness
Association of Free Lutheran Congregations
Back-Country Evangelism, Inc.
Baptist Faith Missions
Baptist Haiti Mission, Inc.
Baptist International Missions, Inc.
Baptist Mid-Missions
Baptist World Mission
Bethany Home, Inc.
Bethany Missionary Association
Bethel Foreign Mission Foundation
Bethel Pentecostal Temple, Inc.
Bible Club Movement of Canada
Bible Club Movement, Inc.
Bible Memory Association International
Bible Protestant Missions, Inc.
Bible Way Chrs. of Our Lord Jesus Christ Worldwide, Inc.
BMMF International/Canada
BMMF/International (U.S.A.)
Brazil Gospel Fellowship Mission
Campus Crusade for Christ, International (Overseas Dept.)
Central Yearly Meeting of Friends Missionary Committee
Christ For The Nations, Inc.
Christian and Missionary Alliance in Canada
Christian Baptist Ch. of God Assn. Wld. for Christ Msns.
Christian Catholic Church
Christian Church (Disciples of Christ) Div. of Oseas. Min.
Christian Evangelical Mission of Indonesia
Christian Mission for the Deaf
Christian Nationals' Evangelism Commission, Inc. (CNEC)
Christian Nationals' Evangelism Commission, Inc. (Canada)
Christian Salvage Mission,

Inc.

Church of God (Anderson,
Indiana) Msny. Brd.

Church of God (Holiness)
For. Msn. Brd.

Church of God in Christ,
Mennonite Gen. Msn. Bd.,
Inc.

Church of God World
Missions

Church of our Lord Jesus
Christ of the Apostolic
Faith, Inc.

Church of the Nazarene,
Gen. Bd. Dept. of Wld.
Msns.

Churches of God, General
Conference Comm. on Wrld.
Msns.

Compassion International,
Inc.

Conservative Baptist
Foreign Mission Society

Cumberland Presbyterian
Church, Board of Missions

David C. Cook Foundation

Evangelical Bible Mission,
Inc.

Evangelical Covenant Church
of America, Bd. of Wld.
Msn.

Evangelical Mennonite
Brethren Commission on
Mission

Evangelical Methodist
Church Bible Methodist
Missions

Evangelistic Faith Mission,
Inc.

Evangelization Society of
the Pittsburgh Bible
Institute

Evangelize China
Fellowship, Inc.

Fellowship of Christian
Assemblies Mission to
Liberia

Fellowship of Grace
Brethren Church, For.
Msny. Soc.

Fellowship of Independent
Missions

Forester Foundation, Inc.

Free Gospel Church, Inc.

Friends For Missions, Inc.

Friends of Indonesia
Fellowship, Inc.

Full Gospel Evangelistic
Association

Full Gospel Grace
Fellowship

Full Gospel Native
Missionary Association

General Conference
Mennonite Church, Comm.
on Oseas. Msn.

Glad Tidings Missionary
Society, Inc.

Global Concern, Inc.

Good Shepherd Agricultural
Mission, Inc.

Gospel Recordings of
Canada, Inc.

Great Commission Crusades,
Inc.

Harvest Fields Missionary
and Evangelistic Assn.,
Inc.

Hindustan Bible Institute,
Inc.

Holy Land Christian Mission

Houses of Refuge, Intl.
Orphanages Assn. Inc.

India Christian Mission,
Inc.

Institute of Holy Land
Studies

International Bible
Institute

International Christian
Mission

Intl. Church of the
Foursquare Gospel--Dept.
of Msns. Intl.

International Church Relief
Fund, Inc.

International Missions,
Inc.

Janz Team

Japan Evangelistic Band

Japan Evangelistic Band
(Canada)

Japan International
Christian Univ. Found.,
Inc.

Japan-North American
Commission on Cooperative
Mission

Jewish Voice Broadcast

John Milton Society for the
Blind

Kansas Yearly Meeting of
Friends Africa Gospel
Mission

Korea Gospel Mission

Latin America Mission, Inc.

Lester Sumrall Evangelistic
Association

Liberty Corner Mission

Lord's Way Inn Ministries,
Inc.

Lott Carey Baptist Foreign
Mission Convention

Mahon Mission

Maranatha Baptist Mission,
Inc.

Mennonite Mission Bd. of
Pacific Coast Conf.
(Mexico Bd.)
Message of Life, Inc.
Mexican Missions, Inc.
Mission Renewal Team, Inc.
Mission to the World
Missionary Dentist, Inc.
Missionary Electronics,
Inc.
Missionary Gospel
Fellowship, Inc.
Missions of Baja
Moody Institute of Science
Mustard Seed, Inc., The
New Life League
Northwest Yearly Meeting of
Friends Ch., Dept. of
Msns.
Open Bible Ministries, Inc.
Pan American Missionary
Society, Inc.
Pentecostal Assemblies of
Canada, Oseas. Msns.
Dept.
Pentecostal Assemblies of
the World, Inc. For.
Msns. Dept.
Pentecostal Free Will
Baptist Church, Inc.
Pilgrim Fellowship, Inc.,
The
Pillar of Fire Missions
Presbyterian Church in the
U.S.A., Div. of Intl.
Msn.
Primitive Methodist Church
in the USA, Intl. Msn.
Bd.
Project Partner, Inc.
Protestant Episcopal Church
(Order of the Holy Cross)
Protestant Episcopal Church
in the USA, Soc. of St.
Margaret
Ramabai Mukti Mission
(American Council of)
Reformed Church in America
General Program Council
Reformed Episcopal Church
Bd. of For. Msns.
Regions Beyond Missionary
Union (Canada)
Regular Baptists of Canada,
Women's Missionary
Society
Rural Gospel and Medical
Missions of India, Inc.
Salvation Army, Canada and
Bermuda
Salvation Army, The
Schwenkfelder Church in the
USA and For. Bd. of Msns.

Society of St. John the
Evangelist
Totonac Bible Center, Inc.
Unevangelized Fields
Mission
United Church Board For
World Ministries
United Evangelical Churches
United Methodist Ch. Wld.
Div. of the Bd. of Global
Min.
United Pentecostal Church
Intl. For. Msns. Div.
United Presbyterian Church
in the USA Program Agency
United World Mission,
Incorporated
Voice of Calvary
Wings of Mercy Missions
Inc.
Word of Life Fellowship
World Gospel Mission
World Mission Prayer League
World Mission Prayer League
Canada
World Missionary
Evangelism, Inc.
World Missions Fellowship
World's Christian Endeavor
Union
World-Wide Missions
International
Worldwide Discipleship
Association, Inc.
Worldwide Fellowship with
Jesus Christ Mission
Youth With A Mission

Education, Medical and Nursing

Ludhiana Christian Medical
College Board, U.S.A.,
Inc.

Education, Missionary

America's Keswick, Inc.
American Advent Mission
Society
American Committee for
KEEP, Inc.
Bethany Fellowship Msns.
(Div. of Bethany
Fellowship, Inc.)
Chiang Mai Mission Board
Christian and Missionary
Alliance in Canada
Christian INFO
Church of the United
Brethren in Christ, Brd.
of Msns.
Committee To Assist

Ministry Education
Overseas (CAMEO)
Episcopal Church Missionary
Community
Evangelical Christian
Education Ministries Inc.
Evangelical Literature
League (T.E.L.L.)
Evangelical Missions
Information Service, Inc.
Evangelization Society of
the Pittsburgh Bible
Institute
Faith Christian Fellowship
World Outreach
Fellowship of Artists For
Cultrual Evangelism
(FACE)
Harvest Fields Missionary
and Evangelistic Assn.,
Inc.
Institute of Chinese
Studies
International Crusades,
Inc.
Korea International
Mission, Inc.
Link Care Center
Ministry of Mission
Services
Mission Services
Association, Inc.
Mission SOS
Mission Training and
Resource Center
Missionary Internship, Inc.
National Baptist
Convention, U.S.A., Inc.
For. Msn. Bd.
Org. of Continuing Educ.
for American Nurses
(OCEAN)
Overseas Ministries Study
Center
Pentecostal Free Will
Baptist Church, Inc.
Presbyterian Church in
Canada, Board of World
Mission
Samuel Zwemer Institute
Spanish-World Gospel
Mission, Inc.
Sundanese Missionary
Fellowship
Toronto Institute of
Linguistics
United Presbyterian Order
for World Evangelization
United States Center for
World Mission

Education, Secular

Africa Evangelical
Fellowship
Africa Evangelical
Fellowship (Canada)
Allegheny Wesleyan
Methodist Missions
American Committee for
KEEP, Inc.
Brethren in Christ Missions
Carver Foreign Missions,
Inc.
Chiang Mai Mission Board
Christian Mission for the
Deaf
Christian Service Corps
Conservative Baptist
Foreign Mission Society
Evangelical Alliance
Mission of Canada, Inc.
Free Gospel Church, Inc.
Free Methodist Church of N.
America Gen. Msny. Bd.
India Evangelical Mission,
Inc.
International Foundation
For EWHA Woman's
University
International Institute,
Inc.
Intl Pentecostal Ch. of
Christ, Global Msns.
Dept.
Janz Team
Korea Gospel Mission
Liebenzell Mission of
U.S.A., Inc.
Mennonite Central Committee
Methodist Protestant
Church, Board of Msns.
Middle East Christian
Outreach--USA Council
Missions of Baja
Mustard Seed, Inc., The
Voice of China and Asia
Missionary Society, Inc.
Wesleyan Church Gen. Dept.
of Wld. Msns.
Wider Ministries Commission

Education, Theological

Africa Evangelical
Fellowship
Africa Evangelical
Fellowship (Canada)
Africa Inland Mission
Africa Inter-Mennonite
Mission, Inc.
African Bible Colleges,
Inc.
American Baptist
Association, Missionary
Committee

AGENCIES LISTED BY PRIMARY TASK

American Baptist Churches
in the U.S.A., Intl. Min.
American Lutheran Ch., Div.
For Wld. Msn.
Andes Evangelical Mission
Armenian Missionary
Association of America,
Inc.
Association of Baptists For
World Evangelism, Inc.
Baptist General Conference
Board of World Missions
Baptist Missionary
Association of America
Berean Mission, Inc.
Bethany Fellowship Msns.
(Div. of Bethany
Fellowship, Inc.)
Bethesda Mission, Inc.
Bible Missionary Church,
World Missions Department
Bible Presbyterian Church,
Ind. Brd. For Presby.
For. Msns.
BMMF International/Canada
Brethren Church, Missionary
Board of The Brethren
Church
California Yearly Meeting
of Friends Church, Bd. of
Msns.
CAM International
Campus Crusade for Christ,
International (Overseas
Dept.)
Canadian Baptist Overseas
Mission Board
Carver Foreign Missions,
Inc.
Chiang Mai Mission Board
Christian and Missionary
Alliance
Christian and Missionary
Alliance in Canada
Christian Church of North
America, Msns. Dept.
Christian Evangelical
Mission of Indonesia
Christian Mission for the
Deaf
Christian Nationals'
Evangelism Commission,
Inc. (CNEC)
Christian Nationals'
Evangelism Commission,
Inc. (Canada)
Church of God World
Missions
Church of the United
Brethren in Christ, Brd.
of Msns.
Committee To Assist
Ministry Education

Overseas (CAMEO)
Congregational Holiness
Church Foreign Mission
Dept.
Conservative Baptist
Foreign Mission Society
Eastern Mennonite Board of
Missions and Charities
Elim Fellowship, Inc.
European Evangelistic
Society
Evangelical Alliance
Mission (TEAM)
Evangelical Alliance
Mission of Canada, Inc.
Evangelical Baptist
Missions, Inc.
Evangelical Bible Mission,
Inc.
Evangelical Christian
Education Ministries Inc.
Evangelical Free Ch. of
America, Bd. of Oseas.
Msn.
Evangelical Friends Church,
Eastern Region, Fr. For.
Msnry.
Evangelical Leadership
International
Evangelical Literature
League (T.E.L.L.)
Evangelical Lutheran
Church, Division of World
Missions
Evangelical Mennonite
Brethren Commission on
Mission
Evangelical Methodist
Church World Missions
Evangelical Scripture
Mission
Evangelization Society of
the Pittsburgh Bible
Institute
Faith Christian Fellowship
World Outreach
Fellowship of Christian
Assemblies Mission to
Liberia
Fellowship of Evangelical
Baptist Chrs. in Canada
Free Gospel Church, Inc.
Free Methodist Church of N.
America Gen. Msny. Bd.
Full Gospel Evangelistic
Association
General Baptist Foreign
Mission Society, Inc.
Gospel Mission of South
America
Grace Mission, Inc.
Greater Europe Mission
Harvest Fields Missionary

84

and Evangelistic Assn.,
Inc.
Independent Faith Mission,
Inc.
India Evangelical Mission,
Inc.
India National Inland
Mission
Institute of Holy Land
Studies
International Bible
Institute
International Evangelism
Crusades, Inc.
International Missions,
Inc.
Intl Pentecostal Ch. of
Christ, Global Msns.
Dept.
Japan Evangelical Mission
Japan Evangelistic Band
Japan Evangelistic Band
(Canada)
Korea International
Mission, Inc.
Liebenzell Mission of
U.S.A., Inc.
Lutheran Church in
America-Div. for Wrld.
Msn. and Ecumenism
Lutheran Church-Missouri
Synod
Macedonian Service
Foundation, Inc.
Mennonite Board of Missions
Mennonite Brethren
Missions/Services
Methodist Protestant
Church, Board of Msns.
Mission to the World
Missionary Church, Div. of
Overseas Ministries
Missionary Evangelistic
Fellowship, Inc.
Moravian Church in America,
Bd. of Wld. Msn.
Morris Cerullo World
Evangelism, Inc.
Natl. Assn. of
Congregational Chr. Chs.
of the U.S.A.
OMI Brotherhood Foundation
of America, Inc.
OMS International, Inc.
Open Bible Ministries, Inc.
Open Bible Standard
Missions, Inc.
Orthodox Presbyterian
Church Committee on
Foreign Missions
Outreach, Inc.
Overseas Ministries Study
Center

Overseas Missionary
Fellowship
Overseas Missionary
Fellowship
Pentecostal Church of God,
World Missions Department
Pentecostal Free Will
Baptist Church, Inc.
Pillar of Fire Missions
Presbyterian Church in
Canada, Board of World
Mission
Presbyterian Church in the
U.S.A., Div. of Intl.
Msn.
Regions Beyond Missionary
Union (U.S.A.)
Schwenkfelder Church in the
USA and For. Bd. of Msns.
Scripture Union, U.S.A.
Society for Europe's
Evangelization (S.E.E.)
South America Mission, Inc.
Sudan Interior Mission,
Inc.
Things to Come Mission,
Inc.
Unevangelized Fields
Mission
United Missionary
Fellowship
Wesleyan Church Gen. Dept.
of Wld. Msns.
Westminister Biblical
Missions, Inc.
Wisconsin Evangelical
Lutheran Synod, Bd. for
Wld. Msns.
Word of Life Fellowship
World Baptist Fellowship
Mission Agency
International
World Gospel Mission
World Mission in Church and
Society
World Outreach
World Presbyterian
Missions, Inc.
Worldwide Evangelization
Crusade
Youth With A Mission

Education, Theological by Extension

Africa Evangelical
Fellowship
Africa Inland Mission
Africa Inland Mission
(Canada)
Andes Evangelical Mission
Anglican Orthodox Church
Assemblies of God, Div. of

AGENCIES LISTED BY PRIMARY TASK

Foreign Mnsn.
Baptist General Conference
  Board of World Missions
Bethesda Mission, Inc.
Bible Alliance Mission,
  Inc.
Bible Literature
  International
Bible Research
  International
BMMF International/Canada
BMMF/International (U.S.A.)
Brethren Church, Missionary
  Board of The Brethren
  Church
California Yearly Meeting
  of Friends Church, Bd. of
  Msns.
CAM International
Christian and Missionary
  Alliance in Canada
Christian Reformed Board
  For World Missions
Christian Union General
  Mission Board
Church of God (Anderson,
  Indiana) Msny. Brd.
Church of God (Holiness)
  For. Msn. Brd.
Church of God World
  Missions
Church of the United
  Brethren in Christ, Brd.
  of Msns.
Committee To Assist
  Ministry Education
  Overseas (CAMEO)
Conservative Baptist
  Association of America
Conservative Baptist
  Foreign Mission Society
Elim Fellowship, Inc.
Evangelical Christian
  Education Ministries Inc.
Evangelical Covenant Church
  of America, Bd. of Wld.
  Msn.
Evangelical Lutheran
  Church, Division of World
  Missions
Evangelical Lutheran Synod
  Board For Missions
Evangelical Mennonite
  Church, Comm. on Oseas.
  Msns.
Far Eastern Gospel Crusade
Franconia Mennonite
  Conference Mission
  Commission
Full Gospel Evangelistic
  Association
Grace Mission, Inc.
Greater Europe Mission

International Bible
  Institute
International Christian
  Fellowship
Liebenzell Mission of
  U.S.A., Inc.
Logoi, Inc.
Lutheran Frontier Missions
Mexican Border Missions
Mexican Mission Ministries,
  Inc.
Mission Mailbag, Inc.
North Africa Mission
Northwest Yearly Meeting of
  Friends Ch., Dept. of
  Msns.
Overseas Missionary
  Fellowship
Pentecostal Church of God,
  World Missions Department
Pentecostal Holiness
  Church-World Missions
  Department
Presbyterian Church in
  Canada, Board of World
  Mission
Regions Beyond Missionary
  Union (Canada)
Seventh Day Baptist
  Missionary Society
Tele-Missions
  International, Inc.
Wider Ministries Commission
World Baptist Fellowship
  Mission Agency
  International
World Mission Prayer League
Worldteam

Evaluation of Mission Efforts

United Presbyterian Center
  for Mission Studies

Evangelism, Child

Chr. Homes Children, Inc.
  Harold Martin Evang.
  Assn., Inc.
Mexican Missions, Inc.
Scripture Union, U.S.A.

Evangelism, Mass

Action International
  Ministries
ACTS International
Adib Eden Evangelistic
  Missionary Society, Inc.
Advent Christian Gen. Conf.
  of America
Africa Inland Mission
Africa Inland Mission

AGENCIES LISTED BY PRIMARY TASK

(Canada)
African Enterprise
African Methodist Episcopal
Zion Ch., Dept. of Oseas.
Msns.
Alberto Mottesi
Evangelistic Association,
Inc.
American Board of Missions
to the Jews, Inc.
American Messianic
Fellowship
American Scripture Gift
Mission
AMG International
(Advancing the Ministries
of the Gospel)
Anis Shorrosh Evangelistic
Association
Apostolic Church of
Pentecost of
Canada-Missionary Dept.
Apostolic Faith Mission of
Portland, Oregon
Apostolic Overcoming Holy
Church of God
Appleman Campaigns, Inc.
Arthur Bradford
Evangelistic Association
Assemblies of God, Div. of
Foreign Mnsn.
Back-Country Evangelism,
Inc.
Baptist Bible Fellowship
International
Baptist World Mission
Bethel Foreign Mission
Foundation
Bethel Pentecostal Temple,
Inc.
Bible Alliance Mission,
Inc.
Bible Christian Union, Inc.
Bible Club Movement of
Canada
Bible Club Movement, Inc.
Bible Holiness Movement
Bible Protestant Missions,
Inc.
Bible Way Chrs. of Our Lord
Jesus Christ Worldwide,
Inc.
Biblical Literature
Fellowship
Billy Graham Evangelistic
Association
Brazil Gospel Fellowship
Mission
Breakthrough Ministries
Campus Crusade for Christ,
International (Overseas
Dept.)
Central Yearly Meeting of

Friends Missionary
Committee
Children of India
Foundation
Chinese for Christ, Inc.
Chinese Gospel Crusade,
Inc.
Christ's Mission
Christian Aid Mission
Christian and Missionary
Alliance in Canada
Christian Baptist Ch. of
God Assn. Wld. for Christ
Msns.
Christian Canadian Mission
to Overseas Students
Chrn. Echoes Natl.
Ministry, Inc. (Chrn.
Crusade)
Chr. Homes Children, Inc.
Harold Martin Evang.
Assn., Inc.
Christian Nationals'
Evangelism Commission,
Inc. (CNEC)
Christian Nationals'
Evangelism Commission,
Inc. (Canada)
Christian Reformed Board
For World Missions
Christians United in
Action, Inc.
Church of God in Christ,
Mennonite Gen. Msn. Bd.,
Inc.
Church of God of Prophecy,
World Mission Committee
Church of God of the
Apostolic Faith, Inc.
Church of God, USA
Headquarters
Church of the Nazarene,
Gen. Bd. Dept. of Wld.
Msns.
Churches of God, General
Conference Comm. on Wrld.
Msns.
Compassion of Canada
Concordia Tract Mission
Crusade Evangelism
International
Eastern European Mission
Evangelical Alliance
Mission of Canada, Inc.
Evangelical Literature
League (T.E.L.L.)
Evangelical Methodist
Church Bible Methodist
Missions
Evangelical Scripture
Mission
Evangelism Resources
Evangelism Resources

Evangelistic Faith Mission, Inc.
Evangelize China Fellowship, Inc.
Faith Christian Fellowship World Outreach
Faith Ministries
Far East Broadcasting Company, Inc.
Fellowship of Christian Assemblies Mission to Liberia
Fellowship of Grace Brethren Church, For. Msny. Soc.
Fellowship of Independent Missions
Forester Foundation, Inc.
Free Gospel Church, Inc.
Free Methodist Church of N. America Gen. Msny. Bd.
Friends For Missions, Inc.
Friends of Indonesia Fellowship, Inc.
Friends of Turkey
Full Gospel Native Missionary Association
Fuller Evangelistic Association
Glad Tidings Missionary Society, Inc.
Global Concern, Inc.
Global Outreach Mission
Globe Missionary Evangelism
Gospel Baptist Missions
Great Commission Crusades, Inc.
Greater Mexican Missions
H.O.P.E. Bible Mission, Inc.
Harvest Fields Missionary and Evangelistic Assn., Inc.
Heritage Village Church and Missionary Fellowship, Inc.
Hermano Pablo, Inc.
Holy Land Christian Mission
Independent Assemblies of God, International
Independent Faith Mission, Inc.
India Evangelical Mission, Inc.
India National Inland Mission
International Board of Jewish Missions, Inc.
Intl. Church of the Foursquare Gospel--Dept. of Msns. Intl.
International Evangelism Crusades, Inc.

International Fellowship of Christians
International Gospel League
International Lutheran Laymen's League
International Messianic Outreach
Janz Team
Jesus to the Communist World, Inc.
Jesus to the Communist World, Inc.
Jewish Voice Broadcast
Jews For Jesus
Kansas Yearly Meeting of Friends Africa Gospel Mission
Latin America Mission, Inc.
Liebenzell Mission of Canada
Ling A. Juane Ministries, Inc.
Lott Carey Baptist Foreign Mission Convention
Luis Palau Evangelistic Team, Inc.
Lutheran Church in America-Div. for Wrld. Msn. and Ecumenism
Mahon Mission
Messengers of the New Covenant, Inc.
Metropolitan Church Association
Mexican Missions, Inc.
Minnesota Bible Fellowship, Inc.
Mission Mailbag, Inc.
Mission to Japan, Inc.
Missionary Electronics, Inc.
Missionary Evangelistic Fellowship, Inc.
Missionary Revival Crusade Missions, Inc.
Moody Institute of Science
Moravian Church in America, Bd. of Wld. Msn.
Morris Cerullo World Evangelism, Inc.
Natl. Baptist Convention of Amer., For. Msn. Bd.
National Religious Broadcasters
New Life League
New Testament Missionary Union
Next Towns Crusade, Inc.
Norma Lam Ministries
O.C. Ministries, Inc.
Open Air Campaigners (USA)
Open Door Missionary Fellowship, Inc.

Operation Mobilization - Canada
Operation Mobilization Send the Light, Inc.
Osborn Foundation
Overseas Radio and Television, Inc.
Pan American Missions, Inc.
Pentecostal Holiness Church-World Missions Department
Petra International, Inc.
Pocket Testament League, Inc.
Presbyterian Church in Canada, Board of World Mission
Primitive Methodist Church in the USA, Intl. Msn. Bd.
Protestant Episcopal Church (Order of the Holy Cross)
R.E.A.P.
Refugee Children, Inc.
Regions Beyond Missionary Union (U.S.A.)
Release the World for Christ
Rural Gospel and Medical Missions of India, Inc.
Salvation Army, Canada and Bermuda
Salvation Army, The
Society for Europe's Evangelization (S.E.E.)
South American Crusades, Inc.
South Pacific Evangelical Fellowship
Southern European Mission, Inc.
Sundanese Missionary Fellowship
Team Ventures International
Tele-Missions International, Inc.
Trans World Missions
Underground Christian Missions, Inc.
United Evangelical Churches
United Fundamentalist Church
United Indian Missions, Inc.
United Pentecostal Church Intl. For. Msns. Div.
Voice of Calvary
We Go, Inc. (World Encounter Gospel Organization)
Wings of Healing
World Evangelism Foundation
World Gospel Mission

World Hope Foundation
World Literature Crusade
World Missionary Assistance Plan
World Missionary Evangelism, Inc.
World Missionary Press, Inc.
World Missions, Inc.
World Opportunities International
World Thrust Films, Inc.
World Vision International
World Vision, Incorporated
Youth For Christ/U.S.A.
Youth For Christ/U.S.A.

Evangelism, Personal and Small Group

Action International Ministries
Afghan Border Crusade
Africa Inland Mission
Africa Inland Mission (Canada)
African Enterprise
Afro-American Missionary Crusade, Inc.
Alberto Mottesi Evangelistic Association, Inc.
All Peoples Baptist Mission
Allegheny Wesleyan Methodist Missions
American Baptist Association, Missionary Committee
American Baptist Churches in the U.S.A., Intl. Min.
American Board of Missions to the Jews, Inc.
American European Bethel Mission, Inc.
American European Fellowship Chrn. Oneness Evang., Inc.
American Lutheran Ch., Div. For Wld. Msn.
American Mc All Association
American Messianic Fellowship
American Missionary Fellowship
American Scripture Gift Mission
Anis Shorrosh Evangelistic Association
Apostolic Church in Canada, The
Armenian Missionary Association of America, Inc.

AGENCIES LISTED BY PRIMARY TASK

Assemblies of God, Div. of
Foreign Mnsn.
Associate Reformed Presb.
Ch., Wld. Witness
Association of Free
Lutheran Congregations
Baptist Bible Fellowship
International
Baptist Faith Missions
Baptist International
Missions, Inc.
Baptist Missionary
Association of America
Berean Mission, Inc.
Bethesda Mission, Inc.
Bible Christian Union, Inc.
Bible Holiness Movement
Bible Missionary Church,
World Missions Department
Bible Presbyterian Church,
Ind. Brd. For Presby.
For. Msns.
BMMF International/Canada
BMMF/International (U.S.A.)
Border Missions
Brethren Church, Missionary
Board of The Brethren
Church
Brethren in Christ Missions
CAM International
Carver Foreign Missions,
Inc.
Child Evangelism
Fellowship, Inc.
Chinese World Mission
Center
Christ's Mission
Christian Business Men's
Committee International
(Canada)
Christian Business Men's
Committee of USA
Christian Literature
Crusade (Ontario) Inc.
Christian Medical Society
Christian Mission for the
Deaf
Christian Missionary
Fellowship
Christian Pilots
Association, Inc.
Christian Salvage Mission,
Inc.
Christian Service Corps
Christians In Action
Church of God (Anderson,
Indiana) Msny. Brd.
Church of God (Seventh
Day), Gen. Conf., Msns.
Abroad
Church of God General
Conference Mission
Department

Church of God of Prophecy,
World Mission Committee
Churches of Christ in
Christian Union: Foreign
Msny. Dept.
Concordia Tract Mission
Conservative Baptist
Association of America
Conservative Baptist
Foreign Mission Society
Conservative Mennonite
Board of Missions and
Charities
Correll Missionary
Ministries
Crusade Evangelism
International
Cumberland Presbyterian
Church, Board of Missions
Defenders of the Christian
Faith Movement, Inc.
Emmanuel International
European Evangelistic
Society
Evangelical Alliance
Mission (TEAM)
Evangelical Baptist
Missions, Inc.
Evangelical Bible Mission,
Inc.
Evangelical Covenant Church
of America, Bd. of Wld.
Msn.
Evangelical Free Ch. of
America, Bd. of Oseas.
Msn.
Evangelical Friends Church,
Eastern Region, Fr. For.
Msnry.
Evangelical Lutheran
Church, Division of World
Missions
Evangelical Lutheran Synod
Board For Missions
Evangelical Mennonite
Brethren Commission on
Mission
Evangelical Mennonite
Conference Board of
Missions
Evangelical Methodist
Church World Missions
Evangelism Resources
Faith Christian Fellowship
World Outreach
Far Eastern Gospel Crusade
Fellowship of Evangelical
Baptist Chrs. in Canada
Foundation For His
Ministry-Orphanage
Committee
Friends of Israel Gospel
Ministry, Inc.

AGENCIES LISTED BY PRIMARY TASK

General Conference
  Mennonite Church, Comm.
  on Oseas. Msn.
Gideons International
Global Outreach Mission
Globe Missionary Evangelism
Go-Ye Fellowship
Good Shepherd Agricultural
  Mission, Inc.
Gospel Mission of South
  America
Gospel Missionary Union
Gospel Outreach
Gospel Outreach to India,
  Inc.
Gospel Recordings
  Incorporated
Great Commission Crusades,
  Inc.
Greater Europe Mission
Harvest Fields Missionary
  and Evangelistic Assn.,
  Inc.
High School Evangelism
  Fellowship, Inc.
Hindustan Bible Institute,
  Inc.
Houses of Refuge, Intl.
  Orphanages Assn. Inc.
Independent Faith Mission,
  Inc.
Independent Gospel Missions
India Evangelical Mission,
  Inc.
Inter-Varsity Christian
  Fellowship of Canada
International Board of
  Jewish Missions, Inc.
International Christian
  Fellowship
Intl. Church of the
  Foursquare Gospel--Dept.
  of Msns. Intl.
International Crusades,
  Inc.
International Evangelism
  Crusades, Inc.
International Missions,
  Inc.
International Needs-USA
Japan Evangelical Mission
Japan Evangelistic
  Association, Inc.
Japan Evangelistic Band
Japan Evangelistic Band
  (Canada)
Jews For Jesus
Jubilee, Inc.
Korea Gospel Mission
Korea International
  Mission, Inc.
Language Institute For
  Evangelism (LIFE)

Liberty Corner Mission
Liebenzell Mission of
  Canada
Liebenzell Mission of
  U.S.A., Inc.
Life For Latins, Inc.
Ling A. Juane Ministries,
  Inc.
Literacy and Evangelism,
  Inc.
Lord's Way Inn Ministries,
  Inc.
Lutheran Church-Missouri
  Synod
Men For Missions
  International
Mennonite Board of Missions
Mennonite Brethren
  Missions/Services
Messengers of the New
  Covenant, Inc.
Methodist Protestant
  Church, Board of Msns.
Mexican Christian Mission,
  Inc.
Middle East Christian
  Outreach--USA Council
Minneapolis Friends of
  Israel
Mission to Europe's
  Millions, Inc.
Mission to the World
Missionary Church, Div. of
  Overseas Ministries
Missionary Dentist, Inc.
Missionary Electronics,
  Inc.
Missionary Evangelistic
  Fellowship, Inc.
Missionary Gospel
  Fellowship, Inc.
Missionary Strategy Agency
Missions, Inc.
Narramore Christian
  Foundation
Natl. Assn. of
  Congregational Chr. Chs.
  of the U.S.A.
Navigators of Canada
  International, The
Navigators, The
Next Towns Crusade, Inc.
North Africa Mission
North American Baptist Gen.
  Msny. Soc., Inc.
Open Bible Ministries, Inc.
Open Bible Standard
  Missions, Inc.
Orthodox Presbyterian
  Church Committee on
  Foreign Missions
Outreach International
Overcomer Press, Inc.

Overseas Christian
  Servicemen's Centers
Overseas Missionary
  Fellowship
Pan American Missionary
  Society, Inc.
Pentecostal Assemblies of
  Canada, Oseas. Msns.
  Dept.
Pilgrim Fellowship, Inc.,
  The
Pillar of Fire Missions
Pioneer Bible Translators
Pocket Testament League,
  Inc.
Ramabai Mukti Mission
  (American Council of)
REACH, Incorporated
Red Sea Mission Team, Inc.,
  U.S.A. Council
Reformed Church in America
  General Program Council
Reformed Presbyterian Ch.
  of N. America, Bd. of
  For. Msns.
Regions Beyond Missionary
  Union (Canada)
Regions Beyond Missionary
  Union (U.S.A.)
Salvation Army, The
Schwenkfelder Church in the
  USA and For. Bd. of Msns.
Scripture Gift Mission
  (Canada), Inc.
Seventh Day Baptist
  Missionary Society
Society for Europe's
  Evangelization (S.E.E.)
South America Mission, Inc.
Sudan Interior Mission,
  Inc.
Sundanese Missionary
  Fellowship
Tainan Evangelical Mission
Team Ventures International
Teen Missions
  International, Inc.
Unevangelized Fields
  Mission
United Fundamentalist
  Church
United Missionary
  Fellowship
United Presbyterian Church
  in the USA Program Agency
United World Mission,
  Incorporated
Vacation Samaritans
Victory Mission of the
  Americas
Virginia Mennonite Board of
  Missions and Charities
Voice of China and Asia

  Missionary Society, Inc.
Wesleyan Church Gen. Dept.
  of Wld. Msns.
Word of Life Fellowship
World Baptist Fellowship
  Mission Agency
  International
World Evangelism Foundation
World Mission Prayer League
World Mission Prayer League
  Canada
World Missions Fellowship
World Missions, Inc.
World Neighbors, Inc.
World Radio Missionary
  Fellowship, Inc.
World Vision of Canada
World's Christian Endeavor
  Union
Worldwide Discipleship
  Association, Inc.
Worldwide Evangelization
  Crusade
Youth For Christ/U.S.A.
Youth With A Mission

Evangelism, Saturation

Air Crusade, Inc.
Alberto Mottesi
  Evangelistic Association,
  Inc.
America's Keswick, Inc.
American Association for
  Jewish Evangelism
American Board of Missions
  to the Jews, Inc.
Andes Evangelical Mission
Calvary Evangelistic
  Mission, Inc./WIVV Msny.
  Radio Station
Christ For The Philippines,
  Inc.
Evangelical Mennonite
  Brethren Commission on
  Mission
Evangelism Resources
Far East Broadcasting
  Company, Inc.
Gospel Crusade World Wide
  Mission Outreach
Gospel Recordings
  Incorporated
Home of Onesiphorus
Japan Evangelistic Band
Japan Evangelistic Band
  (Canada)
Japanese Evangelical
  Missionary Society
Korea International
  Mission, Inc.
Mexican Christian Mission,
  Inc.

Missions, Inc.
Northwest Yearly Meeting of
Friends Ch., Dept. of
Msns.
O.C. Ministries, Inc.
OMS International, Inc.
Oriental Missionary
Crusade, Inc.
Romanian Missionary Society
Sundanese Missionary
Fellowship
Youth With A Mission

Evangelism, Student

Ambassadors For Christ,
Inc.
American Messianic
Fellowship
Anis Shorrosh Evangelistic
Association
BMMF International/Canada
Campus Crusade for Christ,
International (Overseas
Dept.)
Christian Canadian Mission
to Overseas Students
Christian Evangelical
Mission of Indonesia
Christian Medical Society
Conservative Baptist
Association of America
Far Eastern Gospel Crusade
Free Gospel Church, Inc.
Friends of Israel Gospel
Ministry, Inc.
Globe Missionary Evangelism
Harvest Fields Missionary
and Evangelistic Assn.,
Inc.
High School Evangelism
Fellowship, Inc.
India Evangelical Mission,
Inc.
Inter-Varsity Christian
Fellowship
International Fellowship of
Evangelical Students -
USA
International Students,
Inc.
Japan Evangelistic Band
Japan Evangelistic Band
(Canada)
Japanese Evangelical
Missionary Society
Jews For Jesus
Korea Gospel Mission
Language Institute For
Evangelism (LIFE)
Latin America Assistance
Mailbox Club, The
Messengers of the New

Covenant, Inc.
Missionary Dentist, Inc.
Missionary Strategy Agency
Missions, Inc.
Navigators of Canada
International, The
Navigators, The
Oriental Missionary
Crusade, Inc.
Overseas Missionary
Fellowship
Pocket Testament League,
Inc.
REACH, Incorporated
Scripture Union, U.S.A.
Tainan Evangelical Mission
Team Ventures International
Trans World Missions
Welfare of the Blind, Inc.
Worldwide Discipleship
Association, Inc.
Youth Enterprises, Inc.
Youth For Christ/U.S.A.

Evangelism, Youth

Young Life
Youth for Christ (Canada)

Evangelism/Church Growth Workshops Overseas

Evangelical Missions
Information Service, Inc.

Fellowships

MAP International (Medical
Assistance Programs)

Fund Raising

American European
Fellowship Chrn. Oneness
Evang., Inc.
American Leprosy Missions,
Inc.
Apostolic Christian Church
(Nazarene), Apos. Chr.
Ch. Found.
Armenian Missionary
Association of America,
Inc.
Bible Missionary Church,
World Missions Department
Campus Crusade for Christ,
International (Overseas
Dept.)
Canadian Bible Society
Chiang Mai Mission Board
Children of India
Foundation
Children's Haven

International, Inc.
Christian Information
  Service, Inc.
Christian Life Missions
Christian Union General
  Mission Board
Church of God (Holiness)
  For. Msn. Brd.
Church of God World
  Missions
Church of the Lutheran
  Brethren of America, Brd.
  of Wrld. Ms
Compassion of Canada
Correll Missionary
  Ministries
Eastern European Mission
Evangelical Christian
  Education Ministries Inc.
Evangelical Leadership
  International
Evangelical Missions
  Council of Good News
Evangelism Center, Inc.
FARMS International, Inc.
Full Gospel Native
  Missionary Association
Fundamental Evangelistic
  Association
Gospel Crusade World Wide
  Mission Outreach
Haggai Institute for
  Advanced Leadership
  Training, Inc.
Holt International
  Children's Services, Inc.
International Foundation
  For EWHA Woman's
  University
Japan International
  Christian Univ. Found.,
  Inc.
John Milton Society for the
  Blind
Leprosy Mission Canada
Literacy and Evangelism,
  Inc.
Living Bibles International
Macedonian Service
  Foundation, Inc.
Men For Missions
  International
Messengers of the New
  Covenant, Inc.
Middle East Media
Moravian Church in America,
  Bd. of Wld. Msn.
Natl. Baptist Convention of
  Amer., For. Msn. Bd.
North American Baptist Gen.
  Msny. Soc., Inc.
N. American Committee for
  IME, Institut Medical

Evangelique
North East India General
  Mission, Inc.
OMI Brotherhood Foundation
  of America, Inc.
Outreach, Inc.
Pacific Broadcasting
  Association, Inc.
Providence Mission Homes,
  Inc.
R.E.A.P.
Share the Care
  International
Vellore Christian Medical
  College Board, (USA) Inc.
World Vision of Canada
Wycliffe Associates, Inc.

Fund Transmittal

Afro-American Missionary
  Crusade, Inc.
Amazing Grace Missions
Ambassadors For Christ,
  Inc.
American Board of
  International Missions
American European
  Fellowship Chrn. Oneness
  Evang., Inc.
American Mc All Association
Apostolic Christian Church
  (Nazarene), Apos. Chr.
  Ch. Found.
Women's Chrn. Clg. Madras
  Inc./St. Christopher's
  Trng. Clg.
Back to the Bible
  Missionary Agency
Christian Aid Mission
Christian Business Men's
  Committee International
  (Canada)
Christian Information
  Service, Inc.
Christian Missions in Many
  Lands, Inc.
Christian Union General
  Mission Board
Church of God World
  Missions
Correll Missionary
  Ministries
D.M. Stearns Missionary
  Fund, Inc.
Elim Fellowship, Inc.
Evangelical Missions
  Council of Good News
Faith Christian Fellowship
  World Outreach
FARMS International, Inc.
Friends For Missions, Inc.
Friends of Turkey

Fuller Evangelistic
Association
Fundamental Evangelistic
Association
Go-Ye Fellowship
Good Shepherd Agricultural
Mission, Inc.
India Christian Mission,
Inc.
International Christian
Leprosy Mission, Inc.
(Canada)
International Christian
Leprosy Mission, Inc.
(USA)
International Christian
Mission
International Foundation
For EWHA Woman's
University
Lutheran World Federation,
U.S.A. National Committee
Ministry of Mission
Services
Missionary Evangelistic
Fellowship, Inc.
Native Preacher Company,
Inc.
Outreach, Inc.
Pacific Broadcasting
Association, Inc.
Petra International, Inc.
Progressive Natl. Bapt.
Conv. USA, Inc. Bapt.
For. Msn. Bur.
Unevangelized Tribes
Mission, Inc.
United Church of Canada,
Division of World
Outreach
United Fundamentalist
Church
Vellore Christian Medical
College Board, (USA) Inc.
We Go, Inc. (World
Encounter Gospel
Organization)
Welfare of the Blind, Inc.
World Baptist Fellowship
Mission Agency
International
World Wide Prayer and
Missionary Union

Furlough Housing

Cedar Lane Missionary
Homes, Inc.
Home Finders International

Furloughed Missionary Support

AIM, Inc. (Assistance in
Missions)
Baptist Faith Missions
Christian INFO
Christian Services
Fellowship, Inc.
Church of God (Anderson,
Indiana) Msny. Brd.
Faith Ministries
FARMS International, Inc.
General Conference of
Seventh-day Adventists
Men For Missions
International
Missionary Auto-Truck
Service
Missionary Leasing Company
Overseas Ministries Study
Center
Providence Mission Homes,
Inc.
World Concern/Crista
International

Industrial Training

Kansas Yearly Meeting of
Friends Africa Gospel
Mission
Lott Carey Baptist Foreign
Mission Convention

Information Service

AIM, Inc. (Assistance in
Missions)
Ambassadors For Christ,
Inc.
American Board of
International Missions
American Leprosy Missions,
Inc.
American Mc All Association
American Messianic
Fellowship
Christian Amateur Radio
Fellowship
Christian Information
Service, Inc.
Christian Missions in Many
Lands, Inc.
Christian Services
Fellowship, Inc.
Committee To Assist
Ministry Education
Overseas (CAMEO)
Episcopal Church Missionary
Community
Evangelical Friends Mission
Evangelical Missions
Council of Good News
Evangelical Missions
Information Service, Inc.
Far East Broadcasting

Company, Inc.
FARMS International, Inc.
Fellowship of Artists For
Cultrual Evangelism
(FACE)
Fellowship of Faith For
Muslims
Food For The Hungry
International
Friends of Turkey
Intercristo
International Fellowship of
Christians
Japan International
Christian Univ. Found.,
Inc.
Lutheran World Federation,
U.S.A. National Committee
Lutherans For World
Evangelization
Mission Renewal Team, Inc.
Mission Services
Association, Inc.
Mission Training and
Resource Center
Missionary Communications,
Inc.
Missionary Information
Exchange
Missions Advanced Research
and Communication Center
(MARC)
National Association of
Free Will Baptists, Bd.
of For. Msns
National Religious
Broadcasters
Org. of Continuing Educ.
for American Nurses
(OCEAN)
Overcomer Press, Inc.
Providence Mission Homes,
Inc.
Samuel Zwemer Institute
Society of Central Asian
News (SCAN)
Today's Mission
Incorporated
United Presbyterian Center
for Mission Studies
United Presbyterian Order
for World Evangelization
United States Center for
World Mission
World Mission Information
Bank
World Wide Prayer and
Missionary Union

International Summer School

International Foundation
For EWHA Woman's

University

Internship Ministries

Outreach International

Justice

Japan-North American
Commission on Cooperative
Mission

Leadership Training

African Enterprise
Christian Missionary
Fellowship
Christians United in
Action, Inc.
World Missionary Assistance
Plan
World Vision International
World Vision, Incorporated
Young Life

Linguistics

Christian and Missionary
Alliance in Canada
Church of the Lutheran
Brethren of America, Brd.
of Wrld. Ms
Churches of Christ in
Christian Union: Foreign
Msny. Dept.
Comm. on Children's
Literature For Women and
Children
Evangel Bible Translators
Evangelical Alliance
Mission (TEAM)
General Conference of
Seventh-day Adventists
Gospel Recordings
Incorporated
Korea International
Mission, Inc.
Link Care Center
Lutheran Bible Translators,
Inc.
Missionary Internship, Inc.
New Tribes Mission
New Tribes Mission of
Canada
Outreach International
Pioneer Bible Translators
Regions Beyond Missionary
Union (Canada)
Toronto Institute of
Linguistics
Wycliffe Bible Translators
International, Inc.

AGENCIES LISTED BY PRIMARY TASK

Literacy

Action International
Ministries
Advent Christian Gen. Conf.
of America
Africa Inland Mission
(Canada)
African Methodist Episcopal
Zion Ch., Dept. of Oseas.
Msns.
Baptist Haiti Mission, Inc.
Carver Foreign Missions,
Inc.
Christian Literature
International
Christian Reformed World
Relief Committee
Christian Translation
Ministries
Church of the Lutheran
Brethren of America, Brd.
of Wrld. Ms
Churches of Christ in
Christian Union: Foreign
Msny. Dept.
CODEL (Coordination in
Development, Inc.)
Comm. on Children's
Literature For Women and
Children
Conservative Baptist
Foreign Mission Society
David C. Cook Foundation
Evangel Bible Translators
Great Commission Crusades,
Inc.
Literacy and Evangelism,
Inc.
Lutheran Bible Translators,
Inc.
Lutheran Church-Missouri
Synod
Lutheran Frontier Missions
New Tribes Mission
New Tribes Mission of
Canada
Pioneer Bible Translators
Red Sea Mission Team, Inc.,
U.S.A. Council
Regions Beyond Missionary
Union (Canada)
Westminister Biblical
Missions, Inc.
World Literature Crusade
Wycliffe Bible Translators
International, Inc.

Literature Distribution

Action International
Ministries
ACTS International

Adib Eden Evangelistic
Missionary Society, Inc.
Afghan Border Crusade
Africa Evangelical
Fellowship (Canada)
Africa Inland Mission
(Canada)
African Methodist Episcopal
Church, Inc. Dept. of
Msns.
African Methodist Episcopal
Zion Ch., Dept. of Oseas.
Msns.
Air Crusade, Inc.
Ambassadors For Christ,
Inc.
America's Keswick, Inc.
American Advent Mission
Society
American Association for
Jewish Evangelism
American Baptist
Association, Missionary
Committee
American Board of
International Missions
American Board of Missions
to the Jews, Inc.
American European
Fellowship Chrn. Oneness
Evang., Inc.
American Messianic
Fellowship
American Scripture Gift
Mission
American Tract Society
Anchor Bay Evangelistic
Association
Apostolic Faith Mission of
Portland, Oregon
Asian Outreach
Back to the Bible
Missionary Agency
Baptist General Conference
Board of World Missions
Baptist Haiti Mission, Inc.
Baptist International
Missions, Inc.
Bethany Fellowship Msns.
(Div. of Bethany
Fellowship, Inc.)
Bethel Foreign Mission
Foundation
Bible Alliance Mission,
Inc.
Bible Christian Union, Inc.
Bible Holiness Movement
Bible Memory Association
International
Bible Presbyterian Church,
Ind. Brd. For Presby.
For. Msns.
Bookmates International,

Incorporated
Brazil Gospel Fellowship
  Mission
California Yearly Meeting
  of Friends Church, Bd. of
  Msns.
Calvary Evangelistic
  Mission, Inc./WIVV Msny.
  Radio Station
Chinese Christian Mission
Chinese Gospel Crusade,
  Inc.
Christ For The Nations,
  Inc.
Christ For The Philippines,
  Inc.
Christian and Missionary
  Alliance
Christian and Missionary
  Alliance in Canada
Christian Church of North
  America, Msns. Dept.
Chrn. Echoes Natl.
  Ministry, Inc. (Chrn.
  Crusade)
Christian Life Missions
Christian Literature
  Crusade (Ontario) Inc.
Christian Literature
  Crusade, Inc.
Christian Literature
  International
Christian Medical Society
Christian Pilots
  Association, Inc.
Christian Salvage Mission,
  Inc.
Christian Services
  Fellowship, Inc.
Christian Transportation
Christian Union General
  Mission Board
Christian World Publishers,
  Inc.
Church of God (Seventh
  Day), Gen. Conf., Msns.
  Abroad
Church of God General
  Conference Mission
  Department
Church of the Lutheran
  Brethren of America, Brd.
  of Wrld. Ms
Church of the Nazarene,
  Gen. Bd. Dept. of Wld.
  Msns.
Comm. on Children's
  Literature For Women and
  Children
Concordia Tract Mission
Conservative Baptist
  Foreign Mission Society
Correll Missionary

Ministries
Eastern European Mission
Evangelical Baptist
  Missions, Inc.
Evangelical Literature
  League (T.E.L.L.)
Evangelical Literature
  Overseas (ELO)
Evangelical Mennonite
  Church, Comm. on Oseas.
  Msns.
Evangelical Scripture
  Mission
Evangelical Tract
  Distributors (Canada)
Evangelism Center, Inc.
Everyday Publications
Fellowship of Grace
  Brethren Church, For.
  Msny. Soc.
Fellowship of Independent
  Missions
Forester Foundation, Inc.
Friends of Israel Gospel
  Ministry, Inc.
Friends of Turkey
Friendship Ministry
  International
General Conference
  Mennonite Church, Comm.
  on Oseas. Msn.
Global Concern, Inc.
Global Outreach Mission
Gospel Association for the
  Blind, Inc.
Gospel Baptist Missions
Great Commission Crusades,
  Inc.
Greater Europe Mission
Greater Mexican Missions
H.O.P.E. Bible Mission,
  Inc.
Harvesters International
  Mission, Inc.
High School Evangelism
  Fellowship, Inc.
Hindustan Bible Institute,
  Inc.
Independent Assemblies of
  God, International
Independent Gospel Missions
India Christian Mission,
  Inc.
India Evangelical Mission,
  Inc.
Inter-Varsity Christian
  Fellowship
Inter-Varsity Christian
  Fellowship of Canada
International Christian
  Fellowship
International Gospel League
International Needs-USA

AGENCIES LISTED BY PRIMARY TASK

International Prison Ministry
Jesus Evangelism
Jesus to the Communist World, Inc.
Jewish Voice Broadcast
John Milton Society for the Blind
Kansas Yearly Meeting of Friends Africa Gospel Mission
Latin America Mission, Inc.
Lester Sumrall Evangelistic Association
Liberty Corner Mission
Life messengers, Inc.
Living Waters
Logoi, Inc.
Lutheran Frontier Missions
Macedonian Service Foundation, Inc.
Mahon Mission
Media Ministries Division, Mennonite Bd. of Msns.
Message of Life, Inc.
Messengers of the New Covenant, Inc.
Mexican Christian Mission, Inc.
Middle East Christian Outreach--USA Council
Middle East Media
Minnesota Bible Fellowship, Inc.
Mission Possible Foundation, Inc.
Mission Services Association, Inc.
Mission to Europe's Millions, Inc.
Missionary Evangelistic Fellowship, Inc.
Missionary Information Exchange
Missionary Strategy Agency
Missions Advanced Research and Communication Center (MARC)
Moody Literature Ministries
Narramore Christian Foundation
New Testament Missionary Union
Next Towns Crusade, Inc.
Norma Lam Ministries
Open Bible Ministries, Inc.
Open Door Missionary Fellowship, Inc.
Operation Mobilization - Canada
Operation Mobilization Send the Light, Inc.
Org. of Continuing Educ.

for American Nurses (OCEAN)
Outreach, Inc.
Overcomer Press, Inc.
Overseas Missionary Fellowship
Pan American Missions, Inc.
Pentecostal Assemblies of Canada, Oseas. Msns. Dept.
Pentecostal Assemblies of the World, Inc. For. Msns. Dept.
Prison Mission Assn., Inc.
Reformed Episcopal Church Bd. of For. Msns.
Russia for Christ, Inc.
Salvation Army, The
Samaritan's Purse
Scripture Gift Mission (Canada), Inc.
Slavic Gospel Association
Source of Light Ministries, Intl.
South America Mission, Inc.
South American Crusades, Inc.
Spanish Evangelical Literature Fellowship, Inc.
Spanish-World Gospel Mission, Inc.
Sundanese Missionary Fellowship
Today's Mission Incorporated
Trans World Missions
Trans World Radio
Ukrainian Evangelical Alliance of North America
Undenominational Church of the Lord
Underground Christian Missions, Inc.
United Evangelical Churches
United Fundamentalist Church
United Pentecostal Church Intl. For. Msns. Div.
Western Tract Mission
Wings of Healing
World Evangelism Foundation
World Gospel Crusades
World Hope Foundation
World Literature Crusade
World Missionary Press, Inc.
World Missions, Inc.
World Opportunities International
World Radio Missionary Fellowship, Inc.
World Wide Missionary

Crusader, Inc.
World's Christian Endeavor
Union
World-Wide Missions
International
Worldwide Fellowship with
Jesus Christ Mission
Youth Enterprises, Inc.
Youth For Christ/U.S.A.

Literature Production

Action International
Ministries
ACTS International
Adib Eden Evangelistic
Missionary Society, Inc.
Alberto Mottesi
Evangelistic Association,
Inc.
American Leprosy Missions,
Inc.
American Scripture Gift
Mission
American Tract Society
AMG International
(Advancing the Ministries
of the Gospel)
Anchor Bay Evangelistic
Association
Apostolic Church of
Pentecost of
Canada-Missionary Dept.
Apostolic Faith Mission of
Portland, Oregon
Asian Outreach
Bethany Fellowship Msns.
(Div. of Bethany
Fellowship, Inc.)
Bethel Pentecostal Temple,
Inc.
Bethesda Mission, Inc.
Bible Alliance Mission,
Inc.
Bible Christian Union, Inc.
Bible Holiness Movement
Bible Literature
International
Bible Memory Association
International
Biblical Literature
Fellowship
Billy Graham Evangelistic
Association
Bookmates International,
Incorporated
Calvary Evangelistic
Mission, Inc./WIVV Msny.
Radio Station
Canadian Bible Society
Child Evangelism
Fellowship, Inc.
Chinese Christian Mission

Christ For The Nations,
Inc.
Christ's Mission
Christian and Missionary
Alliance
Christian and Missionary
Alliance in Canada
Christian Literature and
Bible Center, Inc.
Christian Literature
Crusade (Ontario) Inc.
Christian Literature
Crusade, Inc.
Christian Medical Society
Christian Translation
Ministries
Christian Transportation
Christian Union General
Mission Board
Christian World Publishers,
Inc.
Conservative Baptist
Foreign Mission Society
Crusade Evangelism
International
David C. Cook Foundation
European Evangelistic
Society
Evangelical Alliance
Mission (TEAM)
Evangelical Literature
League (T.E.L.L.)
Evangelical Literature
Overseas (ELO)
Evangelical Scripture
Mission
Evangelical Tract
Distributors (Canada)
Evangelize China
Fellowship, Inc.
Everyday Publications
Forester Foundation, Inc.
Free Methodist Church of N.
America Gen. Msny. Bd.
Global Concern, Inc.
Gospel Missionary Union
Grace and Truth, Inc.
Grace Mission, Inc.
Harvesters International
Mission, Inc.
Inter-Varsity Christian
Fellowship
International Bible
Translators
International Christian
Fellowship
International Lutheran
Laymen's League
Jesus Evangelism
Latin America Assistance
Life messengers, Inc.
Living Bibles International
Logoi, Inc.

AGENCIES LISTED BY PRIMARY TASK

Lutheran Bible Translators, Inc.
Lutheran Braille Workers
Lutheran Church-Missouri Synod
Lutheran Frontier Missions
Media Ministries Division, Mennonite Bd. of Msns.
Mennonite Board of Missions
Message of Life, Inc.
Messengers of the New Covenant, Inc.
Middle East Media
Mission Services Association, Inc.
Missionary Strategy Agency
Missionary TECH Team
Missions Advanced Research and Communication Center (MARC)
Moody Literature Ministries
Narramore Christian Foundation
National Association of Free Will Baptists, Bd. of For. Msns
New Life International
New Life League
North Africa Mission
Northwest Yearly Meeting of Friends Ch., Dept. of Msns.
Open Door Missionary Fellowship, Inc.
Operation Mobilization - Canada
Operation Mobilization Send the Light, Inc.
Orthodox Presbyterian Church Committee on Foreign Missions
Osborn Foundation
Outreach, Inc.
Overseas Missionary Fellowship
Pentecostal Assemblies of Canada, Oseas. Msns. Dept.
Pilgrim Fellowship, Inc., The
R.E.A.P.
Reformation Translation Fellowship
Romanian Missionary Society
Salvation Army, The
Scripture Gift Mission (Canada), Inc.
Scripture Union, U.S.A.
Source of Light Ministries, Intl.
Spanish Evangelical Literature Fellowship, Inc.

Tainan Evangelical Mission
Today's Mission Incorporated
Undenominational Church of the Lord
United Presbyterian Order for World Evangelization
Western Tract Mission
Wisconsin Evangelical Lutheran Synod, Bd. for Wld. Msns.
World Gospel Crusades
World Literature Crusade
World Missionary Assistance Plan
World Missionary Press, Inc.
World Outreach
World Wide Missionary Crusader, Inc.
World Wide Prayer and Missionary Union
World-Wide Missions International
Worldwide Discipleship Association, Inc.
Youth For Christ/U.S.A.

Management Consulting

Christian Service Fellowship
Evangelical Leadership International
Helps International Ministries, Inc.
Jubilee, Inc.
Mission Training and Resource Center
Missionary TECH Team
Technoserve, Inc.
United Board for Christian Higher Education in Asia

Media Resource Pool

Fellowship of Faith For Muslims

Medical Supplies

Afro-American Missionary Crusade, Inc.
Christian Blind Mission International (CBM Intl.)
Christian Pilots Association, Inc.
Compassion Relief and Development, Inc.
Correll Missionary Ministries
Evangelization Society of the Pittsburgh Bible

Institute
Grace Mission, Inc.
Handclasp International
Inc.
Holt International
Children's Services, Inc.
International Church Relief
Fund, Inc.
Ludhiana Christian Medical
College Board, U.S.A.,
Inc.
MAP International (Medical
Assistance Programs)
Moravian Church in America,
Bd. of Wld. Msn.
Natl. Baptist Convention of
Amer., For. Msn. Bd.
REAP International
Samaritan's Purse
World Concern/Crista
International

Medicine, Dental and Public Health

Action International
Ministries
Afghan Border Crusade
Africa Evangelical
Fellowship
Africa Evangelical
Fellowship (Canada)
Africa Inland Mission
Africa Inland Mission
(Canada)
African Methodist Episcopal
Church, Inc. Dept. of
Msns.
African Methodist Episcopal
Zion Ch., Dept. of Oseas.
Msns.
American Advent Mission
Society
American Baptist Churches
in the U.S.A., Intl. Min.
American Committee for
KEEP, Inc.
American Leprosy Missions,
Inc.
Associate Reformed Presb.
Ch., Wld. Witness
Association of Baptists For
World Evangelism, Inc.
Baptist General Conference
Board of World Missions
Baptist Haiti Mission, Inc.
Baptist Mid-Missions
Berean Mission, Inc.
Bethany Home, Inc.
Bethel Foreign Mission
Foundation
Bible Presbyterian Church,
Ind. Brd. For Presby.

For. Msns.
BMMF International/Canada
BMMF/International (U.S.A.)
Brethren in Christ Missions
Calcutta Mission of Mercy
Campus Crusade for Christ,
International (Overseas
Dept.)
Canadian Baptist Overseas
Mission Board
Christian Baptist Ch. of
God Assn. Wld. for Christ
Msns.
Christian Blind Mission
International (CBM Intl.)
Christian Church (Disciples
of Christ) Div. of Oseas.
Min.
Christian Dental Society
Christian Evangelical
Mission of Indonesia
Christian Medical Society
Christian Pilots
Association, Inc.
Christian Reformed Board
For World Missions
Christian Reformed World
Relief Committee
Christian Service Corps
Christians United in
Action, Inc.
Church of God (Anderson,
Indiana) Msny. Brd.
Church of God in Christ,
Mennonite Gen. Msn. Bd.,
Inc.
Church of our Lord Jesus
Christ of the Apostolic
Faith, Inc.
Church of the Lutheran
Brethren of America, Brd.
of Wrld. Ms
Church of the Nazarene,
Gen. Bd. Dept. of Wld.
Msns.
Church of the United
Brethren in Christ, Brd.
of Msns.
Church World Service
Division of DOM-NCCCUSA
Churches of Christ in
Christian Union: Foreign
Msny. Dept.
Churches of God, General
Conference Comm. on Wrld.
Msns.
CODEL (Coordination in
Development, Inc.)
Compassion International,
Inc.
Conservative Baptist
Foreign Mission Society
Evangelical Alliance

Mission (TEAM)
Evangelical Alliance
Mission of Canada, Inc.
Evangelical Covenant Church
of America, Bd. of Wld.
Msn.
Evangelical Free Ch. of
America, Bd. of Oseas.
Msn.
Evangelical Friends Church,
Eastern Region, Fr. For.
Msnry.
Evangelical Lutheran
Church, Division of World
Missions
Evangelistic Faith Mission,
Inc.
Fellowship of Christian
Assemblies Mission to
Liberia
Fellowship of Evangelical
Baptist Chrs. in Canada
Fellowship of Grace
Brethren Church, For.
Msny. Soc.
Free Methodist Church of N.
America Gen. Msny. Bd.
Friends of Indonesia
Fellowship, Inc.
Frontier Ministries
International
General Baptist Foreign
Mission Society, Inc.
General Conference
Mennonite Church, Comm.
on Oseas. Msn.
General Conference of
Seventh-day Adventists
Glad Tidings Missionary
Society, Inc.
Global Concern, Inc.
Handclasp International
Inc.
Hindustan Bible Institute,
Inc.
Holy Land Christian Mission
Houses of Refuge, Intl.
Orphanages Assn. Inc.
India Evangelical Mission,
Inc.
International Missions,
Inc.
Kansas Yearly Meeting of
Friends Africa Gospel
Mission
Leprosy Mission Canada
Liebenzell Mission of
Canada
Living Waters
Logos Translators
Lott Carey Baptist Foreign
Mission Convention
Ludhiana Christian Medical

College Board, U.S.A.,
Inc.
Lutheran Church in
America-Div. for Wrld.
Msn. and Ecumenism
Lutheran Church-Missouri
Synod
Lutheran Orient Mission
Society
Lutheran World Relief,
Incorporated
MAP International (Medical
Assistance Programs)
Mennonite Brethren
Missions/Services
Mennonite Central Committee
Missionary Church, Div. of
Overseas Ministries
Missionary Dentist, Inc.
Missionary Health
Institute, Inc.
Moravian Church in America,
Bd. of Wld. Msn.
Natl. Assn. of
Congregational Chr. Chs.
of the U.S.A.
National Baptist
Convention, U.S.A., Inc.
For. Msn. Bd.
N. American Committee for
IME, Institut Medical
Evangelique
OMS International, Inc.
Overseas Missionary
Fellowship
Overseas Missionary
Fellowship
Pan American Missions, Inc.
Paul Carlson Medical
Program, Inc.
Pentecostal Assemblies of
the World, Inc. For.
Msns. Dept.
Presbyterian Church in
Canada, Board of World
Mission
Presbyterian Church in the
U.S.A., Div. of Intl.
Msn.
Primitive Methodist Church
in the USA, Intl. Msn.
Bd.
Project Partner with
Christ, Inc.
Ramabai Mukti Mission
(American Council of)
Red Sea Mission Team, Inc.,
U.S.A. Council
Reformed Church in America
General Program Council
Reformed Episcopal Church
Bd. of For. Msns.
Refugee Children, Inc.

Regions Beyond Missionary
Union (Canada)
Romanian Missionary Society
Rural Gospel and Medical
Missions of India, Inc.
Salvation Army, The
Schwenkfelder Church in the
USA and For. Bd. of Msns.
Seventh Day Baptist
Missionary Society
Southern Baptist
Convention, Foreign
Mission Board
Sudan Interior Mission,
Inc.
Totonac Bible Center, Inc.
United Church Board For
World Ministries
United Methodist Church
Comm. on Relief
United Methodist Ch. Wld.
Div. of the Bd. of Global
Min.
United World Mission,
Incorporated
Vacation Samaritans
Voice of Calvary
Wesleyan Church Gen. Dept.
of Wld. Msns.
Wider Ministries Commission
Wings of Mercy Missions
Inc.
World Gospel Mission
World Medical Mission
World Mission Prayer League
World Mission Prayer League
Canada
World Missionary
Evangelism, Inc.
World Presbyterian
Missions, Inc.
World Radio Missionary
Fellowship, Inc.
World-Wide Missions
International
Worldwide Evangelization
Crusade
Worldwide Fellowship with
Jesus Christ Mission

Ministry to Servicemen

Baptist Bible Fellowship
International
Baptist International
Missions, Inc.
Bible Literature
International
Christian and Missionary
Alliance in Canada
Christian Transportation
Conservative Baptist
Association of America

Independent Gospel Missions
Lord's Way Inn Ministries,
Inc.
Moody Institute of Science
Navigators, The
New Life International
Overseas Christian
Servicemen's Centers
Overseas Christian
Servicemen's Centers
Prison Mission Assn., Inc.
United Missionary
Fellowship
Youth With A Mission

Ministry to the Handicapped

Chinese for Christ, Inc.
Christian Blind Mission
International (CBM Intl.)
Christian Blind Mission
International (CBM Intl.)
Erhlin Christian Polio Home
Gospel Association for the
Blind, Inc.
Gospel Association for the
Blind, Inc.
Lutheran Braille Workers
Lutheran Frontier Missions
Operation Eyesight
Universal
United Missionary
Fellowship
Welfare of the Blind, Inc.

Mission Conferences

Macedonian Service
Foundation, Inc.

Mission Strategy Development

Institute of Chinese
Studies

Missionary Orientation
and Training

American Lutheran Ch., Div.
For Wld. Msn.
Bethany Missionary
Association
CAM International Practical
Missionary Training, Inc.
Christian Missions in Many
Lands, Inc.
Christian Reformed Board
For World Missions
Christians In Action
Church of God (Anderson,
Indiana) Msny. Brd.
Church of God of Prophecy,
World Mission Committee

AGENCIES LISTED BY PRIMARY TASK

Cumberland Presbyterian
Church, Board of Missions
Emmanuel International
Episcopal Church Missionary
Community
Evangel Bible Translators
Faith Ministries
Fellowship of Artists For
Cultrual Evangelism
(FACE)
General Conference of
Seventh-day Adventists
Gospel Outreach
Haggai Community
Harvest Fields Missionary
and Evangelistic Assn.,
Inc.
Inter-Varsity Christian
Fellowship
International Crusades,
Inc.
Korea International
Mission, Inc.
Liberty Corner Mission
Link Care Center
Literacy and Evangelism,
Inc.
Lutheran Church-Missouri
Synod
Lutheran World Federation,
U.S.A. National Committee
Mission SOS
Mission Training and
Resource Center
Missionary Internship, Inc.
Missions Outreach, Inc.
Narramore Christian
Foundation
New Tribes Mission
Open Doors With Brother
Andrew
Org. of Continuing Educ.
for American Nurses
(OCEAN)
Outreach International
Overseas Ministries Study
Center
Overseas Missionary
Fellowship
Pentecostal Free Will
Baptist Church, Inc.
Presbyterian Church in
Canada, Board of World
Mission
Regular Baptists of Canada,
Women's Missionary
Society
Samuel Zwemer Institute
Share the Care
International
Society for Europe's
Evangelization (S.E.E.)
Sundanese Missionary

Fellowship
Toronto Institute of
Linguistics
Vacation Samaritans
Victory Mission of the
Americas
World Missionary Assistance
Plan
Youth With A Mission

Motion Pictures

Adib Eden Evangelistic
Missionary Society, Inc.
Anis Shorrosh Evangelistic
Association
Billy Graham Evangelistic
Association
Brazil Gospel Fellowship
Mission
Campus Crusade for Christ,
International (Overseas
Dept.)
Christian Literature and
Bible Center, Inc.
Evangelical Baptist
Missions, Inc.
Gospel Films, Inc.
Hermano Pablo, Inc.
International Films, Inc.
Life For Latins, Inc.
Mennonite Mission Bd. of
Pacific Coast Conf.
(Mexico Bd.)
Moody Institute of Science
Pan American Missions, Inc.
Prison Mission Assn., Inc.
World Neighbors, Inc.
World Thrust Films, Inc.
World Vision of Canada

Nurture or Support of
National Churches

Adib Eden Evangelistic
Missionary Society, Inc.
African Methodist Episcopal
Zion Ch., Dept. of Oseas.
Msns.
African Mission Services,
Inc.
American Advent Mission
Society
American Lutheran Ch., Div.
For Wld. Msn.
American Missionary
Fellowship
American Waldensian Aid
Society
Apostolic Church in Canada,
The
Associate Reformed Presb.
Ch., Wld. Witness

AGENCIES LISTED BY PRIMARY TASK

Association of Free
Lutheran Congregations
Baptist Haiti Mission, Inc.
Bethel Mission of China,
Inc.
Bible Christian Union, Inc.
Bible Way Chrs. of Our Lord
Jesus Christ Worldwide,
Inc.
Bibles For The World, Inc.
Biblical Literature
Fellowship
BMMF International/Canada
Brazil Gospel Fellowship
Mission
Brethren in Christ Missions
Children of India
Foundation
Chinese Christian Mission
Christian Aid Mission
Christian Canadian Mission
to Overseas Students
Christian Catholic Church
Christian Church (Disciples
of Christ) Div. of Oseas.
Min.
Christian Church of North
America, Msns. Dept.
Christian Missionary
Fellowship
Christian Nationals'
Evangelism Commission,
Inc. (CNEC)
Christian Nationals'
Evangelism Commission,
Inc. (Canada)
Church of God (Seventh
Day), Gen. Conf., Msns.
Abroad
Church of God, USA
Headquarters
Church of the Lutheran
Brethren of America, Brd.
of Wrld. Ms
Church of the Nazarene,
Gen. Bd. Dept. of Wld.
Msns.
Church of the United
Brethren in Christ, Brd.
of Msns.
Churches of Christ in
Christian Union: Foreign
Msny. Dept.
Conservative Baptist
Foreign Mission Society
Correll Missionary
Ministries
Crusade Evangelism
International
Daystar Communications,
Inc.
Eastern Mennonite Board of
Missions and Charities

Elim Fellowship, Inc.
Emmanuel International
Evangelical Bible Mission,
Inc.
Evangelical Congregational
Church Division of
Missions
Evangelical Friends Church,
Eastern Region, Fr. For.
Msnry.
Evangelical Latin League,
Inc.
Evangelical Lutheran
Church, Division of World
Missions
Evangelical Mennonite
Church, Comm. on Oseas.
Msns.
Evangelical Methodist
Church Bible Methodist
Missions
Evangelical Scripture
Mission
Evangelize China
Fellowship, Inc.
Far Eastern Gospel Crusade
FARMS International, Inc.
Franconia Mennonite
Conference Mission
Commission
Friends of Indonesia
Fellowship, Inc.
Full Gospel Native
Missionary Association
General Conference
Mennonite Church, Comm.
on Oseas. Msn.
General Conference of the
Evangelical Baptist
Church, Inc.
Good Shepherd Agricultural
Mission, Inc.
Gospel Outreach to India,
Inc.
Harvest Fields Missionary
and Evangelistic Assn.,
Inc.
Houses of Refuge, Intl.
Orphanages Assn. Inc.
Independent Gospel Missions
Japan Evangelical Mission
Japan Evangelistic
Association, Inc.
Japan-North American
Commission on Cooperative
Mission
Japanese Evangelical
Missionary Society
Kansas Yearly Meeting of
Friends Africa Gospel
Mission
Language Institute For
Evangelism (LIFE)

AGENCIES LISTED BY PRIMARY TASK

Logoi, Inc.
Maranatha Baptist Mission,
 Inc.
Men in Action
Mennonite Board of Missions
Moravian Church in America,
 Bd. of Wld. Msn.
Natl. Assn. of
 Congregational Chr. Chs.
 of the U.S.A.
National Baptist
 Convention, U.S.A., Inc.
 For. Msn. Bd.
New Life International
Next Towns Crusade, Inc.
North American Baptist Gen.
 Msny. Soc., Inc.
OMS International, Inc.
Orthodox Presbyterian
 Church Committee on
 Foreign Missions
Osborn Foundation
Overseas Missionary
 Fellowship
Pentecostal Holiness
 Church-World Missions
 Department
Petra International, Inc.
Presbyterian Church in
 Canada, Board of World
 Mission
Progressive Natl. Bapt.
 Conv. USA, Inc. Bapt.
 For. Msn. Bur.
Project Partner with
 Christ, Inc.
Reformed Church in America
 General Program Council
Reformed Episcopal Church
 Bd. of For. Msns.
Salvation Army, The
Seventh Day Baptist
 Missionary Society
Southern European Mission,
 Inc.
Sudan Interior Mission,
 Inc.
Ukrainian Evangelical
 Alliance of North America
United Church Board For
 World Ministries
United Methodist Ch. Wld.
 Div. of the Bd. of Global
 Min.
United Presbyterian Church
 in the USA Program Agency
United World Mission,
 Incorporated
Voice of China and Asia
 Missionary Society, Inc.
We Go, Inc. (World
 Encounter Gospel
 Organization)

Westminister Biblical
 Missions, Inc.
Wisconsin Evangelical
 Lutheran Synod, Bd. for
 Wld. Msns.
Word of Life Fellowship
World Ministries Commission
World Mission in Church and
 Society
World Missionary
 Evangelism, Inc.
World Wide Prayer and
 Missionary Union
World-Wide Missions
 International
Worldteam

Orphanage/Childcare

Action International
 Ministries
Adib Eden Evangelistic
 Missionary Society, Inc.
Africa Inland Mission
 (Canada)
Afro-American Missionary
 Crusade, Inc.
American Board for the
 Syrian Orphanage
American Committee for
 KEEP, Inc.
American Mc All Association
AMG International
 (Advancing the Ministries
 of the Gospel)
Anchor Bay Evangelistic
 Association
Apostolic Christian Church
 (Nazarene), Apos. Chr.
 Ch. Found.
Bethany Home, Inc.
Bibles for the Nations
Bibles For The World, Inc.
BMMF International/Canada
Calcutta Mission of Mercy
Children of India
 Foundation
Children's Haven
 International, Inc.
Chrn. Echoes Natl.
 Ministry, Inc. (Chrn.
 Crusade)
Chr. Homes Children, Inc.
 Harold Martin Evang.
 Assn., Inc.
Christian Service Corps
Christians United in
 Action, Inc.
Church of God (Anderson,
 Indiana) Msny. Brd.
Church of God in Christ,
 Mennonite Gen. Msn. Bd.,
 Inc.

Church of God of Prophecy,
World Mission Committee
Compassion International,
Inc.
Compassion of Canada
Evangelical Free Ch. of
America, Bd. of Oseas.
Msn.
Evangelical Scripture
Mission
Evangelize China
Fellowship, Inc.
Fellowship of Christian
Assemblies Mission to
Liberia
Fellowship of Independent
Missions
Food For The Hungry
International
Foundation For His
Ministry-Orphanage
Committee
Friendship Ministry
International
Full Gospel Evangelistic
Association
Full Gospel Native
Missionary Association
General Baptist Foreign
Mission Society, Inc.
Global Concern, Inc.
Good Shepherd Agricultural
Mission, Inc.
Gospel Outreach to India,
Inc.
Hindustan Bible Institute,
Inc.
Holt International
Children's Services, Inc.
Holy Land Christian Mission
Home of Onesiphorus
Houses of Refuge, Intl.
Orphanages Assn. Inc.
Independent Gospel Missions
India Christian Mission,
Inc.
India Evangelical Mission,
Inc.
India National Inland
Mission
International Church Relief
Fund, Inc.
International Gospel League
Intl Pentecostal Ch. of
Christ, Global Msns.
Dept.
Korea Gospel Mission
Lester Sumrall Evangelistic
Association
Missions of Baja
Mustard Seed, Inc., The
Natl. Assn. of
Congregational Chr. Chs.

of the U.S.A.
Natl. Baptist Convention of
Amer., For. Msn. Bd.
New Life League
Norma Lam Ministries
Ramabai Mukti Mission
(American Council of)
Refugee Children, Inc.
Rural Gospel and Medical
Missions of India, Inc.
Salvation Army, Canada and
Bermuda
Share the Care
International
Southern European Mission,
Inc.
Teen Missions
International, Inc.
Tele-Missions
International, Inc.
Trans World Missions
United Methodist Church
Comm. on Relief
United Methodist Ch. Wld.
Div. of the Bd. of Global
Min.
Victory Mission of the
Americas
Voice of China and Asia
Missionary Society, Inc.
Wings of Healing
Wings of Mercy Missions
Inc.
World Hope Foundation
World Missionary
Evangelism, Inc.
World Missions Fellowship
World Missions, Inc.
World Outreach
World Presbyterian
Missions, Inc.
World Vision International
World Vision of Canada
World Vision, Incorporated
World-Wide Missions
International

Pastoral Support

Greater Mexican Missions

Postal Evangelism

Friends of Turkey

Prayer Fellowship

Fellowship of Faith For
Muslims

Prison Evangelism

Christian Life Missions

AGENCIES LISTED BY PRIMARY TASK

Psychological Counseling

ACTS International
Gospel Association for the
  Blind, Inc.
Great Commission Crusades,
  Inc.
International Evangelism
  Crusades, Inc.
Japan Evangelistic
  Association, Inc.
Link Care Center
Narramore Christian
  Foundation
New Life International
Youth With A Mission

Purchasing Service

African Mission Services,
  Inc.
AIM, Inc. (Assistance in
  Missions)
Gospel Recordings of
  Canada, Inc.
Living Waters
Ludhiana Christian Medical
  College Board, U.S.A.,
  Inc.
MAP International (Medical
  Assistance Programs)
Vellore Christian Medical
  College Board, (USA) Inc.

Recording and Distribution

African Methodist Episcopal
  Zion Ch., Dept. of Oseas.
  Msns.
Bible Alliance Mission,
  Inc.
Bible Translations On Tape,
  Inc.
Brethren Church, Missionary
  Board of The Brethren
  Church
Christ For The Philippines,
  Inc.
Far East Broadcasting
  Company, Inc.
Gospel Recordings
  Incorporated
Gospel Recordings of
  Canada, Inc.
International Bible
  Institute
International Lutheran
  Laymen's League
John Milton Society for the
  Blind
Media Ministries Division,
  Mennonite Bd. of Msns.
Mission Aides, Incorporated

Mission Aides, Incorporated
Mission Aides, Incorporated
Missionary Electronics,
  Inc.
Missionary TECH Team
Overcomer Press, Inc.
Overseas Radio and
  Television, Inc.
Pacific Broadcasting
  Association, Inc.
Pilgrim Fellowship, Inc.,
  The
Portable Recording
  Ministries, Inc.
Sundanese Missionary
  Fellowship
Trans World Radio

Recruiting;

Campus Crusade for Christ,
  International (Overseas
  Dept.)
Christian Missionary
  Fellowship
Christian Union General
  Mission Board
Christians In Action
Church of God (Anderson,
  Indiana) Msny. Brd.
Church of God (Holiness)
  For. Msn. Brd.
Episcopal Church Missionary
  Community
Faith Ministries
General Conference of
  Seventh-day Adventists
Intercristo
International Students,
  Inc.
Laos, Inc.
Literacy and Evangelism,
  Inc.
Lutheran World Federation,
  U.S.A. National Committee
Middle East Christian
  Outreach--USA Council
Middle East Media
Missionary Evangelistic
  Fellowship, Inc.
Missions Outreach, Inc.
Next Towns Crusade, Inc.
N. American Committee for
  IME, Institut Medical
  Evangelique
Operation Mobilization Send
  the Light, Inc.
Outreach International
Youth With A Mission

Reference Board

International Fellowship of

Christians

Refugee Resettlement

United Methodist Church Comm. on Relief

Rehabilitation

United Methodist Church Comm. on Relief

Research (Medical)

Leprosy Mission Canada

Research (Mission Related)

Chinese Gospel Crusade, Inc.
Christian INFO
David C. Cook Foundation
Daystar Communications, Inc.
FARMS International, Inc.
Fellowship of Artists For Cultrual Evangelism (FACE)
Global Concern, Inc.
Haggai Institute for Advanced Leadership Training, Inc.
Institute of Chinese Studies
International Missionary Advance
Link Care Center
Ludhiana Christian Medical College Board, U.S.A., Inc.
Lutheran Church-Missouri Synod
Lutherans For World Evangelization
Mission Services Association, Inc.
Mission SOS
Mission Training and Resource Center
Missionary Information Exchange
Missionary Strategy Agency
Missions Advanced Research and Communication Center (MARC)
New Life International
O.C. Ministries, Inc.
Open Doors With Brother Andrew
Overseas Ministries Study Center
Portable Recording Ministries, Inc.

Presbyterian Church in Canada, Board of World Mission
Samuel Zwemer Institute
Society of Central Asian News (SCAN)
Toronto Institute of Linguistics
United Presbyterian Center for Mission Studies
United Presbyterian Order for World Evangelization
United States Center for World Mission
World Vision International

Scholarships

Lutheran World Federation, U.S.A. National Committee

Schools for Missionary Children

International Institute, Inc.

Scripture Booklet Distribution

World Missionary Press, Inc.

Self-Help Projects

American Friends Service Committee
American Mc All Association
BMMF International/Canada
Christian Reformed World Relief Committee
Church of God (Anderson, Indiana) Msny. Brd.
CODEL (Coordination in Development, Inc.)
Compassion Relief and Development, Inc.
FARMS International, Inc.
Food For The Hungry International
Food for the Hungry/Canada
Friends For Missions, Inc.
Frontier Ministries International
General Baptist Foreign Mission Society, Inc.
Gospel Outreach
Harvest Fields Missionary and Evangelistic Assn., Inc.
Houses of Refuge, Intl. Orphanages Assn. Inc.
Jubilee, Inc.

AGENCIES LISTED BY PRIMARY TASK

Lutheran World Relief,
Incorporated
Mennonite Central Committee
Mennonite Economic
Development Associates
Mexican Christian Mission,
Inc.
Natl. Assn. of
Congregational Chr. Chs.
of the U.S.A.
Operation Eyesight
Universal
Outreach, Inc.
Paul Carlson Medical
Program, Inc.
REACH, Incorporated
Self Help Foundation
Toronto Institute of
Linguistics
World Concern/Crista
International
World Ministries Commission
World Neighbors, Inc.
World Relief Corporation
World Vision of Canada
Wycliffe Associates, Inc.

Serving Other Agencies

African Mission Services,
Inc.
AIM, Inc. (Assistance in
Missions)
Amazing Grace Missions
American Friends Service
Committee
American Scripture Gift
Mission
Back to the Bible
Missionary Agency
Bible Alliance Mission,
Inc.
Bible Literature
International
Bible Translations On Tape,
Inc.
Cedar Lane Missionary
Homes, Inc.
Chiang Mai Mission Board
Christ's Mission
Christian INFO
Christian Pilots
Association, Inc.
Christian Service Corps
Christian Service
Fellowship
Christian Services
Fellowship, Inc.
CODEL (Coordination in
Development, Inc.)
Committee To Assist
Ministry Education
Overseas (CAMEO)

Compassion of Canada
Compassion Relief and
Development, Inc.
Conservative Congregational
Christian Conference
Daystar Communications,
Inc.
Evangelical Missions
Information Service, Inc.
Faith Ministries
Friendship Ministry
International
Fuller Evangelistic
Association
General Association of
Regular Baptist Churches
Gospel Recordings
Incorporated
Gospel Recordings of
Canada, Inc.
Helps International
Ministries, Inc.
Intercristo
International Bible
Translators
International Christian
Mission
International Fellowship of
Christians
International Missionary
Advance
Leprosy Mission Canada
Ministry of Mission
Services
Mission Aides, Incorporated
Mission Aviation Fellowship
Missionary Communications,
Inc.
Missionary Flights
International
Missionary Information
Exchange
Missionary Internship, Inc.
Missionary TECH Team
Missions Outreach, Inc.
New Life International
Org. of Continuing Educ.
for American Nurses
(OCEAN)
Outreach, Inc.
Prison Mission Assn., Inc.
Project Partner with
Christ, Inc.
Project Partner, Inc.
Providence Mission Homes,
Inc.
REAP International
Samaritan's Purse
Samuel Zwemer Institute
Self Help Foundation
Share the Care
International
Steer, Inc.

Teen Missions
International, Inc.
Today's Mission
Incorporated
Toronto Institute of
Linguistics
United Church of Canada,
Division of World
Outreach
United Presbyterian Center
for Mission Studies
United States Center for
World Mission
W. Shabaz Associates, Inc.
World Literature Crusade
World Mission Information
Bank
World Missions Fellowship
World Wide Prayer and
Missionary Union
Wycliffe Associates, Inc.
Wycliffe Associates, Inc.

Serving Other Agencies, Churches

American Bible Society

Serving Other Churches

Tokyo Evangelistic Center

Short-Term Missionary Support Teams

Missions Outreach, Inc.

Short-Term Youth Training

Operation Mobilization -
Canada
Operation Mobilization Send
the Light, Inc.

Social Work

Japan-North American
Commission on Cooperative
Mission

Sports Evangelism

Youth Enterprises, Inc.

Strategies for Evangelism

Daystar Communications,
Inc.

Supplies Ministerial Staff When Needed

Society of St. John the

Evangelist

Supplying Equipment

African Mission Services,
Inc.
AIM, Inc. (Assistance in
Missions)
American Friends Service
Committee
Bible Alliance Mission,
Inc.
Bible Translations On Tape,
Inc.
Christian Amateur Radio
Fellowship
Christian Pilots
Association, Inc.
Christian Services
Fellowship, Inc.
Compassion Relief and
Development, Inc.
Evangelization Society of
the Pittsburgh Bible
Institute
Globe Missionary Evangelism
Gospel Recordings of
Canada, Inc.
Jungle Aviation and Radio
Service, Inc. (JAARS)
Living Waters
Macedonian Service
Foundation, Inc.
Men For Missions
International
Mission Aides, Incorporated
Missionary Auto-Truck
Service
Missionary Auto-Truck
Service
Missionary Electronics,
Inc.
Moravian Church in America,
Bd. of Wld. Msn.
Portable Recording
Ministries, Inc.
REAP International
Refugee Children, Inc.
Samaritan's Purse
Self Help Foundation
Welfare of the Blind, Inc.

Support of Bible College

International Biblical
Baptist Fellowship, Inc.

Support of Missionaries

Chr. Homes Children, Inc.
Harold Martin Evang.
Assn., Inc.
Gospel Baptist Missions

AGENCIES LISTED BY PRIMARY TASK

International Biblical
Baptist Fellowship, Inc.
Maranatha Baptist Mission,
Inc.

Support of National Ministries

Chinese for Christ, Inc.

Support of National Missionaries

Hague Foreign Mission, Inc.

Support of Nationals ✔

African Enterprise
African Methodist Episcopal
Church, Inc. Dept. of
Msns.
African Methodist Episcopal
Zion Ch., Dept. of Oseas.
Msns.
African Mission Services,
Inc.
Agricultural Missions, Inc.
All Peoples Baptist Mission
American Association for
Jewish Evangelism
American Baptist
Association, Missionary
Committee
American Board of
International Missions
American European
Fellowship Chrn. Oneness
Evang., Inc.
AMG International
(Advancing the Ministries
of the Gospel)
Anglican Church of Canada,
Natl. and Wld. Program
Anglican Orthodox Church
Anis Shorrosh Evangelistic
Association
Apostolic Church of
Pentecost of
Canada-Missionary Dept.
Baptist Haiti Mission, Inc.
Bethany Missionary
Association
Bethel Mission of China,
Inc.
Bible Missionary Church,
World Missions Department
Bible Translations On Tape,
Inc.
Bible Way Chrs. of Our Lord
Jesus Christ Worldwide,
Inc.
Bibles for the Nations
BMMF/International (U.S.A.)

Bookmates International,
Incorporated
Campus Crusade for Christ,
International (Overseas
Dept.)
Central Yearly Meeting of
Friends Missionary
Committee
Children of India
Foundation
Christian Aid Mission
Christian Baptist Ch. of
God Assn. Wld. for Christ
Msns.
Christian Business Men's
Committee International
(Canada)
Christian Canadian Mission
to Overseas Students
Christian Church of North
America, Msns. Dept.
Christian Mission for the
Deaf
Church of God (Anderson,
Indiana) Msny. Brd.
Church of God (Seventh
Day), Gen. Conf., Msns.
Abroad
Church of God of the
Apostolic Faith, Inc.
Church of the United
Brethren in Christ, Brd.
of Msns.
Eastern European Mission
Evangelical Christian
Education Ministries Inc.
Evangelical Congregational
Church Division of
Missions
Evangelical Leadership
International
Evangelical Methodist
Church Bible Methodist
Missions
Evangelical Methodist
Church World Missions
Evangelical Missions
Council of Good News
Evangelization Society of
the Pittsburgh Bible
Institute
Evangelize China
Fellowship, Inc.
Faith Center Global
Ministries
Free Gospel Church, Inc.
Friends of Indonesia
Fellowship, Inc.
Friendship Ministry
International
Full Gospel Evangelistic
Association
Full Gospel Native

113

Missionary Association
General Conference of the
 Evangelical Baptist
 Church, Inc.
Glad Tidings Missionary
 Society, Inc.
Gospel Crusade World Wide
 Mission Outreach
Gospel Outreach to India,
 Inc.
Great Commission Crusades,
 Inc.
Houses of Refuge, Intl.
 Orphanages Assn. Inc.
Independent Assemblies of
 God, International
International Christian
 Mission
International Films, Inc.
International Foundation
 For EWHA Woman's
 University
International Needs-USA
Japanese Evangelical
 Missionary Society
Jubilee, Inc.
Lester Sumrall Evangelistic
 Association
Lutheran Orient Mission
 Society
Metropolitan Church
 Association
Mexican Border Missions
Mission Aviation Fellowship
Mission Possible
 Foundation, Inc.
Missionary Evangelistic
 Fellowship, Inc.
Moody Institute of Science
Natl. Baptist Convention of
 Amer., For. Msn. Bd.
New Life League
Next Towns Crusade, Inc.
North East India General
 Mission, Inc.
Open Doors With Brother
 Andrew
Outreach, Inc.
Pan American Missionary
 Society, Inc.
Pentecostal Free Will
 Baptist Church, Inc.
Petra International, Inc.
Progressive Natl. Bapt.
 Conv. USA, Inc. Bapt.
 For. Msn. Bur.
R.E.A.P.
Regular Baptists of Canada,
 Women's Missionary
 Society
Rural Gospel and Medical
 Missions of India, Inc.
Share the Care

International
Slavic Gospel Association
South Pacific Evangelical
 Fellowship
Southern European Mission,
 Inc.
Spanish Evangelical
 Literature Fellowship,
 Inc.
Things to Come Mission,
 Inc.
Ukrainian Evangelical
 Alliance of North America
We Go, Inc. (World
 Encounter Gospel
 Organization)
Welfare of the Blind, Inc.
Wings of Mercy Missions
 Inc.
Wisconsin Evangelical
 Lutheran Synod, Bd. for
 Wld. Msns.
World Hope Foundation
World Missionary
 Evangelism, Inc.
World Missions, Inc.
World Neighbors, Inc.
World-Wide Missions
 International

Supports Higher Education

United Board for Christian
 Higher Education in Asia

Teacher Training

Bible Club Movement of
 Canada
Bible Club Movement, Inc.

Teaching

Advent Christian Gen. Conf.
 of America

Technical Assistance

Agricultural Missions, Inc.
Amateur Radio Missionary
 Service (ARMS)
American Friends Service
 Committee
Christian Amateur Radio
 Fellowship
Compassion Relief and
 Development, Inc.
Evangelical Literature
 Overseas (ELO)
Frontier Ministries
 International
Holt International
 Children's Services, Inc.

International Institute,
   Inc.
Jungle Aviation and Radio
   Service, Inc. (JAARS)
Ludhiana Christian Medical
   College Board, U.S.A.,
   Inc.
Mennonite Economic
   Development Associates
Mission Aides, Incorporated
Mission Aviation Fellowship
Missionary Air Transport,
   Inc.
Missionary Electronics,
   Inc.
Missionary Information
   Exchange
Missionary TECH Team
National Religious
   Broadcasters
Paul Carlson Medical
   Program, Inc.
Portable Recording
   Ministries, Inc.
REAP International
Technical Support Mission
Technoserve, Inc.
United Methodist Church
   Comm. on Relief
World Relief Corporation
World Vision International

Training

Adib Eden Evangelistic
   Missionary Society, Inc.
Agricultural Missions, Inc.
Ambassadors For Christ,
   Inc.
American Board of Missions
   to the Jews, Inc.
American Leprosy Missions,
   Inc.
American Missionary
   Fellowship
Assemblies of God, Div. of
   Foreign Mnsn.
Association of Free
   Lutheran Congregations
Breakthrough Ministries
Campus Crusade for Christ,
   International (Overseas
   Dept.)
Canadian Baptist Overseas
   Mission Board
Child Evangelism
   Fellowship, Inc.
Chinese Christian Mission
Chinese World Mission
   Center
Christian Translation
   Ministries
Church of God of Prophecy,

World Mission Committee
Church World Service
   Division of DOM-NCCCUSA
Cumberland Presbyterian
   Church, Board of Missions
David C. Cook Foundation
Daystar Communications,
   Inc.
Evangelical Literature
   Overseas (ELO)
Evangelical Scripture
   Mission
Forester Foundation, Inc.
Global Concern, Inc.
Globe Missionary Evangelism
Good Shepherd Agricultural
   Mission, Inc.
Gospel Crusade World Wide
   Mission Outreach
Gospel Outreach
Great Commission Crusades,
   Inc.
Haggai Institute for
   Advanced Leadership
   Training, Inc.
High School Evangelism
   Fellowship, Inc.
Independent Assemblies of
   God, International
Institute of Chinese
   Studies
Inter-Varsity Christian
   Fellowship of Canada
Intl. Church of the
   Foursquare Gospel--Dept.
   of Msns. Intl.
International Fellowship of
   Evangelical Students -
   USA
International Films, Inc.
International Gospel League
International Needs-USA
International Students,
   Inc.
Japan Evangelistic
   Association, Inc.
Jungle Aviation and Radio
   Service, Inc. (JAARS)
Leprosy Mission Canada
Life For Latins, Inc.
Ling A. Juane Ministries,
   Inc.
Logoi, Inc.
Mahon Mission
Media Ministries Division,
   Mennonite Bd. of Msns.
Mennonite Economic
   Development Associates
Mexican Mission Ministries,
   Inc.
Mission SOS
Missionary Air Transport,
   Inc.

AGENCIES LISTED BY PRIMARY TASK

Missionary Evangelistic
Fellowship, Inc.
Missionary Gospel
Fellowship, Inc.
Missionary Strategy Agency
National Religious
Broadcasters
Navigators of Canada
International, The
Navigators, The
Next Towns Crusade, Inc.
Open Air Campaigners (USA)
Open Doors With Brother
Andrew
Outreach, Inc.
Overseas Missionary
Fellowship
Overseas Radio and
Television, Inc.
Pillar of Fire Missions
Portable Recording
Ministries, Inc.
REACH, Incorporated
Self Help Foundation
South Pacific Evangelical
Fellowship
Team Ventures International
Tokyo Evangelistic Center
Toronto Institute of
Linguistics
Trans World Missions
United Evangelical Churches
United Indian Missions,
Inc.
United Pentecostal Church
Intl. For. Msns. Div.
United Presbyterian Order
for World Evangelization
United States Center for
World Mission
Vacation Samaritans
Welfare of the Blind, Inc.
Westminister Biblical
Missions, Inc.
Wider Ministries Commission
World Missionary
Evangelism, Inc.
World Neighbors, Inc.
World's Christian Endeavor
Union
Wycliffe Bible Translators
International, Inc.
Youth for Christ (Canada)
Youth For Christ/U.S.A.
Youth With A Mission

Training National Workers

Men in Action

Transfers Material Goods to Missionaries

Missionary Services, Inc.

Translation, Bible

Africa Inter-Mennonite
Mission, Inc.
American Bible Society
Association of Baptists For
World Evangelism, Inc.
Baptist Mid-Missions
Bible Alliance Mission,
Inc.
Biblical Literature
Fellowship
California Yearly Meeting
of Friends Church, Bd. of
Msns.
Canadian Bible Society
Christian and Missionary
Alliance
Christian Literature
International
Christian Translation
Ministries
Christian World Publishers,
Inc.
Church of the Nazarene,
Gen. Bd. Dept. of Wld.
Msns.
Churches of Christ in
Christian Union: Foreign
Msny. Dept.
Evangel Bible Translators
Free Gospel Church, Inc.
Great Commission Crusades,
Inc.
Independent Gospel Missions
International Bible
Translators
Jungle Aviation and Radio
Service, Inc. (JAARS)
Kansas Yearly Meeting of
Friends Africa Gospel
Mission
Liebenzell Mission of
Canada
Living Bibles International
Logos Translators
Lutheran Bible Translators,
Inc.
Lutheran Church-Missouri
Synod
Middle East Media
Mission to the World
New Tribes Mission
New Tribes Mission of
Canada
Pioneer Bible Translators
Reformed Episcopal Church
Bd. of For. Msns.
Regions Beyond Missionary
Union (Canada)
Regions Beyond Missionary

Union (U.S.A.)
Scripture Gift Mission
(Canada), Inc.
Spanish Evangelical
Literature Fellowship,
Inc.
Sudan Interior Mission,
Inc.
Trinitarian Bible Society,
Canada
Unevangelized Fields
Mission
World Home Bible League
World Missionary Press,
Inc.
World Presbyterian
Missions, Inc.
Worldwide Evangelization
Crusade
Wycliffe Associates, Inc.
Wycliffe Bible Translators
International, Inc.

Union
Youth For Christ/U.S.A.

Translation, Other

Anglican Orthodox Church
California Yearly Meeting
of Friends Church, Bd. of
Msns.
Christian Literature
Crusade (Ontario) Inc.
Christian Literature
International
Christian Translation
Ministries
Christian World Publishers,
Inc.
Evangelical Scripture
Mission
Friends of Turkey
Gospel Literature
International
Jesus to the Communist
World, Inc.
Reformation Translation
Fellowship
World Thrust Films, Inc.

Workshops for Nationals

Comm. on Children's
Literature For Women and
Children

Youth Ministry

American European Bethel
Mission, Inc.
Mexican Missions, Inc.
Outreach, Inc.
World Opportunities
International
World's Christian Endeavor

Associations of Agencies

Six associations of mission agencies represent about 40 percent of the total missionary force, with the three largest (DOM, EFMA, IFMA) representing about 39 percent. The six associations are the Commission on World Concerns (CWC) of the Canadian Council of Churches; the Division of Overseas Ministries (DOM) of the National Council of the Churches of Christ in the U.S.A.; the Evangelical Foreign Missions Association (EFMA), an affiliate of the National Association of Evangelicals; the Interdenominational Foreign Mission Association (IFMA); The Associated Missions (TAM); and the Fellowship of Missions (FOM). Although the total number of missionaries in agencies belonging to these asociations as a whole has increased slightly, the percentage they represent has significantly decreased from that reported in the Eleventh Edition.

Valid comparisons over time among associations, based upon number of missionaries and financial data, are difficult because association memberships are not static. Old members leave, new ones join. Some agencies belong to more than one association. Not all agencies reported the same type of information. With these qualifications in mind, the EFMA in 1979 has increased significantly in both missionaries and in income, whereas the IFMA has increased slightly in missionaries and significantly in income. DOM-NCCUSA, while increasing slightly in income, has decreased significantly in the number of missionaries. It is important to note the income shown is not the income of the associations, but is the reported income of member agencies listed in this **Handbook**.

Affiliated agencies now send 40 percent of the overseas personnel and receive about 46 percent of the reported income. This compares with 56 percent of the personnel and 54 percent of the income as reported in the Eleventh Edition.

This rather drastic shift is due to strong growth in a few of the unaffiliated agencies. This should not obscure the fact that member agencies associated with the EFMA have shown an income growth of 89 percent.

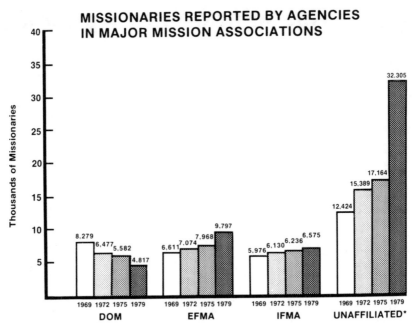

MISSIONARIES REPORTED BY AGENCIES IN MAJOR MISSION ASSOCIATIONS

Thousands of Missionaries

DOM: 1969 8,279 · 1972 6,477 · 1975 5,582 · 1979 4,817

EFMA: 1969 6,611 · 1972 7,074 · 1975 7,968 · 1979 9,797

IFMA: 1969 5,976 · 1972 6,130 · 1975 6,236 · 1979 6,575

UNAFFILIATED*: 1969 12,424 · 1972 15,389 · 1975 17,164 · 1979 32,305

*Note: totals reflect only those msys. unaffiliated with DOM. IFMA and EFMA

The decline in the percentage of the total force and income represented by the DOM-NCCSA and the CCC-CWC was first noted in 1960. It continued in 1968, 1975 and again in 1979. The shift in personnel from the conciliar agencies appears to be continuing. The United Methodist Board of Global Ministries and Church World Service run counter to this overall trend.

For details of membership, finances and personnel, see the individual association descriptions in the Mission Association section which follows immediately.

Although not an association of agencies, the formation of the Association of Church Missions Committees in June 1974 to represent the **lay** interest in mission portends change. A non-denominational organization of local churches, the membership represents about 600 churches from almost 25 denominations with a total church mission budget of over ten million dollars. At the current rate of growth, it is not unreasonable to expect a three-year projection to approximately 25 percent of the total income available to North American Protestant sending agencies.

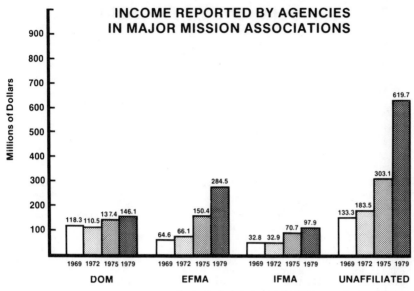

INCOME REPORTED BY AGENCIES
IN MAJOR MISSION ASSOCIATIONS

Income is total reported by member agencies

Associations of Agencies

Since 1893 when the Foreign Missions conference of North America was organized, mission boards and agencies have on occasion formed themselves into associations for coordination and assistance in their ministries. At present, major Protestant missionary associations in North America include: The Canadian Council of Churches, Commission on World Concerns (CCCCWC); Division of Overseas Ministries, National Council of the Churches of Christ in the USA (DOM-NCCCUSA); Evangelical Foreign Missions Association (EFMA); and Interdenominational Foreign Mission Association of North America (IFMA). These four associations represent about 40 percent of the Protestant missionaries from North America.

Two other mission associations exist. The Associated Missions of the International Council of Christian Churches (TAM-ICCC) was formed in 1952. In 1959 several of the agencies included in the TAM-ICCC withdrew and formed a new association known as the Fellowship of Missions (FOM).

It is important to note that the DOM-NCCCUSA and CCC-CWC are not organizationally equivalent to the EFMA, IFMA, FOM and TAM-ICCC. The DOM and CWC are divisions of larger organizations; the National Council of the Churches of Christ in the USA and the Canadian Council of Churches respectively. Agencies are related to DOM-NCCCUSA and CCC-CWC because their parent body is a member communion, or they may be affiliated members, or they may be in "fraternal relationship," involving no organic ties. Member communions are those denominations and agencies in full participation in the work of the National Council of Churches and its program units. Affiliated boards and agencies are those agencies not members of the National Council, but participating in one or more cooperative work projects carried forward by the Division of Overseas Ministries.

The other associations are organizations formed by the component missionary agencies. EFMA includes both denominational and non-denominational agencies while the IFMA is entirely non-denominational in its membership.

THE ASSOCIATED MISSIONS OF THE INTERNATIONAL COUNCIL OF CHRISTIAN CHURCHES (TAM-ICCC)
756 Haddon Ave., Collingswood, NJ   08108

      TELEPHONE   (609) 858-0700

      OFFICERS   Dr. Henry A. Campbell, Pres.
               B.R. Oatley-Willis, Gen. Sec.

ORGANIZED   1948 as Missions Commission of ICCC resolved in-
              to present organization in 1952.

DESCRIPTION   An inter-mission service agency of fundamental
              tradition.

THE CANADIAN COUNCIL OF CHURCHES COMMISSION ON WORLD CONCERNS (CCC-CWC)
40 St. Clair Avenue., E. Toronto, ON, M4T 1M9, Canada

TELEPHONE   (416) 921-4152

OFFICERS   Mrs. Heather Johnston, Pres.
              The Rev. Dr. Donald Anderson, Gen. Sec.

ORGANIZED   1928 as Canadian Overseas Missionary Conference
              merged with CCC in 1948.

DESCRIPTION   The Commission on World Concerns is the program
              unit of the Canadian Council on Churches through
              which the CCC communicates to other councils on
              matters of overseas and ecumenical missions
              projects, and through which Canadian churches
              provide support for such projects. The CCC is
              an ecumenical agency with 11 member churches and
              eight other agencies in fraternal relationship.

EVANGELICAL FOREIGN MISSIONS ASSOCIATION (EFMA)
1430 K Street, N.W., Washington, DC 20005

TELEPHONE   (202) 628-7911

OFFICERS   Dr. Vernon Wiebe, Pres.
              Dr. Wade T. Coggins, Exec. Director

ORGANIZED   1945

PERIODICALS   **Missionary   News   Service**   (semi-monthly);
              Evangelical   Missions   Quarterly   (published
              jointly with IFMA through EMIS).

DESCRIPTION   The EFMA has 72 members (11 are associate mem-
              bers who are not sending agencies), which send
              out 9,308 missionaries. Of that total 8,265
              originate from North America and the remainder
              from other sending countreis.

              EFMA is an association of foreign mission soci-
              eties operating for the purpose of providing:
              (1) united representation before governments,
              (2) a basis for fellowship, (3) a channel for
              promoting cooperative effort, (4) information
              concerning government regulations and interna-
              tional affairs which affect foreign missions,
              (5) services along the following lines: pass-
              port and visa service, processing authentica-
              tion of legal documents, travel, reservations
              (through Universal Travel Service,
              (800) 323-9402), conferences and seminars,
              information services (through EMIS).

              EFMA is the mission affiliate of the National
              Association of Evangelicals.

COMMITTEES
AND AGENCIES   EFMA forms committees and agencies as special
                needs arise.

                Many are formed jointly with the Interdenomina-
                tional Foreign Mission Association. (See
                listing of joint committees following the IFMA
                section.)

CORPORATION   The World Relief Corporation of the National
                Association of Evangelicals is the relief
                organization which represents EFMA. Address
                P.O. Box WRC, Wheaton, IL 60187.

                OCR Committee dealing with matters of "post dif-
                ferential" costs for overseas locations. It
                helps missions cope with the complex economic
                situation in the world. Mr. Fay Richardson,
                Chairman; P.O. Box 5, Wheaton, IL 60187.

THE FELLOWSHIP OF MISSIONS (FOM)
4205 Chester Avenue, Cleveland, OH 44103

TELEPHONE   (216) 432-2200

OFFICERS   William J. Hopewell, Jr., D.D., Pres.
                C. Raymond Buck, Ph.D., Vice-Pres.

ORGANIZED   1969

PERIODICAL   **Focus on Missions,** thrice yearly.

DESCRIPTION   A non-denominational inter-mission service
                agency of fundamental tradition, acting as an
                accrediting agency for its constituents, pro-
                viding an information service, arranging sem-
                inars and similar services, and encouraging the
                formation of missionary and church fellowships.
                FOM is composed of mission agencies (including
                "home" missions) with a total missionary force
                of nearly 1,300.

INTERDENOMINATIONAL FOREIGN MISSION ASSOCIATION OF NORTH AMERICA, INC. (IFMA)
P.O. Box 395, Wheaton, IL 60187

TELEPHONE   (312) 682-9270

CHAIRMAN   W. Elwyn Davies, Pres.

EXEC. OFFICER   Mr. Edwin L. Frizen, Jr., Exec. Director

ORGANIZED   1917

PERIODICALS   **IFMA NEWS** (QUARTERLY)
                Evangelical Missions Quarterly published
                jointly with the EFMA through EMIS).

PUBLICATIONS   **Mission Administration Manual; Accounting and
                Financial Reporting Guide for Missionary Organ-
                izations; IFMA Opportunities** (a listing of per-
                sonnel needs of member missions.)

124

DESCRIPTION   The Interdenominational Foreign Mission Associ-
               ation (IFMA) is an association of 49 foreign
               mission agencies without denominational affili-
               ation, and representing more than 9,000 mis-
               sionaries in over 115 countries. Of the 7,711
               missionaries serving overseas, 5,407 are from
               North America and 2,304 from other countries.
               Also, 1,749 from North America and 11 from over-
               seas serve in North American ministries. In
               addition to these, more than 1000 workers from
               North America serve in summer and under one-year
               assignments.

               The IFMA is incorporated in the United States
               and Canada. It was founded for the purpose of
               strengthening the effectiveness and outreach of
               fatih missions. As stated in the constitution,
               its purpose is "to further spiritual fellowship
               and intercessory prayer; to promote mutual
               helpfulness and conferences concerning mis-
               sionary principles and practice; to make pos-
               sible a united testimony concerning the
               existing need for a speedy and complete evangel-
               ization of the world; and to establish a united
               voice."

               Membership in the IFMA is an indication that the
               societies have met the requirements and stan-
               dards of the Association, and are recommended
               for prayer and financial support, as well as for
               missionary service by conservative evangelical
               Christians. Member missions are governed by
               responsible councils or directorates; exercise
               control over missionaries; publish audited
               financial statements annually; approve each
               other on the field and at home in ethical
               practices; adhere to a strong conservative
               evangelical doctrinal position; and are engaged
               in taking the gospel of the Lord Jesus Christ to
               all people everywhere.

               Besides affording a basis for fellowship for its
               agencies, the IFMA provides:

               1. Accreditation of member missions.

               2. A united voice before government and
                   the public.

               3. Information on social security, tax
                   matters and other government regula-
                   tions.

               4. Avenues for cooperative endeavors.

               5. Counseling on mission issues.

               6. Briefings, conferences and seminars.

               The IFMA Business Administration Committee
               sponsors the biennial Mission Administration
               Seminar, publishes the Mission Administration
               Manual and the Accounting and Financial
               Reporting Guide for Missionary Organizations.

Leadership and assistance are also given through committees representing Africa, Asia, China, Latin America, Islamic areas; Committee to Assist Ministry Education Overseas (CAMEO); Evangelical Mission Information Service (EMIS); Missions Agency Review; and Personnel. All of these are joint with the Evangelical Foreign Missions Association (EFMA).

NATIONAL COUNCIL OF THE CHURCHES OF CHRIST IN THE U.S.A. DIVISION OF OVERSEAS MINISTRIES (DOM-NCCCUSA)
475 Riverside Drive, New York, NY 10027

TELEPHONE (212) 870-2175

ORGANIZED 1893 as the Foreign Missions Conference of North America and reorganized in 1950 as the Division of Foreign Missions, National Council of the Churches of Christ in the U.S.A., continuing the work of Church World Service, Incorporated since 1946.

PERIODICALS Annual Report

INCOME 1978 32,893,337

EXPENDITURES 1978 34,970,765

DIVISION SERVICES Associate General Secretary (of the NCCCUSA)for Overseas Ministries
Eugene L. Stockwell
Associate Secretary (and Executive Director CWS)
Paul F. McCleary
Financial Management
Director, Selma M. Femrite
Interpretation and Promotion
Director, John J. Mullen
Overseas Personnel
Director, John P. Mullenburg
Associated Mission Medical Office (AMMO)
Physician, John D. Frame, M.D.

The Associated Mission Medical Office was organized in August 1933 by six major mission boards in response to the need for more specialized experienced and systematized medical care of missionaries on furlough and for health appraisal of new candidates. It serves mission boards and occasionally missionaries of non-member boards.

DEPARTMENTS Church World Service Department (CWS)
Executive Director, Paul F. McCleary
Material Resources Program
Director, Jan S. F. Van Hoogstraten
CROP-The Community Hunger Appeal of CWS
National Director, Ronald E. Stenning
Immigration and Refugee Program
Director, John W. Schauer, Jr.
Planned Parenthood Program
Director, Iluminada R. Rodriquez

126

The Church World Services Department develops
and maintains the elements of relief, recon-
struction , rehabilitation and social and
economic development in cooperative overseas
ministries program with specific responsibility
to meet requests for assistance in disaster or
other emergency situations to obtain and make
available material resources to plan and con-
duct a program of refugee immigration services,
and to coordinate and act on behalf of cooperative overseas ministries programs of United
States churches with related programs of world
ecumenical bodies other church-related
agencies, government foundations, and private
welfare agencies.

Strategy, Technical and Area Program Department
(STAP)
Executive Director, Robert C.S. Powell
Africa Working Group
Executive Director, Robert C.S. Powell
Church World Service Director,
Jan S. F. Van Hoogstraten
East Asia and the Pacific Working Group
Executive Director, Edwin M. Luidens
China Program Director, Franklin J. Woo
Asia Research Consultants, Hong Kong,
Ray & Rhea Whitehead
Director for Japan & Hong Kong, Robert W.
Northrup
Southern Asia Working Group
Executive Director, Boyd B. Lowry
Latin American and the Caribbean Working Group
Executive Director, William L. Wipfler
Church World Service Director,
H. Dwight Swartzendruber
Middle East and Europe Working Group
Director, J. Richard Butler

The Strategy, Technical and Area Program
Department combines and coordinates the functional and service units which operate with
overseas Christian councils, councils of
churches and assists in the provision of ministries needed by the developing indigenous
churches in Asia, Africa and Latin America as
well as in the service of U.S.A. citizens living
abroad. The units and their services are described below.

Committee on Agriculture and Rural Life
Executive Director, J. Benton Rhoades
Associate Director, Jessie M. Taylor

The purpose of this program is to give help to
North American Protestant churches in their
efforts to provide a Christian witness and service for rural people around the world through
improved food production, rural community development, home improvement and nutrition and
the strengthening of rural church life.

It operates under a program and policy committee
composed of designated representatives of

Protestant mission agencies, and selected persons of competence in the field of agriculture and rural development.

The office is responsible for working relationships between the Division of Overseas Ministries, NCCCUSA and Agricultural Missions, Inc.

Churchmen Overseas Program
  Director, John R. Collins

The program for Churchmen Overseas is divided into three functions:

Overseas Union Churches. English language churches in non-English speaking countries are related to this office. They are almost all interdenominational, international and interracial. Each is fully autonomous, this unit exercising no control over it. The office provides extensive personnel assistance provides certain financial services and grants, and encourages fellowship with similar congregations throughout the world.

American Laymen Overseas. This portion of the program is designed to provide Christian guidance and direction for the approximately one percent of the U.S. population which currently lives overseas and several million Americans who travel overseas each year. Training institutes for laymen have been held in the U.S.A. and at overseas centers in cooperation with other Christians in the area.

Ministry to Service Personnel in the Far East. The committee seeks to find ways whereby U.S. military personnel may relate themselves to the national Christians and churches in Japan, Korea, Okinawa, Thailand, and Hong Kong. Service Centers provide home-like recreation facilities for service men; guide service, conducted tours, information service and an opportunity to spend time in Christian homes and churches.

Ecumenical Scholarships and Theological Education. The Ecumenical Scholarship Program was established in 1946. It cooperates with the Scholarship program of the World Council of Churches. Candidates from Europe and Africa are selected by the Scholarship Committee in Geneva, upon recommendation of their respective National Committees; those from Asia, Latin America and elsewhere are selected by National Christian Councils in direct negotiation with the Program. The scholarship program aims to strengthen the work and to enrich the common life in all lands by an exchange of potential leaders and by providing students with larger opportunities for study and experiences.

Intermedia
 Executive Director, Vern Rossman
 Director, Marion E. Van Horne

It is Intermedia's purpose to assist churches in
Asia, Africa, the Middle East and Latin America
in the cooperative use of communication tools
for evangelism and Christian education. U.S.
and Canadian denominations are related through
Intermedia to literature, broadcasting and
audio-visual   ministries   of   the   overseas
councils of churches, wherever possible. The
productions of Christian council centers include dramatic films, filmstrips, picture-story
cards, records, radio and TV programs and pro-
jectors.

Intermedia assists the advance of literacy and
Christian literature in Africa, Asia, the Near
East and Latin America, and maintains close
relationships with world bodies engaged in
widespread communications ministries.

Leadership Development
 Director, John W. Backer

ORGANIZATION NAME	OVERSEAS PERSONNEL	SHORT TERM	TOTAL INCOME
CANADIAN COUNCIL OF CHURCHES COMMISSION ON WORLD CONCERNS			
Anglican Church of Canada, Natl. and Wld. Program	10	NR	NR
Totals	10	NR	NR
DIVISION OF OVERSEAS MINISTRIES, NATIONAL COUNCIL OF THE CHURCHES OF CHRIST IN THE U.S.A. (DOM-NCCCUSA)			
African Methodist Episcopal Church, Inc. Dept. of Msns.	10	0	$300,000
African Methodist Episcopal Zion Ch., Dept. of Oseas. Msns.	4	2	$174,000
American Baptist Churches in the U.S.A., Intl. Min.	200	1	$8,097,300
American Leprosy Missions, Inc.	6	0	$1,365,692
American Lutheran Ch., Div. For Wld. Msn.	329	18	$31,328,924
Women's Chrn. Clg. Madras Inc./St. Christopher's Trng. Clg.	NR	NR	NR
Christian Church (Disciples of Christ) Div. of Oseas. Min.	75	0	$3,182,445
Church World Service Division of DOM-NCCCUSA	42	0	$41,170,080
Churches of God, General Conference Comm. on Wld. Msns.	19	3	$349,600
CODEL (Coordination in Development, Inc.)	0	0	$1,564,514
Comm. on Children's Literature For Women and Children	0	0	$50,000
Cumberland Presbyterian Church, Board of Missions	7	2	$663,761
International Foundation For EWHA Woman's University	0	0	$100,000
Japan International Christian Univ. Found., Inc.	0	0	$387,782
Laos, Inc.	NR	55	$106,000
Lott Carey Baptist Foreign Mission Convention	7	0	$650,000
Ludhiana Christian Medical College Board, U.S.A., Inc.	20	4	$323,657
Lutheran Church in America-Div. For Wld. Msn. and Ecumenism	148	0	$11,438,261
Lutheran Orient Mission Society	2	0	$120,000
Moravian Church in America, Brd. of Wrld. Msn.	27	3	$700,000
N. American Committee for IME, Institut Medical Evangelique	0	0	$8,187
Presbyterian Church in the U.S.A., Div. of Intl. Msn.	259	32	$7,662,854
Progressive Natl. Bapt. Conv. USA, Inc. Bapt. For. Msn. Bur.	0	NR	NR
Reformed Church in America General Program Council	132	34	$7,103,295
Seventh Day Baptist Missionary Society	6	2	$163,000

ORGANIZATION NAME	OVERSEAS PERSONNEL	SHORT TERM	TOTAL INCOME
United Board for Christian Higher Education in Asia	NR	4	$13,623,501
United Church Board For World Ministries	160	0	$9,495,679
United Methodist Church Comm. on Relief	650	985	$12,800,000
United Methodist Ch. Wld. Div. of the Bd. of Global Min.	938	166	$19,377,430
United Presbyterian Church in the USA Program Agency	359	20	$12,008,328
Wider Ministries Commission	18	2	$424,000
World Ministries Commission	45	21	$ 1,635,259
Totals	3,463	1,354	$186,273,549

EVANGELICAL FOREIGN MISSIONS ASSOCIATION (EFMA)

ORGANIZATION NAME	OVERSEAS PERSONNEL	SHORT TERM	TOTAL INCOME
Action International Ministries	19	9	$422,512
Africa Inter-Mennonite Mission, Inc.	58	6	$713,840
American Advent Mission Society	18	0	$298,205
Assemblies of God, Div. of For. Msns.	1214	170	$29,875,534
Associate Reformed Presb. Ch., Wld. Witness	12	10	$588,628
Baptist General Conference Board of World Missions	101	11	$5,934,347
Bethany Fellowship Msns. (Div. of Bethany Fellowship, Inc.)	111	30	$1,052,851
Bible Literature International	0		$1,500,000
BMMF International/Canada	29	4	$298,000
BMMF/International (U.S.A.)	31	8	$389,634
Brethren Church, Missionary Board of The Brethren Church	8	8	$450,000
Brethren in Christ Missions	34	80	$905,898
California Yearly Meeting of Friends Church, Bd. of Msns.	12	2	$277,551
Calvary Evangelistic Mission, Inc./WIVV Msny. Radio Station	17	14	$891,918
Campus Crusade for Christ, International (Overseas Dept.)	500	77	$50,000,000
Christ's Mission	4	19	$243,000
Christian and Missionary Alliance	809	9	$15,627,269
Christian Church of North America, Msns. Dept.	21	0	$412,193
Christian Literature Crusade, Inc.	22	0	$417,409
Christian Nationals' Evangelism Commission, Inc. (CNEC)	18	6	$2,191,660
Christian Nationals' Evangelism Commission, Inc. (Canada)	4	0	$312,417
Christian Reformed Board For World Missions	258	8	$5,381,910
Christian Reformed World Relief Committee	29	0	$2,600,000

ORGANIZATION NAME	OVERSEAS PERSONNEL	SHORT TERM	TOTAL INCOME
Church of God World Missions	78	0	$5,892,704
Church of the Lutheran Brethren of America, Bd. of Wld. Msns	41	0	$413,000
Church of the Nazarene, Gen. Bd. Dept. of Wld. Msns.	484	70	$14,960,725
Church of the United Brethren in Christ, Bd. of Msns.	26	0	$493,884
Churches of Christ in Christian Union: Foreign Msny. Dept.	54	0	$535,742
Committee To Assist Ministry Education Overseas (CAMEO)	0	0	$22,500
Compassion International, Inc.	17	0	$11,221,207
Conservative Baptist Association of America	33	0	$2,930,000
Conservative Baptist Foreign Mission Society	501	114	$9,057,172
Eastern European Mission	2	0	$178,796
Evangelical Congregational Church Division of Missions	61	24	$615,428
Evangelical Free Ch. of America, Bd. of Oseas. Msn.	204	24	$2,695,321
Evangelical Friends Church, Eastern Region, Fr. For. Msny. S	14	1	$314,256
Evangelical Literature Overseas (ELO)	3	0	$93,500
Evangelical Mennonite Brethren Commission on Mission	145	0	$1,876,918
Evangelical Mennonite Church, Comm. on Oseas. Msns.	27	3	$266,266
Evangelical Mennonite Conference Board of Missions	46	17	$680,000
Evangelical Methodist Church World Missions	12	0	$248,330
Evangelistic Faith Mission, Inc.	28	0	$1,200,000
Far East Broadcasting Company, Inc.	37	0	$5,330,825
Fellowship of Grace Brethren Churches, For. Msny. Soc.	99	11	$1,256,546
Free Methodist Church of N. America Gen. Mssy. Brd.	144	68	$2,300,000
General Baptist Foreign Mission Society, Inc.	11	0	$304,410
Grace Mission, Inc.	24	7	$683,764
Intercristo	0	0	$258,649
Intl. Church of the Foursquare Gospel--Dept. of Msns. Intl.	87	9	$2,639,367
International Students, Inc.	5	3	$1,555,000
Kansas Yearly Meeting of Friends Africa Gospel Mission	17	0	$145,000
Latin America Mission, Inc.	164	60	$1,724,000
Link Care Center	0	0	$144,000
Literacy and Evangelism, Inc.	2	0	$338,050
Logoi, Inc.	3	0	$3,343,651
Mennonite Brethren Missions/Services	158	70	$1,133,996
Mexican Mission Ministries, Inc.	6	0	$197,425
Mission Aviation Fellowship	240	4	$7,170,916
Mission to the World	134	29	$1,781,637

ORGANIZATION NAME	OVERSEAS PERSONNEL	SHORT TERM	TOTAL INCOME
Missionary Church, Div. of Overseas Ministries	122	91	$17,631,285
Missionary Internship, Inc.	0	0	$289,529
National Association of Free Will Baptists, Brd. of For. Msn	98	9	$1,598,672
National Religious Broadcasters	0	0	$485,000
Navigators, The	145	50	$11,303,888
North American Baptist Gen. Msny. Soc., Inc.	93	8	$5,000,000
Northwest Yearly Meeting of Friends Ch., Dept. of Msns.	16	1	$304,960
O.C. Ministries, Inc.	73	207	$3,334,152
OMS International, Inc.	231	40	$7,676,708
Open Bible Standard Missions, Inc.	34	2	$470,000
Org. of Continuing Educ. For American Nurses (OCEAN)	0	0	$68,000
Pentecostal Assemblies of Canada, Oseas. Msns. Dept.	192	18	$4,361,452
Pentecostal Church of God, World Missions Department	29	0	$500,000
Pentecostal Holiness Church-World Missions Department	92	3	$1,520,000
Primitive Methodist Church in the USA, Intl. Msn. Bd.	15	3	$300,082
Reformed Presbyterian Ch. of N. America, Bd. of For. Msns.	8	0	$119,041
Trans World Radio	151	7	$10,000,000
United World Mission, Incorporated	52	10	$1,275,134
Wesleyan Church Gen. Dept. of Wld. Msns.	201	31	$2,255,521
World Concern/Crista International	33	8	$2,592,083
World Gospel Crusades	6	4	$306,153
World Gospel Mission	146	18	$4,811,232
World Missionary Assistance Plan	27	0	$940,300
World Opportunities International	28	20	$3,600,000
World Vision, Incorporated	0	0	$46,681,140
Worldwide Evangelization Crusade	134	7	$980,698
Youth For Christ/U.S.A.	28	1	$ 5,762,781
Totals	8,190	1,515	$336,955,572

FELLOWSHIP OF MISSIONS (FOM)

Association of Baptists For World Evangelism, Inc.	502	18	$5,043,629
Baptist Mid-Missions	608	14	$11,000,060
Bible Protestant Missions, Inc.	2	0	$44,000

ORGANIZATION NAME	OVERSEAS PERSONNEL	SHORT TERM	TOTAL INCOME
Evangelical Methodist Church Bible Methodist Missions	7	NR	$72,000
WEFMinistries, Inc.	132	0	$1,676,123
Totals	1,251	32	$17,836,923

INTERDENOMINATIONAL FOREIGN MISSION ASSOCIATION (IFMA)

ORGANIZATION NAME	OVERSEAS PERSONNEL	SHORT TERM	TOTAL INCOME
Africa Evangelical Fellowship	170	17	$2,004,423
Africa Evangelical Fellowship (Canada)	68	11	$986,100
Africa Inland Mission	511	65	$4,527,149
Africa Inland Mission (Canada)	79	11	$1,071,193
Andes Evangelical Mission	43	NR	$423,814
Berean Mission, Inc.	59	1	$868,000
Bible Christian Union, Inc.	106	2	$1,323,862
Bible Club Movement of Canada	2	0	$326,344
Bible Club Movement, Inc.	30	NR	$2,226,383
BMMF International/Canada	29	4	$298,000
BMMF/International (U.S.A.)	31	8	$389,634
CAM International	228	12	$3,045,419
Christian Nationals' Evangelism Commission, Inc. (CNEC)	18	6	$2,191,660
Christian Nationals' Evangelism Commission, Inc. (Canada)	4	0	$312,417
Committee To Assist Ministry Education Overseas (CAMEO)	0	0	$2,500
Evangelical Alliance Mission (TEAM)	905	197	$10,891,110
Evangelical Alliance Mission of Canada, Inc.	100	7	$1,089,767
Evangelical Literature Overseas (ELO)	3	0	$93,500
Far East Broadcasting Company, Inc.	37	0	$5,330,825
Far Eastern Gospel Crusade	135	25	$2,660,801
Global Outreach Mission	175	16	$1,194,652
Gospel Missionary Union	389	17	$4,016,478
Gospel Recordings Incorporated	4	4	$537,000
Gospel Recordings of Canada, Inc.	4	0	$147,407
Greater Europe Mission	160	25	$4,092,480
Home of Onesiphorus	10	0	$310,560
International Christian Fellowship	31	0	$244,501
International Missions, Inc.	132	3	$1,167,811
Janz Team	64	10	$490,000

ORGANIZATION NAME	OVERSEAS PERSONNEL	SHORT TERM	TOTAL INCOME
Japan Evangelical Mission	49	5	$797,995
Language Institute For Evangelism (LIFE)	7	14	$575,000
Liebenzell Mission of U.S.A., Inc.	20	0	$356,394
Mission Aviation Fellowship	240	4	$7,170,916
Mission Aviation Fellowship of Canada	12	1	$300,000
North Africa Mission	72	4	$884,688
Org. of Continuing Educ. for American Nurses (OCEAN)	0	0	$68,000
Overseas Christian Servicemen's Centers	46	18	$1,023,456
Overseas Missionary Fellowship	96	11	$684,004
Overseas Missionary Fellowship	203	5	$1,426,800
Pocket Testament League, Inc.	20	9	$1,192,485
Portable Recording Ministries, Inc.	0	0	$166,132
Ramabai Mukti Mission (American Council of)	4	1	$614,000
Regions Beyond Missionary Union (Canada)	42	2	$599,430
Regions Beyond Missionary Union (U.S.A.)	125	2	$2,516,835
Slavic Gospel Association	89	4	$1,390,248
South America Mission, Inc.	99	4	NR
South American Crusades, Inc.	NR	0	$13,071,000
Sudan Interior Mission, Inc.	590	28	$3,750,000
Unevangelized Fields Mission	312	4	$1,275,134
United World Mission, Incorporated	52	10	$188,457
World Missions Fellowship	12	4	$4,037,000
World Radio Missionary Fellowship, Inc.	161	43	$2,319,310
Worldteam	173	10	
Totals	5,951	624	$97,874,074

THE ASSOCIATED MISSIONS, INTERNATIONAL COUNCIL OF CHRISTIAN CHURCHES (TAM-ICCC)

ORGANIZATION NAME	OVERSEAS PERSONNEL	SHORT TERM	TOTAL INCOME
Bible Presbyterian Church, Ind. Bd. for Presb. For. Msns.	40	0	$435,984
Christian World-Wide Evang. Msn. of Canada	4	12	$11,500
Independent Gospel Missions	NR	NR	$180,000
International Christian Mission	0	0	NR
Methodist Protestant Church, Board of Msns.	4	0	$45,000
World Baptist Fellowship Mission Agency International	154	0	$1,862,858
Totals	202	12	$2,535,342

Mission Agencies

This section in the book contains a basic directory of North American Protestant agencies engaged in or supporting ministries outside of North America. As indicated in the Introduction, the data listed in this directory basically contains information provided by the respective agencies in response to a survey questionnaire.

It should be noted that many agencies have ministries in North America (including Alaska and Hawaii) which are not indicated in this **Handbook**. Thus, the agency listing does not always reflect the full scope of an organization's work. Where there is a question on this, the agency should be queried directly.

Agencies are listed alphabetically without considering the "the" ahead of a name, even though this may be a part of the official name. Each agency decided whether or not to include "Inc." as part of the official name. Agencies or mission boards appear in the directory under the name of their parent organization or church denomination. Where the individual agency or board name is commonly known, it appears in alphabetic sequence as a cross-reference. Some mission agencies have merged, reorganized, internationalized, or changed their names since their previous directory listing. These prior names are also listed and a cross-reference directs one to the present name. An agency that is a subdivision of a larger organization will be listed if it is perceived to service the larger missions community rather than simply its parent organization. Additional cross-references frequently used secondary or legal names, acronyms and subsidiaries which are not listed separately as an aid to directory users.

The name is followed by the:

Street Address:
P.O. Address: mailing address if different from street address.
Telephone: if in North America.
Executive Officer: executive officer or equivalent.
Organized: date organized or founded.
Affiliation: affiliation, if any, with the major mission associations--DOM/NCCUSA, IFMA, EFMA, TAM/ICC, FOM CCC-CWC. The status of relationship is also indicated (if other than member, e.g., affiliate, associate, etc.). Associations of missions agencies are described on page 61. Current lists of members of these associations are shown on page 373.

Description: clarification of name and organizational changes, ecclesiastical or doctrinal tradition, primary activity and scope of ministries, basically as taken from the questionnaire. An "international" organization is either one employing personnel from North America which has its headquarters outside the US or Canada, or has offices in North America raising funds, or its personnel come from several nations.

Income, 1979: "Cash" - total agency income (excluding gifts-in-kind) for 1979 (or latest fiscal year) for all ministries, programs, services including domestic and overseas administration and fund raising costs. "NR" or "NA" - appearing in place of income or other dollar totals, indicates that the information was not reported on the questionnaire, but may be available on request from the agency. Footnotes indicate the total was estimated by the editor on the basis of current knowledge of agency size and ministry, or by the agency itself. Estimated figures should be seen as indicating general orders of magnitude only whose accuracy is limited by the information at hand.

For Overseas Ministries: that part of the total agency income ("cash") spent outside North America or expended with direct impact on overseas personnel or ministries. Since agencies employ a variety of accounting procedures and have varying financial requirements, categories and ministry methods, direct comparisons of expenditures between agencies is not always possible or advisable.

Personnel:

North Americans Overseas: the number of personnel is reported as per data provided by agencies for 1979. Detail is provided for reference purposes by sex and marital status followed by the total number of North American career personnel overseas under the heading "Total Active."

North American Administrative Staff: personnel and/or employees assigned to administrative duties in North America.

Short Term: personnel reported by agency as non-career missionaries regardless of length of service. These figures represent a wide diversity of ministries and tasks. Persons vary from teenagers spending 2-10 wks on special work or training assignments to mechanics, construction workers or translators spending a designated amount of time, often four to six years, on a specific project which has a definite completion date.

Non-North Americans Overseas: persons who are citizens of countries other than the U.S.A. or Canada, and who serve with the agency in countries other than their homeland, e.g., Brazilians serving in the U.S.A., Koreans serving in Hong Kong, etc., but with North American or international agencies.

NR or NA: indicates data not reported. There may be discrepancies noted between the totals reported here and those shown country by country. This reflects the data as it was reported and no attempt was made to reconcile the two.

Retired: number of personnel reported by the agency presently supported on retirement. This does not indicate active personnel covered by a retirement insurance program.

Fields of Service: countries outside North America in which the agency reports ministry. Since agencies did not always use standard nomenclature when describing their fields of operation, those fields listed by the agency on the questionnaire and those shown in this listing are not always exactly as they were recorded on the questionnaire. Terminology has been made to conform where possible to that used by the United Nations. A country name with no North American personnel listed often indicates that work is being done by nationals and that the agency only provides program support, not personnel.

Year Began Work: the year in which the agency began work in the country.

North American Personnel: "Total Now" - number of North American overseas staff (fully supported including short-term) in or assigned to each respective country as of Jan. 1, 1980. "New" - overseas staff who began working during the reporting period from 1975-79.

Related Churches: "Related Churches" - a country by country report of churches which were planted by the agency or which are related to them currently.

People Groups: number of people groups in each country among which the agency reports ministry.

Notes: additional information on institutions supported, or other comments extracted from the "Comments" section of Part 2 of the questionnaire.

Footnotes: explanatory footnotes may appear in two different places in the agency directory: prior to the beginning of the "Fields of Service" table (the country by country listings) and as the final entry in agency listings. The reader will encounter individual data items which are footnoted and general notes which usually impact on one's perception and use of the overall agency listing.

Action International Ministries
                                              10118 NE 198th Pl.
                                              Bothell WA 98011
                                              P.O. ADDRESS:
                                              Box 2068
                                              Lynnwood WA 98036
Tel. (206) 485-1967
EXECUTIVE OFFICER: Tom Barcanic and Doug Nichols
ORGANIZED: 1974   AFFILIATION: EFMA
DESCRIPTION: Founded in 1974 as Films For Asia. Name changed
   in 1975. An interdenominational sending agency of
   evangelical tradition nurturing national churches and
   engaged in relief, evangelism, literature, correspondence
   courses and motion pictures. Also involved in medical and
   childcare work, training for pastors and laymen, vocational
   training and camps for underpriviledged children.
TOTAL INCOME: $422,512   FOR OVERSEAS MINISTRIES: $422,512
PERSONNEL:
   NORTH AMERICANS OVERSEAS   NON-NORTH AMERICANS OVERSEAS: 0
             MARRIED: 16   NORTH AMERICAN ADM. STAFF: 2
          SINGLE MEN: 2   SHORT TERM: 9
        SINGLE WOMEN: 1   RETIRED: 0

      TOTAL ACTIVE: 19

FIELD OF SERVICE	YEAR BEGAN	PERSONNEL NOW	PERSONNEL NEW	RELATED CHURCHES	PEOPLE GROUPS	NOTES
Philippines	1974	28	24		4	

ACTS International
                                              108 S Clinton
                                              Albion MI 49224
                                              P.O. ADDRESS:
                                              Box 507
                                              Albion MI 49224
Tel. (517) 629-4607
EXECUTIVE OFFICER: Richard W. Innes
ORGANIZED: 1972
DESCRIPTION: An interdenominational sending agency of Baptist
   tradition with emphasis on communications as a means to
   teach the Christian message. Engaged in broadcasting, mass
   evangelism, literature production and distribution and
   psychological counseling.
TOTAL INCOME: $230,000   FOR OVERSEAS MINISTRIES: $230,000
PERSONNEL:
   NORTH AMERICANS OVERSEAS   NON-NORTH AMERICANS OVERSEAS: 1
             MARRIED: 1   NORTH AMERICAN ADM. STAFF: 2
          SINGLE MEN: NR   SHORT TERM: 0
        SINGLE WOMEN: NR   RETIRED: NR

      TOTAL ACTIVE: 1

FIELD OF SERVICE	YEAR BEGAN	PERSONNEL NOW	PERSONNEL NEW	RELATED CHURCHES	PEOPLE GROUPS	NOTES
Australia	1971	11	4	700		
New Zealand	1974	2		50		

   Note: All but one person are nationals.

Adib Eden Evangelistic Missionary Society, Inc.

1500 NW 29th St.
Miami FL 33142
P.O. ADDRESS:
Box 420006
Miami FL 33142

Tel. (305) 635-6366
EXECUTIVE OFFICER: A. Eden
ORGANIZED: 1967
DESCRIPTION: An interdenominational agency supporting national churches and engaged in evangelism, literature production and distribution, training, childcare, motion pictures and radio and TV broadcasting.
TOTAL INCOME: NR   FOR OVERSEAS MINISTRIES: $110,000
PERSONNEL:
```
    NORTH AMERICANS OVERSEAS     NON-NORTH AMERICANS OVERSEAS:     2
            MARRIED:     4          NORTH AMERICAN ADM. STAFF:     3
         SINGLE MEN:     1                        SHORT TERM:     10
       SINGLE WOMEN:     0                           RETIRED:     0
                     -----
       TOTAL ACTIVE:     5
```
NOTES: Overseas income estimated by MARC.

Advancing the Ministries of the Gospel SEE: AMG International
AMG International

Advent Christian General Conference of America

14601 Albermarle Rd.
Charlotte NC 28212
P.O. ADDRESS:
Box 23152
Charlotte NC 28212

Tel. (704) 545-6161
EXECUTIVE OFFICER: J. Edgar Hickel
ORGANIZED: 1865
DESCRIPTION: A denominational sending agency involved in evangelism, teaching, literacy and agriculture.
TOTAL INCOME: $308,000   FOR OVERSEAS MINISTRIES: $308,000
PERSONNEL:
```
    NORTH AMERICANS OVERSEAS     NON-NORTH AMERICANS OVERSEAS:     NR
            MARRIED:     NR         NORTH AMERICAN ADM. STAFF:     2
         SINGLE MEN:     NR                       SHORT TERM:     0
       SINGLE WOMEN:     NR                          RETIRED:     0
                     -----
       TOTAL ACTIVE:     19
```

FIELD OF SERVICE	YEAR BEGAN	PERSONNEL NOW	PERSONNEL NEW	RELATED CHURCHES	PEOPLE GROUPS	NOTES
India		4				
Japan		7				
Malaysia						
Nigeria						
Philippines		8				

Afghan Border Crusade

73 Windermere Ave.
Lansdowne PA 19050

Tel. (215) 622-3639
EXECUTIVE OFFICER: W. J. Ringer
ORGANIZED: 1944
DESCRIPTION: An interdenominational, international sending agency giving aid and/or relief and distributing Bibles among Muslims and Pathans in the frontier area of Pakistan.

Also involved in evangelism, church planting, literature
distribution and medicine.
TOTAL INCOME: $45,000   FOR OVERSEAS MINISTRIES: $45,000
PERSONNEL:
        NORTH AMERICANS OVERSEAS   NON-NORTH AMERICANS OVERSEAS: 6
                    MARRIED: 2   NORTH AMERICAN ADM. STAFF: 1
                SINGLE MEN: 1   SHORT TERM: 3
              SINGLE WOMEN: 4   RETIRED: 0

           TOTAL ACTIVE: 7
NOTES: Income estimated by MARC.

FIELD OF SERVICE	YEAR BEGAN	PERSONNEL NOW	PERSONNEL NEW	RELATED CHURCHES	PEOPLE GROUPS	NOTES
Pakistan	1944	7		5		

Africa Evangelical Fellowship

733 Bloomfield Ave.
Bloomfield NJ 07003
P.O. ADDRESS:
Box 1679
Bloomfield NJ 07003

Tel. (201) 748-9281
EXECUTIVE OFFICER: Robert Fine
ORGANIZED: 1889   AFFILIATION: IFMA
DESCRIPTION: An international, nondenominational sending agency
    of conservative evangelical tradition involved in evangelism,
    literature distribution and church planting. Other ministries
    include aviation, theological education by extension (TEE),
    radio and TV broadcasting and medical work.
TOTAL INCOME: $2,004,423   FOR OVERSEAS MINISTRIES: $2,004,424
PERSONNEL:
        NORTH AMERICANS OVERSEAS   NON-NORTH AMERICANS OVERSEAS: 0
                    MARRIED: 133   NORTH AMERICAN ADM. STAFF: 7
                SINGLE MEN: 4   SHORT TERM: 17
              SINGLE WOMEN: 33   RETIRED: 0

           TOTAL ACTIVE: 170

FIELD OF SERVICE	YEAR BEGAN	PERSONNEL NOW	PERSONNEL NEW	RELATED CHURCHES	PEOPLE GROUPS	NOTES
Angola	1914	10	1	300	5	
Botswana	1972	7	3	3	2	
Malawi	1900	15	1	70	1	
Mauritius	1969	4		2	3	
Mozambique	1936			400	1	
Namibia	1971	3			2	
Portugal	1979	1				
Reunion	1971		2	4	3	1
South Africa	1889	36	7	144	3	
Swaziland	1891	6	2	20		
Zambia	1910	65	10	340	2	
Zimbabwe	1900	14	2	45	2	

Note: 1. Personnel in Reunion have
left. 2. Two people are working in
England as assistants to International
Director and wife.
3. Seven people seconded.

Africa Evangelical Fellowship (Canada)

470 McNicoll Ave.
Willowdale ON M1S 2M5
Canada

Tel. (416) 491-0881
EXECUTIVE OFFICER: Keith Donald
ORGANIZED: 1889   AFFILIATION: IFMA
DESCRIPTION: An international, interdenominational sending
    agency of evangelical tradition involved in church planting
    and Bible teaching. Other ministries include education,
    medical assistance, radio and TV broadcasting and
    literature distribution.
TOTAL INCOME: $986,100   FOR OVERSEAS MINISTRIES: $844,630
PERSONNEL:
    NORTH AMERICANS OVERSEAS   NON-NORTH AMERICANS OVERSEAS: 7
               MARRIED: 53   NORTH AMERICAN ADM. STAFF: 10
            SINGLE MEN: 1   SHORT TERM: 11
          SINGLE WOMEN: 14   RETIRED: 0

          TOTAL ACTIVE: 68

FIELD OF SERVICE	YEAR BEGAN	PERSONNEL NOW	PERSONNEL NEW	RELATED CHURCHES	PEOPLE GROUPS	NOTES
Angola	1912	2	2			
Botswana	1974	2	2	6		
Malawi	1901	3				
Mauritius	1966	2		3		
Mozambique	1936					
Namibia	1972					
Portugal	1980	1	1			
Reunion	1970			6		
South Africa	1894	20	3	40		
Swaziland	1894	6	6	23		
Zambia	1910	40	13	360		
Zimbabwe	1900	5	1			

Africa Inland Mission

135 W Crooked Hill Rd.
Pearl River NY 10965
P.O. ADDRESS:
Box 178
Pearl River NY 10965

Tel. (914) 735-4014
EXECUTIVE OFFICER: Peter Stam
ORGANIZED: 1895   AFFILIATION: IFMA
DESCRIPTION: An international, interdenominational sending
    agency dedicated to the work of evangelism, church
    planting and church growth by means of education, medicine
    and personal witness. Also involved in aviation,
    leadership and missionary outreach in national churches.
TOTAL INCOME: $4,527,149   FOR OVERSEAS MINISTRIES: $4,527,149
PERSONNEL:
    NORTH AMERICANS OVERSEAS   NON-NORTH AMERICANS OVERSEAS: 125
               MARRIED: 380   NORTH AMERICAN ADM. STAFF: 53
            SINGLE MEN: 15   SHORT TERM: 65
          SINGLE WOMEN: 116   RETIRED: 142

          TOTAL ACTIVE: 511

FIELD OF SERVICE	YEAR BEGAN	PERSONNEL NOW	NEW	RELATED CHURCHES	PEOPLE GROUPS	NOTES
Central African Rep.	1924	17	8	70		
Comoro	1975	9	6			
Kenya	1895	430	144	3000		
Reunion	1977	2		2		
Seychelles	1977	6				
Sudan	1949	18	4	15		
Tanzania	1908	45	4	650		
Uganda	1918	15	2	650		
Zaire	1912	111	13	1800		

Africa Inland Mission (Canada)

1641 Victoria Park Ave.
Scarborough ON M1R 1P8
Canada

Tel. (416) 751-6077
EXECUTIVE OFFICER: D. Harris
ORGANIZED: 1953   AFFILIATION: IFMA
DESCRIPTION: An international, interdenominational sending
    agency of Baptist and evangelical tradition establishing
    churches and engaged in medicine, literacy, childcare,
    education, literature distribution and radio and
    TV broadcasting.
TOTAL INCOME: $1,071,193   FOR OVERSEAS MINISTRIES: $1,071,193
PERSONNEL:
    NORTH AMERICANS OVERSEAS   NON-NORTH AMERICANS OVERSEAS: 0
                MARRIED: 53   NORTH AMERICAN ADM. STAFF: 14
             SINGLE MEN: 0   SHORT TERM: 11
           SINGLE WOMEN: 26   RETIRED: 9

           TOTAL ACTIVE: 79
NOTES: Overseas income estimated by MARC.

FIELD OF SERVICE	YEAR BEGAN	PERSONNEL NOW	NEW	RELATED CHURCHES	PEOPLE GROUPS	NOTES
Central African Rep.		3	1			
Comoro	1975					
Kenya	1895	61	16	3000		
Sudan						
Tanzania	1909	3		300		
Uganda						
Zaire		20	2	500		

Africa Inter-Mennonite Mission, Inc.

224 W High St.
Elkhart IN 46514

Tel. (219) 294-3711
EXECUTIVE OFFICER: James E. Bertsche
ORGANIZED: 1911   AFFILIATION: EFMA
DESCRIPTION: A denominational sending agency of Mennonite
    tradition supported by Mennonite churches and conferences.
    Involved in evangelism and church planting, Bible
    translation, radio broadcasting, education, leadership
    training, agricultural assistance and social concern
    projects.
TOTAL INCOME: $713,840   FOR OVERSEAS MINISTRIES: $713,840
PERSONNEL:
    NORTH AMERICANS OVERSEAS   NON-NORTH AMERICANS OVERSEAS: 58
                MARRIED: 48   NORTH AMERICAN ADM. STAFF: 2
             SINGLE MEN: 2   SHORT TERM: 6

```
       SINGLE WOMEN:      8                        RETIRED:    21
                       -----
       TOTAL ACTIVE:     58
```

FIELD OF SERVICE	YEAR BEGAN	PERSONNEL NOW	NEW	RELATED CHURCHES	PEOPLE GROUPS	NOTES
Botswana	1975	9	2	3		
Lesotho	1973	6	2	4		
Upper Volta	1978	4	4	2		
Zaire	1911	39	1	20		

African Bible Colleges, Inc.

P.O. ADDRESS:
Box 103
Clinton MS 39056

EXECUTIVE OFFICER: John W. Chinchen
ORGANIZED: 1976
DESCRIPTION: An interdenominational agency of evangelical
    tradition establishing and funding Bible colleges in
    Africa. Provides general Christian and theological
    education, and radio broadcasts followed-up with
    correspondence courses.
TOTAL INCOME: $172,710   FOR OVERSEAS MINISTRIES: $172,710
PERSONNEL:

```
    NORTH AMERICANS OVERSEAS    NON-NORTH AMERICANS OVERSEAS:    0
              MARRIED:    6        NORTH AMERICAN ADM. STAFF:    0
           SINGLE MEN:    0                       SHORT TERM:    1
         SINGLE WOMEN:    0                         RETIRED:    0
                      -----
         TOTAL ACTIVE:    6
```

FIELD OF SERVICE	YEAR BEGAN	PERSONNEL NOW	NEW	RELATED CHURCHES	PEOPLE GROUPS	NOTES
Liberia	1977	6	6			

African Enterprise

232 N Lake Ave. Ste. 200
Pasadena CA 91102
P.O. ADDRESS:
Box 988
Pasadena CA 91101

Tel. (213) 796-5830
EXECUTIVE OFFICER: Keith Jesson
ORGANIZED: 1962
DESCRIPTION: An interdenominational sending agency whose
    tradition is in keeping with the principles of the
    Lausanne Covenant, engaged in Christian leadership
    training accomplished through the cooperation of local
    churches overseas. Evangelistic teams minister to
    children in South Africa and conduct relief work in
    Uganda. Also supports nationals and is involved in radio
    and TV broadcasting.
TOTAL INCOME: $1,130,000   FOR OVERSEAS MINISTRIES: $1,130,000
PERSONNEL:

```
    NORTH AMERICANS OVERSEAS    NON-NORTH AMERICANS OVERSEAS:    3
              MARRIED:    4        NORTH AMERICAN ADM. STAFF:   25
           SINGLE MEN:    0                       SHORT TERM:    1
         SINGLE WOMEN:    1                         RETIRED:    0
                      -----
         TOTAL ACTIVE:    5
```

FIELD OF SERVICE	YEAR BEGAN	PERSONNEL NOW	PERSONNEL NEW	RELATED CHURCHES	PEOPLE GROUPS	NOTES
Kenya	1975	1	1			
South Africa	1962	4	4			
Tanzania	1974					
Uganda	1971					
Zimbabwe	1976					

African Methodist Episcopal Church, Inc. Department of Missions

475 Riverside Dr. Rm1926
New York NY 10115

Tel. (212) 864-2471
EXECUTIVE OFFICER: John W. P. Collier, Jr.
ORGANIZED: 1844   AFFILIATION: DOM-NCCCUSA
DESCRIPTION: A denominational sending agency of Methodist
    tradition involved in agriculture, education, literature,
    medicine and support of nationals.
TOTAL INCOME: $300,000   FOR OVERSEAS MINISTRIES: $300,000
PERSONNEL:
    NORTH AMERICANS OVERSEAS   NON-NORTH AMERICANS OVERSEAS: NR
            MARRIED: NR   NORTH AMERICAN ADM. STAFF: 28
        SINGLE MEN: NR   SHORT TERM: 0
      SINGLE WOMEN: NR   RETIRED: 0

    TOTAL ACTIVE: 10

FIELD OF SERVICE	YEAR BEGAN	PERSONNEL NOW	PERSONNEL NEW	RELATED CHURCHES	PEOPLE GROUPS	NOTES
Bahamas						
Barbados						
Bermuda						
Botswana						
Dominican Republic						
Ghana						
Guyana						
Haiti						
Jamaica						
Lesotho						
Liberia						
Malawi						
Mozambique						
Namibia						
Nigeria						
Sierra Leone						
South Africa						
Surinam						
Swaziland						
Tanzania						
Trinidad and Tobago						
Zaire						
Zambia						
Zimbabwe						

African Methodist Episcopal Zion Church, Department of Overseas Missions

475 Riverside Dr Ste1910
New York NY 10115

Tel. (212) 749-2952
EXECUTIVE OFFICER: Harold A. L. Clement
ORGANIZED: 1875   AFFILIATION: DOM-NCCCUSA
DESCRIPTION: A denominational sending agency of Methodist
    tradition supporting nationals and national churches.
    Engaged in evangelism, education, literature and literacy.
    Also involved in agriculture and relief, medicine,
    recording, community development and technical assistance.
TOTAL INCOME: $174,000   FOR OVERSEAS MINISTRIES: $174,000
PERSONNEL:

NORTH AMERICANS OVERSEAS		NON-NORTH AMERICANS OVERSEAS:	4
MARRIED:	4	NORTH AMERICAN ADM. STAFF:	1
SINGLE MEN:	0	SHORT TERM:	2
SINGLE WOMEN:	0	RETIRED:	NR
TOTAL ACTIVE:	4		

FIELD OF SERVICE	YEAR BEGAN	PERSONNEL NOW	PERSONNEL NEW	RELATED CHURCHES	PEOPLE GROUPS	NOTES
Bahamas	1877					
Barbados	1971					
Ghana	1896	1				
Guyana	1911					
Jamaica	1966					
Liberia	1876					
Nigeria	1930					
South Africa	1969					
U.S. Virgin Is.	1917					
United Kingdom	1971					

African Mission Services, Inc.

1012 City Ave.
Philadelphia PA 19151

Tel. (215) 642-2255
EXECUTIVE OFFICER: A. E. K. Brenner
ORGANIZED: 1979
DESCRIPTION: An interdenominational agency of evangelical and
    ecumenical tradition providing assistance to missionaries,
    mission stations and other evangelical ministries
    throughout Africa. Engaged in nurture or support
    of national churches, purchasing services, supplying
    equipment and support of nationals.
TOTAL INCOME: $50,000   FOR OVERSEAS MINISTRIES: $40,000
PERSONNEL:

NORTH AMERICANS OVERSEAS		NON-NORTH AMERICANS OVERSEAS:	0
MARRIED:	0	NORTH AMERICAN ADM. STAFF:	1
SINGLE MEN:	0	SHORT TERM:	0
SINGLE WOMEN:	0	RETIRED:	0
TOTAL ACTIVE:	0		

Afro-American Missionary Crusade, Inc.

700 E Church Ln.
Philadelphia PA 19144
P.O. ADDRESS:
Box 6339
Philadelphia PA 19139

Tel. (215) 843-4767
EXECUTIVE OFFICER: Donald E. Dennis
ORGANIZED: 1947
DESCRIPTION: A nondenominational sending agency of evangelical
    and fundamentalist tradition establishing churches and
    engaged in extension education, evangelism, childcare,
    fund transmittal and medical supplies.
TOTAL INCOME: $55,000   FOR OVERSEAS MINISTRIES: $37,400
PERSONNEL:
    NORTH AMERICANS OVERSEAS   NON-NORTH AMERICANS OVERSEAS: 1
                 MARRIED: 2   NORTH AMERICAN ADM. STAFF: 2
              SINGLE MEN: 0   SHORT TERM: 1
            SINGLE WOMEN: 3   RETIRED: 0

        TOTAL ACTIVE: 5

FIELD OF SERVICE	YEAR BEGAN	PERSONNEL NOW	NEW	RELATED CHURCHES	PEOPLE GROUPS	NOTES
Liberia	1948	3		16	2	

Agape Movement SEE: Campus Crusade For Christ International (Overseas Dept.)

Agri-Business Mission Associates SEE: Conservative Mennonite Board of Missions and Charities

Agricultural Missions, Inc.

475 Riverside Dr. Rm.624
New York NY 10115

Tel. (212) 870-2553
EXECUTIVE OFFICER: J. Benton Rhoades
ORGANIZED: 1930
DESCRIPTION: A nondenominational specialzed service agency
    with an ecumenical tradition serving overseas missions and
    churches through consultation and training in rural
    ministries. Provides technical, legal and agricultural
    assistance and aids in community development and funding.
TOTAL INCOME: NR   FOR OVERSEAS MINISTRIES: $417,846
PERSONNEL:
    NORTH AMERICANS OVERSEAS   NON-NORTH AMERICANS OVERSEAS: 0
                 MARRIED: 0   NORTH AMERICAN ADM. STAFF: 0
              SINGLE MEN: 0   SHORT TERM: 0
            SINGLE WOMEN: 0   RETIRED: 0

        TOTAL ACTIVE: 0

Agricultural Missions, Inc. SEE: DOM—NCCUSA, Mission Association Section

AIM, Inc. (Assistance in Missions)

9003 Terhune Ave.
Sun Valley CA 91352

Tel. (213) 257-8969
EXECUTIVE OFFICER: Richard Palmquist
ORGANIZED: 1950
DESCRIPTION: An evangelical, nondenominational agency serving
    furloughed missionaries. Donated automobiles are repaired
    and loaned and alternate energy systems are made available

through missionary organizations when funds are available.
TOTAL INCOME: $5,000   FOR OVERSEAS MINISTRIES: $0
PERSONNEL:
    NORTH AMERICANS OVERSEAS   NON-NORTH AMERICANS OVERSEAS: 0
            MARRIED: 0   NORTH AMERICAN ADM. STAFF: 0
         SINGLE MEN: 0   SHORT TERM: 0
       SINGLE WOMEN: 0   RETIRED: 0

       TOTAL ACTIVE: 0

Air Crusade, Inc.

1407 W Princeton
Ontario CA 91762
P.O. ADDRESS:
Box 1769
Ontario CA 91762

Tel. (714) 986-0677
EXECUTIVE OFFICER: Marvin F. Foster
ORGANIZED: 1958
DESCRIPTION: A nondenominational, evangelical service agency
    distributing gospels by aircraft in Latin America.
    Recipients are encouraged to enroll in free Bible
    correspondence courses with church planting the eventual
    goal.
TOTAL INCOME: $54,413   FOR OVERSEAS MINISTRIES: $54,413
PERSONNEL:
    NORTH AMERICANS OVERSEAS   NON-NORTH AMERICANS OVERSEAS: 5
            MARRIED: 0   NORTH AMERICAN ADM. STAFF: 3
         SINGLE MEN: 0   SHORT TERM: 5
       SINGLE WOMEN: 0   RETIRED: 0

       TOTAL ACTIVE: 0

FIELD OF SERVICE	YEAR BEGAN	PERSONNEL NOW	PERSONNEL NEW	RELATED CHURCHES	PEOPLE GROUPS	NOTES
Guatemala	1959			10		
Honduras	1973					
Mexico	1954			22		

Air Team of Houston

805 Shirlee Dr.
Seabrook TX 77586
DESCRIPTION: No data is reported for this agency for one of the
    following reasons: it is currently inactive or no longer
    exists; it has terminated overseas ministries or has ceased
    to operate as a North American entity.

Alberto Mottesi Evangelistic Association, Inc.

5022 W Hazard Ave.
Santa Ana CA 92703
P.O. ADDRESS:
Box 18588
Irvine CA 92714

Tel. (714) 551-6235
EXECUTIVE OFFICER: Alberto H. Mottesi
ORGANIZED: 1977
DESCRIPTION: A nondenominational agency of evangelical and
    Baptist tradition ministering to Hispanics. Engaged in
    mass crusades, lay training, literature, TV and radio
    broadcasting. Broadcasts over 500 times a day in 18 Latin
    American countries.
TOTAL INCOME: NA   FOR OVERSEAS MINISTRIES: NA

PERSONNEL:
        NORTH AMERICANS OVERSEAS   NON-NORTH AMERICANS OVERSEAS: 0
                      MARRIED: 0   NORTH AMERICAN ADM. STAFF: NR
                   SINGLE MEN: 0   SHORT TERM: 0
                 SINGLE WOMEN: 0   RETIRED: 0

        TOTAL ACTIVE: 0

All Peoples Baptist Mission

1156 N Oliver
Wichita KS 67208

Tel. (316) 682-6545
EXECUTIVE OFFICER: Bruce A. Bell
ORGANIZED: 1980
DESCRIPTION: A denominational sending agency of Baptist
    tradition engaged in establishing churches, evangelism,
    Bible distribution, radio broadcasting and support of
    nationals.
TOTAL INCOME: $107,000   FOR OVERSEAS MINISTRIES: $90,000
PERSONNEL:
        NORTH AMERICANS OVERSEAS   NON-NORTH AMERICANS OVERSEAS: 2
                      MARRIED: 10   NORTH AMERICAN ADM. STAFF: 0
                   SINGLE MEN: 0   SHORT TERM: 0
                 SINGLE WOMEN: 0   RETIRED: 0

        TOTAL ACTIVE: 10
NOTES: Income estimated by agency.

FIELD OF SERVICE	YEAR BEGAN	PERSONNEL NOW	NEW	RELATED CHURCHES	PEOPLE GROUPS	NOTES
El Salvador		6	4	1		
Germany, Fed. Rep.						
Libya			2			

Note: Some data not available
because agency is in process of
reorganization.

Allegheny Wesleyan Methodist Missions

1827 Allen Dr.
Salem OH 44460
P.O. ADDRESS:
Box 357
Salem OH 44460

Tel. (216) 337-9376
EXECUTIVE OFFICER: F. E. Mansell
ORGANIZED: 1969
DESCRIPTION: A denominational sending agency of Wesleyan
    tradition engaged in church planting, evangelism and secular
    and general Christian education.
TOTAL INCOME: $261,729   FOR OVERSEAS MINISTRIES: $123,776
PERSONNEL:
        NORTH AMERICANS OVERSEAS   NON-NORTH AMERICANS OVERSEAS: 0
                      MARRIED: 8   NORTH AMERICAN ADM. STAFF: 1
                   SINGLE MEN: 0   SHORT TERM: 0
                 SINGLE WOMEN: 3   RETIRED: NR

        TOTAL ACTIVE: 11

FIELD OF SERVICE	YEAR BEGAN	PERSONNEL NOW	NEW	RELATED CHURCHES	PEOPLE GROUPS	NOTES
Haiti	1968	6	1	4		

```
Peru            1972      5     2        7
```

Amateur Radio Missionary Service (ARMS)

7135 S Sherman
Littleton CO 80122

EXECUTIVE OFFICER: Charles Cox
ORGANIZED: 1957
DESCRIPTION: A nondenominational specialized volunteer radio
    service of evangelical tradition providing communications
    and Christian fellowship between missionaries and homeland
    through amateur radio facilities.

```
TOTAL INCOME:      $0              FOR OVERSEAS MINISTRIES:      $0
PERSONNEL:
   NORTH AMERICANS OVERSEAS    NON-NORTH AMERICANS OVERSEAS:    0
             MARRIED:   0           NORTH AMERICAN ADM. STAFF:  0
          SINGLE MEN:   0                        SHORT TERM:    0
        SINGLE WOMEN:   0                          RETIRED:     0
                      -----
        TOTAL ACTIVE:   0
```
NOTES: Personnel are volunteer and consist of approximately
    400 licensed and associate members.

Amazing Grace Missions

431 E Pryon Ave.
San Antonio TX 78214

EXECUTIVE OFFICER: Osa Dodson
ORGANIZED: 1938
DESCRIPTION: A specialized service and fund transmitting
    agency of Baptist tradition serving as a channel for
    several churches in fellowship. Missionaries supported
    serve under other approved agencies, and are not fully
    supported by the mission.

```
TOTAL INCOME:        NR           FOR OVERSEAS MINISTRIES:      NR
PERSONNEL:
   NORTH AMERICANS OVERSEAS    NON-NORTH AMERICANS OVERSEAS:    0
             MARRIED:   0           NORTH AMERICAN ADM. STAFF:  NR
          SINGLE MEN:   0                        SHORT TERM:    0
        SINGLE WOMEN:   0                          RETIRED:     0
                      -----
        TOTAL ACTIVE:   0
```


Ambassadors For Christ, Inc.

Highway 30 & Leamon St.
Paradise PA 17562
P.O. ADDRESS:
Box AFC
Paradise PA 17562

Tel. (717) 687-8564
EXECUTIVE OFFICER: Hay-Him Chan
ORGANIZED: 1963
DESCRIPTION: An interdenominational fund transmitting and
    service agency of evangelical tradition supporting
    Christian-Chinese ministries involved in literature
    distribution, information service and training.

```
TOTAL INCOME:   $137,545   FOR OVERSEAS MINISTRIES:   $137,545
PERSONNEL:
   NORTH AMERICANS OVERSEAS    NON-NORTH AMERICANS OVERSEAS:    0
             MARRIED:   8           NORTH AMERICAN ADM. STAFF:  1
          SINGLE MEN:   0                        SHORT TERM:    8
```

SINGLE WOMEN: 0   RETIRED: 0

     TOTAL ACTIVE: 8
NOTES: All overseas personnel are short-term.
        and sent through other agencies.

America's Keswick, Inc.

Keswick Grove
Whiting NJ 08759

Tel. (201) 350-1187
EXECUTIVE OFFICER: William A. Raws
ORGANIZED: 1921
DESCRIPTION: An interdenominational fund transmitting agency
     of evangelical and independent tradition supporting and
     serving independent missionaries. Also involved in aviation,
     Bible distribution, literature distribution, evangelism
     and missionary education.
TOTAL INCOME: $137,273   FOR OVERSEAS MINISTRIES: $125,723
PERSONNEL:
     NORTH AMERICANS OVERSEAS   NON-NORTH AMERICANS OVERSEAS: 0
            MARRIED: 18   NORTH AMERICAN ADM. STAFF: 3
         SINGLE MEN: 0   SHORT TERM: 0
       SINGLE WOMEN: 0   RETIRED: 0

     TOTAL ACTIVE: 18

FIELD OF SERVICE	YEAR BEGAN	PERSONNEL NOW	NEW	RELATED CHURCHES	PEOPLE GROUPS	NOTES
Austria		4	2			
France		2				
Germany, Fed. Rep.		4				
Mexico		4	2			

American Advent Mission Society

14601 Albermarle Rd.
Charlotte NC 28212
P.O. ADDRESS:
Box 23152
Charlotte NC 28212

Tel. (704) 545-6161
EXECUTIVE OFFICER: J. Edgar Hickel
ORGANIZED: 1865   AFFILIATION: EFMA
DESCRIPTION: A denominational sending agency of Adventist
     tradition sponsoring missionaries engaged in establishing
     churches, helping to serve in national churches, teaching
     in Bible schools, distributing literature and serving in
     health clinics.
TOTAL INCOME: NR   FOR OVERSEAS MINISTRIES: $298,205
PERSONNEL:
     NORTH AMERICANS OVERSEAS   NON-NORTH AMERICANS OVERSEAS: 1
            MARRIED: 10   NORTH AMERICAN ADM. STAFF: 4
         SINGLE MEN: 0   SHORT TERM: 0
       SINGLE WOMEN: 8   RETIRED: 6

     TOTAL ACTIVE: 18

Amer. Assoc. Bd. St. Christopher's Trng. Clg. Vepery, Madras, Inc.
SEE: Women's Chrn. Clg. and St. Christopher's Trng. Clg.

153

American Association for Jewish Evangelism

5860 N Lincoln Ave.
Chicago IL 60659

Tel. (312) 275-2133
EXECUTIVE OFFICER: Ralph M. Gade
ORGANIZED: 1944
DESCRIPTION: A nondenominational agency of Baptist tradition
    supporting nationals and carrying on literature
    distribution, radio work and door-to-door evangelism
    focused specifically toward Jewish people in the USA,
    Canada, Mexico and Israel.
TOTAL INCOME: $350,000   FOR OVERSEAS MINISTRIES: NR
PERSONNEL:
    NORTH AMERICANS OVERSEAS   NON-NORTH AMERICANS OVERSEAS: NR
            MARRIED: NR   NORTH AMERICAN ADM. STAFF: NR
         SINGLE MEN: NR   SHORT TERM: NR
       SINGLE WOMEN: NR   RETIRED: NR

        TOTAL ACTIVE: 1

FIELD OF SERVICE	YEAR BEGAN	PERSONNEL NOW	PERSONNEL NEW	RELATED CHURCHES	PEOPLE GROUPS	NOTES
Israel		1				
Mexico						

American Baptist Association, Missionary Committee

4605 State Line Ave.
Texarkana TX 75501
P.O. ADDRESS:
Box 1050
Texarkana TX 75501

Tel. (214) 792-2783
EXECUTIVE OFFICER: Kenneth Bazar
ORGANIZED: 1924
DESCRIPTION: A denominational agency of Baptist tradition
    assisting local churches in sending missionaries and
    establishing churches. Also involved in evangelism,
    theological education, literature distribution and support
    of nationals.
TOTAL INCOME: $800,000   FOR OVERSEAS MINISTRIES: $500,000
PERSONNEL:
    NORTH AMERICANS OVERSEAS   NON-NORTH AMERICANS OVERSEAS: 0
            MARRIED: 65   NORTH AMERICAN ADM. STAFF: 1
         SINGLE MEN: 0   SHORT TERM: 0
       SINGLE WOMEN: 0   RETIRED: 0

        TOTAL ACTIVE: 65
NOTES: Income estimated by agency.

FIELD OF SERVICE	YEAR BEGAN	PERSONNEL NOW	PERSONNEL NEW	RELATED CHURCHES	PEOPLE GROUPS	NOTES
Australia	1968	1		2		
Colombia	1971	2		4		
Costa Rica	1940	7	2	12		
France	1973	1		1		
Germany, Fed. Rep.	1957	1		2		
India	1973	4		11		

FIELD OF SERVICE	YEAR BEGAN	PERSONNEL NOW	PERSONNEL NEW	RELATED CHURCHES	PEOPLE GROUPS	NOTES
Israel	1967	1	1	1		
Japan	1952	6	3	11		
Korea, Rep. of	1972	7	1	15		
Mexico	1955	21	6	32		
Nicaragua	1963	1		1		
Nigeria	1976	1		2		
Peru	1960	2		10		
Philippines	1961	5	4	25		
Solomon Is.	1969	2	1	12		

American Baptist Churches in the U.S.A., International Ministries

Valley Forge PA 19481

Tel. (215) 768-2200
EXECUTIVE OFFICER: Chester J. Jump, Jr.
ORGANIZED: 1814   AFFILIATION: DOM-NCCCUSA
DESCRIPTION: A denominational sending agency of Baptist tradition
    engaged in church planting, development of human resources,
    theological education, evangelism and medicine. Also concerned
    with both professional church leadership and lay leadership
    development.
TOTAL INCOME: $8,097,300   FOR OVERSEAS MINISTRIES: $8,097,300
PERSONNEL:
    NORTH AMERICANS OVERSEAS   NON-NORTH AMERICANS OVERSEAS: 8
             MARRIED: 175   NORTH AMERICAN ADM. STAFF: 20
          SINGLE MEN: 0   SHORT TERM: 1
        SINGLE WOMEN: 25   RETIRED: 248

        TOTAL ACTIVE: 200

FIELD OF SERVICE	YEAR BEGAN	PERSONNEL NOW	PERSONNEL NEW	RELATED CHURCHES	PEOPLE GROUPS	NOTES
Burma	1814			2786		
El Salvador	1911	5	2	44		
Europe-general	1832	8				
Haiti	1923	14	2	86		
Hong-Kong	1842	11	2	8		
India	1836	25	2	3916		
Japan	1872	15	2	65		
Mexico	1870	2		10		
Nicaragua	1917	9	2	42		
Philippines	1900	9	2	387		
Thailand	1952	33	2	96		
Zaire	1884	52	2	283		

American Baptist Convention SEE: American Baptist Churches in the USA Intl. Min.

American Bible Society

1865 Broadway
New York NY 10023

Tel. (212) 581-7400
EXECUTIVE OFFICER: Edmund F. Wagner
ORGANIZED: 1816
DESCRIPTION: A nondenominational specialized agency serving
    churches of all confessions through Scripture translation,
    production and distribution in over 150 countries and
    territories. Cooperates with the United Bible Societies.
TOTAL INCOME: $28,936,379   FOR OVERSEAS MINISTRIES: $7,993,436

PERSONNEL:
```
    NORTH AMERICANS OVERSEAS      NON-NORTH AMERICANS OVERSEAS:   NR
            MARRIED:    NR         NORTH AMERICAN ADM. STAFF:     NR
         SINGLE MEN:    NR                       SHORT TERM:      NR
       SINGLE WOMEN:    NR                         RETIRED:       NR
                     -----
       TOTAL ACTIVE:    NR
```

American Board for the Syrian Orphanage

7314 Boyer St.
Philadelphia PA 19119

Tel. (215) 242-3162
EXECUTIVE OFFICER: Gerhard Krodel
ORGANIZED: 1941
DESCRIPTION: No current information available. Information
   from 1976 directory. An interdenominational sending
   agency of Lutheran tradition supporting education and
   childcare in the Middle East.
TOTAL INCOME: $20,500   FOR OVERSEAS MINISTRIES: $20,500
PERSONNEL:
```
    NORTH AMERICANS OVERSEAS      NON-NORTH AMERICANS OVERSEAS:   NR
            MARRIED:    0          NORTH AMERICAN ADM. STAFF:     NR
         SINGLE MEN:    0                       SHORT TERM:       0
       SINGLE WOMEN:    0                          RETIRED:      NR
                     -----
       TOTAL ACTIVE:    0
```
NOTES: Income estimated by MARC.

FIELD OF SERVICE	YEAR BEGAN	PERSONNEL NOW	NEW	RELATED CHURCHES	PEOPLE GROUPS	NOTES
Jordan	1960					1
Lebanon	1960					

   Note: 1. Orphanage, boarding/day school,
   college prep. and vocational training.

American Board of International Missions

P.O. ADDRESS:
Box 1252
York PA 17405

Tel. (717) 854-5216
EXECUTIVE OFFICER: Grant T. Billett
ORGANIZED: 1929
DESCRIPTION: Affiliated with American Ministerial Association.
   A nondenominational sending agency of independent
   tradition promoting missionary work, serving missionaries
   and nationals, and engaged in fund transmittal,
   information service, literature and education. Many of the
   personnel are volunteer. Agency also works in conjunction
   with individual churches which send their money directly
   to missionaries overseas.
TOTAL INCOME: $100,000   FOR OVERSEAS MINISTRIES: $100,000
PERSONNEL:
```
    NORTH AMERICANS OVERSEAS      NON-NORTH AMERICANS OVERSEAS:   NR
            MARRIED:    NR         NORTH AMERICAN ADM. STAFF:     15
         SINGLE MEN:    NR                      SHORT TERM:       15
       SINGLE WOMEN:    NR                         RETIRED:       NR
                     -----
       TOTAL ACTIVE:   129
```
NOTES: Income estimated by agency.

American Board of Missions to the Jews, Inc.

100 Hunt Rd.
Orangeburg NY 10962
P.O. ADDRESS:
Box 2000
Orangeburg NY 10962

Tel. (914) 359-8535
EXECUTIVE OFFICER: Harold A. Sevener
ORGANIZED: 1894
DESCRIPTION: Founded in 1894 as the Williamsburg Mission to the
    Jews. Name changed in 1924. An independent, non-sending
    agency of Baptist and independent tradition engaged in
    literature distribution, broadcasting, and evangelism focused
    on the Jews.
TOTAL INCOME: $2,000,000   FOR OVERSEAS MINISTRIES: $125,000
PERSONNEL:
    NORTH AMERICANS OVERSEAS   NON-NORTH AMERICANS OVERSEAS: 0
            MARRIED: 0   NORTH AMERICAN ADM. STAFF: 27
        SINGLE MEN: 0   SHORT TERM: NR
      SINGLE WOMEN: 0   RETIRED: NR

      TOTAL ACTIVE: 0

FIELD OF SERVICE	YEAR BEGAN	PERSONNEL NOW	NEW	RELATED CHURCHES	PEOPLE GROUPS	NOTES
Argentina	1942	1				
France	1935	1				
Greece	1969	1				
Israel	1964	4				

American Committee for KEEP, Inc.

2445 Hartrey Ave.
Evanston IL 60201
P.O. ADDRESS:
Box 404
Evanston IL 60204

Tel. (312) 475-1478
EXECUTIVE OFFICER: Thomas L. Harris
ORGANIZED: 1950
DESCRIPTION: A denominational agency of Episcopal tradition
    providing funds for agricultural and technical assistance
    as well as self-help projects at the Kiyosato Educational
    Experiment Project in Japan. Also involved in church
    planting and construction, childcare and medicine.
TOTAL INCOME: $50,000   FOR OVERSEAS MINISTRIES: $50,000
PERSONNEL:
    NORTH AMERICANS OVERSEAS   NON-NORTH AMERICANS OVERSEAS: NR
            MARRIED: 0   NORTH AMERICAN ADM. STAFF: 1
        SINGLE MEN: 0   SHORT TERM: NR
      SINGLE WOMEN: 0   RETIRED: NR

      TOTAL ACTIVE: 0
NOTES: Income estimated by agency.

American Council of the Ramabai Mukti Mission SEE: Ramabai Mukti Mission, American Council of

American European Bethel Mission, Inc.

1911 F De La Vina
Santa Barbara CA 93101
P.O. ADDRESS:
Box 30562
Santa Barbara CA 93105

Tel. (805) 687-4168
EXECUTIVE OFFICER: Eugenia J. Abramow
ORGANIZED: 1927
DESCRIPTION: A nondenominational sending agency maintaining
two youth hostels in Israel and also engaged in evangelism
and radio broadcasting in the USA. Also has ministries to
Jewish college students in California.
TOTAL INCOME: NR FOR OVERSEAS MINISTRIES: $198,000
PERSONNEL:

NORTH AMERICANS OVERSEAS		NON-NORTH AMERICANS OVERSEAS:	NR
MARRIED:	NR	NORTH AMERICAN ADM. STAFF:	NR
SINGLE MEN:	NR	SHORT TERM:	0
SINGLE WOMEN:	NR	RETIRED:	NR

TOTAL ACTIVE: 9
NOTES: Overseas income estimated by MARC.

FIELD OF SERVICE	YEAR BEGAN	PERSONNEL NOW	NEW	RELATED CHURCHES	PEOPLE GROUPS	NOTES
Greece	1963	1				
Israel	1950	8	4			

American European Fellowship for Christian Oneness and Evangelization, Inc.

15 Philipse Pl.
Yonkers NY 10701

Tel. (914) 969-5170
EXECUTIVE OFFICER: Catherine Ruth Smith
ORGANIZED: 1922
DESCRIPTION: No current information available. Information
from 1976 directory. An interdenominational fund
raising and transmitting agency of fundamentalist
tradition involved in supporting nationals, Bible and
literature distribution, aid, and personal and child
evangelism.
TOTAL INCOME: $8,500 FOR OVERSEAS MINISTRIES: $8,500
PERSONNEL:

NORTH AMERICANS OVERSEAS		NON-NORTH AMERICANS OVERSEAS:	2
MARRIED:	0	NORTH AMERICAN ADM. STAFF:	1
SINGLE MEN:	0	SHORT TERM:	NR
SINGLE WOMEN:	0	RETIRED:	NR

TOTAL ACTIVE: 0

American Evangelical Lutheran Church, Suomi Synod SEE: Lutheran Church in America

American Friends Service Committee

1501 Cherry St.
Philadelphia PA 19102

Tel. (215) 241-7000
EXECUTIVE OFFICER: Louis W. Schneider
ORGANIZED: 1917
DESCRIPTION: A specialized service agency of Friends tradition
conducting charitable, social, philanthropic and relief
work for branches of the Quakers in America. Programs
work to increase international understanding, promote non-
violent means to peace and social change, protect human

rights, and conserve and share world resources.   Provides
technical assistance and supports self-help efforts.
Human dignity is stressed and help given without regard
for race, religion, politics.
TOTAL INCOME: $11,221,354   FOR OVERSEAS MINISTRIES: $6,345,370
PERSONNEL:
```
    NORTH AMERICANS OVERSEAS   NON-NORTH AMERICANS OVERSEAS:    NR
              MARRIED:    NR       NORTH AMERICAN ADM. STAFF:    NR
           SINGLE MEN:    NR                     SHORT TERM:    NR
         SINGLE WOMEN:    NR                        RETIRED:    NR
                        -----
        TOTAL ACTIVE:    NR
```
NOTES: Includes income spent for USA ministries.

American Institute of Holy Land Studies
SEE: Institute of Holy Land Studies

American Leprosy Missions, Inc.
1262 Broad St.
Bloomfield NJ 07003

Tel. (201) 338-9197
EXECUTIVE OFFICER: Roger K. Ackley
ORGANIZED: 1906   AFFILIATION: DOM-NCCCUSA-Assoc. member
DESCRIPTION: A nondenominational specialized service agency of
    evangelical tradition providing medical assistance to
    victims of leprosy. Also supplies medicine, supports
    medical and social rehabilitation, ministers to the
    emotional and spiritual needs of leprosy patients, trains
    workers and finances research. Contributes to public
    health and education programs.
TOTAL INCOME: $1,365,692   FOR OVERSEAS MINISTRIES: $1,365,692
PERSONNEL:
```
    NORTH AMERICANS OVERSEAS   NON-NORTH AMERICANS OVERSEAS:     4
              MARRIED:     6       NORTH AMERICAN ADM. STAFF:    16
           SINGLE MEN:     0                     SHORT TERM:     0
         SINGLE WOMEN:     0                        RETIRED:     0
                        -----
        TOTAL ACTIVE:     6
```

FIELD OF SERVICE	YEAR BEGAN	PERSONNEL NOW	NEW	RELATED CHURCHES	PEOPLE GROUPS	NOTES
Angola	1944					
Brazil	1968	4				
Burma	1923					
Cameroon	1935					
Comoro	1978					
Ethiopia	1965	2				
Guyana	1978					
India	1906	2				
Korea, Rep. of	1909					
Liberia	1928					
Malawi	1974					
Paraguay	1951	2	2			
Philippines	1906					
Taiwan Rep of China	1955					
Tanzania	1941	2				
Thailand	1908					
Zaire	1935					

American Lutheran Church, Division
For World Mission and Inter-Church
Cooperation

422 S Fifth St.
Minneapolis MN 55415

Tel. (612) 330-3100
EXECUTIVE OFFICER: Morris A. Sorenson, Jr.
ORGANIZED: 1961   AFFILIATION: DOM-NCCCUSA
DESCRIPTION: A denominational sending agency of Lutheran
    tradition providing personnel and funds for support and
    nurture of national churches. Also engaged in community
    development, theological education, theological education
    by extension (TEE), and medical work.
TOTAL INCOME: $31,328,924   FOR OVERSEAS MINISTRIES: $6,447,944
PERSONNEL:

NORTH AMERICANS OVERSEAS		NON-NORTH AMERICANS OVERSEAS:	0
MARRIED:	295	NORTH AMERICAN ADM. STAFF:	9
SINGLE MEN:	8	SHORT TERM:	18
SINGLE WOMEN:	26	RETIRED:	0
TOTAL ACTIVE:	329		

FIELD OF SERVICE	YEAR BEGAN	PERSONNEL NOW	NEW	RELATED CHURCHES	PEOPLE GROUPS	NOTES
Australia	1974	7	3	1		
Brazil	1958	19	9	1		
Cameroon	1923	36	16	1		
Central African Rep.	1974	16	7	1		
Colombia	1944	10	6	1		
Egypt	1979	1				
Ethiopia	1957	2		1		
Germany, Fed. Rep.	1972	15	6			
Hong-Kong	1890	10	12	1		
India	1865	4		2		
Japan	1898	61	14	1		
Madagascar	1888	35	13	1		
Nepal	1978					
Nigeria	1913	15	5	1		
Papua New Guinea	1886	67	17	1		
Senegal	1976	7	7			
South Africa	1844	10		1		
Taiwan Rep of China	1952	12	1	1		
Tanzania	1948	7	4	1		

American Lutheran Church, Ohio
Synod SEE: American Lutheran Church

Ohio Synod SEE:

American Mc All Association

71 W 23rd St., Rm.1526
New York NY 10010

Tel. (212) 675-1036
EXECUTIVE OFFICER: Mrs. Robert A.L. Beutley
ORGANIZED: 1883
DESCRIPTION: An interdenominational Presbyterian/Congregational
    agency engaged in evangelism, aid and/or relief, development
    of human resources and information service. Also involved
    in self-help projects, fund transmittal and childcare.
TOTAL INCOME: $50,000   FOR OVERSEAS MINISTRIES: $50,000
PERSONNEL:

NORTH AMERICANS OVERSEAS		NON-NORTH AMERICANS OVERSEAS:	0
MARRIED:	0	NORTH AMERICAN ADM. STAFF:	2
SINGLE MEN:	0	SHORT TERM:	0

```
SINGLE WOMEN:      0                              RETIRED:       0
                 -----
   TOTAL ACTIVE:   0
```

FIELD OF SERVICE	YEAR BEGAN	PERSONNEL NOW	PERSONNEL NEW	RELATED CHURCHES	PEOPLE GROUPS	NOTES
France	1883			12		

American Messianic Fellowship

7448 N Damen Ave.
Chicago IL 60645

Tel. (312) 743-3410
EXECUTIVE OFFICER: William E. Currie
ORGANIZED: 1885
DESCRIPTION: A nondenominational, fundamentalist sending agency
   of independent tradition engaged in evangelism, information
   service, correspondence courses and literature distribution.
TOTAL INCOME: $284,648   FOR OVERSEAS MINISTRIES: $51,000

```
PERSONNEL:
   NORTH AMERICANS OVERSEAS   NON-NORTH AMERICANS OVERSEAS:   0
            MARRIED:    6        NORTH AMERICAN ADM. STAFF:    2
         SINGLE MEN:    0                       SHORT TERM:   12
       SINGLE WOMEN:    4                          RETIRED:    6
                      -----
       TOTAL ACTIVE:   10
```

FIELD OF SERVICE	YEAR BEGAN	PERSONNEL NOW	PERSONNEL NEW	RELATED CHURCHES	PEOPLE GROUPS	NOTES
Iran	1977		4	1	1	
Israel	1957	5	5	2	1	
Mexico	1979	2	2	3	1	

American Missionary Fellowship

672 Conestoga Rd.
Villanova PA 19085
P.O. ADDRESS:
Box 368
Villanova PA 19085

Tel. (215) 527-4439
EXECUTIVE OFFICER: E. Eugene Williams
ORGANIZED: 1817
DESCRIPTION: A nondenominational agency of evangelical and
   independent tradition establishing churches and engaged
   in general Christian education, evangelism, nurture or
   support of national churches and training.
TOTAL INCOME: $2,675,000   FOR OVERSEAS MINISTRIES: NR

```
PERSONNEL:
   NORTH AMERICANS OVERSEAS   NON-NORTH AMERICANS OVERSEAS:    2
            MARRIED:    4        NORTH AMERICAN ADM. STAFF:   16
         SINGLE MEN:    0                       SHORT TERM:   21
       SINGLE WOMEN:    0                          RETIRED:   90
                      -----
       TOTAL ACTIVE:    4
NOTES:  Agency also supports a large home mission program.
        Reported overseas personnel serve in Mexico.
        Additional personnel are involved in both
        overseas and home programs.
```

161

```
------------------------------------------------------------
                    YEAR    PERSONNEL   RELATED   PEOPLE
FIELD OF SERVICE    BEGAN   NOW   NEW   CHURCHES  GROUPS  NOTES
------------------------------------------------------------
Mexico              1976     4     4      12
```

American Scripture Gift Mission

1211 Arch St.
Philadelphia PA 19107

Tel. (215) 561-3232
EXECUTIVE OFFICER: David B. Wylie
ORGANIZED: 1915
DESCRIPTION: An interdenominational service agency of
    evangelical tradition involved in Bible and literature
    distribution among the elderly in retirement and nursing
    homes and also in prison ministries. Translations are in
    over 340 languages and agency cooperates with other
    organizations in distribution. Parent agency, Scripture
    Gift Mission, is based in Great Britain.

```
TOTAL INCOME:      $81,640   FOR OVERSEAS MINISTRIES:     $12,000
PERSONNEL:
    NORTH AMERICANS OVERSEAS   NON-NORTH AMERICANS OVERSEAS:    0
               MARRIED:   0       NORTH AMERICAN ADM. STAFF:    0
            SINGLE MEN:   0                    SHORT TERM:      0
          SINGLE WOMEN:   0                       RETIRED:      0
                       -----
         TOTAL ACTIVE:    0
```

American Tract Society

1624 N First St.
Garland TX 75040
P.O. ADDRESS:
Box 40208
Garland TX 75040

Tel. (214) 276-9408
EXECUTIVE OFFICER: Stephen E. Slocom
ORGANIZED: 1825
DESCRIPTION: An interdenominational publishing company engaged
    in literature production and distribution to individuals,
    churches and mission groups.

```
TOTAL INCOME:     $700,000        FOR OVERSEAS MINISTRIES:    NR
PERSONNEL:
    NORTH AMERICANS OVERSEAS   NON-NORTH AMERICANS OVERSEAS:    0
               MARRIED:   0       NORTH AMERICAN ADM. STAFF:   20
            SINGLE MEN:   0                    SHORT TERM:      0
          SINGLE WOMEN:   0                       RETIRED:      0
                       -----
         TOTAL ACTIVE:    0
```

American Waldensian Aid Society

475 Riverside Dr Rm 1850
New York NY 10115

Tel. (212) 870-2671
EXECUTIVE OFFICER: Charles W. Arbuthnot
ORGANIZED: 1906
DESCRIPTION: A specialized service agency supporting the
    Waldensian Church of Italy by providing information to
    supporters and raising and transmitting funds.

```
TOTAL INCOME:      $87,361   FOR OVERSEAS MINISTRIES:     $87,361
PERSONNEL:
    NORTH AMERICANS OVERSEAS   NON-NORTH AMERICANS OVERSEAS:    0
               MARRIED:   0       NORTH AMERICAN ADM. STAFF:    0
            SINGLE MEN:   0                    SHORT TERM:      0
```

SINGLE WOMEN: 0   RETIRED: 0

TOTAL ACTIVE: 0

AMG International (Advancing the Ministries of the Gospel)

6815 Shallowford Rd.
Chattanooga TN 37421

Tel. (615) 894-6062
EXECUTIVE OFFICER: Spiros Zodhiates
ORGANIZED: 1946
DESCRIPTION: A nondenominational sending agency of evangelical
    and Baptist tradition engaged in evangelism, childcare,
    radio and TV broadcasting, support of nationals and
    literature production.
TOTAL INCOME: $4,404,001   FOR OVERSEAS MINISTRIES: $3,159,000
PERSONNEL:
    NORTH AMERICANS OVERSEAS   NON-NORTH AMERICANS OVERSEAS: 2400
            MARRIED: 40   NORTH AMERICAN ADM. STAFF: 80
         SINGLE MEN: 0   SHORT TERM: 5
       SINGLE WOMEN: 6   RETIRED: 2

       TOTAL ACTIVE: 46
NOTES: The large number reported for non-North
    Americans overseas are primarily nationals,
    not expatriates.

FIELD OF SERVICE	YEAR BEGAN	PERSONNEL NOW	NEW	RELATED CHURCHES	PEOPLE GROUPS	NOTES
Bangladesh	1978	2		2		
Belgium	1978			1		
Brazil	1975			4		
Burma	1974	6	4	20		
Colombia	1973	2		10		
Cyprus	1965	4		5		
Egypt	1978			1		
Greece	1946	2		30		
Guatemala	1974	4		10		
Haiti	1976	3		20		
Hong-Kong	1978	2		1		
India	1968	2		2000		
Indonesia		2		300		
Israel	1975			1		
Italy	1973	2		1		
Jamaica	1978	2		1		
Japan	1978					
Korea, Rep. of	1977			1		
Lebanon	1973			1		
Mexico	1975	2		1		
Nepal	1978			1		
Nicaragua	1978			30		
Nigeria	1980	2				
Pakistan	1976	2		2		
Peru	1973			1		
Philippines	1970	5				
South Africa	1979			1		
Spain	1975			1		
Sri Lanka	1970			50		
Taiwan Rep of China	1974					

FIELD OF SERVICE	YEAR BEGAN	PERSONNEL NOW	NEW	RELATED CHURCHES	PEOPLE GROUPS	NOTES
Thailand	1974	1		5		
Turkey	1979	2				
Yugoslavia	1975			1		
Zaire	1978	4		40		

Anchor Bay Evangelistic Association

P.O. ADDRESS:
Box 188
New Baltimore MI 48047

Tel. (313) 725-0821
EXECUTIVE OFFICER: Maurice J. Hart
ORGANIZED: 1940
DESCRIPTION: A sending agency of Pentecostal tradition
    involved in licensing and ordaining ministers,
    establishing churches, childcare, literature work, and
    engaged in aid and relief. Operates Anchor Bay Bible
    Institute.
TOTAL INCOME: NR   FOR OVERSEAS MINISTRIES: $440,000
PERSONNEL:
    NORTH AMERICANS OVERSEAS   NON-NORTH AMERICANS OVERSEAS: NR
              MARRIED: NR   NORTH AMERICAN ADM. STAFF: 2
           SINGLE MEN: NR   SHORT TERM: NR
         SINGLE WOMEN: NR   RETIRED: 0

      TOTAL ACTIVE: 20
NOTES: Overseas personnel estimated by agency.
        Overseas income estimated by MARC.

FIELD OF SERVICE	YEAR BEGAN	PERSONNEL NOW	NEW	RELATED CHURCHES	PEOPLE GROUPS	NOTES
Belize		2				
Brazil		2				
Indonesia		2				
Mexico		6				
Philippines		8				

Andes Evangelical Mission

21 Schoolhouse Rd.
Whiting NJ 08759
P.O. ADDRESS:
Box 155
Whiting NJ 08759

Tel. (201) 350-9292
EXECUTIVE OFFICER: Ronald E. Wiebe
ORGANIZED: 1907   AFFILIATION: IFMA
DESCRIPTION: An interdenominational, evangelical Congregational
    sending agency of fundamentalist tradition engaged in
    radio and TV broadcasting, church planting, theological
    education and theological education by extension (TEE).
    Also involved in student ministries, youth camps and
    conferences and correspondence courses.
TOTAL INCOME: $423,814   FOR OVERSEAS MINISTRIES: $353,919
PERSONNEL:
    NORTH AMERICANS OVERSEAS   NON-NORTH AMERICANS OVERSEAS: 0
              MARRIED: 37   NORTH AMERICAN ADM. STAFF: 4
           SINGLE MEN: 0   SHORT TERM: NR

```
     SINGLE WOMEN:     6                          RETIRED:    13
                     -----
     TOTAL ACTIVE:    43
-----------------------------------------------------------------------
                     YEAR     PERSONNEL   RELATED    PEOPLE
FIELD OF SERVICE     BEGAN    NOW   NEW   CHURCHES   GROUPS   NOTES
-----------------------------------------------------------------------
Bolivia              1907     42    18      370
Peru                 1968      1     1
```

Anglican Church of Canada, National and World Program

600 Jarvis St.
Toronto ON, M4Y 1J6
Canada

Tel. (416) 924-9192
EXECUTIVE OFFICER: E. W. Scott
ORGANIZED: 1893   AFFILIATION: CCC-CWC
DESCRIPTION: An Anglican church sending missionaries and
    supporting national churches.

```
TOTAL INCOME:          NR          FOR OVERSEAS MINISTRIES:    NR
PERSONNEL:
   NORTH AMERICANS OVERSEAS   NON-NORTH AMERICANS OVERSEAS:    NR
            MARRIED:   NR         NORTH AMERICAN ADM. STAFF:   NR
         SINGLE MEN:   NR                      SHORT TERM:     NR
       SINGLE WOMEN:   NR                        RETIRED:      NR
                     -----
     TOTAL ACTIVE:    10
NOTES:  Overseas personnel estimated by MARC.
-----------------------------------------------------------------------
                     YEAR     PERSONNEL   RELATED    PEOPLE
FIELD OF SERVICE     BEGAN    NOW   NEW   CHURCHES   GROUPS   NOTES
-----------------------------------------------------------------------
Ecuador              1979      2
Fiji                 1964
Gambia               1976      1
Ghana                1967      1
India                1912
Jamaica              1972
Japan                1910
Lesotho              1977      1
Malaysia             1973      1
Oceania-general      1976      1
Sudan                1974      2
Trinidad and Tobago  1974
Uganda               1964
Zaire                1979      1
```

Anglican Orthodox Church

323 Walnut St.
Statesville NC 28677
P.O. ADDRESS:
Box 128
Statesville NC 28677

Tel. (704) 873-8365
EXECUTIVE OFFICER: James P. Dees
ORGANIZED: 1963
DESCRIPTION: A denominational agency of orthodox Anglican
    tradition supporting nationals and establishing churches.
    North Americans are not permanently stationed overseas but
    travel to other countries to help temporarily. Involved
    in general Christian education and theological education
    by extension (TEE). Also engaged in translating the Book
    of Common Prayer into other languages and dialects.
TOTAL INCOME: NA   FOR OVERSEAS MINISTRIES: NA

```
PERSONNEL:
    NORTH AMERICANS OVERSEAS     NON-NORTH AMERICANS OVERSEAS:    0
            MARRIED:     0        NORTH AMERICAN ADM. STAFF:      0
         SINGLE MEN:     0                   SHORT TERM:          0
       SINGLE WOMEN:     0                      RETIRED:          0
                     -----
       TOTAL ACTIVE:     0
```

```
                     YEAR    PERSONNEL   RELATED   PEOPLE
FIELD OF SERVICE     BEGAN   NOW   NEW   CHURCHES  GROUPS  NOTES
```

```
Colombia             1972
Fiji                 1974
India                1965
Madagascar           1969
Nigeria              1970
Pakistan             1969
Philippines          1978
Tonga                1976
Zimbabwe             1970
```

Anis Shorrosh Evangelistic Association

154 Country Club Dr.
Daphne AL 36526
P.O. ADDRESS:
Box 440
Spanish Fort AL 36527

Tel. (205) 626-1124
EXECUTIVE OFFICER: Anis A. Shorrosh
ORGANIZED: 1970
DESCRIPTION: An interdenominational agency of Baptist
    tradition supporting national evangelists in India, Nepal,
    Israel and Sri Lanka. Also involved in overseas
    evangelistic trips, general Christian education, motion
    pictures and book production.
TOTAL INCOME: $117,694   FOR OVERSEAS MINISTRIES: $117,694
```
PERSONNEL:
    NORTH AMERICANS OVERSEAS     NON-NORTH AMERICANS OVERSEAS:    NR
            MARRIED:     8        NORTH AMERICAN ADM. STAFF:      3
         SINGLE MEN:     5                   SHORT TERM:          4
       SINGLE WOMEN:     0                      RETIRED:          1
                     -----
       TOTAL ACTIVE:    13
```

Apostolic Christian Church (Nazarene), Apostolic Christian Church Foundation

P.O. ADDRESS:
Box 151
Tremont IL 61568

Tel. (309) 925-3551
EXECUTIVE OFFICER: Walter H. Meyer
ORGANIZED: 1953
DESCRIPTION: A denominational sending agency of evangelical
    tradition supporting national churches and involved in
    orphanages and childcare. Also engaged in church planting,
    fund raising and fund transmittal.
TOTAL INCOME: $235,000   FOR OVERSEAS MINISTRIES: $235,000
```
PERSONNEL:
    NORTH AMERICANS OVERSEAS     NON-NORTH AMERICANS OVERSEAS:    0
            MARRIED:    18        NORTH AMERICAN ADM. STAFF:      2
         SINGLE MEN:     1                   SHORT TERM:          0
```

```
SINGLE WOMEN:    3                           RETIRED:      0
                -----
TOTAL ACTIVE:   22
```

FIELD OF SERVICE	YEAR BEGAN	PERSONNEL NOW	PERSONNEL NEW	RELATED CHURCHES	PEOPLE GROUPS	NOTES
Argentina	1965			15		
Brazil	1959	13	2	20		
Ghana	1972		1	5		
Papua New Guinea	1959	9	3	32		

Apostolic Christian Church in the U.S. SEE: Apostolic Christian Msn. Fund, Apostolic Chrn. Ch. Amer.

Apostolic Christian Mission Fund
3420 N Sheridan Rd.
Peoria IL 61604

```
Tel. (313) 548-2000
EXECUTIVE OFFICER: Ben C. Maibach
ORGANIZED: 1835
DESCRIPTION:  A denominational sending agency of Apostolic
    Christian tradition serving missionaries and engaged in
    education.
TOTAL INCOME:     $50,000   FOR OVERSEAS MINISTRIES:     $25,000
PERSONNEL:
    NORTH AMERICANS OVERSEAS    NON-NORTH AMERICANS OVERSEAS:    NR
            MARRIED:   NR           NORTH AMERICAN ADM. STAFF:   NR
        SINGLE MEN:    NR                        SHORT TERM:      2
        SINGLE WOMEN:  NR                          RETIRED:       0
                       -----
        TOTAL ACTIVE:   2
```

FIELD OF SERVICE	YEAR BEGAN	PERSONNEL NOW	PERSONNEL NEW	RELATED CHURCHES	PEOPLE GROUPS	NOTES
Japan	1952	2				

Apostolic Church in Canada, The
27 Castlefield Ave.
Toronto ON M4R 1G3
Canada

```
Tel. (416) 292-1811
EXECUTIVE OFFICER: David S. Morris
ORGANIZED: 1930
DESCRIPTION:  A denominational sending agency of Pentecostal
    tradition establishing churches and engaged in financing
    church construction, nurture of nationals and national
    churches, evangelism and correspondence courses.
TOTAL INCOME:    $221,094   FOR OVERSEAS MINISTRIES:     $43,985
PERSONNEL:
    NORTH AMERICANS OVERSEAS    NON-NORTH AMERICANS OVERSEAS:    0
            MARRIED:    4            NORTH AMERICAN ADM. STAFF:   2
        SINGLE MEN:     0                        SHORT TERM:      0
        SINGLE WOMEN:   0                          RETIRED:      NR
                       -----
        TOTAL ACTIVE:    4
NOTES:  Administrative personnel are part-time
        and unpaid.
```

FIELD OF SERVICE	YEAR BEGAN	PERSONNEL NOW	PERSONNEL NEW	RELATED CHURCHES	PEOPLE GROUPS	NOTES
Brazil	1970	4	4	7		

Apostolic Church of Pentecost of Canada-Missionary Dept.

3026 Taylor St. E, Ste.4
Saskatoon SK S7H 4J2
Canada

Tel. (306) 374-1944
EXECUTIVE OFFICER: E. G. Bradley
ORGANIZED: 1921
DESCRIPTION: A denominational sending agency of Pentecostal
    tradition establishing churches and engaged in evangelism,
    general Christian education, literature production and
    support of nationals.
TOTAL INCOME: $560,000   FOR OVERSEAS MINISTRIES: $255,000
PERSONNEL:
    NORTH AMERICANS OVERSEAS   NON-NORTH AMERICANS OVERSEAS: NR
            MARRIED: 52   NORTH AMERICAN ADM. STAFF: 3
        SINGLE MEN: 0   SHORT TERM: 5
      SINGLE WOMEN: 8   RETIRED: 1

        TOTAL ACTIVE: 60

FIELD OF SERVICE	YEAR BEGAN	PERSONNEL NOW	PERSONNEL NEW	RELATED CHURCHES	PEOPLE GROUPS	NOTES
Brazil	1972	4	2			
El Salvador	1979	2	2			
Ghana	1979	2	2			
Guatemala	1975	4	2			
India	1946	4				
Israel		1				
Ivory Coast		1				
Japan	1951	2				
Malawi	1947	4				
Mexico	1963	8	2			
South Africa		2				
Taiwan Rep of China		4				
Upper Volta		14				
Zimbabwe	1951	6				

Apostolic Faith Mission of Portland, Oregon

SE 52nd and Duke St.
Portland OR 97206

Tel. (503) 222-9761
EXECUTIVE OFFICER: Loyce C. Carver
ORGANIZED: 1907
DESCRIPTION: A sending agency of conservative Pentecostal
    tradition establishing churches and engaged in evangelism,
    literature production and distribution. Works in Asia,
    Indonesia, Europe and Africa.
TOTAL INCOME: NR   FOR OVERSEAS MINISTRIES: $132,000
PERSONNEL:
    NORTH AMERICANS OVERSEAS   NON-NORTH AMERICANS OVERSEAS: NR
            MARRIED: NR   NORTH AMERICAN ADM. STAFF: 120
        SINGLE MEN: NR   SHORT TERM: NR
      SINGLE WOMEN: NR   RETIRED: NR

        TOTAL ACTIVE: 6
NOTES: The number of personnel on administrative
        duty includes pastors of churches.
        Overseas income estimated by MARC.

Apostolic Overcoming Holy Church of God

2257 St. Steven's Rd.
Mobile AL 36617

Tel. (205) 473-8312
EXECUTIVE OFFICER: James E. Finley
ORGANIZED: 1919
DESCRIPTION: A denominational sending agency of Pentecostal
  and Apostolic tradition that is evangelistic in purpose.
TOTAL INCOME: NR   FOR OVERSEAS MINISTRIES: $44,000
PERSONNEL:

NORTH AMERICANS OVERSEAS		NON-NORTH AMERICANS OVERSEAS:	NR
MARRIED:	NR	NORTH AMERICAN ADM. STAFF:	NR
SINGLE MEN:	NR	SHORT TERM:	0
SINGLE WOMEN:	NR	RETIRED:	0
TOTAL ACTIVE:	2		

NOTES: Overseas income estimated by MARC.

FIELD OF SERVICE	YEAR BEGAN	PERSONNEL NOW	NEW	RELATED CHURCHES	PEOPLE GROUPS	NOTES
Haiti	1975	2				

Appleman Campaigns, Inc.

7337 Broadway
Kansas City MO 64114

Tel. (816) 333-4022
EXECUTIVE OFFICER: Hyman Appleman
ORGANIZED: 1935
DESCRIPTION: No current information available. Information
  from 1976 directory. A nondenominational agency of
  Baptist tradition specializing in evangelistic campaigns
  overseas and also in the USA.
TOTAL INCOME: $27,500   FOR OVERSEAS MINISTRIES: NR
PERSONNEL:

NORTH AMERICANS OVERSEAS		NON-NORTH AMERICANS OVERSEAS:	NR
MARRIED:	NR	NORTH AMERICAN ADM. STAFF:	2
SINGLE MEN:	NR	SHORT TERM:	NR
SINGLE WOMEN:	NR	RETIRED:	NR
TOTAL ACTIVE:	NR		

NOTES: Income estimated by MARC.

Arabic Literature Mission
SEE: Middle East Christian Outreach

Armenian Missionary Association of America, Inc.

140 Forest Ave.
Paramus NJ 07652

Tel. (201) 265-2607
EXECUTIVE OFFICER: G. H. Chopourian
ORGANIZED: 1918
DESCRIPTION: A denominational service agency of evangelical
  and Presbyterian tradition engaged in evangelism,
  education, fund raising and aid/relief.
TOTAL INCOME: $951,183   FOR OVERSEAS MINISTRIES: NR
PERSONNEL:

NORTH AMERICANS OVERSEAS		NON-NORTH AMERICANS OVERSEAS:	NR
MARRIED:	0	NORTH AMERICAN ADM. STAFF:	6
SINGLE MEN:	0	SHORT TERM:	NR

SINGLE WOMEN: 0   RETIRED: NR

TOTAL ACTIVE: 0

Arthur Bradford Evangelistic Association

729 Cleveland
Brooklyn NY 11203

Tel. (212) 257-3773
EXECUTIVE OFFICER: Arthur Bradford
ORGANIZED: 1968
DESCRIPTION: A specialized agency of Pentecostal tradition
    working in evangelistic team campaigns overseas.
TOTAL INCOME: $78,000   FOR OVERSEAS MINISTRIES: NR
PERSONNEL:
    NORTH AMERICANS OVERSEAS   NON-NORTH AMERICANS OVERSEAS: NR
              MARRIED: 0   NORTH AMERICAN ADM. STAFF: 14
          SINGLE MEN: 0   SHORT TERM: 0
        SINGLE WOMEN: 0   RETIRED: NR

        TOTAL ACTIVE: 0

Asian Outreach

1 Sugar St.
Causeway Bay Hong Ko
P.O. ADDRESS:
Box 3448
Hong Kong

EXECUTIVE OFFICER: Paul E. Kauffman
ORGANIZED: 1955
DESCRIPTION: An international, interdenominational service
    and sending agency of evangelical and charismatic
    tradition producing and distributing literature to
    nationals and other agencies in Asia. Also engaged in
    correspondence courses and audio-visual work. Asian based,
    most staff and support are Asian.
TOTAL INCOME: $1,100,000   FOR OVERSEAS MINISTRIES: $1,100,000
PERSONNEL:
    NORTH AMERICANS OVERSEAS   NON-NORTH AMERICANS OVERSEAS: 7
              MARRIED: 4   NORTH AMERICAN ADM. STAFF: 1
          SINGLE MEN: NR   SHORT TERM: 0
        SINGLE WOMEN: NR   RETIRED: NR

        TOTAL ACTIVE: 4
NOTES: The Headquarters is in Hong Kong.

FIELD OF SERVICE	YEAR BEGAN	PERSONNEL NOW	PERSONNEL NEW	RELATED CHURCHES	PEOPLE GROUPS	NOTES
China, People's Rep.	1968					
Hong-Kong	1955	4	2			
Indonesia	1979					
Japan	1975					
Korea, Rep. of	1971					
Malaysia	1971					
Singapore	1965					
Taiwan Rep of China	1975					

Assemblies of God, Division of
Foreign Missions

1445 Boonville Ave.
Springfield MO 65802

Tel. (417) 862-2781
EXECUTIVE OFFICER: J. Philip Hogan
ORGANIZED: 1914   AFFILIATION: EFMA
DESCRIPTION: A denominational sending agency of Pentecostal
    and evangelical tradition doing evangelism, establishing
    churches and training national church workers. Involved in
    personal and mass evangelism, theological education by
    extension (TEE), correspondence courses, publishing and
    distribution of literature.
TOTAL INCOME: $29,875,534   FOR OVERSEAS MINISTRIES: $29,875,534
PERSONNEL:
    NORTH AMERICANS OVERSEAS   NON-NORTH AMERICANS OVERSEAS: 19
            MARRIED: 1098   NORTH AMERICAN ADM. STAFF: 38
        SINGLE MEN: 5   SHORT TERM: 170
      SINGLE WOMEN: 111   RETIRED: 138

      TOTAL ACTIVE: 1214

FIELD OF SERVICE	YEAR BEGAN	PERSONNEL NOW	NEW	RELATED CHURCHES	PEOPLE GROUPS	NOTES
Afghanistan	1972					
American Samoa	1928	2		12		
Argentina	1914	13		106		
Austria	1967	2		31		
Bahamas	1953	2		17		
Bangladesh	1956	13		12		
Belgium	1951	29		31		
Belize	1946	4		6		
Benin	1921	6		35		
Bolivia	1948	14		509		
Botswana	1963	2		17		
Brazil	1911	25				
Bulgaria	1968			217		
Burma	1931			400		
Cameroon	1974	4		1		
Canary Islands		7		4		
Chile	1941	18		69		
Colombia	1932	11		81		
Costa Rica	1942	12		100		
Cuba	1920			115		
Czechoslovakia	1968			92		
Dominican Republic	1933	6		238		
Ecuador	1962	17		27		
Egypt	1910	4		144		
El Salvador	1929	8		535		
Ethiopia	1975					
Fiji	1926	6		105		
France	1964	8		999		
French Polynesia		4				
Germany, Fed. Rep.	1948	27		146		
Ghana	1931	30		230		
Greece	1931	5		11		
Guam	1960	2		3		
Guatemala	1937	9		644		
Guyana	1957	2		35		
Haiti	1957	6		78		

FIELD OF SERVICE	YEAR BEGAN	PERSONNEL NOW	NEW	RELATED CHURCHES	PEOPLE GROUPS	NOTES
Honduras	1937	13		165		
Hong-Kong	1928	17		12		
Hungary	1968			191		
India	1906	35		331		
Indonesia	1945	31		205		
Iran	1965	4		11		
Ireland						
Israel	1908					
Italy	1908	12		755		
Ivory Coast	1927	12		93		
Jamaica	1937	5		35		
Japan	1913	30		93		
Jordan	1908	6		4		
Kenya	1972	26		215		
Korea, Rep. of	1952	13		310		
Lebanon	1920	2		3		
Lesotho	1950	2		27		
Liberia	1908	11		248		
Malawi	1930	16		83		
Malaysia	1957	16		43		
Marshall Is.		4		3		
Mexico	1915	27		811		
Mozambique	1974			50		
Nepal	1973	2				
Netherlands	1965	6		55		
New Caledonia	1969	4		4		
Nicaragua	1926	6		122		
Nigeria	1939	30		1759		
Pacific Trust Terr.		4		2		
Pakistan		2				
Panama	1967	12		16		
Paraguay	1945	9		19		
Peru	1919	7		575		
Philippines	1930	57		520		
Poland	1968			201		
Portugal	1973	8		325		
Romania	1968			835		
Samoa	1928	2		26		
Senegal	1956	15		26		
Sierra Leone	1916	8		32		
Singapore	1957	5		13		
Solomon Is.		4		16		
South Africa	1910	34		137		
Spain	1947	23		25		
Sri Lanka	1925	2		22		
Surinam	1958	2		4		
Switzerland	1967	2		255		
Taiwan Rep of China	1948	16		47		
Tanzania	1930	21		190		
Thailand	1969	8		11		
Togo	1921	18		40		
Tonga	1972	2		16		
Tunisia		2				
Upper Volta	1921	19		500		
Uruguay	1944	6		50		

FIELD OF SERVICE	YEAR BEGAN	PERSONNEL NOW	NEW	RELATED CHURCHES	PEOPLE GROUPS	NOTES
USSR	1958	2				
Vanuatu	1973	4		21		
Venezuela	1919	13		115		
Viet Nam, Soc. Rep.	1972					
Yugoslavia	1968	3		65		
Zaire	1921	15		216		
Zimbabwe		2		7		

Associate Boards for Women's Christian College, Madras, Inc. and St. Christopher's Training College, Vepery, Madras, Inc.

475 Riverside Dr.16th Fl
New York NY 10115

Tel. (212) 749-0700
EXECUTIVE OFFICER: Mrs. Orrin Judd
ORGANIZED: 1915   AFFILIATION: DOM-NCCCUSA, Frat. Rel.
DESCRIPTION: An interdenominational board transmitting funds
    and supported by cooperating denominations.
TOTAL INCOME: NR   FOR OVERSEAS MINISTRIES: NR
PERSONNEL:
    NORTH AMERICANS OVERSEAS   NON-NORTH AMERICANS OVERSEAS: NR
              MARRIED: NR   NORTH AMERICAN ADM. STAFF: NR
           SINGLE MEN: NR   SHORT TERM: NR
         SINGLE WOMEN: NR   RETIRED: NR

        TOTAL ACTIVE: NR

Associate Reformed Presbyterian Church World Witness, the Board of Foreign Missions

1 Cleveland St.
Greenville SC 29601

Tel. (803) 232-8297
EXECUTIVE OFFICER: John E. Mariner
ORGANIZED: 1839   AFFILIATION: EFMA
DESCRIPTION: Founded in 1839 as General Synod Board of Foreign
    Missions. Name changed in 1978. A denominational sending
    agency of Reformed Presbyterian tradition establishing,
    nurturing and supporting national churches, and engaged in
    public health, camping and agricultural ministries.
TOTAL INCOME: $588,628   FOR OVERSEAS MINISTRIES: $588,628
PERSONNEL:
    NORTH AMERICANS OVERSEAS   NON-NORTH AMERICANS OVERSEAS: 0
              MARRIED: 8   NORTH AMERICAN ADM. STAFF: 2
           SINGLE MEN: 1   SHORT TERM: 10
         SINGLE WOMEN: 3   RETIRED: 0

        TOTAL ACTIVE: 12

FIELD OF SERVICE	YEAR BEGAN	PERSONNEL NOW	NEW	RELATED CHURCHES	PEOPLE GROUPS	NOTES
Mexico	1878	11	3	100	4	
Pakistan	1907	17	7	120	5	

Associate Reformed Presbyterian Church, General Synod, Board of Foreign Missions SEE: Associate Reformed Presbyterian Church, World Witness, Board of Foreign Mission

Association of Baptists for World Evangelism, Inc.

1720 Springdale Rd.
Cherry Hill NJ 08034
P.O. ADDRESS:
Box 5000
Cherry Hill NJ 08034

Tel. (609) 424-4606
EXECUTIVE OFFICER: Wendell W. Kempton
ORGANIZED: 1927   AFFILIATION: FOM
DESCRIPTION: A denominational sending agency of Baptist
    tradition engaged in church planting, theological education,
    Bible translation, medicine and aviation.
TOTAL INCOME: $5,043,629   FOR OVERSEAS MINISTRIES: $5,043,629
PERSONNEL:
    NORTH AMERICANS OVERSEAS   NON-NORTH AMERICANS OVERSEAS: 0
             MARRIED: 430   NORTH AMERICAN ADM. STAFF: 14
          SINGLE MEN: 4   SHORT TERM: 18
        SINGLE WOMEN: 68   RETIRED: 36

       TOTAL ACTIVE: 502
NOTES: North American overseas personnel includes
        16 people working in the USA.

FIELD OF SERVICE	YEAR BEGAN	PERSONNEL NOW	PERSONNEL NEW	RELATED CHURCHES	PEOPLE GROUPS	NOTES
Philippines	1927	68	19	400		
Portugal	1979	8	4			
Spain	1968	20	6	2		
Togo	1973	25	15	4		

Association of Free Lutheran Congregations

3110 E Medecine Lake Blvd.
Minneapolis MN 55441

Tel. (612) 545-5631
EXECUTIVE OFFICER: Richard Snipstead
ORGANIZED: 1962
DESCRIPTION: A denominational sending agency of Lutheran
    tradition engaged in church planting, extension and
    general Christian education, personal evangelism,
    training and nurture or support of national churches.
TOTAL INCOME: $218,880   FOR OVERSEAS MINISTRIES: $191,140
PERSONNEL:
    NORTH AMERICANS OVERSEAS   NON-NORTH AMERICANS OVERSEAS: NR
             MARRIED: NR   NORTH AMERICAN ADM. STAFF: 1
          SINGLE MEN: NR   SHORT TERM: 4
        SINGLE WOMEN: NR   RETIRED: 0

       TOTAL ACTIVE: 9

FIELD OF SERVICE	YEAR BEGAN	PERSONNEL NOW	PERSONNEL NEW	RELATED CHURCHES	PEOPLE GROUPS	NOTES
Brazil		9				
India						
Mexico		1				

Audio Bible Studies International
SEE: International Bible Institute

Back to the Bible Missionary Agency

12th and M Sts.
Lincoln NE 68501
P.O. ADDRESS:
Box 82808
Lincoln NE 68501
Tel. (402) 474-4567
EXECUTIVE OFFICER: Eric H. Bowley
ORGANIZED: 1952
DESCRIPTION: A nondenominational agency of independent tradition
    providing Bible teaching, radio broadcasts, literature and
    funding support for nationals, missionaries and mission
    projects. In 1979 assisted more than 50 sending agencies.
TOTAL INCOME: $1,440,659   FOR OVERSEAS MINISTRIES: $1,296,593
PERSONNEL:
NORTH AMERICANS OVERSEAS   NON-NORTH AMERICANS OVERSEAS: 1
         MARRIED: 0   NORTH AMERICAN ADM. STAFF: 5
      SINGLE MEN: 1   SHORT TERM: 0
    SINGLE WOMEN: 1   RETIRED: NA

    TOTAL ACTIVE: 2
NOTES: Income figures include Canada.

FIELD OF SERVICE	YEAR BEGAN	PERSONNEL NOW	PERSONNEL NEW	RELATED CHURCHES	PEOPLE GROUPS	NOTES
Australia	1957					
Ecuador	1970					
India	1970					
Italy	1961	2	2			
Jamaica	1958					
Philippines	1957					
Sri Lanka	1955	1				
United Kingdom	1954					

    Note: North American personnel
    serving in overseas offices are
    on loan from other agencies.

Back-Country Evangelism, Inc.

P.O. ADDRESS:
Box 36
Pasadena CA 91102
EXECUTIVE OFFICER: John E. Huffman
ORGANIZED: 1953
DESCRIPTION: No current information available. Information
    from 1976 directory. A nondenominational sending agency
    of independent tradition with missionaries in Mexico.
    Agency personnel involved in evangelism and education.
TOTAL INCOME: $27,500   FOR OVERSEAS MINISTRIES: NR
PERSONNEL:
NORTH AMERICANS OVERSEAS   NON-NORTH AMERICANS OVERSEAS: NR
         MARRIED: NR   NORTH AMERICAN ADM. STAFF: NR
      SINGLE MEN: NR   SHORT TERM: NR
    SINGLE WOMEN: NR   RETIRED: NR

    TOTAL ACTIVE: NR
NOTES: Income estimated by MARC.

FIELD OF SERVICE	YEAR BEGAN	PERSONNEL NOW	PERSONNEL NEW	RELATED CHURCHES	PEOPLE GROUPS	NOTES
Mexico	1953					1

    1. Training school

Baptist Bible Fellowship
International

730 Kearney
Springfield MO 65801
P.O. ADDRESS:
Box 191
Springfield MO 65801

Tel. (417) 862-5001
EXECUTIVE OFFICER: David Cavin
ORGANIZED: 1950
DESCRIPTION: A nondenominational sending agency of independent,
    Baptist and fundamentalist tradition engaged in church
    planting, church construction or financing, evangelism and
    ministry to servicemen.
TOTAL INCOME: $10,884,000   FOR OVERSEAS MINISTRIES: $559,000
PERSONNEL:
    NORTH AMERICANS OVERSEAS   NON-NORTH AMERICANS OVERSEAS: 0
              MARRIED: 620   NORTH AMERICAN ADM. STAFF: NR
           SINGLE MEN: 0   SHORT TERM: 0
         SINGLE WOMEN: 10   RETIRED: 6

       TOTAL ACTIVE: 630

FIELD OF SERVICE	YEAR BEGAN	PERSONNEL NOW	NEW	RELATED CHURCHES	PEOPLE GROUPS	NOTES
American Samoa	1975	2				
Argentina	1959	12				
Australia	1954	20				
Barbados	1977	2				
Belgium	1962	8				
Belize	1978	2				
Bolivia	1977	4				
Brazil	1952	8				
Chile	1954	8				
Colombia	1972	10				
Costa Rica	1968	13				
Ecuador	1975	8				
Egypt	1974	2				
El Salvador	1976	6				
Ethiopia	1960	26				
France	1970	12				
French Polynesia	1977	2				
Germany, Fed. Rep.	1970	16				
Guam	1975	2				
Guatemala	1975	6				
Honduras	1974	6				
Hong-Kong	1950	2				
India	1955	4				
Indonesia	1972	12				
Iran	1966	2				
Israel	1979	2				
Italy	1978	2				
Jamaica	1972	4				
Japan	1950	27				
Kenya	1962	28				
Korea, Rep. of	1950	28				
Lebanon	1956	2				
Mexico	1950	58				
Netherlands	1978	4				

FIELD OF SERVICE	YEAR BEGAN	PERSONNEL NOW	NEW	RELATED CHURCHES	PEOPLE GROUPS	NOTES
New Zealand	1971	6				
Nicaragua	1969	4				
Norway	1971	8				
Pacific Trust Terr.	1973	2				
Pakistan	1952	2				
Panama	1977	2				
Papua New Guinea	1961	12				
Peru	1958	17				
Philippines	1950	62				
Puerto Rico	1955	10				
Singapore	1967	2				
Spain	1970	8				
Switzerland	1973	2				
Taiwan Rep of China	1950	17				
U.S. Virgin Is.	1972	2				
United Kingdom	1972	18				
Uruguay	1959	8				
Venezuela	1958	4				
Zaire	1957	2				

Baptist Faith Missions

1012 Balsam Dr.
Lexington KY 40504

Tel. (606) 278-8627
EXECUTIVE OFFICER: H.H. Overbey
ORGANIZED: 1923
DESCRIPTION: An independent Baptist organization engaged in
    church planting and construction, education, evangelism and
    furloughed missionary support.
TOTAL INCOME: NR   FOR OVERSEAS MINISTRIES: $321,127
PERSONNEL:
    NORTH AMERICANS OVERSEAS   NON-NORTH AMERICANS OVERSEAS: 0
                MARRIED: 11   NORTH AMERICAN ADM. STAFF: 2
             SINGLE MEN: 0   SHORT TERM: 0
           SINGLE WOMEN: 0   RETIRED: 1

           TOTAL ACTIVE: 11

FIELD OF SERVICE	YEAR BEGAN	PERSONNEL NOW	NEW	RELATED CHURCHES	PEOPLE GROUPS	NOTES
Brazil	1923	9		36		
Honduras	1972			3		
Korea, Rep. of	1971	1		4		
Peru	1935	1		17		

Baptist General Conference Board of
World Missions

1233 Central St.
Evanston IL 60201

Tel. (312) 328-8500
EXECUTIVE OFFICER: Virgil A. Olson
ORGANIZED: 1944   AFFILIATION: EFMA
DESCRIPTION: A denominational sending agency of Baptist and
    evangelical tradition establishing churches and engaged
    in theological education and theological education by
    extension (TEE). Also involved in literature
    distribution and medicine.
TOTAL INCOME: $5,934,347   FOR OVERSEAS MINISTRIES: $2,278,414

PERSONNEL:
```
    NORTH AMERICANS OVERSEAS     NON-NORTH AMERICANS OVERSEAS:     0
              MARRIED:    92         NORTH AMERICAN ADM. STAFF:     4
           SINGLE MEN:     0                        SHORT TERM:    11
         SINGLE WOMEN:     9                           RETIRED:    NA
                       -----
        TOTAL ACTIVE:   101
```

FIELD OF SERVICE	YEAR BEGAN	PERSONNEL NOW	PERSONNEL NEW	RELATED CHURCHES	PEOPLE GROUPS	NOTES
Argentina	1955	12	4	14		
Brazil	1955	12	2			
Cameroon	1979	2	2			
Ethiopia	1950	13		29		
India	1946	1		300		
Ivory Coast	1977	4	4			
Japan	1948	13	2	26		
Kenya	1978	2	2			
Mexico	1951	15	8	12		
Philippines	1950	26	4	33		

Baptist Haiti Mission, Inc.

1537 Plainfield Ave. NE
Grand Rapids MI 49505

Tel. (616) 361-7046
EXECUTIVE OFFICER: W. Glen Campbell
ORGANIZED: 1943
DESCRIPTION: A denominational sending agency of fundamental
    and Baptist tradition engaged in establishing and
    constructing churches, evangelism, literacy, education and
    agriculture. Also involved in aid, self-help projects,
    medicine, and support and training of nationals.
TOTAL INCOME: NR   FOR OVERSEAS MINISTRIES: $313,464
PERSONNEL:
```
    NORTH AMERICANS OVERSEAS     NON-NORTH AMERICANS OVERSEAS:     0
              MARRIED:     2         NORTH AMERICAN ADM. STAFF:     1
           SINGLE MEN:     1                        SHORT TERM:     0
         SINGLE WOMEN:     0                           RETIRED:     0
                       -----
        TOTAL ACTIVE:     3
```

FIELD OF SERVICE	YEAR BEGAN	PERSONNEL NOW	PERSONNEL NEW	RELATED CHURCHES	PEOPLE GROUPS	NOTES
Haiti	1943	17		161	1	

    Note: Personnel include 14 self-
    supporting North American
    volunteers.

Baptist International Missions, Inc.

800 Dodds Ave.
Chattanooga TN 37404
P.O. ADDRESS:
Box 9215
Chattanooga TN 37412

Tel. (615) 698-1523
EXECUTIVE OFFICER: J. R. Faulkner
ORGANIZED: 1960
DESCRIPTION: A nondenominational sending agency of
    fundamentalist and Baptist tradition planting churches
    and engaged in evangelism, general Christian education,
    broadcasting, literature distribution and ministry to
    servicemen.

```
TOTAL INCOME:  $7,500,000    FOR OVERSEAS MINISTRIES:  $6,000,000
PERSONNEL:
   NORTH AMERICANS OVERSEAS    NON-NORTH AMERICANS OVERSEAS:    30
             MARRIED:  506        NORTH AMERICAN ADM. STAFF:    25
          SINGLE MEN:  20                       SHORT TERM:     0
        SINGLE WOMEN:  70                          RETIRED:     1
                      -----
        TOTAL ACTIVE:  596
-----------------------------------------------------------------------
                       YEAR    PERSONNEL    RELATED   PEOPLE
FIELD OF SERVICE       BEGAN   NOW   NEW    CHURCHES  GROUPS  NOTES
-----------------------------------------------------------------------
Argentina                       2
Australia              1970     14
Bahamas                1968     47
Bolivia                1969      8
Brazil                 1967     51
Caribbean-general               32
Chile                           4
Colombia                        4
Costa Rica             1968     14
Dominican Republic     1969      2
El Salvador            1970      4
France                 1969     12
Germany, Fed. Rep.     1969     16
Ghana                  1974     12
Greece                          1
Grenada                         2
Guatemala              1971      2
Haiti                           4
Honduras               1970     10
India                           4
Indonesia              1971      4
Ireland                         6
Italy                           5
Ivory Coast            1970     10
Jamaica                         4
Japan                  1965     40
Korea, Rep. of                  4
Mexico                 1965     28
Netherlands Antilles            4
New Zealand            1973      4
Niger                  1966      4
Norway                 1973      6
Pacific Trust Terr.             4
Panama                          2
Papua New Guinea       1968      6
Peru                   1969      9
Philippines            1970     37
Puerto Rico                     12
Senegal                         8
Singapore                       2
South Africa           1968     10
Spain                  1965     15
Taiwan Rep of China             8
Thailand                        6
Togo                            2
Trinidad and Tobago    1974      2
U.S. Virgin Is.                 14
```

FIELD OF SERVICE	YEAR BEGAN	PERSONNEL NOW	NEW	RELATED CHURCHES	PEOPLE GROUPS	NOTES
United Kingdom	1972	17				
Venezuela		6				

Baptist Mid-Missions   826-3930

4205 Chester Ave.
Cleveland OH 44103

Tel. (216) ~~432-2200~~
EXECUTIVE OFFICER: ~~Allan B. Lewis~~ *Guy Anderson*
ORGANIZED: 1920   AFFILIATION: FOM
DESCRIPTION: A denominational sending agency of Baptist
    tradition establishing churches and engaged in general
    Christian education, aviation, medicine and Bible
    translation.
TOTAL INCOME: $11,000,060   FOR OVERSEAS MINISTRIES: $6,500,000
PERSONNEL:

NORTH AMERICANS OVERSEAS		NON-NORTH AMERICANS OVERSEAS:	0
MARRIED:	NR	NORTH AMERICAN ADM. STAFF:	40
SINGLE MEN:	NR	SHORT TERM:	14
SINGLE WOMEN:	NR	RETIRED:	157
TOTAL ACTIVE:	608		

FIELD OF SERVICE	YEAR BEGAN	PERSONNEL NOW	NEW	RELATED CHURCHES	PEOPLE GROUPS	NOTES
Australia	1968	23				
Austria	1967	7				
Bangladesh	1979	6				
Brazil	1946	140				
Central African Rep.	1920	72				
Chad	1925	17				
Dominican Republic	1950	14				
Finland		2				
France	1948	32				
Germany, Fed. Rep.	1959	17				
Ghana	1946	23				
Haiti	1949	13				
Honduras	1954	6				
Hong-Kong	1958	2				
India	1935	20				
Italy	1951	14				
Ivory Coast	1974	9				
Jamaica	1939	8				
Japan	1949	27				
Jordan	1970	2				
Korea, Rep. of	1966					
Liberia	1938	44				
Mexico	1960	17				
Netherlands	1954	6				
New Zealand	1973	9				
Peru	1937	17				
Puerto Rico	1959	14				
Spain	1979	4				
St. Lucia	1946	8				
St. Vincent	1947	4				

FIELD OF SERVICE	YEAR BEGAN	PERSONNEL NOW	NEW	RELATED CHURCHES	PEOPLE GROUPS	NOTES
Taiwan Rep of China	1972	2				
United Kingdom	1972	29				
Venezuela	1924	13				

Baptist Missionary Association of America

721 Main St.
Little Rock AR 72201

Tel. (501) 376-6788
EXECUTIVE OFFICER: Craig Branham
ORGANIZED: 1950
DESCRIPTION: A denominational sending agency of Baptist
    tradition establishing churches and engaged in evangelism,
    Bible distribution, theological education and aviation.
TOTAL INCOME: $972,400   FOR OVERSEAS MINISTRIES: $972,350
PERSONNEL:
    NORTH AMERICANS OVERSEAS   NON-NORTH AMERICANS OVERSEAS: 0
            MARRIED: 24   NORTH AMERICAN ADM. STAFF: 7
         SINGLE MEN: 0   SHORT TERM: 7
       SINGLE WOMEN: 0   RETIRED: 2

        TOTAL ACTIVE: 24
NOTES: Income estimated by MARC.

FIELD OF SERVICE	YEAR BEGAN	PERSONNEL NOW	NEW	RELATED CHURCHES	PEOPLE GROUPS	NOTES
Australia	1965	3	1			
Bolivia	1965	3				
Brazil	1953	1				
Cape Verde	1956					
Costa Rica	1961	2				
Guatemala	1978	1	1			
Honduras	1976	2	2			
India	1975					
Italy	1953					
Japan	1953	1				
Korea, Rep. of	1978					
Mexico	1953	4	2			
Nicaragua	1965					
Philippines	1974	6	5			
Portugal	1962					
South Africa	1974					
Taiwan Rep of China	1953	1				
Uruguay						

Baptist World Mission

811 Second Ave. SE
Decatur AL 35601

Tel. (205) 353-2221
EXECUTIVE OFFICER: Monroe Parker
ORGANIZED: 1962
DESCRIPTION: An independent sending agency of Baptist and
    fundamentalist tradition engaged in evangelism, church
    planting and education.
TOTAL INCOME: $250,000   FOR OVERSEAS MINISTRIES: $250,000
PERSONNEL:
    NORTH AMERICANS OVERSEAS   NON-NORTH AMERICANS OVERSEAS: NR
            MARRIED: NR   NORTH AMERICAN ADM. STAFF: 4
         SINGLE MEN: NR   SHORT TERM: 0

```
SINGLE WOMEN:    NR                          RETIRED:    0
               -----
    TOTAL ACTIVE:    85
```

FIELD OF SERVICE	YEAR BEGAN	PERSONNEL NOW	NEW	RELATED CHURCHES	PEOPLE GROUPS	NOTES
Argentina						
Australia		1				
Brazil						
Costa Rica		1				
France	1969					
Germany, Fed. Rep.	1969					
Israel						
Japan		6				
Korea, Rep. of		2				
Mexico	1965	4				
Papua New Guinea						
Spain						
Sweden		1				
Thailand		1				
United Kingdom		2				
Uruguay	1964	5				

Beams of Light Missionary Society, Inc.
SEE: Full Gospel Grace Fellowship

Berean Mission, Inc.

3536 Russell Blvd.
St. Louis MO 63104

```
Tel. (314) 773-0110
EXECUTIVE OFFICER: Donald A. Urey
ORGANIZED: 1937    AFFILIATION: IFMA
DESCRIPTION:  A denominational sending agency of fundamentalist
    and independent Baptist tradition engaged in church planting,
    evangelism, medicine, theological education and
    correspondence courses.
TOTAL INCOME:    $868,000    FOR OVERSEAS MINISTRIES:    $555,000
PERSONNEL:
    NORTH AMERICANS OVERSEAS    NON-NORTH AMERICANS OVERSEAS:    0
            MARRIED:    50            NORTH AMERICAN ADM. STAFF:    4
        SINGLE MEN:    0                       SHORT TERM:    1
      SINGLE WOMEN:    9                          RETIRED:    2
                    -----
    TOTAL ACTIVE:    59
```

FIELD OF SERVICE	YEAR BEGAN	PERSONNEL NOW	NEW	RELATED CHURCHES	PEOPLE GROUPS	NOTES
Barbados	1957	3		2		
Brazil	1967	3		1		
Dominica	1971	4		2		
Ecuador	1959	13	7	39		
France	1979	2				
Grenada	1957	13	3	7		
Kenya	1965	5				
Philippines	1953	3		9		
Zaire	1938	13	2	138		

Beth Sar Shalom Mission (Canada)
SEE: American Board of Missions to the Jews

Beth Sar Shalom Mission, Inc.
SEE: American Board of Missions to the Jews, Inc.

Bethany Fellowship Missions
(Div. of Bethany Fellowship, Inc.)
Tel. (612) 944-2121
EXECUTIVE OFFICER: T. A. Hegre
ORGANIZED: 1945   AFFILIATION: EFMA
DESCRIPTION: An interdenominational sending agency of
    evangelical tradition establishing churches, Bible schools
    and seminaries. Engaged in literature production and
    distribution, and missionary and theological education.

6810 Auto Club Rd.
Minneapolis MN 55438

TOTAL INCOME: $1,052,851   FOR OVERSEAS MINISTRIES: $993,031
PERSONNEL:
NORTH AMERICANS OVERSEAS		NON-NORTH AMERICANS OVERSEAS:	4
MARRIED:	101	NORTH AMERICAN ADM. STAFF:	2
SINGLE MEN:	5	SHORT TERM:	30
SINGLE WOMEN:	5	RETIRED:	1

TOTAL ACTIVE: 111
NOTES: Income includes support for 79 missionaries who
    are serving under other agencies.

FIELD OF SERVICE	YEAR BEGAN	PERSONNEL NOW	PERSONNEL NEW	RELATED CHURCHES	PEOPLE GROUPS	NOTES
Bahamas	1968	2				
Brazil	1963	48	7	16		
Dominican Republic	1978	2	2			
Haiti	1975	1	1	6		
Honduras	1979	6	6			
Indonesia	1971	11	7			
Mexico	1971	14	2	1		
Philippines	1971	6	6	2		
Puerto Rico	1965	15	10			
U.S. Virgin Is.	1966	6	2			

Bethany Home, Inc.

420 Winton Rd. North
Rochester NY 14610
P.O. ADDRESS:
Box 3956
Rochester NY 14610

Tel. (716) 482-6069
EXECUTIVE OFFICER: Frank H. Jackson
ORGANIZED: 1946
DESCRIPTION: A nondenominational Baptist sending agency of
    evangelical tradition supporting an orphanage and engaged in
    childcare, adoption programs, Christian education and
    medicine. Also supplies agricultural assistance.
TOTAL INCOME: $155,000   FOR OVERSEAS MINISTRIES: $155,000
PERSONNEL:
NORTH AMERICANS OVERSEAS		NON-NORTH AMERICANS OVERSEAS:	0
MARRIED:	6	NORTH AMERICAN ADM. STAFF:	3
SINGLE MEN:	0	SHORT TERM:	2
SINGLE WOMEN:	3	RETIRED:	0

TOTAL ACTIVE: 9

FIELD OF SERVICE	YEAR BEGAN	PERSONNEL NOW	PERSONNEL NEW	RELATED CHURCHES	PEOPLE GROUPS	NOTES
Philippines	1946	9	7	1		

Bethany Missionary Association

2209 E Sixth St.
Long Beach CA 90814

Tel. (213) 433-5771
EXECUTIVE OFFICER: David E. Schoch
ORGANIZED: 1953
DESCRIPTION: An interdenominational sending agency of
independent tradition supporting nationals and engaged in
broadcasting, general Christian education, and missionary
orientation and training.
TOTAL INCOME: NR   FOR OVERSEAS MINISTRIES: $154,000
PERSONNEL:

NORTH AMERICANS OVERSEAS		NON-NORTH AMERICANS OVERSEAS:	0
MARRIED:	6	NORTH AMERICAN ADM. STAFF:	6
SINGLE MEN:	1	SHORT TERM:	2
SINGLE WOMEN:	0	RETIRED:	5
TOTAL ACTIVE:	7		

NOTES: Overseas income estimated by MARC.

FIELD OF SERVICE	YEAR BEGAN	PERSONNEL NOW	PERSONNEL NEW	RELATED CHURCHES	PEOPLE GROUPS	NOTES
Brazil	1954	2		3		
Denmark	1965	2		1		
Japan	1959	4	1	5		
Mexico	1959	2	3	3		
South Africa	1970	2		1		

Bethel Foreign Mission Foundation

435 S Lincoln Ave.
Rockport IN 47635
P.O. ADDRESS:
Box 174
Rockport IN 47635

Tel. (812) 649-4375
EXECUTIVE OFFICER: David R. Williams
ORGANIZED: 1933
DESCRIPTION: An independent sending agency of Pentecostal
tradition involved in education, evangelism, literature,
medical supplies and establishing churches.
TOTAL INCOME: $85,000   FOR OVERSEAS MINISTRIES: $85,000
PERSONNEL:

NORTH AMERICANS OVERSEAS		NON-NORTH AMERICANS OVERSEAS:	NR
MARRIED:	50	NORTH AMERICAN ADM. STAFF:	2
SINGLE MEN:	3	SHORT TERM:	NR
SINGLE WOMEN:	4	RETIRED:	0
TOTAL ACTIVE:	57		

FIELD OF SERVICE	YEAR BEGAN	PERSONNEL NOW	PERSONNEL NEW	RELATED CHURCHES	PEOPLE GROUPS	NOTES
Guatemala	1969	7		2		

FIELD OF SERVICE	YEAR BEGAN	PERSONNEL NOW	PERSONNEL NEW	RELATED CHURCHES	PEOPLE GROUPS	NOTES
Haiti	1960	4				
Japan	1958	11		4		
Korea, Rep. of	1961	8		16		
Mexico	1956	27		50		
Papua New Guinea	1959	6				

Bethel Mission of China, Inc.

240 S Oakland Ave.
Pasadena CA 91101

Tel. (213) 796-1300
EXECUTIVE OFFICER: Alice Y. Lan
ORGANIZED: 1920
DESCRIPTION: A nondenominational agency of evangelical
   tradition supporting nationals and national churches.
TOTAL INCOME: NR   FOR OVERSEAS MINISTRIES: NR
PERSONNEL:
   NORTH AMERICANS OVERSEAS   NON-NORTH AMERICANS OVERSEAS: NR
           MARRIED: NR   NORTH AMERICAN ADM. STAFF: NR
        SINGLE MEN: NR   SHORT TERM: NR
      SINGLE WOMEN: NR   RETIRED: NR

      TOTAL ACTIVE: NR

FIELD OF SERVICE	YEAR BEGAN	PERSONNEL NOW	PERSONNEL NEW	RELATED CHURCHES	PEOPLE GROUPS	NOTES
Hong-Kong	1940			1		
Indonesia	1940			12		
Taiwan Rep of China	1940			1		

Bethel Pentecostal Temple, Inc.

2033 Second Ave.
Seattle WA 98121
P.O. ADDRESS:
Box 62
Seattle WA 98111

Tel. (206) 345-9160
EXECUTIVE OFFICER: C. Joe McKnight
ORGANIZED: 0
DESCRIPTION: No current information available. Information
    from 1976 directory. A nondenominational sending agency
    of Pentecostal tradition engaged in evangelism and
    establishing churches. Also involved in education and
    literature production.
TOTAL INCOME: $41,400   FOR OVERSEAS MINISTRIES: $41,400
PERSONNEL:
   NORTH AMERICANS OVERSEAS   NON-NORTH AMERICANS OVERSEAS: NR
           MARRIED: 16   NORTH AMERICAN ADM. STAFF: NR
        SINGLE MEN: 0   SHORT TERM: 0
      SINGLE WOMEN: 0   RETIRED: NR

      TOTAL ACTIVE: 16
NOTES: Incomes estimated by MARC.

FIELD OF SERVICE	YEAR BEGAN	PERSONNEL NOW	PERSONNEL NEW	RELATED CHURCHES	PEOPLE GROUPS	NOTES
Indonesia						

Japan

Bethesda Mission, Inc.

3745 26th Ave. South
Minneapolis MN 55406

Tel. (612) 721-3929
EXECUTIVE OFFICER: Harry Rosbottom
ORGANIZED: 1951
DESCRIPTION: A nondenominational sending agency of evangelical tradition engaged in theological education, church planting and literature production.
TOTAL INCOME: $234,700   FOR OVERSEAS MINISTRIES: $234,700
PERSONNEL:

NORTH AMERICANS OVERSEAS		NON-NORTH AMERICANS OVERSEAS:	0
MARRIED:	18	NORTH AMERICAN ADM. STAFF:	2
SINGLE MEN:	0	SHORT TERM:	4
SINGLE WOMEN:	3	RETIRED:	0
TOTAL ACTIVE:	21		

FIELD OF SERVICE	YEAR BEGAN	PERSONNEL NOW	NEW	RELATED CHURCHES	PEOPLE GROUPS	NOTES
Bolivia	1951	9	3	20		
Brazil	1957	8	1	5		
Netherlands Antilles	1953	6		1		

Bible Alliance Mission, Inc.

1200 Aurora Blvd.
Bradenton FL 33508
P.O. ADDRESS:
Box 1549
Bradenton FL 33506

Tel. (813) 778-3659
EXECUTIVE OFFICER: Anthony T. Rossi
ORGANIZED: 1975
DESCRIPTION: An interdenominational specialized agency of evangelical and Baptist tradition providing cassette players and Scripture recordings in 19 languages and dialects for distribution among unreached peoples. Also provides open reel tapes for broadcasting, and is involved in serving other agencies, literature production and distribution, education, and some Bible translation.
TOTAL INCOME: NR   FOR OVERSEAS MINISTRIES: $99,410
PERSONNEL:

NORTH AMERICANS OVERSEAS		NON-NORTH AMERICANS OVERSEAS:	1
MARRIED:	0	NORTH AMERICAN ADM. STAFF:	2
SINGLE MEN:	1	SHORT TERM:	0
SINGLE WOMEN:	0	RETIRED:	0
TOTAL ACTIVE:	1		

FIELD OF SERVICE	YEAR BEGAN	PERSONNEL NOW	NEW	RELATED CHURCHES	PEOPLE GROUPS	NOTES

Central African Rep.

FIELD OF SERVICE	YEAR BEGAN	PERSONNEL NOW	NEW	RELATED CHURCHES	PEOPLE GROUPS	NOTES
Kenya	1978					
Sudan						
Tanzania						
Zaire						

Bible and Medical Missionary Fellowship/Canada SEE: BMMF International/Canada

Bible and Medical Missionary Fellowship/USA SEE: BMMF International/USA

Bible Christian Union, Inc.

418 Chestnut St.
Lebanon PA 17042
P.O. ADDRESS:
Box 718
Lebanon PA 17042

Tel. (717) 273-9791
EXECUTIVE OFFICER: W. Elwyn Davies
ORGANIZED: 1904   AFFILIATION: IFMA
DESCRIPTION: An interdenominational sending agency of
    evangelical tradition establishing churches and supporting
    national churches. Also engaged in broadcasting,
    evangelism and literature production and distribution.
TOTAL INCOME: $1,323,862   FOR OVERSEAS MINISTRIES: $1,323,862
PERSONNEL:
```
    NORTH AMERICANS OVERSEAS    NON-NORTH AMERICANS OVERSEAS:   5
            MARRIED:   80        NORTH AMERICAN ADM. STAFF:    24
        SINGLE MEN:    6                    SHORT TERM:    2
      SINGLE WOMEN:   20                      RETIRED:   10
                     -----
        TOTAL ACTIVE:  106
```
NOTES: Personnel include Europeans and
        North Americans.

FIELD OF SERVICE	YEAR BEGAN	PERSONNEL NOW	NEW	RELATED CHURCHES	PEOPLE GROUPS	NOTES
Austria	1962	4			2	
France	1938	28	10	7	1	
Germany, Fed. Rep.	1910	11	1		5	
Greece	1968	3		2	1	
Ireland	1979	12	12			
Italy	1950	19	8	4	1	
Netherlands	1946	17	6	3	2	
Portugal	1966	2	1		1	
Spain	1934	6	1	3	1	
Switzerland	1954	2			2	
United Kingdom	1927	2		1		

    Note: Ministries also include
    radio broadcasts into Russia and
    Eastern Europe.

Bible Club Movement of Canada

798 Main St. East
Hamilton ON L8M 1L4
Canada

Tel. (416) 549-9810
EXECUTIVE OFFICER: Chloe Chamberlain
ORGANIZED: 1944   AFFILIATION: IFMA-Canada
DESCRIPTION: An interdenominational sending agency of
    evangelical and fundamentalist tradition engaged in
    evangelism, Bible memorization, correspondence courses,
    teacher training, and Christian education. Work with
    children, teens and adults is carried out through
    clubs, camps and Bible school. Also has home mission work.
    Christian education has been partially incorporated
    into the public school system.
TOTAL INCOME: $326,344   FOR OVERSEAS MINISTRIES: NR
PERSONNEL:
    NORTH AMERICANS OVERSEAS   NON-NORTH AMERICANS OVERSEAS: NR
            MARRIED: NR   NORTH AMERICAN ADM. STAFF: 4
        SINGLE MEN: NR   SHORT TERM: 0
      SINGLE WOMEN: NR   RETIRED: 0

        TOTAL ACTIVE: 2
NOTES: Fields of Service and overseas income are
    included in the USA report.

Bible Club Movement, Inc.

237 Fairfield Ave.
Upper Darby PA 19082

Tel. (215) 352-7177
EXECUTIVE OFFICER: Oscar H. Hirt
ORGANIZED: 1936   AFFILIATION: IFMA-member
DESCRIPTION: An interdenominational sending agency of
    evangelical and fundamentalist tradition engaged in
    evangelism, Bible memorization, correspondence courses,
    teacher training and Christian education. Work with
    children, teens and adults is carried out through clubs,
    camps and Bible school. Also has home mission work.
TOTAL INCOME: $2,226,383   FOR OVERSEAS MINISTRIES: $222,500
PERSONNEL:
    NORTH AMERICANS OVERSEAS   NON-NORTH AMERICANS OVERSEAS: NR
            MARRIED: NR   NORTH AMERICAN ADM. STAFF: 213
        SINGLE MEN: NR   SHORT TERM: NR
      SINGLE WOMEN: NR   RETIRED: NR

        TOTAL ACTIVE: 30

FIELD OF SERVICE	YEAR BEGAN	PERSONNEL NOW	NEW	RELATED CHURCHES	PEOPLE GROUPS	NOTES
Cuba	1947					
Germany, Fed. Rep.	1952					
Guatemala						
Ireland	1964					
Italy	1963					
Japan						
Kenya	1948					
Mexico	1960					
Netherlands	1948					
Norway						

FIELD OF SERVICE	YEAR BEGAN	PERSONNEL NOW	NEW	RELATED CHURCHES	PEOPLE GROUPS	NOTES
Pacific Trust Terr.						
Spain	1947					
Surinam	1968					
Tanzania	1948					
United Kingdom	1946					
Zaire	1970					
Zimbabwe	1973					

Bible Holiness Movement

311 Vic Bld 319 W Pender
Vancouver BC
Canada
P.O. ADDRESS:
Box 223 Postal Sta. A
Vancouver BC V6C 2M3
Canada

Tel. (604) 683-1833
EXECUTIVE OFFICER: Wesley H. Wakefield
ORGANIZED: 1949
DESCRIPTION: A nondenominational agency of Wesleyan and
    Holiness tradition supporting national centers and
    churches. Also involved in aid and relief, literature
    production and distribution and evangelism.
TOTAL INCOME: $31,582   FOR OVERSEAS MINISTRIES: $5,247
PERSONNEL:
    NORTH AMERICANS OVERSEAS   NON-NORTH AMERICANS OVERSEAS: 0
                MARRIED: 0   NORTH AMERICAN ADM. STAFF: 4
             SINGLE MEN: 0   SHORT TERM: 0
           SINGLE WOMEN: 0   RETIRED: 0

        TOTAL ACTIVE: 0

FIELD OF SERVICE	YEAR BEGAN	PERSONNEL NOW	NEW	RELATED CHURCHES	PEOPLE GROUPS	NOTES
Ghana	1952			2		
Haiti	1979			3		
Jamaica	1979			1		
Liberia	1979			2		
Nigeria	1952			15		
Philippines	1963			30		

    Note: All personnel are nationals except one North
    American who serves as a short-term overseer.

Bible Land Prophetic Pilgrimage
SEE: American Association for Jewish Evangelism

Bible Literature International

625 E North Broadway
Columbus OH 43214
P.O. ADDRESS:
Box 477
Columbus OH 43216

Tel. (614) 267-3116
EXECUTIVE OFFICER: J. M. Falkenberg
ORGANIZED: 1923   AFFILIATION: EFMA
DESCRIPTION: An interdenominational specialized service agency
    of evangelical tradition working through other agencies to
    provide Christian literature in 227 languages. Also engaged
    in Bible distribution, theological education and ministry to
    servicemen.

```
TOTAL INCOME:  $1,500,000   FOR OVERSEAS MINISTRIES:  $1,028,481
PERSONNEL:
  NORTH AMERICANS OVERSEAS   NON-NORTH AMERICANS OVERSEAS:    0
            MARRIED:   0       NORTH AMERICAN ADM. STAFF:     0
         SINGLE MEN:   0                  SHORT TERM:         0
       SINGLE WOMEN:   0                    RETIRED:          0
                      -----
       TOTAL ACTIVE:   0
```

Bible Memory Association International

1298 Pennsylvania
St. Louis MO 63130
P.O. ADDRESS:
Box 12000
St. Louis MO 63112

```
Tel. (314) 726-1323
EXECUTIVE OFFICER: Robert L. Griffin
ORGANIZED: 1944
DESCRIPTION:  An interdenominational service agency of
    independent tradition encouraging and promoting Scripture
    memorization.
TOTAL INCOME:   $900,000       FOR OVERSEAS MINISTRIES:   NR
PERSONNEL:
  NORTH AMERICANS OVERSEAS   NON-NORTH AMERICANS OVERSEAS:    0
            MARRIED:   4       NORTH AMERICAN ADM. STAFF:    35
         SINGLE MEN:   0                  SHORT TERM:         0
       SINGLE WOMEN:   0                    RETIRED:          0
                      -----
       TOTAL ACTIVE:   4
```

FIELD OF SERVICE	YEAR BEGAN	PERSONNEL NOW	PERSONNEL NEW	RELATED CHURCHES	PEOPLE GROUPS	NOTES
Brazil	1966	3	3			
Ecuador	1974	2				
Germany, Fed. Rep.	1971	2				
Mexico	1974	2	2			
South Africa	1966	3	2			
Zimbabwe	1966	1	1			

Bible Missionary Church, World Missions Department

2611 S Wadsworth
Denver CO 80227

```
Tel. (303) 986-3655
EXECUTIVE OFFICER: Waldon V. Kurtz
ORGANIZED: 1956
DESCRIPTION:  A denominational agency of Holiness tradition
    engaged in theological education, fund raising,
    evangelism, Bible distribution and support of nationals.
TOTAL INCOME:   $250,000   FOR OVERSEAS MINISTRIES:   $250,000
PERSONNEL:
  NORTH AMERICANS OVERSEAS   NON-NORTH AMERICANS OVERSEAS:    2
            MARRIED:  NR       NORTH AMERICAN ADM. STAFF:    NR
         SINGLE MEN:  NR                  SHORT TERM:         0
       SINGLE WOMEN:  NR                    RETIRED:         NR
                      -----
       TOTAL ACTIVE:  NR
```

FIELD OF SERVICE	YEAR BEGAN	PERSONNEL NOW	PERSONNEL NEW	RELATED CHURCHES	PEOPLE GROUPS	NOTES
Barbados	1958	2	2	4	1	

FIELD OF SERVICE	YEAR BEGAN	PERSONNEL NOW	PERSONNEL NEW	RELATED CHURCHES	PEOPLE GROUPS	NOTES
Guyana	1958	2		9	2	
Japan	1965	8		6	2	
Mexico	1965	8	3	15	2	
Nigeria	1969			25	1	
Papua New Guinea	1960	11	2	65	1	
Philippines	1978	2		2	1	
St. Vincent	1958	2		4	1	

Bible Presbyterian Church, Independent Board For Presbyterian Foreign Missions

246 W Walnut Ln.
Philadelphia PA 19144

Tel. (215) 438-0511
EXECUTIVE OFFICER: Lynn Gray Gordon
ORGANIZED: 1933   AFFILIATION: TAM-ICCC
DESCRIPTION: A denominational sending agency of Presbyterian
    tradition establishing churches and engaged in theological
    education, evangelism, literature distribution and
    medicine.
TOTAL INCOME: $435,984   FOR OVERSEAS MINISTRIES: $435,984
PERSONNEL:

NORTH AMERICANS OVERSEAS		NON-NORTH AMERICANS OVERSEAS:	4
MARRIED:	28	NORTH AMERICAN ADM. STAFF:	3
SINGLE MEN:	0	SHORT TERM:	0
SINGLE WOMEN:	12	RETIRED:	2

TOTAL ACTIVE: 40

FIELD OF SERVICE	YEAR BEGAN	PERSONNEL NOW	PERSONNEL NEW	RELATED CHURCHES	PEOPLE GROUPS	NOTES
Brazil	1948	5		4		
Chile	1945	3		22		
Guatemala		2		1		
Israel	1945	8	2	1		
Kenya	1943	7		90		
Korea, Rep. of	1936	3		30		
Saudi Arabia	1940	3				
Singapore	1964	2		28		
Taiwan Rep of China	1935	2		5		
United Kingdom	1956	1		1		

Bible Protestant Church, Inc. Bible Protestant Msns., Inc.
SEE: Bible Protestant Missions, Inc.

Bible Protestant Missions, Inc.

5944 Telegraph Rd.
Alexandria VA 22310
P.O. ADDRESS:
Rd. 1 Box 12
Port Jarvis NY 12771

Tel. (703) 960-1157
EXECUTIVE OFFICER: Harold Haines
ORGANIZED: 1940   AFFILIATION: FOM
DESCRIPTION: A denominational sending agency of fundamentalist
    tradition engaged in evangelism, education and church
    planting. Also engaged in home mission work.
TOTAL INCOME: NA   FOR OVERSEAS MINISTRIES: $44,000

```
PERSONNEL:
    NORTH AMERICANS OVERSEAS    NON-NORTH AMERICANS OVERSEAS:    NR
            MARRIED:    NR         NORTH AMERICAN ADM. STAFF:     3
         SINGLE MEN:    NR                      SHORT TERM:       0
       SINGLE WOMEN:    NR                        RETIRED:        0
                       -----
     TOTAL ACTIVE:     2
NOTES:  Overseas income estimated by MARC.
```

FIELD OF SERVICE	YEAR BEGAN	PERSONNEL NOW	NEW	RELATED CHURCHES	PEOPLE GROUPS	NOTES
Japan		2				1

1. Four national pastors in Japan.

Bible Research International

64 Lansdowne South
Cambridge ON N1R 6C7
Canada
P.O. ADDRESS:
Box 7000
Cambridge ON N1R 6C7
Canada

Tel. (519) 621-3428
EXECUTIVE OFFICER: Harvey Lainson
ORGANIZED: 1974
DESCRIPTION: An association authorized under Indiana and
    Manitoba to grant degrees to Bible Institute and credits
    for courses taken by correspondence including theological
    education by extension (TEE).
TOTAL INCOME: $10,000   FOR OVERSEAS MINISTRIES: $1,000

```
PERSONNEL:
    NORTH AMERICANS OVERSEAS    NON-NORTH AMERICANS OVERSEAS:    NR
            MARRIED:    NR         NORTH AMERICAN ADM. STAFF:     3
         SINGLE MEN:    NR                      SHORT TERM:       0
       SINGLE WOMEN:    NR                        RETIRED:        0
                       -----
     TOTAL ACTIVE:     NR
```

Bible Translations On Tape, Inc.

226 Texas St.
Cedar Hill TX 75104
P.O. ADDRESS:
Box 2500
Cedar Hill TX 75104

Tel. (214) 299-5450
EXECUTIVE OFFICER: W. Paul Smith
ORGANIZED: 1972
DESCRIPTION: An evangelical, interdenominational, specialized
    service agency with the primary goal of reaching illiterates
    through Scripture recordings in vernacular languages. Also
    engaged in church planting, supplying equipment, supporting
    nationals and serving other agencies.
TOTAL INCOME: $243,624   FOR OVERSEAS MINISTRIES: $46,072

```
PERSONNEL:
    NORTH AMERICANS OVERSEAS    NON-NORTH AMERICANS OVERSEAS:    0
            MARRIED:    6          NORTH AMERICAN ADM. STAFF:     1
         SINGLE MEN:    1                      SHORT TERM:        0
       SINGLE WOMEN:    0                        RETIRED:         0
                       -----
     TOTAL ACTIVE:     7
```

FIELD OF SERVICE	YEAR BEGAN	PERSONNEL NOW	PERSONNEL NEW	RELATED CHURCHES	PEOPLE GROUPS	NOTES
Ghana	1979	2	2			
Kenya	1979	1	1			
Mexico	1977	2	2			

Bible Way Churches of Our Lord Jesus Christ Worldwide, Inc., Foreign Missions Board

1100 New Jersey Ave. NW
Washington D.C.   20001

Tel. (202) 723-0505
EXECUTIVE OFFICER: C. A. Bird
ORGANIZED: 1957
DESCRIPTION: A denominational sending agency of Pentecostal
    tradition engaged in evangelism, education and supporting
    of nationals and national churches.
TOTAL INCOME: $150,000   FOR OVERSEAS MINISTRIES: $75,000
PERSONNEL:
    NORTH AMERICANS OVERSEAS   NON-NORTH AMERICANS OVERSEAS: NR
              MARRIED: NR   NORTH AMERICAN ADM. STAFF: 10
           SINGLE MEN: NR   SHORT TERM: 0
         SINGLE WOMEN: NR   RETIRED: 0

       TOTAL ACTIVE: 2

FIELD OF SERVICE	YEAR BEGAN	PERSONNEL NOW	PERSONNEL NEW	RELATED CHURCHES	PEOPLE GROUPS	NOTES
Jamaica	1958					
Liberia	1958	2				
Nigeria						
Trinidad and Tobago	1958					

Bibles for the Nations

P.O. ADDRESS:
Box 1240
Cambridge ON N1R 6C9
Canada

Tel. (519) 621-3428
EXECUTIVE OFFICER: Harvey Lainson
ORGANIZED: 1974
DESCRIPTION: A service agency of evangelical tradition
    involved in Bible distribution, support of national
    evangelists and orphans in India and Burma. Also has a
    home ministry.
TOTAL INCOME: NA   FOR OVERSEAS MINISTRIES: NA
PERSONNEL:
    NORTH AMERICANS OVERSEAS   NON-NORTH AMERICANS OVERSEAS: NR
              MARRIED: 0   NORTH AMERICAN ADM. STAFF: 2
           SINGLE MEN: 0   SHORT TERM: NR
         SINGLE WOMEN: 0   RETIRED: NR

       TOTAL ACTIVE: 0

Bibles For The World, Inc.

1300 Crescent St.
Wheaton IL 60187
P.O. ADDRESS:
Box 805
Wheaton IL 60187

Tel. (312) 668-7733
EXECUTIVE OFFICER: Rochunga Pudiate
ORGANIZED: 1958
DESCRIPTION: A nondenominational agency of evangelical
    tradition supporting the establishment of national
    churches and engaged in Bible distribution. Also involved
    in childcare.
TOTAL INCOME: $2,773,982   FOR OVERSEAS MINISTRIES: $2,212,101
PERSONNEL:

NORTH AMERICANS OVERSEAS		NON-NORTH AMERICANS OVERSEAS:	0
MARRIED:	0	NORTH AMERICAN ADM. STAFF:	25
SINGLE MEN:	0	SHORT TERM:	0
SINGLE WOMEN:	0	RETIRED:	0
TOTAL ACTIVE:	0		

Biblical Literature Fellowship

453 King St.
Redwood City CA 94062
P.O. ADDRESS:
Box 771
Redwood City CA 94064

EXECUTIVE OFFICER: A. F. Kroeker
ORGANIZED: 1953
DESCRIPTION: No current information available. Information
    from 1976 directory. Founded in 1953 as Missionary
    Prayer and Literature Fellowship. A nondenominational
    specialized service agency of independent, fundamentalist
    and evangelical tradition, promoting church growth and
    evangelism through literature and Bible translations.
    Short-term program has been discontinued.
TOTAL INCOME: $42,780   FOR OVERSEAS MINISTRIES: $42,780
PERSONNEL:

NORTH AMERICANS OVERSEAS		NON-NORTH AMERICANS OVERSEAS:	6
MARRIED:	4	NORTH AMERICAN ADM. STAFF:	0
SINGLE MEN:	0	SHORT TERM:	0
SINGLE WOMEN:	2	RETIRED:	0
TOTAL ACTIVE:	6		

NOTES: Income estimated by MARC.

FIELD OF SERVICE	YEAR BEGAN	PERSONNEL NOW	NEW	RELATED CHURCHES	PEOPLE GROUPS	NOTES
Belgium	1959					1

1. Publishing house.

Billy Graham Evangelistic Association

1300 Harmon Pl.
Minneapolis MN 55403

Tel. (612) 338-0500
EXECUTIVE OFFICER: Billy Graham
ORGANIZED: 1950
DESCRIPTION: An interdenominational agency of evangelical
    tradition engaged in mass evangelism plus radio and TV
    evangelism. Also engaged in literature production and
    film ministry through translation.
TOTAL INCOME: $38,405,064   FOR OVERSEAS MINISTRIES: $2,608,981

PERSONNEL:
```
    NORTH AMERICANS OVERSEAS    NON-NORTH AMERICANS OVERSEAS:   NR
              MARRIED:    NR       NORTH AMERICAN ADM. STAFF:   NR
           SINGLE MEN:    NR                      SHORT TERM:   NR
         SINGLE WOMEN:    NR                         RETIRED:   NR
                       -----
         TOTAL ACTIVE:    NR
```
NOTES: Income from 1979 agency annual report.

BMMF International/Canada

4028 Sheppard E, Ste 200
Againcourt ON M1S 1S6
Canada

Tel. (416) 293-9832
EXECUTIVE OFFICER: Mariano Di Gangi
ORGANIZED: 1852   AFFILIATION: IFMA/EFMA
DESCRIPTION: Formerly Bible and Medical Missionary
    Fellowship. Name change in 1978. An international and
    interdenominational sending agency of evangelical
    tradition engaged in evangelism, education, childcare,
    self-help projects, radio and TV broadcasting and
    medicine. Also supports national churches and serves
    other agencies.
TOTAL INCOME: $298,000   FOR OVERSEAS MINISTRIES: $298,000
PERSONNEL:
```
    NORTH AMERICANS OVERSEAS    NON-NORTH AMERICANS OVERSEAS:    0
              MARRIED:    20       NORTH AMERICAN ADM. STAFF:    4
           SINGLE MEN:     1                      SHORT TERM:    4
         SINGLE WOMEN:     8                         RETIRED:    2
                       -----
         TOTAL ACTIVE:    29
```

FIELD OF SERVICE	YEAR BEGAN	PERSONNEL NOW	NEW	RELATED CHURCHES	PEOPLE GROUPS	NOTES
Afghanistan	1966					
Bangladesh	1972	2				
Bhutan	1974					
India	1852	10	8			
Iran	1972	1	2			
Lebanon	1966					
Nepal	1954	6	5			
Pakistan	1852	7	5		1	

BMMF/International (U.S.A.)

241 Fairfield Ave.
Upper Darby PA 19082

Tel. (215) 352-0581
EXECUTIVE OFFICER: T. Laurence Wynne
ORGANIZED: 1852   AFFILIATION: IFMA/EFMA
DESCRIPTION: Previously known as Bible and Medical Missionary
    Fellowship. Name changed 1978. An international,
    interdenominational sending agency of evangelical
    tradition involved in education, medicine and
    broadcasting. Also engaged in the support or nurture of
    national churches, serving other agencies, childcare and
    self-help projects.
TOTAL INCOME: $389,634   FOR OVERSEAS MINISTRIES: $294,786
PERSONNEL:
```
    NORTH AMERICANS OVERSEAS    NON-NORTH AMERICANS OVERSEAS:    0
              MARRIED:    16       NORTH AMERICAN ADM. STAFF:    3
           SINGLE MEN:     2                      SHORT TERM:    8
```

```
SINGLE WOMEN:   13                              RETIRED:    7
                -----
TOTAL ACTIVE:   31
```

FIELD OF SERVICE	YEAR BEGAN	PERSONNEL NOW	NEW	RELATED CHURCHES	PEOPLE GROUPS	NOTES
Asia-general						
Bangladesh	1971	4	4			
India	1852	16	5			
Iran	1970					
Middle East-general	1979	2	2			
Nepal	1954	5	2			
Pakistan	1852	4	2			

Bookmates International, Incorporated

P.O. ADDRESS:
Box 9883
Fresno CA 93795

Tel. (209) 445-1840
EXECUTIVE OFFICER: Helen Wessel
ORGANIZED: 1970
DESCRIPTION: An interdenominational service agency of
    evangelical tradition serving nationals through Christian
    book publishing and distribution. Works with nationals
    serving in their own countries.
TOTAL INCOME: $39,299   FOR OVERSEAS MINISTRIES: NR
PERSONNEL:
    NORTH AMERICANS OVERSEAS   NON-NORTH AMERICANS OVERSEAS: 0
              MARRIED: 0   NORTH AMERICAN ADM. STAFF: 0
           SINGLE MEN: 0   SHORT TERM: 0
         SINGLE WOMEN: 0   RETIRED: 0

         TOTAL ACTIVE: 0

Border Missions

3rd St.
Hidalgo TX 78557

Tel. (512) 843-2125
EXECUTIVE OFFICER: Mrs. H. A. Morgan
ORGANIZED: 1950
DESCRIPTION: A specialized service agency of evangelical
    tradition assisting the needy in Mexico with food and
    clothing. Also engaged in evangelism and assisting with
    church planting.
TOTAL INCOME: NR   FOR OVERSEAS MINISTRIES: $88,000
PERSONNEL:
    NORTH AMERICANS OVERSEAS   NON-NORTH AMERICANS OVERSEAS: NR
              MARRIED: NR   NORTH AMERICAN ADM. STAFF: NR
           SINGLE MEN: NR   SHORT TERM: 100
         SINGLE WOMEN: NR   RETIRED: NR

         TOTAL ACTIVE: 4
NOTES: All personnel are volunteer.
        Overseas income estimated by MARC.

Brazil Christian Mission SEE: Christian Churches/Churches of Christ

Brazil Gospel Fellowship Mission

121 N Glenwood
Springfield IL 62702
P.O. ADDRESS:
Box 355
Springfield IL 62705

Tel. (217) 523-7176
EXECUTIVE OFFICER: Gerald Bergen
ORGANIZED: 1939
DESCRIPTION: An independent sending agency of fundamentalist
    tradition establishing and nurturing churches. Engaged in
    education, broadcasting, evangelism, literature, motion
    pictures and corresponence courses.
TOTAL INCOME: $500,000   FOR OVERSEAS MINISTRIES: $465,000
PERSONNEL:

NORTH AMERICANS OVERSEAS		NON-NORTH AMERICANS OVERSEAS:	NR
MARRIED:	NR	NORTH AMERICAN ADM. STAFF:	3
SINGLE MEN:	NR	SHORT TERM:	1
SINGLE WOMEN:	NR	RETIRED:	0
TOTAL ACTIVE:	39		

Bread for the World

32 Union Sq. East
New York NY 10003

Tel. (212) 260-7000
EXECUTIVE OFFICER: Arthur Simon
ORGANIZED: 1973
DESCRIPTION: An ecumenical Christian citizen's movement that
    works to reduce hunger by influencing public policy
    through citizen lobbies. Now has over 33000 memebers.
TOTAL INCOME: $900,000   FOR OVERSEAS MINISTRIES: $0
PERSONNEL:

NORTH AMERICANS OVERSEAS		NON-NORTH AMERICANS OVERSEAS:	0
MARRIED:	0	NORTH AMERICAN ADM. STAFF:	30
SINGLE MEN:	0	SHORT TERM:	0
SINGLE WOMEN:	0	RETIRED:	0
TOTAL ACTIVE:	0		

Breakthrough Ministries

1157 E Lemon
Bradbury CA 91010

Tel. (213) 359-4775
EXECUTIVE OFFICER: Louis M. Files
ORGANIZED: 1972
DESCRIPTION: An interdenominational agency involved in
    evangelizing North Americans and training Christians for
    missionary work in Mexico. Assists in organizing vacation
    and weekend short-term efforts in Mexico.
TOTAL INCOME: $33,000   FOR OVERSEAS MINISTRIES: NA
PERSONNEL:

NORTH AMERICANS OVERSEAS		NON-NORTH AMERICANS OVERSEAS:	NR
MARRIED:	0	NORTH AMERICAN ADM. STAFF:	2
SINGLE MEN:	0	SHORT TERM:	NR
SINGLE WOMEN:	0	RETIRED:	0
TOTAL ACTIVE:	0		

FIELD OF SERVICE	YEAR BEGAN	PERSONNEL NOW	NEW	RELATED CHURCHES	PEOPLE GROUPS	NOTES
Mexico	1966					

197

Brethren Assemblies

DESCRIPTION: The Brethren Assemblies are also known as
    Plymouth or Christian Brethren. Missionaries are sent
    directly from each assembly and not through a central
    agency. USA and Canadian workers comprise about one third
    of the assembly missionaries in the world which total 1300
    to 1500. Figures include Christian Missions in Many Lands
    (USA) and the Missionary Service Committee, Inc. (Canada),
    which serve the 'open' branch of the Brethren.

TOTAL INCOME: $5,500,000   FOR OVERSEAS MINISTRIES: $5,500,000

PERSONNEL:

NORTH AMERICANS OVERSEAS		NON-NORTH AMERICANS OVERSEAS:	NR
MARRIED:	NR	NORTH AMERICAN ADM. STAFF:	0
SINGLE MEN:	NR	SHORT TERM:	0
SINGLE WOMEN:	NR	RETIRED:	30
TOTAL ACTIVE:	554		

FIELD OF SERVICE	YEAR BEGAN	PERSONNEL NOW	NEW	RELATED CHURCHES	PEOPLE GROUPS	NOTES
Angola		8				
Argentina		22				
Belgium		8				
Bolivia		14				
Brazil		15				
Burundi		9				
Caribbean-general		16				
Chad		3				
Chile		19				
Colombia		31				
Costa Rica		6				
Dominican Republic		18				
Ecuador		21				
El Salvador		7				
France		21				
French Guiana		2				
Germany, Fed. Rep.		12				
Guatemala		4				
Honduras		6				
Hong-Kong		7				
India		10				
Indonesia						
Iran		2				
Ireland		6				
Israel						
Italy		11				
Japan		31				
Kenya		5				
Korea, Rep. of		10				
Lebanon		4				
Mexico		14				
Netherlands		2				
Nicaragua		2				
Nigeria		12				
Pakistan		1				
Papua New Guinea		4				

FIELD OF SERVICE	YEAR BEGAN	PERSONNEL NOW	NEW	RELATED CHURCHES	PEOPLE GROUPS	NOTES
Paraguay		10				
Peru		13				
Philippines		25				
Portugal		6				
Puerto Rico		5				
Rwanda		3				
Senegal		2				
South Africa		20				
Spain		13				
Taiwan Rep of China		4				
Tanzania		2				
Uruguay		6				
Venezuela		11				
Zaire		27				
Zambia		38				
Zimbabwe		6				

Brethren Church, Missionary Board of The Brethren Church

530 College Ave.
Ashland OH 44805

Tel. (419) 289-2195
EXECUTIVE OFFICER: M. Virgil Ingraham
ORGANIZED: 1892   AFFILIATION: EFMA
DESCRIPTION: A denominational sending agency of Brethren
    tradition engaged in church planting, education, medical
    services and serving national churches. Also involved in
    radio program production and audio-visual technical
    assistance.
TOTAL INCOME: $450,000   FOR OVERSEAS MINISTRIES: $260,000
PERSONNEL:
    NORTH AMERICANS OVERSEAS   NON-NORTH AMERICANS OVERSEAS: 0
              MARRIED: 8   NORTH AMERICAN ADM. STAFF: 3
          SINGLE MEN: 0   SHORT TERM: 0
        SINGLE WOMEN: 0   RETIRED: 0

        TOTAL ACTIVE: 8

FIELD OF SERVICE	YEAR BEGAN	PERSONNEL NOW	NEW	RELATED CHURCHES	PEOPLE GROUPS	NOTES
Argentina	1948	4				

Brethren in Christ Church SEE: Brethren in Christ Missions

Brethren in Christ Missions

P.O. ADDRESS:
Box 149
Elizabethtown PA 17022

Tel. (717) 367-7045
EXECUTIVE OFFICER: J. Wilmer Heisey
ORGANIZED: 1895   AFFILIATION: EFMA
DESCRIPTION: A denominational sending agency of Wesleyan and
    Anabaptist tradition engaged in evangelism, establishing
    churches and assisting national churches in education,
    literature and medicine. Denomination is a member of the
    Mennonite Central Committee.
TOTAL INCOME: $905,898   FOR OVERSEAS MINISTRIES: $550,670

PERSONNEL:
```
    NORTH AMERICANS OVERSEAS      NON-NORTH AMERICANS OVERSEAS:    0
              MARRIED:    24          NORTH AMERICAN ADM. STAFF:    2
           SINGLE MEN:     0                         SHORT TERM:   80
         SINGLE WOMEN:    10                            RETIRED:   51
                         -----
         TOTAL ACTIVE:    34
```

FIELD OF SERVICE	YEAR BEGAN	PERSONNEL NOW	NEW	RELATED CHURCHES	PEOPLE GROUPS	NOTES
India	1904	6		28		
Japan	1953	4		7		
Nicaragua	1965	4		31		
Zambia	1906	17	2	75		
Zimbabwe	1898	3				

Calcutta Mission of Mercy

1717 S Puget Sound
Tacoma WA 98405

Tel. (206) 756-5329
EXECUTIVE OFFICER: Joseph N. Ellis
ORGANIZED: 1977
DESCRIPTION: A fund raising agency of Pentecostal tradition
    serving a medical ministry.
TOTAL INCOME: $845,000   FOR OVERSEAS MINISTRIES: $845,000
PERSONNEL:
```
    NORTH AMERICANS OVERSEAS      NON-NORTH AMERICANS OVERSEAS:    0
              MARRIED:     1          NORTH AMERICAN ADM. STAFF:   10
           SINGLE MEN:     0                         SHORT TERM:    0
         SINGLE WOMEN:     0                            RETIRED:    0
                         -----
         TOTAL ACTIVE:     1
```

FIELD OF SERVICE	YEAR BEGAN	PERSONNEL NOW	NEW	RELATED CHURCHES	PEOPLE GROUPS	NOTES
India	1954	1				

California Yearly Meeting of Friends Church, Board of Missions

15915 E Russell St.
Whittier CA 90609
P.O. ADDRESS:
Box 1607
Whittier CA 90609

Tel. (213) 947-2883
EXECUTIVE OFFICER: Keith Sarver
ORGANIZED: 1895   AFFILIATION: EFMA
DESCRIPTION: A denominational sending agency of evangelical and
    Friends tradition serving national churches and involved
    in church planting and construction, radio and TV
    broadcasting and agricultural assistance. Also assisting in
    education, literature distribution and Bible translation.
TOTAL INCOME: $277,551   FOR OVERSEAS MINISTRIES: $143,343
PERSONNEL:
```
    NORTH AMERICANS OVERSEAS      NON-NORTH AMERICANS OVERSEAS:    2
              MARRIED:     8          NORTH AMERICAN ADM. STAFF:    1
           SINGLE MEN:     1                         SHORT TERM:    2
         SINGLE WOMEN:     3                            RETIRED:   10
                         -----
         TOTAL ACTIVE:    12
```
NOTES: The one North American administrator is part-time.
    Retired personnel receive partial support only.

FIELD OF SERVICE	YEAR BEGAN	PERSONNEL NOW	NEW	RELATED CHURCHES	PEOPLE GROUPS	NOTES
El Salvador	1902			6		
Guatemala	1902	11	5	122		
Honduras	1902	1		29		

Calvary Evangelistic Mission, Inc./WIVV Missionary Radio Station

1904 Ponce de Leon
San Juan PR 00907
P.O. ADDRESS:
Box A
San Juan PR 00936

Tel. (809) 724-2727
EXECUTIVE OFFICER: Donald D. Luttrell
ORGANIZED: 1955   AFFILIATION: EFMA
DESCRIPTION: An interdenominational sending agency of Baptist
    tradition engaged in broadcasting and related follow-up
    ministries. Operates radio WIVV. Also involved in
    correspondence courses, evangelism and literature.
TOTAL INCOME: $891,918   FOR OVERSEAS MINISTRIES: $891,918
PERSONNEL:
    NORTH AMERICANS OVERSEAS   NON-NORTH AMERICANS OVERSEAS: 5
                MARRIED: 11   NORTH AMERICAN ADM. STAFF: 0
            SINGLE MEN: 0   SHORT TERM: 14
          SINGLE WOMEN: 6   RETIRED: 0

        TOTAL ACTIVE: 17

FIELD OF SERVICE	YEAR BEGAN	PERSONNEL NOW	NEW	RELATED CHURCHES	PEOPLE GROUPS	NOTES
Netherlands Antilles	1955					
Puerto Rico	1955	17	20			

CAM International

8625 La Prada Dr.
Dallas TX 75228

Tel. (214) 327-8206
EXECUTIVE OFFICER: Albert T. Platt
ORGANIZED: 1890   AFFILIATION: IFMA
DESCRIPTION: Founded in 1890 as the Central American Mission.
    Name changed to CAM International in 1976. A
    nondenominational sending agency of evangelical and
    Fundamentalist tradition planting churches and engaged in
    theological education, theological education by extension
    (TEE), broadcasting and evangelism.
TOTAL INCOME: $3,048,419   FOR OVERSEAS MINISTRIES: $2,672,824
PERSONNEL:
    NORTH AMERICANS OVERSEAS   NON-NORTH AMERICANS OVERSEAS: 6
                MARRIED: 198   NORTH AMERICAN ADM. STAFF: 33
            SINGLE MEN: 1   SHORT TERM: 12
          SINGLE WOMEN: 29   RETIRED: 29

        TOTAL ACTIVE: 228

FIELD OF SERVICE	YEAR BEGAN	PERSONNEL NOW	NEW	RELATED CHURCHES	PEOPLE GROUPS	NOTES
El Salvador	1896	4	2	116	1	

FIELD OF SERVICE	YEAR BEGAN	PERSONNEL NOW	NEW	RELATED CHURCHES	PEOPLE GROUPS	NOTES
Guatemala	1899	97	12	806	1	
Honduras	1896	45	5	146	1	
Mexico	1959	46	7	15	1	
Nicaragua	1900	8		68	1	
Panama	1944	9	2	17	1	
Spain	1971	14	4	6	1	

CAM International Practical Missionary Training, Inc.

216 E Commonwealth Ave.
Fullerton CA 92632
P.O. ADDRESS:
Box 628
Fullerton CA 92632

Tel. (714) 526-5139
EXECUTIVE OFFICER: Kenneth E. Royer
ORGANIZED: 1949
DESCRIPTION: A nondenominational specialized service
    agency of evangelical and fundamentalist traditions
    recruiting and training missionaries for a number of
    agencies. Students are sent to other countries for
    short-term training. Related to CAM International.
TOTAL INCOME: $62,927   FOR OVERSEAS MINISTRIES: $62,927
PERSONNEL:
    NORTH AMERICANS OVERSEAS   NON-NORTH AMERICANS OVERSEAS: 0
        MARRIED: 4   NORTH AMERICAN ADM. STAFF: 4
        SINGLE MEN: 0   SHORT TERM: 69
        SINGLE WOMEN: 0   RETIRED: NR

        TOTAL ACTIVE: 4
NOTES: The four overseas personnel are the same
    four persons serving as administrative
    personnel. They spend two months on the
    field and the rest of the time at
    headquarters.

CAMEO SEE: Committee to Assist Missionary Education Overseas

Campus Crusade for Christ, International (Overseas Dept.)

Arrowhead Springs
San Bernardino CA 92414

Tel. (714) 886-5224
EXECUTIVE OFFICER: William R. Bright
ORGANIZED: 1951   AFFILIATION: EFMA
DESCRIPTION: An interdenominational sending agency of
    evangelical tradition engaged in evangelism and serving
    national churches.
TOTAL INCOME: $50,000,000   FOR OVERSEAS MINISTRIES: $12,500,000
PERSONNEL:
    NORTH AMERICANS OVERSEAS   NON-NORTH AMERICANS OVERSEAS: 5
        MARRIED: 264   NORTH AMERICAN ADM. STAFF: 84
        SINGLE MEN: 83   SHORT TERM: 77
        SINGLE WOMEN: 153   RETIRED: 3

        TOTAL ACTIVE: 500
NOTES: All figures in this report include data
    of Agape Movement, an International
    Division of Campus Crusade for Christ.

FIELD OF SERVICE	YEAR BEGAN	PERSONNEL NOW	NEW	RELATED CHURCHES	PEOPLE GROUPS	NOTES
Argentina	1963	32				
Australia	1967	46				
Bangladesh	1975	48				
Barbados	1979					
Belize	1979					
Bolivia	1965	21				
Bophuthatswana	1978	14				
Brazil	1968	27				
British Virgin Is.	1979					
Chile	1963	40				
Colombia	1963	291				
Costa Rica	1976	10				
Cyprus	1978	20				
Denmark	1973	3				
Dominican Republic	1977	15				
Ecuador	1965	17				
Egypt	1971	9				
El Salvador	1966	20				
Fiji	1974	12				
Finland	1967	28				
France	1970	24				
Germany, Fed. Rep.	1966	99				
Ghana	1966	4				
Gilbert Islands	1974					
Greece	1978	5				
Guam	1976	16				
Guatemala	1963	49				
Haiti	1977					
Honduras	1966	50				
Hong-Kong	1972	18				
India	1963	136				
Indonesia	1968	134				
Iran	1967	4				
Ireland	1972	28				
Italy	1969	18				
Ivory Coast	1975	3				
Jamaica	1977					
Japan	1962	15				
Kenya	1972	80				
Korea, Rep. of	1958	115				
Lebanon	1968	3				
Lesotho	1979	6				
Liberia	1979	5				
Macao	1975	7				
Madagascar	1979	2				
Malawi	1975					
Malaysia	1968	24				
Mali	1972	2				
Mexico	1962	153				
Micronesia	1973	2				
Netherlands	1968	42				
New Zealand	1972	17				
Nicaragua	1976	4				
Nigeria	1969	38				
Norway	1974	2				

FIELD OF SERVICE	YEAR BEGAN	PERSONNEL NOW	NEW	RELATED CHURCHES	PEOPLE GROUPS	NOTES
Pakistan	1960	19				
Panama	1965	29				
Papua New Guinea	1978	4				
Paraguay	1966	7				
Peru	1961	9				
Philippines	1965	207				
Portugal	1975	11				
Puerto Rico	1971	15				
Singapore	1969	38				
Solomon Is.	1974	4				
South Africa	1971	120				
Spain	1970	28				
Sri Lanka	1968	9				
Sudan	1975	14				
Surinam	1979					
Swaziland	1973	60				
Sweden	1972	8				
Switzerland	1969	9				
Taiwan Rep of China	1964	32				
Tanzania	1977					
Thailand	1971	15				
Togo	1979					
Tonga	1974	1				
Trinidad and Tobago	1977	2				
U.S. Virgin Is.	1978	4				
Uganda	1971	17				
United Kingdom	1967	80				
Uruguay	1966	2				
Venezuela	1972	190				
Zambia	1975	2				
Zimbabwe	1978	4				

Note: Overseas personnel include nationals.

Canadian Baptist
Overseas Mission

217 St. George Street
Toronto ON M5R 2M2
Canada

Tel. (416) 922-5163
EXECUTIVE OFFICER: Robert C. Berry
ORGANIZED: 1911
DESCRIPTION: A denominational sending agency of evangelical
    tradition serving four Baptist conventions in Canada.
    Involved in church planting, theolgoical education,
    agricultural assistance, medicine and training.
TOTAL INCOME: $1,912,002   FOR OVERSEAS MINISTRIES: $1,912,002
PERSONNEL:
    NORTH AMERICANS OVERSEAS   NON-NORTH AMERICANS OVERSEAS: 2
            MARRIED: 56   NORTH AMERICAN ADM. STAFF: 13
         SINGLE MEN: 3   SHORT TERM: 3
       SINGLE WOMEN: 23   RETIRED: 39

       TOTAL ACTIVE: 82

FIELD OF SERVICE	YEAR BEGAN	PERSONNEL NOW	NEW	RELATED CHURCHES	PEOPLE GROUPS	NOTES
Bolivia	1898	35	15	200	1	

FIELD OF SERVICE	YEAR BEGAN	PERSONNEL NOW	NEW	RELATED CHURCHES	PEOPLE GROUPS	NOTES
Brazil	1974	10	8	125		
India	1874	23	6	200	2	
Indonesia	1972	4		100	1	
Kenya	1970	12	7		1	
Zaire	1962	9	2	400		

Note: Zaire ministry is in cooperation with American Baptists.

Canadian Bible Society

1835 Yonge St.
Toronto ON M4S 1Y1
Canada

Tel. (419) 482-3081
EXECUTIVE OFFICER: Kenneth George McMillan
ORGANIZED: 1904
DESCRIPTION: An international, nondenominational agency serving churches of all confessions and engaged in translation, publication and distribution of scriptures. Also involved in broadcasting and fund raising.
TOTAL INCOME: $3,690,189   FOR OVERSEAS MINISTRIES: $1,464,585
PERSONNEL:

NORTH AMERICANS OVERSEAS		NON-NORTH AMERICANS OVERSEAS:	NR
MARRIED:	2	NORTH AMERICAN ADM. STAFF:	22
SINGLE MEN:	0	SHORT TERM:	0
SINGLE WOMEN:	0	RETIRED:	28
TOTAL ACTIVE:	2		

Canadian Council of Churches, Commission on World Concerns
SEE: Mission Association Section

Canadian Yearly Meeting of the
Religious Society of Friends
Canadian Friends Service Committee

60 Lowther
Toronto ON M5R 1C7
Canada

DESCRIPTION: No data is reported for this agency for one of the following reasons: it is currently inactive or no longer exists; it has terminated overseas ministries or has ceased to operate as a North American entity.

Carver Foreign Missions, Inc.

65 Haynes St.
Atlanta GA 30313
P.O. ADDRESS:
MB Sta. Box 92091
Atlanta GA 30314

Tel. (404) 525-9747
EXECUTIVE OFFICER: W. D. Hungerpiller
ORGANIZED: 1955
DESCRIPTION: An interdenominational sending agency involved in education, literacy, evangelism and church planting. Agency supports a Christian Academy in Liberia with 425 students and a Bible Institute with 40 students. Serves as a channel for involving blacks in missionary work.
TOTAL INCOME: $92,326   FOR OVERSEAS MINISTRIES: $92,326
PERSONNEL:

NORTH AMERICANS OVERSEAS		NON-NORTH AMERICANS OVERSEAS:	0
MARRIED:	4	NORTH AMERICAN ADM. STAFF:	3
SINGLE MEN:	1	SHORT TERM:	1

```
SINGLE WOMEN:    4                                    RETIRED:    0
              -----
   TOTAL ACTIVE:    9
-----------------------------------------------------------------
                  YEAR      PERSONNEL    RELATED    PEOPLE
FIELD OF SERVICE  BEGAN    NOW   NEW    CHURCHES   GROUPS  NOTES
-----------------------------------------------------------------
Liberia           1956      9                1         1
```

CBM International (Christian Blind Mission)
SEE: Christian Blind Mission International

Cedar Lane Missionary Homes, Inc.
103 Cedar Lane
Laurel Springs NJ 08021

```
Tel. (609) 783-6525
EXECUTIVE OFFICER: Raymond H. VanDerVeer
ORGANIZED: 1949
DESCRIPTION:  An independent, nondenominational service agency
    supplying homes for furloughed missionaries.
TOTAL INCOME:    $49,660        FOR OVERSEAS MINISTRIES:    $0
PERSONNEL:
    NORTH AMERICANS OVERSEAS   NON-NORTH AMERICANS OVERSEAS:    0
            MARRIED:    0         NORTH AMERICAN ADM. STAFF:    5
         SINGLE MEN:    0                       SHORT TERM:    0
       SINGLE WOMEN:    0                         RETIRED:    2
                     -----
       TOTAL ACTIVE:    0
```

Central American Mission SEE: CAM International

Central American Mission, Practical Missionary Training SEE: CAM International, Practical Missionary Training

Central Yearly Meeting of Friends
Missionary Committee
P.O. ADDRESS:
Box 542
Westfield IN 46074

```
Tel. (317) 896-5082
EXECUTIVE OFFICER: Joseph A. Enyart
ORGANIZED: 1925
DESCRIPTION:  A denominational sending agency of Friends
    tradition engaged in church planting, education, Bible
    distribution, evangelism and support of nationals.
TOTAL INCOME:    $55,000   FOR OVERSEAS MINISTRIES:    $51,000
PERSONNEL:
    NORTH AMERICANS OVERSEAS   NON-NORTH AMERICANS OVERSEAS:    NR
            MARRIED:   NR         NORTH AMERICAN ADM. STAFF:    8
         SINGLE MEN:   NR                       SHORT TERM:    2
       SINGLE WOMEN:   NR                         RETIRED:    NR
                     -----
       TOTAL ACTIVE:   10
-----------------------------------------------------------------
                  YEAR      PERSONNEL    RELATED    PEOPLE
FIELD OF SERVICE  BEGAN    NOW   NEW    CHURCHES   GROUPS  NOTES
-----------------------------------------------------------------
Bolivia
```

Chiang Mai Mission Board

1914 Greenview Dr.
Ann Arbor MI 48103

Tel. (313) 761-9320
EXECUTIVE OFFICER: Douglas R. Sherman
ORGANIZED: 1974
DESCRIPTION: A nondenominational specialized Presbyterian
agency engaged in fund raising and education.
Primarily involved in physical development of certain
agencies in Northern Thailand. Supports Payap College in
Chiang Mai and works closely with the Church of Christ in
Thailand.
TOTAL INCOME: $250,000   FOR OVERSEAS MINISTRIES: $250,000
PERSONNEL:
    NORTH AMERICANS OVERSEAS   NON-NORTH AMERICANS OVERSEAS: 0
                MARRIED: 0   NORTH AMERICAN ADM. STAFF: 10
            SINGLE MEN: 0   SHORT TERM: 0
          SINGLE WOMEN: 0   RETIRED: 0

        TOTAL ACTIVE: 0
NOTES: All administrative personnel are
        part-time.

FIELD OF SERVICE	YEAR BEGAN	PERSONNEL NOW	NEW	RELATED CHURCHES	PEOPLE GROUPS	NOTES
Thailand	1974					

Child Evangelism Fellowship, Inc.

P.O. ADDRESS:
Box 348
Warrenton MO 63383

Tel. (314) 456-4321   *Allen George*
EXECUTIVE OFFICER: Rieder M. Kalland
ORGANIZED: 1937
DESCRIPTION: An interdenominational sending agency of Baptist
and evangelical tradition engaged in literature
production, training, radio and TV broadcasting,
correspondence courses and evangelism.
TOTAL INCOME: NR   FOR OVERSEAS MINISTRIES: $1,491,000
PERSONNEL:
    NORTH AMERICANS OVERSEAS   NON-NORTH AMERICANS OVERSEAS: 6
                MARRIED: 67   NORTH AMERICAN ADM. STAFF: 5
            SINGLE MEN: 0   SHORT TERM: 4
          SINGLE WOMEN: 40   RETIRED: NR

        TOTAL ACTIVE: 107

FIELD OF SERVICE	YEAR BEGAN	PERSONNEL NOW	NEW	RELATED CHURCHES	PEOPLE GROUPS	NOTES
Argentina	1947	1				
Australia	1949	3	1			
Austria	1955	15	1			
Barbados						
Belgium	1955					
Bermuda	1974	1	1			
Bolivia	1974					
Brazil	1941	6				

FIELD OF SERVICE	YEAR BEGAN	PERSONNEL NOW	NEW	RELATED CHURCHES	PEOPLE GROUPS	NOTES
Burundi	1956	2				
Chile	1952	3	2			
Colombia	1970	3	1			
Costa Rica	1957	2				
Denmark	1947	1				
Dominican Republic	1958	6	4			
Ecuador	1952	2				
Egypt	1971					
Finland	1966	4	2			
France	1949	12	4			
Germany, Fed. Rep.	1948	5				
Ghana	1970	1				
Greece	1967	1	1			
Guam	1962	1				
Guatemala	1945	2				
Haiti						
Hong-Kong	1963	2				
India	1947	3				
Indonesia	1963					
Iran	1974	3	1			
Ireland	1954					
Israel	1951	2				
Italy	1956	1				
Ivory Coast	1976	2	2			
Japan	1948	6				
Kenya	1966	5	2			
Korea, Rep. of	1957	2				
Liberia	1955	1				
Mexico	1943	6				
Netherlands	1949	2				
New Zealand	1951	1				
Nigeria	1974					
Norway	1950	3				
Paraguay	1973	2				
Philippines	1952	4				
Portugal	1949	1				
Reunion		2	2			
Solomon Is.	1975					
South Africa	1944					
Spain	1967	2				
Sri Lanka	1973					
Surinam	1974					
Switzerland	1950	10	1			
Taiwan Rep of China	1954	2				
Thailand	1957	1				
Trinidad and Tobago	1964	2	2			
United Kingdom	1943	5	1			
Venezuela	1949	4	2			
Zaire	1959					
Zambia	1970	1				
Zimbabwe	1951	1				

Note: The fourteen countries with no personnel
listed are staffed by nationals.

Children of India Foundation

302 WT Bldg, 23 Broad St
Westerly RI 02891

Tel. (401) 596-0846
EXECUTIVE OFFICER: Gert Rune Rohdin
ORGANIZED: 1977
DESCRIPTION: A nondenominational service agency engaged in
    fund raising, orphanage and childcare. Also involved in
    support of nationals and churches.

TOTAL INCOME: NR   FOR OVERSEAS MINISTRIES: $31,168
PERSONNEL:
    NORTH AMERICANS OVERSEAS   NON-NORTH AMERICANS OVERSEAS: 0
              MARRIED: 0   NORTH AMERICAN ADM. STAFF: 1
           SINGLE MEN: 0   SHORT TERM: 0
         SINGLE WOMEN: 0   RETIRED: 0

         TOTAL ACTIVE: 0

FIELD OF SERVICE	YEAR BEGAN	PERSONNEL NOW	NEW	RELATED CHURCHES	PEOPLE GROUPS	NOTES
India						

Children's Haven International, Inc.

514 S Cage Blvd.
Pharr TX 78577

Tel. (512) 787-7378
EXECUTIVE OFFICER: Shirley Mendoza
ORGANIZED: 1972
DESCRIPTION: A nondenominational agency of evangelical
    tradition operating and supporting a children's home in
    Mexico. Also involved in community development and
    aid/relief. All personnel are self-supporting.

TOTAL INCOME: $164,944   FOR OVERSEAS MINISTRIES: $164,944
PERSONNEL:
    NORTH AMERICANS OVERSEAS   NON-NORTH AMERICANS OVERSEAS: 0
              MARRIED: 6   NORTH AMERICAN ADM. STAFF: 11
           SINGLE MEN: 5   SHORT TERM: 19
         SINGLE WOMEN: 21   RETIRED: 0

         TOTAL ACTIVE: 32

FIELD OF SERVICE	YEAR BEGAN	PERSONNEL NOW	NEW	RELATED CHURCHES	PEOPLE GROUPS	NOTES
Mexico	1972	11	71		1	

    Note: New overseas personnel
    includes short and long term for
    1976-1979.

China Missionary and Evangelistic Association

La Tijera Station
Los Angeles CA 90043
P.O. ADDRESS:
Box 43033
Los Angeles CA 90043

DESCRIPTION: No data is reported for this agency for one of the
    following reasons: it is currently inactive or no longer
    exists; it has terminated overseas ministries or has ceased
    to operate as a North American entity.

Chinese Christian Mission

951 Petaluma Blvd. South
Petaluma CA 94952
P.O. ADDRESS:
Box 617
Petaluma CA 94952

Tel. (707) 762-1314
EXECUTIVE OFFICER: Mark Kor Cheng
ORGANIZED: 1961
DESCRIPTION: A nondenominational agency of evangelical and
    independent tradition involved in church planting, training,
    literature production and distribution and support of
    national churches. Major ministry is to promote world
    missions in Chinese Churches.
TOTAL INCOME: $262,214   FOR OVERSEAS MINISTRIES: $47,706
PERSONNEL:
    NORTH AMERICANS OVERSEAS   NON-NORTH AMERICANS OVERSEAS: 2
            MARRIED: 2   NORTH AMERICAN ADM. STAFF: 1
         SINGLE MEN: 0   SHORT TERM: 5
       SINGLE WOMEN: 0   RETIRED: 0

       TOTAL ACTIVE: 2

FIELD OF SERVICE	YEAR BEGAN	PERSONNEL NOW	PERSONNEL NEW	RELATED CHURCHES	PEOPLE GROUPS	NOTES
Hong-Kong	1965	2		150	1	
Panama	1979	2	2	2	1	
Philippines	1970	1		45	1	
Singapore	1977		1	30	1	
Taiwan Rep of China	1961	23	3	200	1	

Chinese for Christ, Inc.

510 N Bunker Hill
Los Angeles CA 90012
P.O. ADDRESS:
Box 29126
Los Angeles CA 90029

Tel. (213) 628-8078
EXECUTIVE OFFICER: Calvin Chad
ORGANIZED: 1959
DESCRIPTION: A nondenominational agency of independent
    tradition concerned mainly with reaching Chinese students
    from Hong-Kong, Taiwan and Mainland China who are now
    living in the USA. Also help support small ministries
    among Chinese in their own countries. Have a radio
    ministry to Mainland China and Taiwan which is partically
    supported by the USA office and a music school for the
    blind in Taiwan.
TOTAL INCOME: $233,107   FOR OVERSEAS MINISTRIES: NR
PERSONNEL:
    NORTH AMERICANS OVERSEAS   NON-NORTH AMERICANS OVERSEAS: NR
            MARRIED: NR   NORTH AMERICAN ADM. STAFF: 4
         SINGLE MEN: NR   SHORT TERM: 0
       SINGLE WOMEN: NR   RETIRED: 0

       TOTAL ACTIVE: 1

FIELD OF SERVICE	YEAR BEGAN	PERSONNEL NOW	PERSONNEL NEW	RELATED CHURCHES	PEOPLE GROUPS	NOTES
Taiwan Rep of China	1970	1				

Note: Taiwan has a school for the blind.

Chinese Gospel Crusade, Inc.

131 NW 143rd St.
Miami FL 33168
P.O. ADDRESS:
Box 42-595
Miami FL 33142

Tel. (305) 681-1971
EXECUTIVE OFFICER: Dwight Porter
ORGANIZED: 1959
DESCRIPTION: No current information available. Information
    from 1976 directory. An interdenominational service
    agency of evangelical and fundamentalist tradition
    supplying Chinese literature and supporting radio
    broadcasting. Also engaged in mass evangelism and
    mission-related research. Cooperates with the Christian
    and Missionary Alliance Press in Hong Kong. Staffed
    by volunteers.
TOTAL INCOME: $1,500   FOR OVERSEAS MINISTRIES: $1,500
PERSONNEL:
    NORTH AMERICANS OVERSEAS   NON-NORTH AMERICANS OVERSEAS: NR
            MARRIED: NR   NORTH AMERICAN ADM. STAFF: 2
        SINGLE MEN: NR   SHORT TERM: NR
      SINGLE WOMEN: NR   RETIRED: 0

      TOTAL ACTIVE: NR
NOTES: Income estimated by MARC.

Chinese Overseas Christian Mission, Inc.

3621 Highland Pl.
Fairfax VA 22030
P.O. ADDRESS:
Box 320
Fairfax VA 22030

Tel. (703) 273-3500
EXECUTIVE OFFICER: Donald Macintosh
ORGANIZED: 0
DESCRIPTION: A specialized service agency broadcasting to
    China in Chinese and English.
TOTAL INCOME: NR   FOR OVERSEAS MINISTRIES: NR
PERSONNEL:
    NORTH AMERICANS OVERSEAS   NON-NORTH AMERICANS OVERSEAS: NR
            MARRIED: 0   NORTH AMERICAN ADM. STAFF: 0
        SINGLE MEN: 0   SHORT TERM: 0
      SINGLE WOMEN: 0   RETIRED: 0

      TOTAL ACTIVE: 0

Chinese World Mission Center

1605 E Elizabeth
Pasadena CA 91104

Tel. (213) 684-0004
EXECUTIVE OFFICER: Danny Yu
ORGANIZED: 1979
DESCRIPTION: A specialized service agency of evangelical
    tradition training people for Chinese missions.
TOTAL INCOME: $65,000   FOR OVERSEAS MINISTRIES: $0
PERSONNEL:
    NORTH AMERICANS OVERSEAS   NON-NORTH AMERICANS OVERSEAS: NR
            MARRIED: 0   NORTH AMERICAN ADM. STAFF: 4
        SINGLE MEN: 0   SHORT TERM: 0

```
SINGLE WOMEN:     0                              RETIRED:     0
                -----
TOTAL ACTIVE:     0
```

Christ Church of North America, General Conference SEE: Christian Church of N. Amer. Gen. Council, Msns. Dept.

Christ for Greater Manila, Inc. SEE: Action International Ministries

Christ For The Nations, Inc.

```
                                        3404 Conway
                                        Dallas TX 75224
                                        P.O. ADDRESS:
                                        Box 24910
                                        Dallas TX 75224
Tel. (214) 376-1711
EXECUTIVE OFFICER: Freda T. Lindsay
ORGANIZED: 1948
DESCRIPTION:  An interdenominational specialized service agency
    of charismatic and evangelical tradition assisting missions
    by fund raising for church construction, literature
    production and distribution, education and aid. Also
    operates Christ For The Nations Institute with an
    enrollment of 1500 students.
TOTAL INCOME:  $5,189,000   FOR OVERSEAS MINISTRIES:  $1,057,000
PERSONNEL:
    NORTH AMERICANS OVERSEAS   NON-NORTH AMERICANS OVERSEAS:     0
              MARRIED:     0       NORTH AMERICAN ADM. STAFF:   150
           SINGLE MEN:     0                     SHORT TERM:     0
         SINGLE WOMEN:     0                        RETIRED:     0
                         -----
         TOTAL ACTIVE:     0
```


Christ For The Philippines, Inc.

```
                                        P.O. ADDRESS:
                                        Box 6172
                                        Grand Rapids MI 49506
Tel. (616) 243-9459
EXECUTIVE OFFICER: Ruperto Alparaque
ORGANIZED: 1975
DESCRIPTION:  An interdenominational agency of Baptist and
    fundamentalist tradition engaged in evangelism,
    broadcasting, correspondence courses and recording and
    literature distribution.
TOTAL INCOME:      $7,298     FOR OVERSEAS MINISTRIES:     $0
PERSONNEL:
    NORTH AMERICANS OVERSEAS   NON-NORTH AMERICANS OVERSEAS:     0
              MARRIED:     0       NORTH AMERICAN ADM. STAFF:     0
           SINGLE MEN:     0                     SHORT TERM:     0
         SINGLE WOMEN:     0                        RETIRED:     0
                         -----
         TOTAL ACTIVE:     0
```

FIELD OF SERVICE	YEAR BEGAN	PERSONNEL NOW	NEW	RELATED CHURCHES	PEOPLE GROUPS	NOTES
Philippines	1975					

Note: Two people are under appointment.

Christ's Mission

275 State St.
Hackensack NJ 07602
P.O. ADDRESS:
Box 176
Hackensack NJ 07602

Tel. (201) 342-6202
EXECUTIVE OFFICER: Royal L. Peck
ORGANIZED: 1883   AFFILIATION: EFMA
DESCRIPTION: An interdenominational sending agency of
   evangelical tradition with the primary objective of using
   short-term missionaries working in teams of 20-30 in a
   cross-cultural context. Involved in establishing churches,
   literature production and serving other agencies.
TOTAL INCOME: $243,000   FOR OVERSEAS MINISTRIES: $98,000
PERSONNEL:

NORTH AMERICANS OVERSEAS		NON-NORTH AMERICANS OVERSEAS:	0
MARRIED:	2	NORTH AMERICAN ADM. STAFF:	6
SINGLE MEN:	1	SHORT TERM:	19
SINGLE WOMEN:	1	RETIRED:	5
TOTAL ACTIVE:	4		

FIELD OF SERVICE	YEAR BEGAN	PERSONNEL NOW	NEW	RELATED CHURCHES	PEOPLE GROUPS	NOTES
Italy	1980	27				

Christian Aid Mission

Route 10, Box 1
Charlottesville VA 22901

Tel. (804) 977-5650
EXECUTIVE OFFICER: R.V. Finley
ORGANIZED: 1953
DESCRIPTION: An independent fund transmitting agency of
   fundamentalist and evangelical tradition providing
   support to nationals and indigenous missions.
TOTAL INCOME: $745,849   FOR OVERSEAS MINISTRIES: $425,862
PERSONNEL:

NORTH AMERICANS OVERSEAS		NON-NORTH AMERICANS OVERSEAS:	0
MARRIED:	0	NORTH AMERICAN ADM. STAFF:	5
SINGLE MEN:	0	SHORT TERM:	0
SINGLE WOMEN:	0	RETIRED:	0
TOTAL ACTIVE:	0		

FIELD OF SERVICE	YEAR BEGAN	PERSONNEL NOW	NEW	RELATED CHURCHES	PEOPLE GROUPS	NOTES
Argentina	1977			200	8	
Botswana	1953			200	8	
Burma	1977			300	19	
Colombia	1953			75	9	
Ghana	1953			100	14	
Haiti	1975			10	3	
Hong-Kong	1953			7	2	
India	1953			4500	84	
Indonesia	1968			120	16	
Kenya	1953			300	12	

FIELD OF SERVICE	YEAR BEGAN	PERSONNEL NOW	NEW	RELATED CHURCHES	PEOPLE GROUPS	NOTES
Korea, Rep. of	1953			600	1	
Lesotho	1953			60	7	
Nepal	1953			29	12	
Nigeria	1953			350	28	
Peru	1977			20	5	
Philippines	1953			390	42	
South Africa	1953			750	14	
Sri Lanka	1953			10	2	
Swaziland	1953			30	6	
Taiwan Rep of China	1953			20	6	
Thailand	1974			8	2	
Transkei	1953			100	4	
Zimbabwe	1953			150	17	

Christian Amateur Radio Fellowship

408 S Pearl
Knox IN 46534

Tel. (219) 772-5165
EXECUTIVE OFFICER: Kenneth Whiles
ORGANIZED: 1967
DESCRIPTION: A nondenominational fellowship of Christian
    tradition which provides information, equipment and
    technical assistance to encourage missionaries to obtain
    license and operate amateur radio.
TOTAL INCOME: $100   FOR OVERSEAS MINISTRIES: $200
PERSONNEL:
    NORTH AMERICANS OVERSEAS   NON-NORTH AMERICANS OVERSEAS: 0
            MARRIED: 0   NORTH AMERICAN ADM. STAFF: 0
        SINGLE MEN: 0   SHORT TERM: 0
      SINGLE WOMEN: 0   RETIRED: 0

      TOTAL ACTIVE: 0

Christian and Missionary Alliance

350 N Highland Ave.
Nyack NY 10960
P.O. ADDRESS:
Box C
Nyack NY 10960

Tel. (914) 353-0750
EXECUTIVE OFFICER: David L. Rambo
ORGANIZED: 1887   AFFILIATION: EFMA
DESCRIPTION: A denominational sending agency of evangelical
    tradition establishing churches and engaged in literature
    production and distribution, theological education, Bible
    translation and radio and TV broadcasting.
TOTAL INCOME: $15,627,269   FOR OVERSEAS MINISTRIES: $13,302,683
PERSONNEL:
    NORTH AMERICANS OVERSEAS   NON-NORTH AMERICANS OVERSEAS: 38
            MARRIED: 642   NORTH AMERICAN ADM. STAFF: 18
        SINGLE MEN: 16   SHORT TERM: 9
      SINGLE WOMEN: 151   RETIRED: 204

      TOTAL ACTIVE: 809

FIELD OF SERVICE	YEAR BEGAN	PERSONNEL NOW	NEW	RELATED CHURCHES	PEOPLE GROUPS	NOTES
Argentina	1897	13	9	47		

FIELD OF SERVICE	YEAR BEGAN	PERSONNEL NOW	NEW	RELATED CHURCHES	PEOPLE GROUPS	NOTES
Asia-general	1976	7	5			4
Australia	1969	14	4	23		
Bahamas	1971	2		1		
Brazil	1962	16	6	14		
Chile	1897	21	4	209		
Colombia	1923	36	8	193		
Costa Rica	1975			4		
Dominican Republic	1969			31	1	
Ecuador	1897	76	29	162		1
France		9	4	8		
Gabon	1934	42	10	124		
Germany, Fed. Rep.	1970	4	4	2		
Guatemala	1970	2		39	2	
Guinea	1918	11		295		
Hong-Kong	1933	27	10	38		
India	1887	33	4	76		
Indonesia	1929	151	9	1407		
Israel	1890	6		2		
Ivory Coast	1930	28	7	716		
Japan	1891	16	7	42		
Jordan	1890	8	5	3		
Kampuchea	1923					
Lao, People's Dem. R	1929					
Lebanon	1890			5		
Malaysia	1965	29	14			2
Mali	1923	39	13	342		
Mexico	1954	2		19	1	
Netherlands		4		3		
New Zealand	1972	8	6	4		
Peru	1925	31	6	135		
Philippines	1902	69	20	987		
Spain	1978	6	8	2		
Surinam	1978	2	2	1		
Syria	1890			13		
Taiwan Rep of China	1952	18	8	15		
Thailand	1929	55	11	121		
United Kingdom	1976			5		
Upper Volta	1923	32	10	204		
Uruguay	1960			8		3
Venezuela	1972	2	2	3		
Viet Nam, Soc. Rep.	1911					
Zaire	1884	31	11	2494		

Note: 1. Includes Alliance Academy.
2. Dalat School.
3. Work begun by Argentine C&MA.
4. Southeast Asia Radio staff (working
with FEBC in Los Angeles, CA.

Christian and Missionary Alliance in Canada

P.O. ADDRESS:
Box 4048
Regina SK S4P 3R9
Canada

Tel. (416) 689-6659
EXECUTIVE OFFICER: Melvin P. Sylvester
ORGANIZED: 1887
DESCRIPTION: An autonomous Canadian denominational sending
agency of evangelical tradition working in association
with C&MA of the USA. See USA listing for
description, aims and statistics.

```
TOTAL INCOME:        NR      FOR OVERSEAS MINISTRIES:  $2,420,000
PERSONNEL:
   NORTH AMERICANS OVERSEAS    NON-NORTH AMERICANS OVERSEAS:      0
          MARRIED:   NR           NORTH AMERICAN ADM. STAFF:      6
       SINGLE MEN:   NR                        SHORT TERM:       NR
     SINGLE WOMEN:   NR                          RETIRED:       NR
                    -----
   TOTAL ACTIVE:    110
NOTES:  Overseas income estimated by MARC.
```

Christian Baptist Church of God
Association World for Christ
Missions

P.O. ADDRESS:
Box 132
Wheelersburg OH 45694

Tel. (614) 574-6042
EXECUTIVE OFFICER: Goldie Taylor
ORGANIZED: 1962
DESCRIPTION: A denominational sending agency of Wesleyan
    tradition establishing churches, supporting nationals and
    engaged in evangelism, medicine, broadcasting and
    education. Affiliated with Faith Bible Institute in USA.

```
TOTAL INCOME:     $75,000   FOR OVERSEAS MINISTRIES:    $37,500
PERSONNEL:
   NORTH AMERICANS OVERSEAS    NON-NORTH AMERICANS OVERSEAS:     NR
          MARRIED:   NR           NORTH AMERICAN ADM. STAFF:    100
       SINGLE MEN:   NR                        SHORT TERM:       0
     SINGLE WOMEN:   NR                          RETIRED:        0
                    -----
   TOTAL ACTIVE:      4
```

Christian Blind Mission
International (CBM Intl.)

1506 E Roosevelt Rd.
Wheaton IL 60187
P.O. ADDRESS:
Box 175
Wheaton Il 60187

Tel. (312) 690-0300
EXECUTIVE OFFICER: Magdalena Wiesinger
ORGANIZED: 1975
DESCRIPTION: A nondenominational specialized service agency
    ministering to the blind and handicapped through practical
    assistance, education and spiritual guidance. An
    independent associate of Christoffel-Blindenmission,
    Bensheim, Germany, cooperating in projects and funds.
    Works in over 70 countries.

```
TOTAL INCOME:    $165,277   FOR OVERSEAS MINISTRIES:   $165,277
PERSONNEL:
   NORTH AMERICANS OVERSEAS    NON-NORTH AMERICANS OVERSEAS:    106
          MARRIED:   NR           NORTH AMERICAN ADM. STAFF:     12
       SINGLE MEN:   NR                        SHORT TERM:       NA
     SINGLE WOMEN:   NR                          RETIRED:        2
                    -----
   TOTAL ACTIVE:     21
```

Christian Brethren SEE: Brethren Assemblies

Christian Broadcasting Network

CBN Center
Virginia Beach VA 23463

Tel. (804) 424-7777
EXECUTIVE OFFICER: Marion G."Pat" Robertson
ORGANIZED: 1960
DESCRIPTION: An interdenominational evangelical broadcasting
    network producing Christian TV and radio programs in 15
    countries plus the Armed Forces Radio and TV Service.
TOTAL INCOME: $56,500,000   FOR OVERSEAS MINISTRIES: $4,068,000
PERSONNEL:
```
    NORTH AMERICANS OVERSEAS    NON-NORTH AMERICANS OVERSEAS:    NR
            MARRIED:    NR         NORTH AMERICAN ADM. STAFF:   771
        SINGLE MEN:    NR                      SHORT TERM:      0
      SINGLE WOMEN:    NR                         RETIRED:     NR
                     -----
      TOTAL ACTIVE:    15
```
NOTES: Administration also has 88 part-time and
    volunteer employees.

FIELD OF SERVICE	YEAR BEGAN	PERSONNEL NOW	PERSONNEL NEW	RELATED CHURCHES	PEOPLE GROUPS	NOTES
Australia						2
Bermuda						1
Brazil						1
Chile						1
Colombia		2				1
Costa Rica		3				1
Dominican Republic						1
Guatemala						1
Honduras						1
India						2
Japan						1
Peru						1
Philippines		2				1
Puerto Rico		2				1
USSR						2

    Note: 1. TV broadcasts.
    2. Radio broadcasts.

Christian Business Men's Committee
International (Canada)

960 Portage Ave.
Winnepeg MB R3G 0R4
Canada

Tel. (615) 698-4444
EXECUTIVE OFFICER: David E. Redekop
ORGANIZED: 1973
DESCRIPTION: A nondenominational agency of evangelical
    tradition engaged in evangelism, fund transmittal and
    support of nationals, working in Africa, Asia and Latin
    America where Christian Businessmen are not represented.
    Related to similar organizations in other countries.
TOTAL INCOME: NR   FOR OVERSEAS MINISTRIES: NR
PERSONNEL:
```
    NORTH AMERICANS OVERSEAS    NON-NORTH AMERICANS OVERSEAS:    NR
            MARRIED:    NR         NORTH AMERICAN ADM. STAFF:    NR
        SINGLE MEN:    NR                      SHORT TERM:       0
      SINGLE WOMEN:    NR                         RETIRED:      NR
                     -----
      TOTAL ACTIVE:    NR
```

Christian Business Men's Committee of USA

P.O. ADDRESS:
Box 3380
Chattanooga TN 37404

Tel. (615) 698-4444
EXECUTIVE OFFICER: Ted DeMoss
ORGANIZED: 0
DESCRIPTION: An interdenominational specialized service agency
    of evangelical tradition seeking to evangelize businessmen
    through other businessmen. There are approximately 600
    active committees in the USA. See Christian Business Men's
    Committee International (Canada) for overseas work.
TOTAL INCOME: $1,000,000   FOR OVERSEAS MINISTRIES: $0
PERSONNEL:

NORTH AMERICANS OVERSEAS		NON-NORTH AMERICANS OVERSEAS:	0
MARRIED:	0	NORTH AMERICAN ADM. STAFF:	0
SINGLE MEN:	0	SHORT TERM:	0
SINGLE WOMEN:	0	RETIRED:	0
TOTAL ACTIVE:	0		

NOTES: Income estimated by agency.

Christian Canadian Mission to Overseas Students

201 Stanton St.
Fort Erie ON L2A 3N8
Canada

Tel. (416) 871-1773
EXECUTIVE OFFICER: R. V. Finley
ORGANIZED: 1953
DESCRIPTION: An independent agency of evangelical and
    fundamentalist tradition engaged in establishing
    churches, evangelism and support of nationals and national
    churches. Funds sent through evangelistic mission boards
    overseas. Fields of service are reported in Christian Aid
    Mission which is the parent organization.
TOTAL INCOME: $65,554   FOR OVERSEAS MINISTRIES: $52,248
PERSONNEL:

NORTH AMERICANS OVERSEAS		NON-NORTH AMERICANS OVERSEAS:	0
MARRIED:	0	NORTH AMERICAN ADM. STAFF:	0
SINGLE MEN:	0	SHORT TERM:	0
SINGLE WOMEN:	0	RETIRED:	0
TOTAL ACTIVE:	0		

Christian Catholic Church

Dowie Memorial Dr.
Zion IL 60099

Tel. (312) 746-1411
EXECUTIVE OFFICER: Roger W. Ottersen
ORGANIZED: 1896
DESCRIPTION: A service and support agency of evangelical
    tradition involved in church planting and nurture. Also
    engaged in general Christian education.
TOTAL INCOME: $571,024   FOR OVERSEAS MINISTRIES: $32,386
PERSONNEL:

NORTH AMERICANS OVERSEAS		NON-NORTH AMERICANS OVERSEAS:	0
MARRIED:	2	NORTH AMERICAN ADM. STAFF:	0
SINGLE MEN:	0	SHORT TERM:	0
SINGLE WOMEN:	0	RETIRED:	4
TOTAL ACTIVE:	2		

FIELD OF SERVICE	YEAR BEGAN	PERSONNEL NOW	NEW	RELATED CHURCHES	PEOPLE GROUPS	NOTES
Australia	1888			2		
Guyana	1945			6		
Israel	1929			3		
Jamaica	1916					
Japan	1951	2		2		
Philippines	1945			35		

Christian Church (Disciples of Christ) Division of Overseas Ministires

P.O. ADDRESS:
Box 1986
Indianapolis IN 46206

Tel. (317) 353-1491
EXECUTIVE OFFICER: Kenneth L. Teegarden
ORGANIZED: 1920   AFFILIATION: DOM-NCCCUSA
DESCRIPTION: A denominational sending agency of Christian
    "Restoration Movement" and ecumenical tradition serving
    national churches and involved in agriculture, education,
    medicine, community service and church development.
TOTAL INCOME: $3,182,445   FOR OVERSEAS MINISTRIES: $1,915,126
PERSONNEL:

NORTH AMERICANS OVERSEAS		NON-NORTH AMERICANS OVERSEAS:	8
MARRIED:	60	NORTH AMERICAN ADM. STAFF:	6
SINGLE MEN:	5	SHORT TERM:	0
SINGLE WOMEN:	10	RETIRED:	0
TOTAL ACTIVE:	75		

FIELD OF SERVICE	YEAR BEGAN	PERSONNEL NOW	NEW	RELATED CHURCHES	PEOPLE GROUPS	NOTES
Argentina	1906	4				
Brazil	1968	2				
Hong-Kong	1963	3				
India	1882	11				
Indonesia	1964	4				
Jamaica	1885	6				
Japan	1883	10				
Mexico	1895	5				
Nepal	1955	2				
Paraguay	1917	6				
Philippines	1901	6				
Puerto Rico	1889	2				
Thailand	1951	11				
Venezuela	1963	1				
Zaire	1899	17				

Christian Church of North America, Missions Dept., General Council

1818 E State, Ste.208
Sharon PA 16146
P.O. ADDRESS:
Box 801
Sharon Pᴬ 16146

Tel. (412) 981-6030
EXECUTIVE OFFICER: Guy Bongiovanni
ORGANIZED: 1927   AFFILIATION: EFMA
DESCRIPTION: A denominational sending agency of Pentecostal

tradition engaged in church planting and nurture. Also
involved in Bible and literature distribution.
TOTAL INCOME: $412,193   FOR OVERSEAS MINISTRIES: $294,000
PERSONNEL:

```
    NORTH AMERICANS OVERSEAS    NON-NORTH AMERICANS OVERSEAS:    2
               MARRIED:    18       NORTH AMERICAN ADM. STAFF:    3
            SINGLE MEN:     2                     SHORT TERM:    0
          SINGLE WOMEN:     1                        RETIRED:    0
                         -----
          TOTAL ACTIVE:    21
```

FIELD OF SERVICE	YEAR BEGAN	PERSONNEL NOW	NEW	RELATED CHURCHES	PEOPLE GROUPS	NOTES
Argentina	1975		2	80		
Australia	1967	10		4		
Barbados						
Belgium						
France						
Germany, Fed. Rep.						
Ghana						
India						
Italy	1949	2		700		
Luxembourg	1954	4		80		
Philippines						
Switzerland						
United Kingdom						
Uruguay						
Venezuela	1963	2		5		

Christian Churches, Direct Support Missions SEE: Christian Churches/Churches of Christ

Christian Churches/Churches of Christ

No central Headquarters

DESCRIPTION: A body of autonomous churches out of the
    "Restoration Movement," which send and support
    missionaries from local congregations. Further
    information can be obtained from World Mission
    Information Bank, P.O. Box 344091, Dallas, Texas,
    75234, Tel. (214) 241-0800. Not to be confused with
    Disciples of Christ, Christian Churches, or Churches
    of Christ using instrumental music in worship.
TOTAL INCOME: NA   FOR OVERSEAS MINISTRIES: $40,000,000
PERSONNEL:

```
    NORTH AMERICANS OVERSEAS    NON-NORTH AMERICANS OVERSEAS:    NR
               MARRIED:    NR       NORTH AMERICAN ADM. STAFF:    NR
            SINGLE MEN:    NR                     SHORT TERM:    NR
          SINGLE WOMEN:    NR                        RETIRED:    NR
                         -----
          TOTAL ACTIVE:   699
```
NOTES: Data from World Mission Information Bank and
         the Directory of the Ministry.
         WMIB estimates overseas expenditure to exceed $40 million.

FIELD OF SERVICE	YEAR BEGAN	PERSONNEL NOW	NEW	RELATED CHURCHES	PEOPLE GROUPS	NOTES
Antigua		2				

FIELD OF SERVICE	YEAR BEGAN	PERSONNEL NOW	PERSONNEL NEW	RELATED CHURCHES	PEOPLE GROUPS	NOTES
Asia-general		17				
Austria	1950	13				
Bahamas	1960	2		1		
Barbados	1965	2				
Belgium	1948	4				
Brazil	1956	54				
Chile	1958	26				
Colombia	1967	10				
Costa Rica	1967	2				
Dominican Republic		9				
Ecuador	1962	5				
Germany, Fed. Rep.		14				
Ghana		3				
Guatemala	1959	2				
Haiti		8				
Honduras		4				
Hong-Kong	1925	11				
India	1963	24				
Indonesia	1967	21				
Italy	1949	13				
Jamaica	1965	3				
Japan	1890	62				
Kenya	1965	26				
Korea, Rep. of	1930	9				
Liberia		5				
Malawi	1908	1				
Mexico	1933	100				
New Guinea		10				
Nigeria	1950	6				
Peru		2				
Philippines	1925	23				
Portugal		2				
Puerto Rico	1953	32				1
South Africa	1950	31				
Spain		4				
St. Vincent		2				
Switzerland	1955	2				
Taiwan Rep of China	1950	14				
Thailand	1957	27				
Transkei		1				
United Kingdom		18				
Zaire		13				
Zambia		24				
Zimbabwe	1896	40				

Note: 1. Missionaries in Puerto Rico are listed with more than one agency and therefore have been counted more than once.

Christian Dental Society

5235 Sky Trail
Littleton CO 80123

Tel. (303) 794-2290
EXECUTIVE OFFICER: Everett C. Claus
ORGANIZED: 1963
DESCRIPTION: An interdenominational specialized service agency recruiting dentists for voluntary service overseas and interfacing with other agencies using dentistry as a tool to carry the Gospel. Volunteers sent for 2-4 weeks.
TOTAL INCOME: $50,000   FOR OVERSEAS MINISTRIES: $50,000

PERSONNEL:
```
    NORTH AMERICANS OVERSEAS      NON-NORTH AMERICANS OVERSEAS:    NR
              MARRIED:      0        NORTH AMERICAN ADM. STAFF:      2
           SINGLE MEN:      0                     SHORT TERM:      0
         SINGLE WOMEN:      0                        RETIRED:     NR
                       -----
         TOTAL ACTIVE:      0
```
NOTES: Income and Administrative personnel estimated by agency.

Christian Echoes National Ministry, Inc. (Christian Crusade)

6555 S Lewis
Tulsa OK 74136
P.O. ADDRESS:
Box 977
Tulsa OK 74101

Tel. (918) 749-0514
EXECUTIVE OFFICER: Billy James Hargis
ORGANIZED: 1947
DESCRIPTION: No current information available. Information
    from 1976 directory. A nondenominational specialized
    service agency of fundamentalist tradition engaged in mass
    evangelism and involved in radio and literature work. Also
    carried out overseas missionary work through the David
    Livingston Missionary Society. Supports more than 30
    overseas orphanages.
TOTAL INCOME: $138,000   FOR OVERSEAS MINISTRIES: NR
PERSONNEL:
```
    NORTH AMERICANS OVERSEAS      NON-NORTH AMERICANS OVERSEAS:    NR
              MARRIED:      0        NORTH AMERICAN ADM. STAFF:     NR
           SINGLE MEN:      0                     SHORT TERM:     NR
         SINGLE WOMEN:      0                        RETIRED:     NR
                       -----
         TOTAL ACTIVE:      0
```

FIELD OF SERVICE	YEAR BEGAN	PERSONNEL NOW	NEW	RELATED CHURCHES	PEOPLE GROUPS	NOTES
Bangladesh						
Brazil					1	
Hong-Kong						
India					1	
Indonesia						
Iran						
Japan						
Kenya						
Korea, Rep. of					1	
Malawi						
Mexico					1	
Nicaragua						
Philippines						
South Africa						
Sri Lanka						
Surinam						
Taiwan Rep of China						
Thailand						

    Note: 1. Orphanages.

Christian Endeavor SEE: World's Christian Endeavor Union

Christian Homes for Children, Inc.
Harold Martin Evangelistic
Association, Inc.

100 Club Ave.
Dorian PQ J7V 2C9
Canada

EXECUTIVE OFFICER: Harold G. Martin
ORGANIZED: 1945
DESCRIPTION: No current information available. Information
    from 1976 directory. A nondenominational fund transmittal
    agency of evangelical tradition involved in childcare,
    support of missionaries, evangelism, radio broadcasting,
    camping and child evangelism. Operates Camp Laurentide,
    Jorstadt Castle, Christ College and Seminary, and a
    retreat center, all in Quebec.

TOTAL INCOME:	NR	FOR OVERSEAS MINISTRIES:	NR
PERSONNEL:			
NORTH AMERICANS OVERSEAS		NON-NORTH AMERICANS OVERSEAS:	NR
MARRIED:	NR	NORTH AMERICAN ADM. STAFF:	NR
SINGLE MEN:	NR	SHORT TERM:	NR
SINGLE WOMEN:	NR	RETIRED:	NR
TOTAL ACTIVE:	NR		

Christian INFO

B2, 223A 10 St. NW
Calgary AB T2N 1V5
Canada

Tel. (403) 283-4114
EXECUTIVE OFFICER: Lois Bromley
ORGANIZED: 1979
DESCRIPTION: A nondenominational information and communication
    service agency active in mission challenge. Seeks to
    involve people in mission and to facilitate linkage of
    churches, missions and individuals.

TOTAL INCOME:	$16,795	FOR OVERSEAS MINISTRIES:	$0
PERSONNEL:			
NORTH AMERICANS OVERSEAS		NON-NORTH AMERICANS OVERSEAS:	0
MARRIED:	0	NORTH AMERICAN ADM. STAFF:	0
SINGLE MEN:	0	SHORT TERM:	0
SINGLE WOMEN:	0	RETIRED:	0
TOTAL ACTIVE:	0		

Christian Information Service, Inc.

117 W Wesley
Wheaton IL 60187
P.O. ADDRESS:
Box 1177
Wheaton IL 60187

Tel. (312) 668-8767
EXECUTIVE OFFICER: W. T. Bray
ORGANIZED: 1966
DESCRIPTION: A service agency of evangelical tradition
    working in mass communications. Involved in the
    development of human resources, broadcasting and
    information service.

TOTAL INCOME:	$20,000	FOR OVERSEAS MINISTRIES:	NR
PERSONNEL:			
NORTH AMERICANS OVERSEAS		NON-NORTH AMERICANS OVERSEAS:	1
MARRIED:	0	NORTH AMERICAN ADM. STAFF:	2
SINGLE MEN:	0	SHORT TERM:	2

```
      SINGLE WOMEN:    0                            RETIRED:      0
                -----
      TOTAL ACTIVE:    0
NOTES:  Overseas income included in total income.
--------------------------------------------------------------------
                      YEAR    PERSONNEL   RELATED   PEOPLE
FIELD OF SERVICE      BEGAN   NOW   NEW   CHURCHES  GROUPS  NOTES
--------------------------------------------------------------------
Bangladesh            1970                            11
Hong-Kong             1970                            11
India                 1966     2     2                11
Indonesia             1970                            11
Kampuchea             1968                            11
Lao, People's Dem. R  1968                            11
Philippines           1970     1     1                11
Spain                 1965                            11
Thailand              1966                            11
Viet Nam, Soc. Rep.   1968                            11
```

Christian Life Missions

396 E St. Charles Rd.
Wheaton IL 60187

Tel. (312) 653-4200
EXECUTIVE OFFICER: Robert Walker
ORGANIZED: 1956
DESCRIPTION: A project-oriented nondenominational service
    agency of evangelical tradition. Projects include aid or
    relief, literature distribution and prison evangelism.
TOTAL INCOME: $15,624   FOR OVERSEAS MINISTRIES: $15,624
PERSONNEL:
```
    NORTH AMERICANS OVERSEAS    NON-NORTH AMERICANS OVERSEAS:    0
              MARRIED:    0        NORTH AMERICAN ADM. STAFF:    0
           SINGLE MEN:    0                      SHORT TERM:    0
         SINGLE WOMEN:    0                         RETIRED:    0
                     -----
       TOTAL ACTIVE:     0
```

Christian Literature and Bible Center, Inc.

3840 Oakley Ave.
Memphis TN 38111

EXECUTIVE OFFICER: Andrew J. Losier
ORGANIZED: 1938
DESCRIPTION: No current information available. Information
    from 1976 directory. A nondenominational service agency
    of fundamentalist tradition producing gospel tracts,
    conversion follow-up material, Christian films and
    cassettes. Material is distributed by volunteers to 50
    different language groups.
TOTAL INCOME: $14,000   FOR OVERSEAS MINISTRIES: NR
PERSONNEL:
```
    NORTH AMERICANS OVERSEAS    NON-NORTH AMERICANS OVERSEAS:    NR
              MARRIED:    NR       NORTH AMERICAN ADM. STAFF:    NR
           SINGLE MEN:    NR                     SHORT TERM:     0
         SINGLE WOMEN:    NR                        RETIRED:    NR
                     -----
       TOTAL ACTIVE:     NR
```
NOTES: Data from agency's publications. Income estimated
        by MARC.

South Africa   1938   1
  1. Literature center

Christian Literature Crusade (Ontario) Inc.

1757 Avenue Rd.
Toronto ON M5M 3Y8
Canada

Tel. (416) 787-2543
EXECUTIVE OFFICER: Percy W. Page
ORGANIZED: 1941
DESCRIPTION: An international, nondenominational service and
    sending agency of fundamentalist and evangelical
    tradition engaged in literature production and
    distribution. Also engaged in Bible distribution and
    translation.
TOTAL INCOME: $34,215   FOR OVERSEAS MINISTRIES: $21,941
PERSONNEL:
  NORTH AMERICANS OVERSEAS   NON-NORTH AMERICANS OVERSEAS: 0
        MARRIED: 4   NORTH AMERICAN ADM. STAFF: 1
     SINGLE MEN: 0   SHORT TERM: 0
   SINGLE WOMEN: 0   RETIRED: 0

    TOTAL ACTIVE: 4
NOTES: Funds are not designated specifically for
    support of the 4 Canadian missionaries but
    are disbursed through the North American
    headquarters and are used where needed.
    Fields of service are listed with the North
    American agency report.

Christian Literature Crusade, Inc.

701 Pennsylvania Ave.
Ft. Washington PA 19034
P.O. ADDRESS:
Box C
Ft. Washington PA 19034

Tel. (215) 542-1242
EXECUTIVE OFFICER: Robert J. Gerry
ORGANIZED: 1941   AFFILIATION: EFMA
DESCRIPTION: An interdenominational service and sending agency
    of evangelical tradition engaged in literature production
    and distribution.
TOTAL INCOME: $417,409   FOR OVERSEAS MINISTRIES: $373,292
PERSONNEL:
  NORTH AMERICANS OVERSEAS   NON-NORTH AMERICANS OVERSEAS: 55
        MARRIED: 20   NORTH AMERICAN ADM. STAFF: 10
     SINGLE MEN: 0   SHORT TERM: 0
   SINGLE WOMEN: 2   RETIRED: 4

    TOTAL ACTIVE: 22

Antigua   1961

FIELD OF SERVICE	YEAR BEGAN	PERSONNEL NOW	NEW	RELATED CHURCHES	PEOPLE GROUPS	NOTES
Argentina	1959					
Australia	1945					
Austria	1957					
Barbados	1957					
Brazil	1958					
Cameroon	1972					
Chile	1958					
Colombia	1973	2				
Dominica	1947					
France	1952					
French Guiana	1972					
Germany, Fed. Rep.	1948					
Gibraltar	1974					
Guinea-Bissau	1964					
Hong-Kong	1974	5				
India	1946					
Indonesia	1954	3				
Italy	1956					
Ivory Coast	1962					
Jamaica	1951					
Japan	1950					
Korea, Rep. of	1974					
Liberia	1946	2				
Martinique	1979					
Middle East-general	1976	2				
Netherlands	1962					
New Zealand	1961					
Pakistan	1960	2				
Panama	1976					
Papua New Guinea	1959					
Philippines	1957					
Sierra Leone	1967					
Spain	1966					
Sri Lanka	1975					
St. Lucia	1960					
St. Vincent	1977					
Thailand	1958	2				
Trinidad and Tobago	1950	2				
United Kingdom	1941	1	1			
Uruguay	1951					
Venezuela	1970					

Christian Literature International

P.O. ADDRESS:
Box 777
Canby OR 97013

Tel. (503) 266-9734
EXECUTIVE OFFICER: Gleason H. Wedyard
ORGANIZED: 1967
DESCRIPTION: A nondenominational agency of evangelical
    tradition specializing in the translation, publication and
    distribution of Bibles and literature using controlled
    vocabulary designed for new readers.
TOTAL INCOME: NR   FOR OVERSEAS MINISTRIES: NR
PERSONNEL:
    NORTH AMERICANS OVERSEAS   NON-NORTH AMERICANS OVERSEAS: 0
            MARRIED: 0   NORTH AMERICAN ADM. STAFF: 7
        SINGLE MEN: 0   SHORT TERM: 0

```
SINGLE WOMEN:     0                          RETIRED:     0
              -----
TOTAL ACTIVE:     0
```

Christian Medical Society

```
                                             1616 Gateway Blvd.
                                             Richardson TX 75080
                                             P.O. ADDRESS:
                                             Box 689
                                             Richardson TX 75080
Tel. (214) 783-8384
EXECUTIVE OFFICER: Joseph Bayly
ORGANIZED: 1931
DESCRIPTION:  A nondenominational professional organization of
    Ecumenical and evangelical tradition made up of Christian
    medical osteopathic doctors, dentists and medical and
    dental students. Their Medical Group Missions are short
    term medical and dental missions serving underdeveloped
    areas in the Dominican Republic, Haiti, Honduras,
    Colombia and Guatemala.
TOTAL INCOME:     $484,542   FOR OVERSEAS MINISTRIES:    $152,774
PERSONNEL:
    NORTH AMERICANS OVERSEAS    NON-NORTH AMERICANS OVERSEAS:    NR
            MARRIED:    4           NORTH AMERICAN ADM. STAFF:    4
         SINGLE MEN:    0                      SHORT TERM:    NR
       SINGLE WOMEN:    0                         RETIRED:    NR
                     -----
       TOTAL ACTIVE:    4
```

```
                    YEAR      PERSONNEL   RELATED   PEOPLE
FIELD OF SERVICE    BEGAN     NOW   NEW   CHURCHES  GROUPS  NOTES
```

FIELD OF SERVICE	YEAR BEGAN	PERSONNEL NOW	NEW	RELATED CHURCHES	PEOPLE GROUPS	NOTES
Dominican Republic	1960	2	1			
Honduras	1960	1				

Christian Methodist Episcopal
Church Board of Missions

```
                                             1301 Orleans St. Apt 911
                                             Detroit MI 48207
DESCRIPTION:  No data is reported for this agency for one of the
    following reasons: it is currently inactive or no longer
    exists; it has terminated overseas ministries or has ceased
    to operate as a North American entity.
```

Christian Mission for Deaf Africans
SEE: Christian Mission for the Deaf

Christian Mission for the Deaf

```
                                             P.O. ADDRESS:
                                             Box 1254
                                             Flint MI 48501
EXECUTIVE OFFICER: Andrew Foster
ORGANIZED: 1956
DESCRIPTION:  Originally known as Christian Mission For Deaf
    Africans.  Name changed in 1978.  A nondenominational
    sending agency of "Plymouth Brethren" tradition engaged in
    evangelism and education of the deaf. Also involved in
    preparing teachers for schools for the deaf and in Bible
    institutes.
TOTAL INCOME:       NR      FOR OVERSEAS MINISTRIES:     $44,000
PERSONNEL:
    NORTH AMERICANS OVERSEAS    NON-NORTH AMERICANS OVERSEAS:     0
            MARRIED:    2           NORTH AMERICAN ADM. STAFF:     1
         SINGLE MEN:    0                      SHORT TERM:     0
```

```
      SINGLE WOMEN:    0                          RETIRED:    0
                 -----
      TOTAL ACTIVE:    2
NOTES:  Overseas income estimated by MARC.
----------------------------------------------------------------
                      YEAR    PERSONNEL   RELATED   PEOPLE
FIELD OF SERVICE      BEGAN   NOW   NEW   CHURCHES  GROUPS  NOTES
----------------------------------------------------------------
Benin                 1976
Cameroon              1977
Central African Rep.  1977
Chad                  1976
Gabon                 1980
Ghana                 1957
Ivory Coast           1974
Nigeria               1959
Senegal               1977
Sierra Leone          1978
Togo                  1976
Upper Volta           1979
Zaire                 1978
```

Christian Mission to the Republic of Korea SEE: Christian Churches/Churches of Christ

Christian Missionary Fellowship

4540 N Franklin Rd.
Indianapolis IN 46226
P.O. ADDRESS:
Box 26306
Indianapolis IN 46226

```
Tel. (317) 542-9256
EXECUTIVE OFFICER: James C. Smith
ORGANIZED: 1949
DESCRIPTION:  A nondenominational sending fellowship of Christian
    "Restoration Movement" tradition engaged in recruiting,
    sending and supporting missionaries, church planting,
    evangelism, support of national churches and training
    nationals for leadership.
TOTAL INCOME:    $900,000   FOR OVERSEAS MINISTRIES:    $674,000
PERSONNEL:
    NORTH AMERICANS OVERSEAS   NON-NORTH AMERICANS OVERSEAS:    0
                MARRIED:  34        NORTH AMERICAN ADM. STAFF:   3
             SINGLE MEN:   0                    SHORT TERM:      2
           SINGLE WOMEN:   0                      RETIRED:      NR
                           -----
      TOTAL ACTIVE:    34
----------------------------------------------------------------
                      YEAR    PERSONNEL   RELATED   PEOPLE
FIELD OF SERVICE      BEGAN   NOW   NEW   CHURCHES  GROUPS  NOTES
----------------------------------------------------------------
Brazil                1957    10    6       12
Indonesia             1978     4    4                 1
Kenya                 1977    20   10                 2
```

Christian Missions in Many Lands, Inc.

Bailey's Corner/18th Ave
Wall Township NJ 07719
P.O. ADDRESS:

228

Box 13
Spring Lake NJ 07762

Tel. (201) 449-8880
EXECUTIVE OFFICER: Fred G. MacKenzie
ORGANIZED: 1921
DESCRIPTION: A nondenominational service agency of "Plymouth
    Brethren" tradition assisting individual missionaries
    through fund transmittal and receipt, orientation,
    repatriation arrangements, planning home itineraries,
    promotional activities and underwriting children's
    educational costs.
TOTAL INCOME: NR   FOR OVERSEAS MINISTRIES: NR
PERSONNEL:
    NORTH AMERICANS OVERSEAS   NON-NORTH AMERICANS OVERSEAS: 0
             MARRIED: 0   NORTH AMERICAN ADM. STAFF: NR
          SINGLE MEN: 0   SHORT TERM: 0
        SINGLE WOMEN: 0   RETIRED: 0

        TOTAL ACTIVE: 0

Christian Missions, Inc.

12405 Littleton St.
Wheaton MD 20906

DESCRIPTION: No data is reported for this agency for one of the
    following reasons: it is currently inactive or no longer
    exists; it has terminated overseas ministries or has ceased
    to operate as a North American entity.

Christian Nationals' Evangelism
Commission, Inc. (CNEC)

1470 N Fourth St.
San Jose CA 95112

Tel. (408) 298-0965
EXECUTIVE OFFICER: Allen B. Finley
ORGANIZED: 1943   AFFILIATION: EFMA/IFMA-Assoc. Member
DESCRIPTION: A nondenominational service agency of evangelical
    tradition establishing and supporting national churches.
    Also engaged in education and evangelism.
TOTAL INCOME: $2,191,660   FOR OVERSEAS MINISTRIES: $1,715,176
PERSONNEL:
    NORTH AMERICANS OVERSEAS   NON-NORTH AMERICANS OVERSEAS: 7
             MARRIED: 18   NORTH AMERICAN ADM. STAFF: 8
          SINGLE MEN: 0   SHORT TERM: 6
        SINGLE WOMEN: 0   RETIRED: 0

        TOTAL ACTIVE: 18

FIELD OF SERVICE	YEAR BEGAN	PERSONNEL NOW	PERSONNEL NEW	RELATED CHURCHES	PEOPLE GROUPS	NOTES
Argentina	1979					
Bangladesh	1975			7		
Bolivia	1977					
Brazil	1969	2		9		
Burma	1978			17		
Chile	1977					
China, People's Rep.	1943					
Fiji	1974					
France	1980	2	2			
Ghana	1973					

FIELD OF SERVICE	YEAR BEGAN	PERSONNEL NOW	NEW	RELATED CHURCHES	PEOPLE GROUPS	NOTES
Guatemala	1964	2				
Hong-Kong	1950	4	2	16		
India	1969	2	2	38		
Indonesia	1971			43		
Ivory Coast	1972					
Jamaica	1977					
Japan	1977					
Kenya	1972	1	1			
Korea, Rep. of	1976			35		
Liberia	1964	2		108		
Macao	1962			1		
Malaysia	1954			7		
Mexico	1968	2				
Nigeria	1963					
Pakistan	1975					
Philippines	1968					
Singapore	1952	3	2	30		
South Africa	1975					
Sri Lanka	1972			1		
Sudan	1973					
Taiwan Rep of China	1959			3		
Thailand	1955			7		
Zaire	1969					
Zambia	1972					

Christian Nationals' Evangelism Commission, Inc. (CNEC) (Canada)

5140 Dundas St. W
Islington ON M9A 1C2
Canada
P.O. ADDRESS:
Box 215
Islington ON M9A 4X2
Canada

Tel. (416) 236-2705
EXECUTIVE OFFICER: George Doxsee
ORGANIZED: 1943   AFFILIATION: EFMA/IFMA-Assoc. Member
DESCRIPTION: A nondenominational service agency of evangelical
    tradition establishing and supporting national churches.
    Also engaged in education and evangelism.
TOTAL INCOME: $312,417   FOR OVERSEAS MINISTRIES: $312,417
PERSONNEL:
    NORTH AMERICANS OVERSEAS   NON-NORTH AMERICANS OVERSEAS: 2
               MARRIED: 4   NORTH AMERICAN ADM. STAFF: 2
            SINGLE MEN: 0   SHORT TERM: 0
          SINGLE WOMEN: 0   RETIRED: 0

        TOTAL ACTIVE: 4

FIELD OF SERVICE	YEAR BEGAN	PERSONNEL NOW	NEW	RELATED CHURCHES	PEOPLE GROUPS	NOTES
Argentina	1979					
Bangladesh	1975					
Bolivia	1977					
Brazil	1969	2				

FIELD OF SERVICE	YEAR BEGAN	PERSONNEL NOW	PERSONNEL NEW	RELATED CHURCHES	PEOPLE GROUPS	NOTES
Burma	1978					
Chile	1977					
China, People's Rep.	1943					
Fiji	1974					
France	1980					
Ghana	1973					
Guatemala	1964					
Hong-Kong	1950					
India	1969	2	2			
Indonesia	1971					
Ivory Coast	1972					
Jamaica	1977					
Japan	1977					
Kenya	1972					
Korea, Rep. of	1976					
Liberia	1964					
Macao	1962					
Malaysia	1954					
Mexico	1968					
Nigeria	1963					
Pakistan	1975					
Philippines	1968					
Singapore	1952					
South Africa	1975					
Sri Lanka	1972					
Sudan	1973					
Taiwan Rep of China	1959					
Thailand	1955					
Zaire	1969					
Zambia	1972					

Christian Pilots Association, Inc.

802 N Foxdale
West Covina CA 91790
P.O. ADDRESS:
Box 2092
Irwindale CA 91706

Tel. (213) 962-7591
EXECUTIVE OFFICER: Howard Payne
ORGANIZED: 1972
DESCRIPTION: An interdenominational service agency of
    evangelical tradition providing aviation support on a
    voluntary basis to agencies and churches engaged in
    agricultural assistance, aid, relief, evangelism,
    literature and medicine. Also involved in construction
    in remote areas. Limited to Western Hemisphere.
TOTAL INCOME: $50,000   FOR OVERSEAS MINISTRIES: $150,000
PERSONNEL:
    NORTH AMERICANS OVERSEAS   NON-NORTH AMERICANS OVERSEAS: 0
            MARRIED: 0   NORTH AMERICAN ADM. STAFF: 0
         SINGLE MEN: 0   SHORT TERM: 0
       SINGLE WOMEN: 0   RETIRED: 0

       TOTAL ACTIVE: 0
NOTES: Overseas income is estimated value of
        two million lbs. of relief goods
        distributed.

Kampuchea

Christian Reformed Board For World Missions

2850 Kalamazoo Ave. SE
Grand Rapids MI 49560

Tel. (616) 241-6568
EXECUTIVE OFFICER: Eugene Rubingh
ORGANIZED: 1888   AFFILIATION: EFMA
DESCRIPTION: A denominational sending agency of Reformed
    tradition engaged in aviation, broadcasting, church
    planting, education, mass evangelism, Bible translation
    and medicine.
TOTAL INCOME: $5,381,910   FOR OVERSEAS MINISTRIES: $5,381,900
PERSONNEL:
    NORTH AMERICANS OVERSEAS   NON-NORTH AMERICANS OVERSEAS: 4
            MARRIED: 230   NORTH AMERICAN ADM. STAFF: 16
         SINGLE MEN: 3   SHORT TERM: 8
       SINGLE WOMEN: 25   RETIRED: 5

       TOTAL ACTIVE: 258
NOTES: Income figures represent both USA and
        Canada.

FIELD OF SERVICE	YEAR BEGAN	PERSONNEL NOW	NEW	RELATED CHURCHES	PEOPLE GROUPS	NOTES
Argentina	1930	15	3			
Australia	1978	2	2			
Brazil	1934	6	6			
El Salvador	1978	6	6			
Guam	1962	4	4			
Guatemala	1978	4	4			
Honduras	1971	10	10			
Japan	1951	24	2			
Jordan	1979	2	2			
Liberia	1975	7	5			
Mexico	1962	23	5			
Nicaragua	1973	5	1			
Nigeria	1940	97	41			
Philippines	1961	18	10			
Puerto Rico	1967	10	2			
Taiwan Rep of China	1953	7				

Christian Reformed World Relief Committee

2850 Kalamazoo SE
Grand Rapids MI 49560

Tel. (616) 241-1691
EXECUTIVE OFFICER: John DeHaan
ORGANIZED: 1962   AFFILIATION: EFMA
DESCRIPTION: A denominational service agency of Reformed
    tradition engaged in agriculture, community development,
    literacy, medicine and self-help projects.
TOTAL INCOME: $2,600,000   FOR OVERSEAS MINISTRIES: $1,500,000
PERSONNEL:
    NORTH AMERICANS OVERSEAS   NON-NORTH AMERICANS OVERSEAS: 29
            MARRIED: 19   NORTH AMERICAN ADM. STAFF: 6
         SINGLE MEN: 7   SHORT TERM: 0

```
SINGLE WOMEN:    3                           RETIRED:      0
                -----
   TOTAL ACTIVE:   29
----------------------------------------------------------------
                   YEAR    PERSONNEL    RELATED    PEOPLE
FIELD OF SERVICE   BEGAN   NOW   NEW    CHURCHES   GROUPS   NOTES
----------------------------------------------------------------
Bangladesh         1973     5    5                   14
Costa Rica         1975
Guatemala          1976     1    1        12          3
Haiti              1975     5    5        54
Honduras           1973     3    3        40
Mexico             1969     4    3        35         12
Nicaragua          1972
Niger              1975     2    1
Nigeria            1970     2    1       150
Philippines        1970     4    3        15
```

Christian Salvage Mission, Inc.

200 Free St.
Fowlerville MI 48836

Tel. (517) 223-3193
EXECUTIVE OFFICER: David Brown
ORGANIZED: 1958
DESCRIPTION: A nondenominational specialized service agency of
    Baptist tradition involved in the collection and
    distribution of used and surplus Christian literature
    and materials. Agency recycles literature and sends it
    to 139 different countries.

```
TOTAL INCOME:      $61,861     FOR OVERSEAS MINISTRIES:     $0
PERSONNEL:
   NORTH AMERICANS OVERSEAS   NON-NORTH AMERICANS OVERSEAS:    0
              MARRIED:    0       NORTH AMERICAN ADM. STAFF:    8
           SINGLE MEN:    0                    SHORT TERM:      0
         SINGLE WOMEN:    0                      RETIRED:       0
                         -----
         TOTAL ACTIVE:    0
```

Christian Service Corps

1509 Sixteenth St. NW
Washington D.C. 20036

Tel. (202) 462-8822
EXECUTIVE OFFICER: Robert N. Meyers
ORGANIZED: 1965
DESCRIPTION: An interdenominational service agency which
    recruits, trains and places short-term missionaries as
    well as assisting them with fund raising. All personnel
    are on loan to other agencies.

```
TOTAL INCOME:      $500,000   FOR OVERSEAS MINISTRIES:    $400,000
PERSONNEL:
   NORTH AMERICANS OVERSEAS   NON-NORTH AMERICANS OVERSEAS:    0
              MARRIED:    0       NORTH AMERICAN ADM. STAFF:   32
           SINGLE MEN:    0                    SHORT TERM:     53
         SINGLE WOMEN:    0                      RETIRED:       8
                         -----
         TOTAL ACTIVE:    0
----------------------------------------------------------------
                   YEAR    PERSONNEL    RELATED    PEOPLE
FIELD OF SERVICE   BEGAN   NOW   NEW    CHURCHES   GROUPS   NOTES
----------------------------------------------------------------
Bolivia            1974     4
```

FIELD OF SERVICE	YEAR BEGAN	PERSONNEL NOW	NEW	RELATED CHURCHES	PEOPLE GROUPS	NOTES
Cameroon		1				
Cayman Islands		2				
Ecuador	1973	1				
Gambia		1				
Guatemala	1974	3				
Haiti	1975	4				
Ireland	1974	1				
Jamaica	1974	3				
Kenya		5				
Korea, Rep. of		3				
Liberia		1				
Mali						
Nigeria		1				
Pacific Trust Terr.		4				
Papua New Guinea		2				
Philippines		5				
Puerto Rico		3				
Senegal	1973	1				
Switzerland		1				
Zaire		1				

Christian Service Fellowship

6500 Xerxes Ave. South
Minneapolis MN 55423

Tel. (612) 920-0574
EXECUTIVE OFFICER: Spencer Bower
ORGANIZED: 1950
DESCRIPTION: An interdenominational specialized service agency
    which gives management counsel and service to other
    agencies through its staff and other supplemental persons.
TOTAL INCOME: NR   FOR OVERSEAS MINISTRIES: NR
PERSONNEL:
    NORTH AMERICANS OVERSEAS   NON-NORTH AMERICANS OVERSEAS: 0
            MARRIED: 0   NORTH AMERICAN ADM. STAFF: 5
         SINGLE MEN: 0   SHORT TERM: 0
       SINGLE WOMEN: 0   RETIRED: NR

       TOTAL ACTIVE: 0

Christian Services Fellowship, Inc.

5716 Benton Ave. South
Minneapolis MN 55436

Tel. (612) 926-4616
EXECUTIVE OFFICER: Donald D. Moore
ORGANIZED: 1973
DESCRIPTION: An interdenominational service agency of evangelical
    tradition which assists missionaries on furlough providing
    distribution of missionary newsletters, supply equipment,
    computer/data processing services.
TOTAL INCOME: $105,052   FOR OVERSEAS MINISTRIES: $80,000
PERSONNEL:
    NORTH AMERICANS OVERSEAS   NON-NORTH AMERICANS OVERSEAS: 0
            MARRIED: 0   NORTH AMERICAN ADM. STAFF: 2
         SINGLE MEN: 0   SHORT TERM: 0
       SINGLE WOMEN: 0   RETIRED: 0

       TOTAL ACTIVE: 0

Christian Translation Ministries

Ilima St.
Orchid Land Est HI 96778
P.O. ADDRESS:
Box 1485
Pahoa HI 96778

EXECUTIVE OFFICER: Daniel Dodenhoff
ORGANIZED: 1977
DESCRIPTION: An interdenominational specialized agency of
    evangelical tradition engaged in Bible translation.
    Establishing a school to teach bilingual nationals to
    translate the Scriptures into their mother tongue. Also
    engaged in literature production.
TOTAL INCOME: $16,476   FOR OVERSEAS MINISTRIES: $0
PERSONNEL:
    NORTH AMERICANS OVERSEAS   NON-NORTH AMERICANS OVERSEAS: 0
             MARRIED: 0   NORTH AMERICAN ADM. STAFF: 2
          SINGLE MEN: 0   SHORT TERM: 0
        SINGLE WOMEN: 0   RETIRED: 0

        TOTAL ACTIVE: 0

Christian Transportation

512 Yonge St.
Toronto ON M4Y 1X9
Canada

Tel. (416) 922-5626
EXECUTIVE OFFICER: Leslie M. Nimigan
ORGANIZED: 1930
DESCRIPTION: A nondenominational agency engaged in outreach
    to those in transportation industries and also to postal
    workers. Involved in Christian literature publications.
    Overseas distribution is to naval personnel.
TOTAL INCOME: $73,000   FOR OVERSEAS MINISTRIES: $1,000
PERSONNEL:
    NORTH AMERICANS OVERSEAS   NON-NORTH AMERICANS OVERSEAS: 0
             MARRIED: 0   NORTH AMERICAN ADM. STAFF: 5
          SINGLE MEN: 0   SHORT TERM: 0
        SINGLE WOMEN: 0   RETIRED: 0

        TOTAL ACTIVE: 0
NOTES: Income reported for overseas ministry is
        spent on shipment of publications.

Christian Union
General Mission Board

347 Maple
Liberty Center OH 43532
P.O. ADDRESS:
Box 454
Liberty Center OH 43532

Tel. (419) 533-2381
EXECUTIVE OFFICER: Bernard A. Clymer
ORGANIZED: 1864
DESCRIPTION: A denominational sending agency of evangelical
    tradition establishing churches and involved in
    correspondence courses, Bible distribution, fund raising
    and transmittal, literature production and distribution,
    and recruiting.
TOTAL INCOME: $40,000   FOR OVERSEAS MINISTRIES: $40,000
PERSONNEL:
    NORTH AMERICANS OVERSEAS   NON-NORTH AMERICANS OVERSEAS: 5
             MARRIED: 11   NORTH AMERICAN ADM. STAFF: 3
          SINGLE MEN: 0   SHORT TERM: 1

```
      SINGLE WOMEN:     1                              RETIRED:      0
                        -----
      TOTAL ACTIVE:    12
```

FIELD OF SERVICE	YEAR BEGAN	PERSONNEL NOW	NEW	RELATED CHURCHES	PEOPLE GROUPS	NOTES
Colombia	1978	2	2			
Indonesia	1975	2			1	
Japan	1962	2		1	1	
Liberia	1964	3			11	
Nigeria	1943	1			2	
Philippines	1969	2				

Christian World Publishers, Inc.

3688 Mt. Diablo Blvd.
Lafayette CA 94549

Tel. (415) 284-1070
EXECUTIVE OFFICER: E. Peter Cunliffe
ORGANIZED: 1974
DESCRIPTION: A nondenominational agency of evangelical
    tradition training nationals to produce and distribute
    Christian literature overseas.
TOTAL INCOME: $55,700   FOR OVERSEAS MINISTRIES: $55,700
PERSONNEL:

```
   NORTH AMERICANS OVERSEAS    NON-NORTH AMERICANS OVERSEAS:    0
            MARRIED:    2          NORTH AMERICAN ADM. STAFF:    0
         SINGLE MEN:    0                         SHORT TERM:    1
       SINGLE WOMEN:    0                            RETIRED:    0
                        -----
       TOTAL ACTIVE:    2
```

FIELD OF SERVICE	YEAR BEGAN	PERSONNEL NOW	NEW	RELATED CHURCHES	PEOPLE GROUPS	NOTES
Brazil	1964	2				

Christian World-Wide Evangelical Mission of Canada

3606 W 14th Ave.
Vancouver BC V6R 2W5
Canada
P.O. ADDRESS:
Jl. Kebon Jeruk 17/1A
Hayam Wuruk Jakarta
Indonesia

Tel. (604) 224-6524
EXECUTIVE OFFICER: Paul Tambunan
ORGANIZED: 1950   AFFILIATION: TAM-ICCC
DESCRIPTION: A nondenominational agency of evangelical and
    Presbyterian tradition aiding in the support of
    The Christian Evangelical Mission of Indonesia which is
    engaged in community development, education, medicine and
    evangelism.
TOTAL INCOME: $11,500   FOR OVERSEAS MINISTRIES: $8,500
PERSONNEL:

```
   NORTH AMERICANS OVERSEAS    NON-NORTH AMERICANS OVERSEAS:    NR
            MARRIED:    2          NORTH AMERICAN ADM. STAFF:    3
         SINGLE MEN:    2                         SHORT TERM:   12
       SINGLE WOMEN:    0                            RETIRED:    5
                        -----
       TOTAL ACTIVE:    4
```

FIELD OF SERVICE	YEAR BEGAN	PERSONNEL NOW	NEW	RELATED CHURCHES	PEOPLE GROUPS	NOTES
Hong-Kong	1950	3	4			
Indonesia	1949	5	7			
Taiwan Rep of China	1965	2	2			

Christians In Action

350 E Market St.
Long Beach CA 90805
P.O. ADDRESS:
Box 7271
Long Beach CA 90807

Tel. (213) 428-2022
EXECUTIVE OFFICER: Lee Shelley
ORGANIZED: 1958
DESCRIPTION: Founded in 1958 as Missionary and Soul Winning
    Fellowship. Name changed in 1974 to Christians In Action.
    An international, interdenominational sending agency of
    evangelical tradition establishing churches and engaged
    in missionary orientation and training, radio and TV
    broadcasting and recruiting. Have developed a unique system
    of "circuit-riding" involving teams assigned to more than
    one country.
TOTAL INCOME: $734,032   FOR OVERSEAS MINISTRIES: $599,968
PERSONNEL:
```
    NORTH AMERICANS OVERSEAS    NON-NORTH AMERICANS OVERSEAS:   14
              MARRIED:   66          NORTH AMERICAN ADM. STAFF:   21
           SINGLE MEN:   15                      SHORT TERM:    6
         SINGLE WOMEN:   16                         RETIRED:    4
                        -----
         TOTAL ACTIVE:   97
```

FIELD OF SERVICE	YEAR BEGAN	PERSONNEL NOW	NEW	RELATED CHURCHES	PEOPLE GROUPS	NOTES
Brazil	1957	7	2	2	1	
Chile	1978	7	8	1		
Colombia	1969	2		2		
Ecuador	1976	5	5	2		
Germany, Fed. Rep.	1976	6	4	2	1	
Guam	1979	2	2	1		
Guatemala	1970	8	2	6		
Honduras	1978	2	2	1		
Japan	1957	13	6	11	3	
Korea, Rep. of	1957	7	7	2		
Macao	1973	3	3	1	1	
Mexico	1957	7	7	5		
Peru	1979	2	2	1		
Philippines	1977	4	4	1		
Sierra Leone	1969	7	7	3	1	
Switzerland	1957	2		2		
United Kingdom	1965	4	2	3	1	
Uruguay	1979	4	4	1	1	

Christian United in Action SEE: United Evangelical Churches

Christians United in Action, Inc.

303 S Alta Vista Ave.
Monrovia CA 91016
P.O. ADDRESS:
Box 88
Monrovia CA 91016

Tel. (213) 359-8285
EXECUTIVE OFFICER: Charles J. Hardin
ORGANIZED: 1976
DESCRIPTION: An international interdenominational sending
    agency of evangelical tradition involved in evangelism and
    training of national leaders. Also active in orphanage and
    medical clinic work.
TOTAL INCOME: NR   FOR OVERSEAS MINISTRIES: $440,000
PERSONNEL:
    NORTH AMERICANS OVERSEAS   NON-NORTH AMERICANS OVERSEAS: NR
              MARRIED: NR   NORTH AMERICAN ADM. STAFF: 5
           SINGLE MEN: NR   SHORT TERM: 12
         SINGLE WOMEN: NR   RETIRED: 0

        TOTAL ACTIVE: 20
NOTES: Overseas income estimated by MARC.

FIELD OF SERVICE	YEAR BEGAN	PERSONNEL NOW	NEW	RELATED CHURCHES	PEOPLE GROUPS	NOTES
Australia		2				
Austria		1				
France		2				
Kenya		2				
Philippines		1				

    Note: Teams travel extensively and
    reach ministers and individuals in
    72 countries.

Church of God (Anderson, Indiana)
Missionary Board of the
Church of God

1303 E 5th St.
Anderson IN 46011
P.O. ADDRESS:
Box 2498
Anderson IN 46011

Tel. (317) 642-0258
EXECUTIVE OFFICER: Donald D. Johnson
ORGANIZED: 1909
DESCRIPTION: A denominational sending agency of evangelical,
    Holiness and Wesleyan tradition establishing churches
    and involved in missionary orientation and training,
    furloughed missionary support and recruiting. Also
    engaged in evangelism, medicine, education, childcare,
    self-help projects and support of nationals.
TOTAL INCOME: $2,359,692   FOR OVERSEAS MINISTRIES: $2,267,447
PERSONNEL:
    NORTH AMERICANS OVERSEAS   NON-NORTH AMERICANS OVERSEAS: 1
              MARRIED: 79   NORTH AMERICAN ADM. STAFF: 5
           SINGLE MEN: 1   SHORT TERM: 8
         SINGLE WOMEN: 2   RETIRED: NA

        TOTAL ACTIVE: 82

FIELD OF SERVICE	YEAR BEGAN	PERSONNEL NOW	PERSONNEL NEW	RELATED CHURCHES	PEOPLE GROUPS	NOTES
Argentina	1927	2		20		
Australia		6	6	3		
Bangladesh	1925		2	35		
Bermuda	1905	2		2		
Bolivia	1974	2		96		
Brazil	1923	6	2	34		
Costa Rica	1920		2	5		
Egypt	1908	2	2	12		
Guam	1958	2	2	1		
Hong-Kong	1953	3				
Japan	1906	8		18		
Kenya	1905	9	3	400		
Korea, Rep. of	1936	4	4	27		
Mexico	1946	5	4	31		
Panama	1910	2	2	22		
Peru	1962	1		25		
Puerto Rico	1966	4	4	3		
St. Kitts-Nevis	1946	2	2	7		
Tanzania	1968	8	4	54		
Thailand	1975	4	2	5		
Venezuela	1980	2	2			

Church of God (Holiness) Foreign Mission Board

7415 Metcalf
Overland Park KS 66204
P.O. ADDRESS:
Box 4060
Overland Park KS 66204

Tel. (913) 432-0303
EXECUTIVE OFFICER: David H. Mauck
ORGANIZED: 1922
DESCRIPTION: A nondenominational sending agency of Baptist,
    Holiness and Wesleyan tradition establishing churches and
    engaged in fund raising, recruiting, general Christian
    education and theological education by extension (TEE).
TOTAL INCOME: NR   FOR OVERSEAS MINISTRIES: $180,000
PERSONNEL:
    NORTH AMERICANS OVERSEAS   NON-NORTH AMERICANS OVERSEAS: 1
            MARRIED: 16   NORTH AMERICAN ADM. STAFF: 2
         SINGLE MEN: 0   SHORT TERM: 0
       SINGLE WOMEN: 6   RETIRED: 2

        TOTAL ACTIVE: 22

FIELD OF SERVICE	YEAR BEGAN	PERSONNEL NOW	PERSONNEL NEW	RELATED CHURCHES	PEOPLE GROUPS	NOTES
Anguilla	1975	2		1		
Bolivia	1945	2		105		
British Virgin Is.	1947	2		5		
Cayman Islands	1933	2		3		
Haiti	1966	1		4		
Jamaica	1933	4		38		
Mexico	1967	4		8		
U.S. Virgin Is.	1963	6		2		

Church of God (Seventh Day), General Conference, Missions Abroad

330 W 152nd Ave.
Broomfield CO 80233
P.O. ADDRESS:
Box 33677
Denver CO 80233

Tel. (303) 452-7973
EXECUTIVE OFFICER: Robert Coulter
ORGANIZED: 1860
DESCRIPTION: A denominational sending agency of Adventist and
    fundamentalist tradition engaged in establishing churches and
    personal and small group evangelism. Also involved in
    literature distribution, support of nationals and nurture or
    support of national churches.
TOTAL INCOME: $40,000   FOR OVERSEAS MINISTRIES: $40,000
PERSONNEL:
    NORTH AMERICANS OVERSEAS   NON-NORTH AMERICANS OVERSEAS: 0
               MARRIED: 2   NORTH AMERICAN ADM. STAFF: 3
            SINGLE MEN: 0   SHORT TERM: 0
          SINGLE WOMEN: 0   RETIRED: 0

          TOTAL ACTIVE: 2

FIELD OF SERVICE	YEAR BEGAN	PERSONNEL NOW	PERSONNEL NEW	RELATED CHURCHES	PEOPLE GROUPS	NOTES
Colombia	1976	1		1		
Germany, Fed. Rep.	1961					
India	1936			15		
Jamaica	1931			50		
Nigeria	1939			50		
Philippines	1935			12		
Trinidad and Tobago	1931			4		

Church of God at Baden, I.H.P.

8375 N Broadway
St. Louis MO 63147

Tel. (314) 261-1376
EXECUTIVE OFFICER: Paul and William Finke
ORGANIZED: 1920
DESCRIPTION: A nondenominational sending agency of evangelical
    tradition establishing new churches.
TOTAL INCOME: NA   FOR OVERSEAS MINISTRIES: $44,000
PERSONNEL:
    NORTH AMERICANS OVERSEAS   NON-NORTH AMERICANS OVERSEAS: NR
               MARRIED: NR   NORTH AMERICAN ADM. STAFF: 6
            SINGLE MEN: NR   SHORT TERM: NR
          SINGLE WOMEN: NR   RETIRED: NR

          TOTAL ACTIVE: 2

FIELD OF SERVICE	YEAR BEGAN	PERSONNEL NOW	PERSONNEL NEW	RELATED CHURCHES	PEOPLE GROUPS	NOTES
Japan	1951	2				

Church of God General Conference
Mission Department

131 N 3rd St.
Oregon IL 61061
P.O. ADDRESS:
Box 100
Oregon IL 61061

Tel. (815) 732-7991
EXECUTIVE OFFICER: S.O. Ross
ORGANIZED: 1921
DESCRIPTION: A denominational sending agency of Adventist
    tradition engaged in Bible distribution, church planting,
    correspondence courses, evangelism and literature
    distribution.
TOTAL INCOME: $225,000   FOR OVERSEAS MINISTRIES: $100,978
PERSONNEL:

NORTH AMERICANS OVERSEAS		NON-NORTH AMERICANS OVERSEAS:	0
MARRIED:	0	NORTH AMERICAN ADM. STAFF:	2
SINGLE MEN:	1	SHORT TERM:	0
SINGLE WOMEN:	0	RETIRED:	0
TOTAL ACTIVE:	1		

FIELD OF SERVICE	YEAR BEGAN	PERSONNEL NOW	NEW	RELATED CHURCHES	PEOPLE GROUPS	NOTES
Ghana	1970	1		4		
India	1964	5		8		
Liberia	1967	2		2		
Mexico	1963	1		1		
Nigeria	1967	6		8		
Philippines	1961	9		8		

Church of God in Christ, Mennonite
General Mission Board, Inc.

420 N Wedel Ave.
Moundridge KS 67107
P.O. ADDRESS:
Box 313
Moundridge KS 67107

Tel. (316) 345-2533
EXECUTIVE OFFICER: Curt Ensz
ORGANIZED: 1933
DESCRIPTION: A denominational sending agency of Mennonite
    tradition establishing churches and engaged in evangelism,
    medicine, childcare and education.
TOTAL INCOME: $669,521   FOR OVERSEAS MINISTRIES: $505,925
PERSONNEL:

NORTH AMERICANS OVERSEAS		NON-NORTH AMERICANS OVERSEAS:	NR
MARRIED:	NR	NORTH AMERICAN ADM. STAFF:	20
SINGLE MEN:	NR	SHORT TERM:	8
SINGLE WOMEN:	NR	RETIRED:	NR
TOTAL ACTIVE:	91		

FIELD OF SERVICE	YEAR BEGAN	PERSONNEL NOW	NEW	RELATED CHURCHES	PEOPLE GROUPS	NOTES
Belize						
Dominican Republic	1976	4				
Guatemala	1976	4				

FIELD OF SERVICE	YEAR BEGAN	PERSONNEL NOW	NEW	RELATED CHURCHES	PEOPLE GROUPS	NOTES
Haiti	1966	15				
India						
Mexico	1933	45				
Nigeria	1963	8				
Philippines	1974	10				

Church of God of Prophecy, World Mission Committee

Bible Pl.
Cleveland TN 37311

Tel. (615) 472-4511
EXECUTIVE OFFICER: M. A. Tomlinson
ORGANIZED: 1903
DESCRIPTION: A denominational sending agency of Holiness and
    Pentecostal tradition engaged in personal and mass
    evangelism, missionary orientation and training, church
    planting, and orphanage and childcare.
TOTAL INCOME: $1,103,014   FOR OVERSEAS MINISTRIES: $960,320
PERSONNEL:
    NORTH AMERICANS OVERSEAS   NON-NORTH AMERICANS OVERSEAS: 39
            MARRIED: 20   NORTH AMERICAN ADM. STAFF: 12
         SINGLE MEN: 0   SHORT TERM: 6
       SINGLE WOMEN: 0   RETIRED: 0

       TOTAL ACTIVE: 20

FIELD OF SERVICE	YEAR BEGAN	PERSONNEL NOW	NEW	RELATED CHURCHES	PEOPLE GROUPS	NOTES
Argentina	1955			11		
Australia	1956		2	4		
Bahamas	1923			55		
Bermuda	1955	1		1		
Bolivia	1974			20		
Botswana	1965			10		
Brazil	1965					
British Virgin Is.	1951			24		
Cayman Islands	1978			1		
Chile	1975			7		
Colombia	1973			5		
Costa Rica	1932		2	7		
Cuba	1935			4		
Cyprus	1935			1		
Dominican Republic	1940			79		
Egypt	1935			11		
El Salvador	1954			38		
Germany, Fed. Rep.	1959		2	2		
Greece	1931			1		
Guatemala	1951		2	94		
Guyana	1956			5		
Haiti	1931			185		
Honduras	1942			47		
India	1957			206		
Indonesia	1971			108		
Israel	1965		2	3		
Ivory Coast	1978			4		

FIELD OF SERVICE	YEAR BEGAN	PERSONNEL NOW	NEW	RELATED CHURCHES	PEOPLE GROUPS	NOTES
Jamaica	1923			260		
Jordan	1976			1		
Kenya	1978			6		
Korea, Rep. of	1969			29		
Malawi	1977			16		
Mexico	1944			126		
Mozambique	1979			9		
Netherlands Antilles	1935	2		21		
Nicaragua	1962			30		
Nigeria	1971			17		
Panama	1946			16		
Paraguay	1977			2		
Peru	1955			57		
Philippines	1952			17		
Portugal	1976			1		
Puerto Rico	1940			20		
Sierra Leone	1934			24		
South Africa	1967			8		
Swaziland	1977			7		
Tanzania	1978			1		
Thailand	1968		2	6		
Trinidad and Tobago	1961		2	11		
Turks and Caicos Is.	1932			6		
U.S. Virgin Is.	1926		2	12		
United Kingdom	1952	2		97		
Uruguay	1957	2		8		
Venezuela	1968			16		
Zaire	1979			13		
Zambia	1977			24		
Zimbabwe	1976			13		

Church of God of the Apostolic Faith, Inc.

13334 E 14th St.
Tulsa OK 74108

Tel. (918) 583-2882
EXECUTIVE OFFICER: Joe L. Edmonson
ORGANIZED: 1951
DESCRIPTION: A denominational agency of Pentecostal tradition
    engaged in church planting, evangelism and support of
    nationals.
TOTAL INCOME: $35,000   FOR OVERSEAS MINISTRIES: $35,000
PERSONNEL:
    NORTH AMERICANS OVERSEAS   NON-NORTH AMERICANS OVERSEAS: NR
           MARRIED: NR   NORTH AMERICAN ADM. STAFF: 3
        SINGLE MEN: NR   SHORT TERM: 0
      SINGLE WOMEN: NR   RETIRED: 0

      TOTAL ACTIVE: 2

FIELD OF SERVICE	YEAR BEGAN	PERSONNEL NOW	NEW	RELATED CHURCHES	PEOPLE GROUPS	NOTES
Mexico						

Church of God World Missions

Keith at 25th Sts., NW
Cleveland TN 37311

Tel. (615) 472-3361
EXECUTIVE OFFICER: Robert White
ORGANIZED: 1886   AFFILIATION: EFMA
DESCRIPTION: A denominational sending agency of evangelical,
    Holiness and Pentecostal tradition involved in church
    planting, church construction and education. Also engaged
    in fund raising and transmittal.
TOTAL INCOME: $5,892,704   FOR OVERSEAS MINISTRIES: $5,031,504
PERSONNEL:
```
      NORTH AMERICANS OVERSEAS    NON-NORTH AMERICANS OVERSEAS:   36
              MARRIED:   74        NORTH AMERICAN ADM. STAFF:      9
           SINGLE MEN:   0                       SHORT TERM:       0
         SINGLE WOMEN:   4                          RETIRED:       0
                      -----
         TOTAL ACTIVE:  78
```

FIELD OF SERVICE	YEAR BEGAN	PERSONNEL NOW	PERSONNEL NEW	RELATED CHURCHES	PEOPLE GROUPS	NOTES
Antigua	1966			3		
Argentina	1944			125		
Australia	1968			3		
Bahamas	1944			57		
Barbados	1944			48		
Belgium	1974	2	2	1		
Belize	1944			5		
Bermuda	1944			4		
Bolivia	1960	1	1	14		
Bophuthatswana	1978	2		19		1
Botswana	1966			2		
Brazil	1954			73		
British Virgin Is.	1968			1		
Burundi	1978			7		
Cameroon	1970			40		
Cayman Islands	1972			3		
Chad	1968			3		
Chile	1956			117		
Colombia	1960	2		31		
Costa Rica	1950	2		50		
Cuba	1944			9		
Dominican Republic	1944			136		
Ecuador	1972			10		
Egypt	1946			23		
El Salvador	1944	4		200		
France	1960			7		
Germany, Fed. Rep.	1944	4		54		
Ghana	1966	2		16		
Gilbert Islands	1956	2	2	18		
Greece	1964	2	2	2		
Grenada	1964			6		
Guadeloupe	1968			1		
Guatemala	1944	8	2	529		
Guyana	1966			16		
Haiti	1944	5	2	284		
Honduras	1946	6	4	140		
India	1944			409		

FIELD OF SERVICE	YEAR BEGAN	PERSONNEL NOW	PERSONNEL NEW	RELATED CHURCHES	PEOPLE GROUPS	NOTES
Indonesia	1968	2		564		
Israel	1968	4		1		
Italy	1960	2		8		
Ivory Coast	1978			1		
Jamaica	1944			272		
Japan	1954			6		
Kenya	1978	2	2	4		
Korea, Rep. of	1966			38		
Lesotho	1968	4		26		1
Liberia	1968	4	2	20		
Malawi	1966	2		15		
Mexico	1944	4	2	712		
Mozambique	1966			150		1
Namibia		2		23		1
Netherlands	1966			1		
Netherlands Antilles	1948			3		
Nicaragua	1952	2		48		
Nigeria	1952	2		58		
Pakistan	1978			2		
Panama	1944	9	2	37		
Paraguay	1954	2		30		
Peru	1950	2		86		
Philippines	1948	6	2	189		
Portugal	1966			3		
Puerto Rico	1944			131		
South Africa	1951	2		660		1
Spain	1960	2		4	2	
St. Kitts-Nevis	1944			8		
St. Vincent	1944			14		
Swaziland	1966	2		4		1
Tanzania	1972	1		40		
Thailand	1972	2	2	2		
Togo	1976			3		
Transkei	1966	4		17		1
Trinidad and Tobago	1956	2		35		
Turks and Caicos Is.	1944			1		
U.S. Virgin Is.	1966	2		3		
United Kingdom	1972			87		
Uruguay	1946	4		20		
Venezuela	1966	2		5		
Yugoslavia	1968			10		
Zaire	1970			62		
Zambia	1966			222		
Zimbabwe	1966	2	2	52		

Note: 1. Countries in which the Full Gospel
- Church of God of South Africa World Missions
Board makes the appointment. Personnel include
nationals and one North American.

Church of God, USA Headquarters

2504 Arrow Wood Dr. SE
Huntsville AL 35803

Tel. (205) 881-9629
EXECUTIVE OFFICER: Voy M. Bullen
ORGANIZED: 1903
DESCRIPTION: No current information available. Information
from 1976 directory. A denominational sending agency
of Pentecostal tradition engaged in evangelism, church
planting and support of national churches.
TOTAL INCOME: $69,000   FOR OVERSEAS MINISTRIES: NR

```
PERSONNEL:
    NORTH AMERICANS OVERSEAS      NON-NORTH AMERICANS OVERSEAS:      NR
              MARRIED:    0        NORTH AMERICAN ADM. STAFF:      NR
           SINGLE MEN:    0                      SHORT TERM:      NR
         SINGLE WOMEN:    0                         RETIRED:      NR
                      -----
       TOTAL ACTIVE:    0
NOTES:  Income estimated by MARC.
```

FIELD OF SERVICE	YEAR BEGAN	PERSONNEL NOW	NEW	RELATED CHURCHES	PEOPLE GROUPS	NOTES
Nigeria						
Panama						
United Kingdom						

Church of our Lord Jesus Christ of the Apos. Faith Chrn. For. Msn. Bd. SEE: Church of our Lord Jesus Christ of the Apos. Faith, Inc.

Church of our Lord Jesus Christ of the Apostolic Faith, Inc.

2801 A.C. Powell Jr Blvd
New York NY 10027
P.O. ADDRESS:
Triborough Box 108
New York New York 10035

```
Tel. (212) 866-1700
EXECUTIVE OFFICER: William L. Booner
ORGANIZED: 1919
DESCRIPTION:  A service agency involved in medicine and general
    Christian education. Maintains two schools and one medical
    clinic.
TOTAL INCOME:        NR    FOR OVERSEAS MINISTRIES:    $176,000
PERSONNEL:
    NORTH AMERICANS OVERSEAS      NON-NORTH AMERICANS OVERSEAS:      NR
              MARRIED:   NR        NORTH AMERICAN ADM. STAFF:      15
           SINGLE MEN:   NR                      SHORT TERM:       2
         SINGLE WOMEN:   NR                         RETIRED:       0
                      -----
       TOTAL ACTIVE:    8
NOTES:  Overseas income estimated by MARC.
```

Church of the Brethren World SEE: World Ministries Commission Ministries Commission

Church of the Lutheran Brethren of America, Board of World Missions

1007 West Side Dr.
Fergus Falls MN 56537
P.O. ADDRESS:
Box 655
Fergus Falls MN 56537

```
Tel. (218) 736-5666
EXECUTIVE OFFICER: Robert Overgaard
ORGANIZED: 1900    AFFILIATION: EFMA
DESCRIPTION:  A denominational sending agency of Lutheran
    tradition establishing churches and engaged in community
    development, education, fund raising, literature and
    support of national churches. Also involved in Bible
    translation and distribution.
TOTAL INCOME:    $413,000    FOR OVERSEAS MINISTRIES:    $413,000
```

```
PERSONNEL:
     NORTH AMERICANS OVERSEAS    NON-NORTH AMERICANS OVERSEAS:    0
               MARRIED:    38        NORTH AMERICAN ADM. STAFF:    2
            SINGLE MEN:     0                      SHORT TERM:    0
          SINGLE WOMEN:     3                         RETIRED:    3
                        -----
          TOTAL ACTIVE:    41
```

FIELD OF SERVICE	YEAR BEGAN	PERSONNEL NOW	PERSONNEL NEW	RELATED CHURCHES	PEOPLE GROUPS	NOTES
Cameroon	1920	19	4	402	12	
Chad	1920	8	2	420	11	
Japan	1950	8	6	15		
Taiwan Rep of China	1951	6		15	2	

Church of the Nazarene, General Board Department of World Missions

704 Vernon Ave. West
Fergus Falls MN 56537
P.O. ADDRESS:
Box 655
Fergus Falls MN 56537

Tel. (218) 736-5666
EXECUTIVE OFFICER: Jerald Johnson
ORGANIZED: 1900   AFFILIATION: EFMA
DESCRIPTION: A denominational sending agency of Wesleyan
    tradition engaged in evangelism, church planting and
    support of national churches. Also involved in relief,
    Bible translation and distribution, education, literature
    and medicine.

```
TOTAL INCOME:        NR    FOR OVERSEAS MINISTRIES: $14,960,725
PERSONNEL:
     NORTH AMERICANS OVERSEAS    NON-NORTH AMERICANS OVERSEAS:    36
               MARRIED:   400        NORTH AMERICAN ADM. STAFF:    7
            SINGLE MEN:    NR                      SHORT TERM:   70
          SINGLE WOMEN:    NR                         RETIRED:  103
                        -----
          TOTAL ACTIVE:   484
```

FIELD OF SERVICE	YEAR BEGAN	PERSONNEL NOW	PERSONNEL NEW	RELATED CHURCHES	PEOPLE GROUPS	NOTES
Argentina	1919	11		44		
Australia	1946			24		
Bahamas	1971			5		
Barbados	1926			32		
Belize	1934	4		21		
Bolivia	1945	8				
Bophuthatswana		46		95		
Brazil	1958	16		23		
Cape Verde	1903	4		17		
Caribbean-general		5				
Chile	1962	12		13		
Colombia	1975	8		2		
Costa Rica	1948	14		10		
Cuba	1902			10		
Denmark	1959			2		

FIELD OF SERVICE	YEAR BEGAN	PERSONNEL NOW	NEW	RELATED CHURCHES	PEOPLE GROUPS	NOTES
Dominican Republic	1975	8		23		
Ecuador	1972	9		6		
El Salvador	1964	2		7		
France		4				
Germany, Fed. Rep.	1958			14		2
Guatemala	1976	10		75		
Guyana	1946	2		38		
Haiti	1950	8		117		
Honduras	1971	4		3		
Hong-Kong	1971	2		1		
India	1902	12		28		
Indonesia	1974	8		7		
Israel	1952	4		1		
Italy	1948	5		14		
Jamaica	1966	22				
Japan	1905	17		77		
Jordan	1948	8		4		
Korea, Rep. of	1948	4		46		
Lebanon	1954			7		
Malawi	1957	10		47		
Mexico	1903			219		
Mozambique	1922	8		203		
Namibia		4		1		
Netherlands	1967			3		
New Zealand	1952			13		
Nicaragua	1943	5		52		
Nigeria	1976			20		
Panama	1953	2		11		
Papua New Guinea	1955	46		30		
Peru	1917	13		107		
Philippines	1948	17		89		
Portugal	1974	4		2		
Puerto Rico	1944	4		25		
Samoa	1960	6		8		
South Africa	1919	29		147		
Swaziland	1910	59		77		
Switzerland	1958			14		
Syria	1920			7		1
Taiwan Rep of China	1956	8		28		
Trinidad and Tobago	1926	7		20		
Uruguay	1949	4		12		
Zambia	1964	6		7		
Zimbabwe	1963	8		18		

Note: 1. Lebanon and Syria statistics have
been combined.
2. Germany and Switzerland statistics have
been combined.

Church of the United Brethren in Christ, Board of Missions

302 Lake St.
Huntington IN 46750

Tel. (219) 356-2312
EXECUTIVE OFFICER: Duane A. Reahm
ORGANIZED: 1853   AFFILIATION: EFMA
DESCRIPTION: A denominational sending agency of evangelical
    Methodist tradition engaged in church planting and
    construction. Also involved in missionary education,
    theological education, medicine and nurture and support of
    nationals and national churches.
TOTAL INCOME: $493,884   FOR OVERSEAS MINISTRIES: $493,884

```
PERSONNEL:
    NORTH AMERICANS OVERSEAS    NON-NORTH AMERICANS OVERSEAS:   26
              MARRIED:   16          NORTH AMERICAN ADM. STAFF:    5
           SINGLE MEN:    0                        SHORT TERM:    0
         SINGLE WOMEN:   10                           RETIRED:    3
                       -----
         TOTAL ACTIVE:   26
```

FIELD OF SERVICE	YEAR BEGAN	PERSONNEL NOW	NEW	RELATED CHURCHES	PEOPLE GROUPS	NOTES
Honduras	1945	4		29		
Hong-Kong	1949			5		
India	1974	1				
Jamaica	1945			19		
Nicaragua	1966			5		
Sierra Leone	1855	22	5	52		

Church World Service Division of
DOM-NCCCUSA

475 Riverside Dr.
New York NY 10115

Tel. (212) 870-2257
EXECUTIVE OFFICER: Paul F. McCleary
ORGANIZED: 1946   AFFILIATION: DOM-NCCCUSA
DESCRIPTION: An interdenominational service agency within the
    Division of Overseas Ministries, NCCCUSA, which is an
    emergency relief, development and refugee agency for 31
    Protestant and Orthodox churches. Carries out programs of
    food production, livestock/poultry, water resources,
    family planning, public health care and training of
    leadership through indigenous church organizations in 75
    countries.
TOTAL INCOME: $41,170,080   FOR OVERSEAS MINISTRIES: $41,170,080

```
PERSONNEL:
    NORTH AMERICANS OVERSEAS    NON-NORTH AMERICANS OVERSEAS:   NR
              MARRIED:   NR          NORTH AMERICAN ADM. STAFF:   NR
           SINGLE MEN:   NR                        SHORT TERM:    0
         SINGLE WOMEN:   NR                           RETIRED:    0
                       -----
         TOTAL ACTIVE:   42
```

FIELD OF SERVICE	YEAR BEGAN	PERSONNEL NOW	NEW	RELATED CHURCHES	PEOPLE GROUPS	NOTES
Bangladesh		1				
Dominican Republic		3				
Ecuador		1				
Germany, Fed. Rep.		1				
Guatemala		1				
Haiti		2				
India		2				
Indonesia		1				
Kampuchea		3				
Kenya		1				
Madagascar		1				
Malaysia		13				
Niger		2				
Pakistan		2				
Senegal		1				

FIELD OF SERVICE	YEAR BEGAN	PERSONNEL NOW	NEW	RELATED CHURCHES	PEOPLE GROUPS	NOTES
Sudan		1				
Tanzania		1				
Thailand		2				
Trinidad and Tobago		1				
Viet Nam, Soc. Rep.		1				
Zaire		1				

Churches of Christ in Christian Union: Foreign Missionary Department

459 E Ohio St.
Circleville OH 43113

Tel. (614) 474-8856
EXECUTIVE OFFICER: Carl E. Waggoner
ORGANIZED: 1909   AFFILIATION: EFMA
DESCRIPTION: A denominational sending agency of Wesleyan
    tradition engaged in evangelism, education and medicine.
    Also involved in disaster relief, nurturing national
    churches and linguistics.
TOTAL INCOME: $535,742   FOR OVERSEAS MINISTRIES: $456,289
PERSONNEL:
   NORTH AMERICANS OVERSEAS   NON-NORTH AMERICANS OVERSEAS: 1
         MARRIED: 46   NORTH AMERICAN ADM. STAFF: 8
      SINGLE MEN: 0   SHORT TERM: 0
    SINGLE WOMEN: 8   RETIRED: 1
     TOTAL ACTIVE: 54

FIELD OF SERVICE	YEAR BEGAN	PERSONNEL NOW	NEW	RELATED CHURCHES	PEOPLE GROUPS	NOTES
Antigua	1962			2		
Barbados	1961	2		7		
Burundi		1	1			
Dominica	1943	4	2	16		
Honduras		4				
Kenya		4				
Korea, Rep. of	1975	2	2			
Mexico	1944	6		8		
Papua New Guinea	1963	21	5	75		

Churches of God, General Conference Commission on World Missions

2200 Jennifer Ln.
Findlay OH 45840
P.O. ADDRESS:
Box 926
Findlay OH 45840

Tel. (419) 424-1961
EXECUTIVE OFFICER: Richard E. Wilkin
ORGANIZED: 1898   AFFILIATION: DOM-NCCCUSA
DESCRIPTION: A denominational sending agency of evangelical
    tradition establishing churches and involved in community
    development, general Christian education and medicine.
TOTAL INCOME: $349,600   FOR OVERSEAS MINISTRIES: $225,600
PERSONNEL:
   NORTH AMERICANS OVERSEAS   NON-NORTH AMERICANS OVERSEAS: 0
         MARRIED: 9   NORTH AMERICAN ADM. STAFF: 1
      SINGLE MEN: 1   SHORT TERM: 3

```
     SINGLE WOMEN:    9                          RETIRED:    2
                   -----
     TOTAL ACTIVE:   19
```

```
                    YEAR     PERSONNEL   RELATED    PEOPLE
FIELD OF SERVICE    BEGAN    NOW  NEW    CHURCHES   GROUPS  NOTES
```

FIELD OF SERVICE	YEAR BEGAN	PERSONNEL NOW	NEW	RELATED CHURCHES	PEOPLE GROUPS	NOTES
Bangladesh	1898	5		26		
Haiti	1967	13	2	10		
India	1898	1		1		
Venezuela	1979					1

Note: 1. Ministry in cooperation
with Church of God, Anderson, IN.

CLW Broadcasters, Inc. SEE: AMG International

CODEL (Coordination in Development, Inc.)

79 Madison Ave.
New York NY 10016

Tel. (212) 685-2030
EXECUTIVE OFFICER: Boyd Lowry
ORGANIZED: 1969   AFFILIATION: DOM-NCCCUSA
DESCRIPTION: An interdenominational, ecumenical Protestant-
    Catholic non-sending consortium involved in cooperative
    socio-economic development projects. Involved in agricultural
    assistance, development of human resources, literature, self-
    help projects and medicine. Also serves member agencies.
TOTAL INCOME: $1,564,514   FOR OVERSEAS MINISTRIES: $1,564,514
PERSONNEL:
```
     NORTH AMERICANS OVERSEAS    NON-NORTH AMERICANS OVERSEAS:    0
                MARRIED:    0        NORTH AMERICAN ADM. STAFF:    9
             SINGLE MEN:    0                      SHORT TERM:    0
           SINGLE WOMEN:    0                         RETIRED:   NR
                         -----
           TOTAL ACTIVE:    0
```

Committee on Children's Literature For Women and Children in Mission Fields, Inc.

475 Riverside Dr, Rm 670
New York NY 10115

Tel. (212) 870-2378
EXECUTIVE OFFICER: Marion Van Horne
ORGANIZED: 1912   AFFILIATION: DOM-NCCCUSA
DESCRIPTION: An interdenominational specialized service agency
    providing for the distribution of magazines and books for
    women and children overseas. Also conducts workshops for
    nationals using books/materials indigenous to those
    attending. Countries include Indonesia, Ireland and areas
    in the Middle East.
TOTAL INCOME: $50,000   FOR OVERSEAS MINISTRIES: $50,000
PERSONNEL:
```
     NORTH AMERICANS OVERSEAS    NON-NORTH AMERICANS OVERSEAS:    0
                MARRIED:    0        NORTH AMERICAN ADM. STAFF:    2
             SINGLE MEN:    0                      SHORT TERM:    0
           SINGLE WOMEN:    0                         RETIRED:    0
                         -----
           TOTAL ACTIVE:    0
```
NOTES: Income estimated by agency.

**Committee To Assist Ministry
Education Overseas (CAMEO)**

370 S Schmale Rd.
Carol Stream IL 60187
P.O. ADDRESS:
Box 852
Wheaton IL 60187

Tel. (312) 690-6177
EXECUTIVE OFFICER: Lois McKinney
ORGANIZED: 1965   AFFILIATION: EFMA/IFMA
DESCRIPTION: An interdenominational specialized educational
    service agency of the EFMA and IFMA assisting in
    theological education, theological education by extension
    (TEE), and workshops, consultations and information
    services.

TOTAL INCOME: $22,500   FOR OVERSEAS MINISTRIES: NR
PERSONNEL:

NORTH AMERICANS OVERSEAS		NON-NORTH AMERICANS OVERSEAS:	0
MARRIED:	0	NORTH AMERICAN ADM. STAFF:	NR
SINGLE MEN:	0	SHORT TERM:	0
SINGLE WOMEN:	0	RETIRED:	0
TOTAL ACTIVE:	0		

**Committee to Assist Missionary Education Overseas SEE: Committee
to Assist Ministry Education Overseas (CAMEO)**

Compassion International, Inc.

3955 Cragwood Dr.
Colorado Spgs CO 80933
P.O. ADDRESS:
Box 7000
Colorado Spgs CO 80933

Tel. (303) 596-5460
EXECUTIVE OFFICER: W. H. Erickson
ORGANIZED: 1952   AFFILIATION: EFMA-Assoc. member
DESCRIPTION: A denominational sending agency of evangelical
    tradition involved in aid and relief, education, medicine,
    community development and childcare. Provides special
    assistance for children through basic programs of family
    helper plans, children's homes, schools, special care
    centers, hostels, meals sponsorships, relief and
    community development.

TOTAL INCOME: $11,221,207   FOR OVERSEAS MINISTRIES: $11,133,846
PERSONNEL:

NORTH AMERICANS OVERSEAS		NON-NORTH AMERICANS OVERSEAS:	3
MARRIED:	14	NORTH AMERICAN ADM. STAFF:	18
SINGLE MEN:	0	SHORT TERM:	0
SINGLE WOMEN:	3	RETIRED:	1
TOTAL ACTIVE:	17		

FIELD OF SERVICE	YEAR BEGAN	PERSONNEL NOW	NEW	RELATED CHURCHES	PEOPLE GROUPS	NOTES
Belize	1979					
Bolivia	1975	1	1			
Brazil	1975					
Burma	1972	6	4			1
Burundi	1979	1	1			

252

FIELD OF SERVICE	YEAR BEGAN	PERSONNEL NOW	NEW	RELATED CHURCHES	PEOPLE GROUPS	NOTES
Colombia	1973	4				2
Dominican Republic	1970	4	3			
Ecuador	1975					
El Salvador	1976	2	2			
Haiti	1968	5	5			
Honduras	1974					
Hong-Kong	1974					
India	1968	7	3			3
Indonesia	1968	17	3			4
Jamaica	1970					
Korea, Rep. of	1952	10	7			5
Liberia	1975					
Malaysia	1973					
Mexico	1979					
Nicaragua	1974					
Papua New Guinea	1978					
Paraguay	1975					
Peru	1979					
Philippines	1974					
Rwanda	1979					
Singapore	1969					
Spain	1973					
Thailand	1970	1	1			
Venezuela	1973					

Note: 1. Has 3 part-time personnel.
2. Has 1 part-time person.
3. Has 3 part-time personnel.
4. Has 14 part-time personnel.
5. Has 2 part-time personnel.

Compassion of Canada

551 Knightshill Rd.
London ON N6J 3A1
Canada
P.O. ADDRESS:
Box 5591
London ON N6A 5G8
Canada

Tel. (519) 686-6788
EXECUTIVE OFFICER: James Somerville
ORGANIZED: 1964
DESCRIPTION: A nondenominational service organization of
    evangelical tradition engaged in aid and/or relief,
    community development, evangelism, fund raising, serving
    other agencies and a special emphasis on childcare.
TOTAL INCOME: $1,360,228   FOR OVERSEAS MINISTRIES: $1,293,028
PERSONNEL:

NORTH AMERICANS OVERSEAS		NON-NORTH AMERICANS OVERSEAS:	NR
MARRIED:	0	NORTH AMERICAN ADM. STAFF:	12
SINGLE MEN:	0	SHORT TERM:	0
SINGLE WOMEN:	0	RETIRED:	NR
TOTAL ACTIVE:	0		

Compassion Relief and Development, Inc.

3955 Cragwood Dr.
Colorado Spgs CO 80933
P.O. ADDRESS:
Box 7000
Colorado Spgs CO 80933

Tel. (303) 596-5460
EXECUTIVE OFFICER: Donald J. Smith
ORGANIZED: 1972
DESCRIPTION: An interdenominational specialized service agency
   of evangelical tradition engaged in aid and relief in
   disaster. Also offers technical and agricultural
   assistance, aids in development of human resources and
   community development and serves other agencies.
TOTAL INCOME: $682,469   FOR OVERSEAS MINISTRIES: $649,300
PERSONNEL:

NORTH AMERICANS OVERSEAS		NON-NORTH AMERICANS OVERSEAS:	15
MARRIED:	NR	NORTH AMERICAN ADM. STAFF:	3
SINGLE MEN:	NR	SHORT TERM:	2
SINGLE WOMEN:	NR	RETIRED:	2
TOTAL ACTIVE:	12		

Compassion, Inc. SEE: Compassion International, Inc.

Concordia Tract Mission

P.O. ADDRESS:
Box 201
St. Louis MO 63166

Tel. (314) 664-7000
EXECUTIVE OFFICER: Emil W. Benz
ORGANIZED: 1958
DESCRIPTION: A denominational specialized service agency of
   Lutheran tradition engaged in evangelism and distributing
   Christian literature in 35 languages.
TOTAL INCOME: $65,000   FOR OVERSEAS MINISTRIES: $0
PERSONNEL:

NORTH AMERICANS OVERSEAS		NON-NORTH AMERICANS OVERSEAS:	0
MARRIED:	0	NORTH AMERICAN ADM. STAFF:	4
SINGLE MEN:	0	SHORT TERM:	0
SINGLE WOMEN:	0	RETIRED:	0
TOTAL ACTIVE:	0		

Congregational Christian Churches of the U.S. SEE: National Association of Congregational Christian Churches

Congregational Holiness Church
Foreign Mission Dept.

3888 Fayetteville Hwy.
Griffin GA 30223

Tel. (404) 228-4833
EXECUTIVE OFFICER: Leon M. Reese
ORGANIZED: 1921
DESCRIPTION: A denominational sending agency of Pentecostal
   tradition establishing churches and engaged in Bible
   distribution, radio and TV broadcasting, church construction
   or financing and theological education.
TOTAL INCOME: $110,000   FOR OVERSEAS MINISTRIES: $110,000
PERSONNEL:

NORTH AMERICANS OVERSEAS		NON-NORTH AMERICANS OVERSEAS:	2
MARRIED:	6	NORTH AMERICAN ADM. STAFF:	4
SINGLE MEN:	0	SHORT TERM:	2

```
     SINGLE WOMEN:      0                           RETIRED:    NR
                     -----
     TOTAL ACTIVE:      6
----------------------------------------------------------------------
                    YEAR    PERSONNEL   RELATED   PEOPLE
FIELD OF SERVICE    BEGAN   NOW    NEW  CHURCHES  GROUPS  NOTES
----------------------------------------------------------------------
Brazil              1972                   15
Costa Rica          1966                   10
Cuba                1955                    7
Guatemala           1974                    7
Honduras            1967                   47
Mexico              1963    5      1       75
```

Congregational Holiness Church, World Missions Department SEE: Congregational Holiness Church, Foreign Missions Department

Conservative Baptist Association of America

25 W 560 Geneva Rd.
Wheaton IL 60187
P.O. ADDRESS:
Box 828
Wheaton IL 60187

```
Tel. (312) 653-4900
EXECUTIVE OFFICER: Rufus Jones
ORGANIZED: 1950   AFFILIATION: EFMA
DESCRIPTION:  A denominational sending agency of Baptist
    tradition engaged in evangelism, church planting, education
    and ministry to servicemen.
TOTAL INCOME:   $2,930,000      FOR OVERSEAS MINISTRIES:    NR
PERSONNEL:
    NORTH AMERICANS OVERSEAS   NON-NORTH AMERICANS OVERSEAS:    4
           MARRIED:   32          NORTH AMERICAN ADM. STAFF:   14
        SINGLE MEN:    0                        SHORT TERM:     0
      SINGLE WOMEN:    1                           RETIRED:     9
                     -----
      TOTAL ACTIVE:   33
----------------------------------------------------------------------
                    YEAR    PERSONNEL   RELATED   PEOPLE
FIELD OF SERVICE    BEGAN   NOW    NEW  CHURCHES  GROUPS  NOTES
----------------------------------------------------------------------
Belize              1960    2               6
Costa Rica          1967    2      2        6
Guam                1957    2      2        2
Honduras            1951    10     4       78
Mexico              1952    9              34
Puerto Rico                 2               4
```

Conservative Baptist Foreign Mission Society

25 West 560 Geneva Rd.
Wheaton IL 60187
P.O. ADDRESS:
Box 5
Wheaton IL 60187

```
Tel. (312) 665-1200
EXECUTIVE OFFICER: Warren W. Webster
ORGANIZED: 1943   AFFILIATION: EFMA
DESCRIPTION:  A denominational sending agency of Baptist
    tradition engaged in evangelism, establishing churches and
    serving national churches. Also involved in education,
    literature, linguistics, medicine, radio and support
    of nationals.
TOTAL INCOME:   $9,057,172   FOR OVERSEAS MINISTRIES:  $9,057,172
```

PERSONNEL:
NORTH AMERICANS OVERSEAS   NON-NORTH AMERICANS OVERSEAS: 2
       MARRIED: 414   NORTH AMERICAN ADM. STAFF: 0
    SINGLE MEN: 7   SHORT TERM: 114
  SINGLE WOMEN: 80   RETIRED: 16

  TOTAL ACTIVE: 501

FIELD OF SERVICE	YEAR BEGAN	PERSONNEL NOW	NEW	RELATED CHURCHES	PEOPLE GROUPS	NOTES
Argentina	1948	40	5	99	4	
Austria	1970	10	2	1	2	
Brazil	1946	56	8	38	6	
France	1962	12	2	5	3	
Hong-Kong	1963	10	4	5	3	
India	1945	13	1	177	4	
Indonesia	1961	40	9	61	4	
Italy	1947	19	5	10	2	
Ivory Coast	1947	75	12	133	5	
Japan	1947	39	13	42	3	
Jordan	1956	8	4	5	2	
Kenya	1975	6		6	3	
Madagascar	1965	8		7	3	
Middle East-general	1977	2	2		1	
Pakistan	1954	15		8	6	
Philippines	1952	47	6	82	9	
Portugal	1949	4		4	1	
Rwanda	1972	8	2	93	2	
Senegal	1962	14		2	2	
Taiwan Rep of China	1952	27	5	20	4	
Zaire	1946	45	10	557	6	

Conservative Baptist Haiti Mission
SEE: Baptist Haiti Mission, Inc.

Conservative Congregational
Christian Conference

25 W 626 St. Charles Rd.
Wheaton IL 60187

Tel. (312) 682-3110
EXECUTIVE OFFICER: George S. Buhl
ORGANIZED: 1948
DESCRIPTION: A denominational agency of Congregational
    tradition involved in overseas work only through its
    member churches. These in turn support other agencies.
TOTAL INCOME: $63,991   FOR OVERSEAS MINISTRIES: $0
PERSONNEL:
NORTH AMERICANS OVERSEAS   NON-NORTH AMERICANS OVERSEAS: 0
       MARRIED: 0   NORTH AMERICAN ADM. STAFF: 0
    SINGLE MEN: 0   SHORT TERM: 0
  SINGLE WOMEN: 0   RETIRED: 0

  TOTAL ACTIVE: 0
NOTES: Total contributions to missions by churches
        belonging to Conference is $1,849,258 distributed
        through other agencies.

Conservative Mennonite Board of
Missions and Charities

9920 Rosedale M.C. Rd.
Irwin OH 43029

Tel. (614) 857-1366
EXECUTIVE OFFICER: David I. Miller
ORGANIZED: 1919
DESCRIPTION: A denominational sending agency of Mennonite and
    Anabaptist tradition engaged in evangelism, agricultural
    assistance, aid and/or relief, church planting and community
    development.
TOTAL INCOME: $434,330   FOR OVERSEAS MINISTRIES: $225,850
PERSONNEL:
    NORTH AMERICANS OVERSEAS   NON-NORTH AMERICANS OVERSEAS: 2
            MARRIED: 26   NORTH AMERICAN ADM. STAFF: 8
         SINGLE MEN: 6   SHORT TERM: 19
       SINGLE WOMEN: 11   RETIRED: 0

       TOTAL ACTIVE: 43

FIELD OF SERVICE	YEAR BEGAN	PERSONNEL NOW	NEW	RELATED CHURCHES	PEOPLE GROUPS	NOTES
Costa Rica	1962	11	7	12	1	
Germany, Fed. Rep.	1952	6	3			
Nicaragua	1968	26	19	9		

Correll Missionary Ministries

4742 Old Woods Rd.
Charlotte NC 28209
P.O. ADDRESS:
Box 11793
Charlotte NC 28220

Tel. (704) 527-1195
EXECUTIVE OFFICER: Sidney Correll
ORGANIZED: 1978
DESCRIPTION: A denominational specialized service agency of
    evangelical tradition engaged in aid and/or relief, Bible
    distribution, broadcasting, fund raising and transmittal,
    literature distribution, medical supplies and nurture or
    support of national churches.
TOTAL INCOME: $31,336   FOR OVERSEAS MINISTRIES: $31,336
PERSONNEL:
    NORTH AMERICANS OVERSEAS   NON-NORTH AMERICANS OVERSEAS: 0
            MARRIED: 0   NORTH AMERICAN ADM. STAFF: 0
         SINGLE MEN: 0   SHORT TERM: 0
       SINGLE WOMEN: 0   RETIRED: 0

       TOTAL ACTIVE: 0

Council for Cooperation with the
Dominican Evangelical Church

475 Riverside Dr. Rm 301
New York NY 10115

DESCRIPTION: No data is reported for this agency for one of the
    following reasons: it is currently inactive or no longer
    exists; it has terminated overseas ministries or has ceased
    to operate as a North American entity.

CROP SEE: Church World Service, Division of DOM-NCCCUSA

Crusade Evangelism International

1106 Dearness Dr. Unit 5B
London ON N6E 1N9
Canada
P.O. ADDRESS:
Box 2
London ON N6A 4V3
Canada

Tel. (519) 681-3137
EXECUTIVE OFFICER: E. Barry Moore
ORGANIZED: 1960
DESCRIPTION: An interdenominational service agency of
evangelical tradition engaged in mass evangelism. Also
involved in pre-crusade education for evangelism.
TOTAL INCOME: $522,000   FOR OVERSEAS MINISTRIES: $87,000
PERSONNEL:

NORTH AMERICANS OVERSEAS		NON-NORTH AMERICANS OVERSEAS:	0
MARRIED:	0	NORTH AMERICAN ADM. STAFF:	8
SINGLE MEN:	0	SHORT TERM:	0
SINGLE WOMEN:	0	RETIRED:	0
TOTAL ACTIVE:	0		

Cumberland Presbyterian Church, Board of Missions

1978 Union Ave.
Memphis TN 38104
P.O. ADDRESS:
Box 40149
Memphis TN 38104

Tel. (901) 274-7513
EXECUTIVE OFFICER: Joe Matlock
ORGANIZED: 1880   AFFILIATION: DOM-NCCCUSA
DESCRIPTION: A denominational sending agency of evangelical
and Presbyterian tradition. The Board's Division of
World Missions, responsible for work outside the USA, is
engaged in church planting, missionary orientation and
training, evangelism and general Christian education.
TOTAL INCOME: $663,761   FOR OVERSEAS MINISTRIES: $265,678
PERSONNEL:

NORTH AMERICANS OVERSEAS		NON-NORTH AMERICANS OVERSEAS:	4
MARRIED:	6	NORTH AMERICAN ADM. STAFF:	1
SINGLE MEN:	0	SHORT TERM:	2
SINGLE WOMEN:	1	RETIRED:	1
TOTAL ACTIVE:	7		

FIELD OF SERVICE	YEAR BEGAN	PERSONNEL NOW	NEW	RELATED CHURCHES	PEOPLE GROUPS	NOTES
Hong-Kong	1949	1		4		1

Note: 1. Also serves in Macau.

D.M. Stearns Missionary Fund, Inc.

147 W School House Ln.
Philadelphia PA 19144

Tel. (215) 438-5040
EXECUTIVE OFFICER: Charles F. Magel
ORGANIZED: 1922
DESCRIPTION: No current information available. Information
from 1976 directory. A nondenominational fund
transmitting agency of evangelical tradition channeling
funds to approximately 805 mission agencies and
individuals.
TOTAL INCOME: $690,000   FOR OVERSEAS MINISTRIES: NR

PERSONNEL:

NORTH AMERICANS OVERSEAS		NON-NORTH AMERICANS OVERSEAS:	NR
MARRIED:	0	NORTH AMERICAN ADM. STAFF:	NR
SINGLE MEN:	0	SHORT TERM:	NR
SINGLE WOMEN:	0	RETIRED:	NR
TOTAL ACTIVE:	0		

NOTES: Income estimated by MARC.

David C. Cook Foundation

Cook Square
Elgin IL 60120

Tel. (312) 741-2400
EXECUTIVE OFFICER: David C. Cook, III
ORGANIZED: 1944
DESCRIPTION: A nondenominational, non-sending operating
    foundation involved in research and development of
    Christian programs in literacy, literature and
    communications training. Cooperates internationally with
    other Christian publishers and media agencies.
TOTAL INCOME: $368,449   FOR OVERSEAS MINISTRIES: $198,759
PERSONNEL:

NORTH AMERICANS OVERSEAS		NON-NORTH AMERICANS OVERSEAS:	0
MARRIED:	0	NORTH AMERICAN ADM. STAFF:	0
SINGLE MEN:	0	SHORT TERM:	0
SINGLE WOMEN:	0	RETIRED:	0
TOTAL ACTIVE:	0		

Daystar Communications, Inc.

392 E Third Ave.
Eugene OR 97401
P.O. ADDRESS:
Box 10123
Eugene OR 97440

Tel. (503) 342-6712
EXECUTIVE OFFICER: Stephen Talitwala
ORGANIZED: 1963
DESCRIPTION: A nondenominational, international sending and
    specialized agency of evangelical tradition providing
    mission related research assistance to other agencies.
    Research is conducted in communications, church growth,
    literature, education and development. Trains national
    workers and missionaries in communication and Christian
    leadership. Sponsors Daystar International Institute.
TOTAL INCOME: $326,700   FOR OVERSEAS MINISTRIES: $326,700
PERSONNEL:

NORTH AMERICANS OVERSEAS		NON-NORTH AMERICANS OVERSEAS:	10
MARRIED:	11	NORTH AMERICAN ADM. STAFF:	2
SINGLE MEN:	0	SHORT TERM:	5
SINGLE WOMEN:	2	RETIRED:	0
TOTAL ACTIVE:	13		

FIELD OF SERVICE	YEAR BEGAN	PERSONNEL NOW	PERSONNEL NEW	RELATED CHURCHES	PEOPLE GROUPS	NOTES
Kenya	1974	22	11		15	
Zimbabwe	1963	1			1	

259

**Defenders of the Christian Faith
Movement, Inc.**

800 Flushing Ave.
Brooklyn NY 11237
P.O. ADDRESS:
Box 547 Wycoff Hgt. Sta.
Brooklyn NY 11206

Tel. (212) 455-7035
EXECUTIVE OFFICER: Rafel Matos
ORGANIZED: 1946
DESCRIPTION: A denominational agency of evangelical, Baptist
    and Pentecostal tradition engaged in evangelism to
    Spanish-speaking peoples and the establishment of
    churches. Also involved in aid and/or relief, broadcasting
    and Bible distribution.

TOTAL INCOME: $8,000   FOR OVERSEAS MINISTRIES: NR
PERSONNEL:
    NORTH AMERICANS OVERSEAS   NON-NORTH AMERICANS OVERSEAS: 0
                MARRIED: 0   NORTH AMERICAN ADM. STAFF: 0
             SINGLE MEN: 0   SHORT TERM: 0
           SINGLE WOMEN: 0   RETIRED: 0

        TOTAL ACTIVE: 0
NOTES: Income estimated by agency.

FIELD OF SERVICE	YEAR BEGAN	PERSONNEL NOW	PERSONNEL NEW	RELATED CHURCHES	PEOPLE GROUPS	NOTES
Colombia	1978			4		
Guatemala	1958			20		

Dominion Food for the Hungry SEE: Food for the Hungry/Canada

Douglas Memorial Children's Homes SEE: World Missionary Evangelism, Inc.

Eastern European Mission

232 N Lake Ave.
Pasadena CA 91101

Tel. (213) 796-5425
EXECUTIVE OFFICER: Walter E. Zurfluh
ORGANIZED: 1927   AFFILIATION: EFMA
DESCRIPTION: A nondenominational sending agency of evangelical
    tradition supporting nationals and engaged in radio and TV
    broadcasting, literature distribution, fund raising, mass
    evangelism and support of nationals.

TOTAL INCOME: $178,796   FOR OVERSEAS MINISTRIES: $154,622
PERSONNEL:
    NORTH AMERICANS OVERSEAS   NON-NORTH AMERICANS OVERSEAS: 0
                MARRIED: 2   NORTH AMERICAN ADM. STAFF: 4
             SINGLE MEN: 0   SHORT TERM: 0
           SINGLE WOMEN: 0   RETIRED: 1

        TOTAL ACTIVE: 2

FIELD OF SERVICE	YEAR BEGAN	PERSONNEL NOW	PERSONNEL NEW	RELATED CHURCHES	PEOPLE GROUPS	NOTES
Austria	1962	2	2	1		

FIELD OF SERVICE	YEAR BEGAN	PERSONNEL NOW	PERSONNEL NEW	RELATED CHURCHES	PEOPLE GROUPS	NOTES
Germany, Fed. Rep.	1951	2	1		1	
Greece	1953	5		1		
Netherlands	1955	2	1	1		
Poland	1927	7	4		1	
Yugoslavia	1946	6		2		

Eastern Mennonite Board of Missions and Charities

Oak Lane and Brandt Blvd
Salunga PA 17538

Tel. (717) 898-2251
EXECUTIVE OFFICER: Paul G. Landis
ORGANIZED: 1914
DESCRIPTION: A denominational sending agency of Mennonite
   tradition establishing churches and engaged in community
   development, aid and/or relief, theological education
   and support of national churches.
TOTAL INCOME: $3,300,000 FOR OVERSEAS MINISTRIES: $1,800,000
PERSONNEL:
   NORTH AMERICANS OVERSEAS   NON-NORTH AMERICANS OVERSEAS: 0
           MARRIED: 70   NORTH AMERICAN ADM. STAFF: 0
        SINGLE MEN: 2   SHORT TERM: 49
      SINGLE WOMEN: 16   RETIRED: 18

      TOTAL ACTIVE: 88

FIELD OF SERVICE	YEAR BEGAN	PERSONNEL NOW	PERSONNEL NEW	RELATED CHURCHES	PEOPLE GROUPS	NOTES
Belize	1960	12	8	5		
Brazil	1975	2				
Ethiopia	1948	7	3	14		
France	1955	2		2		
Germany, Fed. Rep.	1957	3	2	8		
Guatemala	1968	17	2	29		
Haiti	1968	2				
Honduras	1950	17	7	35		
Hong-Kong	1965	2		1		
Indonesia	1974	2		5		
Kenya	1964	33	17	48		
Philippines	1971	4	2	22		
Poland		2	2			
Sudan	1972	1				
Swaziland	1971	5	3			
Tanzania	1934	31	14	650		
Venezuela	1978	2	2	1		
Yugoslavia	1971	3	2			

EFMA Purchasing Division SEE: EFMA, Mission Association Section

Elim Fellowship, Inc.

7245 College St.
Lima NY 14485

Tel. (716) 582-1230
EXECUTIVE OFFICER: Carlton Spencer
ORGANIZED: 1947
DESCRIPTION: An interdenominational/denominational sending
   agency of Pentecostal tradition engaged in radio and TV
   broadcasting, church planting, fund transmittal, education
   and nurture or support of national churches.

TOTAL INCOME: $677,917   FOR OVERSEAS MINISTRIES: $574,267
PERSONNEL:
   NORTH AMERICANS OVERSEAS   NON-NORTH AMERICANS OVERSEAS: 0
         MARRIED: 105   NORTH AMERICAN ADM. STAFF: 7
     SINGLE MEN: 1   SHORT TERM: 10
   SINGLE WOMEN: 8   RETIRED: 0

    TOTAL ACTIVE: 114

FIELD OF SERVICE	YEAR BEGAN	PERSONNEL NOW	PERSONNEL NEW	RELATED CHURCHES	PEOPLE GROUPS	NOTES
Argentina	1956	4		20		
Burundi	1968	4	4	50		
Colombia	1964	5		10		
Costa Rica	1966	8	4	20		
Germany, Fed. Rep.	1973	2				
Guatemala	1974	6	4			
Haiti	1969	2				
Indonesia	1972	2	2			
Israel	1977	2	2			
Japan	1975	4	2			
Kenya	1940	34	11	600		
Korea, Rep. of	1942	3				
Mexico	1962	10	4			
Nigeria	1975	4	3			
Paraguay	1974	3	2			
Peru	1964	5	1	40		
Philippines	1966	8		30		
Spain	1966	4	2			
Tanzania	1955	4		100		
Uganda	1962	3		300		
Zaire	1962	2		600		

Emmanuel International

R.R. 4
Stouffville ON L0H 1L0
Canada
P.O. ADDRESS:
Box 50
Stouffville ON L0H 1L0
Canada

Tel. (416) 640-2111
EXECUTIVE OFFICER: George G. Middleton
ORGANIZED: 1975
DESCRIPTION: An interdenominational agency of evangelical
   tradition sending short-term missionaries to provide
   relief and support of national churches. Also engaged in
   evangelism, community development and missionary
   orientation and training.
TOTAL INCOME: $508,353   FOR OVERSEAS MINISTRIES: $426,816
PERSONNEL:
   NORTH AMERICANS OVERSEAS   NON-NORTH AMERICANS OVERSEAS: 2
         MARRIED: 8   NORTH AMERICAN ADM. STAFF: 9
     SINGLE MEN: 9   SHORT TERM: 22
   SINGLE WOMEN: 7   RETIRED: 0

    TOTAL ACTIVE: 24
NOTES: All overseas staff are short-term except
   one couple.

FIELD OF SERVICE	YEAR BEGAN	PERSONNEL NOW	NEW	RELATED CHURCHES	PEOPLE GROUPS	NOTES
Dominica	1979	2				
Ethiopia	1975					
Guatemala	1977	6				
Haiti	1978	12				
Nigeria	1979	6				
Philippines	1980	11				
Upper Volta	1980	1				

Episcopal Church Missionary Community (Anglican Missionary Training and Fellowship Center)

1567 Elizabeth St.
Pasadena CA 91104

Tel. (213) 797-8323
EXECUTIVE OFFICER: Walter W. Hannum
ORGANIZED: 1974
DESCRIPTION: A denominational service agency of Episcopal
    tradition providing missionary orientation and training
    and information services for those going overseas. Also
    engaged in missionary education and recruiting.
TOTAL INCOME: $30,000   FOR OVERSEAS MINISTRIES: $0
PERSONNEL:
    NORTH AMERICANS OVERSEAS   NON-NORTH AMERICANS OVERSEAS: NR
           MARRIED: 0   NORTH AMERICAN ADM. STAFF: NR
        SINGLE MEN: 0   SHORT TERM: 0
      SINGLE WOMEN: 0   RETIRED: 0

       TOTAL ACTIVE: 0

Episcopal Church SEE: Protestant Episcopal Church

Erhlin Christian Polio Home

1021 Santa Fe Ave.
Albany CA 94706

EXECUTIVE OFFICER: Donald R. Roberts
ORGANIZED: 1964
DESCRIPTION: A nondenominational special service agency of
    evangelical tradition ministering to children with polio
    in Taiwan. Provides medical assistance, living
    accomodations and contributes to their social welfare.
TOTAL INCOME: $9,495   FOR OVERSEAS MINISTRIES: $9,495
PERSONNEL:
    NORTH AMERICANS OVERSEAS   NON-NORTH AMERICANS OVERSEAS: 0
           MARRIED: 0   NORTH AMERICAN ADM. STAFF: 0
        SINGLE MEN: 0   SHORT TERM: 0
      SINGLE WOMEN: 1   RETIRED: 0

       TOTAL ACTIVE: 1
NOTES: Overseas income estimated by MARC.

FIELD OF SERVICE	YEAR BEGAN	PERSONNEL NOW	NEW	RELATED CHURCHES	PEOPLE GROUPS	NOTES
Taiwan Rep of China	1964	1		10	1	

European Christian Mission SEE: Mission to Europe's Millions

European Evangelistic Crusade SEE: Fellowship of Evangelical Churches in Canada

European Evangelistic Soceity

113 Sherman Ave.
Montgomery IL 60538
P.O. ADDRESS:
Box 268
Aurora IL 60507

Tel. (312) 896-4333
EXECUTIVE OFFICER: W.L. Thompson
ORGANIZED: 1932
DESCRIPTION: A nondenominational sending agency of Christian
    "Restoration Movement" tradition establishing churches
    and engaged in theological education, evangelism and
    literature production. Also involved in research on New
    Testament and church origins.
TOTAL INCOME: $114,250   FOR OVERSEAS MINISTRIES: $114,250
PERSONNEL:
    NORTH AMERICANS OVERSEAS   NON-NORTH AMERICANS OVERSEAS: 2
             MARRIED: 2   NORTH AMERICAN ADM. STAFF: 1
          SINGLE MEN: 0   SHORT TERM: 0
        SINGLE WOMEN: 0   RETIRED: 0

        TOTAL ACTIVE: 2

FIELD OF SERVICE	YEAR BEGAN	PERSONNEL NOW	NEW	RELATED CHURCHES	PEOPLE GROUPS	NOTES
Germany, Fed. Rep.	1949	2		1		1

    Note: 1. Has research institute.

Evangel Bible Translators

226 S Glassell
Orange CA 92667
P.O. ADDRESS:
Box 5070
Orange CA 92667

Tel. (714) 997-3703
EXECUTIVE OFFICER: H. Syvelle Phillips
ORGANIZED: 1976
DESCRIPTION: A nondenominational sending agency of Pentecostal
    tradition engaged in missionary orientation and training,
    Bible translation and distribution, linguistics and
    literacy.
TOTAL INCOME: $199,000   FOR OVERSEAS MINISTRIES: $70,000
PERSONNEL:
    NORTH AMERICANS OVERSEAS   NON-NORTH AMERICANS OVERSEAS: 1
             MARRIED: 8   NORTH AMERICAN ADM. STAFF: 7
          SINGLE MEN: 0   SHORT TERM: 3
        SINGLE WOMEN: 1   RETIRED: 0

        TOTAL ACTIVE: 9

FIELD OF SERVICE	YEAR BEGAN	PERSONNEL NOW	NEW	RELATED CHURCHES	PEOPLE GROUPS	NOTES
France	1978	2				
Haiti	1978	2				
India	1978	1				

FIELD OF SERVICE	YEAR BEGAN	PERSONNEL NOW	PERSONNEL NEW	RELATED CHURCHES	PEOPLE GROUPS	NOTES
Peru	1979	2				

Evangelical Alliance Mission (TEAM)

400 S Main Place
Carol Stream IL 60187
P.O. ADDRESS:
Box 969
Wheaton IL 60187

708

Tel. (312) 653-5300
EXECUTIVE OFFICER: Richard M. Winchell *Res. 668-5918*
ORGANIZED: 1890   AFFILIATION: IFMA
DESCRIPTION: An interdenominational sending agency of
    evangelical tradition committed primarily to evangelism,
    church planting and development. Involved in education,
    literature, linguistics, medicine, radio and other
    specialized services.
TOTAL INCOME: $10,899,110   FOR OVERSEAS MINISTRIES: $10,899,110
PERSONNEL:

NORTH AMERICANS OVERSEAS		NON-NORTH AMERICANS OVERSEAS:	26
MARRIED:	711	NORTH AMERICAN ADM. STAFF:	79
SINGLE MEN:	10	SHORT TERM:	197
SINGLE WOMEN:	184	RETIRED:	82
TOTAL ACTIVE:	905		

FIELD OF SERVICE	YEAR BEGAN	PERSONNEL NOW	PERSONNEL NEW	RELATED CHURCHES	PEOPLE GROUPS	NOTES
Austria	1965	21	2	3	2	
Chad	1969	29	7	537	8	
Colombia	1923	30	6	130	1	
Europe-general	1960	4		1	1	
France	1953	37	9	1	2	
India	1892	53	3	83	4	
Indonesia	1952	63	21	300	9	
Japan	1891	149	35	227	1	
Korea, Rep. of	1953	22	4		1	
Netherlands Antilles	1931	23	5	10	1	
Pakistan	1946	49	7	19	1	
Peru	1962	9	1	1	1	
Portugal	1936	9		9	1	
South Africa	1892	96	7	309	7	
Spain	1953	17	3	11	1	
Sri Lanka	1955	2	2	1	1	
Taiwan Rep of China	1951	74	19	27	1	
Trinidad and Tobago	1964	14	6	10	1	
United Arab Emirates	1960	37	15	8	3	
Venezuela	1906	117	25	136	1	
Zimbabwe	1942	56	10	65	2	

Evangelical Alliance Mission of Canada, Inc.

70 Froom Crescent
Regina SK S4N 1S7
Canada
P.O. ADDRESS:
Box 890
Regina SK S4P 3B2
Canada

Tel. (306) 525-5444
EXECUTIVE OFFICER: Richard Winchell

ORGANIZED: 1890   AFFILIATION: IFMA
DESCRIPTION: An interdenominational sending agency of
    evangelical and fundamentalist tradition establishing
    churches and engaged in secular and theological education,
    radio and TV broadcasting, correspondence courses,
    evangelism and medicine.
TOTAL INCOME: $1,089,767   FOR OVERSEAS MINISTRIES: $937,562
PERSONNEL:
    NORTH AMERICANS OVERSEAS   NON-NORTH AMERICANS OVERSEAS: 0
              MARRIED: 66   NORTH AMERICAN ADM. STAFF: 9
           SINGLE MEN: 0   SHORT TERM: 7
         SINGLE WOMEN: 34   RETIRED: 6

        TOTAL ACTIVE: 100

FIELD OF SERVICE	YEAR BEGAN	PERSONNEL NOW	NEW	RELATED CHURCHES	PEOPLE GROUPS	NOTES
Austria	1965	1		4		
Chad	1969	20	4	600		
Colombia	1918	1	1	119		
France	1952	4	4	15		
India	1903	18		58		
Japan	1891	10		125		
Netherlands Antilles	1931	1		12		
Pakistan	1947	6	2	6		
Peru	1961	1				
South Africa	1892	5		150		
Taiwan Rep of China	1951	5	2	20		
United Arab Emirates	1961	5	1	3		
Venezuela	1906	12	3	133		
Zimbabwe	1939	10	2	100		

Evangelical Baptist Churches in Canada SEE: Fellowship of Evangelical Baptist Churches in Canada

Evangelical Baptist Missions, Inc.

426 S U.S. Highway 31
Kokomo IN 46901
P.O. ADDRESS:
Box 2225
Kokomo IN 46901

Tel. (317) 453-4488
EXECUTIVE OFFICER: David L. Marshall
ORGANIZED: 1928
DESCRIPTION: A denominational sending agency of Baptist and
    fundamentalist tradition establishing churches and engaged
    in evangelism, theological education, literature distribution
    and motion pictures.
TOTAL INCOME: $1,357,847   FOR OVERSEAS MINISTRIES: $1,357,847
PERSONNEL:
    NORTH AMERICANS OVERSEAS   NON-NORTH AMERICANS OVERSEAS: 0
              MARRIED: 96   NORTH AMERICAN ADM. STAFF: 7
           SINGLE MEN: 0   SHORT TERM: 1
         SINGLE WOMEN: 10   RETIRED: 0

        TOTAL ACTIVE: 106

FIELD OF SERVICE	YEAR BEGAN	PERSONNEL NOW	NEW	RELATED CHURCHES	PEOPLE GROUPS	NOTES
Argentina	1974	6	4	2		

266

FIELD OF SERVICE	YEAR BEGAN	PERSONNEL NOW	PERSONNEL NEW	RELATED CHURCHES	PEOPLE GROUPS	NOTES
Australia	1972	6	4	3		
Benin	1966	3		7	1	
France	1956	22	8	7	1	
Germany, Fed. Rep.	1977	2	2			
Ivory Coast	1979	2	2			
Mali	1951	12	4	4	2	
Martinique	1946	8		7		
Niger	1929	19	4	6	1	
Sweden	1975	2		1		
United Kingdom	1976	5	5	1		
Zambia	1979	2	2	1		

Evangelical Bible Mission, Inc.

Danks Corner Rd.
Summerfield FL 32691
P.O. ADDRESS:
Drawer 189
Summerfield FL 32691

Tel. (904) 245-2560
EXECUTIVE OFFICER: Jacob A. Miller
ORGANIZED: 1939
DESCRIPTION: An interdenominational sending agency of Wesleyan
    and Holiness tradition engaged in church planting,
    evangelism, general Christian education, theological
    education and aviation.
TOTAL INCOME: $244,751   FOR OVERSEAS MINISTRIES: $172,394
PERSONNEL:
    NORTH AMERICANS OVERSEAS   NON-NORTH AMERICANS OVERSEAS: 0
        MARRIED: 30   NORTH AMERICAN ADM. STAFF: 6
    SINGLE MEN: 0   SHORT TERM: 0
    SINGLE WOMEN: 6   RETIRED: 0

    TOTAL ACTIVE: 36

FIELD OF SERVICE	YEAR BEGAN	PERSONNEL NOW	PERSONNEL NEW	RELATED CHURCHES	PEOPLE GROUPS	NOTES
Haiti	1943	4		5		
Nigeria	1970			10		
Papua New Guinea	1948	32	12	100	3	

Evangelical Christian Education Ministries Inc.

845 Chicago Ave. Ste 224
Evanston IL 60202
P.O. ADDRESS:
Box 3009
Evanston IL 60204

Tel. (312) 328-4060
EXECUTIVE OFFICER: Jerry Owsley
ORGANIZED: 1968
DESCRIPTION: An interdenominational fund raising and support
    agency of evangelical tradition assisting Christian
    educational institutions overseas, primarily theological
    seminaries and indigenous Bible schools.
TOTAL INCOME: $75,000   FOR OVERSEAS MINISTRIES: $75,000
PERSONNEL:
    NORTH AMERICANS OVERSEAS   NON-NORTH AMERICANS OVERSEAS: 0
        MARRIED: 2   NORTH AMERICAN ADM. STAFF: 1
    SINGLE MEN: 0   SHORT TERM: 2

```
            SINGLE WOMEN:      0                          RETIRED:      0
                            -----
               TOTAL ACTIVE:   2
--------------------------------------------------------------------------
                            YEAR      PERSONNEL   RELATED   PEOPLE
FIELD OF SERVICE            BEGAN     NOW   NEW   CHURCHES  GROUPS  NOTES
--------------------------------------------------------------------------
France                      1971       2
```

Evangelical Congregational Church
Division of Missions

100 W Park Ave.
Myerstown PA 17067

Tel. (717) 866-2181
EXECUTIVE OFFICER: Richard A. Cattermole
ORGANIZED: 1922   AFFILIATION: EFMA
DESCRIPTION: A denominational sending agency of evangelical
    and Wesleyan tradition establishing churches and
    supporting national churches and workers. Missionaries
    are sent both directly and through other agencies.
    Fifty-four missionaries are serving under boards in 16
    countries.
TOTAL INCOME: $615,428   FOR OVERSEAS MINISTRIES: $334,145
PERSONNEL:

```
    NORTH AMERICANS OVERSEAS    NON-NORTH AMERICANS OVERSEAS:      0
            MARRIED:   36           NORTH AMERICAN ADM. STAFF:      3
          SINGLE MEN:   4                       SHORT TERM:     24
        SINGLE WOMEN:  21                          RETIRED:      4
                       -----
       TOTAL ACTIVE:   61
--------------------------------------------------------------------------
                            YEAR      PERSONNEL   RELATED   PEOPLE
FIELD OF SERVICE            BEGAN     NOW   NEW   CHURCHES  GROUPS  NOTES
--------------------------------------------------------------------------
Japan                       1963       1     1
```

Evangelical Covenant Church of
America, Board of World Mission

5101 N Francisco Ave.
Chicago IL 60625

Tel. (312) 784-3000
EXECUTIVE OFFICER: Raymond L. Dahlberg
ORGANIZED: 1885
DESCRIPTION: A denominational sending agency of evangelical
    tradition establishing churches and involved in general
    Christian education and theological education by
    extension (TEE), evangelism and medicine.
TOTAL INCOME: NR   FOR OVERSEAS MINISTRIES: $1,132,000
PERSONNEL:

```
    NORTH AMERICANS OVERSEAS    NON-NORTH AMERICANS OVERSEAS:      0
            MARRIED:   84           NORTH AMERICAN ADM. STAFF:      6
          SINGLE MEN:   0                       SHORT TERM:     24
        SINGLE WOMEN:  19                          RETIRED:     13
                       -----
       TOTAL ACTIVE:  103
--------------------------------------------------------------------------
                            YEAR      PERSONNEL   RELATED   PEOPLE
FIELD OF SERVICE            BEGAN     NOW   NEW   CHURCHES  GROUPS  NOTES
--------------------------------------------------------------------------
Colombia                    1968       8     6
```

FIELD OF SERVICE	YEAR BEGAN	PERSONNEL NOW	NEW	RELATED CHURCHES	PEOPLE GROUPS	NOTES
Ecuador	1947	11				
Japan	1949	15	3			
Mexico	1946	10	4			
Taiwan Rep of China	1952	4	2			
Thailand	1971	4	2			
Zaire	1937	48	7			

Evangelical Foreign Missions Association SEE: EFMA, Mission Association Section

Evangelical Free Church of America, Board of Overseas Mission

1515 E 66th St.
Minneapolis MN 55423

Tel. (612) 866-3343
EXECUTIVE OFFICER: Robert Dillon
ORGANIZED: 1887   AFFILIATION: EFMA
DESCRIPTION: A denominational sending agency of evangelical
    tradition establishing churches and engaged in theological
    education, medicine and orphanage/childcare.
TOTAL INCOME: $2,695,321   FOR OVERSEAS MINISTRIES: $2,398,836
PERSONNEL:

NORTH AMERICANS OVERSEAS		NON-NORTH AMERICANS OVERSEAS:	0
MARRIED:	170	NORTH AMERICAN ADM. STAFF:	9
SINGLE MEN:	0	SHORT TERM:	24
SINGLE WOMEN:	34	RETIRED:	0
TOTAL ACTIVE:	204		

Evangelical Friends Church, Eastern Region, Friends Foreign Missionary Society

P.O. ADDRESS:
Box 671
Arvada CO 80001

Tel. (303) 421-8100
EXECUTIVE OFFICER: Robert Hess
ORGANIZED: 1884   AFFILIATION: EFMA
DESCRIPTION: A denominational sending agency of Friends
    tradition establishing churches, serving national churches,
    and engaged in theological education, evangelism and
    medicine.
TOTAL INCOME: $314,256   FOR OVERSEAS MINISTRIES: $211,054
PERSONNEL:

NORTH AMERICANS OVERSEAS		NON-NORTH AMERICANS OVERSEAS:	1
MARRIED:	10	NORTH AMERICAN ADM. STAFF:	0
SINGLE MEN:	0	SHORT TERM:	1
SINGLE WOMEN:	4	RETIRED:	1
TOTAL ACTIVE:	14		

Evangelical Friends Mission

1201 30th St. NW
Canton OH 44709

Tel. (216) 492-1577
EXECUTIVE OFFICER: James E. Morris
ORGANIZED: 1978
DESCRIPTION: A denominational agency of Friends and
    evangelical tradition engaged in the coordination and
    promotion for missions of four Evangelical Friends yearly
    meetings. Also establishes churches and serves as an

information service. Is sole administrator of the mission in Mexico to which all four yearly meetings contribute.

TOTAL INCOME: $74,370   FOR OVERSEAS MINISTRIES: $33,310

PERSONNEL:

NORTH AMERICANS OVERSEAS		NON-NORTH AMERICANS OVERSEAS:	0
MARRIED:	4	NORTH AMERICAN ADM. STAFF:	2
SINGLE MEN:	0	SHORT TERM:	0
SINGLE WOMEN:	0	RETIRED:	0

TOTAL ACTIVE:	4		

NOTES: One couple in Mexico is completely supported by Iowa Yearly Meeting Mission Board whose funds are not included in amount spent overseas.

FIELD OF SERVICE	YEAR BEGAN	PERSONNEL NOW	NEW	RELATED CHURCHES	PEOPLE GROUPS	NOTES
Mexico	1967	4	4	3		

Evangelical Furlough Missionary Housing Services, Inc. SEE: Home Finders International

Evangelical Latin League, Inc.
Rt. 1 Box 18J
San Juan TX 78589

EXECUTIVE OFFICER: Thomas Haughey
ORGANIZED: 1961
DESCRIPTION: No current information available. Information from 1976 directory. A nondenominational sending agency of Baptist tradition primarily assisting Mexican churches with special projects. Projects include areas of training and publication.

TOTAL INCOME: $276,000   FOR OVERSEAS MINISTRIES: $276,000

PERSONNEL:

NORTH AMERICANS OVERSEAS		NON-NORTH AMERICANS OVERSEAS:	NR
MARRIED:	NR	NORTH AMERICAN ADM. STAFF:	NR
SINGLE MEN:	NR	SHORT TERM:	NR
SINGLE WOMEN:	NR	RETIRED:	NR

TOTAL ACTIVE:	16		

NOTES: Income estimated by MARC.

FIELD OF SERVICE	YEAR BEGAN	PERSONNEL NOW	NEW	RELATED CHURCHES	PEOPLE GROUPS	NOTES
Mexico						

Evangelical Leadership International
124 S Berkeley
Pasadena CA 91107
P.O. ADDRESS:
Box 4497
Pasadena CA 91106

Tel. (213) 795-3632
EXECUTIVE OFFICER: Gadiel T. Isidro
ORGANIZED: 1975
DESCRIPTION: An interdenominational specialized service agency of evangelical tradition supporting nationals and engaged in fund raising, management counseling, theological education, church construction or financing and support of nationals.

TOTAL INCOME: NR   FOR OVERSEAS MINISTRIES: NR

PERSONNEL:

	NORTH AMERICANS OVERSEAS		NON-NORTH AMERICANS OVERSEAS:	0
MARRIED:	0		NORTH AMERICAN ADM. STAFF:	2
SINGLE MEN:	0		SHORT TERM:	0
SINGLE WOMEN:	0		RETIRED:	NR

TOTAL ACTIVE:	0			

Evangelical Literature League
(T.E.L.L.)

941 Wealthy St. SE
Grand Rapids MI 49506
P.O. ADDRESS:
Box 6219
Grand Rapids MI 49506

Tel. (616) 454-3196
EXECUTIVE OFFICER: Hubert VanTol
ORGANIZED: 1961
DESCRIPTION: An interdenominational specialized service agency
    of Reformed tradition assisting missionaries and national
    churches in production and distribution of theological and
    educational literature in Spanish.
TOTAL INCOME: $125,000   FOR OVERSEAS MINISTRIES: $0
PERSONNEL:

	NORTH AMERICANS OVERSEAS		NON-NORTH AMERICANS OVERSEAS:	0
MARRIED:	0		NORTH AMERICAN ADM. STAFF:	3
SINGLE MEN:	0		SHORT TERM:	0
SINGLE WOMEN:	0		RETIRED:	0

TOTAL ACTIVE:	0			

Evangelical Literature Overseas
(ELO)

207 N Washington
Wheaton IL 60187
P.O. ADDRESS:
Box 725
Wheaton IL 60187

Tel. (312) 653-4820
EXECUTIVE OFFICER: James L. Johnson
ORGANIZED: 1953   AFFILIATION: EFMA-Assoc./IFMA-Assoc.
DESCRIPTION: An interdenominational specialized service agency
    of evangelical tradition providing funds and technical
    assistance in writing, production and distribution of
    Christian literature. Also trains nationals.
TOTAL INCOME: $93,500   FOR OVERSEAS MINISTRIES: $68,000
PERSONNEL:

	NORTH AMERICANS OVERSEAS		NON-NORTH AMERICANS OVERSEAS:	NR
MARRIED:	NR		NORTH AMERICAN ADM. STAFF:	3
SINGLE MEN:	NR		SHORT TERM:	0
SINGLE WOMEN:	NR		RETIRED:	1

TOTAL ACTIVE:	3			

FIELD OF SERVICE	YEAR BEGAN	PERSONNEL NOW	NEW	RELATED CHURCHES	PEOPLE GROUPS	NOTES
Hong-Kong		1				
Kenya		2				

Evangelical Lutheran Church of Canada, Bd. of Wld. Msns.
SEE: Evangelical Lutheran Church, Div. of Wld. Msns.

Evangelical Lutheran Church, Division of World Missions

247 1st Ave. North
Saskatoon SK S7K 4H5
Canada

Tel. (306) 653-0133
EXECUTIVE OFFICER: Paul Nostbakken
ORGANIZED: 1967
DESCRIPTION: A denominational agency of Lutheran tradition
    sending personnel through other agencies. Member of the
    Lutheran World Federation.
TOTAL INCOME: $232,971   FOR OVERSEAS MINISTRIES: $217,475
PERSONNEL:

NORTH AMERICANS OVERSEAS		NON-NORTH AMERICANS OVERSEAS:		NR
MARRIED:	10	NORTH AMERICAN ADM. STAFF:		2
SINGLE MEN:	0	SHORT TERM:		0
SINGLE WOMEN:	2	RETIRED:		5
TOTAL ACTIVE:	12			

FIELD OF SERVICE	YEAR BEGAN	PERSONNEL NOW	NEW	RELATED CHURCHES	PEOPLE GROUPS	NOTES
Cameroon	1979	3	1	1		
Colombia	1979	2		1		
India	1979	2		1		
Papua New Guinea	1979	3		1		

Evangelical Lutheran Synod Board For Missions

1825 Windom Way
Madison WI 53704

Tel. (608) 244-6340
EXECUTIVE OFFICER: Steven Quist
ORGANIZED: 1918
DESCRIPTION: A denominational sending agency of Lutheran
    tradition engaged in evangelism and theological education
    by extension (TEE).
TOTAL INCOME: $120,000   FOR OVERSEAS MINISTRIES: $78,000
PERSONNEL:

NORTH AMERICANS OVERSEAS		NON-NORTH AMERICANS OVERSEAS:		8
MARRIED:	8	NORTH AMERICAN ADM. STAFF:		0
SINGLE MEN:	0	SHORT TERM:		0
SINGLE WOMEN:	0	RETIRED:		4
TOTAL ACTIVE:	8			

FIELD OF SERVICE	YEAR BEGAN	PERSONNEL NOW	NEW	RELATED CHURCHES	PEOPLE GROUPS	NOTES
Peru	1968	8				

Evangelical Mennonite Brethren Commission on Mission

5800 S. 14th St.
Omaha NE 68107

Tel. (402) 731-4780
EXECUTIVE OFFICER: Rev. Allan Wiebe
ORGANIZED: 1936   AFFILIATION: EFMA
DESCRIPTION: A denominational sending agency of Mennonite
    tradition sending most of its personnel through 20 other
    agencies. Involved in establishing churches, evangelism,
    and general Christian and theological education.
TOTAL INCOME: $1,876,918   FOR OVERSEAS MINISTRIES: $447,837

PERSONNEL:
```
    NORTH AMERICANS OVERSEAS     NON-NORTH AMERICANS OVERSEAS:    0
              MARRIED:  112       NORTH AMERICAN ADM. STAFF:     12
           SINGLE MEN:    2                     SHORT TERM:       0
         SINGLE WOMEN:   31                        RETIRED:       5
                       -----
         TOTAL ACTIVE:  145
```

Evangelical Mennonite Church, Commission on Overseas Missions

1420 Kerrway Ct.
Fort Wayne IN 46805

Tel. (219) 423-3649
EXECUTIVE OFFICER: Andrew M. Rupp
ORGANIZED: 1943   AFFILIATION: EFMA
DESCRIPTION: A denominational sending agency of evangelical
    tradition establishing churches, supporting national
    churches and engaged in community development, education
    and literature distribution. Also participates in Africa
    Inter-Mennonite Mission in Zaire and Lesotho, and sends
    personnel through six other boards.
TOTAL INCOME: $266,266   FOR OVERSEAS MINISTRIES: $266,266
PERSONNEL:
```
    NORTH AMERICANS OVERSEAS     NON-NORTH AMERICANS OVERSEAS:    0
              MARRIED:   22       NORTH AMERICAN ADM. STAFF:      1
           SINGLE MEN:    2                     SHORT TERM:       3
         SINGLE WOMEN:    3                        RETIRED:       4
                       -----
         TOTAL ACTIVE:   27
```

FIELD OF SERVICE	YEAR BEGAN	PERSONNEL NOW	PERSONNEL NEW	RELATED CHURCHES	PEOPLE GROUPS	NOTES
Dominican Republic	1946	10	5	30		
Lesotho	1972					
Zaire	1912					

    Note: Nine missionaries are sent to Zaire and
    Lesotho in conjunction with Africa Inter-Mennonite
    Mission. Eleven more are sent through other
    boards.

Evangelical Mennonite Conference Board of Missions

440 Main St.
Steinbach MB R0A 2A0
Canada
P.O. ADDRESS:
Box 1268
Steinbach MB R0A 2A0
Canada

Tel. (204) 326-6401
EXECUTIVE OFFICER: Henry Klassen
ORGANIZED: 1953   AFFILIATION: EFMA
DESCRIPTION: A denominational sending agency of Mennonite
    tradition establishing churches and engaged in radio and
    TV broadcasting, community development and evangelism.
    Agency also supports 52 career missionaries serving with
    other organizations.
TOTAL INCOME: $680,000   FOR OVERSEAS MINISTRIES: $580,000
PERSONNEL:
```
    NORTH AMERICANS OVERSEAS     NON-NORTH AMERICANS OVERSEAS:    0
              MARRIED:   36       NORTH AMERICAN ADM. STAFF:      2
           SINGLE MEN:    1                     SHORT TERM:      17
```

```
   SINGLE WOMEN:    9                      RETIRED:    1
                 -----
   TOTAL ACTIVE:    46
----------------------------------------------------------------
                  YEAR    PERSONNEL   RELATED   PEOPLE
FIELD OF SERVICE  BEGAN   NOW   NEW   CHURCHES  GROUPS  NOTES
----------------------------------------------------------------
Germany, Fed. Rep. 1975    4     2       1        2
Mexico             1954   19     6      10       40
Nicaragua          1966    9     2       4        3
Paraguay           1959   25     8       7        3
```

Evangelical Methodist Church Bible Methodist Missions

Rt. 4 Box 4-T
Leesville SC 29070

Tel. (803) 532-3027
EXECUTIVE OFFICER: L. Milton Cutchen
ORGANIZED: 1948   AFFILIATION: FOM
DESCRIPTION: No current information available. Information
    from 1976 directory. A denominational sending agency of
    Wesleyan and fundamentalist tradition engaged in church
    planting, education, evangelism and the support of
    nationals and national churches.
TOTAL INCOME: $72,000   FOR OVERSEAS MINISTRIES: $72,000
PERSONNEL:
    NORTH AMERICANS OVERSEAS   NON-NORTH AMERICANS OVERSEAS: 41
            MARRIED: 7   NORTH AMERICAN ADM. STAFF: 3
         SINGLE MEN: 0   SHORT TERM: NR
       SINGLE WOMEN: 0   RETIRED: NR

       TOTAL ACTIVE: 7
NOTES: Income estimated by MARC.

```
----------------------------------------------------------------
                  YEAR    PERSONNEL   RELATED   PEOPLE
FIELD OF SERVICE  BEGAN   NOW   NEW   CHURCHES  GROUPS  NOTES
----------------------------------------------------------------
Argentina
Chile                                    3
Guyana                                   2
Jamaica                                  4
Pakistan                               100
Paraguay                                 7
Surinam                                  4
```
    1. Guyana work will close in 1976.
    2. Jamaica has Bible camp grounds.

Evangelical Methodist Church World Missions

3000 W Kellogg Dr.
Wichita KS 67213

Tel. (316) 943-3278
EXECUTIVE OFFICER: Vernon W. Perkins
ORGANIZED: 1946   AFFILIATION: EFMA
DESCRIPTION: A denominational sending agency of Wesleyan
    tradition engaged in evangelism, church planting and
    support of nationals. Also involved in theological
    education and aviation.
TOTAL INCOME: $248,330   FOR OVERSEAS MINISTRIES: $180,278
PERSONNEL:
    NORTH AMERICANS OVERSEAS   NON-NORTH AMERICANS OVERSEAS: 0
            MARRIED: 10   NORTH AMERICAN ADM. STAFF: 2
         SINGLE MEN: 0   SHORT TERM: 0

SINGLE WOMEN: 2   RETIRED: 2

     TOTAL ACTIVE: 12
NOTES: Partial support is received by 50 missionaries under
        other agencies.n

                    YEAR   PERSONNEL   RELATED   PEOPLE
FIELD OF SERVICE   BEGAN   NOW   NEW   CHURCHES GROUPS NOTES

Bolivia   1975   6   6   6   3
Mexico   1946   6   6   35   3

Evangelical Missions Council of
Good News
308 E Main St.
Wilmore KY 40390

Tel. (606) 858-4661
EXECUTIVE OFFICER: V.E. Maybray
ORGANIZED: 1974
DESCRIPTION: An unofficial group within the United Methodist
    Church which recruits and supports missionaries through
    identification of evangelical resources.
TOTAL INCOME: $50,000   FOR OVERSEAS MINISTRIES: $50,000
PERSONNEL:
    NORTH AMERICANS OVERSEAS   NON-NORTH AMERICANS OVERSEAS: 0
              MARRIED: 0   NORTH AMERICAN ADM. STAFF: 0
           SINGLE MEN: 0   SHORT TERM: 0
         SINGLE WOMEN: 0   RETIRED: 0

         TOTAL ACTIVE: 0

Evangelical Missions Information
Service, Inc.
25 W 560 Geneva Rd.
Wheaton IL 60187
P.O. ADDRESS:
Box 794
Wheaton IL 60187

Tel. (312) 653-2158
EXECUTIVE OFFICER: Vergil Gerber
ORGANIZED: 1964
DESCRIPTION: An interdenominational specialized service agency
    of evangelical tradition providing information service to
    mission executives, missionaries, professors, pastors,
    laymen, church and school libraries and overseas church
    leaders through publications, consultations and
    workshops. A cooperative office representing the EFMA and
    IFMA.
TOTAL INCOME: $79,000   FOR OVERSEAS MINISTRIES: $0
PERSONNEL:
    NORTH AMERICANS OVERSEAS   NON-NORTH AMERICANS OVERSEAS: 0
              MARRIED: 0   NORTH AMERICAN ADM. STAFF: 0
           SINGLE MEN: 0   SHORT TERM: 0
         SINGLE WOMEN: 0   RETIRED: 0

         TOTAL ACTIVE: 0

Evangelical Scripture Mission
P.O. Box 518
Monroe WA 98272

Tel. (206) 794-7810
EXECUTIVE OFFICER: Howard M. Gering
ORGANIZED: 1923
DESCRIPTION: An interdenominational agency of independent
    tradition supporting indigenous churches and groups.
    Involved in theological education, childcare, evangelism

and training. Major outreach is Scripture production, distribution and translation.
TOTAL INCOME: $44,200   FOR OVERSEAS MINISTRIES: $44,200
PERSONNEL:
   NORTH AMERICANS OVERSEAS   NON-NORTH AMERICANS OVERSEAS: 0
           MARRIED: 0   NORTH AMERICAN ADM. STAFF: 5
      SINGLE MEN: 0   SHORT TERM: 0
    SINGLE WOMEN: 0   RETIRED: 0

    TOTAL ACTIVE: 0
NOTES: Total income includes Canada.

FIELD OF SERVICE	YEAR BEGAN	PERSONNEL NOW	NEW	RELATED CHURCHES	PEOPLE GROUPS	NOTES
Colombia	1967			15		
Haiti	1975			200		
India	1952			350	11	
Indonesia	1923			655	9	
Jamaica	1975			11		
Japan	1947			10		
Kenya	1970			225	3	
Nigeria	1970			3	3	
Taiwan Rep of China	1947			25		

    Note: Outreaches in Taiwan, Philippines, Malaysia, Sri Lanka, Nagaland, Burma, Nepal, Ghana and Mexico.

Evangelical Tract Distributors (Canada)

P.O. ADDRESS:
Box 146
Edmonton AB T5J 2G9
Canada

Tel. (403) 477-1538
EXECUTIVE OFFICER: Mr. Stout
ORGANIZED: 1935
DESCRIPTION: A mission service agency that publishes and distributes free literature to nearly half of the countries of the world in various languages.
TOTAL INCOME: $500,000   FOR OVERSEAS MINISTRIES: $500,000
PERSONNEL:
   NORTH AMERICANS OVERSEAS   NON-NORTH AMERICANS OVERSEAS: 0
           MARRIED: 0   NORTH AMERICAN ADM. STAFF: 12
      SINGLE MEN: 0   SHORT TERM: 0
    SINGLE WOMEN: 0   RETIRED: 0

    TOTAL ACTIVE: 0

Evangelical Union of South America SEE: Gospel Missionary Union

Evangelism Center, Inc.

800 W Colorado Blvd.
Los Angeles CA 90041
P.O. ADDRESS:
Box 250
Glendale CA 91209

Tel. (213) 254-4371
EXECUTIVE OFFICER: L. Joe Bass
ORGANIZED: 1960
DESCRIPTION: Previously known as Underground Evangelism. Name changed in 1979. An interdenominational agency of evangelical tradition assisting national Christians and churches in

Communist countries. Engaged in aid and/or relief, fund
raising, literature distribution, Bible distribution, and
radio and TV broadcasting.
TOTAL INCOME: $11,048,283   FOR OVERSEAS MINISTRIES: $10,821,503
PERSONNEL:
    NORTH AMERICANS OVERSEAS   NON-NORTH AMERICANS OVERSEAS: 50
              MARRIED: 1   NORTH AMERICAN ADM. STAFF: 45
           SINGLE MEN: 0   SHORT TERM: 70
         SINGLE WOMEN: 0   RETIRED: 0

         TOTAL ACTIVE: 1

| | YEAR | PERSONNEL | | RELATED | PEOPLE | |
FIELD OF SERVICE	BEGAN	NOW	NEW	CHURCHES	GROUPS	NOTES
Pakistan	1980					1
Portugal	1978					1
Thailand	1979					1

    Note: 1. Relief work now in progress.
    2. For security reasons, other
    ministries cannot be named.

Evangelism International, Inc. SEE: Haggai Institute for Advanced Leadership Training, Inc.

Evangelism Resources

2123 Deauville Dr.
Lexington KY 40504

Tel. (606) 254-1067
EXECUTIVE OFFICER: Willys K. Braun
ORGANIZED: 1976
DESCRIPTION: An interdenominational service agency engaged in
    support of saturation evangelism movements in Africa.
TOTAL INCOME: $49,387   FOR OVERSEAS MINISTRIES: $49,387
PERSONNEL:
    NORTH AMERICANS OVERSEAS   NON-NORTH AMERICANS OVERSEAS: 0
              MARRIED: 2   NORTH AMERICAN ADM. STAFF: 0
           SINGLE MEN: 0   SHORT TERM: 0
         SINGLE WOMEN: 0   RETIRED: 0

         TOTAL ACTIVE: 2

| | YEAR | PERSONNEL | | RELATED | PEOPLE | |
FIELD OF SERVICE	BEGAN	NOW	NEW	CHURCHES	GROUPS	NOTES
Nigeria	1980	2	2			

Evangelism to Communist Lands

P.O. ADDRESS:
Box 303
Glendale CA 91209

Tel. (213) 247-5496
EXECUTIVE OFFICER: Paul Popov
ORGANIZED: 1972
DESCRIPTION: A nondenominational service agency of independent
    tradition engaged in Bible printing and distribution,
    broadcasting and assistance to Christians in communist
    lands.
TOTAL INCOME: $733,564   FOR OVERSEAS MINISTRIES: NR
PERSONNEL:
    NORTH AMERICANS OVERSEAS   NON-NORTH AMERICANS OVERSEAS: NR
              MARRIED: NR   NORTH AMERICAN ADM. STAFF: 14
           SINGLE MEN: NR   SHORT TERM: NR

SINGLE WOMEN: NR   RETIRED: NR

TOTAL ACTIVE: NR

Evangelistic Faith Mission, Inc.

US Rte. 50 East
Bedford IN 47421
P.O. ADDRESS:
Box 609
Bedford IN 47421

Tel. (812) 275-7531
EXECUTIVE OFFICER: Victor Glenn
ORGANIZED: 1905   AFFILIATION: EFMA
DESCRIPTION: An interdenominational sending agency of Wesleyan
    tradition establishing churches and engaged in evangelism,
    education, broadcasting and medicine.
TOTAL INCOME: $1,200,000   FOR OVERSEAS MINISTRIES: $900,000
PERSONNEL:
    NORTH AMERICANS OVERSEAS   NON-NORTH AMERICANS OVERSEAS: NR
        MARRIED: NR   NORTH AMERICAN ADM. STAFF: 9
     SINGLE MEN: NR   SHORT TERM: 0
   SINGLE WOMEN: NR   RETIRED: 0

    TOTAL ACTIVE: 28

FIELD OF SERVICE	YEAR BEGAN	PERSONNEL NOW	NEW	RELATED CHURCHES	PEOPLE GROUPS	NOTES
Bolivia		3				
Egypt	1905					
El Salvador	1964					
Ethiopia	1950					
Guatemala	1960					
Honduras	1968					
Korea, Dem. P. Rep.	1971					
Sudan						

Evangelization Society of the Pittsburgh Bible Institute

R.D. 1, Box 391
Gibsonia PA 15044

Tel. (412) 935-1304
EXECUTIVE OFFICER: Ralph T. Kemper
ORGANIZED: 1920
DESCRIPTION: A nondenominational sending agency of Pentecostal
    and fundamentalist tradition establishing churches and
    engaged in education, supporting nationals, supplying
    equipment and correspondence courses. Also involved in
    Bible distribution and medical supply.
TOTAL INCOME: NR   FOR OVERSEAS MINISTRIES: $330,000
PERSONNEL:
    NORTH AMERICANS OVERSEAS   NON-NORTH AMERICANS OVERSEAS: NR
        MARRIED: NR   NORTH AMERICAN ADM. STAFF: 0
     SINGLE MEN: NR   SHORT TERM: 0
   SINGLE WOMEN: NR   RETIRED: 0

    TOTAL ACTIVE: 15
NOTES: Overseas income estimated by MARC.

FIELD OF SERVICE	YEAR BEGAN	PERSONNEL NOW	NEW	RELATED CHURCHES	PEOPLE GROUPS	NOTES
Taiwan Rep of China	1951	4		9		

FIELD OF SERVICE	YEAR BEGAN	PERSONNEL NOW	NEW	RELATED CHURCHES	PEOPLE GROUPS	NOTES
Zaire	1922			200	3	

Evangelization Society SEE: Evangelization Society of the Pittsburgh Bible Institute

Evangelize China Fellowship, Inc.

490 E Walnut St. Ste. 14
Pasadena CA 91101
P.O. ADDRESS:
Box 550, Main P.O.
Los Angeles CA 90053

Tel. (213) 793-0153
EXECUTIVE OFFICER: Paul C. C. Szeto
ORGANIZED: 1947
DESCRIPTION: An interdenominational agency of evangelical
   tradition supporting nationals and national churches,
   engaged in evangelism, education, literature production
   and orphanage and childcare work. Agency is composed of
   Chinese Christians and helps support 500 national workers
   overseas.
TOTAL INCOME: $177,287   FOR OVERSEAS MINISTRIES: $76,000
PERSONNEL:

NORTH AMERICANS OVERSEAS		NON-NORTH AMERICANS OVERSEAS:	NR
MARRIED:	0	NORTH AMERICAN ADM. STAFF:	5
SINGLE MEN:	0	SHORT TERM:	0
SINGLE WOMEN:	0	RETIRED:	0
TOTAL ACTIVE:	0		

FIELD OF SERVICE	YEAR BEGAN	PERSONNEL NOW	NEW	RELATED CHURCHES	PEOPLE GROUPS	NOTES
Hong-Kong	1949			7		
Indonesia	1951			20		
Macao	1949					
Malaysia	1951			2		
Singapore	1951			1		
Taiwan Rep of China	1948					
Thailand	1958			1		

Everyday Publications

230 Glebemount Ave.
Toronto ON M4C 3T4
Canada

Tel. (416) 421-4845
EXECUTIVE OFFICER: R. E. Harlow
ORGANIZED: 1964
DESCRIPTION: A nondenominational service agency of evangelical
   tradition publishing books about the Bible, specializing
   in books written in common English for use in English-
   speaking fields. Also publishes in Swahili, Spanish,
   French and Portuguese.
TOTAL INCOME: $43,893   FOR OVERSEAS MINISTRIES: NR
PERSONNEL:

NORTH AMERICANS OVERSEAS		NON-NORTH AMERICANS OVERSEAS:	0
MARRIED:	0	NORTH AMERICAN ADM. STAFF:	5
SINGLE MEN:	0	SHORT TERM:	0

```
         SINGLE WOMEN:      0                        RETIRED:     0
                        -----
         TOTAL ACTIVE:      0
```

Executive Commission on Overseas Evangelism of the Presbyterian Evangelistic Fellowship, Inc. SEE: Mission to the World

Faith Center Global Ministries

```
                                          1615 S Glendale Ave.
                                          Glendale CA 91205
Tel. (213) 246-8121
EXECUTIVE OFFICER: W. Eugene Scott
ORGANIZED:    0
DESCRIPTION:  A nondenominational sending agency of Pentecostal
    tradition supporting nationals and engaged in
    broadcasting.
TOTAL INCOME:         NR      FOR OVERSEAS MINISTRIES:     $22,000
PERSONNEL:
    NORTH AMERICANS OVERSEAS   NON-NORTH AMERICANS OVERSEAS:     NR
             MARRIED:    NR        NORTH AMERICAN ADM. STAFF:    NR
          SINGLE MEN:    NR                      SHORT TERM:     NR
        SINGLE WOMEN:    NR                        RETIRED:      0
                        -----
        TOTAL ACTIVE:      1
NOTES:  Overseas income estimated by MARC.
```

FIELD OF SERVICE	YEAR BEGAN	PERSONNEL NOW	PERSONNEL NEW	RELATED CHURCHES	PEOPLE GROUPS	NOTES
Brazil		1				

Faith Christian Fellowship
World Outreach

```
                                          2121 E Third St.
                                          Tulsa OK 74150
                                          P.O. ADDRESS:
                                          Box 35443
                                          Tulsa OK 74135
Tel. (918) 599-7224
EXECUTIVE OFFICER: Buddy Harrison
ORGANIZED: 1978
DESCRIPTION:  A nondenominational agency of Pentecostal
    tradition supporting Pastors' conferences and Bible
    schools. Also engaged in missionary and theological
    education, evangelism, establishment of churches and
    fund transmittal.
TOTAL INCOME:    $750,000   FOR OVERSEAS MINISTRIES:     $20,000
PERSONNEL:
    NORTH AMERICANS OVERSEAS   NON-NORTH AMERICANS OVERSEAS:     0
             MARRIED:     0        NORTH AMERICAN ADM. STAFF:    3
          SINGLE MEN:     0                      SHORT TERM:     17
        SINGLE WOMEN:     0                        RETIRED:      0
                        -----
        TOTAL ACTIVE:      0
```

FIELD OF SERVICE	YEAR BEGAN	PERSONNEL NOW	PERSONNEL NEW	RELATED CHURCHES	PEOPLE GROUPS	NOTES
Australia	1979	2		2		
India	1979			40		

FIELD OF SERVICE	YEAR BEGAN	PERSONNEL NOW	NEW	RELATED CHURCHES	PEOPLE GROUPS	NOTES
Jamaica	1979	1		1		
Mexico	1979	3		50		
Philippines	1979	6		1		
United Kingdom	1978	4		1		

Note: Personnel are short term and only partially supported.

Faith Ministries

5415 Wynnefield Ave.
Philadelphia PA 19131
P.O. ADDRESS:
Box 4581
Philadelphia PA 19131

Tel. (215) 877-2734
EXECUTIVE OFFICER: Edward S. Armstrong
ORGANIZED: 1979
DESCRIPTION: An interdenominational Baptist agency of evangelical tradition engaged in mass evangelism, furloughed
missionary support, missionary orientation and training,
recruiting and serving other agencies. Agency has no overseas personnel but helps support missionaries of other
boards that send to Liberia, West Africa.

TOTAL INCOME: NR   FOR OVERSEAS MINISTRIES: NR
PERSONNEL:
   NORTH AMERICANS OVERSEAS   NON-NORTH AMERICANS OVERSEAS: 0
        MARRIED: 0   NORTH AMERICAN ADM. STAFF: 6
     SINGLE MEN: 0   SHORT TERM: 0
   SINGLE WOMEN: 0   RETIRED: 0

    TOTAL ACTIVE: 0

Far Corners Ministries SEE: World Missions, Inc.

Far East Broadcasting Company, Inc.

15700 Imperial Hwy.
La Mirada CA 90638
P.O. ADDRESS:
Box 1
La Mirada CA 90637

Tel. (213) 947-4651
EXECUTIVE OFFICER: Robert H. Bowman
ORGANIZED: 1945   AFFILIATION: EFMA/IFMA
DESCRIPTION: An international, nondenominational specialized
service agency of evangelical tradition with radio
broadcasts in 72 languages (primarily to Asia), providing
follow-up and Bible correspondence courses.

TOTAL INCOME: $5,330,825   FOR OVERSEAS MINISTRIES: $4,191,740
PERSONNEL:
   NORTH AMERICANS OVERSEAS   NON-NORTH AMERICANS OVERSEAS: 20
        MARRIED: 30   NORTH AMERICAN ADM. STAFF: 41
     SINGLE MEN: 4   SHORT TERM: 0
   SINGLE WOMEN: 3   RETIRED: NR

    TOTAL ACTIVE: 37
NOTES: Number of Non-North Americans overseas
      estimated by agency.

FIELD OF SERVICE	YEAR BEGAN	PERSONNEL NOW	NEW	RELATED CHURCHES	PEOPLE GROUPS	NOTES
Burma	1973					
Hong-Kong	1959	1				
Indonesia	1962					
Japan	1959					
Korea, Rep. of	1972	6	2			
Pacific Trust Terr.	1976	8	10			
Philippines	1947	22	6			
Singapore	1962	2	4			
Thailand	1960					
United Kingdom	1960	2	2			

Far East Missionary Society
Interdenominational, Inc.

1204 N Howard St.
Glendale CA 91207

DESCRIPTION: No data is reported for this agency for one of the
    following reasons: it is currently inactive or no longer
    exists; it has terminated overseas ministries or has ceased
    to operate as a North American entity.

Far Eastern Gospel Crusade

36200 Freedom Rd.
Farmington MI 48024
P.O. ADDRESS:
Box 513
Farmington MI 48024

Tel. (313) 477-4210
EXECUTIVE OFFICER: Frank M. Severn
ORGANIZED: 1947   AFFILIATION: IFMA
DESCRIPTION: A nondenominational sending agency of evangelical
    and Baptist tradition establishing churches and engaged
    in education, evangelism, including student evangelism and
    support of national churches.
TOTAL INCOME: $2,660,801   FOR OVERSEAS MINISTRIES: $1,616,327
PERSONNEL:
    NORTH AMERICANS OVERSEAS   NON-NORTH AMERICANS OVERSEAS: 14
             MARRIED: 108   NORTH AMERICAN ADM. STAFF: 20
          SINGLE MEN: 2   SHORT TERM: 25
        SINGLE WOMEN: 25   RETIRED: 6

        TOTAL ACTIVE: 135

FIELD OF SERVICE	YEAR BEGAN	PERSONNEL NOW	NEW	RELATED CHURCHES	PEOPLE GROUPS	NOTES
Japan	1947	68	17	33	2	
Philippines	1947	69	32	23	7	
Taiwan Rep of China	1967	11	7	3	3	

FARMS International, Inc.

123 W 57th St.
New York NY 10019

Tel. (212) 246-9692
EXECUTIVE OFFICER: Gareth B. Miller
ORGANIZED: 1961
DESCRIPTION: An interdenominational specialized service agency
    of evangelical tradition working with missions and national
    churches in agricultural evangelism through training,
    community development, extension education and self-help
    projects.
TOTAL INCOME: $133,000   FOR OVERSEAS MINISTRIES: $25,014

```
PERSONNEL:
    NORTH AMERICANS OVERSEAS    NON-NORTH AMERICANS OVERSEAS:    2
              MARRIED:    2         NORTH AMERICAN ADM. STAFF:    3
           SINGLE MEN:    0                      SHORT TERM:    0
         SINGLE WOMEN:    0                         RETIRED:    0
                        -----
         TOTAL ACTIVE:    2
```

FIELD OF SERVICE	YEAR BEGAN	PERSONNEL NOW	NEW	RELATED CHURCHES	PEOPLE GROUPS	NOTES
Costa Rica	1967	2	1			
Haiti	1975	1				
India	1977	2	2			
Mexico	1977	2	2			
Sri Lanka	1972	1				

Fellowship Deaconry, Inc. SEE: Liberty Corner Mission

Fellowship of Artists For Cultural Evangelism (FACE)

1605 E Elizabeth St.
Pasadena CA 91104

Tel. (213) 794-7970
EXECUTIVE OFFICER: Eugene C. Totten
ORGANIZED: 1973
DESCRIPTION: A nondenominational specialized agency of evangel-
    ical tradition engaged in developing ethnic art researchers
    for mission strategy. Also involved in information service
    and missionary education, orientation and training.

```
TOTAL INCOME:    $16,500         FOR OVERSEAS MINISTRIES:    NR
PERSONNEL:
    NORTH AMERICANS OVERSEAS    NON-NORTH AMERICANS OVERSEAS:    0
              MARRIED:    0         NORTH AMERICAN ADM. STAFF:    7
           SINGLE MEN:    0                      SHORT TERM:    0
         SINGLE WOMEN:    0                         RETIRED:    0
                        -----
         TOTAL ACTIVE:    0
```

Fellowship of Christian Assemblies Mission to Liberia

657 W 18th St.
Los Angeles CA 10314

Tel. (212) 442-2874
EXECUTIVE OFFICER: Paul Zetersten
ORGANIZED: 1968
DESCRIPTION: No current information available. Information
    from 1976 directory. A denominational sending agency of
    Pentecostal tradition involved in evangelism, medicine,
    education, childcare and ministerial training in Liberia.

```
TOTAL INCOME:    $200,000   FOR OVERSEAS MINISTRIES:    $200,000
PERSONNEL:
    NORTH AMERICANS OVERSEAS    NON-NORTH AMERICANS OVERSEAS:    NR
              MARRIED:    NR        NORTH AMERICAN ADM. STAFF:    NR
           SINGLE MEN:    NR                     SHORT TERM:    0
         SINGLE WOMEN:    NR                        RETIRED:    NR
                        -----
         TOTAL ACTIVE:    28
```

FIELD OF SERVICE	YEAR BEGAN	PERSONNEL NOW	NEW	RELATED CHURCHES	PEOPLE GROUPS	NOTES
Liberia	1920					

Fellowship of Evangelical Baptist Churches in Canada, Foreign Mission Board

74 Sheppard Ave. W
Willowdale ON M2N 1M3
Canada

Tel. (416) 223-8696
EXECUTIVE OFFICER: W. H. MacBain
ORGANIZED: 1964
DESCRIPTION: A denominational sending agency of Baptist and
    evangelical tradition establishing churches and engaged
    in theological education, evangelism, medicine and
    aid/relief.
TOTAL INCOME: $645,000   FOR OVERSEAS MINISTRIES: $602,000
PERSONNEL:

NORTH AMERICANS OVERSEAS		NON-NORTH AMERICANS OVERSEAS:	0
MARRIED:	32	NORTH AMERICAN ADM. STAFF:	1
SINGLE MEN:	1	SHORT TERM:	5
SINGLE WOMEN:	7	RETIRED:	1
TOTAL ACTIVE:	40		

FIELD OF SERVICE	YEAR BEGAN	PERSONNEL NOW	NEW	RELATED CHURCHES	PEOPLE GROUPS	NOTES
Belgium	1977	2		5		
Colombia	1969	21	8	20		
France	1978	2	2	1		
Japan	1950	9	2	8	1	
Nigeria	1979	2	2	830	3	
Pakistan	1971	4	2	15	3	

Fellowship of Faith For Muslims

205 Yonge St., Rm. 25
Toronto ON M5B 1N2
Canada

Tel. (416) 364-5054
EXECUTIVE OFFICER: Raymond H. Joyce
ORGANIZED: 1951
DESCRIPTION: A nondenominational specialized service agency of
    evangelical tradition acting as a prayer fellowship and
    information service for those seeking to reach Muslims.
TOTAL INCOME: $16,530   FOR OVERSEAS MINISTRIES: $0
PERSONNEL:

NORTH AMERICANS OVERSEAS		NON-NORTH AMERICANS OVERSEAS:	0
MARRIED:	0	NORTH AMERICAN ADM. STAFF:	3
SINGLE MEN:	0	SHORT TERM:	0
SINGLE WOMEN:	0	RETIRED:	0
TOTAL ACTIVE:	0		

NOTES: Agency's total income does not include
        money received from book sales.

Fellowship of Grace Brethren Churches, Foreign Missionary Society of the Brethren Church

Kings Hwy.
Winona Lake IN 46590
P.O. ADDRESS:
Box 588
Winona Lake IN 46590

Tel. (219) 267-5161
EXECUTIVE OFFICER: John W. Zielasko
ORGANIZED: 1900   AFFILIATION: EFMA

DESCRIPTION: A denominational sending agency of Brethren
    tradition establishing churches and engaged in education,
    evangelism, literature and medicine.
TOTAL INCOME: $1,256,546   FOR OVERSEAS MINISTRIES: $1,226,804
PERSONNEL:
```
    NORTH AMERICANS OVERSEAS     NON-NORTH AMERICANS OVERSEAS:    4
          MARRIED:     78          NORTH AMERICAN ADM. STAFF:    11
       SINGLE MEN:      2                       SHORT TERM:      11
     SINGLE WOMEN:     19                          RETIRED:      17
                     -----
     TOTAL ACTIVE:     99
```
NOTES: Two of the non-North Americans are
    partially supported.

FIELD OF SERVICE	YEAR BEGAN	PERSONNEL NOW	PERSONNEL NEW	RELATED CHURCHES	PEOPLE GROUPS	NOTES
Argentina	1909	11	9	17		
Brazil	1949	13	2	15		
Central African Rep.	1921	51	10	450	2	
Chad		1	1	38		
France	1951	11	7	2		
Germany, Fed. Rep.	1969	7	5	1		
Mexico	1951	6		7		
Puerto Rico	1958	2	2	2		

Fellowship of Independent Missions

P.O. ADDRESS:
Box 72
Fairless Hills PA 19030

Tel. (215) 946-2229
EXECUTIVE OFFICER: Philip Weiss
ORGANIZED: 1950
DESCRIPTION: No current information available. Information
    from 1976 directory. Founded in 1950 as Morocco
    Evangelistic Fellowship. Name changed 1959. Merged with
    Cedar Lane Missionary Homes since 1973. A
    nondenominational sending agency of fundamentalist
    tradition engaged in evangelism, church planting,
    education, childcare, and literature distribution.
TOTAL INCOME: $455,500   FOR OVERSEAS MINISTRIES: $455,500
PERSONNEL:
```
    NORTH AMERICANS OVERSEAS     NON-NORTH AMERICANS OVERSEAS:    2
          MARRIED:     48          NORTH AMERICAN ADM. STAFF:     3
       SINGLE MEN:      2                       SHORT TERM:      NR
     SINGLE WOMEN:      8                          RETIRED:      NR
                     -----
     TOTAL ACTIVE:     58
```

FIELD OF SERVICE	YEAR BEGAN	PERSONNEL NOW	PERSONNEL NEW	RELATED CHURCHES	PEOPLE GROUPS	NOTES
Argentina	1964					
Austria	1971					
Brazil	1964					
Ecuador	1967					
France	1970					
Lebanon	1965					
Mexico	1971					

FIELD OF SERVICE	YEAR BEGAN	PERSONNEL NOW	PERSONNEL NEW	RELATED CHURCHES	PEOPLE GROUPS	NOTES
Morocco	1950					
Niger	1971					
Peru	1962					
South Africa	1968					
Sweden	1972					
Venezuela	1968					

Fellowship of Missions SEE: FOM, Mission Association Section

Films for Asia SEE: Action International Ministries

Focus, Friendship for Overseas Citizens and University Students SEE: International Students, Inc.

Food For The Hungry International

7729 E Greenway
Scottsdale AZ 85260
P.O. ADDRESS:
Box E
Scottsdale AZ 85252

Tel. (602) 998-3100
EXECUTIVE OFFICER: Larry Ward
ORGANIZED: 1971
DESCRIPTION: A nondenominational, international specialized
    service agency of evangelical tradition providing food,
    emergency relief supplies, equipment and agricultural
    assistance. Also supports programs in the areas of
    self-help projects and childcare and serves as an
    information service.
TOTAL INCOME: $3,950,000   FOR OVERSEAS MINISTRIES: $2,904,000
PERSONNEL:
      NORTH AMERICANS OVERSEAS   NON-NORTH AMERICANS OVERSEAS: 2
               MARRIED: 14   NORTH AMERICAN ADM. STAFF: 25
            SINGLE MEN: 4   SHORT TERM: 52
          SINGLE WOMEN: 0   RETIRED: 0

          TOTAL ACTIVE: 18
NOTES: Short-term personnel are
        all student volunteers.

FIELD OF SERVICE	YEAR BEGAN	PERSONNEL NOW	PERSONNEL NEW	RELATED CHURCHES	PEOPLE GROUPS	NOTES
Bangladesh	1972	1	1			
Bolivia	1978	4	4			
El Salvador	1979					
Guatemala	1976	2	2			
Haiti	1971	1	1			
Honduras	1974					
Hong-Kong	1979					
India	1973					
Kenya	1976	3	3			
Mexico	1978					

```
------------------------------------------------------------------
                  YEAR      PERSONNEL   RELATED   PEOPLE
FIELD OF SERVICE  BEGAN    NOW   NEW    CHURCHES  GROUPS  NOTES
------------------------------------------------------------------
Panama            1975
Peru              1979      2     2
Thailand          1975      5     2
     Note: All personnel are expatriate.
```

Food for the Hungry/Canada

8400 Main St. No.211
Vancouver BC V5X 3L3
Canada
P.O. ADDRESS:
Box 67800
Vancouver BC V5W 3W3
Canada

Tel. (604) 324-7885
EXECUTIVE OFFICER: David McKenzie
ORGANIZED: 1970
DESCRIPTION: Formerly Dominion Food for the Hungry. Name
    changed in 1976. A nondenominational specialized service
    agency of evangelical tradition providing food, emergency
    relief supplies and research and development projects
    designed to help the needy become self-reliant. Also
    engaged in training and providing an information service.
TOTAL INCOME: $746,616   FOR OVERSEAS MINISTRIES: $436,648
PERSONNEL:
    NORTH AMERICANS OVERSEAS   NON-NORTH AMERICANS OVERSEAS: NR
            MARRIED: 0   NORTH AMERICAN ADM. STAFF: 5
         SINGLE MEN: 0   SHORT TERM: 3
       SINGLE WOMEN: 0   RETIRED: NR

       TOTAL ACTIVE: 0
NOTES: Personnel sent through international
    agency.

Forester Foundation, Inc.

2545 N Madera Ave.
Kerman CA 93630
P.O. ADDRESS:
Box 11971
Fresno CA 93776

Tel. (209) 222-9325
EXECUTIVE OFFICER: Robert C. Forester
ORGANIZED: 1970
DESCRIPTION: A nondenominational agency of independent and
    charismatic tradition engaged in evangelism, training for
    missionary service, literature and education.
TOTAL INCOME: $38,000   FOR OVERSEAS MINISTRIES: $0
PERSONNEL:
    NORTH AMERICANS OVERSEAS   NON-NORTH AMERICANS OVERSEAS: NR
            MARRIED: 0   NORTH AMERICAN ADM. STAFF: 2
         SINGLE MEN: 0   SHORT TERM: 0
       SINGLE WOMEN: 0   RETIRED: 0

       TOTAL ACTIVE: 0
NOTES: No overseas income reported due to
    reorganization of agency.

POINTER NAME:Foundation for a Better World SEE:
Christian Church of North America, General Council

Foundation For His
Ministry-Orphanage Committee

P.O. ADDRESS:
Box 675
Garden Grove CA 92626

Tel. (714) 547-5846
EXECUTIVE OFFICER: David L. Taylor
ORGANIZED: 1967
DESCRIPTION: A nondenominational sending agency of independent
    and evangelical tradition engaged in evangelism and
    childcare.
TOTAL INCOME: $192,219   FOR OVERSEAS MINISTRIES: $187,677
PERSONNEL:
    NORTH AMERICANS OVERSEAS   NON-NORTH AMERICANS OVERSEAS: 1
                 MARRIED: 17   NORTH AMERICAN ADM. STAFF: 0
              SINGLE MEN: 4   SHORT TERM: 12
            SINGLE WOMEN: 5   RETIRED: 0

        TOTAL ACTIVE: 26

FIELD OF SERVICE	YEAR BEGAN	PERSONNEL NOW	NEW	RELATED CHURCHES	PEOPLE GROUPS	NOTES
Mexico	1967	26	17			

Foursquare Gospel Church SEE: International Church of the Foursquare Gospel

Franconia Mennonite Conference
Mission Commission

Rt. 113 & Bethlehem Pike
Souderton PA 18964
P.O. ADDRESS:
Box 116
Souderton PA 18964

Tel. (215) 723-5513
EXECUTIVE OFFICER: Henry P. Yoder
ORGANIZED: 1917
DESCRIPTION: A denominational sending agency of Mennonite
    tradition establishing and supporting national churches
    and engaged in radio and TV broadcasting, correspondence
    courses and theological education by extension (TEE).
TOTAL INCOME: $262,314   FOR OVERSEAS MINISTRIES: $99,977
PERSONNEL:
    NORTH AMERICANS OVERSEAS   NON-NORTH AMERICANS OVERSEAS: 0
                 MARRIED: 6   NORTH AMERICAN ADM. STAFF: 1
              SINGLE MEN: 0   SHORT TERM: 2
            SINGLE WOMEN: 0   RETIRED: 1

        TOTAL ACTIVE: 6

FIELD OF SERVICE	YEAR BEGAN	PERSONNEL NOW	NEW	RELATED CHURCHES	PEOPLE GROUPS	NOTES
Mexico	1958	6		8	1	

Free Gospel Church, Inc.

P.O. ADDRESS:
Box 477
Export PA 15632

Tel. (412) 327-5454
EXECUTIVE OFFICER: Chester H. Heath
ORGANIZED: 1916
DESCRIPTION: A denominational sending agency of Pentecostal
    tradition supporting nationals and engaged in church
    construction, student evangelism, Bible distribution, and

secular and theological education.
```
TOTAL INCOME:          NR      FOR OVERSEAS MINISTRIES:      $31,644
PERSONNEL:
   NORTH AMERICANS OVERSEAS    NON-NORTH AMERICANS OVERSEAS:       6
              MARRIED:    8         NORTH AMERICAN ADM. STAFF:     0
           SINGLE MEN:    0                        SHORT TERM:     0
         SINGLE WOMEN:    0                           RETIRED:     2
                      -----
         TOTAL ACTIVE:    8
```

FIELD OF SERVICE	YEAR BEGAN	PERSONNEL NOW	NEW	RELATED CHURCHES	PEOPLE GROUPS	NOTES
India	1940	2		3		
Philippines	1925	2	2	8		
Sierra Leone	1925	4	2	12		

Free Methodist Church of North America General Missionary Board

901 College Ave.
Winona Lake IN 46590

Tel. (219) 267-6287
EXECUTIVE OFFICER: C. D. Kirkpatrick
ORGANIZED: 1885   AFFILIATION: EFMA
DESCRIPTION: A denominational sending agency of Wesleyan and
    Episcopal tradition engaged in secular and theological
    education, evangelism, literature production and medicine.
```
TOTAL INCOME:  $2,300,000   FOR OVERSEAS MINISTRIES:  $2,237,000
PERSONNEL:
   NORTH AMERICANS OVERSEAS    NON-NORTH AMERICANS OVERSEAS:       2
              MARRIED:  119         NORTH AMERICAN ADM. STAFF:     5
           SINGLE MEN:    1                        SHORT TERM:    68
         SINGLE WOMEN:   24                           RETIRED:    31
                      -----
         TOTAL ACTIVE:  144
```

FIELD OF SERVICE	YEAR BEGAN	PERSONNEL NOW	NEW	RELATED CHURCHES	PEOPLE GROUPS	NOTES
Brazil	1928	8		24		
Burundi	1935	24		9	49	
Dominican Republic	1889	3		55		
Egypt	1899	3		120		
Haiti	1964	4	3	24		
Hong-Kong	1951	2	2	8		
India	1885	2		18		
Indonesia	1974	4	4	9		
Japan	1895	4	2	31		
Latin America-gen.		2				
Malawi	1973	2	2	13		
Mexico	1917	6	2	11		
Mozambique	1885			80		
Paraguay	1946	3		6		
Philippines	1949	6		38		
Rwanda	1942	17	9	97		
South Africa	1885	20		90		
Taiwan Rep of China	1952	7	1	28		
Zaire	1963	14	2	176		

FIELD OF SERVICE	YEAR BEGAN	PERSONNEL NOW	NEW	RELATED CHURCHES	PEOPLE GROUPS	NOTES
Zimbabwe	1938	3		18		

Free Will Baptists, National Association of SEE: National Association of Free Will Baptists

French Baptist Association, American Council

175 Fifth Ave.
New York NY 10010

DESCRIPTION: No data is reported for this agency for one of the following reasons: it is currently inactive or no longer exists; it has terminated overseas ministries or has ceased to operate as a North American entity.

Friends For Missions, Inc.

514 Lynnhaven Dr. SW
Atlanta GA 30310
P.O. ADDRESS:
Box 10942
Atlanta GA 30310

Tel. (404) 758-8410
EXECUTIVE OFFICER: Mary E. Gullick
ORGANIZED: 1968
DESCRIPTION: An interdenominational, multi-ethnic fund transmittal agency supporting evangelism, education, self-help projects, Bible distribution, aid and relief and medical and nutritional programs, primarily in Haiti. Work is conducted by Haitians. Have 3 schools and 2 nutrition centers.

TOTAL INCOME: $76,000   FOR OVERSEAS MINISTRIES: $34,000
PERSONNEL:
   NORTH AMERICANS OVERSEAS   NON-NORTH AMERICANS OVERSEAS: NR
         MARRIED: 0   NORTH AMERICAN ADM. STAFF: 0
      SINGLE MEN: 0   SHORT TERM: 0
    SINGLE WOMEN: 0   RETIRED: 0

    TOTAL ACTIVE: 0

FIELD OF SERVICE	YEAR BEGAN	PERSONNEL NOW	NEW	RELATED CHURCHES	PEOPLE GROUPS	NOTES
Haiti	1969					

Friends of Indonesia Fellowship, Inc.

18331 Grand Ave.
Lakeland Village, Elsinore CA

Tel. (714) 678-3122
EXECUTIVE OFFICER: John G. Breman
ORGANIZED: 1926
DESCRIPTION: No current information available. Information from 1976 directory. A nondenominational sending agency of fundamentalist tradition involved in support of nationals, church planting and support, evangelism, education, and medical and agricultural assistance.

TOTAL INCOME: $55,000   FOR OVERSEAS MINISTRIES: NR
PERSONNEL:
   NORTH AMERICANS OVERSEAS   NON-NORTH AMERICANS OVERSEAS: NR
         MARRIED: NR   NORTH AMERICAN ADM. STAFF: NR
      SINGLE MEN: NR   SHORT TERM: NR

```
    SINGLE WOMEN:   NR                           RETIRED:    NR
                  -----
    TOTAL ACTIVE:   NR
NOTES:   Income estimated by MARC.
------------------------------------------------------------------
                      YEAR      PERSONNEL    RELATED   PEOPLE
FIELD OF SERVICE      BEGAN    NOW   NEW    CHURCHES  GROUPS  NOTES
------------------------------------------------------------------
Indonesia             1926
```

Friends of Israel Gospel Ministry, *635 2*   475 White Horse Pike
Inc. *609 845, 362*   W. Collingswood NJ 08107
     853 5590   P.O. ADDRESS:
                                                      Box 123
                                                      W. Collingswood NJ 08107
Tel. (609) 854-1120   *Westfeld.*
EXECUTIVE OFFICER: Marvin J. Rosenthal
ORGANIZED: 1938
DESCRIPTION: A nondenominational agency of fundamentalist
    tradition engaged in evangelism, aid and/or relief, Bible
    teaching and literature distribution.
TOTAL INCOME: $1,038,539   FOR OVERSEAS MINISTRIES: $773,300
PERSONNEL:
```
    NORTH AMERICANS OVERSEAS   NON-NORTH AMERICANS OVERSEAS:    0
              MARRIED:   0        NORTH AMERICAN ADM. STAFF:    0
          SINGLE MEN:    0                      SHORT TERM:    0
        SINGLE WOMEN:    0                        RETIRED:    0
                       -----
    TOTAL ACTIVE:       0
```
NOTES: Income estimated by MARC from
         agency financial statement.

**Friends of Israel Missionary and Relief Society SEE: Friends of
Israel Gospel Ministry, Inc.**

Friends of Turkey   P.O. ADDRESS:
                                               Box 3098
                                               Grand Junction CO 81502
Tel. (303) 241-0682
EXECUTIVE OFFICER: Steven E. Hagerman
ORGANIZED: 1970
DESCRIPTION: Originally called Friends of Turkey and Postal
    Evangelism, Inc. Name changed in 1975. An
    interdenominational service agency of evangelical and
    independent tradition engaged in evangelism, literature
    production, fund transmittal and information service.
    Focus of ministry is on postal evangelism and pen pal
    exchange with Turkish-speaking people.
TOTAL INCOME: $21,115   FOR OVERSEAS MINISTRIES: $9,500
PERSONNEL:
```
    NORTH AMERICANS OVERSEAS   NON-NORTH AMERICANS OVERSEAS:    0
              MARRIED:   2        NORTH AMERICAN ADM. STAFF:    3
          SINGLE MEN:    0                      SHORT TERM:    0
        SINGLE WOMEN:    1                        RETIRED:    0
                       -----
    TOTAL ACTIVE:       3
```

```
                      YEAR      PERSONNEL    RELATED   PEOPLE
FIELD OF SERVICE      BEGAN    NOW   NEW    CHURCHES  GROUPS  NOTES
------------------------------------------------------------------
Turkey                1970      3     1         4             1
```
    Note: 1. Also affiliated with independent offices

in the United Kingdom, Germany, Fed. Rep.,
the Netherlands, Sweden and India.

Friends of Turkey and Postal Evangelism, Inc. SEE: Friends of Turkey

Friends United Meeting SEE: Wider Ministries Commission

Friendship Ministry International

2216 W Burbank Blvd.
Burbank CA 91506
P.O. ADDRESS:
Box 32
Hollywood CA 90028

Tel. (213) 848-7996
EXECUTIVE OFFICER: Dorothy C. Haskin
ORGANIZED: 1970
DESCRIPTION: A nondenominational service agency of evangelical
    tradition supplying food and vitamins to missionaries
    overseas and also engaged in childcare, literature
    distribution, aid and relief, Bible distribution, support
    of nationals and serving other agencies. Associated with
    Evangelistic Fellowship of Orissa (India), Evangelize
    India Fellowship, and India National Inland Mission.
TOTAL INCOME: $65,852   FOR OVERSEAS MINISTRIES: $42,643
PERSONNEL:
    NORTH AMERICANS OVERSEAS   NON-NORTH AMERICANS OVERSEAS: 0
             MARRIED: 0   NORTH AMERICAN ADM. STAFF: 4
          SINGLE MEN: 0   SHORT TERM: 0
        SINGLE WOMEN: 0   RETIRED: 0

        TOTAL ACTIVE: 0

Frontier Ministries International

530 W 7th Ave.
Junction City OR 97448

Tel. (503) 998-3015
EXECUTIVE OFFICER: Gordon W. Johnson
ORGANIZED: 1979
DESCRIPTION: A nondenominational sending agency of evangelical
    and charismatic tradition establishing churches and
    engaged in agricultural assistance, medicine, self-help
    projects and technical assistance.
TOTAL INCOME: $22,000   FOR OVERSEAS MINISTRIES: $22,000
PERSONNEL:
    NORTH AMERICANS OVERSEAS   NON-NORTH AMERICANS OVERSEAS: 0
             MARRIED: 2   NORTH AMERICAN ADM. STAFF: 0
          SINGLE MEN: 0   SHORT TERM: NR
        SINGLE WOMEN: 0   RETIRED: 0

        TOTAL ACTIVE: 2

FIELD OF SERVICE	YEAR BEGAN	PERSONNEL NOW	PERSONNEL NEW	RELATED CHURCHES	PEOPLE GROUPS	NOTES
Kenya	1979	2	2		1	

Full Gospel Evangelistic Association

5828 Chippewa
Houston TX 77086

Tel. (713) 448-5125
EXECUTIVE OFFICER: Fred Franks
ORGANIZED: 1951
DESCRIPTION: An interdenominational agency of Pentecostal and
    Holiness tradition engaged in church construction,
    general Christian education, childcare and support of
    nationals.
TOTAL INCOME: NR   FOR OVERSEAS MINISTRIES: $484,000
PERSONNEL:
    NORTH AMERICANS OVERSEAS   NON-NORTH AMERICANS OVERSEAS: 0
            MARRIED: 20   NORTH AMERICAN ADM. STAFF: 2
         SINGLE MEN: 0   SHORT TERM: NR
       SINGLE WOMEN: 2   RETIRED: 0

       TOTAL ACTIVE: 22
NOTES: Overseas income estimated by MARC.

Full Gospel Grace Fellowship

1704 S Harvard Ave.
Tulsa OK 74104
P.O. ADDRESS:
Box 4300
Tulsa OK 74104

Tel. (918) 939-4651
EXECUTIVE OFFICER: Tommy J. Scott
ORGANIZED:
DESCRIPTION: A nondenominational agency of evangelical
    tradition supporting missionaries engaged in evangelism in
    Latin America.
TOTAL INCOME: $78,000   FOR OVERSEAS MINISTRIES: $78,000
PERSONNEL:
    NORTH AMERICANS OVERSEAS   NON-NORTH AMERICANS OVERSEAS: NR
            MARRIED: NR   NORTH AMERICAN ADM. STAFF: NR
         SINGLE MEN: NR   SHORT TERM: 0
       SINGLE WOMEN: NR   RETIRED: NR

       TOTAL ACTIVE: 14
NOTES: Overseas income estimated by MARC.

FIELD OF SERVICE	YEAR BEGAN	PERSONNEL NOW	PERSONNEL NEW	RELATED CHURCHES	PEOPLE GROUPS	NOTES
Argentina						
Belize						
Mexico						
Paraguay						
Surinam						

Full Gospel Native Missionary Association

P.O. ADDRESS:
Box 1240
Joplin MO 64801

Tel. (417) 781-0811
EXECUTIVE OFFICER: C. T. Buchanan
ORGANIZED: 1958
DESCRIPTION: No current information available. Information
    from 1976 directory. An interdenominational fund-raising
    agency of Pentecostal tradition supporting national
    workers, and involved in evangelism, support of orphans
    and children's homes, and education. Also supports
    national churches, pastors and evangelists.

TOTAL INCOME: NR   FOR OVERSEAS MINISTRIES: NR
PERSONNEL:
    NORTH AMERICANS OVERSEAS   NON-NORTH AMERICANS OVERSEAS: NR
               MARRIED: NR   NORTH AMERICAN ADM. STAFF: NR
            SINGLE MEN: NR   SHORT TERM: NR
          SINGLE WOMEN: NR   RETIRED: NR

          TOTAL ACTIVE: NR

FIELD OF SERVICE	YEAR BEGAN	PERSONNEL NOW	NEW	RELATED CHURCHES	PEOPLE GROUPS	NOTES
Haiti				70		2
India				100		1
Indonesia						
Korea, Rep. of						2
Mexico						2
Philippines						
Sri Lanka						
Thailand						

    1. Home for girls and orphanage.
    2. Orphanage.

Fuller Evangelistic Association

44 S Mentor Ave.
Pasadena CA 91106
P.O. ADDRESS:
Box 989
Pasadena CA 91102

Tel. (213) 449-0425
EXECUTIVE OFFICER: Carl F. George
ORGANIZED: 1943
DESCRIPTION: A nondenominational service agency of evangelical
    tradition providing a channel for funds to support
    evangelism and church planting ministries overseas. Also
    sponsors a radio ministry and offers church growth
    consultation services in the USA.
TOTAL INCOME: $1,016,000   FOR OVERSEAS MINISTRIES: $0
PERSONNEL:
    NORTH AMERICANS OVERSEAS   NON-NORTH AMERICANS OVERSEAS: 0
               MARRIED: 0   NORTH AMERICAN ADM. STAFF: 0
            SINGLE MEN: 0   SHORT TERM: 0
          SINGLE WOMEN: 0   RETIRED: 0

          TOTAL ACTIVE: 0

Fundamental Evangelistic Association

P.O. ADDRESS:
Box 6278
Los Osos CA 90026

Tel. (805) 528-3534
EXECUTIVE OFFICER: M. H. Reynolds, Jr.
ORGANIZED: 1947
DESCRIPTION: A nondenominational agency of fundamentalist
    tradition which, while mainly active in the USA, is
    raising and transmitting funds for mission work.
    Missionaries sent through other agencies, primarily
    Independent Faith Mission, Inc. (Pittsburgh, PA).
TOTAL INCOME: $138,000   FOR OVERSEAS MINISTRIES: NR
PERSONNEL:
    NORTH AMERICANS OVERSEAS   NON-NORTH AMERICANS OVERSEAS: NR
               MARRIED: 0   NORTH AMERICAN ADM. STAFF: 8
            SINGLE MEN: 0   SHORT TERM: 0

SINGLE WOMEN: 0   RETIRED: NR

     TOTAL ACTIVE: 0
NOTES: Income estimated by MARC.

General Association of Regular Baptist Churches

1300 N Meacham Rd.
Schaumburg IL 60195

Tel. (312) 843-1600
EXECUTIVE OFFICER: John G. Balyo
ORGANIZED: 1932
DESCRIPTION: Maintains no overseas agency as such but approves
     other Baptist agencies as recipients of personnel and funds.
TOTAL INCOME: NR   FOR OVERSEAS MINISTRIES: NR
PERSONNEL:
     NORTH AMERICANS OVERSEAS   NON-NORTH AMERICANS OVERSEAS: 0
            MARRIED: 0   NORTH AMERICAN ADM. STAFF: NR
         SINGLE MEN: 0   SHORT TERM: 0
       SINGLE WOMEN: 0   RETIRED: NR

     TOTAL ACTIVE: 0

General Baptist Foreign Mission Society, Inc.

Hwy. 67 North
Poplar Bluff MO 63901
P.O. ADDRESS:
Box 537
Poplar Bluff MO 63901

Tel. (314) 785-7975
EXECUTIVE OFFICER: Charles L. Carr
ORGANIZED: 1905   AFFILIATION: EFMA
DESCRIPTION: A denominational sending agency of Baptist
     tradition establishing churches and involved in theological
     education, medicine, orphanage and childcare, and self-help
     projects.
TOTAL INCOME: $304,410   FOR OVERSEAS MINISTRIES: $304,410
PERSONNEL:
     NORTH AMERICANS OVERSEAS   NON-NORTH AMERICANS OVERSEAS: 2
            MARRIED: 10   NORTH AMERICAN ADM. STAFF: 2
         SINGLE MEN: 0   SHORT TERM: 0
       SINGLE WOMEN: 1   RETIRED: 8

        TOTAL ACTIVE: 11

FIELD OF SERVICE	YEAR BEGAN	PERSONNEL NOW	NEW	RELATED CHURCHES	PEOPLE GROUPS	NOTES
Jamaica	1965	2		8		
Oceania-general	1947	2		1		
Philippines	1961	7	5	75	1	

General Conference Mennonite Church SEE: Mennonite Brethren Missions/Services

General Conference Mennonite Church, Commission on Overseas Mission

722 Main St.
Newton KS 67114

P.O. ADDRESS:
Box 347
Newton KS 67114

Tel. (316) 283-5100
EXECUTIVE OFFICER: Howard J. Habegger
ORGANIZED: 1872
DESCRIPTION: A denominational sending agency of Mennonite
 tradition establishing churches and involved in agricultural
 assistance, general Christian education, evangelism, nurture
 or support of national churches, literature distribution
 and medicine.
TOTAL INCOME: $2,062,168   FOR OVERSEAS MINISTRIES: $2,062,168
PERSONNEL:
 NORTH AMERICANS OVERSEAS   NON-NORTH AMERICANS OVERSEAS: 1
       MARRIED: 102   NORTH AMERICAN ADM. STAFF: 10
    SINGLE MEN: 1   SHORT TERM: 19
  SINGLE WOMEN: 19   RETIRED: 33

  TOTAL ACTIVE: 122

FIELD OF SERVICE	YEAR BEGAN	PERSONNEL NOW	NEW	RELATED CHURCHES	PEOPLE GROUPS	NOTES
Bolivia	1974	4	2	6		
Botswana	1974	7	5			
Brazil	1975	4	2	24		
Colombia	1945	7	4	10		
Costa Rica	1977	2				
Hong-Kong	1980	2	2	1		
India	1900	7	5	10		
Japan	1950	19	9	16		
Lesotho	1973	4	4			
Mexico	1950	13	16	3		
Paraguay	1948	3	3			
Taiwan Rep of China	1954	21	29	17		
Upper Volta	1977	4	4			
Uruguay	1956	2		4		
Zaire	1912	28	16	50		

General Conference of Seventh-day Adventists

6840 Eastern Ave. NW
Washington D.C. 20012

Tel. (202) 723-0800
EXECUTIVE OFFICER: Neal C. Wilson
ORGANIZED: 1863
DESCRIPTION: The denominational sending agency of the Seventh-
 day Adventist Church, responsible for promotion of
 missions and the recruitment, specialized training and
 sending of church workers for medical, educational,
 publishing and evangelistic ministries.
TOTAL INCOME: $60,000,000   FOR OVERSEAS MINISTRIES: $60,000,000
PERSONNEL:
 NORTH AMERICANS OVERSEAS   NON-NORTH AMERICANS OVERSEAS: NR
       MARRIED: 924   NORTH AMERICAN ADM. STAFF: NA
    SINGLE MEN: 4   SHORT TERM: 111
  SINGLE WOMEN: 68   RETIRED: NA

  TOTAL ACTIVE: 996

FIELD OF SERVICE	YEAR BEGAN	PERSONNEL NOW	NEW	RELATED CHURCHES	PEOPLE GROUPS	NOTES
Argentina	1890	6	4	197		

296

FIELD OF SERVICE	YEAR BEGAN	PERSONNEL NOW	NEW	RELATED CHURCHES	PEOPLE GROUPS	NOTES
Australia	1885	5	4	422		
Bangladesh	1906	10	6	24		
Belize	1929	2		23		
Bolivia	1907	6	2	59		
Botswana	1921	3	3	21		
Brazil	1894	36	12	772		
Burundi	1925	10	2	109		
Cameroon	1928	4	2	69		
Chad	1977	2	2	3		
Chile	1895	6	6	133		
Colombia	1921	6	4	199		
Costa Rica	1903	2		49		
Cyprus	1932	14	5			
Ecuador	1905	2		20		
Egypt	1879	2		14		
Ethiopia	1907	13	11	87		
Gambia	1978	4	4	1		
Germany, Fed. Rep.	1875	2		392		
Ghana	1894	8	6	216		
Greece	1907	7	3	10		
Guam	1948	38	18	8		
Guatemala	1908	4		68		
Haiti	1905	12	10	154		
Honduras	1891	13	5	399		
Hong-Kong	1888	37	18	14		
India	1895	39	4	589		
Indonesia	1900	26	10	662		
Iran	1911	6	2	6		
Jamaica	1893	10	6	235		
Japan	1896	37	15	90		
Kenya	1906	50	34	491		
Korea, Rep. of	1904	17	7	310		
Lebanon	1908	6	2	10		
Lesotho	1960	5	2	14		
Liberia	1927	8	8	28		
Malawi	1902	26	13	202		
Malaysia	1961	10	4	138		
Mexico	1893	31	16	378		
Nepal	1960	2	2	1		
Netherlands Antilles	1934	2	2	5		
Nigeria	1914	14	10	270		
Pacific Trust Terr.	1930	7	7			
Pakistan	1914	39	13	36		
Panama	1906	2	2	70		
Papua New Guinea	1949	2	2	382		
Peru	1898	16	10	151		
Philippines	1906	25	8	1600		
Pitcairn Islands	1895	2	2	1		
Portugal	1904	2	2	43		
Puerto Rico	1901	67	37	219		
Rwanda	1920	6	2	366		
Sierra Leone	1905	8	5	19		
Singapore	1904	63	31	6		
South Africa	1887	4	4	167		
Sri Lanka	1922	8	2	23		

FIELD OF SERVICE	YEAR BEGAN	PERSONNEL NOW	NEW	RELATED CHURCHES	PEOPLE GROUPS	NOTES
Surinam	1945	2	2	9		
Swaziland	1968	2		7		
Switzerland	1870	2	2	59		
Taiwan Rep of China	1909	31	8	29		
Tanzania	1903	15	8	236		
Thailand	1919	19	12	13		
Trinidad and Tobago	1893	11	5	117		
United Kingdom	1898	14	6	157		
Upper Volta	1972	2		1		
Venezuela	1910	4	4	42		
Zaire	1921	24	10	283		
Zambia	1905	33	19	190		
Zimbabwe	1894	43	16	267		

General Conference of the Church of God Seventh Day SEE: Church of God, Seventh Day, General Conference

General Conference of the Evangelical Baptist Church, Inc.

2400 E Ash St.
Goldsboro NC 37530

Tel. (919) 735-0831
EXECUTIVE OFFICER: William H. Carter
ORGANIZED: 1935
DESCRIPTION: A denominational sending agency of Baptist
    tradition supporting national churches and national
    workers and missionaries sent through other agencies.
TOTAL INCOME: NR   FOR OVERSEAS MINISTRIES: NR
PERSONNEL:
    NORTH AMERICANS OVERSEAS   NON-NORTH AMERICANS OVERSEAS: NR
              MARRIED: NR   NORTH AMERICAN ADM. STAFF: NR
           SINGLE MEN: NR   SHORT TERM: NR
         SINGLE WOMEN: NR   RETIRED: NR

        TOTAL ACTIVE: NR

FIELD OF SERVICE	YEAR BEGAN	PERSONNEL NOW	NEW	RELATED CHURCHES	PEOPLE GROUPS	NOTES
India	1937					
Mexico	1965					

Gen. Conf. of the Mennonite Brethren Chrs., Bd. of Msns. and Services SEE: Mennonite Brethren Missions/Services

Gideons International

2900 Lebanon Rd.
Nashville TN 37214

Tel. (615) 883-8533
EXECUTIVE OFFICER: R. Don Efird
ORGANIZED: 1899
DESCRIPTION: An international, interdenominational Christian
    business and professional association engaged in Bible
    distribution and personal evangelism. Active in 124
    countries, 15 of which have their own national offices.
    Ministry carried out by national Christians; in the last
    3 years membership increased by 7,500 and ministry was
    established in 18 more countries.
TOTAL INCOME: $23,000,000   FOR OVERSEAS MINISTRIES: $15,000,000

PERSONNEL:
```
     NORTH AMERICANS OVERSEAS    NON-NORTH AMERICANS OVERSEAS:    3
          MARRIED:       0          NORTH AMERICAN ADM. STAFF:   46
       SINGLE MEN:       0                      SHORT TERM:       0
     SINGLE WOMEN:       0                         RETIRED:       4
                        -----
     TOTAL ACTIVE:       0
```
NOTES: Administrative personnel consist of 41 full
        time and five part-time.

Glad Tidings Missionary Society, Inc.

3456 Fraser St.
Vancouver BC V5V 4C4
Canada

Tel. (604) 873-3621
EXECUTIVE OFFICER: Maureen Gaglandi
ORGANIZED: 1948
DESCRIPTION: A nondenominational sending agency of independent
    tradition engaged in evangelism and establishing churches.
    Also involved in education, medicine and support of
    nationals.
TOTAL INCOME: $500,000   FOR OVERSEAS MINISTRIES: $500,000
PERSONNEL:
```
     NORTH AMERICANS OVERSEAS    NON-NORTH AMERICANS OVERSEAS:   NR
          MARRIED:      NR          NORTH AMERICAN ADM. STAFF:   20
       SINGLE MEN:      NR                      SHORT TERM:       6
     SINGLE WOMEN:      NR                         RETIRED:       0
                        -----
     TOTAL ACTIVE:      40
```

FIELD OF SERVICE	YEAR BEGAN	PERSONNEL NOW	NEW	RELATED CHURCHES	PEOPLE GROUPS	NOTES
Hong-Kong	1959					
India	1965					
Israel	1976					
Jamaica	1970					
Japan	1965					
Malawi	1976					
Mexico	1972					
Singapore	1965					
Taiwan Rep of China	1952					
Uganda	1960					

Global Concern, Inc.

Midland Bank Bldg.
Minneapolis MN 55402
P.O. ADDRESS:
Postal Drawer 7
Montrose CA 91020

Tel. (213) 352-3083
EXECUTIVE OFFICER: Mervin E. Rosell
ORGANIZED: 1951
DESCRIPTION: An interdenominational specialized service agency
    of evangelical tradition expediting mercy projects and
    engaged in evangelism and training. Projects include
    relief, broadcasting, church construction and education.
    Also involved in literature, research and supplying
    equipment.
TOTAL INCOME: $167,246   FOR OVERSEAS MINISTRIES: $128,922
PERSONNEL:
```
     NORTH AMERICANS OVERSEAS    NON-NORTH AMERICANS OVERSEAS:    0
          MARRIED:       0          NORTH AMERICAN ADM. STAFF:    4
       SINGLE MEN:       0                      SHORT TERM:       0
```

```
SINGLE WOMEN:     0                          RETIRED:     0
        -----
TOTAL ACTIVE:     0
```
NOTES: Agency has no overseas personnel because they
        work with established missionary organizations
        overseas.

Global Orphanages, Inc.

1012 City Line Ave.
Philadelphia PA 19151

Tel. (215) 642-2255
EXECUTIVE OFFICER: A.E.K. Brenner
ORGANIZED: 1951
DESCRIPTION: An interdenominational service agency of
    evangelical tradition providing funds and services to
    orphanages in the USA and overseas.
TOTAL INCOME: $25,000   FOR OVERSEAS MINISTRIES: $25,000
PERSONNEL:

```
NORTH AMERICANS OVERSEAS    NON-NORTH AMERICANS OVERSEAS:    NR
          MARRIED:    0        NORTH AMERICAN ADM. STAFF:     3
       SINGLE MEN:    0                      SHORT TERM:      0
     SINGLE WOMEN:    0                         RETIRED:     NR
                   -----
     TOTAL ACTIVE:    0
```


Global Outreach Mission

496 Pearl Street
Buffalo NY 14203
P.O. ADDRESS:
Box 711
Buffalo NY 14240

Tel. (716) 842-2220
EXECUTIVE OFFICER: J. O. Blackwood
ORGANIZED: 1943   AFFILIATION: IFMA
DESCRIPTION: A nondenominational sending agency of
    evangelical and independent tradition establishing
    churches and engaged in radio and TV broadcasting,
    correspondence courses and literature distribution. Also
    engaged in evangelism on a personal and small group scale
    and Bible distribution.
TOTAL INCOME: $1,194,652   FOR OVERSEAS MINISTRIES: $1,194,652
PERSONNEL:

```
NORTH AMERICANS OVERSEAS    NON-NORTH AMERICANS OVERSEAS:    82
          MARRIED:   158       NORTH AMERICAN ADM. STAFF:     0
       SINGLE MEN:    2                      SHORT TERM:     16
     SINGLE WOMEN:   15                         RETIRED:     0
                   -----
     TOTAL ACTIVE:  175
```

FIELD OF SERVICE	YEAR BEGAN	PERSONNEL NOW	NEW	RELATED CHURCHES	PEOPLE GROUPS	NOTES
Bahamas	1974	2				
Bangladesh	1975	2				
Belgium	1946	7				
Brazil	1973	2				
Congo	1974	2				
Egypt	1974	8				
France	1946	47				

FIELD OF SERVICE	YEAR BEGAN	PERSONNEL NOW	NEW	RELATED CHURCHES	PEOPLE GROUPS	NOTES
Germany, Fed. Rep.	1946	8				
Ghana	1974	2				
Greece	1960	3				
India	1974	18				
Ireland	1965	8				
Jordan		4				
Korea, Rep. of	1974	2				
Namibia		2				
Netherlands		8				
Netherlands Antilles	1946	4				
Peru	1975	2				
Portugal	1952	3				
Spain	1946	9				
Sweden	1975	2				
United Kingdom		2				
Yugoslavia		2				

Global Outreach Incorporated
SEE: Global Outreach Mission

Globe Missionary Evangelism

8600 Hwy. 98 West
Pensacola FL 32506
P.O. ADDRESS:
Box 3138
Pensacola FL 32506

Tel. (904) 453-3451
EXECUTIVE OFFICER: Ken Sumrall
ORGANIZED: 1973
DESCRIPTION: A nondenominational sending agency of charismatic
    tradition involved in evangelism, training and supplying
    equipment.
TOTAL INCOME: $383,630   FOR OVERSEAS MINISTRIES: $167,000
PERSONNEL:
    NORTH AMERICANS OVERSEAS   NON-NORTH AMERICANS OVERSEAS: 0
            MARRIED: 42   NORTH AMERICAN ADM. STAFF: 2
          SINGLE MEN: 1   SHORT TERM: 30
        SINGLE WOMEN: 1   RETIRED: 0

        TOTAL ACTIVE: 44
NOTES: One of the two North American
        administrators works part-time.

FIELD OF SERVICE	YEAR BEGAN	PERSONNEL NOW	NEW	RELATED CHURCHES	PEOPLE GROUPS	NOTES
Australia	1978	2	2			
France	1978	2	2			
Guatemala	1971	4				
Honduras	1976	9	9			
Kenya	1974	2				
Mexico	1971	14	4			
Taiwan Rep of China	1975	2				
United Kingdom	1978	7	7			

Go-Ye Fellowship

1600 Morton Ave.
Los Angeles CA 90026
P.O. ADDRESS:
Box 26405
Los Angeles CA 90026

Tel. (213) 680-9166
EXECUTIVE OFFICER: Hubert Mitchell
ORGANIZED: 1944
DESCRIPTION: An interdenominational sending agency of
    evangelical and independent tradition establishing
    churches and engaged in fund transmittal, radio
    broadcasting, correspondence courses and evangelism.
TOTAL INCOME: $311,718   FOR OVERSEAS MINISTRIES: $290,401
PERSONNEL:
    NORTH AMERICANS OVERSEAS   NON-NORTH AMERICANS OVERSEAS: 0
            MARRIED: 16   NORTH AMERICAN ADM. STAFF: 3
        SINGLE MEN: 1   SHORT TERM: 1
      SINGLE WOMEN: 8   RETIRED: 0

      TOTAL ACTIVE: 25

FIELD OF SERVICE	YEAR BEGAN	PERSONNEL NOW	PERSONNEL NEW	RELATED CHURCHES	PEOPLE GROUPS	NOTES
Argentina	1969	3				
Brazil	1956	6	1	1		
Germany, Fed. Rep.	1976	2				1
India	1951	2				
Indonesia	1938	5		100		
Japan	1957	4	2			
South Africa	1953	1				
Taiwan Rep of China	1951	1		1		

Note: This couple was formerly in Iran but now
uses Germany, Fed. Rep. as headquarters area
for ministry to muslims throughout Europe and
Mid-East (when possible to enter those
countries).

Good Shepherd Agricultural Mission, Inc.

822 Main St.
Fontanelle IA 50846
P.O. ADDRESS:
Box 116
Fontanelle IA 50846

Tel. (515) 745-4041
EXECUTIVE OFFICER: Hilda L. Dahlke
ORGANIZED: 1948
DESCRIPTION: A nondenominational sending agency of evangelical
    tradition training national youth using a Christian farm
    home as the training center. Engaged in agriculture,
    community development, education, personal evangelism and
    medicine. Also supporting national churches and involved
    in fund transmittal.
TOTAL INCOME: $76,400   FOR OVERSEAS MINISTRIES: $52,130
PERSONNEL:
    NORTH AMERICANS OVERSEAS   NON-NORTH AMERICANS OVERSEAS: 0
            MARRIED: 2   NORTH AMERICAN ADM. STAFF: 2
        SINGLE MEN: 0   SHORT TERM: 0
      SINGLE WOMEN: 1   RETIRED: 0

      TOTAL ACTIVE: 3

```
------------------------------------------------------------
                    YEAR     PERSONNEL  RELATED   PEOPLE
FIELD OF SERVICE    BEGAN    NOW   NEW  CHURCHES  GROUPS  NOTES
------------------------------------------------------------
India               1948     3              4        5
```

Gospel Association for the Blind, Inc.

4705 N Federal Highway
Boca Raton FL 33432
P.O. ADDRESS:
Box 62
Delray Beach FL 33444

Tel. (305) 395-0022
EXECUTIVE OFFICER: Ralph Montanus
ORGANIZED: 1947
DESCRIPTION: A nondenominational home and specialized service
    agency of evangelical tradition providing braille
    publications and Gospel recordings in 47 languages.   Also
    involved in aid, psychological counseling and camp
    programs. Operates a free circulating library for the
    blind.

```
TOTAL INCOME:         NR          FOR OVERSEAS MINISTRIES:    NR
PERSONNEL:
  NORTH AMERICANS OVERSEAS    NON-NORTH AMERICANS OVERSEAS:   0
          MARRIED:    0          NORTH AMERICAN ADM. STAFF:   0
       SINGLE MEN:    0                       SHORT TERM:     0
     SINGLE WOMEN:    0                         RETIRED:      0
                    -----
     TOTAL ACTIVE:    0
```

Gospel Baptist Missions

412 Laura Lee
Tallahassee FL 32301

DESCRIPTION: No current information available. Information
    from 1976 directory. A nondenominational sending agency
    of Baptist tradition supporting missionaries engaged in
    church planting, literature distribution, and evangelism.

```
TOTAL INCOME:         NR          FOR OVERSEAS MINISTRIES:    NR
PERSONNEL:
  NORTH AMERICANS OVERSEAS    NON-NORTH AMERICANS OVERSEAS:   NR
          MARRIED:    NR         NORTH AMERICAN ADM. STAFF:   NR
       SINGLE MEN:    NR                      SHORT TERM:     NR
     SINGLE WOMEN:    NR                        RETIRED:      NR
                    -----
     TOTAL ACTIVE:    NR
```

Gospel Crusade World Wide Mission Outreach

P.O. ADDRESS:
Box 279, Rt. 2
Brandenton FL 33508

Tel. (813) 747-6481
EXECUTIVE OFFICER: Gerald Derstine
ORGANIZED: 1953
DESCRIPTION: An interdenominational sending agency of
    evangelical tradition primarily concerned with assisting
    nationals in the indigenous church. Also involved in
    church planting, evangelism, fund raising and pastor's
    training.

```
TOTAL INCOME:   $200,000   FOR OVERSEAS MINISTRIES:    $178,000
PERSONNEL:
  NORTH AMERICANS OVERSEAS    NON-NORTH AMERICANS OVERSEAS:   0
          MARRIED:    12         NORTH AMERICAN ADM. STAFF:   1
       SINGLE MEN:    0                       SHORT TERM:     4
```

```
SINGLE WOMEN:    1                           RETIRED:    9
                -----
    TOTAL ACTIVE:   13
----------------------------------------------------------------
                   YEAR    PERSONNEL    RELATED   PEOPLE
FIELD OF SERVICE   BEGAN   NOW   NEW    CHURCHES  GROUPS  NOTES
----------------------------------------------------------------
Haiti              1953    2              115
Honduras           1965    3     2        14        2
Indonesia          1962
Israel             1975    4     2
Jamaica            1968                     7
Mexico             1972    2
Philippines        1962                   244        5
Sweden             1974    2
Yugoslavia         1977                     4
```

Gospel Films, Inc.

2735 Apple Ave.
Muskegon MI 49442
P.O. ADDRESS:
Box 455
Muskegon MI 49443

Tel. (616) 773-3361
EXECUTIVE OFFICER: Billy Zeoli
ORGANIZED: 1950
DESCRIPTION: A nondenominational specialized service agency of
     evangelical tradition which produces and distributes
     Christian films in 164 countries using 40 languages.
TOTAL INCOME: NR   FOR OVERSEAS MINISTRIES: NR
PERSONNEL:
     NORTH AMERICANS OVERSEAS   NON-NORTH AMERICANS OVERSEAS: NR
            MARRIED: 0   NORTH AMERICAN ADM. STAFF: 36
         SINGLE MEN: 0   SHORT TERM: 0
       SINGLE WOMEN: 0   RETIRED: 0

       TOTAL ACTIVE: 0
NOTES: Income figures are available to the
        public upon written request.

Gospel Literature International

2126 Knoll Dr. Unit C
Ventura CA 93003
P.O. ADDRESS:
Box 6688
Ventura CA 93003

Tel. (805) 644-3929
EXECUTIVE OFFICER: Paul R. Fretz
ORGANIZED: 1961
DESCRIPTION: An interdenominational service organization
     providing copyrighted English Christian education
     curriculum materials for translation and adaptation into
     other languages. Material is provided in more than 90
     languages and support is provided to Christian publishers
     in more than 30 nations.
TOTAL INCOME: $150,000   FOR OVERSEAS MINISTRIES: $65,000
PERSONNEL:
     NORTH AMERICANS OVERSEAS   NON-NORTH AMERICANS OVERSEAS: 0
            MARRIED: 0   NORTH AMERICAN ADM. STAFF: 0
         SINGLE MEN: 0   SHORT TERM: 0

```
SINGLE WOMEN:    0                          RETIRED:    0
                -----
TOTAL ACTIVE:    0
```

Gospel Mission of South America

1401 SW 21st Ave.
Ft. Lauderdale FL 33312

Tel. (305) 587-2975
EXECUTIVE OFFICER: Hudson Shedd
ORGANIZED: 1923
DESCRIPTION: A nondenominational sending agency of Baptist
    tradition establishing churches and involved in radio and
    TV broadcasting, correspondence courses, theological
    education and evangelism.
TOTAL INCOME: $367,728   FOR OVERSEAS MINISTRIES: $330,998
PERSONNEL:

```
    NORTH AMERICANS OVERSEAS    NON-NORTH AMERICANS OVERSEAS:    9
            MARRIED:   41          NORTH AMERICAN ADM. STAFF:    6
          SINGLE MEN:   0                        SHORT TERM:    2
        SINGLE WOMEN:   6                           RETIRED:    1
                      -----
        TOTAL ACTIVE:  47
```

FIELD OF SERVICE	YEAR BEGAN	PERSONNEL NOW	PERSONNEL NEW	RELATED CHURCHES	PEOPLE GROUPS	NOTES
Argentina	1971	10	3	4	1	
Chile	1923	38	2	57	3	
Uruguay	1971	10		5	1	

Gospel Missionary Union

10000 North Oak
Kansas City MO 64155

Tel. (816) 734-8500
EXECUTIVE OFFICER: Dick Darr
ORGANIZED: 1892   AFFILIATION: IFMA
DESCRIPTION: A nondenominational sending agency of evangelical
    and Baptist tradition establishing churches and engaged
    in evangelism, literature production, radio and TV
    production and development of human resourses.
TOTAL INCOME: $4,016,478   FOR OVERSEAS MINISTRIES: $2,687,248
PERSONNEL:

```
    NORTH AMERICANS OVERSEAS    NON-NORTH AMERICANS OVERSEAS:    2
            MARRIED:  314          NORTH AMERICAN ADM. STAFF:   32
          SINGLE MEN:   4                        SHORT TERM:   17
        SINGLE WOMEN:  71                           RETIRED:   34
                      -----
        TOTAL ACTIVE: 389
```

FIELD OF SERVICE	YEAR BEGAN	PERSONNEL NOW	PERSONNEL NEW	RELATED CHURCHES	PEOPLE GROUPS	NOTES
Argentina	1956	22		13		
Austria	1966	9		4		
Bahamas	1956	18	3			
Belgium	1966	8	2	4		
Belize	1955	13	3	9		
Bolivia	1937	32	1	23	2	
Brazil	1911	31	2	19		

FIELD OF SERVICE	YEAR BEGAN	PERSONNEL NOW	NEW	RELATED CHURCHES	PEOPLE GROUPS	NOTES
Colombia	1908	25	4	80	1	
Ecuador	1896	72	8	177	2	
France	1960	13	4	7		
Germany, Fed. Rep.	1961	6	2	1		
Greece	1959	3		13		
Italy	1950	8	3	3		
Mali	1919	37	3	37	1	
Mexico	1956	19	4	5		
Morocco	1894	23	3	4	1	
Panama	1953	15	4		1	
Spain	1967	4	2	2		

Gospel Outreach

430 B Street
Eureka CA 95501
P.O. ADDRESS:
Box 1022
Eureka CA 95501

Tel. (707) 445-2135
EXECUTIVE OFFICER: James Durkin
ORGANIZED: 1971
DESCRIPTION: A nondenominational sending agency of charismatic tradition engaged in church planting and evangelism. Also involved in missionary orientation and training and self-help projects.
TOTAL INCOME: $3,000,000   FOR OVERSEAS MINISTRIES: $80,000
PERSONNEL:

NORTH AMERICANS OVERSEAS		NON-NORTH AMERICANS OVERSEAS:	0
MARRIED:	20	NORTH AMERICAN ADM. STAFF:	2
SINGLE MEN:	9	SHORT TERM:	0
SINGLE WOMEN:	5	RETIRED:	0
TOTAL ACTIVE:	34		

FIELD OF SERVICE	YEAR BEGAN	PERSONNEL NOW	NEW	RELATED CHURCHES	PEOPLE GROUPS	NOTES
Germany, Fed. Rep.	1973	14	20	1		
Guatemala	1974	14	21	1		
Nicaragua	1980					
United Kingdom	1979	2	2	1		

Gospel Outreach SEE: Missionary Electronics, Inc.

Gospel Outreach to India, Inc.

5721 N Kostner Ave.
Chicago IL 60646

Tel. (312) 725-0047
EXECUTIVE OFFICER: LeRoy F. Clark
ORGANIZED: 1976
DESCRIPTION: An interdenominational agency of evangelical and independent tradition nurturing and supporting national churches and engaged in childcare and evangelism. Supports 22 national missionaries and workers in India and is related to 46 churches.
TOTAL INCOME: $6,151   FOR OVERSEAS MINISTRIES: $6,151

PERSONNEL:
```
    NORTH AMERICANS OVERSEAS      NON-NORTH AMERICANS OVERSEAS:   0
            MARRIED:     0         NORTH AMERICAN ADM. STAFF:     0
         SINGLE MEN:     0                       SHORT TERM:      0
       SINGLE WOMEN:     0                          RETIRED:      0
                       -----
       TOTAL ACTIVE:     0
```

Gospel Recordings Incorporated

122 Glendale Blvd.
Los Angeles CA 90026

Tel. (213) 624-7461
EXECUTIVE OFFICER: Larry D. Allmon
ORGANIZED: 1939   AFFILIATION: IFMA-Assoc. member
DESCRIPTION: A nondenominational specialized service agency
    of evangelical tradition producing and distributing audio
    and visual recordings and equipment for communicating the
    Gospel to peoples in their own language, especially those
    less likely to be exposed to other forms of Gospel
    presentation.
```
TOTAL INCOME:     $537,000        FOR OVERSEAS MINISTRIES:    NR
PERSONNEL:
    NORTH AMERICANS OVERSEAS      NON-NORTH AMERICANS OVERSEAS:   1
            MARRIED:     2         NORTH AMERICAN ADM. STAFF:    13
         SINGLE MEN:     0                       SHORT TERM:      4
       SINGLE WOMEN:     2                          RETIRED:      3
                       -----
       TOTAL ACTIVE:     4
```

FIELD OF SERVICE	YEAR BEGAN	PERSONNEL NOW	PERSONNEL NEW	RELATED CHURCHES	PEOPLE GROUPS	NOTES
Brazil	1977	5				
France	1965					
Germany, Fed. Rep.	1965	2				
Mexico	1961	2				
Netherlands	1965					
Switzerland	1965					

Note: Attempting to reach,
through recordings, over 4000
language and dialect groups less
than three per cent Christian.

Gospel Recordings of Canada, Inc.

2 Audley St.
Toronto ON M8Y 2X2
Canada

Tel. (416) 251-1861
EXECUTIVE OFFICER: Robert Phillips
ORGANIZED: 1939   AFFILIATION: IFMA-Assoc. member
DESCRIPTION: A nondenominational specialized service agency
    producing and distributing audio and visual recordings
    and equipment for communicating the Gospel to peoples in
    their own tongue, especially for those less likely to be
    exposed to other forms of Gospel presentation. An agency
    of Gospel Recordings International.
```
TOTAL INCOME:     $147,407        FOR OVERSEAS MINISTRIES:    NR
PERSONNEL:
    NORTH AMERICANS OVERSEAS      NON-NORTH AMERICANS OVERSEAS:   3
            MARRIED:     2         NORTH AMERICAN ADM. STAFF:    12
         SINGLE MEN:     2                       SHORT TERM:      0
```

```
         SINGLE WOMEN:     0                              RETIRED:     0
                         -----
         TOTAL ACTIVE:     4
------------------------------------------------------------------------
                       YEAR     PERSONNEL   RELATED    PEOPLE
FIELD OF SERVICE       BEGAN    NOW   NEW   CHURCHES   GROUPS   NOTES
------------------------------------------------------------------------
Kenya                  1977      2     2
Sudan                  1978      1     1
```

Grace and Truth, Inc.

215 Oak St.
Danville IL 61832

Tel. (217) 442-1120
EXECUTIVE OFFICER: Sam O. Hadley
ORGANIZED: 1931
DESCRIPTION: A nondenominational specialized agency of
   Plymouth Brethren tradition producing literature,
   largely tracts, for distribution on request.

```
TOTAL INCOME:    $150,000        FOR OVERSEAS MINISTRIES:    $0
PERSONNEL:
   NORTH AMERICANS OVERSEAS    NON-NORTH AMERICANS OVERSEAS:    0
          MARRIED:    0           NORTH AMERICAN ADM. STAFF:   NR
       SINGLE MEN:    0                       SHORT TERM:       0
     SINGLE WOMEN:    0                          RETIRED:      NR
                    -----
     TOTAL ACTIVE:    0
```

Grace Mission, Inc.

2125 Martindale Ave. SW
Grand Rapids MI 49509

Tel. (616) 241-5666
EXECUTIVE OFFICER: Daniel C. Bultema
ORGANIZED: 1939   AFFILIATION: EFMA
DESCRIPTION: An interdenominational sending agency of
   evangelical tradition engaged in radio and TV
   broadcasting, literature production, medical supplies,
   theological education and theological education by
   extension (TEE).

```
TOTAL INCOME:    $683,764   FOR OVERSEAS MINISTRIES:    $429,954
PERSONNEL:
   NORTH AMERICANS OVERSEAS    NON-NORTH AMERICANS OVERSEAS:    0
          MARRIED:   23           NORTH AMERICAN ADM. STAFF:   13
       SINGLE MEN:    0                       SHORT TERM:       7
     SINGLE WOMEN:    1                          RETIRED:     22
                    -----
     TOTAL ACTIVE:   24
```

Grand Old Gospel Fellowship, Inc.

610 E Mt. Pleasant Ave.
Philadelphia PA 19119

Tel. (215) 242-5550
DESCRIPTION: No current information available. Information
   from 1976 directory. A nondenominational agency of
   Plymouth Brethren tradition engaged in a radio, camping
   and crusade ministry. A radio program
   called "The Grand Old Gospel Hour" is broadcast in
   South America, Africa and Asia. There are eight
   affiliated churches along the Eastern seaboard of the USA.

```
TOTAL INCOME:     NR      FOR OVERSEAS MINISTRIES:    $31,200
PERSONNEL:
   NORTH AMERICANS OVERSEAS    NON-NORTH AMERICANS OVERSEAS:   NR
          MARRIED:   NR           NORTH AMERICAN ADM. STAFF:   NR
       SINGLE MEN:   NR                       SHORT TERM:      NR
```

SINGLE WOMEN: NR   RETIRED: NR

     TOTAL ACTIVE: 0
NOTES: Data from agency material.
         Overseas income estimated by MARC.

Great Commission Crusades, Inc.

W. Myakka Ave.
IntercessionCty FL 33848
P.O. ADDRESS:
Box 55
IntercessionCty FL 33848

Tel. (305) 348-5206
EXECUTIVE OFFICER: Edward E. Hayes
ORGANIZED: 1949
DESCRIPTION: An interdenominational agency of evangelical and
   Wesleyan tradition engaged in Bible distribution, church
   planting, education, literacy, literature production and
   distribution, support of nationals and psychological
   counseling.
TOTAL INCOME: $14,638   FOR OVERSEAS MINISTRIES: $13,580
PERSONNEL:
   NORTH AMERICANS OVERSEAS   NON-NORTH AMERICANS OVERSEAS: 0
             MARRIED: 0   NORTH AMERICAN ADM. STAFF: 4
          SINGLE MEN: 0   SHORT TERM: 2
        SINGLE WOMEN: 2   RETIRED: 3

      TOTAL ACTIVE: 2

FIELD OF SERVICE	YEAR BEGAN	PERSONNEL NOW	PERSONNEL NEW	RELATED CHURCHES	PEOPLE GROUPS	NOTES
Haiti	1946	4	2		1	

Greater Europe Mission

330 Schmale Rd.
Wheaton IL 60187
P.O. ADDRESS:
Box 668
Wheaton IL 60187

Tel. (312) 462-8050
EXECUTIVE OFFICER: Don Brugmann
ORGANIZED: 1949   AFFILIATION: IFMA
DESCRIPTION: A denominational sending agency establishing
   churches and engaged in evangelism, literature disribution,
   theological education and theological education by
   extension (TEE).
TOTAL INCOME: $4,092,480   FOR OVERSEAS MINISTRIES: $3,236,233
PERSONNEL:
   NORTH AMERICANS OVERSEAS   NON-NORTH AMERICANS OVERSEAS: 1
             MARRIED: 150   NORTH AMERICAN ADM. STAFF: 34
          SINGLE MEN: 1   SHORT TERM: 25
        SINGLE WOMEN: 9   RETIRED: 0

      TOTAL ACTIVE: 160

FIELD OF SERVICE	YEAR BEGAN	PERSONNEL NOW	PERSONNEL NEW	RELATED CHURCHES	PEOPLE GROUPS	NOTES
Austria	1965	10	6			

FIELD OF SERVICE	YEAR BEGAN	PERSONNEL NOW	PERSONNEL NEW	RELATED CHURCHES	PEOPLE GROUPS	NOTES
Belgium	1972	12	4			
Denmark	1976	2	2			
Europe-general	1973	4	2			
France	1949	47	15			
Germany, Fed. Rep.	1954	41	8			
Greece	1966	8	2			
Ireland	1974	6	5			
Italy	1954	14	8			
Portugal	1971	9	3			
Spain	1960	14	11			
Sweden	1956	15	4			
United Kingdom	1971	4	2			

Greater Mexican Missions

c/o Christian Resource Management
P.O. ADDRESS:
Box 2120
Orange CA 92669

Tel. (714) 997-3920
EXECUTIVE OFFICER: Emil Aanderud
ORGANIZED: 1951
DESCRIPTION: A nondenominational service agency of Baptist and
    fundamentalist tradition engaged in evangelism, literature
    distribution and a pastoral support and discipling
    ministry among nationals and national leaders.
TOTAL INCOME: $62,000   FOR OVERSEAS MINISTRIES: NR
PERSONNEL:
    NORTH AMERICANS OVERSEAS   NON-NORTH AMERICANS OVERSEAS: NR
            MARRIED: NR   NORTH AMERICAN ADM. STAFF: 0
        SINGLE MEN: NR   SHORT TERM: 0
      SINGLE WOMEN: NR   RETIRED: 0

      TOTAL ACTIVE: 2
NOTES: Agency no longer in Nebraska
        Must now be contacted through Christian
        Resource Management or to Mr. Aanderud
        directly at: Felix para 134, Mexico 19,
        D.F., Mexico

H.O.P.E. Bible Mission, Inc.

P.O. ADDRESS:
Box 161M
Morristown NH 07960

Tel. (201) 543-4492
EXECUTIVE OFFICER: I.M. Hone
ORGANIZED: 1950
DESCRIPTION: A nondenominational sending agency engaged in
    evangelism and Scripture distribution.
TOTAL INCOME: $114,900   FOR OVERSEAS MINISTRIES: $114,900
PERSONNEL:
    NORTH AMERICANS OVERSEAS   NON-NORTH AMERICANS OVERSEAS: NR
            MARRIED: NR   NORTH AMERICAN ADM. STAFF: NR
        SINGLE MEN: NR   SHORT TERM: NR
      SINGLE WOMEN: NR   RETIRED: NR

      TOTAL ACTIVE: 21

France
Germany, Fed. Rep.
Spain

Haggai Community

1774 N Sierra Bonita
Pasadena CA 91104

Tel. (213) 797-1389
EXECUTIVE OFFICER: Steve Hawthorne
ORGANIZED: 1977
DESCRIPTION: A nondenominational agency engaged in missionary
    orientation and training and motivating pre-candidate
    missionaries.
TOTAL INCOME: $1,300   FOR OVERSEAS MINISTRIES: $1,300
PERSONNEL:

NORTH AMERICANS OVERSEAS	NON-NORTH AMERICANS OVERSEAS:	0
MARRIED: 0	NORTH AMERICAN ADM. STAFF:	2
SINGLE MEN: 0	SHORT TERM:	0
SINGLE WOMEN: 0	RETIRED:	0

TOTAL ACTIVE: 0

Haggai Institute for Advanced
Leadership Training, Inc.

2751 Buford HwyNE Ste530
Atlanta GA 30324
P.O. ADDRESS:
Box 13
Atlanta GA 30370

Tel. (404) 325-2580
EXECUTIVE OFFICER: John Haggai
ORGANIZED: 1962
DESCRIPTION: A nondenominational specialized service agency
    serving national churches with training in evangelism.
    Training is conducted in Singapore with faculty, materials
    and methods of the Third World. Those trainees then teach
    techniques to others in their homeland.
TOTAL INCOME: $2,129,880   FOR OVERSEAS MINISTRIES: $2,129,880
PERSONNEL:

NORTH AMERICANS OVERSEAS	NON-NORTH AMERICANS OVERSEAS:	0
MARRIED: 1	NORTH AMERICAN ADM. STAFF:	15
SINGLE MEN: 0	SHORT TERM:	0
SINGLE WOMEN: 0	RETIRED:	0

TOTAL ACTIVE: 1

FIELD OF SERVICE	YEAR BEGAN	PERSONNEL NOW	NEW	RELATED CHURCHES	PEOPLE GROUPS	NOTES
Australia	1973					
Brazil	1979					
India	1979					
Ireland	1979					
Korea, Rep. of	1978					
Nigeria	1979					
Singapore	1970	1				

Haggai Institute SEE: Haggai Institute for Advanced
Leadership Training, Inc.

Hague Foreign Mission, Inc.

R.R. 1
East Omega MN 56569

Tel. (813) 525-4729
EXECUTIVE OFFICER: Alvin Larson
ORGANIZED: 1950
DESCRIPTION: No current information available. Information
    from 1976 directory. A nondenominational international
    service agency of Lutheran tradition supporting Norwegian
    missionaries in Japan and Ethiopia. Most of these
    missionaries are from the Mission Samband or Norwegian
    Lutheran Mission.

TOTAL INCOME: $96,600   FOR OVERSEAS MINISTRIES: NR
PERSONNEL:
    NORTH AMERICANS OVERSEAS   NON-NORTH AMERICANS OVERSEAS: NR
            MARRIED: NR   NORTH AMERICAN ADM. STAFF: NR
        SINGLE MEN: NR   SHORT TERM: NR
      SINGLE WOMEN: NR   RETIRED: NR

    TOTAL ACTIVE: NR
NOTES: Income estimated by MARC.

Handclasp International Inc.

3110 W Harvard Ste. 12
Santa Ana CA 92704
P.O. ADDRESS:
Box 1496
Santa Ana CA 92704

Tel. (714) 549-1859
EXECUTIVE OFFICER: Maurice R. Henrich
ORGANIZED: 1970
DESCRIPTION: A nondenominational service agency providing
    medical supplies, supporting clinics and hospitals,
    assisting with medical relief and supplying equipment.

TOTAL INCOME: NR   FOR OVERSEAS MINISTRIES: NR
PERSONNEL:
    NORTH AMERICANS OVERSEAS   NON-NORTH AMERICANS OVERSEAS: 0
            MARRIED: 0   NORTH AMERICAN ADM. STAFF: 0
        SINGLE MEN: 0   SHORT TERM: 0
      SINGLE WOMEN: 0   RETIRED: 0

    TOTAL ACTIVE: 0

Harvest Fields Missionary and Evangelistic Association, Inc.

3411 First Ave.
Sacramento CA 95817

Tel. (916) 452-6745
EXECUTIVE OFFICER: Joseph R. Morse
ORGANIZED: 1949
DESCRIPTION: A nondenominational agency of Pentecostal
    tradition engaged in training and sending missionaries.
    Also establishing churches and involved in education,
    evangelism and nurture of national churches.

TOTAL INCOME: NA   FOR OVERSEAS MINISTRIES: $242,000
PERSONNEL:
    NORTH AMERICANS OVERSEAS   NON-NORTH AMERICANS OVERSEAS: 0
            MARRIED: 10   NORTH AMERICAN ADM. STAFF: 3
        SINGLE MEN: 1   SHORT TERM: 0
      SINGLE WOMEN: 0   RETIRED: 2

    TOTAL ACTIVE: 11
NOTES: Overseas income estimated by MARC.

312

FIELD OF SERVICE	YEAR BEGAN	PERSONNEL NOW	NEW	RELATED CHURCHES	PEOPLE GROUPS	NOTES
Egypt		2		1	1	
Indonesia		2		1	1	
Israel		2		1	1	
Philippines		2	1	2	2	
Taiwan Rep of China		1		1	1	

Harvest Production SEE: Evangelical Baptist Missions, Inc.

Harvesters International Mission, Inc.

6417 N Figueroa
Los Angeles CA 90042
P.O. ADDRESS:
Box 42008
Los Angeles CA 90042

Tel. (213) 256-2885
EXECUTIVE OFFICER: David Morsey
ORGANIZED: 0
DESCRIPTION: Harvesters International publishes and
    distributes Christian literature free of charge to
    Christians throughout the world. Literature is sent to
    Portugal, Spain, France, South America and Africa.
TOTAL INCOME: NA   FOR OVERSEAS MINISTRIES: NA
PERSONNEL:
    NORTH AMERICANS OVERSEAS   NON-NORTH AMERICANS OVERSEAS: NR
           MARRIED: 0   NORTH AMERICAN ADM. STAFF: 4
        SINGLE MEN: 0   SHORT TERM: 0
      SINGLE WOMEN: 0   RETIRED: 0

      TOTAL ACTIVE: 0

POINTER NAME:HCJB Radio SEE:
World Radio Missionary Fellowship

Hearthstone Ministries, Inc.

915 Fifth Ave.
Williamsport PA 17701

EXECUTIVE OFFICER: OLD DATA
ORGANIZED: 0
TOTAL INCOME: $0   FOR OVERSEAS MINISTRIES: $0
PERSONNEL:
    NORTH AMERICANS OVERSEAS   NON-NORTH AMERICANS OVERSEAS: 0
           MARRIED: 0   NORTH AMERICAN ADM. STAFF: 0
        SINGLE MEN: 0   SHORT TERM: 0
      SINGLE WOMEN: 0   RETIRED: 0

      TOTAL ACTIVE: 0

POINTER NAME:Help for a Hungry World SEE:
International Students Inc.

Helps International Ministries, Inc.

P.O. ADDRESS:
Box 836
Harlem GA 30814

Tel. (404) 556-9361
EXECUTIVE OFFICER: David P. DeJong
ORGANIZED: 1976
DESCRIPTION: A nondenominational service agency of
    fundamentalist tradition assisting missions and

313

missionaries with church construction and management
consulting.
TOTAL INCOME: $46,303   FOR OVERSEAS MINISTRIES: $0
PERSONNEL:
  NORTH AMERICANS OVERSEAS   NON-NORTH AMERICANS OVERSEAS: 0
          MARRIED: 0   NORTH AMERICAN ADM. STAFF: 1
      SINGLE MEN: 0   SHORT TERM: 0
    SINGLE WOMEN: 0   RETIRED: 0

    TOTAL ACTIVE: 0

Heritage Village Church and
Missionary Fellowship, Inc. (PTL
Television network)

7224 Park Rd.
Charlotte NC 28210

Tel. (704) 554-6080
EXECUTIVE OFFICER: Jim Bakker
ORGANIZED: 1973
DESCRIPTION: Founded in 1973 as Trinity Broadcasting Systems,
  Inc. Name changed in 1976. A nondenominational television
  broadcasting ministry of evangelical tradition supporting
  productions in the USA and overseas. Also involved in
  Bible distribution, correspondence courses and aid/relief.
TOTAL INCOME: $51,000,000   FOR OVERSEAS MINISTRIES: $500,000
PERSONNEL:
  NORTH AMERICANS OVERSEAS   NON-NORTH AMERICANS OVERSEAS: 0
          MARRIED: 0   NORTH AMERICAN ADM. STAFF: 0
      SINGLE MEN: 0   SHORT TERM: 0
    SINGLE WOMEN: 0   RETIRED: 0

    TOTAL ACTIVE: 0
NOTES: Overseas income estimated by agency.

FIELD OF SERVICE	YEAR BEGAN	PERSONNEL NOW	NEW	RELATED CHURCHES	PEOPLE GROUPS	NOTES
Australia						
France						
India						
Japan						
Latin America-gen.						
Thailand						

Note: The amounts given to these countries are
not consistent and monies given are not specified
for any particular purpose. Monies are given,
except in India, for the production of TV
programs.

Hermano Pablo, Inc.

2080 Placentia Blvd.
Costa Mesa CA 92626
P.O. ADDRESS:
Box 100
Costa Mesa CA 92626

Tel. (714) 645-0676
EXECUTIVE OFFICER: Paul Finkenbinder
ORGANIZED: 1955
DESCRIPTION: No current information available. Information
  from 1976 directory. Founded in 1955 as Latin America
  Radio Evangelism. Name changed in 1971. A
  nondenominational service agency producing radio
  broadcasts and gospel films in Spanish. Also involved
  in overseas crusades and disaster relief. Publishes
  Christian columns in 10 Latin American daily newspapers.
TOTAL INCOME: $290,000   FOR OVERSEAS MINISTRIES: NR

PERSONNEL:
```
    NORTH AMERICANS OVERSEAS    NON-NORTH AMERICANS OVERSEAS:   NR
              MARRIED:    0        NORTH AMERICAN ADM. STAFF:    8
           SINGLE MEN:    0                      SHORT TERM:    0
         SINGLE WOMEN:    0                         RETIRED:   NR
                       -----
         TOTAL ACTIVE:    0
```
NOTES: Income estimated by MARC.
         Has work in every Spanish-speaking country.
         Total income includes support of 300 radio stations.

High School Evangelism Fellowship, Inc.

10 Garber Square
Ridgewood NJ 07450
P.O. ADDRESS:
Box 780
Tenafly NJ 07670

Tel. (201) 652-1405
EXECUTIVE OFFICER: A. Brandt Reed
ORGANIZED: 1938
DESCRIPTION: A nondenominational sending agency of independent
    tradition involved in high school student evangelism.
TOTAL INCOME: $323,250   FOR OVERSEAS MINISTRIES: $180,646
PERSONNEL:
```
    NORTH AMERICANS OVERSEAS    NON-NORTH AMERICANS OVERSEAS:    0
              MARRIED:   10        NORTH AMERICAN ADM. STAFF:    4
           SINGLE MEN:    0                      SHORT TERM:    2
         SINGLE WOMEN:    0                         RETIRED:    0
                       -----
         TOTAL ACTIVE:   10
```

FIELD OF SERVICE	YEAR BEGAN	PERSONNEL NOW	NEW	RELATED CHURCHES	PEOPLE GROUPS	NOTES
Japan	1950	10	2			

Hindustan Bible Institute, Inc.

800 W Carson, Ste. 22
Torrance CA 90502
P.O. ADDRESS:
Box 2815, Terminal Annex
Los Angeles CA 90051

Tel. (213) 533-6097
EXECUTIVE OFFICER: Len Shockey
ORGANIZED: 1950
DESCRIPTION: A nondenominational agency of Baptist and
    independent tradition engaged in theological education and
    training of Indian nationals through its Bible Institute.
    Related ministries in which students are involved are
    literature distribution, medicine, evangelism and
    childcare.
TOTAL INCOME: $174,477   FOR OVERSEAS MINISTRIES: $174,477
PERSONNEL:
```
    NORTH AMERICANS OVERSEAS    NON-NORTH AMERICANS OVERSEAS:    0
              MARRIED:    0        NORTH AMERICAN ADM. STAFF:    2
           SINGLE MEN:    0                      SHORT TERM:    0
         SINGLE WOMEN:    0                         RETIRED:    0
                       -----
         TOTAL ACTIVE:    0
```

Holt International Children's Services, Inc.

1195 City View
Eugene OR 97402
P.O. ADDRESS:
Box 2880
Eugene OR 97402

Tel. (503) 687-2202
EXECUTIVE OFFICER: John E. Adams
ORGANIZED: 1956
DESCRIPTION: Founded as Orphan's Foundation Fund. Name changed
    in 1975. A nondenominational service agency with emphasis
    on childcare, adoption programs, technical assistance,
    fund raising and providing medical supplies. Assists with
    child welfare services in foreign countries and provides
    adoption services in the USA.
TOTAL INCOME: $2,309,098   FOR OVERSEAS MINISTRIES: $2,309,098
PERSONNEL:

NORTH AMERICANS OVERSEAS		NON-NORTH AMERICANS OVERSEAS:	0
MARRIED:	1	NORTH AMERICAN ADM. STAFF:	17
SINGLE MEN:	2	SHORT TERM:	0
SINGLE WOMEN:	0	RETIRED:	NR
TOTAL ACTIVE:	3		

FIELD OF SERVICE	YEAR BEGAN	PERSONNEL NOW	PERSONNEL NEW	RELATED CHURCHES	PEOPLE GROUPS	NOTES
India	1979	1				
Korea, Rep. of	1956					
Nicaragua	1978					
Philippines	1976					
Thailand	1976					

Holy Land Christian Mission

2000 E Red Bridge Rd.
Kansas City MO 64131
P.O. ADDRESS:
Box 55
Kansas City MO 64141

Tel. (816) 942-2000
EXECUTIVE OFFICER: R. Joseph Gripkey
ORGANIZED: 1936
DESCRIPTION: Founded in 1936 as Society of Christian Approach
    to the Jews. Merged with Holy Land Christian Approach
    Mission in 1970. Name changed from Holy Land Mission to
    Holy Land Christian Mission in 1974. A nondenominational
    sending agency engaged in evangelism, education, aid and
    relief, medicine and childcare.
TOTAL INCOME: $4,050,313   FOR OVERSEAS MINISTRIES: $2,651,460
PERSONNEL:

NORTH AMERICANS OVERSEAS		NON-NORTH AMERICANS OVERSEAS:	NR
MARRIED:	NR	NORTH AMERICAN ADM. STAFF:	40
SINGLE MEN:	NR	SHORT TERM:	0
SINGLE WOMEN:	NR	RETIRED:	0
TOTAL ACTIVE:	4		

FIELD OF SERVICE	YEAR BEGAN	PERSONNEL NOW	PERSONNEL NEW	RELATED CHURCHES	PEOPLE GROUPS	NOTES
Chile						2

FIELD OF SERVICE	YEAR BEGAN	PERSONNEL NOW	NEW	RELATED CHURCHES	PEOPLE GROUPS	NOTES
Colombia						2
Guatemala						2
India						2
Israel						1

Note: 1. Ministry includes an Orphan Home School and Trade Schools, Crippled Children's Hospital, Widow and Refugee Aid Program and 6 day-care centers in refugee camps.
2. Each of these countries has a child sponsorship program.

Home Finders International

933 Glen Forest
Rockford IL 61111

Tel. (815) 654-0900
EXECUTIVE OFFICER: Arthur S. Fowler
ORGANIZED: 1975
DESCRIPTION: Founded as Evangelical Furlough Missionary Housing Services, Inc. Name changed in 1979. An interdenominational specialized service agency of evangelical tradition finding housing in the USA and Canada for furloughed and retiring missionaries. Utilizes existing missionary housing and parsonages as well as rental and seasonal homes owned by individuals.

TOTAL INCOME: $3,500   FOR OVERSEAS MINISTRIES: $0
PERSONNEL:

NORTH AMERICANS OVERSEAS		NON-NORTH AMERICANS OVERSEAS:	0
MARRIED:	0	NORTH AMERICAN ADM. STAFF:	NR
SINGLE MEN:	0	SHORT TERM:	0
SINGLE WOMEN:	0	RETIRED:	0
TOTAL ACTIVE:	0		

Home of Onesiphorus

3939 N Hamlin Ave.
Chicago IL 60618

Tel. (312) 478-4092
EXECUTIVE OFFICER: George E. Hedberg
ORGANIZED: 1916   AFFILIATION: IFMA
DESCRIPTION: An interdenominational sending agency of evangelical tradition engaged in evangelism and childcare.

TOTAL INCOME: $310,560   FOR OVERSEAS MINISTRIES: $236,045
PERSONNEL:

NORTH AMERICANS OVERSEAS		NON-NORTH AMERICANS OVERSEAS:	1
MARRIED:	8	NORTH AMERICAN ADM. STAFF:	4
SINGLE MEN:	0	SHORT TERM:	0
SINGLE WOMEN:	2	RETIRED:	0
TOTAL ACTIVE:	10		

FIELD OF SERVICE	YEAR BEGAN	PERSONNEL NOW	NEW	RELATED CHURCHES	PEOPLE GROUPS	NOTES
Hong-Kong	1949	2		1	1	
Israel	1951	2	2		1	

FIELD OF SERVICE	YEAR BEGAN	PERSONNEL NOW	NEW	RELATED CHURCHES	PEOPLE GROUPS	NOTES
Lebanon	1950	2				
Taiwan Rep of China	1971	3			1	

Houses of Refuge, International Orphanages Association, Inc.

1100 Texas
El Paso TX 79901
P.O. ADDRESS:
Box 9285
El Paso TX 79983

EXECUTIVE OFFICER: B.T. Claiborne
ORGANIZED: 1968
DESCRIPTION: An interdenominational sending agency of
    independent tradition involved in general Christian
    education, childcare, community development, evangelism
    and self-help projects. Also supports nationals and
    national churches.

TOTAL INCOME: $50,000   FOR OVERSEAS MINISTRIES: $50,000
PERSONNEL:
```
    NORTH AMERICANS OVERSEAS    NON-NORTH AMERICANS OVERSEAS:    4
             MARRIED:     8         NORTH AMERICAN ADM. STAFF:    1
          SINGLE MEN:     2                       SHORT TERM:    2
        SINGLE WOMEN:     2                          RETIRED:    0
                      -----
        TOTAL ACTIVE:    12
```

FIELD OF SERVICE	YEAR BEGAN	PERSONNEL NOW	NEW	RELATED CHURCHES	PEOPLE GROUPS	NOTES
Mexico	1977	12	12	5	1	

Independent Assemblies of God, International

3840 5th Ave.
San Diego CA 92103

Tel. (714) 295-1028
EXECUTIVE OFFICER: A. W. Rasmussen
ORGANIZED: 1918
DESCRIPTION: A denominational agency of Pentecostal tradition
    supporting missionaries sent from individual churches
    engaged in evangelism and establishing churches. Also
    involved in literature distribution, training and support
    of nationals.

TOTAL INCOME: NR   FOR OVERSEAS MINISTRIES: NR
PERSONNEL:
```
    NORTH AMERICANS OVERSEAS    NON-NORTH AMERICANS OVERSEAS:    NR
             MARRIED:    NR         NORTH AMERICAN ADM. STAFF:    NR
          SINGLE MEN:    NR                       SHORT TERM:    0
        SINGLE WOMEN:    NR                          RETIRED:    0
                      -----
        TOTAL ACTIVE:    NR
```
NOTES: There are 2000 individual churches,
        all of which are indigenous.

Independent Assemblies of God, Mission to Liberia SEE: Fellowship of Christian Assemblies Mission to Liberia

Independent Bible Baptist Mission

Rt. 2
Sedalia CO 80135

DESCRIPTION: No data is reported for this agency for one of the
following reasons: it is currently inactive or no longer
exists; it has terminated overseas ministries or has ceased
to operate as a North American entity.

Independent Board for Presbyterian Foreign Missions SEE: Bible Presbyterian Church

Independent Faith Mission, Inc.

2301 S Holden Rd.
Greensboro NC 27407
P.O. ADDRESS:
Box 7791
Greensboro NC 27407

Tel. (919) 292-1255
EXECUTIVE OFFICER: Robert F. Kurtz
ORGANIZED: 1950
DESCRIPTION: A nondenominational, independent Baptist board of
fundamentalist tradition serving local churches by sending
missionaries. Engaged in establishing churches,
evangelism and theological education.

```
TOTAL INCOME:        NR     FOR OVERSEAS MINISTRIES:    $880,000
PERSONNEL:
   NORTH AMERICANS OVERSEAS   NON-NORTH AMERICANS OVERSEAS:    NR
            MARRIED:   32       NORTH AMERICAN ADM. STAFF:     NR
         SINGLE MEN:    1                     SHORT TERM:       0
       SINGLE WOMEN:    7                        RETIRED:      NR
                     -----
       TOTAL ACTIVE:   40
```
NOTES: Overseas income estimated by MARC.

FIELD OF SERVICE	YEAR BEGAN	PERSONNEL NOW	NEW	RELATED CHURCHES	PEOPLE GROUPS	NOTES
France		4				
Italy		6				
Kenya		10				
South Africa		2				
Surinam		12				
Switzerland		2				
Zimbabwe		4				

Independent Gospel Missions

P.O. ADDRESS:
Box 1507
New Castle PA 16103

Tel. (412) 946-2711
EXECUTIVE OFFICER: D.L. Bovard
ORGANIZED: 1969   AFFILIATION: TAM-ICCC
DESCRIPTION: A nondenominational, non-sending training agency
of independent Baptist tradition establishing and serving
home and national churches. Involved in evangelism, Bible
translation and distribution, servicemen's centers,
childcare and relief.

```
TOTAL INCOME:    $180,000        FOR OVERSEAS MINISTRIES:    NR
PERSONNEL:
   NORTH AMERICANS OVERSEAS   NON-NORTH AMERICANS OVERSEAS:    NR
            MARRIED:   NR       NORTH AMERICAN ADM. STAFF:      3
         SINGLE MEN:   NR                     SHORT TERM:      NR
```

India Christian Mission, Inc.

67 Glenlawn Ave.
Sea Cliff, L.I. NY 11579

Tel. (516) 676-5260
EXECUTIVE OFFICER: John Binns
ORGANIZED: 1897
DESCRIPTION: A nondenominational fund transmitting agency of
    evangelical tradition supporting agriculture, education,
    literature and orphanage work.
TOTAL INCOME: $28,000   FOR OVERSEAS MINISTRIES: $28,000
PERSONNEL:
    NORTH AMERICANS OVERSEAS   NON-NORTH AMERICANS OVERSEAS: 2
              MARRIED: 0   NORTH AMERICAN ADM. STAFF: 2
           SINGLE MEN: 0   SHORT TERM: 0
         SINGLE WOMEN: 0   RETIRED: 0

        TOTAL ACTIVE: 0

FIELD OF SERVICE	YEAR BEGAN	PERSONNEL NOW	NEW	RELATED CHURCHES	PEOPLE GROUPS	NOTES
India	1897					
Sri Lanka	1924					

India Evangelical Mission, Inc.

12613 213th St.
Lakewood CA 90715
P.O. ADDRESS:
Box 1633
Lakewood CA 90715

Tel. (213) 865-8913
EXECUTIVE OFFICER: G.V. Mathai
ORGANIZED: 1966
DESCRIPTION: An interdenominational agency of evangelical
    tradition establishing churches and engaged in evangelism,
    Bible distribution and correspondence courses. Also
    involved in education, medicine and support of nationals.
    Operates public Christian reading rooms.
TOTAL INCOME: $94,000   FOR OVERSEAS MINISTRIES: $80,000
PERSONNEL:
    NORTH AMERICANS OVERSEAS   NON-NORTH AMERICANS OVERSEAS: 35
              MARRIED: 2   NORTH AMERICAN ADM. STAFF: 1
           SINGLE MEN: 0   SHORT TERM: 0
         SINGLE WOMEN: 0   RETIRED: 0

        TOTAL ACTIVE: 2

FIELD OF SERVICE	YEAR BEGAN	PERSONNEL NOW	NEW	RELATED CHURCHES	PEOPLE GROUPS	NOTES
India	1970	45		15		

India National Inland Mission

P.O. ADDRESS:
Box 42584
Los Angeles CA 90050

Tel. (213) 257-9970
EXECUTIVE OFFICER: Paul Pillai
ORGANIZED: 1964
DESCRIPTION: An interdenominational agency of evangelical

tradition involved in Bible distribution, establishing
churches, theological education, evangelism and
orphanage/childcare work. Also has a Bible college and a
small medical clinic.
TOTAL INCOME: $180,000   FOR OVERSEAS MINISTRIES: $180,000
PERSONNEL:
  NORTH AMERICANS OVERSEAS   NON-NORTH AMERICANS OVERSEAS: 0
        MARRIED: 0   NORTH AMERICAN ADM. STAFF: 0
    SINGLE MEN: 0   SHORT TERM: 0
  SINGLE WOMEN: 0   RETIRED: 0

    TOTAL ACTIVE: 0

FIELD OF SERVICE	YEAR BEGAN	PERSONNEL NOW	PERSONNEL NEW	RELATED CHURCHES	PEOPLE GROUPS	NOTES
India	1964	80	25	28	28	

Institut Medical Evangelique, North American Committee SEE: North American Committee for IME

Institute of Chinese Studies

1605 E Elizabeth St.
Pasadena CA 91104

Tel. (213) 798-9151
EXECUTIVE OFFICER: James A. Ziervogel
ORGANIZED: 1977
DESCRIPTION: An interdenominational specialized agency of
evangelical tradition engaged in mission strategy
development, mission related research involving unreached
groups of Chinese, and missionary education and training.
TOTAL INCOME: $4,389   FOR OVERSEAS MINISTRIES: $0
PERSONNEL:
  NORTH AMERICANS OVERSEAS   NON-NORTH AMERICANS OVERSEAS: 0
        MARRIED: 0   NORTH AMERICAN ADM. STAFF: 0
    SINGLE MEN: 0   SHORT TERM: 0
  SINGLE WOMEN: 0   RETIRED: 0

    TOTAL ACTIVE: 0
NOTES: Six personnel are assigned to
administrative duties but all are seconded
from other mission agencies.

Institute of Holy Land Studies

460 Central Ave.
Highland Park IL 60035
P.O. ADDRESS:
Box 456
Highland Park IL 60035

Tel. (312) 433-4060
EXECUTIVE OFFICER: George Giacumakis
ORGANIZED: 1957
DESCRIPTION: A nondenominational specialized educational
institution of evangelical tradition providing theological
and Christian education at collegiate and post-graduate
levels in Jerusalem.
TOTAL INCOME: $415,049   FOR OVERSEAS MINISTRIES: $415,049
PERSONNEL:
  NORTH AMERICANS OVERSEAS   NON-NORTH AMERICANS OVERSEAS: 10
        MARRIED: 12   NORTH AMERICAN ADM. STAFF: 2
    SINGLE MEN: 0   SHORT TERM: 0

| | SINGLE WOMEN: | 2 | | | RETIRED: | 1 |
| TOTAL ACTIVE: | 14 | | | | | |

FIELD OF SERVICE	YEAR BEGAN	PERSONNEL NOW	NEW	RELATED CHURCHES	PEOPLE GROUPS	NOTES
Israel	1959	19	9	50		

Inter-Varsity Christian Fellowship

233 Langdon St.
Madison WI 53703

Tel. (608) 257-0263
EXECUTIVE OFFICER: John W. Alexander
ORGANIZED: 1939
DESCRIPTION: An interdenominational specialized agency of
evangelical tradition seeking to establish chapters of
Inter-Varsity Christian Fellowship (IVCF), Student Foreign
Missions Fellowship (SFMF), and Nurses Christian
Fellowship (NCF) on college and university campuses and in
schools of nursing. Engaged in evangelism, discipleship,
literature and missions. While not a sending agency in
the traditional sense, it is involved in seconding campus
student missionaries to overseas agencies and the
International Fellowship of Evangelical Students. Sponsors
the world student missions convention commonly known
as Urbana.
TOTAL INCOME: $10,443,887   FOR OVERSEAS MINISTRIES: $558,000
PERSONNEL:
NORTH AMERICANS OVERSEAS		NON-NORTH AMERICANS OVERSEAS:	NR
MARRIED:	NR	NORTH AMERICAN ADM. STAFF:	26
SINGLE MEN:	NR	SHORT TERM:	0
SINGLE WOMEN:	NR	RETIRED:	0
TOTAL ACTIVE:	10		

Inter-Varsity Christian Fellowship of Canada

745 Mount Pleasant Rd.
Toronto ON M4S 2N5
Canada

Tel. (416) 487-3431
EXECUTIVE OFFICER: A. Donald MacLeod
ORGANIZED: 1929
DESCRIPTION: An international, interdenominational agency of
evangelical tradition with the primary goal of fostering
evangelism, spiritual development and missionary service
among students and faculty in universities, secondary
schools and professional schools. Also involved in
literature distribution, training and camping.
TOTAL INCOME: $1,740,000   FOR OVERSEAS MINISTRIES: $56,550
PERSONNEL:
NORTH AMERICANS OVERSEAS		NON-NORTH AMERICANS OVERSEAS:	0
MARRIED:	0	NORTH AMERICAN ADM. STAFF:	25
SINGLE MEN:	0	SHORT TERM:	0
SINGLE WOMEN:	0	RETIRED:	3
TOTAL ACTIVE:	0		

Interamerican Gospel Communications SEE: Portable Recording Ministries, Inc.

Intercristo

19303 Fremont Ave. North
Seattle WA 98133

Tel. (206) 623-0715
EXECUTIVE OFFICER: R. A. Harlan
ORGANIZED: 1967   AFFILIATION: EFMA-Assoc. member
DESCRIPTION: An interdenominational specialzed service agency
    of evangelical tradition providing computerized personnel
    information and guidance to match individuals to specific
    Christian agency personnel needs in North America and
    abroad. Functions as an information link between the
    potential missionary and the sending agency.
TOTAL INCOME: $258,649   FOR OVERSEAS MINISTRIES: $0
PERSONNEL:
    NORTH AMERICANS OVERSEAS   NON-NORTH AMERICANS OVERSEAS: 0
              MARRIED: 0   NORTH AMERICAN ADM. STAFF: 0
           SINGLE MEN: 0   SHORT TERM: 0
         SINGLE WOMEN: 0   RETIRED: 0

       TOTAL ACTIVE: 0

Intermedia SEE: DOM-NCCCUSA, Mission Association Section

International Bible Institute

9926 Pioneer Blvd., #107
Santa Fe Spgs CA 90670
P.O. ADDRESS:
Box 2473
Santa Fe Spgs CA 90670

Tel. (213) 949-9537
EXECUTIVE OFFICER: Earle E. Williams
ORGANIZED: 1971
DESCRIPTION: A nondenominational agency of evangelical
    tradition supplying a complete three year Bible Institute
    study program on cassettes for use on the mission field.
    Includes general Christian education, theological
    education and theological education by extension (TEE).
TOTAL INCOME: $21,176   FOR OVERSEAS MINISTRIES: $10,955
PERSONNEL:
    NORTH AMERICANS OVERSEAS   NON-NORTH AMERICANS OVERSEAS: 0
              MARRIED: 2   NORTH AMERICAN ADM. STAFF: 2
           SINGLE MEN: 0   SHORT TERM: 0
         SINGLE WOMEN: 0   RETIRED: 0

       TOTAL ACTIVE: 2

FIELD OF SERVICE	YEAR BEGAN	PERSONNEL NOW	PERSONNEL NEW	RELATED CHURCHES	PEOPLE GROUPS	NOTES
Mexico	1976	1				
Philippines	1979	1	1	18		

International Bible Translators

P.O. ADDRESS:
Box 344091
Dallas TX 75234

Tel. (214) 241-0800
EXECUTIVE OFFICER: Stanley L. Morris
ORGANIZED: 1972
DESCRIPTION: A nondenominational service agency of evangelical
    tradition that works with various churches and mission
    organizations in all aspects of Bible translation,
    computer utilization in translation, English and foreign

323

language typesetting and publishing.
```
TOTAL INCOME:          NR           FOR OVERSEAS MINISTRIES:    NR
PERSONNEL:
   NORTH AMERICANS OVERSEAS    NON-NORTH AMERICANS OVERSEAS:    0
           MARRIED:     0       NORTH AMERICAN ADM. STAFF:      3
        SINGLE MEN:     0                    SHORT TERM:        0
      SINGLE WOMEN:     0                       RETIRED:        0
                      -----
      TOTAL ACTIVE:    0
```

International Biblical Baptist
Fellowship, Inc.

4616 61st St.
Camrose AB T4V 2H8
Canada

DESCRIPTION: No current information available. Information
   from 1976 directory. A nondenominational sending agency
   of fundamental, Baptist tradition supporting missionaries
   and the educational ministry of the Berean Baptist Bible
   College of Bangalore, India.
```
TOTAL INCOME:      $27,500           FOR OVERSEAS MINISTRIES:    NR
PERSONNEL:
   NORTH AMERICANS OVERSEAS    NON-NORTH AMERICANS OVERSEAS:    NR
           MARRIED:    NR       NORTH AMERICAN ADM. STAFF:      NR
        SINGLE MEN:    NR                    SHORT TERM:        NR
      SINGLE WOMEN:    NR                       RETIRED:        NR
                      -----
      TOTAL ACTIVE:    NR
```
NOTES: Income estimated by MARC.

FIELD OF SERVICE	YEAR BEGAN	PERSONNEL NOW	NEW	RELATED CHURCHES	PEOPLE GROUPS	NOTES
India	1962					

International Board of Jewish
Missions, Inc.

1805 Bailey Ave.
Chattanooga TN 37404
P.O. ADDRESS:
Box 3307
Chattanooga TN 37404

Tel. (615) 698-3417
EXECUTIVE OFFICER: Jacob Gardenhouse
ORGANIZED: 1940
DESCRIPTION: A nondenominational service agency of evangelical
   and fundamentalist tradition ministering to Jews in the
   USA and overseas. Countries of service include Brazil,
   Uruguay, Argentina, Canada and Israel. Also involved in
   radio broadcasting.
```
TOTAL INCOME:          NR     FOR OVERSEAS MINISTRIES:    $660,000
PERSONNEL:
   NORTH AMERICANS OVERSEAS    NON-NORTH AMERICANS OVERSEAS:    NR
           MARRIED:    NR       NORTH AMERICAN ADM. STAFF:      15
        SINGLE MEN:    NR                    SHORT TERM:        0
      SINGLE WOMEN:    NR                       RETIRED:        NR
                      -----
      TOTAL ACTIVE:    30
```
NOTES: Overseas income estimated by MARC.

International Christian Fellowship

213 Naperville St.
Wheaton IL 60187

Tel. (312) 668-8569
EXECUTIVE OFFICER: Phil Parshall
ORGANIZED: 1893   AFFILIATION: IFMA
DESCRIPTION: An international, interdenominational sending
    agency of evangelical tradition establishing churches and
    engaged in evangelism, theological education by extension
    (TEE), correspondence courses and literature production
    and distribution.
TOTAL INCOME: $244,501   FOR OVERSEAS MINISTRIES: $226,248
PERSONNEL:
    NORTH AMERICANS OVERSEAS   NON-NORTH AMERICANS OVERSEAS: 65
            MARRIED: 25   NORTH AMERICAN ADM. STAFF: 6
        SINGLE MEN: 0   SHORT TERM: 0
      SINGLE WOMEN: 6   RETIRED: NR

      TOTAL ACTIVE: 31

FIELD OF SERVICE	YEAR BEGAN	PERSONNEL NOW	PERSONNEL NEW	RELATED CHURCHES	PEOPLE GROUPS	NOTES
Bangladesh	1958	11		2	2	
India	1893	10		38	4	
Indonesia	1973				1	
Iran	1969					
Nepal	1969	1			1	
Pakistan	1953	9			3	

International Christian Leprosy Mission, Inc. (Canada)

P.O. ADDRESS:
Box 91564
W. Vancouver BC V7V 3P2
Canada

Tel. (604) 926-1390
EXECUTIVE OFFICER: R. Ben Gullison
ORGANIZED: 1943
DESCRIPTION: An interdenominational fund transmitting agency
    supporting leprosy patients and their families.
TOTAL INCOME: $13,070   FOR OVERSEAS MINISTRIES: NR
PERSONNEL:
    NORTH AMERICANS OVERSEAS   NON-NORTH AMERICANS OVERSEAS: NR
            MARRIED: 0   NORTH AMERICAN ADM. STAFF: 1
        SINGLE MEN: 0   SHORT TERM: 0
      SINGLE WOMEN: 0   RETIRED: 0

      TOTAL ACTIVE: 0

International Christian Leprosy Mission, Inc. (USA)

6917 SW Oak St.
Portland OR 97223
P.O. ADDRESS:
Box 23353
Portland OR 97223

Tel. (503) 244-5935
EXECUTIVE OFFICER: Hattie A. Metcalf
ORGANIZED: 1943
DESCRIPTION: An interdenominational fund transmitting agency
    supporting leprosy patients and their families.
TOTAL INCOME: $28,221   FOR OVERSEAS MINISTRIES: $8,978

PERSONNEL:
```
        NORTH AMERICANS OVERSEAS    NON-NORTH AMERICANS OVERSEAS:   NR
                     MARRIED:   0      NORTH AMERICAN ADM. STAFF:    1
                  SINGLE MEN:   0                     SHORT TERM:    0
                SINGLE WOMEN:   0                        RETIRED:    0
                             -----
                TOTAL ACTIVE:   0
```
NOTES: All overseas personnel are nationals.

International Christian Mission

P.O. ADDRESS:
Box 154
Kingston NS B0P 1R0
Canada

Tel. (902) 765-4517
EXECUTIVE OFFICER: William Freeman
ORGANIZED: 1940   AFFILIATION: TAM-ICCC
DESCRIPTION: A nondenominational agency engaged in general
    Christian education in Kingston and also supporting
    missionaries in India and Spain. Associated with Baptist
    Mid-Missions in New Zealand.
TOTAL INCOME: NA   FOR OVERSEAS MINISTRIES: NA
PERSONNEL:
```
        NORTH AMERICANS OVERSEAS    NON-NORTH AMERICANS OVERSEAS:   NR
                     MARRIED:   0      NORTH AMERICAN ADM. STAFF:    0
                  SINGLE MEN:   0                     SHORT TERM:    0
                SINGLE WOMEN:   0                        RETIRED:    0
                             -----
                TOTAL ACTIVE:   0
```

International Christian Organization SEE: Intercristo

International Church of the
Foursquare Gospel—Department of
Missions International

1100 Glendale Blvd.
Los Angeles CA 90026

Tel. (213) 484-1100
EXECUTIVE OFFICER: Rolf K. McPherson
ORGANIZED: 1923   AFFILIATION: EFMA
DESCRIPTION: A denominational sending agency of evangelical
    and Pentecostal tradition establishing churches and
    engaged in evangelism, training, extension education and
    general Christian education.
TOTAL INCOME: $2,639,367   FOR OVERSEAS MINISTRIES: $2,622,899
PERSONNEL:
```
        NORTH AMERICANS OVERSEAS    NON-NORTH AMERICANS OVERSEAS:    8
                     MARRIED:  76      NORTH AMERICAN ADM. STAFF:   10
                  SINGLE MEN:   2                     SHORT TERM:    9
                SINGLE WOMEN:   9                        RETIRED:   17
                             -----
                TOTAL ACTIVE:  87
```

FIELD OF SERVICE	YEAR BEGAN	PERSONNEL NOW	NEW	RELATED CHURCHES	PEOPLE GROUPS	NOTES
Argentina	1970	4		139		
Australia	1953	2		24		

FIELD OF SERVICE	YEAR BEGAN	PERSONNEL NOW	NEW	RELATED CHURCHES	PEOPLE GROUPS	NOTES
Bolivia	1928	2		38		
Brazil	1946	6		1685		
Chile	1949	3	1	79		
Colombia	1943	5		578		
Costa Rica	1954	4	1	73		
Ecuador	1956	4		73		
El Salvador	1973	2		5		
Greece		2		7		
Guatemala	1955	3		67		
Honduras	1952	4		70		
Hong-Kong	1936	4	2	4	2	
Jamaica	1962	2		40		
Japan	1951	1	1	18		
Korea, Rep. of	1969	2		12		
Mexico	1943	3		110	1	
Nicaragua	1955	2		22		
Nigeria	1954	2		69		
Panama	1928	4	2	361		
Papua New Guinea	1956	5	3	213		
Philippines	1926	9	6	988	13	
Spain	1974	4	2	4		
Sri Lanka	1979	2	2		2	
Transkei	1929	3		105	2	
United Kingdom	1979	2	2			
Venezuela	1955	2		44		

International Church Relief Fund, Inc.

315 N Weber St.
Colorado Spgs CO 80903
P.O. ADDRESS:
Box 426
Colorado Spgs CO 80901

Tel. (303) 635-7744
EXECUTIVE OFFICER: Peter Nel
ORGANIZED: 1975
DESCRIPTION: A nondenominational agency of independent
    tradition providing agricultural assistance and aid or
    relief in underdeveloped nations, especially in the
    aftermath of natural and/or uncontrollable disasters.
    Also assisting with childcare, medical supplies and
    Christian education.
TOTAL INCOME: $629,785   FOR OVERSEAS MINISTRIES: $629,785
PERSONNEL:
    NORTH AMERICANS OVERSEAS   NON-NORTH AMERICANS OVERSEAS: 0
              MARRIED: 0   NORTH AMERICAN ADM. STAFF: 4
           SINGLE MEN: 0   SHORT TERM: 0
         SINGLE WOMEN: 0   RETIRED: 0

         TOTAL ACTIVE: 0

International Crusades, Inc.

515 Schoenbeck Rd.
Prospect Hgts IL 60070
P.O. ADDRESS:
Box 203
Prospect Heights IL 60070

Tel. (312) 870-3800
EXECUTIVE OFFICER: Kevin G. Dyer
ORGANIZED: 1960
DESCRIPTION: A nondenominational sending agency of "Plymouth

Brethren" tradition establishing churches and engaged in
missionary education, personal and small group evangelism
and missionary orientation and training. Also involved in
discipling new believers.
TOTAL INCOME: $880,535   FOR OVERSEAS MINISTRIES: $233,929
PERSONNEL:
```
    NORTH AMERICANS OVERSEAS    NON-NORTH AMERICANS OVERSEAS:    0
            MARRIED:    30          NORTH AMERICAN ADM. STAFF:   25
         SINGLE MEN:    16                         SHORT TERM:   64
       SINGLE WOMEN:    26                            RETIRED:    0
                     -----
       TOTAL ACTIVE:    72
```

FIELD OF SERVICE	YEAR BEGAN	PERSONNEL NOW	PERSONNEL NEW	RELATED CHURCHES	PEOPLE GROUPS	NOTES
Austria	1973	17	15	1		
Belgium	1979	1	1	1		
Bolivia	1977	13	13	4		
France	1969	8	8	4		
Japan	1979	5	5	12		
Netherlands	1979	6	6	1		
St. Lucia	1978	18	18	2		
St. Vincent	1978	4	4	4		

International Evangelism Crusades, Inc.

7970 Woodman Ave.
Van Nuys CA 91402
P.O. ADDRESS:
Box 5
Van Nuys CA 91408

Tel. (213) 781-7704
EXECUTIVE OFFICER: Frank E. Stranges
ORGANIZED: 1959
DESCRIPTION: An interdenominational fellowship of independent
and evangelical tradition providing supportive services
to individual ministers and workers in several countries
who are engaged in theological education, radio and TV
broadcasting, psychological counseling and evangelism.
TOTAL INCOME: $10,000   FOR OVERSEAS MINISTRIES: $10,000
PERSONNEL:
```
    NORTH AMERICANS OVERSEAS    NON-NORTH AMERICANS OVERSEAS:    0
            MARRIED:    20          NORTH AMERICAN ADM. STAFF:    0
         SINGLE MEN:     0                         SHORT TERM:    0
       SINGLE WOMEN:     0                            RETIRED:    0
                     -----
       TOTAL ACTIVE:    20
```
NOTES: Total income estimated by agency. Overseas income
estimated by MARC.

FIELD OF SERVICE	YEAR BEGAN	PERSONNEL NOW	PERSONNEL NEW	RELATED CHURCHES	PEOPLE GROUPS	NOTES
Jamaica	1960	10		60		
Korea, Rep. of	1975	10		36		

International Everlasting Gospel

1250 Broadway
New York NY 10001
P.O. ADDRESS:

Box 8722 G.P.O.
New York NY 10001

Tel. (212) 736-2805
EXECUTIVE OFFICER: Young Il Kim
ORGANIZED: 1978
DESCRIPTION: A sending agency of evangelical tradition
    involved in church planting. Sends missionaries to India,
    Kenya, Japan and South America.
TOTAL INCOME: $20,000   FOR OVERSEAS MINISTRIES: $20,000
PERSONNEL:

NORTH AMERICANS OVERSEAS		NON-NORTH AMERICANS OVERSEAS:	NR
MARRIED:	NR	NORTH AMERICAN ADM. STAFF:	6
SINGLE MEN:	NR	SHORT TERM:	0
SINGLE WOMEN:	NR	RETIRED:	0
TOTAL ACTIVE:	2		

International Fellowship of Christians

P.O. ADDRESS:
Box 404
Grand Haven MI 49417

Tel. (313) 227-4071
EXECUTIVE OFFICER: Ronald C. Smeenge
ORGANIZED: 1978
DESCRIPTION: An interdenominational association serving other
    agencies through recommending and processing placements of
    personnel for overseas congregations; compiling and
    maintaining a directory of English-speaking congregations
    abroad; and acting in an advisory and orientation capacity
    for cross-cultural ministries. Suscribes to the Lausanne
    Covenant as statement of faith.
TOTAL INCOME: NR   FOR OVERSEAS MINISTRIES: $66,000
PERSONNEL:

NORTH AMERICANS OVERSEAS		NON-NORTH AMERICANS OVERSEAS:	NR
MARRIED:	NR	NORTH AMERICAN ADM. STAFF:	NR
SINGLE MEN:	NR	SHORT TERM:	NR
SINGLE WOMEN:	NR	RETIRED:	NR
TOTAL ACTIVE:	3		

NOTES: Overseas income estimated by MARC.

International Fellowship of Evangelical Students—USA

233 Langdon
Madison WI 53701
P.O. ADDRESS:
Box 270
Madison WI 53701

Tel. (608) 257-0263
EXECUTIVE OFFICER: Brian Rust
ORGANIZED: 1947
DESCRIPTION: USA office is part of an international agency of
    evangelical tradition engaged in student evangelism and
    training. IFES is a fellowship of autonomous evangelical
    student movements that all have a common purpose and basis
    of faith, of which Inter-Varsity Christian Fellowship is
    the North American member.
TOTAL INCOME: $558,000   FOR OVERSEAS MINISTRIES: NR
PERSONNEL:

NORTH AMERICANS OVERSEAS		NON-NORTH AMERICANS OVERSEAS:	NR
MARRIED:	NR	NORTH AMERICAN ADM. STAFF:	4
SINGLE MEN:	NR	SHORT TERM:	0

```
    SINGLE WOMEN:    NR                          RETIRED:    0
                    -----
    TOTAL ACTIVE:    10
---------------------------------------------------------------------
                    YEAR      PERSONNEL   RELATED   PEOPLE
FIELD OF SERVICE    BEGAN    NOW   NEW    CHURCHES  GROUPS  NOTES
---------------------------------------------------------------------
Brazil                       1
Germany, Fed. Rep.           1
Italy                        1
Kenya                        1
Mexico                       2
South Africa                 2
United Kingdom               1
Zimbabwe                     1
    Note: Student personnel overseas
    are seconded from Inter-Varsity
    Christian Fellowship.
```

International Films, Inc.

1610 E Elizabeth Ste 214
Pasadena CA 91104
P.O. ADDRESS:
Box 767-C
Pasadena CA 91104

Tel. (213) 681-2229
EXECUTIVE OFFICER: C. Ray Carlson
ORGANIZED: 1963   AFFILIATION: U.S. Center For World Mission
DESCRIPTION: A nondenominational, international specialized
    service agency of evangelical tradition producing films
    and videotapes in many languages, primarily for use
    overseas. Also establishing indigenous agencies abroad
    with similar objectives, and conducting training programs
    in mass media.

```
TOTAL INCOME:    $100,000    FOR OVERSEAS MINISTRIES:    $100,000
PERSONNEL:
    NORTH AMERICANS OVERSEAS    NON-NORTH AMERICANS OVERSEAS:    1
            MARRIED:    0          NORTH AMERICAN ADM. STAFF:    5
         SINGLE MEN:    0                       SHORT TERM:    0
       SINGLE WOMEN:    0                          RETIRED:    0
                       -----
    TOTAL ACTIVE:    0
---------------------------------------------------------------------
                    YEAR      PERSONNEL   RELATED   PEOPLE
FIELD OF SERVICE    BEGAN    NOW   NEW    CHURCHES  GROUPS  NOTES
---------------------------------------------------------------------
Germany, Fed. Rep.  1972
India               1977      1
Japan               1974
United Kingdom      1972
```

International Foundation for EWHA
Woman's University

475 Riverside Dr. Rm1221
New York NY 10115

Tel. (212) 666-7414
EXECUTIVE OFFICER: Moon Phong
ORGANIZED: 1969   AFFILIATION: DOM-NCCCUSA-Frat. Rel.
DESCRIPTION: An interdenominational service agency providing
    financial and other support to EWHA Woman's University in
    Korea. Also operates an exchange program of professors
    and sponsors an international summer school. Agency is
    supported by various denominations and individuals.
TOTAL INCOME: $100,000   FOR OVERSEAS MINISTRIES: $100,000

PERSONNEL:
```
   NORTH AMERICANS OVERSEAS   NON-NORTH AMERICANS OVERSEAS:   NR
          MARRIED:   0         NORTH AMERICAN ADM. STAFF:   NR
        SINGLE MEN:  0                        SHORT TERM:    0
      SINGLE WOMEN:  0                           RETIRED:   NR
                    -----
       TOTAL ACTIVE:   0
```
NOTES: Affiliated/World Div. Global Ministries
        United Methodist Church

International Gospel League

854 E Washington Blvd.
Pasadena CA 91104
P.O. ADDRESS:
Box 519
Pasadena CA 91102

Tel. (213) 798-0551
EXECUTIVE OFFICER: Howard T. Lewis
ORGANIZED: 1906
DESCRIPTION: A nondenominational sending agency of evangelical
    tradition engaged in training and supporting national
    pastors, evangelists, teachers and medical personnel. Also
    engaged in mass evangelism, literature distribution and
    childcare work.
```
TOTAL INCOME:       NR          FOR OVERSEAS MINISTRIES:    NR
PERSONNEL:
   NORTH AMERICANS OVERSEAS   NON-NORTH AMERICANS OVERSEAS:   NR
          MARRIED:  NR         NORTH AMERICAN ADM. STAFF:   15
        SINGLE MEN: NR                        SHORT TERM:  100
      SINGLE WOMEN: NR                           RETIRED:    5
                    -----
       TOTAL ACTIVE:   0
```

FIELD OF SERVICE	YEAR BEGAN	PERSONNEL NOW	NEW	RELATED CHURCHES	PEOPLE GROUPS	NOTES
Ghana	1968					
Greece	1975					
Haiti	1970					
Hong-Kong	1975					
India	1906					
Japan	1949					
Kenya	1978					
Korea, Rep. of	1954					
Liberia	1947					
Nigeria	1958					
Panama	1972					
Philippines	1960					
Puerto Rico	1949					
Sierra Leone	1960					
Taiwan Rep of China	1955					
Uganda	1979					

International Institute of Christian Communications
SEE: Daystar Communications, Inc.

International Institute, Inc.

240 Kathleen Dr.
Park Ridge IL 60068
P.O. ADDRESS:

Box 99
Park Ridge IL 60068

Tel. (312) 823-7416
EXECUTIVE OFFICER: Richard E. Wager,
ORGANIZED: 1960
DESCRIPTION: A nondenominational specialized service agency of
    evangelical and Baptist tradition providing elementary
    school correspondence courses for missionary children.
    Also assists in establishing Christian schools overseas,
    and helps with organization and curriculum.
TOTAL INCOME: $100,000   FOR OVERSEAS MINISTRIES: $0
PERSONNEL:

NORTH AMERICANS OVERSEAS		NON-NORTH AMERICANS OVERSEAS:		0
MARRIED:	0	NORTH AMERICAN ADM. STAFF:		0
SINGLE MEN:	0		SHORT TERM:	0
SINGLE WOMEN:	0		RETIRED:	0
TOTAL ACTIVE:	0			

International Lutheran Laymen's
League

2185 Hampton Ave.
St. Louis MO 63139

Tel. (314) 647-4900
EXECUTIVE OFFICER: John A. Daniels
ORGANIZED: 1917
DESCRIPTION: A denominational specialized service agency of
    Lutheran tradition producing "The Lutheran Hour" radio
    program, broadcast overseas in 39 languages and supported
    through 18 overseas branch offices and production centers.
    The program "This is the Life" is shown in 21 nations.
    Also engaged in evangelism, correspondence courses and
    literature production.
TOTAL INCOME: $8,659,057   FOR OVERSEAS MINISTRIES: $149,700
PERSONNEL:

NORTH AMERICANS OVERSEAS		NON-NORTH AMERICANS OVERSEAS:		0
MARRIED:	2	NORTH AMERICAN ADM. STAFF:		115
SINGLE MEN:	0		SHORT TERM:	0
SINGLE WOMEN:	0		RETIRED:	7
TOTAL ACTIVE:	2			

International Messianic Outreach

2055 E Lake Rd.
Atlanta GA 30307

Tel. (404) 377-2612
EXECUTIVE OFFICER: David Couture
ORGANIZED: 1974
DESCRIPTION: An independent agency of evangelical tradition
    involved in mass evangelism to the Jews.
TOTAL INCOME: $91,000   FOR OVERSEAS MINISTRIES: $0
PERSONNEL:

NORTH AMERICANS OVERSEAS		NON-NORTH AMERICANS OVERSEAS:		NR
MARRIED:	NR	NORTH AMERICAN ADM. STAFF:		2
SINGLE MEN:	NR		SHORT TERM:	0
SINGLE WOMEN:	NR		RETIRED:	0
TOTAL ACTIVE:	NR			

International Missionary Advance

1605 E Elizabeth St.
Pasadena CA 91104

Tel. (213) 794-4102
EXECUTIVE OFFICER: Ben A. Jennings
ORGANIZED: 1975
DESCRIPTION: An interdenominational sending agency of
    evangelical tradition assisting churches in developing
    their own indigenous missionary agencies.
TOTAL INCOME: $70,000   FOR OVERSEAS MINISTRIES: $21,561
PERSONNEL:

NORTH AMERICANS OVERSEAS		NON-NORTH AMERICANS OVERSEAS:	0
MARRIED:	1	NORTH AMERICAN ADM. STAFF:	2
SINGLE MEN:	1	SHORT TERM:	0
SINGLE WOMEN:	0	RETIRED:	0
TOTAL ACTIVE:	2		

FIELD OF SERVICE	YEAR BEGAN	PERSONNEL NOW	PERSONNEL NEW	RELATED CHURCHES	PEOPLE GROUPS	NOTES
Japan	1975			75		
Korea, Rep. of	1973	1		3000		
Taiwan Rep of China	1978			1000		

International Missions, Inc.

62 Sandra Lane
Wayne NJ 07470
P.O. ADDRESS:
Box 323
Wayne NJ 07470

Tel. (201) 696-4804
EXECUTIVE OFFICER: Bill Tarter
ORGANIZED: 1930   AFFILIATION: IFMA
DESCRIPTION: An interdenominational sending agency of
    independent tradition establishing churches and engaged
    in evangelism and medicine. Also involved in general
    Christian education and theological education.
TOTAL INCOME: $1,167,811   FOR OVERSEAS MINISTRIES: $103,557
PERSONNEL:

NORTH AMERICANS OVERSEAS		NON-NORTH AMERICANS OVERSEAS:	2
MARRIED:	102	NORTH AMERICAN ADM. STAFF:	13
SINGLE MEN:	5	SHORT TERM:	3
SINGLE WOMEN:	25	RETIRED:	13
TOTAL ACTIVE:	132		

FIELD OF SERVICE	YEAR BEGAN	PERSONNEL NOW	PERSONNEL NEW	RELATED CHURCHES	PEOPLE GROUPS	NOTES
Hong-Kong	1950	7	3	8	1	
India	1930	16		100	3	
Iran	1955	2		1	3	
Japan	1950	10	4	3	1	
Kenya	1956	19	13	2	2	
Netherlands	1976	2		1	3	
Pakistan	1954	14	4	5	2	
Philippines	1951	14	5	36	3	
Surinam	1961	6	2	2	3	

FIELD OF SERVICE	YEAR BEGAN	PERSONNEL NOW	NEW	RELATED CHURCHES	PEOPLE GROUPS	NOTES
Turkey	1975					
United Kingdom	1966	6	2	2	2	

International Needs-USA

1156 N 80th St.
Seattle WA 98103
P.O. ADDRESS:
Box 15420
Seattle WA 98115

Tel. (206) 524-9000
EXECUTIVE OFFICER: Ray Harrison
ORGANIZED: 1975
DESCRIPTION: An interdenominational service agency of
    evangelical tradition working through nationals to provide
    training and aid/relief.
TOTAL INCOME: $300,000   FOR OVERSEAS MINISTRIES: $275,000
PERSONNEL:
    NORTH AMERICANS OVERSEAS   NON-NORTH AMERICANS OVERSEAS: 80
                MARRIED: 0   NORTH AMERICAN ADM. STAFF: 0
             SINGLE MEN: 0   SHORT TERM: 0
           SINGLE WOMEN: 0   RETIRED: 0

       TOTAL ACTIVE: 0

FIELD OF SERVICE	YEAR BEGAN	PERSONNEL NOW	NEW	RELATED CHURCHES	PEOPLE GROUPS	NOTES
Bangladesh	1974					
India	1974					
Korea, Rep. of	1975					
Nepal	1974					
Philippines	1975					

    Note: All overseas personnel are nationals.

International Opportunities Unlimited

DESCRIPTION: No data is reported for this agency for one of the
    following reasons: it is currently inactive or no longer
    exists; it has terminated overseas ministries or has ceased
    to operate as a North American entity.

International Pentecostal Assemblies World Missions Dept.

SEE: Intl. Pentecostal Church of Christ, Global Msns. Dept.

International Pentecostal Church of Christ, Global Missions Dept.

892 Berne St. SE
Atlanta GA 30316
P.O. ADDRESS:
Box 18145
Atlanta GA 30316

Tel. (404) 627-2681
EXECUTIVE OFFICER: James B. Keiller
ORGANIZED: 1917
DESCRIPTION: Founded as International Pentecostal Assemblies,
    World Missions Dept. Name changed in 1976. A denominational
    sending agency of Pentecostal tradition establishing
    churches and involved in both secular and theological
    education and childcare.
TOTAL INCOME: $78,507   FOR OVERSEAS MINISTRIES: $53,000

PERSONNEL:
```
     NORTH AMERICANS OVERSEAS    NON-NORTH AMERICANS OVERSEAS:    0
             MARRIED:    14          NORTH AMERICAN ADM. STAFF:    1
          SINGLE MEN:     0                        SHORT TERM:    0
        SINGLE WOMEN:     6                           RETIRED:    0
                      -----
        TOTAL ACTIVE:    20
```

FIELD OF SERVICE	YEAR BEGAN	PERSONNEL NOW	NEW	RELATED CHURCHES	PEOPLE GROUPS	NOTES
Brazil	1938			200		
Hong-Kong	1930	1		1		
India	1943	2	1	2		
Italy	1952			1		
Japan		1				
Kenya	1938	14	3	300		
Mexico	1952	2		6		
Puerto Rico	1962			2		
United Kingdom	1975					

International Prison Ministry

3606 Cavalier
Garland TX 75042
P.O. ADDRESS:
Box 63
Dallas TX 74221

Tel. (214) 494-2302
EXECUTIVE OFFICER: Ray Hoekstra
ORGANIZED: 1970
DESCRIPTION: A specialized agency that provides Bibles and
    literature to state and federal prisons and juvenile
    halls in the Philippines, Caribbean-General, Mexico and
    the Virgin Islands.
TOTAL INCOME: NA   FOR OVERSEAS MINISTRIES: NR
PERSONNEL:
```
     NORTH AMERICANS OVERSEAS    NON-NORTH AMERICANS OVERSEAS:    NR
             MARRIED:     0          NORTH AMERICAN ADM. STAFF:   13
          SINGLE MEN:     0                        SHORT TERM:    1
        SINGLE WOMEN:     0                           RETIRED:    NR
                      -----
        TOTAL ACTIVE:     0
```

International Society of Christian Endeavor SEE: World's Christian Endeavor Union

International Students, Inc.

P.O. ADDRESS:
Box C
Colorado Springs CO 80901

Tel. (303) 475-9500
EXECUTIVE OFFICER: Hal Guffey
ORGANIZED: 1953   AFFILIATION: EFMA
DESCRIPTION: A nondenominational service agency of evangelical
    tradition engaged in student evangelism, training and
    church planting. It ministers specifically to the
    internationals in the USA, including foreign students and
    trainees.
TOTAL INCOME: $1,555,000   FOR OVERSEAS MINISTRIES: $25,900
PERSONNEL:
```
     NORTH AMERICANS OVERSEAS    NON-NORTH AMERICANS OVERSEAS:    NR
             MARRIED:    NR          NORTH AMERICAN ADM. STAFF:  130
          SINGLE MEN:    NR                        SHORT TERM:    3
```

```
SINGLE WOMEN:    NR                          RETIRED:      0
                 -----
   TOTAL ACTIVE:   5
```

FIELD OF SERVICE	YEAR BEGAN	PERSONNEL NOW	NEW	RELATED CHURCHES	PEOPLE GROUPS	NOTES
Costa Rica						
Ecuador						
Egypt						
Japan						

Janz Brothers Gospel Association SEE: Janz Team

Janz Team

2081 Henderson Hwy.
Winnipeg MAN R2G 1P7
Canada
P.O. ADDRESS:
Box 4004, Station B
Winnipeg MAN R2G 1P7
Canada

Tel. (204) 334-0055
EXECUTIVE OFFICER: Leo Janz
ORGANIZED: 1954   AFFILIATION: IFMA-Assoc. member
DESCRIPTION: Founded as Janz Brothers Gospel Association.
    Name changed in 1977. An interdenominational sending
    agency of evangelical tradition engaged in mass
    evangelism and secular and general Christian education.
TOTAL INCOME: $490,000   FOR OVERSEAS MINISTRIES: $490,000
PERSONNEL:
```
   NORTH AMERICANS OVERSEAS     NON-NORTH AMERICANS OVERSEAS:     0
             MARRIED:    52          NORTH AMERICAN ADM. STAFF:    1
          SINGLE MEN:    2                          SHORT TERM:   10
        SINGLE WOMEN:   10                             RETIRED:    0
                      -----
        TOTAL ACTIVE:   64
```

FIELD OF SERVICE	YEAR BEGAN	PERSONNEL NOW	NEW	RELATED CHURCHES	PEOPLE GROUPS	NOTES
Brazil	1975	9				
Germany, Fed. Rep.	1954	73				

Japan Evangelical Mission

306 6th Ave. North
Three Hills AB TOM 2A0
Canada
P.O. ADDRESS:
Box 640
Three Hills AB TOM 2A0
Canada

Tel. (403) 443-5591
EXECUTIVE OFFICER: Ben Ichikawa
ORGANIZED: 1951   AFFILIATION: IFMA
DESCRIPTION: A nondenominational sending agency of independent
    and evangelical tradition establishing churches and
    involved in theological education and evangelism. Also
    conducts camps and conferences and is engaged in teaching
    English to Japanese.
TOTAL INCOME: $797,995   FOR OVERSEAS MINISTRIES: $393,810

```
PERSONNEL:
   NORTH AMERICANS OVERSEAS   NON-NORTH AMERICANS OVERSEAS:    2
             MARRIED:    38      NORTH AMERICAN ADM. STAFF:     5
          SINGLE MEN:     1                  SHORT TERM:        5
        SINGLE WOMEN:    10                     RETIRED:        0
                        -----
        TOTAL ACTIVE:   49
```

FIELD OF SERVICE	YEAR BEGAN	PERSONNEL NOW	NEW	RELATED CHURCHES	PEOPLE GROUPS	NOTES
Brazil	1972	10	5	1	1	
Japan	1951	40	8	18	1	

Japan Evangelistic Association, Inc.

1717 Norfolk Ave. #1373
Lubbock TX 79416
P.O. ADDRESS:
Box 3310
Lubbock TX 79452

```
Tel. (806) 793-3829
EXECUTIVE OFFICER: Joe R. Gooden
ORGANIZED: 1959
DESCRIPTION:  An interdenominational agency of evangelical and
     Baptist tradition specializing in the training of young
     Japanese pastors.  Also engaged in church planting and
     nurturing, evangelism and psychological counseling.
TOTAL INCOME:    $98,000   FOR OVERSEAS MINISTRIES:    $98,000
PERSONNEL:
   NORTH AMERICANS OVERSEAS   NON-NORTH AMERICANS OVERSEAS:    0
             MARRIED:     4      NORTH AMERICAN ADM. STAFF:     0
          SINGLE MEN:     0                  SHORT TERM:        0
        SINGLE WOMEN:     0                     RETIRED:        0
                        -----
        TOTAL ACTIVE:    4
NOTES:  One volunteer helps with administrative
        duties in USA office.
```

FIELD OF SERVICE	YEAR BEGAN	PERSONNEL NOW	NEW	RELATED CHURCHES	PEOPLE GROUPS	NOTES
Japan	1950	4		18		

Japan Evangelistic Band

2237 Manhattan Ave.
Hermosa Beach CA 90254

```
Tel. (213) 376-5867
EXECUTIVE OFFICER: Tudor J. Jones
ORGANIZED: 1903
DESCRIPTION:  An interdenominational sending agency of Holiness
     tradition engaged in evangelism and education. Also
     operates a Bible college in Japan.
TOTAL INCOME:        NR     FOR OVERSEAS MINISTRIES:    $39,092
PERSONNEL:
   NORTH AMERICANS OVERSEAS   NON-NORTH AMERICANS OVERSEAS:   NR
             MARRIED:     2      NORTH AMERICAN ADM. STAFF:     3
          SINGLE MEN:     0                  SHORT TERM:        0
        SINGLE WOMEN:     1                     RETIRED:        1
                        -----
        TOTAL ACTIVE:    3
```

FIELD OF SERVICE	YEAR BEGAN	PERSONNEL NOW	NEW	RELATED CHURCHES	PEOPLE GROUPS	NOTES
Japan	1903	3				

Japan Evangelistic Band (Canada)

4225 Grant St.
Burnaby BC V5C 3P1
Canada

Tel. (604) 298-6317
EXECUTIVE OFFICER: Tudor J. Jones
ORGANIZED: 1903
DESCRIPTION: An interdenominational sending agency of Holiness
    tradition engaged in evangelism and education. Also
    operates a Bible college in Japan.
TOTAL INCOME: $4,780   FOR OVERSEAS MINISTRIES: $4,366
PERSONNEL:

NORTH AMERICANS OVERSEAS		NON-NORTH AMERICANS OVERSEAS:	NR
MARRIED:	2	NORTH AMERICAN ADM. STAFF:	3
SINGLE MEN:	0	SHORT TERM:	0
SINGLE WOMEN:	1	RETIRED:	1
TOTAL ACTIVE:	3		

FIELD OF SERVICE	YEAR BEGAN	PERSONNEL NOW	NEW	RELATED CHURCHES	PEOPLE GROUPS	NOTES
Japan	1903	3				

Japan International Christian University Foundation, Inc.

475 Riverside Dr. Rm.720
New York NY 10115

Tel. (212) 870-2893
EXECUTIVE OFFICER: Ruth Miller
ORGANIZED: 1949   AFFILIATION: DOM-NCCCUSA
DESCRIPTION: An interdenominational organization assisting the
    development of International Christian University in Japan
    (ICU). Engaged in fund raising and transmittal, information
    service and general Christian education.
TOTAL INCOME: $387,782   FOR OVERSEAS MINISTRIES: $277,553
PERSONNEL:

NORTH AMERICANS OVERSEAS		NON-NORTH AMERICANS OVERSEAS:	0
MARRIED:	0	NORTH AMERICAN ADM. STAFF:	0
SINGLE MEN:	0	SHORT TERM:	0
SINGLE WOMEN:	0	RETIRED:	0
TOTAL ACTIVE:	0		
supported.			

FIELD OF SERVICE	YEAR BEGAN	PERSONNEL NOW	NEW	RELATED CHURCHES	PEOPLE GROUPS	NOTES
Japan	1949	11				

Japan-North American Commission on Cooperative Mission

475 Riverside Dr. Rm.618
New York NY 10115

Tel. (212) 870-2021
EXECUTIVE OFFICER: Robert W. Northup
ORGANIZED: 1947
DESCRIPTION: Founded in 1947 as Interboard Committee for
    Christian Work in Japan. Name changed in 1973.
    An interdenominational agency of ecumenical tradition for

two-way cooperative mission between churches and agencies
in Japan and North America. Members include 2 churches in
Japan, 7 churches in Canada, and one board in the USA.
Involved in education, development of human resources,
support of national churches and minority issues.
TOTAL INCOME: $377,000   FOR OVERSEAS MINISTRIES: $377,000
PERSONNEL:
  NORTH AMERICANS OVERSEAS   NON-NORTH AMERICANS OVERSEAS: 180
         MARRIED: 180   NORTH AMERICAN ADM. STAFF: 2
      SINGLE MEN: 18   SHORT TERM: 75
    SINGLE WOMEN: 57   RETIRED: 0

     TOTAL ACTIVE: 255
NOTES: Overseas income is estimated by agency.

                   YEAR   PERSONNEL   RELATED   PEOPLE
FIELD OF SERVICE   BEGAN   NOW   NEW   CHURCHES   GROUPS   NOTES

Japan   1859   235   30   1715
    Note: New personnel is estimated by agency.
    agency.

Japanese Evangelical Missionary Society

112 N San Pedro, No.317
Los Angeles CA 90012

Tel. (213) 629-1089
EXECUTIVE OFFICER: O. S. Tonomura
ORGANIZED: 1951
DESCRIPTION: An interdenominational sending agency of
    evangelical tradition engaged in support of nationals and
    national churches, and student and saturation evangelism,
    especially among the Japanese.
TOTAL INCOME: $90,000   FOR OVERSEAS MINISTRIES: $25,000
PERSONNEL:
  NORTH AMERICANS OVERSEAS   NON-NORTH AMERICANS OVERSEAS: 0
         MARRIED: 2   NORTH AMERICAN ADM. STAFF: 4
      SINGLE MEN: 0   SHORT TERM: 7
    SINGLE WOMEN: 0   RETIRED: 0

     TOTAL ACTIVE: 2

                   YEAR   PERSONNEL   RELATED   PEOPLE
FIELD OF SERVICE   BEGAN   NOW   NEW   CHURCHES   GROUPS   NOTES

Brazil   1966   2

Jesus Evangelism

402 Bradley St.
Santa Paula CA 93060
P.O. ADDRESS:
Box 665
Santa Paula CA 93060

Tel. (805) 525-2901
EXECUTIVE OFFICER: Lenard Galster
ORGANIZED: 1976
DESCRIPTION: A nondenominational agency of evangelical
    tradition involved in literature distribution and
    production.
TOTAL INCOME: $10,000   FOR OVERSEAS MINISTRIES: $5,000
                                                              ?
PERSONNEL:
  NORTH AMERICANS OVERSEAS   NON-NORTH AMERICANS OVERSEAS: 0
         MARRIED: 0   NORTH AMERICAN ADM. STAFF: 0
      SINGLE MEN: 0   SHORT TERM: 0

SINGLE WOMEN: 0   RETIRED: 0

    TOTAL ACTIVE: 0
NOTES: All personnel are volunteer.

Jesus to the Communist World, Inc.

116 S Louise St.
Glendale CA 91205
P.O. ADDRESS:
Box 11
Glendale CA 91209

Tel. (213) 253-5558
EXECUTIVE OFFICER: Michael Wurmbrand
ORGANIZED: 1967
DESCRIPTION: An interdenominational sending agency of
    evangelical and fundamentalist tradition seeking to aid
    Christians in communist nations. Engaged in Bible
    distribution and translation, evangelism and literature
    distribution.
TOTAL INCOME: $6,655,928   FOR OVERSEAS MINISTRIES: $5,425,548
PERSONNEL:
    NORTH AMERICANS OVERSEAS   NON-NORTH AMERICANS OVERSEAS: NR
            MARRIED: NR   NORTH AMERICAN ADM. STAFF: 10
         SINGLE MEN: NR   SHORT TERM: NR
       SINGLE WOMEN: NR   RETIRED: 3

       TOTAL ACTIVE: NR

                    YEAR   PERSONNEL   RELATED   PEOPLE
FIELD OF SERVICE   BEGAN   NOW   NEW   CHURCHES   GROUPS NOTES

Argentina
Australia
Austria
Belgium
Bolivia
Botswana
Brazil
Chile
Colombia
Denmark
Ecuador
Fiji
Finland
France
Germany, Fed. Rep.
Ghana
Greece
Guatemala
Honduras
Hong-Kong
Iceland
India
Ireland
Italy
Ivory Coast
Japan
Korea, Rep. of
Lesotho

```
----------------------------------------------------------------
                   YEAR     PERSONNEL   RELATED   PEOPLE
FIELD OF SERVICE   BEGAN    NOW   NEW   CHURCHES  GROUPS  NOTES
----------------------------------------------------------------
Malaysia
Malta
Netherlands
New Zealand
Nigeria
Norway
Peru
Portugal
Singapore
South Africa
Spain
Sri Lanka
Swaziland
Sweden
Switzerland
Transkei
United Kingdom
Upper Volta
Zaire
Zimbabwe
```

Jewish Voice Broadcast

16001 N 34 St.
Phoenix AZ 85032
P.O. ADDRESS:
Box 6
Phoenix AZ 85001

Tel. (602) 971-8501
EXECUTIVE OFFICER: Louis Caplan
ORGANIZED: 1967
DESCRIPTION: A specialized agency of evangelical tradition
    involved in mass evangelism to Jews, general Christian
    education, literature distribution and radio and TV
    broadcasting. They also send a team to Israel short-term.

```
TOTAL INCOME:         NR        FOR OVERSEAS MINISTRIES:   NR
PERSONNEL:
   NORTH AMERICANS OVERSEAS   NON-NORTH AMERICANS OVERSEAS:  NR
         MARRIED:   NR         NORTH AMERICAN ADM. STAFF:    12
      SINGLE MEN:   NR                       SHORT TERM:      5
    SINGLE WOMEN:   NR                          RETIRED:      0
                   -----
    TOTAL ACTIVE:   NR
```

Jews For Jesus

60 Haight St.
San Francisco CA 94102

Tel. (415) 864-2600
EXECUTIVE OFFICER: Moishe Rosen
ORGANIZED: 1973
DESCRIPTION: An independent agency of evangelical tradition
    sending short-term missionaries to Israel and other
    countries where they chiefly minister to Jews. Agency is
    primarily concerned with student evangelism.

```
TOTAL INCOME: $2,435,000       FOR OVERSEAS MINISTRIES:   NR
PERSONNEL:
   NORTH AMERICANS OVERSEAS   NON-NORTH AMERICANS OVERSEAS:   0
         MARRIED:    0         NORTH AMERICAN ADM. STAFF:     0
      SINGLE MEN:    0                       SHORT TERM:     25
```

```
          SINGLE WOMEN:     0                              RETIRED:     0
                         -----
          TOTAL ACTIVE:     0
---------------------------------------------------------------------
                         YEAR    PERSONNEL   RELATED   PEOPLE
FIELD OF SERVICE         BEGAN   NOW   NEW   CHURCHES  GROUPS  NOTES
---------------------------------------------------------------------
Argentina                1976
Australia                1977
Brazil                   1976
Germany, Dem. Rep.       1979
Germany, Fed. Rep.       1979
Ireland                  1976
Israel                   1975
New Zealand              1978
Switzerland              1975
United Kingdom           1976
```

John Milton Society for the Blind

29 W 34th St., 6th Fl.
New York NY 10001

Tel. (212) 736-4162
EXECUTIVE OFFICER: Chenoweth J. Watson
ORGANIZED: 1928
DESCRIPTION: An interdenominational specialized service agency
    publishing and providing Christian literature for the
    blind. Financial grants are also sent overseas to church
    related schools and homes for the blind.
TOTAL INCOME: $275,000   FOR OVERSEAS MINISTRIES: $20,000
PERSONNEL:
    NORTH AMERICANS OVERSEAS   NON-NORTH AMERICANS OVERSEAS: 0
              MARRIED: 0   NORTH AMERICAN ADM. STAFF: 0
           SINGLE MEN: 0   SHORT TERM: 0
         SINGLE WOMEN: 0   RETIRED: 0

         TOTAL ACTIVE: 0

Jubilee, Inc.: The Other Side Magazine, Jubilee Crafts, Jubilee Fund

300 W Apsley St.
Philadelphia PA 19144
P.O. ADDRESS:
Box 12236
Philadelphia PA 19144

Tel. (215) 849-2178
EXECUTIVE OFFICER: Mary Jane Heisey
ORGANIZED: 1965
DESCRIPTION: Founded as Freedom Now. Name changed to Jubilee,
    Inc. in 1977. Nondenominational service agencies of
    evangelical tradition engaged in support of nationals,
    self-help projects and community development. The Other
    Side is a magazine emphasizing responsibility to social
    issues; Jubilee Crafts sells handicrafts made by third
    world communities; Jubilee Fund supports third world
    ministries run by nationals with focus on development and
    non-violent structural change.
TOTAL INCOME: $81,585   FOR OVERSEAS MINISTRIES: $0
PERSONNEL:
    NORTH AMERICANS OVERSEAS   NON-NORTH AMERICANS OVERSEAS: 0
              MARRIED: 0   NORTH AMERICAN ADM. STAFF: 3
           SINGLE MEN: 0   SHORT TERM: 0

342

SINGLE WOMEN: 0   RETIRED: 0

TOTAL ACTIVE: 0
NOTES: Total income does not include money received for
         magazine. Total of North American administrators
         does not include magazine personnel.

Jungle Aviation and Radio Service, Inc. (JAARS)

P.O. ADDRESS:
Box 248
Waxhaw NC 28173

Tel. (704) 843-2185
EXECUTIVE OFFICER: James Baptista
ORGANIZED: 1947
DESCRIPTION: A nondenominational specialized service agency
    giving aviation and radio support to Wycliffe Bible
    Translators/Summer Institute of Linguistics. Personnel are
    sent through WBT board.
TOTAL INCOME: $600,000   FOR OVERSEAS MINISTRIES: $250,000
PERSONNEL:
    NORTH AMERICANS OVERSEAS   NON-NORTH AMERICANS OVERSEAS: 0
            MARRIED: 0   NORTH AMERICAN ADM. STAFF: 0
         SINGLE MEN: 0   SHORT TERM: 0
       SINGLE WOMEN: 0   RETIRED: 0

        TOTAL ACTIVE: 0

Kansas Yearly Meeting of Friends Africa Gospel Mission

Rt. 2
Macksville KS 67557

EXECUTIVE OFFICER: John Robinson
ORGANIZED: 1932   AFFILIATION: EFMA
DESCRIPTION: No current information available. Information
    from 1976 directory. A denominational sending agency of
    Friends tradition serving national churches and involved
    in evangelism, agricultural assistance, education,
    industrial training, literature, medicine, radio and
    translation.
TOTAL INCOME: $145,000   FOR OVERSEAS MINISTRIES: $145,000
PERSONNEL:
    NORTH AMERICANS OVERSEAS   NON-NORTH AMERICANS OVERSEAS: NR
            MARRIED: 16   NORTH AMERICAN ADM. STAFF: 1
         SINGLE MEN: 0   SHORT TERM: 0
       SINGLE WOMEN: 1   RETIRED: NR

        TOTAL ACTIVE: 17
NOTES: Income estimated by MARC.

FIELD OF SERVICE	YEAR BEGAN	PERSONNEL NOW	NEW	RELATED CHURCHES	PEOPLE GROUPS	NOTES
Burundi	1932			6		

King's Garden, Inc. SEE: World Concern/Crista International

Kiyosato Educational Experiment Project SEE: American Committee for Keep, Inc.

Korea Gospel Mission

1629 W Fairmount
Phoenix AZ 85015
P.O. ADDRESS:
Box 20044
Phoenix AZ 85036

Tel. (602) 266-4637
EXECUTIVE OFFICER: LeRoy Thomas
ORGANIZED: 1952
DESCRIPTION: An interdenominational agency of Baptist and
    Presbyterian tradition engaged in education, evangelism
    and childcare. Sends one USA representative to Korea for
    3 months per year. Has over 75 national workers.
TOTAL INCOME: $36,267   FOR OVERSEAS MINISTRIES: NR
PERSONNEL:
    NORTH AMERICANS OVERSEAS   NON-NORTH AMERICANS OVERSEAS: NR
            MARRIED: 0   NORTH AMERICAN ADM. STAFF: 1
         SINGLE MEN: 0   SHORT TERM: NR
       SINGLE WOMEN: 0   RETIRED: 0

       TOTAL ACTIVE: 0

FIELD OF SERVICE	YEAR BEGAN	PERSONNEL NOW	PERSONNEL NEW	RELATED CHURCHES	PEOPLE GROUPS	NOTES
Korea, Rep. of	1952					

Korea International Mission, Inc.

3423 Chapman
Orange CA 92669
P.O. ADDRESS:
Box 2070
Orange CA 92669

Tel. (714) 997-3920
EXECUTIVE OFFICER: Dale Kietzman
ORGANIZED: 1968
DESCRIPTION: KIM, Inc. is the USA agency supporting the
    East-West Center for Missionary Research and Development
    in Korea, an organ of the Asia Mission Association.
    Involved in church planting, education, evangelism and
    missionary orientation and training. All overseas
    personnel are non-North American.
TOTAL INCOME: $150,000   FOR OVERSEAS MINISTRIES: $150,000
PERSONNEL:
    NORTH AMERICANS OVERSEAS   NON-NORTH AMERICANS OVERSEAS: 16
            MARRIED: 0   NORTH AMERICAN ADM. STAFF: 0
         SINGLE MEN: 0   SHORT TERM: 0
       SINGLE WOMEN: 0   RETIRED: 0

       TOTAL ACTIVE: 0

FIELD OF SERVICE	YEAR BEGAN	PERSONNEL NOW	PERSONNEL NEW	RELATED CHURCHES	PEOPLE GROUPS	NOTES
Germany, Fed. Rep.	1977	2		1		
Hong-Kong	1979			2	1	
Indonesia	1974	2		10	1	
Korea, Rep. of	1968	8		100		
Thailand	1956	6			2	

Kuang Ming Vocational Institute SEE: Tainan Evangelical Mission

Language Institute For Evangelism (LIFE)

32 N Curtis
Alhambra CA 91801
P.O. ADDRESS:
Box 200
Alhambra CA 91802

Tel. (213) 289-5031
EXECUTIVE OFFICER: Kenneth P. Wendling
ORGANIZED: 1965   AFFILIATION: IFMA
DESCRIPTION: A nondenominational specialized service agency of
    evangelical tradition establishing churches and involved
    in evangelism and encouragement of national Christian
    leadership through teaching of conversational English to
    Japanese college students. Agency has an active short-term
    summer program involving 102 student evangelists.
TOTAL INCOME: $575,000   FOR OVERSEAS MINISTRIES: $575,000
PERSONNEL:
  NORTH AMERICANS OVERSEAS   NON-NORTH AMERICANS OVERSEAS: 0
        MARRIED: 4   NORTH AMERICAN ADM. STAFF: 10
    SINGLE MEN: 2   SHORT TERM: 14
  SINGLE WOMEN: 1   RETIRED: 11

    TOTAL ACTIVE: 7

FIELD OF SERVICE	YEAR BEGAN	PERSONNEL NOW	NEW	RELATED CHURCHES	PEOPLE GROUPS	NOTES
Japan	1967	20	10	4	1	

Note: Summer outreach will involve 130 churches.

Laos Team SEE: Laos, Inc.

Laos, Inc.

4920 Piney Branch Rd. NW
Washington D.C. 20011

Tel. (202) 723-8273
EXECUTIVE OFFICER: Morris Bratton
ORGANIZED: 1962   AFFILIATION: DOM-NCCCUSA, Frat. Rel.
DESCRIPTION: Formerly, Laymen's Overseas Service. Name
    changed to Laos Team, Inc. than to Laos, Inc. A
    nondenominational specialized service agency of
    independent tradition recruiting laymeen for short-term
    assignments overseas and in the USA, and organizing
    workshops on contemporary social issues. Laymen include
    teachers, secretaries, doctors and childcare specialists.
TOTAL INCOME: $106,000   FOR OVERSEAS MINISTRIES: NR
PERSONNEL:
  NORTH AMERICANS OVERSEAS   NON-NORTH AMERICANS OVERSEAS: NR
        MARRIED: NR   NORTH AMERICAN ADM. STAFF: 6
    SINGLE MEN: NR   SHORT TERM: 55
  SINGLE WOMEN: NR   RETIRED: NR

    TOTAL ACTIVE: NR
NOTES: Averages between 50 to 60 short-termers per year.

Latin America Assistance

735 State St.
Santa Barbara CA 93101
P.O. ADDRESS:

Box 2361
Santa Barbara CA 93102

Tel. (805) 966-9062
EXECUTIVE OFFICER: Joseph B. Pent
ORGANIZED: 1976
DESCRIPTION: A nondemoninational service agency of evangelical
     tradition involved in literature production and the
     Biblical training and discipleship of Latin American
     youth. Also has correspondence courses.
TOTAL INCOME: NR   FOR OVERSEAS MINISTRIES: $22,000
PERSONNEL:
   NORTH AMERICANS OVERSEAS   NON-NORTH AMERICANS OVERSEAS: NR
         MARRIED: NR   NORTH AMERICAN ADM. STAFF: 1
      SINGLE MEN: NR   SHORT TERM: NR
    SINGLE WOMEN: NR   RETIRED: 0

      TOTAL ACTIVE: 1
NOTES: Overseas income estimated by MARC.

Latin America Mission, Inc.

1826 Ponce de Leon Blvd.
Coral Gables FL 33134
P.O. ADDRESS:
Box 341368
Coral Gables FL 33134

Tel. (305) 444-6228
EXECUTIVE OFFICER: Clayton L. Berg, Jr.
ORGANIZED: 1921   AFFILIATION: EFMA
DESCRIPTION: Founded as Latin American Evangelization
     Campaign, Inc. Name changed in 1938. An
     interdenominational service agency of evangelical
     tradition working in the Latin church by means of
     evangelization, education, mass media and social services.
     Most of the Latin America Mission personnel are seconded
     to other ministries in the Latin world. Most of those
     ministries are members of the Community of Latin American
     Evangelical Ministries.
TOTAL INCOME: $1,724,000   FOR OVERSEAS MINISTRIES: $1,724,000
PERSONNEL:
   NORTH AMERICANS OVERSEAS   NON-NORTH AMERICANS OVERSEAS: 7
         MARRIED: 131   NORTH AMERICAN ADM. STAFF: 22
      SINGLE MEN: 1   SHORT TERM: 60
    SINGLE WOMEN: 32   RETIRED: 21

      TOTAL ACTIVE: 164
NOTES: Out of the total overseas personnel, 142
        were sent through other agencies.

FIELD OF SERVICE	YEAR BEGAN	PERSONNEL NOW	NEW	RELATED CHURCHES	PEOPLE GROUPS	NOTES
Argentina	1976	2	2			
Brazil	1973	1	1			
Colombia	1937	24	7			
Costa Rica	1921	92	10			
Ecuador	1975	2				
Honduras	1976	2	2			
Mexico	1970	10	2			
Panama	1955	2	2			

FIELD OF SERVICE	YEAR BEGAN	PERSONNEL NOW	PERSONNEL NEW	RELATED CHURCHES	PEOPLE GROUPS	NOTES
Peru	1975	2				

Lebanon Evangelical Mission SEE: Middle East Christian Outreach

Leprosy Mission Canada

67 Yonge St., Ste. 1128
Toronto ON M5E 1J8
Canada

Tel. (416) 364-3736
EXECUTIVE OFFICER: Douglas Graham
ORGANIZED: 1892
DESCRIPTION: An interdenominational, international agency of
    evangelical tradition ministering to leprosy patients and
    their families. Engaged in fund raising, training, serving
    other agencies and medical research.
TOTAL INCOME: $615,145   FOR OVERSEAS MINISTRIES: $541,000
PERSONNEL:
    NORTH AMERICANS OVERSEAS   NON-NORTH AMERICANS OVERSEAS: 1
            MARRIED: 0   NORTH AMERICAN ADM. STAFF: 7
         SINGLE MEN: 0   SHORT TERM: 2
       SINGLE WOMEN: 1   RETIRED: 6

        TOTAL ACTIVE: 1

FIELD OF SERVICE	YEAR BEGAN	PERSONNEL NOW	PERSONNEL NEW	RELATED CHURCHES	PEOPLE GROUPS	NOTES
Bangladesh	1913					
Bhutan	1966					
Burma	1899					
India	1874	1				
Indonesia	1969					
Korea, Rep. of						
Lesotho	1976					
Nepal	1963					
Papua New Guinea	1965					
Thailand	1960					
Zaire	1931					
Zambia	1942					

    Note: Overseas staff consists of over 95 percent nationals.

Leprosy Relief, Canada, Inc.

#110, 405 Deguire Blvd.
Montreal PQ H4N 1P9
Canada

Tel. (514) 336-9492
EXECUTIVE OFFICER: Paul E. Legault
ORGANIZED: 1961
DESCRIPTION: A service organization committed to combating
    leprosy by maintaining leprosy centers, aiding victims,
    early detection for children and supporting medical
    research centers.
TOTAL INCOME: $1,511,640   FOR OVERSEAS MINISTRIES: $1,319,640
PERSONNEL:
    NORTH AMERICANS OVERSEAS   NON-NORTH AMERICANS OVERSEAS: NR
            MARRIED: 0   NORTH AMERICAN ADM. STAFF: 6
         SINGLE MEN: 0   SHORT TERM: 0

```
SINGLE WOMEN:     0                          RETIRED:      0
                -----
    TOTAL ACTIVE:     0
--------------------------------------------------------------------
                  YEAR    PERSONNEL   RELATED   PEOPLE
FIELD OF SERVICE  BEGAN   NOW   NEW   CHURCHES  GROUPS   NOTES
--------------------------------------------------------------------
Belgium               1970                                        1
Botswana              1979
Brazil                1975
Cameroon              1975
Central African Rep.  1974
Congo                 1976
Dominican Republic    1979
Egypt                 1979
Ethiopia              1979
Hong-Kong             1979
India                 1961
Indonesia             1979
Israel                1977                                        1
Kenya                 1979
Korea, Rep. of        1977
Lesotho               1979
Malawi                1979
Paraguay              1979
Peru                  1974
Philippines           1976
Samoa                 1977                                        1
Senegal               1975
Sri Lanka             1979
Sudan                 1976
Taiwan Rep of China   1976
Tanzania              1979
Thailand              1979
Upper Volta           1979
Zaire                 1975
Zambia                1979
     Note: 1. Has research center.
```

Lester Sumrall Evangelistic Association

530 E Ireland Rd.
South Bend IN 46624
P.O. ADDRESS:
Box 12
South Bend IN 46624

Tel. (219) 291-3292
EXECUTIVE OFFICER: Lester Sumrall
ORGANIZED: 1957
DESCRIPTION: A nondenominational sending agency of independent
    and Pentecostal tradition establishing churches and
    engaged in education, literature and support of nationals.
    Also supports 14 orphanges in 11 countries. Ministries in
    USA include radio and TV broadcasting, a school of
    evangelism and World Harvest Bible College.
TOTAL INCOME: $100,000   FOR OVERSEAS MINISTRIES: $100,000
PERSONNEL:
    NORTH AMERICANS OVERSEAS   NON-NORTH AMERICANS OVERSEAS: NR
            MARRIED: NR   NORTH AMERICAN ADM. STAFF: 40
         SINGLE MEN: NR   SHORT TERM: 6
       SINGLE WOMEN: NR   RETIRED: 0

        TOTAL ACTIVE: 4

348

FIELD OF SERVICE	YEAR BEGAN	PERSONNEL NOW	NEW	RELATED CHURCHES	PEOPLE GROUPS	NOTES
Brazil	1966					
Guatemala						
Haiti						
Hong-Kong	1959					
India						
Indonesia						
Israel						
Italy						
Mexico						
Philippines	1952					

Liberty Corner Mission

Valley/Martinsville Rds.
Liberty Corner NJ 07938
P.O. ADDRESS:
Box 204
Liberty Corner NJ 07938

Tel. (201) 647-1777
EXECUTIVE OFFICER: Edwin E. Achenbach
ORGANIZED: 1933
DESCRIPTION: A nondenominational, international sending agency
    of evangelical and Holiness tradition engaged in
    preparing deconesses for working among the blind,
    handicapped and leprosy victims in Asian countries.
    Liberty Corner Mission is the foreign mission branch of
    the Fellowship Deaconry, Inc. which has Evangelical
    Fellowship Chapels in various cities of the USA and
    Canada.
TOTAL INCOME: $203,457   FOR OVERSEAS MINISTRIES: $193,832
PERSONNEL:
    NORTH AMERICANS OVERSEAS   NON-NORTH AMERICANS OVERSEAS: 14
              MARRIED: 0   NORTH AMERICAN ADM. STAFF: 2
           SINGLE MEN: 0   SHORT TERM: 0
         SINGLE WOMEN: 1   RETIRED: 0

         TOTAL ACTIVE: 1

FIELD OF SERVICE	YEAR BEGAN	PERSONNEL NOW	NEW	RELATED CHURCHES	PEOPLE GROUPS	NOTES
Japan	1951	8	2	4		
Taiwan Rep of China	1952	10	3	9		

Liebenzell Mission of Canada

236 Finch Ave. East
Willowdale ON M2N 4S2
Canada
P.O. ADDRESS:
R.R. 1
Moffat ON L0P 1J0
Canada

Tel. (416) 223-3182
EXECUTIVE OFFICER: Hans Knauer
ORGANIZED: 1966
DESCRIPTION: An interdenominational agency of evangelical and
    Lutheran tradition engaged in church planting, education,
    evangelism, medicine and Bible translation.
TOTAL INCOME: $18,500   FOR OVERSEAS MINISTRIES: $18,500

PERSONNEL:
```
    NORTH AMERICANS OVERSEAS   NON-NORTH AMERICANS OVERSEAS:   0
            MARRIED:  NR          NORTH AMERICAN ADM. STAFF:    1
         SINGLE MEN:  NR                        SHORT TERM:     0
       SINGLE WOMEN:  NR                          RETIRED:      0
                      -----
       TOTAL ACTIVE:  NR
```
NOTES: Funds left over from their home-base
        development are added to overseas income.

FIELD OF SERVICE	YEAR BEGAN	PERSONNEL NOW	NEW	RELATED CHURCHES	PEOPLE GROUPS	NOTES
Bangladesh	1973					
Japan	1923					
Oceania-general	1920					
Papua New Guinea	1914					
Taiwan Rep of China	1955					

Liebenzell Mission of U.S.A., Inc.

Heath Lane
Schooley's Mtn. NJ 07870

Tel. (201) 852-3044
EXECUTIVE OFFICER: Norman Dietsch
ORGANIZED: 1941   AFFILIATION: IFMA
DESCRIPTION: An international, interdenominational sending
   agency of evangelical tradition establishing churches and
   engaged in education, medicine, translation and Bible
   school ministries.
TOTAL INCOME: $356,394   FOR OVERSEAS MINISTRIES: $203,766
PERSONNEL:
```
    NORTH AMERICANS OVERSEAS   NON-NORTH AMERICANS OVERSEAS:   0
            MARRIED:  16         NORTH AMERICAN ADM. STAFF:    6
         SINGLE MEN:  1                        SHORT TERM:     0
       SINGLE WOMEN:  3                          RETIRED:      0
                      -----
       TOTAL ACTIVE:  20
```

FIELD OF SERVICE	YEAR BEGAN	PERSONNEL NOW	NEW	RELATED CHURCHES	PEOPLE GROUPS	NOTES
Guam	1952	2		1	1	
Pacific Trust Terr.	1906	13	3	29	3	
Papua New Guinea	1914	3		16	2	
Philippines	1970	2				

Life For Latins, Inc.

P.O. ADDRESS:
Box 48
Azusa CA 91702

Tel. (602) 963-9512
EXECUTIVE OFFICER: Dale Cook
ORGANIZED: 1977
DESCRIPTION: A nondenominational sending agency of evangelical
   tradition establishing churches and engaged in evangelism,
   training, broadcasting and motion pictures.
TOTAL INCOME: $39,000   FOR OVERSEAS MINISTRIES: $37,800
PERSONNEL:
```
    NORTH AMERICANS OVERSEAS   NON-NORTH AMERICANS OVERSEAS:   0
            MARRIED:  2          NORTH AMERICAN ADM. STAFF:    1
         SINGLE MEN:  0                        SHORT TERM:     0
```

```
         SINGLE WOMEN:    0                          RETIRED:      0
                        -----
         TOTAL ACTIVE:    2
--------------------------------------------------------------------------
                        YEAR     PERSONNEL   RELATED    PEOPLE
FIELD OF SERVICE        BEGAN    NOW   NEW   CHURCHES   GROUPS   NOTES
--------------------------------------------------------------------------
Mexico                  1978      2     2
```

Life Messengers, Inc.

3530 Bagley Ave. North
Seattle WA 98103
P.O. ADDRESS:
Box 1967
Seattle WA 98111

Tel. (206) 632-8500
EXECUTIVE OFFICER: Wayne W. Galvin
ORGANIZED: 1945
DESCRIPTION: A nondenominational agency of evangelical
    tradition producing Christian literature for use in the
    USA and overseas. Overseas distribution is handled by
    existing mission organizations, while USA distribution is
    through individual Christians.

```
TOTAL INCOME:         NR          FOR OVERSEAS MINISTRIES:    NR
PERSONNEL:
    NORTH AMERICANS OVERSEAS   NON-NORTH AMERICANS OVERSEAS:  NR
             MARRIED:   NR          NORTH AMERICAN ADM. STAFF: NR
         SINGLE MEN:    NR                      SHORT TERM:    NR
         SINGLE WOMEN:  NR                       RETIRED:      NR
                      -----
         TOTAL ACTIVE: NR
```

Ling A. Juane Ministries, Inc.

1383 Chartrand Ave.
Orleans ON K1E 1H9
Canada
P.O. ADDRESS:
Box 8631
Ottawa ON K1G 3H9
Canada

Tel. (613) 824-6923
EXECUTIVE OFFICER: H.A. Braunberger
ORGANIZED: 1975
DESCRIPTION: A nondenominational agency ministering in the
    Philippines with radio broadcasts, personal and mass
    evangelism and training.

```
TOTAL INCOME:      $25,000   FOR OVERSEAS MINISTRIES:    $24,000
PERSONNEL:
    NORTH AMERICANS OVERSEAS   NON-NORTH AMERICANS OVERSEAS:    2
             MARRIED:   2           NORTH AMERICAN ADM. STAFF:  0
         SINGLE MEN:    0                      SHORT TERM:       0
         SINGLE WOMEN:  0                       RETIRED:         0
                      -----
         TOTAL ACTIVE:  2
--------------------------------------------------------------------------
                        YEAR     PERSONNEL   RELATED    PEOPLE
FIELD OF SERVICE        BEGAN    NOW   NEW   CHURCHES   GROUPS   NOTES
--------------------------------------------------------------------------
Philippines             1975      2
```

Link Care Center

1734 W Shaw
Fresno CA 93711

Tel. (209) 439-5920
EXECUTIVE OFFICER: Stanley E. Lindquist
ORGANIZED: 1964   AFFILIATION: EFMA
DESCRIPTION: Founded as Link Care Foundation, Inc. Name
    changed in 1979. An interdenominational specialized
    service agency of evangelical tradition providing Christ-
    centered psychological counseling, testing and consultant
    services to missionaries and mission agencies
    internationally. Programs include pre-field, on-the-field,
    and furlough orientation, para-professional training, tape
    ministry and retirement housing.
TOTAL INCOME: $144,000   FOR OVERSEAS MINISTRIES: $0
PERSONNEL:

NORTH AMERICANS OVERSEAS		NON-NORTH AMERICANS OVERSEAS:	0
MARRIED:	0	NORTH AMERICAN ADM. STAFF:	0
SINGLE MEN:	0	SHORT TERM:	0
SINGLE WOMEN:	0	RETIRED:	0
TOTAL ACTIVE:	0		

Link Care Foundation, Inc. SEE: Link Care Center

Literacy and Evangelism, Inc.

1800 S Jackson Ave.
Tulsa OK 74107

Tel. (918) 585-3826
EXECUTIVE OFFICER: Robert F. Rice
ORGANIZED: 1967   AFFILIATION: EFMA
DESCRIPTION: An interdenominational consulting agency of
    evangelical and independent traditions engaged in training
    literacy workers for evangelism in the USA and overseas.
    Assists churches and missions in establishing adult
    literacy programs and preparation of literacy primers. Work
    has, to date, been carried on in 50 languages.
TOTAL INCOME: $338,050   FOR OVERSEAS MINISTRIES: $27,149
PERSONNEL:

NORTH AMERICANS OVERSEAS		NON-NORTH AMERICANS OVERSEAS:	0
MARRIED:	2	NORTH AMERICAN ADM. STAFF:	10
SINGLE MEN:	0	SHORT TERM:	0
SINGLE WOMEN:	0	RETIRED:	0
TOTAL ACTIVE:	2		

NOTES: Three personnel assigned to administrative
    duties are part-time.

Literature Crusades, Inc. SEE: International Crusades, Inc.

Living Bibles International

1809 Mill St.
Naperville IL 60540
P.O. ADDRESS:
Box 800
Naperville IL 60540

Tel. (312) 690-9360
EXECUTIVE OFFICER: Lars B. Dunberg
ORGANIZED: 1968
DESCRIPTION: A nondenominational specialized service agency of
    evangelical tradition developing living, contemporary
    Bible translations in many languages. Also engaged in fund

```
       raising.
TOTAL INCOME:  $1,954,579        FOR OVERSEAS MINISTRIES:    NR
PERSONNEL:
    NORTH AMERICANS OVERSEAS    NON-NORTH AMERICANS OVERSEAS:   12
              MARRIED:    5        NORTH AMERICAN ADM. STAFF:   12
           SINGLE MEN:    0                   SHORT TERM:        0
         SINGLE WOMEN:    0                      RETIRED:        0
                       -----
         TOTAL ACTIVE:    5
```

FIELD OF SERVICE	YEAR BEGAN	PERSONNEL NOW	NEW	RELATED CHURCHES	PEOPLE GROUPS	NOTES
Bangladesh	1974	1			1	
Brazil	1972	2			1	
Burma	1971	1			1	
Czechoslovakia	1972	2			1	
Denmark	1975	2			1	
Finland	1973	2			1	
France	1973	2			1	
Germany, Fed. Rep.	1970	2			1	
Ghana	1973	17			7	
Greece	1977	2			1	
Hong-Kong	1972				1	
Hungary	1977	1			1	
Iceland	1973	1			1	
India	1971	35			13	
Indonesia	1972	2			1	
Italy	1975	2			1	
Japan	1972	6			1	
Kenya	1973	18			5	
Korea, Rep. of	1972	2			1	
Lebanon	1973	2			1	
Nepal	1973	6			1	
Netherlands	1973	2			1	
Nigeria	1973	18			7	
Norway	1973	2			1	
Philippines	1972	2			2	
Poland	1977	1			1	
Portugal	1972	2			1	
Romania	1975	1			1	
South Africa	1972	11			3	
Spain	1973	2			1	
Sri Lanka	1971	2			1	
Sweden	1972	5			1	
Taiwan Rep of China	1972					
Thailand	1973	2			1	
Turkey	1977	1			1	
Yugoslavia	1973	9			2	
Zimbabwe	1972	3			1	

Note: Only five of the overseas
personnel are North Americans.

Living Waters

8307 Dragon
San Antonio TX 78250
Tel. (512) 684-3020
EXECUTIVE OFFICER: Lane L. Roberts
ORGANIZED: 1979
DESCRIPTION: An interdenominational specialized service agency
    of charismatic tradition supporting and aiding
    missionaries. Involved in literature production, radio
    and TV broadcasting, purchasing service, supplying
    equipment and medicine.

TOTAL INCOME: NA   FOR OVERSEAS MINISTRIES: NA
PERSONNEL:
    NORTH AMERICANS OVERSEAS   NON-NORTH AMERICANS OVERSEAS: 0
              MARRIED: 0   NORTH AMERICAN ADM. STAFF: 5
           SINGLE MEN: 0   SHORT TERM: 0
         SINGLE WOMEN: 0   RETIRED: 0

         TOTAL ACTIVE: 0

Livingstone Memorial Mission

P.O. ADDRESS:
Box 1
Perkasie PA 18944

DESCRIPTION: No data is reported for this agency for one of the
    following reasons: it is currently inactive or no longer
    exists; it has terminated overseas ministries or has ceased
    to operate as a North American entity.

Logoi, Inc.

4100 W Flagler Ste. B-3
Miami FL 33134
P.O. ADDRESS:
Box 350128 Riverside Stn
Miami FL 33135

Tel. (305) 446-8297
EXECUTIVE OFFICER: Mr. Leslie J. Thompson
ORGANIZED: 1965   AFFILIATION: EFMA
DESCRIPTION: An interdenominational agency of evangelical and
    Reformed tradition conducting a Bible education program
    for pastors in Latin America. Also engaged in literature
    production and distribution, nurture or support of national
    churches and theological education by extenion (TEE).
TOTAL INCOME: NR   FOR OVERSEAS MINISTRIES: $343,651
PERSONNEL:
    NORTH AMERICANS OVERSEAS   NON-NORTH AMERICANS OVERSEAS: NR
              MARRIED: 2   NORTH AMERICAN ADM. STAFF: 6
           SINGLE MEN: 1   SHORT TERM: 0
         SINGLE WOMEN: 0   RETIRED: 0

         TOTAL ACTIVE: 3

FIELD OF SERVICE	YEAR BEGAN	PERSONNEL NOW	NEW	RELATED CHURCHES	PEOPLE GROUPS	NOTES
Argentina	1978	2				
Chile	1977	3				
Mexico	1980	2				
Paraguay	1978					
Uruguay	1978	2				

Logos Translators

P.O. ADDRESS:
Box 772
Melbourne FL 32935

Tel. (305) 254-5751
EXECUTIVE OFFICER: Claire Reise
ORGANIZED: 1971
DESCRIPTION: A nondenominational specialized agency of
    charismatic tradition involved in Bible translation and
    medical clinic work.
TOTAL INCOME: $28,000   FOR OVERSEAS MINISTRIES: $24,360

PERSONNEL:
```
    NORTH AMERICANS OVERSEAS     NON-NORTH AMERICANS OVERSEAS:   NR
              MARRIED:   NR        NORTH AMERICAN ADM. STAFF:    NR
           SINGLE MEN:   NR                     SHORT TERM:      NR
         SINGLE WOMEN:   NR                        RETIRED:      NR
                       -----
         TOTAL ACTIVE:   2
```

FIELD OF SERVICE	YEAR BEGAN	PERSONNEL NOW	NEW	RELATED CHURCHES	PEOPLE GROUPS	NOTES
Venezuela		1				

Lord's Way Inn Ministries, Inc.

1933 L Ave., #6
National City CA 92050

Tel. (714) 474-1971
EXECUTIVE OFFICER: Craig La Caille
ORGANIZED: 1972
DESCRIPTION: A nondenominational service agency of evangelical
    tradition engaged in personal and small group evangelism
    and Christian education, ministering to servicemen and
    women from many countries. Maintains a servicemen's
    center.

```
TOTAL INCOME:        NR         FOR OVERSEAS MINISTRIES:   NR
PERSONNEL:
    NORTH AMERICANS OVERSEAS     NON-NORTH AMERICANS OVERSEAS:    0
              MARRIED:    0        NORTH AMERICAN ADM. STAFF:     0
           SINGLE MEN:    0                     SHORT TERM:       0
         SINGLE WOMEN:    0                        RETIRED:       0
                       -----
         TOTAL ACTIVE:    0
```

Lott Carey Baptist Foreign Mission Convention

1501 11th St. NW
Washington DC 20001

Tel. (202) 667-8493
EXECUTIVE OFFICER: Wendell S. Somerville
ORGANIZED: 1897   AFFILIATION: DOM-NCCCUSA
DESCRIPTION: A denominational sending agency of Baptist
    tradition emphasizing evangelism, education, medicine and
    industrial training.

```
TOTAL INCOME:    $650,000   FOR OVERSEAS MINISTRIES:   $520,000
PERSONNEL:
    NORTH AMERICANS OVERSEAS     NON-NORTH AMERICANS OVERSEAS:   NR
              MARRIED:   NR        NORTH AMERICAN ADM. STAFF:     4
           SINGLE MEN:   NR                     SHORT TERM:       0
         SINGLE WOMEN:   NR                        RETIRED:       1
                       -----
         TOTAL ACTIVE:   7
```

FIELD OF SERVICE	YEAR BEGAN	PERSONNEL NOW	NEW	RELATED CHURCHES	PEOPLE GROUPS	NOTES
Guyana		2				
India		1				
Liberia	1900	4				
Nigeria		3				

Note: Most personnel are nationals.

Ludhiana Christian Medical College Board, U.S.A., Inc.

475 Riverside Dr. Rm.250
New York NY 10115

Tel. (212) 870-2641
EXECUTIVE OFFICER: Charles Reynolds
ORGANIZED: 1894   AFFILIATION: DOM-NCCCUSA
DESCRIPTION: An international, nondenominational center for
   medical education, research and service with a Christian
   environment. Operates Ludhiana College in India.
TOTAL INCOME: $323,657   FOR OVERSEAS MINISTRIES: $261,749
PERSONNEL:
    NORTH AMERICANS OVERSEAS   NON-NORTH AMERICANS OVERSEAS: 0
            MARRIED: NR   NORTH AMERICAN ADM. STAFF: 2
         SINGLE MEN: NR   SHORT TERM: 4
       SINGLE WOMEN: NR   RETIRED: 2

       TOTAL ACTIVE: 20
NOTES: All personnel are seconded from other
         agencies.

FIELD OF SERVICE	YEAR BEGAN	PERSONNEL NOW	PERSONNEL NEW	RELATED CHURCHES	PEOPLE GROUPS	NOTES
India	1894	20				

Luis Palau Evangelistic Team, Inc.

1100 NW Murray Rd.
Portland OR 97229
P.O. ADDRESS:
Box 1173
Portland OR 97207

Tel. (503) 643-0777
EXECUTIVE OFFICER: Luis Palau
ORGANIZED: 1978
DESCRIPTION: Originally under Overseas Crusades, Inc. since
   1950. Became separate organization in 1978. An
   interdenominational sending agency of evangelical
   tradition establishing churches and engaged in
   pre-conversion Biblical counseling.
TOTAL INCOME: $1,150,000   FOR OVERSEAS MINISTRIES: $610,615
PERSONNEL:
    NORTH AMERICANS OVERSEAS   NON-NORTH AMERICANS OVERSEAS: 3
            MARRIED: 4   NORTH AMERICAN ADM. STAFF: 14
         SINGLE MEN: 1   SHORT TERM: 0
       SINGLE WOMEN: 0   RETIRED: 21

       TOTAL ACTIVE: 5

FIELD OF SERVICE	YEAR BEGAN	PERSONNEL NOW	PERSONNEL NEW	RELATED CHURCHES	PEOPLE GROUPS	NOTES
Argentina	1974	6	2			
Ecuador	1965	1				
Guatemala	1970	2				
Mexico	1967	11	2			
Paraguay	1979					
Peru	1971	1				
United Kingdom	1976	3	2			

Note: Most personnel are nationals.

Lutheran Bible Translators, Inc.

1114 N Batavia St.
Orange CA 92667
P.O. ADDRESS:
Box 92667
Orange CA 92667

Tel. (714) 639-2850
EXECUTIVE OFFICER: Roy Gesch
ORGANIZED: 1964
DESCRIPTION: A sending agency of Lutheran tradition engaged
    in linguistics, literature production, literacy and Bible
    translation. Also has 65 mission personnel working under
    Wycliffe Bible Translators.
TOTAL INCOME: $1,850,000   FOR OVERSEAS MINISTRIES: $1,064,800
PERSONNEL:
```
    NORTH AMERICANS OVERSEAS    NON-NORTH AMERICANS OVERSEAS:    0
              MARRIED:    46        NORTH AMERICAN ADM. STAFF:    5
           SINGLE MEN:     0                     SHORT TERM:    3
         SINGLE WOMEN:     4                        RETIRED:    0
                     -----
         TOTAL ACTIVE:    50
```

FIELD OF SERVICE	YEAR BEGAN	PERSONNEL NOW	PERSONNEL NEW	RELATED CHURCHES	PEOPLE GROUPS	NOTES
Liberia	1969	25	10		9	
Sierra Leone	1974	23	21		9	

Lutheran Braille Workers

11735 Peach Tree Circle
Yucaipa CA 92399

Tel. (714) 797-3093
EXECUTIVE OFFICER: Helen Loewe Koehler
ORGANIZED: 1944
DESCRIPTION: An interdenominational specialized service agency
    of Lutheran tradition producing braille materials in
    almost 40 languages for the blind, and sight-saving
    materials in 8 languages for the visually handicapped.
    Ministry conducted by 12000 volunteers in 135 work
    centers. Materials are free upon request.
TOTAL INCOME: NA   FOR OVERSEAS MINISTRIES: NA
PERSONNEL:
```
    NORTH AMERICANS OVERSEAS    NON-NORTH AMERICANS OVERSEAS:    NR
              MARRIED:     0        NORTH AMERICAN ADM. STAFF:    6
           SINGLE MEN:     0                     SHORT TERM:    0
         SINGLE WOMEN:     0                        RETIRED:    0
                     -----
         TOTAL ACTIVE:     0
```

Lutheran Church in America-Division
for World Mission and Ecumenism

231 Madison Ave.
New York NY 10016

Tel. (212) 481-9630
EXECUTIVE OFFICER: David L. Vikner
ORGANIZED: 1842   AFFILIATION: DOM-NCCCUSA
DESCRIPTION: A denominational sending agency of Lutheran
    tradition establishing churches and engaged in evangelism,
    theological education, medicine and radio and TV
    broadcasting.
TOTAL INCOME: $11,438,261   FOR OVERSEAS MINISTRIES: $7,174,795

PERSONNEL:
        NORTH AMERICANS OVERSEAS   NON-NORTH AMERICANS OVERSEAS: 0
                MARRIED: 107   NORTH AMERICAN ADM. STAFF: 12
             SINGLE MEN: 8   SHORT TERM: 0
           SINGLE WOMEN: 33   RETIRED: NR

           TOTAL ACTIVE: 148

FIELD OF SERVICE	YEAR BEGAN	PERSONNEL NOW	NEW	RELATED CHURCHES	PEOPLE GROUPS	NOTES
Argentina	1948	5	4			
Belgium	1976	1	1			
Chile	1962	3	3			
Finland	1978	1	1			
Germany, Fed. Rep.	1975	5	4			
Guyana	1943	4	1			
Hong-Kong	1948	4	2			
India	1842	19	6			
Indonesia	1970	5	3			
Japan	1892	26	11			
Kenya	1969	1	1			
Liberia	1862	21	10			
Malaysia	1949	4	1			
Middle East-general	1967	6	5			
Nepal	1974	2	1			
Netherlands	1977	1	1			
Peru	1966	6	2			
Singapore	1966	3				
Sweden	1974	1	1			
Switzerland	1979	1	1			
Taiwan Rep of China	1951	2				
Tanzania	1924	20	5			
Thailand	1975	3	1			
Trinidad and Tobago	1966	1	1			
United Kingdom	1973	2	1			
USSR	1978	1	1			

Lutheran Church-Missouri Synod

500 N Broadway
St. Louis MO 63102

Tel. (314) 231-6969
EXECUTIVE OFFICER: Wilbert J. Sohns
ORGANIZED: 1847
DESCRIPTION: A denominational sending agency of Lutheran
    tradition establishing churches and engaged in education
    broadcasting, correspondence courses, literature, literacy
    and mission-related research.
TOTAL INCOME: $9,532,142   FOR OVERSEAS MINISTRIES: $6,877,332
PERSONNEL:
        NORTH AMERICANS OVERSEAS   NON-NORTH AMERICANS OVERSEAS: 4
                MARRIED: 210   NORTH AMERICAN ADM. STAFF: 11
             SINGLE MEN: 15   SHORT TERM: 25
           SINGLE WOMEN: 29   RETIRED: NR

           TOTAL ACTIVE: 254

FIELD OF SERVICE	YEAR BEGAN	PERSONNEL NOW	NEW	RELATED CHURCHES	PEOPLE GROUPS	NOTES
Argentina	1905			187		

FIELD OF SERVICE	YEAR BEGAN	PERSONNEL NOW	NEW	RELATED CHURCHES	PEOPLE GROUPS	NOTES
Brazil	1901	2		998		
Chile	1954			2		
Costa Rica	1964					
Cuba	1947			1		
El Salvador	1952			14		
Ghana	1961	5	1	19	1	
Guatemala	1947	4		15		
Honduras	1964	1	1	3		
Hong-Kong	1950	23	9	28		
India	1895	11	2	664	2	
Japan	1948	29	28	32		
Kenya	1970	1				
Korea, Rep. of	1958	4	1	9		
Liberia	1978	1	1		2	
Mexico	1940	3		15		
Middle East-general	1960	2				
Nigeria	1936	17	6	250	4	
Panama	1942					
Papua New Guinea	1948	25	5	335	5	
Paraguay	1935			5		
Philippines	1946	17	16	81	5	
Sri Lanka	1927	2	2	6	1	
Taiwan Rep of China	1952	4	3	27		
Togo	1979	1	1		1	
Uruguay	1936			1		
Venezuela	1951	7	5	11		

Lutheran Frontier Missions

1605 E Elizabeth St.
Pasadena CA 91104
P.O. ADDRESS:
Box 446
Pasadena CA 91102

Tel. (213) 794-7116
EXECUTIVE OFFICER: Morris G. Watkins
ORGANIZED: 1972
DESCRIPTION: A denominational sending agency of Lutheran
    tradition producing and distributing literacy materials and
    involved in education and teaching English as a second
    language. Also engaged in church planting and ministry to
    the deaf.
TOTAL INCOME: $150,000   FOR OVERSEAS MINISTRIES: $80,000
PERSONNEL:
    NORTH AMERICANS OVERSEAS   NON-NORTH AMERICANS OVERSEAS: 0
            MARRIED: 10   NORTH AMERICAN ADM. STAFF: 3
        SINGLE MEN: 1   SHORT TERM: 0
      SINGLE WOMEN: 0   RETIRED: 0

        TOTAL ACTIVE: 11

FIELD OF SERVICE	YEAR BEGAN	PERSONNEL NOW	NEW	RELATED CHURCHES	PEOPLE GROUPS	NOTES
Colombia	1972	3		4	4	
Ecuador	1978	2	2	1	1	

FIELD OF SERVICE	YEAR BEGAN	PERSONNEL NOW	PERSONNEL NEW	RELATED CHURCHES	PEOPLE GROUPS	NOTES
Guatemala	1974	2	2	1	3	
Hong-Kong	1978	2	2	1	1	

Lutheran Hour SEE: International Lutheran Laymen's League

Lutheran Medical Mission Association SEE: Lutheran Church, Missouri Synod, Board for Missions

Lutheran Missionary Training Committee SEE: Lutheran World Federation, U.S.A. National Committee

Lutheran Orient Mission Society
1575 Charlton St.
West St. Paul MN 55118

Tel. (612) 227-3191
EXECUTIVE OFFICER: Norman G. Anderson
ORGANIZED: 1910   AFFILIATION: DOM-NCCCUSA
DESCRIPTION: A sending agency of Lutheran tradition engaged in
    medical work and support of nationals.
TOTAL INCOME: $120,000   FOR OVERSEAS MINISTRIES: NR
PERSONNEL:
    NORTH AMERICANS OVERSEAS   NON-NORTH AMERICANS OVERSEAS: NR
          MARRIED: 2   NORTH AMERICAN ADM. STAFF: 4
        SINGLE MEN: 0   SHORT TERM: 0
      SINGLE WOMEN: 0   RETIRED: NR

      TOTAL ACTIVE: 2
NOTES: Two employees working in administration are
        part-time.

FIELD OF SERVICE	YEAR BEGAN	PERSONNEL NOW	PERSONNEL NEW	RELATED CHURCHES	PEOPLE GROUPS	NOTES
Egypt		2				

Lutheran World Federation, U.S.A.
National Committee
360 Park Ave. South
New York NY 10010

Tel. (212) 532-6350
EXECUTIVE OFFICER: Paul A. Wee
ORGANIZED: 1918
DESCRIPTION: A denominational specialized liaison service
    agency for Lutheran churches supplying aid and relief
    through fund transmittal, information service, recruiting,
    scholarships and missionary orientation and training.
    Represents the USA Lutheran member churches in the
    Lutheran World Federation. (Also known as Lutheran World
    Ministries.)
TOTAL INCOME: $4,254,030   FOR OVERSEAS MINISTRIES: $3,389,818
PERSONNEL:
    NORTH AMERICANS OVERSEAS   NON-NORTH AMERICANS OVERSEAS: 0
          MARRIED: 0   NORTH AMERICAN ADM. STAFF: 0
        SINGLE MEN: 0   SHORT TERM: 0
      SINGLE WOMEN: 0   RETIRED: 0

      TOTAL ACTIVE: 0

Lutheran World Ministries SEE: Lutheran World Federation USA Natl. Committee

Lutheran World Relief, Incorporated

360 Park Ave. South
New York NY 10010

Tel. (212) 532-6350
EXECUTIVE OFFICER: Bernard A. Confer
ORGANIZED: 1945
DESCRIPTION: A denominational specialized service agency of
    Lutheran tradition engaged in aid and relief, agricultural
    assistance, medicine, self-help projects and development
    of human resources. The overseas aid and development arm
    of The American Lutheran Church, Association of
    Evangelical Lutheran Churches, the Lutheran Church in
    America and the Lutheran Church-Missouri Synod.
TOTAL INCOME: $10,110,090   FOR OVERSEAS MINISTRIES: $9,437,014
PERSONNEL:

NORTH AMERICANS OVERSEAS		NON-NORTH AMERICANS OVERSEAS:	0
MARRIED:	7	NORTH AMERICAN ADM. STAFF:	15
SINGLE MEN:	2	SHORT TERM:	0
SINGLE WOMEN:	2	RETIRED:	0

TOTAL ACTIVE:	11		

NOTES: Figure for overseas ministries includes
    $5,171,777 which is the value of gifts in
    kind.

FIELD OF SERVICE	YEAR BEGAN	PERSONNEL NOW	PERSONNEL NEW	RELATED CHURCHES	PEOPLE GROUPS	NOTES
Bangladesh	1972					
Bolivia	1977					
Botswana	1974					
Brazil	1961	1				
Cameroon	1971					
Chile	1961					
Dominican Republic	1979					
El Salvador	1975					
Ethiopia	1963					
Guatemala	1965					
Honduras	1978					
Hong-Kong	1954					
India	1951	1				
Jordan	1948					
Kampuchea	1974					
Kenya	1976	1	1			
Liberia	1960					
Madagascar	1959					
Mauritania	1974					
Mozambique	1975					
Nicaragua	1973					
Niger	1974	4	2			
Nigeria	1968					
Papua New Guinea	1960					
Peru	1970	1	1			
Philippines	1967					
Sudan	1972	1	1			
Taiwan Rep of China	1959					
Tanzania	1961	1	1			
Togo	1975	1	1			

FIELD OF SERVICE	YEAR BEGAN	PERSONNEL NOW	NEW	RELATED CHURCHES	PEOPLE GROUPS	NOTES
Uganda	1979					
Viet Nam, Soc. Rep.	1965					
Zambia	1967					

Lutherans For World Evangelization

1605 E Elizabeth St.
Pasadena CA 91104

Tel. (213) 794-7116
EXECUTIVE OFFICER: John N. Ottesen
ORGANIZED: 1979
DESCRIPTION: A specialized service agency of Lutheran
    tradition engaged in research and information service on
    the task of evangelization of unreached peoples.
TOTAL INCOME: $300   FOR OVERSEAS MINISTRIES: $61
PERSONNEL:
    NORTH AMERICANS OVERSEAS   NON-NORTH AMERICANS OVERSEAS: 0
                 MARRIED: 0   NORTH AMERICAN ADM. STAFF: 0
             SINGLE MEN: 0   SHORT TERM: 0
           SINGLE WOMEN: 0   RETIRED: 0

        TOTAL ACTIVE: 0

Macedonian Service Foundation, Inc.

4710 New Tampa Hwy.
Lakeland FL 33801
P.O. ADDRESS:
Box 1116
Lakeland FL 33802

Tel. (813) 682-6249
EXECUTIVE OFFICER: Leon Jasper
ORGANIZED: 1973
DESCRIPTION: A denominational agency of fundamentalist and
    Baptist tradition serving as liaison between churches and
    missionaries. Promotes missions through fund raising,
    supplying equipment, literature distribution and
    theological education. Conducts mission conferences and
    field trips.
TOTAL INCOME: $40,000   FOR OVERSEAS MINISTRIES: $27,000
PERSONNEL:
    NORTH AMERICANS OVERSEAS   NON-NORTH AMERICANS OVERSEAS: 0
                 MARRIED: 0   NORTH AMERICAN ADM. STAFF: 4
             SINGLE MEN: 0   SHORT TERM: 3
           SINGLE WOMEN: 0   RETIRED: 0

        TOTAL ACTIVE: 0
NOTES: All personnel are volunteer.

Manon Mission

2405 Elisha Ave.
Zion IL 60099

EXECUTIVE OFFICER: Gerry Mahon
ORGANIZED: 1904
DESCRIPTION: No current information available. Information
    from 1976 directory. Originally Zulu and Basutoland
    Mission. Name changed in 1947. A nondenominational
    sending agency of evangelical tradition engaged in
    evangelism, church planting, literature, education and
    training. There are S. African missionaries.
TOTAL INCOME: $41,500   FOR OVERSEAS MINISTRIES: NR

PERSONNEL:
```
    NORTH AMERICANS OVERSEAS    NON-NORTH AMERICANS OVERSEAS:   NR
             MARRIED:   NR          NORTH AMERICAN ADM. STAFF:   NR
          SINGLE MEN:   NR                       SHORT TERM:   NR
        SINGLE WOMEN:   NR                          RETIRED:   NR
                      -----
        TOTAL ACTIVE:   NR
```
NOTES: Income estimated by MARC.
```
                     YEAR     PERSONNEL    RELATED   PEOPLE
FIELD OF SERVICE     BEGAN    NOW    NEW   CHURCHES  GROUPS   NOTES
```
```
Angola                                       8
South Africa         1904                                      1
```
    1. T.B. Hospital.

Mailbox Club, The

404 Eager Rd.
Valdosta GA 31601

Tel. (912) 244-6812
EXECUTIVE OFFICER: George B. Eager
ORGANIZED: 1965
DESCRIPTION: An interdenominational special service agency of
    fundamentalist tradition involved in writing, publishing
    and distribution of Bible correspondence courses. Also
    operates a correspondence school of its own.
TOTAL INCOME: $107,155   FOR OVERSEAS MINISTRIES: NA
PERSONNEL:
```
    NORTH AMERICANS OVERSEAS    NON-NORTH AMERICANS OVERSEAS:    0
             MARRIED:    0          NORTH AMERICAN ADM. STAFF:    2
          SINGLE MEN:    0                       SHORT TERM:    2
        SINGLE WOMEN:    0                          RETIRED:    0
                      -----
        TOTAL ACTIVE:    0
```
NOTES: Overseas income is included in total
        income and cannot be delineated.

MAP International (Medical
Assistance Programs)

327 Gunderson Dr.
Carol Stream IL 60187
P.O. ADDRESS:
Box 50
Wheaton IL 60187

Tel. (312) 653-6010
EXECUTIVE OFFICER: J. Raymond Knighton
ORGANIZED: 1954
DESCRIPTION: Founded as Medical Assistance Programs. Name
    changed in 1976. An interdenominational sending agency of
    evangelical tradition providing medical supplies and
    assistance, emergency relief, community development and
    serves as a purchasing service. Agency distributes grants
    through MAP/Reader's Digest International Fellowships and
    operates a large short-term program. Cooperates with
    existing Christian missions in 84 developing countries.
TOTAL INCOME: $9,638,825   FOR OVERSEAS MINISTRIES: $2,487,373
PERSONNEL:
```
    NORTH AMERICANS OVERSEAS    NON-NORTH AMERICANS OVERSEAS:    0
             MARRIED:    4          NORTH AMERICAN ADM. STAFF:    6
          SINGLE MEN:    0                       SHORT TERM:   66
        SINGLE WOMEN:    0                          RETIRED:   NR
                      -----
        TOTAL ACTIVE:    4
```

FIELD OF SERVICE	YEAR BEGAN	PERSONNEL NOW	NEW	RELATED CHURCHES	PEOPLE GROUPS	NOTES
Afghanistan	1965					
Angola						
Antigua						
Bahrain						
Bangladesh						
Belize						
Benin						
Bhutan						
Bolivia						
Botswana						
Brazil						
Burma	1972					
Burundi						
Cameroon						
Caribbean-general						
Central African Rep.						
Chad						
Colombia						
Costa Rica						
Dominican Republic						
Ecuador						
Egypt						
Ghana						
Guatemala						
Haiti						
Honduras						
Hong-Kong						
India						
Indonesia						
Iran						
Israel						
Ivory Coast						
Japan						
Jordan						
Kenya						
Korea, Rep. of						
Lao, People's Dem. R						
Lebanon						
Lesotho						
Liberia						
Madagascar						
Malawi						
Mali						
Mexico						
Morocco						
Mozambique						
Nepal						
Nicaragua						
Niger						
Nigeria						
Pakistan						
Papua New Guinea						
Paraguay						
Peru						
Philippines						

FIELD OF SERVICE	YEAR BEGAN	PERSONNEL NOW	PERSONNEL NEW	RELATED CHURCHES	PEOPLE GROUPS	NOTES
Puerto Rico						
Rwanda						
Sierra Leone						
Somalia						
South Africa						
Sudan	1974					
Swaziland						
Taiwan Rep of China						
Tanzania						
Thailand						
Uganda						
United Arab Emirates						
Upper Volta						
Yemen Arab Republic						
Zaire						
Zambia						

Note: 1. Service to countries, other than those noted, began between 1954 and present.
2. Agency works through over 100 missions.

Maranatha Baptist Mission, Inc.

808 Myrtle Ave.
Natchez MS 39120
P.O. ADDRESS:
Drawer 1425
Natchez MS 39120

Tel. (601) 442-0141
EXECUTIVE OFFICER: James W. Crumpton
ORGANIZED: 1961
DESCRIPTION: No current information available. Information from 1976 directory. A Baptist sending agency, conservative, fundamental and independent, serving as a clearinghouse for direct support of missionaries. Also engaged in church planting and nurture, Bible memorization, community development, education and development of human resources.
TOTAL INCOME: $919,500   FOR OVERSEAS MINISTRIES: $919,500
PERSONNEL:

NORTH AMERICANS OVERSEAS		NON-NORTH AMERICANS OVERSEAS:	NR
MARRIED:	79	NORTH AMERICAN ADM. STAFF:	7
SINGLE MEN:	0	SHORT TERM:	NR
SINGLE WOMEN:	3	RETIRED:	0

TOTAL ACTIVE: 82
NOTES: Income estimated by MARC.

FIELD OF SERVICE	YEAR BEGAN	PERSONNEL NOW	PERSONNEL NEW	RELATED CHURCHES	PEOPLE GROUPS	NOTES
Africa-general				1		
American Samoa				2		
Argentina						
Australia				1		
Bolivia	14			14		
Brazil				3		

FIELD OF SERVICE	YEAR BEGAN	PERSONNEL NOW	NEW	RELATED CHURCHES	PEOPLE GROUPS	NOTES
C. America-general						
Chile				2		
Dominica				2		
Haiti				2		
Jamaica						
Japan				2		
Korea, Rep. of				2		
Mexico				10		1
Netherlands						
Panama				2		
Papua New Guinea						
Peru				3		
Philippines						
Thailand						
U.S. Virgin Is.						

MARC SEE: Missions Advanced Research and Communication Center

Media Ministries Division, Mennonite Board of Missions

1251 Edom Rd.
Harrisonburg VA 22801
P.O. ADDRESS:
Box 1252
Harrisonburg VA 22801

Tel. (703) 434-6701
EXECUTIVE OFFICER: Kenneth J. Weaver
ORGANIZED: 1951
DESCRIPTION: Previously known as Mennonite Broadcasts, Inc.
    Name changed 1979. A denominational service agency of
    Mennonite tradition for the production and distribution
    of mass media materials. Works jointly with national
    churches and local missions.
TOTAL INCOME: $672,111   FOR OVERSEAS MINISTRIES: $233,452
PERSONNEL:

NORTH AMERICANS OVERSEAS		NON-NORTH AMERICANS OVERSEAS:	0
MARRIED:	0	NORTH AMERICAN ADM. STAFF:	0
SINGLE MEN:	0	SHORT TERM:	0
SINGLE WOMEN:	0	RETIRED:	0
TOTAL ACTIVE:	0		

FIELD OF SERVICE	YEAR BEGAN	PERSONNEL NOW	NEW	RELATED CHURCHES	PEOPLE GROUPS	NOTES
Argentina	1950			28		
Belgium	1962					
Belize	1972			4		
Costa Rica	1950			7		
Dominican Republic	1950			25		
Honduras	1950			35		
Italy	1957			1		
Jamaica	1957			9		
Japan	1956			16		
Mexico	1950			12		

```
Puerto Rico          1953                 15
Trinidad and Tobago  1969                  3
Uruguay              1950                  4
    Note: Finance, counsel or program
    material provided in these countries.
    Personnel sent through Mennonite
    mission agencies and reported by such.
```

Medical Ambassadors SEE: O.C. Ministries, Inc.

Medical Assistance Programs, Inc. SEE: MAP International

Medical Group Missions SEE: Christian Medical Society

Medical Supplies for Missions, Inc. SEE: World Concern/Crista International

Men For Missions International

```
                                      1200 Fry Rd.
                                      Greenwood IN 46142
                                      P.O. ADDRESS:
                                      Box A
                                      Greenwood IN 46142
Tel. (317) 881-6752
EXECUTIVE OFFICER: Harry Burr
ORGANIZED: 1954
DESCRIPTION:  A nondenominational agency of evangelical
    tradition raising funds for and creating interest in
    missions. Supplies equipment, provides furloughed
    missionary support, and is engaged in development of
    human resources, fund raising, aviation and evangelism.
    A laymen's ministry affiliated with OMS International.
    Supports a short-term program.
TOTAL INCOME:        NR      FOR OVERSEAS MINISTRIES:    $150,000
PERSONNEL:
    NORTH AMERICANS OVERSEAS   NON-NORTH AMERICANS OVERSEAS:     0
             MARRIED:    0     NORTH AMERICAN ADM. STAFF:        6
          SINGLE MEN:    0                    SHORT TERM:      243
        SINGLE WOMEN:    0                      RETIRED:       NR
                       -----
       TOTAL ACTIVE:    0
```

Men in Action

```
                                      7500 Red Rd. Ste. C
                                      Miami FL 33143
                                      P.O. ADDRESS:
                                      Box 340-325
                                      Coral Gables FL 33134
Tel. (305) 666-1038
EXECUTIVE OFFICER: E. Walford Thompson
ORGANIZED: 1961
DESCRIPTION:  An interdenominational service agency of Reformed
    tradition helping churches and training national workers
    for evangelism and leadership in the USA and Caribbean.
TOTAL INCOME:   $105,000          FOR OVERSEAS MINISTRIES:    NR
```

```
PERSONNEL:
    NORTH AMERICANS OVERSEAS    NON-NORTH AMERICANS OVERSEAS:    NR
            MARRIED:    NR          NORTH AMERICAN ADM. STAFF:     3
         SINGLE MEN:    NR                      SHORT TERM:        0
       SINGLE WOMEN:    NR                         RETIRED:        0
                       -----
       TOTAL ACTIVE:     2
------------------------------------------------------------------------
                       YEAR    PERSONNEL    RELATED    PEOPLE
FIELD OF SERVICE       BEGAN   NOW    NEW   CHURCHES   GROUPS   NOTES
------------------------------------------------------------------------
Cayman Islands         1973
Haiti                  1969
Jamaica                1969
```

Men with Vision SEE: World Gospel Mission

Mennonite Board of Missions

500 S Main St.
Elkhart IN 46515
P.O. ADDRESS:
Box 370
Elkhart IN 46515

Tel. (219) 294-7523
EXECUTIVE OFFICER: Paul M. Gingrich
ORGANIZED: 1906
DESCRIPTION: A denominational sending agency of Mennonite
    tradition establishing churches and engaged in evangelism,
    theological education, nurture of national churches and
    literature production.
TOTAL INCOME: $5,068,000   FOR OVERSEAS MINISTRIES: $1,659,000

```
PERSONNEL:
    NORTH AMERICANS OVERSEAS    NON-NORTH AMERICANS OVERSEAS:     1
            MARRIED:   112          NORTH AMERICAN ADM. STAFF:     7
         SINGLE MEN:     3                      SHORT TERM:        7
       SINGLE WOMEN:    10                         RETIRED:       36
                       -----
       TOTAL ACTIVE:   125
------------------------------------------------------------------------
                       YEAR    PERSONNEL    RELATED    PEOPLE
FIELD OF SERVICE       BEGAN   NOW    NEW   CHURCHES   GROUPS   NOTES
------------------------------------------------------------------------
```

FIELD OF SERVICE	YEAR BEGAN	PERSONNEL NOW	PERSONNEL NEW	RELATED CHURCHES	PEOPLE GROUPS	NOTES
Afghanistan	1975	1				
Algeria	1957	1				
Argentina	1917	12		29		
Belgium	1950	2		6		
Bolivia	1959	6	6	5		
Brazil	1954	17		24		
France	1953	6		1		
Ghana	1957	6	2	16		
India	1899	10		37		
Ireland	1979	2	2			
Israel	1953	8	2	1		
Ivory Coast	1978	4	4			
Japan	1949	15		16		
Mexico	1976	2	2			
Nepal	1957	3				
Nigeria	1959	2	2	53		

FIELD OF SERVICE	YEAR BEGAN	PERSONNEL NOW	PERSONNEL NEW	RELATED CHURCHES	PEOPLE GROUPS	NOTES
Peru	1965	2				
Puerto Rico	1945	5		16		
Spain	1975	6	2	1		
United Kingdom	1952	7	5	1		
Uruguay	1954	3	1	7		
Zaire	1975	2				

Mennonite Brethren
Missions/Services

315 S Lincoln
Hillsboro KS 67063
P.O. ADDRESS:
Box V
Hillsboro KS 67063

Tel. (316) 947-3151
EXECUTIVE OFFICER: Vernon R. Wiebe
ORGANIZED: 1878   AFFILIATION: EFMA
DESCRIPTION: A denominational sending agency of Mennonite
    tradition establishing churches and engaged in community
    development, theological education, evangelism and
    medicine.
TOTAL INCOME: $1,133,996   FOR OVERSEAS MINISTRIES: $1,133,996
PERSONNEL:
    NORTH AMERICANS OVERSEAS   NON-NORTH AMERICANS OVERSEAS: 2
            MARRIED: 134   NORTH AMERICAN ADM. STAFF: 6
         SINGLE MEN: 0   SHORT TERM: 70
       SINGLE WOMEN: 24   RETIRED: 31

        TOTAL ACTIVE: 158

FIELD OF SERVICE	YEAR BEGAN	PERSONNEL NOW	PERSONNEL NEW	RELATED CHURCHES	PEOPLE GROUPS	NOTES
Afghanistan	1969	2	2		1	
Austria	1953	8	9	6		
Bangladesh	1974	1			1	
Botswana	1976	4	4			
Brazil	1944	14	4	25		
Colombia	1945	22	27	23		
Ecuador	1953	5	1			
Germany, Fed. Rep.	1953	8	11	5		
India	1899	6	17	700	4	
Indonesia	1975	4			2	
Japan	1950	17	18	23	1	
Mexico	1950	11	15	1		
Nepal	1969	2			1	
Nigeria	1944	1				
Panama	1958	4	5	10	2	
Paraguay	1935	8	5	19		
Peru	1946	5	4		1	
Sierra Leone	1979	2	2			
Spain		8	18			
Uruguay	1966	8	5	6		
Zaire	1912	28	21	74	2	

Mennonite Broadcasts, Inc. SEE: Media Ministries Division
Mennonite Board of Missions

Mennonite Central Committee

21 S 12th St.
Akron PA 17501

Tel. (717) 859-1151
EXECUTIVE OFFICER: William T. Snyder
ORGANIZED: 1920
DESCRIPTION: A denominational specialized sending agency of
    Mennonite tradition acting as a relief and service agency
    of the Mennonite and Brethern in Christ churches in North
    America. Ministries include community development, secular
    education and agricultural assistance. Also engaged in aid
    and/or relief, medicine and self-help projects.
TOTAL INCOME: $13,330,000   FOR OVERSEAS MINISTRIES: $7,800,000
PERSONNEL:
    NORTH AMERICANS OVERSEAS   NON-NORTH AMERICANS OVERSEAS: 13
                MARRIED: 277   NORTH AMERICAN ADM. STAFF: 32
             SINGLE MEN: 82   SHORT TERM: 0
           SINGLE WOMEN: 72   RETIRED: 7

    TOTAL ACTIVE: 431
NOTES: Of the overseas personnel 166 are sent through
        other agencies.

FIELD OF SERVICE	YEAR BEGAN	PERSONNEL NOW	NEW	RELATED CHURCHES	PEOPLE GROUPS	NOTES
Bangladesh	1970	35				
Belgium	1965	2				
Bolivia	1959	51				
Botswana	1968	32				
Brazil	1968	27				
Chad	1973	2				
Egypt	1968	11				
Ethiopia	1962	2				
France	1946	1				
Germany, Fed. Rep.	1946	14				
Grenada	1976	8				
Guatemala	1976	6				
Haiti	1959	10				
Hungary	1947	1				
India	1942	9				
Indonesia	1948	5				
Ireland	1978	2				
Italy	1976	1				
Jamaica	1970	17				
Jordan	1950	11				
Kenya	1962	6				
Lao, People's Dem. R	1975	4				
Lebanon	1976	2				
Lesotho	1973	13				
Malawi	1963	5				
Nepal	1957	18				
Nicaragua	1978	2				
Nigeria	1963	15				
Paraguay	1930	5				
Philippines	1977	3				
Poland	1971	1				
Sudan	1972	4				
Swaziland	1971	23				

FIELD OF SERVICE	YEAR BEGAN	PERSONNEL NOW	NEW	RELATED CHURCHES	PEOPLE GROUPS	NOTES
Switzerland	1950	2				
Tanzania	1962	3				
Thailand	1975	3				
Transkei	1978	2				
Uganda	1979	3				
United Kingdom	1973	1				
Upper Volta	1975	16				
Zaire	1960	37				
Zambia	1962	18				

Note: Figures for Jordan include West Bank.

Mennonite Church Eastern Mennonite Board of Missions and Charities
SEE: Eastern Mennonite Board of Missions and Charities
Mennonite Church, Mennonite Board of Missions
SEE: Mennonite Board of Missions

Mennonite Economic Development Associates

21 S 12th St.
Akron PA 17501

Tel. (717) 859-1151
EXECUTIVE OFFICER: LLoyd J. Fisher
ORGANIZED: 1953
DESCRIPTION: A denominational specialized agency of Mennonite
    tradition providing capital funds and limited training in
    business methods to help establish small business
    enterprises within the Christian community. Engaged in
    self-help projects, technical assistance and community
    development.
TOTAL INCOME: $341,300   FOR OVERSEAS MINISTRIES: $341,300
PERSONNEL:

NORTH AMERICANS OVERSEAS		NON-NORTH AMERICANS OVERSEAS:	2
MARRIED:	1	NORTH AMERICAN ADM. STAFF:	4
SINGLE MEN:	0	SHORT TERM:	0
SINGLE WOMEN:	0	RETIRED:	NR
TOTAL ACTIVE:	1		

FIELD OF SERVICE	YEAR BEGAN	PERSONNEL NOW	NEW	RELATED CHURCHES	PEOPLE GROUPS	NOTES
Argentina	1974					
Belize	1972	1				1
Bolivia	1973	1				
Colombia	1971					
Costa Rica	1970					
Ethiopia	1969					
Ghana	1974					
Guatemala	1973					
Honduras	1970					
India	1972					
Indonesia	1970					
Jamaica	1979					
Kenya	1971	1				1

FIELD OF SERVICE	YEAR BEGAN	PERSONNEL NOW	NEW	RELATED CHURCHES	PEOPLE GROUPS	NOTES
Nicaragua	1972					
Nigeria	1970					
Paraguay	1954					
Philippines	1972					
Tanzania	1965	1				1
Uruguay	1963					
Zaire	1968	1				2

Note: 1. Supported by EMBMC
2. Supported by BOMAS

Mennonite Mission Board of Pacific Coast Conference (Mexico Board)

9000 Wallace Rd. NW
Salem OR 97304

Tel. (503) 362-8195
EXECUTIVE OFFICER: Willard Kennel
ORGANIZED: 0
DESCRIPTION: A denominational sending agency of Mennonite
    tradition establishing churches and engaged in general
    Christian education and correspondence courses. Also
    involved in a cassette ministry and motion pictures.
TOTAL INCOME: $18,000   FOR OVERSEAS MINISTRIES: $18,000
PERSONNEL:

NORTH AMERICANS OVERSEAS		NON-NORTH AMERICANS OVERSEAS:	0
MARRIED:	2	NORTH AMERICAN ADM. STAFF:	0
SINGLE MEN:	0	SHORT TERM:	0
SINGLE WOMEN:	0	RETIRED:	0
TOTAL ACTIVE:	2		

FIELD OF SERVICE	YEAR BEGAN	PERSONNEL NOW	NEW	RELATED CHURCHES	PEOPLE GROUPS	NOTES
Mexico	1950	2		7		

Mercy, Inc. SEE: World Gospel Crusades, Inc.

Message of Life, Inc.

58607 Road 601
Ahwahnee CA 93601

Tel. (209) 683-7028
EXECUTIVE OFFICER: Joseph C. Sanders
ORGANIZED: 1961
DESCRIPTION: An interdenominational specialized service agency
    of evangelical tradition engaged in the printing,
    preparation and dissemination of Christian education
    materials in English and Spanish.
TOTAL INCOME: $76,602   FOR OVERSEAS MINISTRIES: $45,911
PERSONNEL:

NORTH AMERICANS OVERSEAS		NON-NORTH AMERICANS OVERSEAS:	0
MARRIED:	0	NORTH AMERICAN ADM. STAFF:	1
SINGLE MEN:	0	SHORT TERM:	0
SINGLE WOMEN:	0	RETIRED:	0
TOTAL ACTIVE:	0		

Message to Israel SEE: Bible Christian Union, Inc.

Messengers of the New Covenant, Inc.

242 Shunpike Rd.
Springfield NJ 07081

Tel. (201) 467-0311
EXECUTIVE OFFICER: Edward N. Cleaveland
ORGANIZED: 1943
DESCRIPTION: An interdenominational agency of Baptist
    tradition ministering to Jewish people through Bible
    distribution, correspondence courses, student, mass and
    small group evangelism, and literature production and
    distribution. Also involved in fund raising. Work is
    carried out by nationals.
TOTAL INCOME: $48,000   FOR OVERSEAS MINISTRIES: $1,000
PERSONNEL:

NORTH AMERICANS OVERSEAS		NON-NORTH AMERICANS OVERSEAS:	0
MARRIED:	0	NORTH AMERICAN ADM. STAFF:	2
SINGLE MEN:	0	SHORT TERM:	0
SINGLE WOMEN:	0	RETIRED:	0
TOTAL ACTIVE:	0		

FIELD OF SERVICE	YEAR BEGAN	PERSONNEL NOW	NEW	RELATED CHURCHES	PEOPLE GROUPS	NOTES
Israel	1965					

Methodist Church, The SEE: United Methodist Church Committee on Relief and/or Board of Global Ministries

Methodist Protestant Church, Board of Missions

2810 Greenwood Ave.
Jackson MS 39212
P.O. ADDRESS:
Box 1468
Jackson MS 39205

EXECUTIVE OFFICER: F. E. Sellers
ORGANIZED: 0   AFFILIATION: TAM-ICCC
DESCRIPTION: A denominational sending agency of Wesleyan
    tradition supporting national workers and churches. Also
    engaged in agriculture, education and evangelism.
TOTAL INCOME: $45,000   FOR OVERSEAS MINISTRIES: $45,000
PERSONNEL:

NORTH AMERICANS OVERSEAS		NON-NORTH AMERICANS OVERSEAS:	0
MARRIED:	4	NORTH AMERICAN ADM. STAFF:	0
SINGLE MEN:	0	SHORT TERM:	0
SINGLE WOMEN:	0	RETIRED:	0
TOTAL ACTIVE:	4		

FIELD OF SERVICE	YEAR BEGAN	PERSONNEL NOW	NEW	RELATED CHURCHES	PEOPLE GROUPS	NOTES
Belize		2		5		
Jamaica				5		
Korea, Rep. of		2		75		

Metropolitan Church Association

323 Broad St.
Lake Geneva WI 53147

Tel. (414) 248-6786
EXECUTIVE OFFICER: Murdo Mackay
ORGANIZED: 1894
DESCRIPTION: A denominational sending agency of Wesleyan
    tradition planting churches and engaged in evangelism and
    support of nationals.
TOTAL INCOME: $50,000   FOR OVERSEAS MINISTRIES: $33,000
PERSONNEL:
    NORTH AMERICANS OVERSEAS   NON-NORTH AMERICANS OVERSEAS: NR
            MARRIED: NR   NORTH AMERICAN ADM. STAFF: 4
        SINGLE MEN: NR   SHORT TERM: 0
      SINGLE WOMEN: NR   RETIRED: 0

        TOTAL ACTIVE: 6
NOTES: Income estimated by agency.

FIELD OF SERVICE	YEAR BEGAN	PERSONNEL NOW	NEW	RELATED CHURCHES	PEOPLE GROUPS	NOTES
India	1910	4				
Mexico	1930	1				
South Africa		1				

Mexican Border Missions

2235 Mirasol
Brownsville TX 78520
P.O. ADDRESS:
Box 1131
Brownsville TX 78520

Tel. (512) 542-4911
EXECUTIVE OFFICER: Robert Blodget
ORGANIZED: 1961
DESCRIPTION: A nondenominational sending agency of evangelical
    and independent tradition establishing churches and
    engaged in church construction or financing, support of
    nationals, radio and TV broadcasting and theological
    education by extension (TEE).
TOTAL INCOME: $39,900   FOR OVERSEAS MINISTRIES: $39,900
PERSONNEL:
    NORTH AMERICANS OVERSEAS   NON-NORTH AMERICANS OVERSEAS: 0
            MARRIED: 4   NORTH AMERICAN ADM. STAFF: 0
        SINGLE MEN: 0   SHORT TERM: 0
      SINGLE WOMEN: 0   RETIRED: 0

        TOTAL ACTIVE: 4
NOTES: Overseas income estimated by MARC.

FIELD OF SERVICE	YEAR BEGAN	PERSONNEL NOW	NEW	RELATED CHURCHES	PEOPLE GROUPS	NOTES
Mexico	1961	4	2	500		1

Note: 1. Also work with Mexican National Fellowship
of Independent Churches with 500 congregations.

Mexican Christian Mission, Inc.

8240 Parkway Dr. Ste.209
LaMesa CA 92041

Tel. (714) 463-8664
EXECUTIVE OFFICER: Marc McGuire
ORGANIZED: 1956
DESCRIPTION: An interdenominational agency of evangelical
    tradition establishing churches and engaged in literature

distribution, self-help projects and evangelism.
TOTAL INCOME: $150,000   FOR OVERSEAS MINISTRIES: $73,000
PERSONNEL:
```
     NORTH AMERICANS OVERSEAS      NON-NORTH AMERICANS OVERSEAS:      0
             MARRIED:    3          NORTH AMERICAN ADM. STAFF:        0
          SINGLE MEN:    0                        SHORT TERM:         0
        SINGLE WOMEN:    0                           RETIRED:         0
                       -----
        TOTAL ACTIVE:    3
```

FIELD OF SERVICE	YEAR BEGAN	PERSONNEL NOW	NEW	RELATED CHURCHES	PEOPLE GROUPS	NOTES
Mexico	1956	3		55		

Mexican Fellowship, Inc. SEE: Share the Care International

Mexican Mission Ministries, Inc.

415 N Sugar Rd.
Pharr TX 78577
P.O. ADDRESS:
Box 636
Pharr TX 78577

Tel. (512) 787-3543
EXECUTIVE OFFICER: Walter Gomez
ORGANIZED: 1954   AFFILIATION: EFMA
DESCRIPTION: An interdenominational sending agency of
    evangelical and Baptist tradition establishing churches
    and engaged in radio and TV broadcasting, correspondence
    courses, theological education by extension (TEE) and
    training.
TOTAL INCOME: $197,425   FOR OVERSEAS MINISTRIES: $102,000
PERSONNEL:
```
     NORTH AMERICANS OVERSEAS      NON-NORTH AMERICANS OVERSEAS:      0
             MARRIED:    4          NORTH AMERICAN ADM. STAFF:        2
          SINGLE MEN:    0                        SHORT TERM:         0
        SINGLE WOMEN:    2                           RETIRED:         0
                       -----
        TOTAL ACTIVE:    6
```

FIELD OF SERVICE	YEAR BEGAN	PERSONNEL NOW	NEW	RELATED CHURCHES	PEOPLE GROUPS	NOTES
Mexico	1954	5		35		

Mexican Missions, Inc.

213 Peking St.
McAllen TX 78501
P.O. ADDRESS:
Box 3126
McAllen TX 78501

Tel. (512) 682-2165
EXECUTIVE OFFICER: Edgar L. Stone
ORGANIZED: 1960
DESCRIPTION: A nondenominational sending agency of Pentecostal
    tradition engaged in evangelism, church planting, youth
    work and a Bible school. Also involved in child evangelism
    and sponsoring of youth camps and seminars.
TOTAL INCOME: NA   FOR OVERSEAS MINISTRIES: $22,000
PERSONNEL:
```
     NORTH AMERICANS OVERSEAS      NON-NORTH AMERICANS OVERSEAS:     NR
             MARRIED:   NR          NORTH AMERICAN ADM. STAFF:        3
          SINGLE MEN:   NR                        SHORT TERM:         1
```

```
SINGLE WOMEN:    NR                              RETIRED:      0
                 -----
     TOTAL ACTIVE:    1
NOTES:  Overseas income estimated by MARC.
-------------------------------------------------------------------
                    YEAR       PERSONNEL   RELATED    PEOPLE
FIELD OF SERVICE    BEGAN      NOW   NEW   CHURCHES   GROUPS   NOTES
-------------------------------------------------------------------
Mexico              1960        1
     Note: Mexico has a youth camp.
```

Middle East Christian Outreach—USA Council

P.O. ADDRESS:
Box 1742
Aberdeen SD 57401

Tel. (412) 846-5100
EXECUTIVE OFFICER: George J. Jennings
ORGANIZED: 1860
DESCRIPTION: Founded as Lebanon Evangelical Mission which
     became the Middle East Christian Outreach USA council in
     1976. An interdenominational agency of evangelical and
     Baptist tradition establishing churches and engaged in
     education, evangelism, recruiting and literature
     distribution.

```
TOTAL INCOME:       $6,000      FOR OVERSEAS MINISTRIES:    $0
PERSONNEL:
   NORTH AMERICANS OVERSEAS    NON-NORTH AMERICANS OVERSEAS:    50
           MARRIED:    0           NORTH AMERICAN ADM. STAFF:    2
        SINGLE MEN:    0                       SHORT TERM:    0
      SINGLE WOMEN:    0                          RETIRED:    0
                     -----
      TOTAL ACTIVE:    0
-------------------------------------------------------------------
                    YEAR       PERSONNEL   RELATED    PEOPLE
FIELD OF SERVICE    BEGAN      NOW   NEW   CHURCHES   GROUPS   NOTES
-------------------------------------------------------------------
Cyprus
Egypt
Ethiopia            1956
Jordan
Lebanon             1860
Sudan
Syria
United Arab Emirates 1979
```

Middle East General Mission SEE: Middle East Christian Outreach

Middle East Media

218 W Willow St.
Wheaton IL 60187
P.O. ADDRESS:
Box 263
Glen Ellyn IL 60137

Tel. (312) 653-6550
EXECUTIVE OFFICER: Charles Fizer
ORGANIZED: 1976
DESCRIPTION: A nondenominational sending agency of evangelical
     tradition engaged in literature production and
     distribution, fund raising, recruiting and Bible
     translation.
```
TOTAL INCOME:     $35,636   FOR OVERSEAS MINISTRIES:     $34,273
```

PERSONNEL:
```
       NORTH AMERICANS OVERSEAS    NON-NORTH AMERICANS OVERSEAS:    0
              MARRIED:     6          NORTH AMERICAN ADM. STAFF:    1
           SINGLE MEN:     0                      SHORT TERM:       0
         SINGLE WOMEN:     0                         RETIRED:       0
                         -----
         TOTAL ACTIVE:     6
```
NOTES: Administrative employee is a part-time
         volunteer.

FIELD OF SERVICE	YEAR BEGAN	PERSONNEL NOW	NEW	RELATED CHURCHES	PEOPLE GROUPS	NOTES
Egypt	1976	4	4			
Lebanon	1976	2				

Million Testaments Campaigns, Inc.

1505 Race St.
Philadelphia PA 19102

DESCRIPTION: No data is reported for this agency for one of the
    following reasons: it is currently inactive or no longer
    exists; it has terminated overseas ministries or has ceased
    to operate as a North American entity.

Ministry of Mission Services

1704 Raleo Ave.
Rowland Heights CA 91748
P.O. ADDRESS:
Box 222
Apple Valley CA 92307

Tel. (213) 964-6014
EXECUTIVE OFFICER: Jack Wilburn
ORGANIZED: 1968
DESCRIPTION: A nondenominational agency of Baptist tradition
    engaged in fund transmittal, education, Bible distribution
    and development of human resources. Also serves other
    agencies and supports deaf-mute schools in Baja, Mexico.
TOTAL INCOME: $10,000   FOR OVERSEAS MINISTRIES: $2,000
PERSONNEL:
```
       NORTH AMERICANS OVERSEAS    NON-NORTH AMERICANS OVERSEAS:    2
              MARRIED:     4          NORTH AMERICAN ADM. STAFF:    3
           SINGLE MEN:     1                      SHORT TERM:       2
         SINGLE WOMEN:     1                         RETIRED:       0
                         -----
         TOTAL ACTIVE:     6
```

FIELD OF SERVICE	YEAR BEGAN	PERSONNEL NOW	NEW	RELATED CHURCHES	PEOPLE GROUPS	NOTES
Mexico	1968	5	2	3	1	

Minneapolis Friends of Israel

Kyllo Ln.
St. Paul MN 55122

Tel. (612) 454-2791
EXECUTIVE OFFICER: Rose Kyllo
ORGANIZED: 1948
DESCRIPTION: A nondenominational agency of evangelical and
    fundamentalist tradition supporting one couple in Israel
    who are citizens of that country, with donations from
    North Americans.
TOTAL INCOME: NR   FOR OVERSEAS MINISTRIES: NR

PERSONNEL:
    NORTH AMERICANS OVERSEAS   NON-NORTH AMERICANS OVERSEAS: 0
              MARRIED: 0   NORTH AMERICAN ADM. STAFF: 0
           SINGLE MEN: 0   SHORT TERM: 0
         SINGLE WOMEN: 0   RETIRED: 0

         TOTAL ACTIVE: 0

Minnesota Bible Fellowship, Inc.

1211 E Franklin
Minneapolis MN 55404
P.O. ADDRESS:
Box 8295
Minneapolis MN 55408

Tel. (612) 729-4133
EXECUTIVE OFFICER: A. M. Anfinsen
ORGANIZED: 1962
DESCRIPTION: A nondenominational agency of evangelical
    tradition shipping Christian literatue to missions,
    schools, prisons and the military in over 70 countries.
    Accepts new, used, outdated and unsalable Christian
    literature for shipment. Team called Evangelism Associates
    International is engaged in evangelism. All workers are
    volunteer.
TOTAL INCOME: $12,000   FOR OVERSEAS MINISTRIES: $11,400
PERSONNEL:
    NORTH AMERICANS OVERSEAS   NON-NORTH AMERICANS OVERSEAS: 0
              MARRIED: NR   NORTH AMERICAN ADM. STAFF: 8
           SINGLE MEN: NR   SHORT TERM: 0
         SINGLE WOMEN: NR   RETIRED: 0

         TOTAL ACTIVE: 1
NOTES: Income estimated by agency.

Mission Aides, Incorporated

100 E Montecito St.
Sierra Madre CA 91024
P.O. ADDRESS:
Box 1
Sierra Madre CA 91024

Tel. (213) 355-3346
EXECUTIVE OFFICER: Hugh S. Bell, Jr.
ORGANIZED: 1954
DESCRIPTION: A nondenominational service agency of evangelical
    tradition involved in recording, serving other agencies,
    supplying equipment and technical assistance. Also
    provides magnetic tape duplication and radio broadcast
    tape duplication and distribution.
TOTAL INCOME: $28,846   FOR OVERSEAS MINISTRIES: $25,030
PERSONNEL:
    NORTH AMERICANS OVERSEAS   NON-NORTH AMERICANS OVERSEAS: 0
              MARRIED: 4   NORTH AMERICAN ADM. STAFF: 3
           SINGLE MEN: 0   SHORT TERM: 0
         SINGLE WOMEN: 0   RETIRED: 0

         TOTAL ACTIVE: 4

FIELD OF SERVICE	YEAR BEGAN	PERSONNEL NOW	NEW	RELATED CHURCHES	PEOPLE GROUPS	NOTES
Mexico	1978	4	4			

Mission Aviation Fellowship

1849 Wabash Ave.
Redlands CA 92373
P.O. ADDRESS:
Box 202
Redlands CA 92373

Tel. (714) 794-1151
EXECUTIVE OFFICER: Charles T. Bennett
ORGANIZED: 1944   AFFILIATION: IFMA/EFMA
DESCRIPTION: An interdenominational specialized service agency
    of evangelical tradition supplying aviation, radio, health
    and technical assistance to national churches. Also serves
    other agencies.
TOTAL INCOME: $7,170,916   FOR OVERSEAS MINISTRIES: $6,138,000
PERSONNEL:
    NORTH AMERICANS OVERSEAS   NON-NORTH AMERICANS OVERSEAS: 6
            MARRIED: 236   NORTH AMERICAN ADM. STAFF: 65
         SINGLE MEN: 2   SHORT TERM: 4
       SINGLE WOMEN: 2   RETIRED: 1

       TOTAL ACTIVE: 240

FIELD OF SERVICE	YEAR BEGAN	PERSONNEL NOW	NEW	RELATED CHURCHES	PEOPLE GROUPS	NOTES
Botswana	1979	2	2			
Brazil	1956	30	4		35	
Cameroon	1974	2				
Central African Rep.	1977	4	2			
Colombia	1971	4	2			
Costa Rica	1978	4				
Ecuador	1948	10	6		2	
Guatemala	1976	8	2		3	
Honduras	1949	13	9			
Indonesia	1954	98	27		82	
Kenya	1959	2				
Mexico	1946	6	8		25	
South Africa		2				
Sudan	1973	2				
Surinam	1963	10	3		7	
Venezuela	1965	6	2			
Zaire	1961	35	12		10	
Zimbabwe	1964	2			6	

Mission Aviation Fellowship of Canada

10 Suffolk St. East
Guelph ON N1H 2H6
Canada
P.O. ADDRESS:
Box 368
Guelph ON N1H 6K5
Canada

Tel. (519) 821-3914
EXECUTIVE OFFICER: Herbert Morgan
ORGANIZED: 1972   AFFILIATION: IFMA
DESCRIPTION: A denominational specialized service agency of
    evangelical tradition supplying aviation assistance to
    national churches.
TOTAL INCOME: $300,000   FOR OVERSEAS MINISTRIES: $260,000
PERSONNEL:
    NORTH AMERICANS OVERSEAS   NON-NORTH AMERICANS OVERSEAS: 0
            MARRIED: 12   NORTH AMERICAN ADM. STAFF: 2
         SINGLE MEN: 0   SHORT TERM: 1

```
        SINGLE WOMEN:    0                              RETIRED:    0
                       -----
        TOTAL ACTIVE:   12
---------------------------------------------------------------------
                    YEAR    PERSONNEL    RELATED   PEOPLE
FIELD OF SERVICE    BEGAN   NOW   NEW    CHURCHES  GROUPS  NOTES
---------------------------------------------------------------------
Brazil              1972    4     2
Honduras            1978    2     2
Indonesia           1972    2
Sudan               1977    2
Zaire               1973    2
```

Mission Mailbag, Inc.

2902 Clanton Terr.
Del City OK 73115
P.O. ADDRESS:
Box 15237
Del City OK 73155

```
Tel. (405) 672-4989
EXECUTIVE OFFICER: Eunice Peevey
ORGANIZED: 1962
DESCRIPTION:  A nondenominational specialized service agency of
    Baptist tradition assisting in the support of missionaries
    who are sent through other boards. Involved in mass
    evangelism, Bible distribution, radio and TV broadcasting
    and theological education by extension (TEE).
TOTAL INCOME:     $71,970   FOR OVERSEAS MINISTRIES:     $63,162
PERSONNEL:
    NORTH AMERICANS OVERSEAS   NON-NORTH AMERICANS OVERSEAS:   0
              MARRIED:    0       NORTH AMERICAN ADM. STAFF:   0
          SINGLE MEN:    0                     SHORT TERM:   0
        SINGLE WOMEN:    0                        RETIRED:   0
                       -----
        TOTAL ACTIVE:    0
```

Mission Minded Men SEE: Churches of Christ in Christian Union

Mission Possible Foundation, Inc.

516 N Locust
Denton TX 76201
P.O. ADDRESS:
Box 2014
Denton TX 76201

```
Tel. (817) 382-1508
EXECUTIVE OFFICER: W. Ralph Mann
ORGANIZED: 1974
DESCRIPTION:  A nondenominational agency of evangelical
    tradition engaged in literature and Bible distribution
    among nationals.
TOTAL INCOME:     $137,000   FOR OVERSEAS MINISTRIES:     $137,000
PERSONNEL:
    NORTH AMERICANS OVERSEAS   NON-NORTH AMERICANS OVERSEAS:   1
              MARRIED:    0       NORTH AMERICAN ADM. STAFF:   3
          SINGLE MEN:    2                     SHORT TERM:   0
        SINGLE WOMEN:    0                        RETIRED:   0
                       -----
        TOTAL ACTIVE:    2
NOTES:  Income estimated by agency.
```

Mission Renewal Team, Inc.

1605 E Elizabeth St.
Pasadena CA 91104
P.O. ADDRESS:
Box 3564
Pasadena CA 91103

Tel. (213) 798-9665
EXECUTIVE OFFICER: William Goheen
ORGANIZED: 1974
DESCRIPTION: An interdenominational service agency of
  evangelical tradition aiding missions through challenge
  to local churches. Conducts a missions seminar and
  provides an information service.

TOTAL INCOME:	$7,545	FOR OVERSEAS MINISTRIES:	$0

PERSONNEL:

NORTH AMERICANS OVERSEAS		NON-NORTH AMERICANS OVERSEAS:	0
MARRIED:	0	NORTH AMERICAN ADM. STAFF:	1
SINGLE MEN:	0	SHORT TERM:	0
SINGLE WOMEN:	0	RETIRED:	0
TOTAL ACTIVE:	0		

Mission Services Association, Inc.

County Rd. 400N at 900W
Tipton County IN 46049
P.O. ADDRESS:
Box 177
Kempton IN 46049

Tel. (317) 947-5127
EXECUTIVE OFFICER: Howard E. Ray
ORGANIZED: 1946
DESCRIPTION: A nondenominational specialized service bureau
  which assists missionaries belonging to the Churches of
  Christ/Christian Churches. Provides information service,
  literature production and distribution, missionary
  education and mission related research.

TOTAL INCOME:	NR	FOR OVERSEAS MINISTRIES:	NR

PERSONNEL:

NORTH AMERICANS OVERSEAS		NON-NORTH AMERICANS OVERSEAS:	0
MARRIED:	0	NORTH AMERICAN ADM. STAFF:	0
SINGLE MEN:	0	SHORT TERM:	0
SINGLE WOMEN:	0	RETIRED:	0
TOTAL ACTIVE:	0		

Mission SOS

1605 E Elizabeth
Pasadena CA 91104

Tel. (213) 798-8084
EXECUTIVE OFFICER: Erik Soren Stadell
ORGANIZED: 1976
DESCRIPTION: An interdenominational sending agency
  establishing churches and engaged in missionary education,
  missionary orientation and training, and mission related
  research.

TOTAL INCOME:	NR	FOR OVERSEAS MINISTRIES:	$110,000

PERSONNEL:

NORTH AMERICANS OVERSEAS		NON-NORTH AMERICANS OVERSEAS:	20
MARRIED:	2	NORTH AMERICAN ADM. STAFF:	3
SINGLE MEN:	2	SHORT TERM:	0

```
        SINGLE WOMEN:    1                          RETIRED:   NR
                 -----
        TOTAL ACTIVE:    5
NOTES:  Overseas income estimated by MARC.
------------------------------------------------------------------
                    YEAR    PERSONNEL    RELATED    PEOPLE
FIELD OF SERVICE    BEGAN   NOW   NEW    CHURCHES   GROUPS   NOTES
------------------------------------------------------------------
Germany, Fed. Rep.  1977    2
Mexico              1976    2
Philippines         1979    4
Spain               1977    4
Sweden              1976    2
```

Mission Steers, Inc. SEE: Steer, Inc.

Mission to Europe's Millions, Inc.

B3-223A-10th St. NW
Calgary AB T2N 1V5
Canada

```
Tel. (403) 283-6768
EXECUTIVE OFFICER: Willie Murray
ORGANIZED: 1904
DESCRIPTION:  An international, interdenominational sending
    agency of independent tradition establishing churches and
    engaged in evangelism, literature and Bible distribution,
    and support of natio.al churches.
TOTAL INCOME:    $110,000   FOR OVERSEAS MINISTRIES:    $110,000
PERSONNEL:
    NORTH AMERICANS OVERSEAS    NON-NORTH AMERICANS OVERSEAS:    60
              MARRIED:    8        NORTH AMERICAN ADM. STAFF:     5
           SINGLE MEN:    1                    SHORT TERM:       40
         SINGLE WOMEN:    4                    RETIRED:           0
                       -----
        TOTAL ACTIVE:   13
------------------------------------------------------------------
                    YEAR    PERSONNEL    RELATED    PEOPLE
FIELD OF SERVICE    BEGAN   NOW   NEW    CHURCHES   GROUPS   NOTES
------------------------------------------------------------------
Albania
Australia                                    3         3
Austria                      6     6         9         1
Bulgaria
Czechoslovakia
Denmark
France                       2               7         1
Germany, Dem. Rep.
Germany, Fed. Rep.           2     2
Greece                       1     1         2
Hungary
Ireland                                      1
Italy                                        5
Netherlands                                  2
Poland
Romania
Spain                        2     2         2
Sweden
Switzerland                                  1
```

Mission to Japan, Inc.

1211 Park Ave. Ste. 101
San Jose CA 95126
P.O. ADDRESS:
Box 1203
Campbell CA 95008

Tel. (408) 371-3071
EXECUTIVE OFFICER: Ray T. Pedigo
ORGANIZED: 1950
DESCRIPTION: A service agency of evangelical tradition
   involved in mass evangelism and radio broadcasting. Has a
   boat in the Philippines and one in Japan which are used
   for transportation between islands. One in Japan also has
   evangelistic services held on board.
TOTAL INCOME: NR   FOR OVERSEAS MINISTRIES: $44,000
PERSONNEL:
   NORTH AMERICANS OVERSEAS   NON-NORTH AMERICANS OVERSEAS: NR
              MARRIED: NR   NORTH AMERICAN ADM. STAFF: 3
          SINGLE MEN: NR   SHORT TERM: 0
        SINGLE WOMEN: NR   RETIRED: 0

       TOTAL ACTIVE: 2
NOTES: Overseas income estimated by MARC.

Mission to the World

4151 Memorial Dr Ste209C
Decatur GA 30032
P.O. ADDRESS:
Box 1744
Decatur GA 30031

Tel. (404) 292-8345
EXECUTIVE OFFICER: Paul E. McKaughan
ORGANIZED: 1973   AFFILIATION: EFMA
DESCRIPTION: A denominational sending agency of Presbyterian
   and Reformed tradition establishing churches and engaged
   in Bible translation, evangelism and theological and
   general Christian education.
TOTAL INCOME: $1,781,637   FOR OVERSEAS MINISTRIES: $1,781,637
PERSONNEL:
   NORTH AMERICANS OVERSEAS   NON-NORTH AMERICANS OVERSEAS: 6
              MARRIED: 118   NORTH AMERICAN ADM. STAFF: 19
          SINGLE MEN: 2   SHORT TERM: 29
        SINGLE WOMEN: 14   RETIRED: NR

       TOTAL ACTIVE: 134

FIELD OF SERVICE	YEAR BEGAN	PERSONNEL NOW	NEW	RELATED CHURCHES	PEOPLE GROUPS	NOTES
Bolivia	1976	2	6			

FIELD OF SERVICE	YEAR BEGAN	PERSONNEL NOW	PERSONNEL NEW	RELATED CHURCHES	PEOPLE GROUPS	NOTES
Brazil	1973	3	2			
Central African Rep.	1979	2	2			
Colombia	1976	4	4			
Ecuador	1975	14	14			
El Salvador	1978	2	2			
France	1973	11	9			
Greece	1978	2	2			
Guatemala	1975	2	4			
Haiti	1975	3	5			
Indonesia	1976	7	7			
Italy	1979	1	1			
Ivory Coast	1976	2	2			
Jordan	1977	1	1			
Kenya	1979	2	2			
Korea, Rep. of	1974	11	11			
Mexico	1973	16	9			
Nigeria	1975	4	2			
Papua New Guinea	1975	3	7			
Philippines	1975	4	6			
Portugal	1979	5	5			
Surinam	1976	1	1			
Taiwan Rep of China	1974	18	15			

Note: Also have 10 missionaries serving internationally and 28 under appointment.

Mission Training and Resource Center

221 E Walnut Ste. 271
Pasadena CA 91101

Tel. (213) 577-1733
EXECUTIVE OFFICER: Kenneth A. Ross, III
ORGANIZED: 1979
DESCRIPTION: A nondenominational service agency offering research and training for the purpose of mission. Involved in on-the-field seminars for missionaries, congregations and church leaders, and offers a consultant/information service.
TOTAL INCOME: $250,000   FOR OVERSEAS MINISTRIES: $50,000
PERSONNEL:

NORTH AMERICANS OVERSEAS		NON-NORTH AMERICANS OVERSEAS:	0
MARRIED:	0	NORTH AMERICAN ADM. STAFF:	0
SINGLE MEN:	0	SHORT TERM:	0
SINGLE WOMEN:	0	RETIRED:	0
TOTAL ACTIVE:	0		

Missionary Air Transport, Inc.

820 Chicago Ave.
McAllen TX 78501

Tel. (512) 686-7660
EXECUTIVE OFFICER: David Marple
ORGANIZED: 1972
DESCRIPTION: A nondenominational service agency of independent and fundamentalist tradition involved in aviation and church planting. Also provides training and technical assistance to evangelists and missionaries.
TOTAL INCOME: NR   FOR OVERSEAS MINISTRIES: NR

```
PERSONNEL:
   NORTH AMERICANS OVERSEAS     NON-NORTH AMERICANS OVERSEAS:    NR
           MARRIED:     0           NORTH AMERICAN ADM. STAFF:     3
        SINGLE MEN:     0                        SHORT TERM:       3
      SINGLE WOMEN:     0                           RETIRED:      NR
                    -----
      TOTAL ACTIVE:     0
------------------------------------------------------------------------
                        YEAR     PERSONNEL    RELATED   PEOPLE
FIELD OF SERVICE        BEGAN    NOW   NEW    CHURCHES  GROUPS   NOTES
------------------------------------------------------------------------
Guatemala               1975
Honduras                1974
Nicaragua               1975
```

Missionary and Soul Winning Fellowship SEE: Christians in Action

Missionary Auto-Truck Service
1716 Spruce St.
Philadelphia PA 19103

```
Tel. (215) 735-5133
EXECUTIVE OFFICER: C. Everett Koop
ORGANIZED: 1978
DESCRIPTION:  A nondenominational specialized service agency
   offering assistance to missionaries seeking transportation.
TOTAL INCOME:        NR          FOR OVERSEAS MINISTRIES:    NR
PERSONNEL:
   NORTH AMERICANS OVERSEAS     NON-NORTH AMERICANS OVERSEAS:    0
           MARRIED:     0           NORTH AMERICAN ADM. STAFF:    NR
        SINGLE MEN:     0                        SHORT TERM:       0
      SINGLE WOMEN:     0                           RETIRED:       0
                    -----
      TOTAL ACTIVE:     0
```

Missionary Church Association SEE: Missionary Church, Division of Overseas Ministries

Missionary Church, Division of Overseas Ministries
3901 S Wayne Ave.
Ft. Wayne Avenue IN 46807

```
Tel. (219) 744-1291
EXECUTIVE OFFICER: Eugene Ponchot
ORGANIZED: 1898    AFFILIATION: EFMA
DESCRIPTION:  A denominational sending agency of evangelical
   tradition engaged in establishing churches, community
   development, education and medicine.
TOTAL INCOME: $17,631,285   FOR OVERSEAS MINISTRIES:   $1,390,000
PERSONNEL:
   NORTH AMERICANS OVERSEAS     NON-NORTH AMERICANS OVERSEAS:    0
           MARRIED:   105           NORTH AMERICAN ADM. STAFF:    2
        SINGLE MEN:     0                        SHORT TERM:      91
      SINGLE WOMEN:    17                           RETIRED:     130
                    -----
      TOTAL ACTIVE:   122
------------------------------------------------------------------------
                        YEAR     PERSONNEL    RELATED   PEOPLE
FIELD OF SERVICE        BEGAN    NOW   NEW    CHURCHES  GROUPS   NOTES
------------------------------------------------------------------------
Bangladesh                       2
```

FIELD OF SERVICE	YEAR BEGAN	PERSONNEL NOW	NEW	RELATED CHURCHES	PEOPLE GROUPS	NOTES
Brazil	1955	17		30	1	
Cyprus		2				
Dominican Republic	1945	16	6	87		
Ecuador	1945	21	12	25	2	
France	1979	2	2		1	
Haiti	1952	18	9	71		
India	1908			29	2	
Jamaica	1949	4		38		
Japan		1				
Nigeria	1905	12		235		
Philippines		2				
Sierra Leone	1945	30	12	45	3	

Missionary Church, Division of Overseas Missions SEE: Missionary Church, Division of Overseas Ministries

Missionary Communications, Inc.

914 W Redwood Rd.
Sterling VA 22170
P.O. ADDRESS:
Box 261
Sterling VA 22170

Tel. (701) 430-0336
EXECUTIVE OFFICER: William P. Holsinger
ORGANIZED: 1979
DESCRIPTION: A nondenominational specialized service agency of
    independent tradition providing communications, mass media
    products and consultation assistance to evangelical
    missions worldwide.
TOTAL INCOME: $18,818   FOR OVERSEAS MINISTRIES: $0
PERSONNEL:
    NORTH AMERICANS OVERSEAS   NON-NORTH AMERICANS OVERSEAS: 0
             MARRIED: 0   NORTH AMERICAN ADM. STAFF: 3
          SINGLE MEN: 0   SHORT TERM: 0
        SINGLE WOMEN: 0   RETIRED: 0

        TOTAL ACTIVE: 0

Missionary Dentist, Inc.

20065 10th NW
Seattle WA 98177
P.O. ADDRESS:
Box 7002
Seattle WA 98133

Tel. (206) 546-1200
EXECUTIVE OFFICER: Vaughn V. Chapman
ORGANIZED: 1950
DESCRIPTION: An interdenominational sending agency of
    evangelical tradition engaged in full time dental
    evangelism. Also involved in Bible distribution and
    general Christian education.
TOTAL INCOME: $117,000   FOR OVERSEAS MINISTRIES: $84,000
PERSONNEL:
    NORTH AMERICANS OVERSEAS   NON-NORTH AMERICANS OVERSEAS: 0
             MARRIED: 4   NORTH AMERICAN ADM. STAFF: 2
          SINGLE MEN: 1   SHORT TERM: 20

```
    SINGLE WOMEN:    2                        RETIRED:      0
                 -----
    TOTAL ACTIVE:    7
NOTES:   In addition to the seven overseas personnel,
         six full-time associates are sent through other
         agencies.
```

FIELD OF SERVICE	YEAR BEGAN	PERSONNEL NOW	NEW	RELATED CHURCHES	PEOPLE GROUPS	NOTES
Ecuador	1959	1	1		11	
Haiti	1958	1			3	
India	1950	2			16	
Liberia	1973	2	1		23	

Missionary Electronics, Inc.

1061-D N Shepard St.
Anaheim CA 92806

Tel. (714) 630-0600
EXECUTIVE OFFICER: James R. Ford
ORGANIZED: 1948
DESCRIPTION: An interdenominational service agency of
    evangelical tradition providing technical assistance
    (electronic teaching aids) to developing countries,
    particularly India and Nigeria. Also establishing a church
    planting program.

```
TOTAL INCOME:     $23,400   FOR OVERSEAS MINISTRIES:     $10,600
PERSONNEL:
    NORTH AMERICANS OVERSEAS    NON-NORTH AMERICANS OVERSEAS:     0
            MARRIED:   0            NORTH AMERICAN ADM. STAFF:    1
         SINGLE MEN:   0                         SHORT TERM:      0
       SINGLE WOMEN:   0                            RETIRED:      0
                     -----
       TOTAL ACTIVE:   0
```

Missionary Evangelistic Fellowship, Inc.

54-179 Kawaeku St.
Hauula HI 96717

Tel. (808) 293-5960
EXECUTIVE OFFICER: John H. Rhoads
ORGANIZED: 1940
DESCRIPTION: An interdenominational, specialized agency of
    Baptist and evangelical tradition recruiting, training
    and sending national evangelists from seven Asian nations.
    Operates Asian School of Evangelism in Hawaii.

```
TOTAL INCOME:     $30,000   FOR OVERSEAS MINISTRIES:     $30,000
PERSONNEL:
    NORTH AMERICANS OVERSEAS    NON-NORTH AMERICANS OVERSEAS:    NR
            MARRIED:   4            NORTH AMERICAN ADM. STAFF:    2
         SINGLE MEN:   0                         SHORT TERM:     NR
       SINGLE WOMEN:   0                            RETIRED:      0
                     -----
       TOTAL ACTIVE:   4
```

FIELD OF SERVICE	YEAR BEGAN	PERSONNEL NOW	NEW	RELATED CHURCHES	PEOPLE GROUPS	NOTES
Hong-Kong	1979	2	2			
India	1970	6	2			

FIELD OF SERVICE	YEAR BEGAN	PERSONNEL NOW	NEW	RELATED CHURCHES	PEOPLE GROUPS	NOTES
Indonesia	1970	18	6			
Japan	1951	6	2			
Korea, Rep. of	1970	2				
Philippines	1970	6	4			
Taiwan Rep of China	1979	3	3			

Note: All but 4 overseas personnel are nationals.

Missionary Flights International

1015 S Congress Ave.
West Palm Beach FL 33406
P.O. ADDRESS:
Box 15665
West Palm Beach FL 33406

Tel. (305) 967-3682
EXECUTIVE OFFICER: D. H. Beldin
ORGANIZED: 1964
DESCRIPTION: An interdenominational and inter-mission agency
    of Baptist tradition providing a program of air support to
    mission boards in the West Indies and Latin America.
TOTAL INCOME: $400,000   FOR OVERSEAS MINISTRIES: NR
PERSONNEL:
    NORTH AMERICANS OVERSEAS   NON-NORTH AMERICANS OVERSEAS: 0
              MARRIED: 0   NORTH AMERICAN ADM. STAFF: 11
          SINGLE MEN: 0   SHORT TERM: 0
        SINGLE WOMEN: 0   RETIRED: 0

        TOTAL ACTIVE: 0
NOTES: Use P.O. Box for mail.
        USA Based personnel serve overseas.

Missionary Gospel Fellowship, Inc.

200 W Main St.
Turlock CA 95380
P.O. ADDRESS:
Dwr W
Turlock CA 95380

Tel. (209) 634-8575
EXECUTIVE OFFICER: Alfred J. Pratt
ORGANIZED: 1939
DESCRIPTION: Formerly Migrant Gospel Fellowship. Name changed
    in 1942. An interdenominational sending agency of
    evangelical tradition. Primarily a USA home mission,
    engaged in personal evangelism, youth camps, broadcasting,
    education and literature distribution.
TOTAL INCOME: $281,122   FOR OVERSEAS MINISTRIES: $0
PERSONNEL:
    NORTH AMERICANS OVERSEAS   NON-NORTH AMERICANS OVERSEAS: 0
              MARRIED: 0   NORTH AMERICAN ADM. STAFF: 0
          SINGLE MEN: 0   SHORT TERM: 0
        SINGLE WOMEN: 0   RETIRED: 0

        TOTAL ACTIVE: 0

Missionary Health Institute, Inc.

4000 Leslie St.
Willowdale ON M2K 2R9
Canada

Tel. (416) 494-7511
EXECUTIVE OFFICER: R. C. Warren
ORGANIZED: 1936
DESCRIPTION: A nondenominational specialized service agency of
    evangelical tradition offering health care to mission
    personnel, and dealing specifically with tropical and
    parasitic diseases.

TOTAL INCOME:	$127,000	FOR OVERSEAS MINISTRIES:		$0
PERSONNEL:				
NORTH AMERICANS OVERSEAS		NON-NORTH AMERICANS OVERSEAS:		0
MARRIED:	0	NORTH AMERICAN ADM. STAFF:		NR
SINGLE MEN:	0	SHORT TERM:		0
SINGLE WOMEN:	0	RETIRED:		1
TOTAL ACTIVE:	0			

Missionary Information Exchange

23225 Berkley
Oak Park MI 48237
P.O. ADDRESS:
Box 664
Warren MI 48090

Tel. (313) 541-3688
EXECUTIVE OFFICER: Robert Byrum Hicks
ORGANIZED: 1967
DESCRIPTION: A nondenominational specialized service agency
    of Wesleyan and charismatic tradition serving missionaries
    and agencies with technical assistance, literature
    production and distribution, mission related research and
    information service.

TOTAL INCOME:	$85	FOR OVERSEAS MINISTRIES:		NR
PERSONNEL:				
NORTH AMERICANS OVERSEAS		NON-NORTH AMERICANS OVERSEAS:		0
MARRIED:	0	NORTH AMERICAN ADM. STAFF:		0
SINGLE MEN:	0	SHORT TERM:		0
SINGLE WOMEN:	0	RETIRED:		0
TOTAL ACTIVE:	0			

Missionary Internship, Inc.

36200 Freedom Rd.
Farmington MI 48024
P.O. ADDRESS:
Box 457
Farmington MI 48024

Tel. (313) 474-9110
EXECUTIVE OFFICER: Charles J. Mellis
ORGANIZED: 1952   AFFILIATION: EFMA-Assoc. member
DESCRIPTION: An interdenominational service agency of
    evangelical tradition providing pre-service and in-service
    cultural and language orientation for missionaries and
    other church-related personnel. Programs include a
    variety of learning experiences related to effective
    communication of the Gospel in other cultures.

TOTAL INCOME:	$289,529	FOR OVERSEAS MINISTRIES:		$0
PERSONNEL:				
NORTH AMERICANS OVERSEAS		NON-NORTH AMERICANS OVERSEAS:		0
MARRIED:	0	NORTH AMERICAN ADM. STAFF:		0
SINGLE MEN:	0	SHORT TERM:		0

```
SINGLE WOMEN:      0                          RETIRED:     0
                -----
TOTAL ACTIVE:      0
```

Missionary Leasing Company

25 W 560 Geneva Rd.
Wheaton IL 60187
P.O. ADDRESS:
Box 66
Wheaton IL 60187

Tel. (312) 653-5350
EXECUTIVE OFFICER: Russell Shive
ORGANIZED: 1948
DESCRIPTION: An interdenominational service agency of Baptist
    tradition leasing cars to furloughed missionaries.

```
TOTAL INCOME:        $1,950      FOR OVERSEAS MINISTRIES:    $0
PERSONNEL:
    NORTH AMERICANS OVERSEAS   NON-NORTH AMERICANS OVERSEAS:    0
            MARRIED:    0        NORTH AMERICAN ADM. STAFF:     0
        SINGLE MEN:    0                       SHORT TERM:      0
      SINGLE WOMEN:    0                         RETIRED:       0
                    -----
        TOTAL ACTIVE:    0
```

Missionary Revival Crusade

102 E Lyon
Laredo TX 78040

Tel. (512) 722-2646
EXECUTIVE OFFICER: Daniel Ost
ORGANIZED: 1959
DESCRIPTION: A service and sending agency of charismatic
    tradition engaged in church planting, evangelism and drug
    rehabilitation. Has drug rehabilitation centers.

```
TOTAL INCOME: $1,000,000    FOR OVERSEAS MINISTRIES:    $950,000
PERSONNEL:
    NORTH AMERICANS OVERSEAS   NON-NORTH AMERICANS OVERSEAS:    NR
            MARRIED:    NR       NORTH AMERICAN ADM. STAFF:      2
        SINGLE MEN:    NR                      SHORT TERM:      60
      SINGLE WOMEN:    NR                        RETIRED:        0
                    -----
        TOTAL ACTIVE:    52
```
NOTES: North Americans overseas and short-term
    personnel include nationals.

FIELD OF SERVICE	YEAR BEGAN	PERSONNEL NOW	PERSONNEL NEW	RELATED CHURCHES	PEOPLE GROUPS	NOTES
Colombia						
Mexico						

Missionary Service Committee, Inc. SEE: Brethren Assemblies

Missionary Service Organization, Inc.

207 N Broadway
Santa Ana CA 92701

DESCRIPTION: No data is reported for this agency for one of the
    following reasons: it is currently inactive or no longer
    exists; it has terminated overseas ministries or has ceased
    to operate as a North American entity.

Missionary Services, Inc.

327 Gundersen Dr.
Carol Stream IL 92701

EXECUTIVE OFFICER: Larry Dixon
ORGANIZED: 1952
DESCRIPTION: Founded as Missionary Equipment Services.
   Name changed 1966. An interdenominational specialized
   service agency of evangelical tradition distributing
   materials and clothing for missionary personnel.
   Operates in conjunction with MAP, International.

TOTAL INCOME:	NR	FOR OVERSEAS MINISTRIES:	NR
PERSONNEL:			
NORTH AMERICANS OVERSEAS		NON-NORTH AMERICANS OVERSEAS:	NR
MARRIED:	NR	NORTH AMERICAN ADM. STAFF:	NR
SINGLE MEN:	NR	SHORT TERM:	NR
SINGLE WOMEN:	NR	RETIRED:	NR
TOTAL ACTIVE:	NR		

Missionary Strategy Agency

1054 N St. Andrews Pl.
Los Angeles CA 90038

Tel. (213) 465-2267
EXECUTIVE OFFICER: Masumi Toyotome
ORGANIZED: 1964
DESCRIPTION: A nondenominational service agency of evangelical
   tradition involved in research and development of
   evangelistic strategy. Also engaged in evangelism,
   training and literature distribution and production.

TOTAL INCOME:	NR	FOR OVERSEAS MINISTRIES:	NR
PERSONNEL:			
NORTH AMERICANS OVERSEAS		NON-NORTH AMERICANS OVERSEAS:	0
MARRIED:	0	NORTH AMERICAN ADM. STAFF:	0
SINGLE MEN:	0	SHORT TERM:	0
SINGLE WOMEN:	0	RETIRED:	0
TOTAL ACTIVE:	0		

Missionary Tapes, Inc.

1721 N Lake
Pasadena CA 91104

DESCRIPTION: No data is reported for this agency for one of the
   following reasons: it is currently inactive or no longer
   exists; it has terminated overseas ministries or has ceased
   to operate as a North American entity.

Missionary TECH Team

25 FRJ Dr.
Longview TX 75602

Tel. (214) 757-4530
EXECUTIVE OFFICER: Birne D. Wiley
ORGANIZED: 1969
DESCRIPTION: A nondenominational specialized service agency
   of evangelical and fundamentalist tradition providing
   technical, engineering and consulting help to missionary
   agencies. Currently operates in areas of
   communications, facilities planning and special
   ministries. Has worked in 19 countries.

TOTAL INCOME:	$306,500	FOR OVERSEAS MINISTRIES:	$199,225
PERSONNEL:			
NORTH AMERICANS OVERSEAS		NON-NORTH AMERICANS OVERSEAS:	2
MARRIED:	2	NORTH AMERICAN ADM. STAFF:	3
SINGLE MEN:	0	SHORT TERM:	3

```
SINGLE WOMEN:     0                          RETIRED:     0
                -----
    TOTAL ACTIVE:     2
-----------------------------------------------------------------
                  YEAR      PERSONNEL   RELATED    PEOPLE
FIELD OF SERVICE  BEGAN     NOW   NEW   CHURCHES   GROUPS  NOTES
-----------------------------------------------------------------
Guatemala         1978       2     2
```

Missions Advanced Research and Communication Center (MARC)

919 W Huntington Dr.
Monrovia CA 91016

Tel. (213) 357-1111
EXECUTIVE OFFICER: Samuel Wilson
ORGANIZED: 1966
DESCRIPTION: A nondenominational specialized service agency
    of evangelical tradition involved in missions related
    information and evangelism research, publications,
    strategy training and consultation. Functions as an
    information center on world evangelization.

```
TOTAL INCOME:    $304,000          FOR OVERSEAS MINISTRIES:    NR
PERSONNEL:
    NORTH AMERICANS OVERSEAS   NON-NORTH AMERICANS OVERSEAS:    0
            MARRIED:    0        NORTH AMERICAN ADM. STAFF:     3
         SINGLE MEN:    0                     SHORT TERM:       0
       SINGLE WOMEN:    0                        RETIRED:      0
                     -----
    TOTAL ACTIVE:      0
```
NOTES: Income shown included in World Vision
        International listing.

POINTER NAME:Missions Investment Associates SEE:
Conservative Mennonite Board of Missions and Charities

Missions of Baja

2221 E Winston Unit C
Anaheim CA 92803
P.O. ADDRESS:
Box 4646
Anaheim CA 92803

Tel. (714) 776-2740
EXECUTIVE OFFICER: Carlos Freyer
ORGANIZED: 1967
DESCRIPTION: An interdenominational sending agency of
    evangelical tradition involved in orphanage work, church
    planting and education.

```
TOTAL INCOME:    $60,000   FOR OVERSEAS MINISTRIES:    $150,000
PERSONNEL:
    NORTH AMERICANS OVERSEAS   NON-NORTH AMERICANS OVERSEAS:   NR
            MARRIED:   NR        NORTH AMERICAN ADM. STAFF:     2
         SINGLE MEN:   NR                     SHORT TERM:       0
       SINGLE WOMEN:   NR                        RETIRED:      0
                     -----
    TOTAL ACTIVE:      5
```
NOTES: Contributions and gifts make overseas
        income larger than total income.
```
-----------------------------------------------------------------
                  YEAR      PERSONNEL   RELATED    PEOPLE
FIELD OF SERVICE  BEGAN     NOW   NEW   CHURCHES   GROUPS  NOTES
-----------------------------------------------------------------
Mexico            1967       5
```

Missions Outreach, Inc.

P.O. ADDRESS:
Box 73
Bethany MO 64424

Tel. (816) 425-3777
EXECUTIVE OFFICER: Delmar E. Caulkins
ORGANIZED: 1976
DESCRIPTION: An interdenominational specialized service agency
   of evangelical tradition sending short-term missionary
   support teams to the field to help with building
   construction. Youth teams are sent in the summer, adult
   teams in winter. Also engaged in recruiting and Bible
   memorization.
TOTAL INCOME: $335,658   FOR OVERSEAS MINISTRIES: $100,590
PERSONNEL:

NORTH AMERICANS OVERSEAS		NON-NORTH AMERICANS OVERSEAS:	0
MARRIED:	0	NORTH AMERICAN ADM. STAFF:	0
SINGLE MEN:	0	SHORT TERM:	294
SINGLE WOMEN:	0	RETIRED:	0
TOTAL ACTIVE:	0		

Missions to Japan, Inc.

6122 S Zunia
Tulsa OK 74105

DESCRIPTION: No data is reported for this agency for one of the
   following reasons: it is currently inactive or no longer
   exists; it has terminated overseas ministries or has ceased
   to operate as a North American entity.

Missions Today, Inc.

1161 N Ballenger Hwy.
Flint MI 48504

DESCRIPTION: No data is reported for this agency for one of the
   following reasons: it is currently inactive or no longer
   exists; it has terminated overseas ministries or has ceased
   to operate as a North American entity.

Missions, Inc.

RD 5
Bellefonte PA 16823

Tel. (814) 355-7419
EXECUTIVE OFFICER: Richard L. Shope
ORGANIZED: 1959
DESCRIPTION: An independent specialized agency of
   fundamentalist tradition providing a prayer letter service
   for missionaries.
TOTAL INCOME: $13,000   FOR OVERSEAS MINISTRIES: $13,000
PERSONNEL:

NORTH AMERICANS OVERSEAS		NON-NORTH AMERICANS OVERSEAS:	0
MARRIED:	0	NORTH AMERICAN ADM. STAFF:	2
SINGLE MEN:	0	SHORT TERM:	0
SINGLE WOMEN:	0	RETIRED:	0
TOTAL ACTIVE:	0		

Moody Institute of Science

12000 E Washington Blvd.
Whittier CA 90606

Tel. (213) 698-8256
EXECUTIVE OFFICER: James W. Adams
ORGANIZED: 1945
DESCRIPTION: A nondenominational specialized service agency of
   evangelical tradition producing and distributing

audio-visuals in various languages for use in evangelism
and Christian education. Also has a platform ministry to
American military personnel and an outreach at public
exhibitions and world fairs using the general backdrop of
science.

```
TOTAL INCOME:         NR          FOR OVERSEAS MINISTRIES:    NR
PERSONNEL:
   NORTH AMERICANS OVERSEAS    NON-NORTH AMERICANS OVERSEAS:    0
              MARRIED:    0        NORTH AMERICAN ADM. STAFF:   32
           SINGLE MEN:    0                      SHORT TERM:    0
         SINGLE WOMEN:    0                         RETIRED:    7
                        -----
         TOTAL ACTIVE:    0
```

Moody Literature Ministries

820 N LaSalle St.
Chicago IL 60610

Tel. (312) 329-4364
EXECUTIVE OFFICER: Albert J. Abuhl
ORGANIZED: 1894
DESCRIPTION: A nondenominational specialized service agency of
    evangelical tradition producing and distributing
    literature in 85 languages and 120 countries through
    established overseas agencies.

```
TOTAL INCOME:         NR          FOR OVERSEAS MINISTRIES:    NR
PERSONNEL:
   NORTH AMERICANS OVERSEAS    NON-NORTH AMERICANS OVERSEAS:    0
              MARRIED:    0        NORTH AMERICAN ADM. STAFF:    2
           SINGLE MEN:    0                      SHORT TERM:    0
         SINGLE WOMEN:    0                         RETIRED:    0
                        -----
         TOTAL ACTIVE:    0
```

Moody Literature Mission SEE:
Moody Literature Ministries

Moravian Church in America, Board
of World Mission

69 W Church St.
Bethlehem PA 18018
P.O. ADDRESS:
Box 1245
Bethlehem PA 18018

Tel. (215) 868-1732
EXECUTIVE OFFICER: Theodore F. Hartmann
ORGANIZED: 1949 AFFILIATION: DOM-NCCCUSA
DESCRIPTION: A denominational sending agency of Moravian
    tradition supporting national churches and engaged in
    evangelism, education, agriculture and medical programs.
    Also involved in community development and aid and relief.

```
TOTAL INCOME:    $700,000   FOR OVERSEAS MINISTRIES:    $640,000
PERSONNEL:
   NORTH AMERICANS OVERSEAS    NON-NORTH AMERICANS OVERSEAS:    0
              MARRIED:   24        NORTH AMERICAN ADM. STAFF:    3
           SINGLE MEN:    2                      SHORT TERM:    3
         SINGLE WOMEN:    1                         RETIRED:   29
                        -----
         TOTAL ACTIVE:   27
```

FIELD OF SERVICE	YEAR BEGAN	PERSONNEL NOW	NEW	RELATED CHURCHES	PEOPLE GROUPS	NOTES
Antigua	1732					

FIELD OF SERVICE	YEAR BEGAN	PERSONNEL NOW	NEW	RELATED CHURCHES	PEOPLE GROUPS	NOTES
Barbados	1732					
Dominican Republic	1907			25		
Guyana	1878			8		
Honduras	1930	8		34		
Jamaica	1732	1				
Nicaragua	1849	2	3	118		
St. Kitts-Nevis	1732					
Tanzania	1892	2		200		
Trinidad and Tobago	1732					
U.S. Virgin Is.	1732	10	2	38		

Morris Cerullo World Evangelism, Inc.

P.O. ADDRESS:
Box 700
San Diego CA 92138

Tel. (714) 230-7000
EXECUTIVE OFFICER: Morris Cerullo
ORGANIZED: 1961
DESCRIPTION: A service and sending agency of charismatic and
    evangelical tradition involved in mass evangelism,
    national ministers training institutes and providing
    scholarships for national ministers. Also has a School of
    Ministry in San Diego.
TOTAL INCOME: NA   FOR OVERSEAS MINISTRIES: $22,000
PERSONNEL:
    NORTH AMERICANS OVERSEAS   NON-NORTH AMERICANS OVERSEAS: NR
            MARRIED: NR   NORTH AMERICAN ADM. STAFF: 200
         SINGLE MEN: NR   SHORT TERM: 100
       SINGLE WOMEN: NR   RETIRED: NR

        TOTAL ACTIVE: 10
NOTES: Overseas income estimated by MARC.

Movimiento Misionero Mundial, Inc

Ctera Est. 846 Km.0 HM 4
San Juan PR 00936
P.O. ADDRESS:
Apartado 3644
San Juan PR 00936

Tel. (809) 761-8806
EXECUTIVE OFFICER: Luis Jaime Ortiz
ORGANIZED: 1964
DESCRIPTION: An independent agency relating to churches of
    Pentecostal tradition, particularly Sinai Pentecostal,
    active in church planting.
TOTAL INCOME: NR   FOR OVERSEAS MINISTRIES: $80,000
PERSONNEL:
    NORTH AMERICANS OVERSEAS   NON-NORTH AMERICANS OVERSEAS: NR
            MARRIED: NR   NORTH AMERICAN ADM. STAFF: 7
         SINGLE MEN: NR   SHORT TERM: 0
       SINGLE WOMEN: NR   RETIRED: NR

        TOTAL ACTIVE: 300
NOTES: The mission sends personnel to 21 countries.

Muslim World Evangelical Literature Service SEE: Fellowship of Faith for the Muslims

Mustard Seed, Inc., The

1377 E Colorado St.
Glendale CA 91205
P.O. ADDRESS:
Box 400
Glendale CA 91209

Tel. (213) 241-3811
EXECUTIVE OFFICER: Lillian R. Dickson
ORGANIZED: 1954
DESCRIPTION: An interdenominational agency of evangelical and
    Presbyterian tradition engaged in adoption, aid and
    relief, education and childcare.
TOTAL INCOME: $1,446,000   FOR OVERSEAS MINISTRIES: $1,446,000
PERSONNEL:

NORTH AMERICANS OVERSEAS		NON-NORTH AMERICANS OVERSEAS:	16
MARRIED:	1	NORTH AMERICAN ADM. STAFF:	5
SINGLE MEN:	1	SHORT TERM:	0
SINGLE WOMEN:	1	RETIRED:	0
TOTAL ACTIVE:	3		

Narramore Christian Foundation

1409 N Walnut Grove Ave.
Rosemead CA 91770
P.O. ADDRESS:
Box 5000
Rosemead CA 91770

Tel. (213) 288-7000
EXECUTIVE OFFICER: Clyde M. Narramore
ORGANIZED: 1958
DESCRIPTION: A nondenominational specialized service agency of
    evangelical tradition providing psychological testing and
    counseling, consultation services and counseling seminars
    for missionaries and mission agencies in the USA and
    overseas. Works in cooperation with the Rosemead Graduate
    School of Psychology and the Rosemead Counseling Service.
TOTAL INCOME: $50,000   FOR OVERSEAS MINISTRIES: NA
PERSONNEL:

NORTH AMERICANS OVERSEAS		NON-NORTH AMERICANS OVERSEAS:	0
MARRIED:	0	NORTH AMERICAN ADM. STAFF:	0
SINGLE MEN:	0	SHORT TERM:	0
SINGLE WOMEN:	0	RETIRED:	0
TOTAL ACTIVE:	0		

NOTES: Income is estimated by MARC.

**National Association of
Congregational Christian Churches
of the U.S.A. Missionary Society**

P.O. ADDRESS:
Box 1620
Oak Creek WI 53154

Tel. (414) 764-1620
EXECUTIVE OFFICER: A. Ray Appelquist
ORGANIZED: 1953
DESCRIPTION: A denominational agency of Congregational
    tradition supporting nationals and national churches. Also
    involved in self-help projects, childcare, theological
    education, medicine, evangelism and Bible distribution.
TOTAL INCOME: $224,547   FOR OVERSEAS MINISTRIES: $64,470
PERSONNEL:

NORTH AMERICANS OVERSEAS		NON-NORTH AMERICANS OVERSEAS:	0
MARRIED:	0	NORTH AMERICAN ADM. STAFF:	2
SINGLE MEN:	0	SHORT TERM:	0

```
       SINGLE WOMEN:    0                          RETIRED:      0
                      -----
       TOTAL ACTIVE:    0
------------------------------------------------------------------------
                      YEAR      PERSONNEL    RELATED    PEOPLE
FIELD OF SERVICE      BEGAN     NOW    NEW   CHURCHES   GROUPS   NOTES
------------------------------------------------------------------------
Germany, Fed. Rep.    1958
Greece                1961
Guatemala             1976
Honduras              1975
Hong-Kong
India
Italy
Japan
Korea, Rep. of
Morocco
Nigeria
Philippines
Taiwan Rep of China
United Kingdom        1975
```

National Association of Free Will Baptists, Board of Foreign Missions

1134 Murfreesboro Rd.
Nashville TN 37217
P.O. ADDRESS:
Box 1088
Nashville TN 37202

```
Tel. (615) 361-1010
EXECUTIVE OFFICER: Rolla D. Smith
ORGANIZED: 1935    AFFILIATION: EFMA
DESCRIPTION:  A denominational sending agency of fundamentalist
    and Baptist tradition establishing churches and engaged
    in literature production and information service.
TOTAL INCOME:  $1,598,672   FOR OVERSEAS MINISTRIES:  $1,295,219
PERSONNEL:
    NORTH AMERICANS OVERSEAS    NON-NORTH AMERICANS OVERSEAS:      0
               MARRIED:   90        NORTH AMERICAN ADM. STAFF:    10
            SINGLE MEN:    0                     SHORT TERM:       9
          SINGLE WOMEN:    8                        RETIRED:     106
                       -----
       TOTAL ACTIVE:   98
------------------------------------------------------------------------
                      YEAR      PERSONNEL    RELATED    PEOPLE
FIELD OF SERVICE      BEGAN     NOW    NEW   CHURCHES   GROUPS   NOTES
------------------------------------------------------------------------
Brazil                1958      24     4        12
France                1966      12     3         3
India                 1935       2              14
Ivory Coast           1957      31     9        35         5
Japan                 1954       9              10                 1
Panama                1962       5              10
Spain                 1974       6     2         1
Uruguay               1962       5               6
```

397

National Baptist Convention of America, Foreign Mission Board

777 S RL Thornton Ste210
Dallas TX 75203
P.O. ADDRESS:
Drawer 223665
Dallas TX 75222

Tel. (214) 942-3311
EXECUTIVE OFFICER: Robert H. Wilson
ORGANIZED: 1880
DESCRIPTION: An interdenominational sending agency of Baptist
    tradition engaged in church construction, mass evangelism,
    fund raising and providing medical supplies. Also involved
    in childcare and support of nationals.
TOTAL INCOME: $500,000   FOR OVERSEAS MINISTRIES: $290,703
PERSONNEL:

NORTH AMERICANS OVERSEAS		NON-NORTH AMERICANS OVERSEAS:	0
MARRIED:	6	NORTH AMERICAN ADM. STAFF:	4
SINGLE MEN:	1	SHORT TERM:	12
SINGLE WOMEN:	1	RETIRED:	2
TOTAL ACTIVE:	8		

FIELD OF SERVICE	YEAR BEGAN	PERSONNEL NOW	NEW	RELATED CHURCHES	PEOPLE GROUPS	NOTES
Cameroon	1977	2	3	42		
Ghana	1980	1	1	15		
Haiti				8		
Jamaica				25		
Liberia	1959	2		2		
Panama		1		4		
U.S. Virgin Is.				11		

National Baptist Convention, U.S.A., Inc., Foreign Mission Board

701 South 19th St.
Philadelphia PA 19146
P.O. ADDRESS:
Box 3873 Station D
Philadelphia PA 19146

Tel. (215) 735-7868
EXECUTIVE OFFICER: William J. Harvey, III
ORGANIZED: 1880
DESCRIPTION: A denominational sending agency of Baptist
    tradition establishing churches and engaged in education,
    medicine, agricultural assistance, and supporting national
    churches.
TOTAL INCOME: $1,396,785   FOR OVERSEAS MINISTRIES: $1,396,785
PERSONNEL:

NORTH AMERICANS OVERSEAS		NON-NORTH AMERICANS OVERSEAS:	NR
MARRIED:	6	NORTH AMERICAN ADM. STAFF:	NR
SINGLE MEN:	1	SHORT TERM:	NR
SINGLE WOMEN:	7	RETIRED:	2
TOTAL ACTIVE:	14		

FIELD OF SERVICE	YEAR BEGAN	PERSONNEL NOW	NEW	RELATED CHURCHES	PEOPLE GROUPS	NOTES
Bahamas	1942			172		

FIELD OF SERVICE	YEAR BEGAN	PERSONNEL NOW	NEW	RELATED CHURCHES	PEOPLE GROUPS	NOTES
Barbados	1978	1		3		
Ghana	1950			3		
Jamaica	1972			21		
Lesotho	1961			19		
Liberia	1880	11		19		
Malawi	1900			472		
Nicaragua	1958			3		
Sierra Leone	1951			1		
South Africa	1898			154		
Swaziland	1971	2	2	9		

National Council of the Churches of Christ in the USA, Division of Overseas Ministries SEE: DOM-NCCCUSA, Mission Association Section

National Fellowship of Brethren Churches SEE: Fellowship Grace Brethren Chs., For. Msny. Soc. Breth. Ch.

National Religious Broadcasters

38 Speedwell Ave.
Morristown NJ 07960
P.O. ADDRESS:
Box 2254R
Morristown NJ 07960

Tel. (201) 540-8500
EXECUTIVE OFFICER: Benjamin L. Armstrong
ORGANIZED: 1944   AFFILIATION: EFMA
DESCRIPTION: An interdenominational specialized service
    association of 900 religious broadcasting organizations
    national and international. Represents 75% of religious
    broadcasters in the USA advancing the cause of Gospel
    broadcasting, radio/TV and cable TV worldwide.
    cable TV worldwide.
TOTAL INCOME: $485,000   FOR OVERSEAS MINISTRIES: NA
PERSONNEL:
    NORTH AMERICANS OVERSEAS   NON-NORTH AMERICANS OVERSEAS: 0
              MARRIED: 0   NORTH AMERICAN ADM. STAFF: 25
           SINGLE MEN: 0   SHORT TERM: 0
         SINGLE WOMEN: 0   RETIRED: 0

         TOTAL ACTIVE: 0

Native Preacher Company, Inc.

888 7th Ave., No.400
New York NY 10019

Tel. (212) 265-4300
EXECUTIVE OFFICER: G. L. Gremmels
ORGANIZED: 1924
DESCRIPTION: A nondenominational fund transmitting agency of
    independent tradition channeling contributions to native
    missionaries, some missionary agencies and faith missions
    on the field.
TOTAL INCOME: $4,000   FOR OVERSEAS MINISTRIES: NR
PERSONNEL:
    NORTH AMERICANS OVERSEAS   NON-NORTH AMERICANS OVERSEAS: 0
              MARRIED: 0   NORTH AMERICAN ADM. STAFF: 0
           SINGLE MEN: 0   SHORT TERM: 0

SINGLE WOMEN: 0   RETIRED: 0

    TOTAL ACTIVE: 0
NOTES: Income is estimated by agency.

Navigators of Canada International, The

12-270 Esna Park Rd.
Markham ON L3R 1H3
Canada

Tel. (416) 495-0300
EXECUTIVE OFFICER: Alan Andrews
ORGANIZED: 1968
DESCRIPTION: An international, nondenominational recruiting,
    training and sending agency of evangelical tradition
    emphasizing disciplemaking, particularly by man-to-man
    teamwork and small group methods. Ministry is primarily
    to university students and church laymen.
TOTAL INCOME: $467,196   FOR OVERSEAS MINISTRIES: $58,512
PERSONNEL:
    NORTH AMERICANS OVERSEAS   NON-NORTH AMERICANS OVERSEAS: 0
              MARRIED: 2   NORTH AMERICAN ADM. STAFF: 6
           SINGLE MEN: 0   SHORT TERM: 1
         SINGLE WOMEN: 1   RETIRED: 0

       TOTAL ACTIVE: 3

Navigators, The

3820 N 30th St.
Colorado Spgs CO 80904
P.O. ADDRESS:
Box 20
Colorado Spgs CO 80904

Tel. (303) 598-1212
EXECUTIVE OFFICER: Jack Mayhall
ORGANIZED: 1933   AFFILIATION: EFMA
DESCRIPTION: A nondenominational sending agency of evangelical
    tradition engaged in personal, small group and student
    evangelism, Bible memorization, ministry to servicemen and
    training. Also involved in lay discipling.
TOTAL INCOME: $11,303,888   FOR OVERSEAS MINISTRIES: $3,234,200
PERSONNEL:
    NORTH AMERICANS OVERSEAS   NON-NORTH AMERICANS OVERSEAS: 82
              MARRIED: 134   NORTH AMERICAN ADM. STAFF: 163
           SINGLE MEN: 1   SHORT TERM: 50
         SINGLE WOMEN: 10   RETIRED: 0

       TOTAL ACTIVE: 145

FIELD OF SERVICE	YEAR BEGAN	PERSONNEL NOW	NEW	RELATED CHURCHES	PEOPLE GROUPS	NOTES
Argentina	1973	2				
Australia	1964	6				
Austria	1973	12	6			
Brazil	1963	8	2			
Costa Rica	1957					
Denmark	1957					
Egypt	1975	3				
Finland	1970	2				

FIELD OF SERVICE	YEAR BEGAN	PERSONNEL NOW	NEW	RELATED CHURCHES	PEOPLE GROUPS	NOTES
France	1972	3	1			
Germany, Fed. Rep.	1951	10	2			
Ghana	1974	7	1			
Indonesia	1967	12	2			
Japan	1951	12	4			
Jordan	1976	2	2			
Kenya	1968	4	4			
Korea, Rep. of	1966	4	4			
Lebanon	1960	2				
Malaysia	1966	2				
Mexico	1966	12	4			
Netherlands	1950					
New Zealand	1953	6				
Nigeria	1976					
Norway	1957					
Philippines	1961	5				
Singapore	1962	7	2			
Spain	1970	4				
Sweden	1955	2				
Taiwan Rep of China	1971	2				
United Kingdom	1950	9	2			
Venezuela	1975	6	2			

Nazarene Church SEE: Church of the Nazarene

New Life International

P.O. ADDRESS:
Box 11511
Fresno CA 93773

EXECUTIVE OFFICER: Larry Southwick
ORGANIZED: 1975
DESCRIPTION: A denominational specialized service agency of
    Pentecostal and charismatic tradition assisting local and
    national sister fellowships of the Pentecostal Assemblies
    of God. Engaged in literature production, radio and TV
    broadcasting, mission related research and in supporting
    national churches. Also involved in psychological
    counseling and ministry to servicemen.
TOTAL INCOME: NR   FOR OVERSEAS MINISTRIES: $66,000
PERSONNEL:
    NORTH AMERICANS OVERSEAS   NON-NORTH AMERICANS OVERSEAS: 0
            MARRIED: 0   NORTH AMERICAN ADM. STAFF: 1
          SINGLE MEN: 2   SHORT TERM: 0
         SINGLE WOMEN: 1   RETIRED: 0

        TOTAL ACTIVE: 3
NOTES: There are also four part-time personnel on
        administrative staff.
        Overseas income estimated by MARC.

FIELD OF SERVICE	YEAR BEGAN	PERSONNEL NOW	NEW	RELATED CHURCHES	PEOPLE GROUPS	NOTES
Europe-general	1979					

FIELD OF SERVICE	YEAR BEGAN	PERSONNEL NOW	NEW	RELATED CHURCHES	PEOPLE GROUPS	NOTES
Germany, Fed. Rep.	1979		1	30	1	
Sweden	1979		1	600		
United Kingdom	1980		1	925	1	

New Life League

7654 W Berwyn Ave.
Chicago IL 60656

Tel. (312) 631-9767
EXECUTIVE OFFICER: Fred D. Jarvis
ORGANIZED: 1954
DESCRIPTION: A nondenominational sending and service agency of
    independent tradition engaged in evangelism, education,
    literature production, childcare, support of national
    workers, Bible correspondence courses and broadcasting.
TOTAL INCOME: $100,000   FOR OVERSEAS MINISTRIES: $99,000
PERSONNEL:
NORTH AMERICANS OVERSEAS   NON-NORTH AMERICANS OVERSEAS: NR
          MARRIED: NR   NORTH AMERICAN ADM. STAFF: 2
       SINGLE MEN: NR   SHORT TERM: 40
     SINGLE WOMEN: NR   RETIRED: 0

     TOTAL ACTIVE: 25

FIELD OF SERVICE	YEAR BEGAN	PERSONNEL NOW	NEW	RELATED CHURCHES	PEOPLE GROUPS	NOTES
Bhutan						
Brazil		2				
Colombia		3				
Guatemala	1976					
Haiti		2				
Hong-Kong						
India						
Japan	1954					
Mexico		1				
Nepal						
Papua New Guinea		2				
Taiwan Rep of China						

New Testament Missionary Union

514 Banner Ave.
Winston-Salem NC 27107

EXECUTIVE OFFICER: Blanche Davis
ORGANIZED: 1902
DESCRIPTION: An international, interdenominational sending
    agency of evangelical tradition establishing churches and
    engaged in evangelism and literature. Founded in 1902 as
    the South American Missionary Union. Name changed in 1932.
TOTAL INCOME: NR   FOR OVERSEAS MINISTRIES: NR
PERSONNEL:
NORTH AMERICANS OVERSEAS   NON-NORTH AMERICANS OVERSEAS: NR
          MARRIED: NR   NORTH AMERICAN ADM. STAFF: NR
       SINGLE MEN: NR   SHORT TERM: NR
     SINGLE WOMEN: NR   RETIRED: NR

     TOTAL ACTIVE: NR

New Tribes Mission

1000 E First St.
Sanford FL 32771

Tel. (305) 323-3430
EXECUTIVE OFFICER: Kenneth J. Johnson
ORGANIZED: 1942
DESCRIPTION: A nondenominational sending agency of
    fundamentalist tradition seeking to evangelize and
    establish churches among unreached tribal people.
    Involved in linguistics, literacy, missionary orientation
    and training, aviation, broadcasting and Bible translation.
TOTAL INCOME: $6,995,256   FOR OVERSEAS MINISTRIES: $6,995,256
PERSONNEL:

NORTH AMERICANS OVERSEAS		NON-NORTH AMERICANS OVERSEAS:	87
MARRIED:	NR	NORTH AMERICAN ADM. STAFF:	NR
SINGLE MEN:	NR	SHORT TERM:	30
SINGLE WOMEN:	NR	RETIRED:	0

TOTAL ACTIVE: 1385

FIELD OF SERVICE	YEAR BEGAN	PERSONNEL NOW	NEW	RELATED CHURCHES	PEOPLE GROUPS	NOTES
Australia	1956	27				
Bolivia	1942	113				
Brazil	1945	206				
Colombia	1945	54				
India	1945	3				
Indonesia	1970	115				
Japan	1949	5				
Mexico	1943	27				
Panama	1953	60				
Papua New Guinea	1950	175				
Paraguay	1946	76				
Philippines	1951	127				
Senegal	1954	64				
Thailand	1951	48				
United Kingdom	1970	10				
Venezuela	1946	99				

New Tribes Mission of Canada

P.O. ADDRESS:
Box 707
Durham ON N0G 1R0
Canada

Tel. (519) 369-2622
EXECUTIVE OFFICER: Chester Plimtton
ORGANIZED: 1968
DESCRIPTION: A nondenominational sending agency of
    fundamentalist tradition seeking to evangelize and
    establish churches among unreached tribal people. Involved
    in linguistics, literacy training and Bible translation.
TOTAL INCOME: $821,888   FOR OVERSEAS MINISTRIES: $607,698
PERSONNEL:

NORTH AMERICANS OVERSEAS		NON-NORTH AMERICANS OVERSEAS:	NR
MARRIED:	NR	NORTH AMERICAN ADM. STAFF:	23
SINGLE MEN:	NR	SHORT TERM:	2
SINGLE WOMEN:	NR	RETIRED:	3

TOTAL ACTIVE: 148

New York International Bible Society

144 Tices Ln.
East Brunswick NJ 08816

Tel. (201) 238-5454
EXECUTIVE OFFICER: Y. R. Kindberg
ORGANIZED: 1809
DESCRIPTION: A specialized agency involved in Bible
    publication and world-wide Bible distribution. Limited to
    publication of Scripture.
TOTAL INCOME: $1,973,500   FOR OVERSEAS MINISTRIES: NR
PERSONNEL:
    NORTH AMERICANS OVERSEAS   NON-NORTH AMERICANS OVERSEAS: 0
          MARRIED: 0   NORTH AMERICAN ADM. STAFF: 20
       SINGLE MEN: 0   SHORT TERM: 0
     SINGLE WOMEN: 0   RETIRED: 4

     TOTAL ACTIVE: 0

Next Towns Crusade, Inc.

3015 Gainsborough
San Antonio TX 78230

Tel. (512) 344-7467
EXECUTIVE OFFICER: John M. Bell
ORGANIZED: 1957
DESCRIPTION: A nondenominational sending agency of Pentecostal
    and charismatic tradition establishing and constructing
    churches and engaged in Bible and literature distribution,
    evangelism, training and recruiting. Also supports
    nationals and promotes an apostolic team ministry.
TOTAL INCOME: $155,000   FOR OVERSEAS MINISTRIES: $152,000
PERSONNEL:
    NORTH AMERICANS OVERSEAS   NON-NORTH AMERICANS OVERSEAS: 8
          MARRIED: 6   NORTH AMERICAN ADM. STAFF: 0
       SINGLE MEN: 0   SHORT TERM: 0
     SINGLE WOMEN: 2   RETIRED: 0

     TOTAL ACTIVE: 8

FIELD OF SERVICE	YEAR BEGAN	PERSONNEL NOW	PERSONNEL NEW	RELATED CHURCHES	PEOPLE GROUPS	NOTES
Japan	1957	2		15		
Mexico	1957	6		14		

Nora Lam Ministries

3595 Almaden Rd.
San Jose CA 95118
P.O. ADDRESS:
Box 24466
San Jose CA 95154

Tel. (408) 267-5451
EXECUTIVE OFFICER: Fred Choeck
ORGANIZED: 1971
DESCRIPTION: A nondenominational agency of independent and
    charismatic tradition using mass media, mass evangelism,
    childcare programs, literature and Bible distribution to
    reach Chinese people worldwide.
TOTAL INCOME: NA   FOR OVERSEAS MINISTRIES: NA
PERSONNEL:
    NORTH AMERICANS OVERSEAS   NON-NORTH AMERICANS OVERSEAS: NR
          MARRIED: 0   NORTH AMERICAN ADM. STAFF: 12
       SINGLE MEN: 0   SHORT TERM: NR

```
SINGLE WOMEN:     0                          RETIRED:      0
                -----
TOTAL ACTIVE:     0
```

North Africa Mission

239 Fairfield Ave.
Upper Darby PA 19082

Tel. (215) 352-2003
EXECUTIVE OFFICER: Greg Livingston
ORGANIZED: 1881   AFFILIATION: IFMA
DESCRIPTION: An interdenominational sending agency of
   evangelical tradition establishing churches and engaged in
   radio broadcasting, correspondence courses, literature
   production and theological education by extension (TEE).
TOTAL INCOME: $884,688   FOR OVERSEAS MINISTRIES: $726,672
PERSONNEL:
   NORTH AMERICANS OVERSEAS   NON-NORTH AMERICANS OVERSEAS: 0
           MARRIED: 48   NORTH AMERICAN ADM. STAFF: 14
        SINGLE MEN: 4   SHORT TERM: 4
      SINGLE WOMEN: 20   RETIRED: 4

      TOTAL ACTIVE: 72

                   YEAR   PERSONNEL   RELATED   PEOPLE
FIELD OF SERVICE   BEGAN   NOW   NEW   CHURCHES GROUPS NOTES

Algeria   1881   7   3   2
France   1963   45   19   2
Morocco   1884   9   2   7   2
Tunisia   1885   11   2   2   1
```

## North American Baptist General
## Missionary Society, Inc.

1 S. 210 Summit Ave.
Oakbrook Terrace IL 60181

Tel. (312) 495-2000
EXECUTIVE OFFICER: Fred Folkerts
ORGANIZED: 1883   AFFILIATION: EFMA
DESCRIPTION:  A denominational sending agency of Baptist
   tradition establishing and nurturing national churches.
   Also engaged in church construction, fund raising,
   evangelism and aid/relief.
TOTAL INCOME: $3,000,000   FOR OVERSEAS MINISTRIES: $1,200,000
PERSONNEL:
   NORTH AMERICANS OVERSEAS    NON-NORTH AMERICANS OVERSEAS:    0
           MARRIED:   62          NORTH AMERICAN ADM. STAFF:    5
        SINGLE MEN:    4                         SHORT TERM:    8
      SINGLE WOMEN:   27                           RETIRED:    4
                     -----
      TOTAL ACTIVE:   93
NOTES:  Income includes USA and Canadian offices.

--------------------------------------------------------------
                   YEAR    PERSONNEL    RELATED   PEOPLE
FIELD OF SERVICE   BEGAN   NOW   NEW    CHURCHES  GROUPS  NOTES
--------------------------------------------------------------
Brazil             1966    8     2       41        5
Cameroon           1936    49    18      572       40
Japan              1951    20    7       6         5
Nigeria            1961    16    3       115       20
```

North American Committee for IME, Institut Medical Evangelique

3063 Virginia Ave S. Apt6
Minneapolis MN 55426

Tel. (612) 933-5436
EXECUTIVE OFFICER: Glen W. Tuttle
ORGANIZED: 1951   AFFILIATION: DOM-NCCCUSA
DESCRIPTION: An interdenominational fund raising agency of
    evangelical tradition supporting a medical ministry in
    Zaire.
TOTAL INCOME: $8,187   FOR OVERSEAS MINISTRIES: $8,187
PERSONNEL:
    NORTH AMERICANS OVERSEAS   NON-NORTH AMERICANS OVERSEAS: 0
           MARRIED: 0   NORTH AMERICAN ADM. STAFF: 0
      SINGLE MEN: 0   SHORT TERM: 0
    SINGLE WOMEN: 0   RETIRED: 0

    TOTAL ACTIVE: 0

North Burma Christian Mission SEE: Christian Churches/Churches of Christ

North East India General Mission, Inc.

100 W Park Ave.
Myerstown PA 10767
P.O. ADDRESS:
Box 186
Myerstown PA 10767

Tel. (717) 866-2181
EXECUTIVE OFFICER: Duane M. Ray
ORGANIZED: 1910
DESCRIPTION: A nondenominational fund raising agency of
    evangelical tradition supporting national workers in
    Manipur, North East India.
TOTAL INCOME: $97,000   FOR OVERSEAS MINISTRIES: $90,000
PERSONNEL:
    NORTH AMERICANS OVERSEAS   NON-NORTH AMERICANS OVERSEAS: NR
           MARRIED: 0   NORTH AMERICAN ADM. STAFF: 2
      SINGLE MEN: 0   SHORT TERM: 0
    SINGLE WOMEN: 0   RETIRED: NR

    TOTAL ACTIVE: 0

Northwest Yearly Meeting of Friends Church, Department of Missions

600 E Third St.
Newberg OR 97132
P.O. ADDRESS:
Box 190
Newberg OR 97132

Tel. (503) 538-9419
EXECUTIVE OFFICER: Roger G. Knox
ORGANIZED: 1893   AFFILIATION: EFMA
DESCRIPTION: A denominational sending agency of Friends
    tradition establishing churches, supporting national
    churches and involved in evangelism, education and
    literature.
TOTAL INCOME: $304,960   FOR OVERSEAS MINISTRIES: $247,852
PERSONNEL:
    NORTH AMERICANS OVERSEAS   NON-NORTH AMERICANS OVERSEAS: 0
           MARRIED: 16   NORTH AMERICAN ADM. STAFF: 1
      SINGLE MEN: 0   SHORT TERM: 1

```
SINGLE WOMEN:     0                          RETIRED:    NR
                -----
     TOTAL ACTIVE:   16
-------------------------------------------------------------------
                    YEAR     PERSONNEL    RELATED   PEOPLE
FIELD OF SERVICE    BEGAN    NOW   NEW    CHURCHES  GROUPS   NOTES
-------------------------------------------------------------------
Bolivia             1931      8     2       160
Peru                1961      8     4        27
```

Nurses Christian Fellowship SEE: Inter-Varsity Christian Fellowship

O.C. Ministries, Inc.

3033 Scott Blvd.
Santa Clara CA 95052
P.O. ADDRESS:
Box 66
Santa Clara CA 95052

```
Tel. (408) 727-7111
EXECUTIVE OFFICER: Clyde Cook
ORGANIZED: 1950     AFFILIATION: EFMA
DESCRIPTION:  Founded as Overseas Crusades, Inc. Name changed
   in 1979. An interdenominational sending agency of
   evangelical tradition engaged in evangelism and mission
   related research. Primarily dedicated to motivating,
   training and mobilizing churches for church planting and
   disciple making.
TOTAL INCOME:  $3,334,152   FOR OVERSEAS MINISTRIES:  $3,334,152
PERSONNEL:
   NORTH AMERICANS OVERSEAS   NON-NORTH AMERICANS OVERSEAS:    2
              MARRIED:   70       NORTH AMERICAN ADM. STAFF:    7
          SINGLE MEN:    1                      SHORT TERM:  207
        SINGLE WOMEN:    2                         RETIRED:    2
                       -----
     TOTAL ACTIVE:   73
-------------------------------------------------------------------
                    YEAR     PERSONNEL    RELATED   PEOPLE
FIELD OF SERVICE    BEGAN    NOW   NEW    CHURCHES  GROUPS   NOTES
-------------------------------------------------------------------
Brazil              1963     20     8
Colombia            1963      8     8
France              1979      2     2
Greece              1966      3     1
Guatemala           1979      2     2
Indonesia           1968      8     4
Mexico              1979      2     2
Philippines         1952     18     6
Sri Lanka           1979      6     6
Taiwan Rep of China 1950      4     2
```

OMI Brotherhood Foundation of America, Inc.

248 Highland Dr.
Findlay OH 45840

```
Tel. (419) 423-2760
EXECUTIVE OFFICER: Robert B. Balcomb
ORGANIZED: 1905
DESCRIPTION:  A nondenominational fund raising agency of
   ecumenical tradition for the OMI Brotherhood of Japan.
   Funds now used for scholarships to support both USA and
   foreign students at United Theological Seminary in
   Dayton, Ohio.
TOTAL INCOME:         $554        FOR OVERSEAS MINISTRIES:    $0
```

PERSONNEL:
```
    NORTH AMERICANS OVERSEAS    NON-NORTH AMERICANS OVERSEAS:    0
             MARRIED:    0          NORTH AMERICAN ADM. STAFF:    0
          SINGLE MEN:    0                       SHORT TERM:    0
        SINGLE WOMEN:    0                          RETIRED:    0
                     -----
        TOTAL ACTIVE:    0
```

OMS International, Inc.

1200 Fry Rd.
Greenwood IN 46142
P.O. ADDRESS:
Box A
Greenwood IN 46142

Tel. (317) 881-6751
EXECUTIVE OFFICER: Wesley L. Duewel
ORGANIZED: 1901   AFFILIATION: EFMA
DESCRIPTION: Founded as Oriental Missionary Society. Name
   changed in 1973. A nondenominational sending agency of
   evangelical and Wesleyan tradition engaged in radio and TV
   broadcasting, theological education, evangelism, medicine
   and nurture or support of national churches.
TOTAL INCOME: $7,676,708   FOR OVERSEAS MINISTRIES: $5,248,055
PERSONNEL:
```
    NORTH AMERICANS OVERSEAS    NON-NORTH AMERICANS OVERSEAS:    19
             MARRIED:  193          NORTH AMERICAN ADM. STAFF:  138
          SINGLE MEN:    2                       SHORT TERM:   40
        SINGLE WOMEN:   36                          RETIRED:   33
                     -----
        TOTAL ACTIVE:  231
```

FIELD OF SERVICE	YEAR BEGAN	PERSONNEL NOW	NEW	RELATED CHURCHES	PEOPLE GROUPS	NOTES
Brazil	1950	23	10	50	3	
Colombia	1943	29	19	49	3	
Ecuador	1952	40	26	10	2	
Greece	1947	4	2	3		
Haiti	1958	39	21	44		
Hong-Kong	1954	6	2	8	1	
India	1941	11	4	128	7	
Indonesia	1970	20	11	17	2	
Japan	1901	20	2	135	1	
Korea, Rep. of	1907	12	7	956	2	
Spain	1972	25	17	1	1	
Taiwan Rep of China	1951	21	24	59	1	

Open Air Campaigners (USA)

1028 College Ave.
Wheaton IL 60187
P.O. ADDRESS:
Box 469
Wheaton IL 60187

Tel. (312) 665-0313
EXECUTIVE OFFICER: Urban Meyer
ORGANIZED: 1956
DESCRIPTION: An interdenominational sending agency of
   fundamentalist tradition engaged in open-air evangelism,
   correspondence courses and training. Also works to
   recruit nationals.
TOTAL INCOME: $187,000   FOR OVERSEAS MINISTRIES: $51,653

```
PERSONNEL:
   NORTH AMERICANS OVERSEAS      NON-NORTH AMERICANS OVERSEAS:    1
              MARRIED:    3         NORTH AMERICAN ADM. STAFF:    5
           SINGLE MEN:    0                      SHORT TERM:      0
         SINGLE WOMEN:    0                        RETIRED:      NR
                      -----
        TOTAL ACTIVE:    3
```

FIELD OF SERVICE	YEAR BEGAN	PERSONNEL NOW	NEW	RELATED CHURCHES	PEOPLE GROUPS	NOTES
Germany, Fed. Rep.	1963	4				
Italy	1969	1				

Open Bible Ministries, Inc.

P.O. ADDRESS:
Box 148
Honesdale PA 18431

Tel. (717) 253-1544
EXECUTIVE OFFICER: Bruce R. Burke
ORGANIZED: 1971
DESCRIPTION: A nondenominational sending agency of evangelical
   and Baptist tradition establishing churches and engaged
   in evangelism, education and literature distribution.
TOTAL INCOME: $30,000   FOR OVERSEAS MINISTRIES: $19,000

```
PERSONNEL:
   NORTH AMERICANS OVERSEAS      NON-NORTH AMERICANS OVERSEAS:    4
              MARRIED:   NR         NORTH AMERICAN ADM. STAFF:    3
           SINGLE MEN:  NR                      SHORT TERM:      0
         SINGLE WOMEN:  NR                        RETIRED:      0
                      -----
        TOTAL ACTIVE:    3
```

FIELD OF SERVICE	YEAR BEGAN	PERSONNEL NOW	NEW	RELATED CHURCHES	PEOPLE GROUPS	NOTES
Bophuthatswana	1974					
South Africa	1971	2				
Transkei	1976	2				

Open Bible Standard Missions, Inc.

2020 Bell Ave.
Des Moines IA 50315

Tel. (515) 288-6761
EXECUTIVE OFFICER: Paul V. Canfield
ORGANIZED: 1935   AFFILIATION: EFMA
DESCRIPTION: A denominational sending agency of evangelical
   and Pentecostal tradition establishing churches and
   involved in evangelism, radio and TV broadcasting,
   theological education and correspondence courses.
TOTAL INCOME: NR   FOR OVERSEAS MINISTRIES: $470,000

```
PERSONNEL:
   NORTH AMERICANS OVERSEAS      NON-NORTH AMERICANS OVERSEAS:    0
              MARRIED:   26         NORTH AMERICAN ADM. STAFF:    2
           SINGLE MEN:    0                      SHORT TERM:      2
         SINGLE WOMEN:    8                        RETIRED:      0
                      -----
        TOTAL ACTIVE:   34
```

FIELD OF SERVICE	YEAR BEGAN	PERSONNEL NOW	NEW	RELATED CHURCHES	PEOPLE GROUPS	NOTES
Cuba				11		

FIELD OF SERVICE	YEAR BEGAN	PERSONNEL NOW	PERSONNEL NEW	RELATED CHURCHES	PEOPLE GROUPS	NOTES
El Salvador	1975	2	2	7		
Ghana	1971	1		7		
Guatemala	1975			6		
Haiti	1976	2	2			
Jamaica	1948			23		
Japan				8		
Liberia	1935	9	1	18		
Mexico	1965	2	2	3		
Papua New Guinea	1973	2		6		
Philippines	1978	4	4			
Puerto Rico	1958	4	2	1		
Spain	1969	2		3		
Trinidad and Tobago	1953			65		

Open Door Missionary Fellowship, Inc.

1044 Pershall Rd.
East St. Louis MO 63137
P.O. ADDRESS:
Box 13619
East St. Louis MO 63137

Tel. (314) 868-2203
EXECUTIVE OFFICER: Herbert H. Peters
ORGANIZED: 1952
DESCRIPTION: A service agency of evangelical tradition
    involved in evangelism in black communities, literature
    distribution and production. The literature is sent to
    every state in the USA and any English-speaking country in
    Africa.

TOTAL INCOME: NR   FOR OVERSEAS MINISTRIES: NR
PERSONNEL:
    NORTH AMERICANS OVERSEAS   NON-NORTH AMERICANS OVERSEAS: NR
            MARRIED: NR   NORTH AMERICAN ADM. STAFF: 23
        SINGLE MEN: NR   SHORT TERM: 1
      SINGLE WOMEN: NR   RETIRED: 0

        TOTAL ACTIVE: NR

Open Doors With Brother Andrew

3423 E Chapman Ave.
Orange CA 92669
P.O. ADDRESS:
Box 2020
Orange CA 92669

Tel. (714) 639-6802
EXECUTIVE OFFICER: Brother Andrew
ORGANIZED: 1955
DESCRIPTION: A denominational service and sending agency of
    evangelical tradition involved primarily in Bible
    distribution in limited access or closed countries. Also
    engaged in missionary orientation and training, mission
    related research and support of nationals.

TOTAL INCOME: $5,000,000   FOR OVERSEAS MINISTRIES: $3,600,000
PERSONNEL:
    NORTH AMERICANS OVERSEAS   NON-NORTH AMERICANS OVERSEAS: 16
            MARRIED: 12   NORTH AMERICAN ADM. STAFF: 10
        SINGLE MEN: 1   SHORT TERM: 100

```
SINGLE WOMEN:    3                        RETIRED:      0
                 -----
     TOTAL ACTIVE:   16
NOTES:  Income estimated by agency.
--------------------------------------------------------------------
                   YEAR     PERSONNEL    RELATED    PEOPLE
FIELD OF SERVICE   BEGAN    NOW   NEW    CHURCHES   GROUPS  NOTES
--------------------------------------------------------------------
Brazil
Cyprus
Netherlands
Philippines
South Africa
```

Operation Eyesight Universal

916 36th Street NW
Calgary AB T2N 3A8
Canada
P.O. ADDRESS:
Box 123
Calgary AB T2P 2H6
Canada

Tel. (403) 283-6323
EXECUTIVE OFFICER: Arthur T. Jenkyns
ORGANIZED: 1963
DESCRIPTION: A nondenominational, nonsectarian service agency
     assisting developing countries in the prevention and cure
     of blindness by supporting hospitals and medical
     personnel.

```
TOTAL INCOME:  $1,030,324   FOR OVERSEAS MINISTRIES:  $1,030,324
PERSONNEL:
    NORTH AMERICANS OVERSEAS   NON-NORTH AMERICANS OVERSEAS:    0
              MARRIED:   0        NORTH AMERICAN ADM. STAFF:    2
           SINGLE MEN:   0                     SHORT TERM:      0
         SINGLE WOMEN:   0                      RETIRED:        0
                       -----
         TOTAL ACTIVE:   0
--------------------------------------------------------------------
                   YEAR     PERSONNEL    RELATED    PEOPLE
FIELD OF SERVICE   BEGAN    NOW   NEW    CHURCHES   GROUPS  NOTES
--------------------------------------------------------------------
Bangladesh         1972
Caribbean-general  1977
Haiti              1977
India              1963
Kenya              1973
Liberia            1979
Nepal              1977
Pakistan           1976
Peru               1978
Tanzania           1979
Upper Volta        1980
```

Operation Mobilization—Canada

P.O. ADDRESS:
Box 9
Port Colborne ON L3K 5V7
Canada

Tel. (416) 835-2546
EXECUTIVE OFFICER: Bert Kamphuis
ORGANIZED: 1957
DESCRIPTION: An interdenominational sending agency of
     evangelical tradition engaged primariliy in short-term
     youth training using two ocean-going ships to evangelize,

train and disciple in 35 countries. Also involved in
establishing churches and literature production and
distribution.
TOTAL INCOME: $255,000   FOR OVERSEAS MINISTRIES: $255,000
PERSONNEL:
   NORTH AMERICANS OVERSEAS   NON-NORTH AMERICANS OVERSEAS: 400
         MARRIED: 22   NORTH AMERICAN ADM. STAFF: 6
     SINGLE MEN: 17   SHORT TERM: 25
   SINGLE WOMEN: 17   RETIRED: 0

   TOTAL ACTIVE: 56
NOTES: Total for short-termers includes USA
      and Canada. There are 2500 summer program
      short-termers worldwide.

FIELD OF SERVICE	YEAR BEGAN	PERSONNEL NOW	PERSONNEL NEW	RELATED CHURCHES	PEOPLE GROUPS	NOTES
Austria	1962	40		50		
Bangladesh	1972	30		10		
Belgium	1962	92		50		
Cyprus						
Egypt						
Finland	1970	4		30		
France	1962	39				
Germany, Fed. Rep.	1962	27		100		
India	1963	332		100	10	
Israel	1966	17		10		
Middle East-general	1963	63		20		
Nepal	1964	2		5		
Netherlands	1962	5		100		
Pakistan	1978	49		10		
Singapore	1971	5		50		
Sudan						
Sweden	1964	10		50		
Switzerland	1963	7		30		
Turkey	1963	26		5		
United Kingdom	1962	168				

   Note: 1. Figures reflect both
Canadian and nationals.
2. Two ships, the Doulos and Logos,
carry 392 people for ocean-going
evangelism and training.

Operation Mobilization Send the Light, Inc.

244 Godwin Ave.
Ridgewood NJ 07450
P.O. ADDRESS:
Box 148
Midland Park NJ 07432

Tel. (201) 447-3715
EXECUTIVE OFFICER: Paul Troper
ORGANIZED: 1958
DESCRIPTION: An interdenominational sending agency of
   evangelical tradition engaged in evangelism and literature,
   primarily using short-term personnel. Involved in
   recruiting and training of young people for evangelism.
   Two ocean-going ships are used as an evangelism and
   training center. The fellowship includes workers in 40
   countries. Short-term assignments are for two months to
   two years.
TOTAL INCOME: $1,000,000   FOR OVERSEAS MINISTRIES: $1,000,000

```
PERSONNEL:
      NORTH AMERICANS OVERSEAS      NON-NORTH AMERICANS OVERSEAS:    NR
                MARRIED:  120          NORTH AMERICAN ADM. STAFF:    20
             SINGLE MEN:  100                       SHORT TERM:     200
           SINGLE WOMEN:   75                          RETIRED:       0
                         -----
           TOTAL ACTIVE:  295
NOTES:   Total income estimated by agency.
         Overseas income estimated by MARC.
```

FIELD OF SERVICE	YEAR BEGAN	PERSONNEL NOW	NEW	RELATED CHURCHES	PEOPLE GROUPS	NOTES
Austria	1961	10				
Belgium	1961	30				
Finland						
France	1961	25				
Germany, Fed. Rep.						
India	1964	50				
Iran	1964	10				
Jordan						
Lebanon	1965	20				
Mexico	1958	20				
Nepal						
Singapore						
Sweden						
Switzerland						
United Kingdom						

```
     Note: Much of the information is
     from the 1976 directory.
```

Organization of Continuing Education for American Nurses (OCEAN)

6219 St. Andrews Rd.
Columbia SC 29210
P.O. ADDRESS:
Box 21276
Columbia SC 29221

Tel. (803) 772-4273
EXECUTIVE OFFICER: Sharon Smith
ORGANIZED: 1975   AFFILIATION: IFMA-Candidate/EFMA-Assoc.
DESCRIPTION: An interdenominational specialized service agency
    of evangelical tradition providing continuing education
    for American nurses serving overseas, and also working
    toward unifying national and expatriate nurses in emerging
    nations of the world. Provides nursing education
    workshops, distributes professional literature and works
    with mission societies concerning pre-field medical
    orientation. Membership is approximately 1000. Have
    presented 17 workshops in 16 countries, reaching over 500
    nurses from 50 nations.

```
TOTAL INCOME:      $68,000          FOR OVERSEAS MINISTRIES:    NR
PERSONNEL:
      NORTH AMERICANS OVERSEAS      NON-NORTH AMERICANS OVERSEAS:    0
                MARRIED:    0          NORTH AMERICAN ADM. STAFF:   18
             SINGLE MEN:    0                       SHORT TERM:      0
           SINGLE WOMEN:    0                          RETIRED:      0
                         -----
           TOTAL ACTIVE:    0
```

Oriental Missionary Crusade, Inc.

126 North Oak Knoll
Pasadena CA 91101
P.O. ADDRESS:
Box 507
Pasadena CA 91102

Tel. (213) 796-3568
EXECUTIVE OFFICER: Gene C. Forrest
ORGANIZED: 1958
DESCRIPTION: An interdenominational sending and service agency
    of evangelical and charismatic tradition ministering in
    the Philippines by establishing churches and conducting
    student evangelism. Also have a boat ministry to remote
    islands and seek to reach forgotten tribes.
TOTAL INCOME: $201,441   FOR OVERSEAS MINISTRIES: $173,239
PERSONNEL:

NORTH AMERICANS OVERSEAS		NON-NORTH AMERICANS OVERSEAS:	0
MARRIED:	12	NORTH AMERICAN ADM. STAFF:	3
SINGLE MEN:	0	SHORT TERM:	1
SINGLE WOMEN:	0	RETIRED:	0
TOTAL ACTIVE:	12		

FIELD OF SERVICE	YEAR BEGAN	PERSONNEL NOW	NEW	RELATED CHURCHES	PEOPLE GROUPS	NOTES
Philippines	1958	12	2	300		

Orinoco River Mission SEE: Evangelical Alliance Mission (TEAM)

Orthodox Presbyterian Church
Committee on Foreign Missions

7401 Old York Rd.
Philadelphia PA 19126

Tel. (215) 635-0700
EXECUTIVE OFFICER: Laurence N. Vail
ORGANIZED: 1937
DESCRIPTION: A denominational sending agency of Presbyterian
    tradition establishing new churches and engaged in
    evangelism, education, literature production and support
    of national churches.
TOTAL INCOME: $5,200,000   FOR OVERSEAS MINISTRIES: $456,000
PERSONNEL:

NORTH AMERICANS OVERSEAS		NON-NORTH AMERICANS OVERSEAS:	2
MARRIED:	22	NORTH AMERICAN ADM. STAFF:	3
SINGLE MEN:	1	SHORT TERM:	7
SINGLE WOMEN:	2	RETIRED:	8
TOTAL ACTIVE:	25		

FIELD OF SERVICE	YEAR BEGAN	PERSONNEL NOW	NEW	RELATED CHURCHES	PEOPLE GROUPS	NOTES
Egypt	1975	4	4	1	1	
Japan	1951	6	2	50	1	
Kenya	1979	2	2	22	1	1
Korea, Rep. of	1937	6	3	4000	1	
Lebanon	1974		3	1	2	
Taiwan Rep of China	1950	6	4	20	1	

1. Two medical personnel seconded
to World Presbyterian Missions.

Osborn Foundation

1400 E Skelly Dr.
Tulsa OK 74105
P.O. ADDRESS:
Box 10
Tulsa OK 74102

EXECUTIVE OFFICER: T. L. Osborn
ORGANIZED: 1949
DESCRIPTION: An interdenominational missionary church agency
    of evangelical tradition engaged in mass evangelism,
    support of nationals and production of literature and
    audio-visual evangelism aids in over 100 languages.
TOTAL INCOME: $50,000   FOR OVERSEAS MINISTRIES: NR
PERSONNEL:
    NORTH AMERICANS OVERSEAS   NON-NORTH AMERICANS OVERSEAS: NR
               MARRIED: NR   NORTH AMERICAN ADM. STAFF: NR
            SINGLE MEN: NR   SHORT TERM: NR
          SINGLE WOMEN: NR   RETIRED: NR

          TOTAL ACTIVE: NR
NOTES: Income estimated by agency.

Ost Evangelistic Ministries SEE: Missionary Revival Crusade

Other Side SEE: Jubilee, Inc.; The Other Side Magazine; Jubilee Crafts; Jubilee Fund

Outreach International

1718 Northcrest Dr.
Arlington TX 76102

Tel. (817) 460-0579
EXECUTIVE OFFICER: Al Hamilton
ORGANIZED: 1977
DESCRIPTION: A nondenominational recruiting service of the
    Christian "Restoration Movement" tradition engaged in
    linguistics, Bible distribution, evangelism, and
    missionary orientation and training. Emphasis on
    recruitment and internship ministries.
TOTAL INCOME: $56,321   FOR OVERSEAS MINISTRIES: $20,000
PERSONNEL:
    NORTH AMERICANS OVERSEAS   NON-NORTH AMERICANS OVERSEAS: 0
               MARRIED: 2   NORTH AMERICAN ADM. STAFF: 5
            SINGLE MEN: 0   SHORT TERM: 0
          SINGLE WOMEN: 0   RETIRED: 0

          TOTAL ACTIVE: 2

FIELD OF SERVICE	YEAR BEGAN	PERSONNEL NOW	NEW	RELATED CHURCHES	PEOPLE GROUPS	NOTES
South Africa	1979	2	2	1	2	

Outreach, Inc.

875 16th St. NE
Salem OR 97301
P.O. ADDRESS:
Box 6
Salem OR 97308

Tel. (503) 363-0097
EXECUTIVE OFFICER: Dave Adams
ORGANIZED: 1965
DESCRIPTION: An interdenominational service agency of
    evangelical tradition involved in fund raising and

transmittal, developing local leadership training and
assisting in outreach projects, particularly with youth
and in prison work.
TOTAL INCOME: $35,000   FOR OVERSEAS MINISTRIES: $20,000
PERSONNEL:
   NORTH AMERICANS OVERSEAS   NON-NORTH AMERICANS OVERSEAS: NR
        MARRIED: NR   NORTH AMERICAN ADM. STAFF: 3
     SINGLE MEN: NR   SHORT TERM: 0
   SINGLE WOMEN: NR   RETIRED: 0

    TOTAL ACTIVE: 1
NOTES: Administrative personnel are volunteers.
       One national supported full time in the
       Philippines.

Outreach, Incorporated

1553 Plainfield Ave. NE
Grand Rapids MI 49505
P.O. ADDRESS:
Box 1000
Grand Rapids MI 49501

Tel. (616) 363-7817
EXECUTIVE OFFICER: Harold Van Broekhoven
ORGANIZED: 1966
DESCRIPTION: A nondenominational service agency of evangelical
    tradition engaged in education through the Institute of
    Theological Studies. Also distributes recorded tapes and
    engaged in the production and distribution of foreign
    language Christian literature. Serves other overseas
    agencies through technical assistance and fund raising.
TOTAL INCOME: $95,385   FOR OVERSEAS MINISTRIES: $60,282
PERSONNEL:
   NORTH AMERICANS OVERSEAS   NON-NORTH AMERICANS OVERSEAS: 0
        MARRIED: 0   NORTH AMERICAN ADM. STAFF: 1
     SINGLE MEN: 0   SHORT TERM: 0
   SINGLE WOMEN: 0   RETIRED: 0

    TOTAL ACTIVE: 0

Overcomer Press, Inc.

310 W Main St.
Owosso MI 48867
P.O. ADDRESS:
Box 177
Owosso MI 48867

Tel. (517) 725-9550
EXECUTIVE OFFICER: Gordon H. Bennett
ORGANIZED: 1963
DESCRIPTION: A nondenominational publishing agency of
    "Plymouth Brethren" tradition producing a missions
    magazine in English, distributed in 45 countries. Also
    provides Spanish literature and is engaged in a
    tape cassette ministry, evangelism and information
    services.
TOTAL INCOME: $24,000   FOR OVERSEAS MINISTRIES: $0
PERSONNEL:
   NORTH AMERICANS OVERSEAS   NON-NORTH AMERICANS OVERSEAS: 0
        MARRIED: 0   NORTH AMERICAN ADM. STAFF: 2
     SINGLE MEN: 0   SHORT TERM: 0
   SINGLE WOMEN: 0   RETIRED: 0

    TOTAL ACTIVE: 0

Overseas Ambassadors SEE: O.C. Ministries, Inc.

Overseas Christian Servicemen's Centers

2100 S Lincoln
Denver CO 80210
P.O. ADDRESS:
Box 10308
Denver CO 80210

Tel. (303) 778-1910
EXECUTIVE OFFICER: David L. Meschke
ORGANIZED: 1954   AFFILIATION: IFMA
DESCRIPTION: A nondenominational sending agency of evangelical
    tradition ministering to servicemen and women overseas
    and on furlough.
TOTAL INCOME: $1,023,456   FOR OVERSEAS MINISTRIES: $839,630
PERSONNEL:
   NORTH AMERICANS OVERSEAS   NON-NORTH AMERICANS OVERSEAS: 0
          MARRIED: 42   NORTH AMERICAN ADM. STAFF: 12
       SINGLE MEN: 2   SHORT TERM: 18
     SINGLE WOMEN: 2   RETIRED: 0

     TOTAL ACTIVE: 46

FIELD OF SERVICE	YEAR BEGAN	PERSONNEL NOW	PERSONNEL NEW	RELATED CHURCHES	PEOPLE GROUPS	NOTES
Germany, Fed. Rep.	1972	19	14			
Japan	1962	13	5			
Korea, Rep. of	1975	3	1			
Panama	1958	2	2			
Philippines	1955	4	2			
Spain	1974	4				

Overseas Crusades, Inc. SEE: O.C. Ministries, Inc.

Overseas Ministries Study Center

6315 Ocean Ave.
Ventnor NJ 08406
P.O. ADDRESS:
Box 2057
Ventnor NJ 08406

Tel. (609) 823-6671
EXECUTIVE OFFICER: Gerald H. Anderson
ORGANIZED: 1923
DESCRIPTION: A nondenominational specialized service agency of
    independent tradition providing continuing education for
    missionaries on furlough and overseas church leaders.
    OMSC is a center for residence and non-residence education
    conducting special study groups and providing guidance to
    mission boards in study and research.
TOTAL INCOME: $495,353   FOR OVERSEAS MINISTRIES: $495,353
PERSONNEL:
   NORTH AMERICANS OVERSEAS   NON-NORTH AMERICANS OVERSEAS: 0
          MARRIED: 0   NORTH AMERICAN ADM. STAFF: 13
       SINGLE MEN: 0   SHORT TERM: 0
     SINGLE WOMEN: 0   RETIRED: NR

     TOTAL ACTIVE: 0

Overseas Missionary Fellowship

1058 Avenue Rd.
Toronto ON M5N 2C6
Canada

Tel. (416) 485-0427
EXECUTIVE OFFICER: David J. Michell
ORGANIZED: 1865   AFFILIATION: IFMA
DESCRIPTION: An international, interdenominational sending
   agency of evangelical tradition establishing churches and
   engaged in student and personal evangelism. Also involved
   in radio and TV broadcasting, literature production and
   distribution, correspondence courses, missionary
   orientation and training and theological education.
TOTAL INCOME: $684,004   FOR OVERSEAS MINISTRIES: $684,004
PERSONNEL:

NORTH AMERICANS OVERSEAS		NON-NORTH AMERICANS OVERSEAS:	630
MARRIED:	49	NORTH AMERICAN ADM. STAFF:	12
SINGLE MEN:	4	SHORT TERM:	11
SINGLE WOMEN:	43	RETIRED:	32
TOTAL ACTIVE:	96		

NOTES: The breakdown of overseas personnel into
   areas of service is reported by Overseas
   Missionary Fellowship (USA).

FIELD OF SERVICE	YEAR BEGAN	PERSONNEL NOW	PERSONNEL NEW	RELATED CHURCHES	PEOPLE GROUPS	NOTES
France	1979	2	2			
Hong-Kong	1954	14	4			
Indonesia	1954	89	24			
Japan	1951	82	19			
Korea, Rep. of	1968	5	2			
Malaysia	1928	62	17			
Philippines	1951	131	60			
Singapore	1951	19	2			
Taiwan Rep of China	1952	56	20			
Thailand	1952	263	46			

Overseas Missionary Fellowship

404 S Church St.
Robesonia PA 19551

Tel. (215) 693-5881
EXECUTIVE OFFICER: Daniel W. Bacon
ORGANIZED: 1865   AFFILIATION: IFMA
DESCRIPTION: An international sending agency of evangelical
   tradition establishing churches and engaged in evangelism
   and support of national churches. Also involved in
   medicine, Bible translation and literature production and
   distribution.
TOTAL INCOME: $1,426,800   FOR OVERSEAS MINISTRIES: $1,426,800
PERSONNEL:

NORTH AMERICANS OVERSEAS		NON-NORTH AMERICANS OVERSEAS:	580
MARRIED:	115	NORTH AMERICAN ADM. STAFF:	6
SINGLE MEN:	8	SHORT TERM:	5
SINGLE WOMEN:	80	RETIRED:	60
TOTAL ACTIVE:	203		

FIELD OF SERVICE	YEAR BEGAN	PERSONNEL NOW	PERSONNEL NEW	RELATED CHURCHES	PEOPLE GROUPS	NOTES
France	1979	2	2			

418

FIELD OF SERVICE	YEAR BEGAN	PERSONNEL NOW	NEW	RELATED CHURCHES	PEOPLE GROUPS	NOTES
Hong-Kong	1954	14	4			
Indonesia	1954	89	24			
Japan	1951	82	19			
Korea, Rep. of	1968	5	2			
Malaysia	1928	62	17			
Philippines	1951	131	60			
Singapore	1951	19	2			
Taiwan Rep of China	1952	56	20			
Thailand	1952	263	46			

Overseas Radio and Television, Inc.

2306 Yale Ave. East
Seattle WA 98102
P.O. ADDRESS:
Box 118
Seattle WA 98111

Tel. (206) 324-0676
EXECUTIVE OFFICER: Leland Haggerty
ORGANIZED: 1960
DESCRIPTION: An interdenominational, specialized service
    agency in Christian arts and media, providing radio and TV
    productions for Asia. Active with music, drama, records,
    youth rallies and evangelistic outreach. Training
    nationals in all phases of mass communications.
TOTAL INCOME: NR   FOR OVERSEAS MINISTRIES: $88,000
PERSONNEL:
    NORTH AMERICANS OVERSEAS   NON-NORTH AMERICANS OVERSEAS: 2
            MARRIED: 2   NORTH AMERICAN ADM. STAFF: 1
          SINGLE MEN: 0   SHORT TERM: 3
        SINGLE WOMEN: 2   RETIRED: 0

        TOTAL ACTIVE: 4
NOTES: Overseas income estimated by MARC.

FIELD OF SERVICE	YEAR BEGAN	PERSONNEL NOW	NEW	RELATED CHURCHES	PEOPLE GROUPS	NOTES
Taiwan Rep of China	1960	4	1		3	

Overseas Students Mission SEE: Christian Aid Mission

Pacific Broadcasting Association, Inc.

106 N Dorchester
Wheaton IL 60187
P.O. ADDRESS:
Box 941
Wheaton IL 60187

Tel. (312) 653-6967
EXECUTIVE OFFICER: Bernard E. Holritz
ORGANIZED: 1951
DESCRIPTION: A nondenominational service agency which is the
    North American representative of the Japan-based parent
    organization. Produces radio and TV programs directed to
    Japanese-speaking people. Overseas North American staff
    are on loan from other agencies.
TOTAL INCOME: $87,397   FOR OVERSEAS MINISTRIES: $87,397

```
PERSONNEL:
     NORTH AMERICANS OVERSEAS    NON-NORTH AMERICANS OVERSEAS:    0
             MARRIED:    0          NORTH AMERICAN ADM. STAFF:    0
          SINGLE MEN:    0                         SHORT TERM:    0
        SINGLE WOMEN:    0                            RETIRED:    0
                        -----
        TOTAL ACTIVE:    0
```

| | YEAR | PERSONNEL | | RELATED | PEOPLE | |
FIELD OF SERVICE	BEGAN	NOW	NEW	CHURCHES	GROUPS	NOTES
Japan	1951	4				

Missionary personnel are on loan
from other organizations.

Pan American Missionary Society, Inc.

P.O. ADDRESS:
Box 4598
Pensacola FL 32507

Tel. (904) 944-2886
EXECUTIVE OFFICER: David L. Bergman
ORGANIZED: 1958
DESCRIPTION: A nondenominational sending agency of evangelical
    and independent tradition engaged in church planting,
    radio and TV broadcasting, education, evangelism and
    support of nationals.

```
TOTAL INCOME:    $34,933   FOR OVERSEAS MINISTRIES:    $34,933
PERSONNEL:
     NORTH AMERICANS OVERSEAS    NON-NORTH AMERICANS OVERSEAS:    0
             MARRIED:    2          NORTH AMERICAN ADM. STAFF:    3
          SINGLE MEN:    0                         SHORT TERM:    0
        SINGLE WOMEN:    0                            RETIRED:    0
                        -----
        TOTAL ACTIVE:    2
```
NOTES: Administrative personnel are part-time
        volunteers.

| | YEAR | PERSONNEL | | RELATED | PEOPLE | |
FIELD OF SERVICE	BEGAN	NOW	NEW	CHURCHES	GROUPS	NOTES
Colombia	1974					
Costa Rica	1961	2				
Mexico	1958	1	1	3	1	1
Panama	1958			7	4	

Note: 1. Receives only partial support.

Pan American Missions, Inc.

155 Gardenia Ct.
Ontario CA 91762
P.O. ADDRESS:
Box 4128
Whittier CA 90605

Tel. (714) 983-2889
EXECUTIVE OFFICER: Claud Cook
ORGANIZED: 1959
DESCRIPTION: A nondenominational agency of Baptist tradition
    involved in evangelism and field ministry in Mexico. Also
    provides medical care (including dentistry), aid and
    relief, and distribution of literature and Bibles.

```
TOTAL INCOME:    $7,000        FOR OVERSEAS MINISTRIES:    NR
PERSONNEL:
     NORTH AMERICANS OVERSEAS    NON-NORTH AMERICANS OVERSEAS:    NR
             MARRIED:    2          NORTH AMERICAN ADM. STAFF:    2
          SINGLE MEN:    0                         SHORT TERM:    3
```

```
      SINGLE WOMEN:     0                          RETIRED:    NR
                      -----
      TOTAL ACTIVE:     2
    ---------------------------------------------------------------
                        YEAR      PERSONNEL   RELATED    PEOPLE
    FIELD OF SERVICE    BEGAN     NOW   NEW   CHURCHES   GROUPS  NOTES
    ---------------------------------------------------------------
    Mexico              1959       2
```

Paul Carlson Medical Program, Inc.

3305 W Foster Ave.
Chicago IL 60625

Tel. (312) 539-5181
EXECUTIVE OFFICER: Arthur M. Lundblad
ORGANIZED: 1966
DESCRIPTION: A nondenominational sending agency of evangelical
    tradition primarily serving in the area of medicine but
    also involved in community development, self-help
    projects, technical and agricultural assistance.
TOTAL INCOME: $201,381   FOR OVERSEAS MINISTRIES: $160,896
PERSONNEL:

```
    NORTH AMERICANS OVERSEAS    NON-NORTH AMERICANS OVERSEAS:    0
              MARRIED:   10        NORTH AMERICAN ADM. STAFF:    3
           SINGLE MEN:   2                      SHORT TERM:    3
         SINGLE WOMEN:   1                        RETIRED:    0
                       -----
         TOTAL ACTIVE:  13
    ---------------------------------------------------------------
                        YEAR      PERSONNEL   RELATED    PEOPLE
    FIELD OF SERVICE    BEGAN     NOW   NEW   CHURCHES   GROUPS  NOTES
    ---------------------------------------------------------------
    Zaire               1968      13     7        1
```

Pentecostal Assemblies of Canada, O

Pentecostal Assemblies of Canada, Overseas Missions Department

10 Overlea Blvd.
Toronto, ON, M4H 1A5 Canada
Canada

Tel. (416) 425-1010
EXECUTIVE OFFICER: C. W. Lynn
ORGANIZED: 1919   AFFILIATION: EFMA
DESCRIPTION: A denominational sending agency of Pentecostal
    tradition engaged in evangelism, education and the estab-
    lishment of churches. Also involved with literature
    production and distribution.
TOTAL INCOME: $4,361,452   FOR OVERSEAS MINISTRIES: $3,720,336
PERSONNEL:

```
    NORTH AMERICANS OVERSEAS    NON-NORTH AMERICANS OVERSEAS:   10
              MARRIED:  170        NORTH AMERICAN ADM. STAFF:   12
           SINGLE MEN:   1                      SHORT TERM:   18
         SINGLE WOMEN:  21                        RETIRED:   21
                       -----
         TOTAL ACTIVE:  192
    ---------------------------------------------------------------
                        YEAR      PERSONNEL   RELATED    PEOPLE
    FIELD OF SERVICE    BEGAN     NOW   NEW   CHURCHES   GROUPS  NOTES
    ---------------------------------------------------------------
    Argentina           1925       6     2       309        1
```

FIELD OF SERVICE	YEAR BEGAN	PERSONNEL NOW	PERSONNEL NEW	RELATED CHURCHES	PEOPLE GROUPS	NOTES
Brazil	1963	12	2	112	1	
Caribbean-general	1918	8	2	167	1	
Europe-general	1976	1				
Hong-Kong	1948	6		19		
Kenya	1921	48	20	1618	5	
Liberia	1915	18	7	313	2	
Macao	1961			1		
Malawi	1978	2		25		
Mozambique	1938	1		370		
South Africa	1915	12	1	1400	1	
Taiwan Rep of China	1963	8	2	14		
Tanzania	1921	14	4	372	4	
Thailand	1961	15	2	29	1	
Uganda	1956			265	1	
Zambia	1955	14	6	28	1	
Zimbabwe	1948	2		63	1	

Pentecostal Assemblies of the World, Inc. Foreign Missions Department

3040 N Illinois St.
Indianapolis IN 46208
P.O. ADDRESS:
Box 88271
Indianapolis IN 46208

Tel. (317) 923-3371
EXECUTIVE OFFICER: Joseph Morris
ORGANIZED: 1912
DESCRIPTION: A denominational sending agency of Pentecostal
    tradition involved in education, literature and medicine.
TOTAL INCOME: $166,233   FOR OVERSEAS MINISTRIES: $166,233
PERSONNEL:

NORTH AMERICANS OVERSEAS		NON-NORTH AMERICANS OVERSEAS:	NR
MARRIED:	NR	NORTH AMERICAN ADM. STAFF:	4
SINGLE MEN:	NR	SHORT TERM:	0
SINGLE WOMEN:	NR	RETIRED:	2
TOTAL ACTIVE:	22		

FIELD OF SERVICE	YEAR BEGAN	PERSONNEL NOW	PERSONNEL NEW	RELATED CHURCHES	PEOPLE GROUPS	NOTES
Bahamas		1				
Barbados		2				
Egypt		1				
Ghana		1				
Haiti		4				
India	1976	1				
Liberia		4				
Montserrat	1976	2				
Nigeria		2				
Philippines	1980	2				
United Kingdom	1978	1				

Pentecostal Church of God in America SEE: Pentecostal Church of God-World Missions

Pentecostal Church of God, World Missions Department

2nd and Main Sts.
Joplin MO 64801
P.O. ADDRESS:
Box 816
Joplin MO 64801

Tel. (417) 624-7050
EXECUTIVE OFFICER: Robert W. Boyle
ORGANIZED: 1919   AFFILIATION: EFMA
DESCRIPTION: A denominational sending agency of Pentecostal
    and evangelical tradition establishing churches and
    engaged in church construction, Bible distribution,
    theological education and theological education by
    extension (TEE).
TOTAL INCOME: $500,000   FOR OVERSEAS MINISTRIES: $450,000
PERSONNEL:
    NORTH AMERICANS OVERSEAS   NON-NORTH AMERICANS OVERSEAS: 0
            MARRIED: 28   NORTH AMERICAN ADM. STAFF: 7
         SINGLE MEN: 0   SHORT TERM: 0
       SINGLE WOMEN: 1   RETIRED: 6

       TOTAL ACTIVE: 29

FIELD OF SERVICE	YEAR BEGAN	PERSONNEL NOW	PERSONNEL NEW	RELATED CHURCHES	PEOPLE GROUPS	NOTES
Belize	1956	2		10		
Brazil	1956	2		52		
Cuba	1957			7		
Guatemala	1965	2		65		
Haiti	1952	4		150		
Indonesia	1950	2		75		
Jamaica	1954	2		50		
Japan	1953	2		5		
Mexico	1949	2		55		
Philippines	1950	10		250		
Portugal	1960	2		2		
Trinidad and Tobago	1969			5		

Pentecostal Free Will Baptist Church, Inc.

P.O. ADDRESS:
Box 1081
Dunn NC 28334

Tel. (919) 892-4161
EXECUTIVE OFFICER: Herbert F. Carter
ORGANIZED: 1959
DESCRIPTION: A denominational sending agency of Pentecostal
    tradition establishing churches and engaged in radio
    broadcasting, education, missionary orientation and
    training and support of nationals.
TOTAL INCOME: $265,151   FOR OVERSEAS MINISTRIES: $265,151
PERSONNEL:
    NORTH AMERICANS OVERSEAS   NON-NORTH AMERICANS OVERSEAS: 1
            MARRIED: 1   NORTH AMERICAN ADM. STAFF: 4
         SINGLE MEN: 1   SHORT TERM: 0
       SINGLE WOMEN: 0   RETIRED: 30

       TOTAL ACTIVE: 2

FIELD OF SERVICE	YEAR BEGAN	PERSONNEL NOW	PERSONNEL NEW	RELATED CHURCHES	PEOPLE GROUPS	NOTES
Costa Rica	1978	1	1			

FIELD OF SERVICE	YEAR BEGAN	PERSONNEL NOW	PERSONNEL NEW	RELATED CHURCHES	PEOPLE GROUPS	NOTES
India	1962	1				
Mexico	1963	2				
Nicaragua	1971	1				
Philippines	1969	2				
Puerto Rico	1963	1				
Venezuela	1974	2				

Note: All but two of the overseas personnel are nationals.

Pentecostal Holiness Church-World Missions Department

7300 NW 39th Expressway
Bethany OK 73008
P.O. ADDRESS:
Box 12609
Oklahoma City OK 73159

Tel. (405) 787-7114
EXECUTIVE OFFICER: B. E. Underwood
ORGANIZED: 1904   AFFILIATION: EFMA
DESCRIPTION: A denominational sending agency of Pentecostal
    and Holiness tradition establishing churches and engaged
    in church construction/financing, evangelism and support
    of national churches.
TOTAL INCOME: $1,520,000   FOR OVERSEAS MINISTRIES: $1,520,000
PERSONNEL:
```
        NORTH AMERICANS OVERSEAS    NON-NORTH AMERICANS OVERSEAS:    4
            MARRIED:   76               NORTH AMERICAN ADM. STAFF:   7
         SINGLE MEN:    1                           SHORT TERM:      3
       SINGLE WOMEN:   15                              RETIRED:      9
                      -----
        TOTAL ACTIVE:  92
```

FIELD OF SERVICE	YEAR BEGAN	PERSONNEL NOW	PERSONNEL NEW	RELATED CHURCHES	PEOPLE GROUPS	NOTES
Argentina	1965	4	2	72		
Botswana	1972	2	2	18		
Costa Rica	1930	2	2	26		
Cuba	1952			13		
Haiti	1978	2	2	17		
Hong-Kong	1910	11	5	14	2	
India	1920	10	2	67	3	
Israel	1979	1	1		1	
Kenya	1973	6	6	78	1	
Korea, Rep. of	1979	2	2	142		
Malawi	1950	4	2	24		
Mexico	1931	2		112		
Nigeria	1955			30		
Philippines	1975	6	6	126	1	
South Africa	1913	14	20	300		
United Kingdom	1977	4	4	8	3	
Venezuela	1979	3	3	1		
Zambia	1950	6	4	24		
Zimbabwe	1950	4	4	39		

Peruvian Fellowship SEE: Evangelical Alliance Mission

Petra International, Inc.

406 Heritage
Rockwall TX 75087

Tel. (214) 722-6697
EXECUTIVE OFFICER: Paul Shirley
ORGANIZED: 1977
DESCRIPTION: An interdenominational sending agency of
    evangelical tradition engaged in evangelism, fund
    transmittal and support of nationals and national churches.
TOTAL INCOME: $15,000   FOR OVERSEAS MINISTRIES: $15,000
PERSONNEL:

NORTH AMERICANS OVERSEAS		NON-NORTH AMERICANS OVERSEAS:	0
MARRIED:	7	NORTH AMERICAN ADM. STAFF:	0
SINGLE MEN:	0	SHORT TERM:	0
SINGLE WOMEN:	1	RETIRED:	0
TOTAL ACTIVE:	8		

FIELD OF SERVICE	YEAR BEGAN	PERSONNEL NOW	NEW	RELATED CHURCHES	PEOPLE GROUPS	NOTES
Kenya	1977			6		
Mexico	1977	5		2		
South Africa	1977			1		
United Kingdom	1977					
Zimbabwe	1977	1		4		

Pilgrim Fellowship, Inc., The

1211 Arch St.
Philadelphia PA 19107

Tel. (215) 563-5093
EXECUTIVE OFFICER: E. Schuyler English
ORGANIZED: 1954
DESCRIPTION: An interdenominational sending agency of
    evangelical tradition engaged in recording, broadcasting
    (radio and TV), general Christian education, evangelism
    and literature production.
TOTAL INCOME: $141,430   FOR OVERSEAS MINISTRIES: $113,234
PERSONNEL:

NORTH AMERICANS OVERSEAS		NON-NORTH AMERICANS OVERSEAS:	1
MARRIED:	15	NORTH AMERICAN ADM. STAFF:	2
SINGLE MEN:	0	SHORT TERM:	0
SINGLE WOMEN:	4	RETIRED:	0
TOTAL ACTIVE:	19		

FIELD OF SERVICE	YEAR BEGAN	PERSONNEL NOW	NEW	RELATED CHURCHES	PEOPLE GROUPS	NOTES
Brazil	1948	6				
Japan	1948	8				
South Africa	1949	2	2			
Spain	1976	2	2			
Taiwan Rep of China	1978	1	1			

Pillar of Fire Missions

622 Oakdale Ave.
Chicago IL 60657

Tel. (312) 248-3637
EXECUTIVE OFFICER: Wilbur Konkel
ORGANIZED: 1960
DESCRIPTION: An interdenominational sending agency of
    Episcopal and fundamentalist tradition involved in
    theological and general Christian education, evangelism,

broadcasting and training.
```
TOTAL INCOME:        NA     FOR OVERSEAS MINISTRIES:    $110,000
PERSONNEL:
   NORTH AMERICANS OVERSEAS    NON-NORTH AMERICANS OVERSEAS:    2
            MARRIED:    4         NORTH AMERICAN ADM. STAFF:    5
         SINGLE MEN:    0                      SHORT TERM:    4
       SINGLE WOMEN:    1                        RETIRED:    0
                      -----
       TOTAL ACTIVE:    5
```
NOTES: Overseas income estimated by MARC.

FIELD OF SERVICE	YEAR BEGAN	PERSONNEL NOW	NEW	RELATED CHURCHES	PEOPLE GROUPS	NOTES
Liberia	1960	3	2	16		
Nigeria	1979	2		4		
Spain	1978	5	5	2		
United Kingdom	1930	15	3	2		

Pillar of Fire Society and Schools West African Missions SEE: Pillar of Fire Missions

Pioneer Bible Translators

N Limit St.
Lincoln IL 62656
P.O. ADDRESS:
Box 828
Lincoln IL 62656

Tel. (217) 735-4161
EXECUTIVE OFFICER: Barton McElroy
ORGANIZED: 1974
DESCRIPTION: A denominational service agency of Christian
   "Restoration Movement" tradition operating an institute
   for training Bible translators for the field. Also
   involved in linguistics and literacy, evangelism and
   church planting. Members raise their own support. Funds
   reported are only for institute expenses.
```
TOTAL INCOME:     $28,983        FOR OVERSEAS MINISTRIES:    $0
PERSONNEL:
   NORTH AMERICANS OVERSEAS    NON-NORTH AMERICANS OVERSEAS:    0
            MARRIED:    14        NORTH AMERICAN ADM. STAFF:    2
         SINGLE MEN:    0                      SHORT TERM:    0
       SINGLE WOMEN:    0                        RETIRED:    0
                      -----
       TOTAL ACTIVE:    14
```
NOTES: No overseas income reported because
     members raise their own support.

FIELD OF SERVICE	YEAR BEGAN	PERSONNEL NOW	NEW	RELATED CHURCHES	PEOPLE GROUPS	NOTES
Papua New Guinea	1977	17			5	
Zaire	1980	2			1	

Plymouth Brethren SEE: Brethren Assemblies

Pocket Testament League, Inc.

117 Main St.
Lincoln Park NJ 07035
P.O. ADDRESS:
Box 368
Lincoln Park NJ 07035

Tel. (201) 696-1900
EXECUTIVE OFFICER: Kenneth T. Durman
ORGANIZED: 1908   AFFILIATION: IFMA
DESCRIPTION: A nondenominational, international sending agency
    of evangelical tradition engaged in Scripture distribution
    combined with personal, small group, mass and student
    evangelism.
TOTAL INCOME: $1,192,485   FOR OVERSEAS MINISTRIES: $925,845
PERSONNEL:

NORTH AMERICANS OVERSEAS		NON-NORTH AMERICANS OVERSEAS:	2
MARRIED:	14	NORTH AMERICAN ADM. STAFF:	4
SINGLE MEN:	3	SHORT TERM:	9
SINGLE WOMEN:	3	RETIRED:	2
TOTAL ACTIVE:	20		

FIELD OF SERVICE	YEAR BEGAN	PERSONNEL NOW	NEW	RELATED CHURCHES	PEOPLE GROUPS	NOTES
Brazil	1964	4				
Germany, Fed. Rep.	1960	4				
India	1979					
Indonesia	1965					
Korea, Rep. of	1975					
Philippines	1974					
Portugal	1979					
Spain	1968	1				
Sweden	1973	5				
Taiwan Rep of China	1940	1				
Yugoslavia	1966	3				

Portable Recording Ministries, Inc.

681 Windcrest Dr.
Holland MI 49423

Tel. (616) 396-5291
EXECUTIVE OFFICER: Ronald W. Beery
ORGANIZED: 1967   AFFILIATION: IFMA-Assoc. member
DESCRIPTION: A nondenominational specialized service agency of
    evangelical tradition providing technical assistance to
    missions, missionaries and church workers, particularly in
    the area of tape recording, equipment, supplies and
    overseas technical training programs.
TOTAL INCOME: $1,172,000   FOR OVERSEAS MINISTRIES: $350,000
PERSONNEL:

NORTH AMERICANS OVERSEAS		NON-NORTH AMERICANS OVERSEAS:	0
MARRIED:	0	NORTH AMERICAN ADM. STAFF:	4
SINGLE MEN:	0	SHORT TERM:	0
SINGLE WOMEN:	0	RETIRED:	0
TOTAL ACTIVE:	0		

Practical Missionary Training SEE: CAM International, Practical Missionary Training

Presbyterian Church in America SEE: Mission to the World

Presbyterian Church in America, Mission to the World SEE: Mission to the World

Presbyterian Church in Canada, Board of World Mission

50 Wynford Dr.
Don Mills ON M3C 1J7
Canada

Tel. (416) 441-1111
EXECUTIVE OFFICER: G. A. Malcolm
ORGANIZED: 1875
DESCRIPTION: A denominational sending agency of Presbyterian
    tradition establishing churches and engaged in education,
    evangelism, medicine and research. Also supporting
    national churches and involved in missionary orientation
    and training.
TOTAL INCOME: $2,557,791   FOR OVERSEAS MINISTRIES: $852,591
PERSONNEL:

NORTH AMERICANS OVERSEAS		NON-NORTH AMERICANS OVERSEAS:	1
MARRIED:	22	NORTH AMERICAN ADM. STAFF:	8
SINGLE MEN:	2	SHORT TERM:	11
SINGLE WOMEN:	14	RETIRED:	7
TOTAL ACTIVE:	38		

FIELD OF SERVICE	YEAR BEGAN	PERSONNEL NOW	NEW	RELATED CHURCHES	PEOPLE GROUPS	NOTES
Afghanistan	1974					
Guyana						
India	1898	8				
Japan	1927	7	2			
Malawi		2				
Nepal	1973	3	1			
Nigeria	1956	4	4			
Taiwan Rep of China	1872	11	2			

Presbyterian Church in the United States, Division of International Mission

341 Ponce de Leon Ave.NE
Atlanta GA 30308

Tel. (404) 873-1531
EXECUTIVE OFFICER: G. Thompson Brown
ORGANIZED: 1861   AFFILIATION: DOM-NCCCUSA
DESCRIPTION: A denominational sending agency of Presbyterian
    tradition establishing churches and engaged in medicine,
    theological and general Christian education, and
    agricultural assistance.
TOTAL INCOME: $7,662,854   FOR OVERSEAS MINISTRIES: $4,333,523
PERSONNEL:

NORTH AMERICANS OVERSEAS		NON-NORTH AMERICANS OVERSEAS:	19
MARRIED:	226	NORTH AMERICAN ADM. STAFF:	0
SINGLE MEN:	2	SHORT TERM:	32
SINGLE WOMEN:	31	RETIRED:	NR
TOTAL ACTIVE:	259		

FIELD OF SERVICE	YEAR BEGAN	PERSONNEL NOW	NEW	RELATED CHURCHES	PEOPLE GROUPS	NOTES
Bangladesh	1974	17	15			

FIELD OF SERVICE	YEAR BEGAN	PERSONNEL NOW	PERSONNEL NEW	RELATED CHURCHES	PEOPLE GROUPS	NOTES
Belgium	1973	2				
Brazil	1869	92	10			
Ecuador	1946	6	2			
Fiji	1974	2				
Guatemala	1972	1	1			
Haiti	1974	5	2			
Honduras	1973	2				
India	1976	2	2			
Indonesia	1968	6	2			
Japan	1885	33	4			
Korea, Rep. of	1892	62	17			
Lebanon	1971	2				
Lesotho	1977	2	2			
Mexico	1874	8	3			
Nigeria	1974	2	2			
Rwanda	1975	2	2			
Taiwan Rep of China	1953	18	4			
Zaire	1891	44	19			

Primitive Methodist Church in the USA, International Mission Board

30 Linda Ln.
Lebanon PA 17042

Tel. (717) 273-5951
EXECUTIVE OFFICER: Harold J. Barrett
ORGANIZED: 1921   AFFILIATION: EFMA
DESCRIPTION: A denominational sending agency of Methodist and
     evangelical tradition establishing churches and engaged
     in evangelism, training of nationals, clinic and hospital
     work, primary and secondary Christian education and youth
     camping among nationals.
TOTAL INCOME: $300,082   FOR OVERSEAS MINISTRIES: $290,484
PERSONNEL:
NORTH AMERICANS OVERSEAS		NON-NORTH AMERICANS OVERSEAS:	0
MARRIED:	12	NORTH AMERICAN ADM. STAFF:	2
SINGLE MEN:	1	SHORT TERM:	3
SINGLE WOMEN:	2	RETIRED:	NR
TOTAL ACTIVE:	15		

FIELD OF SERVICE	YEAR BEGAN	PERSONNEL NOW	PERSONNEL NEW	RELATED CHURCHES	PEOPLE GROUPS	NOTES
Guatemala	1921	15	2	80	1	
Spain	1977	2	2	80		

Prison Mission Association Bible Correspondence Fellowship
SEE: Prison Mission Association, Inc.

Prison Mission Association, Inc.

3711 Wallace
Riverside CA 92519
P.O. ADDRESS:
Box 3397
Riverside CA 92519

EXECUTIVE OFFICER: Joe B. Mason
ORGANIZED: 1955
DESCRIPTION: A nondenominational service agency promoting
     Bible study through correspondence courses, particularly

in prisons and to servicemen. Other ministries include
radio broadcasting, motion pictures and literature
distribution.
TOTAL INCOME: $127,432   FOR OVERSEAS MINISTRIES: $13,011
PERSONNEL:
    NORTH AMERICANS OVERSEAS   NON-NORTH AMERICANS OVERSEAS: 1
              MARRIED: 0   NORTH AMERICAN ADM. STAFF: 2
           SINGLE MEN: 0   SHORT TERM: 0
         SINGLE WOMEN: 0   RETIRED: 0

         TOTAL ACTIVE: 0

FIELD OF SERVICE	YEAR BEGAN	PERSONNEL NOW	PERSONNEL NEW	RELATED CHURCHES	PEOPLE GROUPS	NOTES
Cameroon	1972	3			1	
United Kingdom	1967	2			1	

Progressive National Baptist
Convention USA, Inc. Baptist
Foreign Mission Bureau

163 N 60
Philadelphia PA 19139

Tel. (215) 474-3939
EXECUTIVE OFFICER: Goerge S. Bell
ORGANIZED: 1961   AFFILIATION: DOM-NCCCUSA
DESCRIPTION: A denominational agency of Baptist tradition
    supporting education, medical work and nationals.
TOTAL INCOME: NR   FOR OVERSEAS MINISTRIES: NR
PERSONNEL:
    NORTH AMERICANS OVERSEAS   NON-NORTH AMERICANS OVERSEAS: NR
              MARRIED: 0   NORTH AMERICAN ADM. STAFF: NR
           SINGLE MEN: 0   SHORT TERM: NR
         SINGLE WOMEN: 0   RETIRED: NR

         TOTAL ACTIVE: 0

Project Partner with Christ, Inc.

701 N University Blvd.
Middletown OH 45042
P.O. ADDRESS:
Box 1054
Middletown OH 45042

Tel. (513) 425-0938
EXECUTIVE OFFICER: Charles F. Thomas
ORGANIZED: 1968
DESCRIPTION: A nondenominational service and support agency of
    evangelical tradition assisting with aid and relief,
    church construction/financing, medicine and support of
    national churches. Also serves other agencies. (A sister
    organization to Project Partner, Inc.)
TOTAL INCOME: $597,510   FOR OVERSEAS MINISTRIES: $388,020
PERSONNEL:
    NORTH AMERICANS OVERSEAS   NON-NORTH AMERICANS OVERSEAS: 1
              MARRIED: 4   NORTH AMERICAN ADM. STAFF: NR
           SINGLE MEN: 2   SHORT TERM: NR
         SINGLE WOMEN: 2   RETIRED: 0

         TOTAL ACTIVE: 8

Project Partner, Inc.

1007 E Dulle
Marion IL 62959

Tel. (618) 997-1550

EXECUTIVE OFFICER: Charles F. Thomas
ORGANIZED: 1976
DESCRIPTION: A nondenominational service and support agency of
    evangelical tradition engaged primarily in transportation
    and aid through aircraft and medical ship, but also
    involved in aid and relief, education and serving other
    agencies. (A sister organization to Project Partner With
    Christ, Inc.)

TOTAL INCOME:	NR	FOR OVERSEAS MINISTRIES:		NR
PERSONNEL:				
NORTH AMERICANS OVERSEAS		NON-NORTH AMERICANS OVERSEAS:		0
MARRIED:	0	NORTH AMERICAN ADM. STAFF:		3
SINGLE MEN:	0		SHORT TERM:	NR
SINGLE WOMEN:	0		RETIRED:	0
TOTAL ACTIVE:	0			

Protestant Episcopal Church (Order
of the Holy Cross)
Westpark NY 12493

Tel. (914) 384-6660
EXECUTIVE OFFICER: Father Connor Lynn
ORGANIZED: 1884
DESCRIPTION: A denominational sending agency of Episcopal
    tradition involved in education and evangelism in Liberia.
    Order has 70 members worldwide.

TOTAL INCOME:	NR	FOR OVERSEAS MINISTRIES:		$264,000
PERSONNEL:				
NORTH AMERICANS OVERSEAS		NON-NORTH AMERICANS OVERSEAS:		NR
MARRIED:	NR	NORTH AMERICAN ADM. STAFF:		NR
SINGLE MEN:	NR		SHORT TERM:	NR
SINGLE WOMEN:	NR		RETIRED:	NR
TOTAL ACTIVE:	12			

NOTES: Overseas income estimated by MARC.

Prot. Epis, Chr. in the USA Liberian Msn, Order of the Holy Cross
SEE: Prot. Epis. Chr. in the USA (Order of the Holy Cross)

Protestant Episcopal Church in the USA, Section for National and World Mission SEE: World Mission in Church and Society

Protestant Episcopal Church in the
USA, Society of St. Margaret
17 Louisburg Sq.
Boston MA 02108

Tel. (617) 648-6200
EXECUTIVE OFFICER: Sister Ann Marie
ORGANIZED: 1855
DESCRIPTION: A denominational sending agency of Episcopal
    tradition engaged in education.

TOTAL INCOME:	NA	FOR OVERSEAS MINISTRIES:		$88,000
PERSONNEL:				
NORTH AMERICANS OVERSEAS		NON-NORTH AMERICANS OVERSEAS:		NR
MARRIED:	NR	NORTH AMERICAN ADM. STAFF:		NR
SINGLE MEN:	NR		SHORT TERM:	0
SINGLE WOMEN:	NR		RETIRED:	0
TOTAL ACTIVE:	4			

NOTES: Overseas income estimated by MARC.

FIELD OF SERVICE	YEAR BEGAN	PERSONNEL NOW	NEW	RELATED CHURCHES	PEOPLE GROUPS	NOTES
Haiti		4				

Protestant Reformed Churches in America

2016 Tekonsha St. SE
Grand Rapids MI 49506

Tel. (616) 247-0638
EXECUTIVE OFFICER: Meindert Joostens,
ORGANIZED: 1926
DESCRIPTION: A denominational sending agency of Reformed
    tradition involved in church planting.

TOTAL INCOME: $40,000   FOR OVERSEAS MINISTRIES: NR
PERSONNEL:
    NORTH AMERICANS OVERSEAS   NON-NORTH AMERICANS OVERSEAS: NR
            MARRIED: NR   NORTH AMERICAN ADM. STAFF: 12
        SINGLE MEN: NR   SHORT TERM: 2
      SINGLE WOMEN: NR   RETIRED: 2

    TOTAL ACTIVE: NR

FIELD OF SERVICE	YEAR BEGAN	PERSONNEL NOW	PERSONNEL NEW	RELATED CHURCHES	PEOPLE GROUPS	NOTES
Jamaica	1980					
New Zealand						
Singapore	1979	1				

Providence Mission Homes, Inc.

1421 Glengarry Rd.
Pasadena CA 91105

Tel. (213) 255-2043
EXECUTIVE OFFICER: Wm. Jacquet Gribble
ORGANIZED: 1973
DESCRIPTION: An interdenominational service agency of
    evangelical tradition providing housing for missionaries
    on furlough. Provides rent subsidy when needed and locates
    furnishings for missionaries both living in and outside
    the apartment complex. Automobiles and a van are available
    for use.

TOTAL INCOME: $30,000   FOR OVERSEAS MINISTRIES: $0
PERSONNEL:
    NORTH AMERICANS OVERSEAS   NON-NORTH AMERICANS OVERSEAS: 0
            MARRIED: 0   NORTH AMERICAN ADM. STAFF: 0
        SINGLE MEN: 0   SHORT TERM: 0
      SINGLE WOMEN: 0   RETIRED: 0

    TOTAL ACTIVE: 0

PTL Television Network SEE: Heritage Village Church and Msny. Fellowship, Inc.

R.E.A.P. Mission, Inc.

P.O. ADDRESS:
BOX 11600
Costa Mesa CA 92627

Tel. (714) 645-5050
EXECUTIVE OFFICER: Kenny Joseph
ORGANIZED: 1951
DESCRIPTION: An interdenominational service and sending agency
    of fundamentalist tradition reinforcing evangelists and
    aiding pastors in Japan, Korea, Indonesia and India. Also
    engaged in church planting, mass evangelism, fund raising,
    literature production and support of nationals.

TOTAL INCOME: $39,800   FOR OVERSEAS MINISTRIES: $39,800
PERSONNEL:
    NORTH AMERICANS OVERSEAS   NON-NORTH AMERICANS OVERSEAS: 2
            MARRIED: 3   NORTH AMERICAN ADM. STAFF: 2
        SINGLE MEN: 2   SHORT TERM: 4

```
    SINGLE WOMEN:    1                        RETIRED:      0
                  -----
    TOTAL ACTIVE:    6
-----------------------------------------------------------------------
                    YEAR    PERSONNEL    RELATED   PEOPLE
FIELD OF SERVICE    BEGAN   NOW   NEW    CHURCHES  GROUPS   NOTES
-----------------------------------------------------------------------
India               1964
Indonesia           1964                    56
Japan               1951    3               2
Korea, Dem. P. Rep. 1959
Taiwan Rep of China 1959
```

Ramabal Mukti Mission (American Council of)

55 Leigh St.
Clinton NJ 08809
P.O. ADDRESS:
Box 4912
Clinton NJ 08809

Tel. (201) 735-8770
EXECUTIVE OFFICER: Donald Kitchen
ORGANIZED: 1929   AFFILIATION: IFMA-Assoc. member
DESCRIPTION: An interdenominational agency of evangelical,
    fundamentalist tradition establishing churches and
    involved in education, small group evangelism, medicine
    and providing homes for orphans.
TOTAL INCOME: $166,132   FOR OVERSEAS MINISTRIES: $166,132
PERSONNEL:
    NORTH AMERICANS OVERSEAS   NON-NORTH AMERICANS OVERSEAS: 0
              MARRIED: 0   NORTH AMERICAN ADM. STAFF: 4
           SINGLE MEN: 0   SHORT TERM: 1
         SINGLE WOMEN: 4   RETIRED: NR

        TOTAL ACTIVE: 4

                    YEAR   PERSONNEL   RELATED   PEOPLE
FIELD OF SERVICE   BEGAN   NOW   NEW   CHURCHES GROUPS   NOTES

India   1929   4   4   3

REACH, Incorporated

15703 Lujon St.
Hacienda Hgts. CA 91745
P.O. ADDRESS:
Box 5591
Hacienda Hgts. CA 91745

Tel. (213) 968-3165
EXECUTIVE OFFICER: Gene Tabor
ORGANIZED: 1976
DESCRIPTION: A nondenominational service agency of evangelical
    tradition engaged in the development of human resources,
    evangelism, self-help projects and discipleship training.
TOTAL INCOME: NR   FOR OVERSEAS MINISTRIES: NR
PERSONNEL:
    NORTH AMERICANS OVERSEAS   NON-NORTH AMERICANS OVERSEAS: 1
              MARRIED: 2   NORTH AMERICAN ADM. STAFF: 0
           SINGLE MEN: 1   SHORT TERM: 1
         SINGLE WOMEN: 0   RETIRED: 0

        TOTAL ACTIVE: 3
NOTES: Income is currently channeled through home
         churches or other organizations to missionary
         personnel.

433
```
```

| Philippines | | 3 | | | |

REAP International

992 W Ninth St.
Upland CA 91786

Tel. (714) 981-5777
EXECUTIVE OFFICER: James D. Sharp
ORGANIZED: 1973
DESCRIPTION: An interdenominational specialized service agency
    of evangelical tradition serving other agencies by
    offering technical assistance with radiological equipment
    in medical facilities overseas.
TOTAL INCOME: $175,000   FOR OVERSEAS MINISTRIES: $175,000
PERSONNEL:
    NORTH AMERICANS OVERSEAS   NON-NORTH AMERICANS OVERSEAS: 0
        MARRIED: 0   NORTH AMERICAN ADM. STAFF: 0
        SINGLE MEN: 0   SHORT TERM: 0
        SINGLE WOMEN: 0   RETIRED: 0

        TOTAL ACTIVE: 0

Red Sea Mission Team, Inc., U.S.A.

944 Barnett St.
Kerrville TX 78028
P.O. ADDRESS:
Box 990
Kerrville TX 78028

Tel. (512) 257-3534
EXECUTIVE OFFICER: Rusty Maynard
ORGANIZED: 1953
DESCRIPTION: An international, nondenominational sending
    agency of evangelical tradition offering agricultural
    assistance and engaged in evangelism, medicine, literacy
    and church planting.
TOTAL INCOME: $79,621   FOR OVERSEAS MINISTRIES: $52,000
PERSONNEL:
    NORTH AMERICANS OVERSEAS   NON-NORTH AMERICANS OVERSEAS: 0
        MARRIED: 4   NORTH AMERICAN ADM. STAFF: 2
        SINGLE MEN: 0   SHORT TERM: 3
        SINGLE WOMEN: 4   RETIRED: 2

        TOTAL ACTIVE: 8

FIELD OF SERVICE	YEAR BEGAN	PERSONNEL NOW	NEW	RELATED CHURCHES	PEOPLE GROUPS	NOTES
Djibouti	1975				3	
Pakistan	1977				1	
Sudan	1978	2	2		2	
United Kingdom	1977				1	
Yemen Arab Republic	1969	1	1		1	

Reformation Translation Fellowship

P.O. ADDRESS:
Drawer G
Winchester KS 66097

Tel. (913) 774-4242
EXECUTIVE OFFICER: Samuel E. Boyle
ORGANIZED: 1950
DESCRIPTION: No current information available. Information

from 1976 directory. A nondenominational sending agency of
Reformed and Presbyterian tradition translating and
publishing Chinese Christian literature, particularly of a
Calvinist orientation.
TOTAL INCOME: $24,788   FOR OVERSEAS MINISTRIES: $24,788
PERSONNEL:
    NORTH AMERICANS OVERSEAS   NON-NORTH AMERICANS OVERSEAS: NR
              MARRIED: 1   NORTH AMERICAN ADM. STAFF: 1
           SINGLE MEN: 0   SHORT TERM: NR
         SINGLE WOMEN: 0   RETIRED: NR

         TOTAL ACTIVE: 1
NOTES: Spouses not included in total overseas personnel.

                       YEAR   PERSONNEL   RELATED   PEOPLE
FIELD OF SERVICE   BEGAN   NOW   NEW   CHURCHES   GROUPS NOTES

Taiwan Rep of China   1965

Reformed Church in America General
Program Council
475 Riverside Dr.
New York NY 10115
Tel. (212) 870-2265
EXECUTIVE OFFICER: John R. Walchenbach
ORGANIZED: 1857   AFFILIATION: DOM-NCCCUSA
DESCRIPTION: A denominational sending agency of Reformed
    tradition establishing churches and supporting national
    churches. Also engaged in education, medicine,
    agriculture, evangelism and development.
TOTAL INCOME: $7,103,295   FOR OVERSEAS MINISTRIES: $2,938,000
PERSONNEL:
    NORTH AMERICANS OVERSEAS   NON-NORTH AMERICANS OVERSEAS: 0
              MARRIED: 119   NORTH AMERICAN ADM. STAFF: 10
           SINGLE MEN: 1   SHORT TERM: 34
         SINGLE WOMEN: 12   RETIRED: 77

         TOTAL ACTIVE: 132
NOTES: Administrative staff are not all full-time.
        Short-term staff includes volunteers and interns.

FIELD OF SERVICE	YEAR BEGAN	PERSONNEL NOW	PERSONNEL NEW	RELATED CHURCHES	PEOPLE GROUPS	NOTES
Bahrain	1889	8	4			
Egypt	1972	2				
Ethiopia	1963	2				
Hong-Kong	1951	2				
India	1853	8	2			
Japan	1860	18	2			
Kenya	1977	4	2			
Kuwait	1900	5	4			
Lebanon	1967	2				
Mexico	1925	16	2			
Oman	1892	12	3			
Philippines	1950	2	2			
Sudan	1949	2				
Taiwan Rep of China	1952	8	4			
Venezuela	1977	2	2			
Zambia	1978	1				

Reformed Episcopal Church Board of Foreign Missions

25 S 43rd St.
Philadelphia PA 19104

Tel. (215) 222-5158
EXECUTIVE OFFICER: Samuel M. Forster
ORGANIZED: 1892
DESCRIPTION: A denominational sending agency of Biblical and
    Reformed tradition engaged in education, literature,
    supporting national churches, medicine and translation.
TOTAL INCOME: $59,800   FOR OVERSEAS MINISTRIES: $59,800
PERSONNEL:
```
    NORTH AMERICANS OVERSEAS    NON-NORTH AMERICANS OVERSEAS:    NR
                MARRIED:    NR        NORTH AMERICAN ADM. STAFF:     3
             SINGLE MEN:    NR                     SHORT TERM:     0
           SINGLE WOMEN:    NR                       RETIRED:    NR
                        -----
        TOTAL ACTIVE:    15
```

FIELD OF SERVICE	YEAR BEGAN	PERSONNEL NOW	NEW	RELATED CHURCHES	PEOPLE GROUPS	NOTES
France	1964	4				
Germany, Fed. Rep.	1953	5				
India	1890	2				
Kenya	1956	2				
Uganda	1956	2				
Zaire	1951	1				

Reformed Presbyterian Church of North America, Board of Foreign Missions

7418 Penn Ave.
Pittsburgh PA 15208

Tel. (412) 731-1177
EXECUTIVE OFFICER: Robert Henning
ORGANIZED: 1856   AFFILIATION: EFMA
DESCRIPTION: A denominational sending agency of Presbyterian
    and Reformed tradition establishing churches and engaged
    in personal and small group evangelism.
TOTAL INCOME: $119,041   FOR OVERSEAS MINISTRIES: $119,041
PERSONNEL:
```
    NORTH AMERICANS OVERSEAS    NON-NORTH AMERICANS OVERSEAS:    0
                MARRIED:     4        NORTH AMERICAN ADM. STAFF:    0
             SINGLE MEN:     0                     SHORT TERM:     0
           SINGLE WOMEN:     4                       RETIRED:     4
                        -----
        TOTAL ACTIVE:     8
```

FIELD OF SERVICE	YEAR BEGAN	PERSONNEL NOW	NEW	RELATED CHURCHES	PEOPLE GROUPS	NOTES
Japan	1950	6	2	69		

Reformed Presbyterian Church, Evangelical Synod, World Presbyterian Missions, Inc. SEE: World Presbyterian Missions, Inc.

Refugee Children, Inc.

P.O. ADDRESS:
Box 106
Stamford CT 06904

Tel. (203) 323-4900
EXECUTIVE OFFICER: Majken Broby
ORGANIZED: 1953
DESCRIPTION: An interdenominational specialized service agency

supporting children, working in refugee relief and
rehabilitation, medical work, evangelism, and providing
equipment.
TOTAL INCOME: $25,000   FOR OVERSEAS MINISTRIES: $25,000
PERSONNEL:
   NORTH AMERICANS OVERSEAS   NON-NORTH AMERICANS OVERSEAS: 0
           MARRIED: NR   NORTH AMERICAN ADM. STAFF: 1
        SINGLE MEN: NR   SHORT TERM: 0
      SINGLE WOMEN: NR   RETIRED: 0

      TOTAL ACTIVE: 2
NOTES: Income estimated by agency.
         One of the overseas personnel is only partially
         supported.

FIELD OF SERVICE	YEAR BEGAN	PERSONNEL NOW	PERSONNEL NEW	RELATED CHURCHES	PEOPLE GROUPS	NOTES
Germany, Fed. Rep.	1953					
Honduras	1974					
Morocco	1967	1				

Regions Beyond Missionary Union (Canada)

3251 Sheppard Ave. E
Scarborough ON M1T 3K1
Canada

Tel. (416) 494-9904
EXECUTIVE OFFICER: Elmer Austring
ORGANIZED: 1948   AFFILIATION: IFMA
DESCRIPTION: An international, nondenominational sending
   agency of Baptist and evangelical tradition establishing
   churches and engaged in education, evangelism,
   linguistics, literacy and medicine. Also involved in
   church construction, Bible translation and aviation.
TOTAL INCOME: $614,000   FOR OVERSEAS MINISTRIES: $614,000
PERSONNEL:
   NORTH AMERICANS OVERSEAS   NON-NORTH AMERICANS OVERSEAS: 2
           MARRIED: 34   NORTH AMERICAN ADM. STAFF: 4
        SINGLE MEN: 0   SHORT TERM: 2
      SINGLE WOMEN: 8   RETIRED: 0

      TOTAL ACTIVE: 42

FIELD OF SERVICE	YEAR BEGAN	PERSONNEL NOW	PERSONNEL NEW	RELATED CHURCHES	PEOPLE GROUPS	NOTES
Indonesia	1948	31	14	100	1	
Peru		7	5	70	3	
Zaire		3				

Regions Beyond Missionary Union (U.S.A.)

8102 Elberon Ave.
Philadelphia PA 19111

Tel. (215) 745-0680
EXECUTIVE OFFICER: Joseph F. Conley
ORGANIZED: 1873   AFFILIATION: IFMA
DESCRIPTION: An international, interdenominational sending
   agency of Baptist and evangelical tradition establishing
   churches and engaged in theological education, evangelism
   and Bible translation.
TOTAL INCOME: $599,430   FOR OVERSEAS MINISTRIES: $599,430

PERSONNEL:
```
     NORTH AMERICANS OVERSEAS    NON-NORTH AMERICANS OVERSEAS:    0
                MARRIED:  100       NORTH AMERICAN ADM. STAFF:   14
             SINGLE MEN:    6                      SHORT TERM:    2
           SINGLE WOMEN:   19                         RETIRED:    0
                        -----
        TOTAL ACTIVE:  125
```
NOTES: Five of the administrative personnel are
        part-time.

FIELD OF SERVICE	YEAR BEGAN	PERSONNEL NOW	NEW	RELATED CHURCHES	PEOPLE GROUPS	NOTES
India	1899	4				1
Indonesia	1948	100	44	246	15	
Nepal	1954	11	4			1
Peru	1922	34	15	75	2	
Zaire	1878	10	1	400		1

Note: 1. These fields are under
sponsorship of British RBMU which
is an organizationally separate
entity from RBMU International.

Regular Baptist Churches, General Association of SEE: General Association Regular Baptist Churches

Regular Baptist Churches, General Association of SEE: General Association of Regular Baptist Churches

Regular Baptists of Canada, Women's Missionary Society

75 Lowther Ave.
Toronto ON M5R 1C9
Canada

Tel. (416) 923-6112
EXECUTIVE OFFICER: Mrs. J. I. Moore
ORGANIZED: 1926
DESCRIPTION: An independent organization of Baptist tradition
     supporting nationals and engaged in missionary orientation
     and training, correspondence courses, education and Bible
     distribution.
TOTAL INCOME: $40,917   FOR OVERSEAS MINISTRIES: $7,752
PERSONNEL:
```
     NORTH AMERICANS OVERSEAS    NON-NORTH AMERICANS OVERSEAS:    0
                MARRIED:    1       NORTH AMERICAN ADM. STAFF:    0
             SINGLE MEN:    0                      SHORT TERM:    1
           SINGLE WOMEN:    3                         RETIRED:   NR
                        -----
        TOTAL ACTIVE:    4
```

FIELD OF SERVICE	YEAR BEGAN	PERSONNEL NOW	NEW	RELATED CHURCHES	PEOPLE GROUPS	NOTES
Colombia	1962	4		1		

Note: Only one of the overseas
personnel is North American.

Reinforcing Evangelists and Aiding Pastors SEE: R.E.A.P. Mission, Inc.

Release the World for Christ

11950 Airline Dr Ste.210
Houston TX 77060

Tel. (713) 931-7100
EXECUTIVE OFFICER: Chris Panos
ORGANIZED: 1966
DESCRIPTION: An interdenominational agency of Greek Orthodox
    tradition holding evangelistic and healing crusades
    primarily in India.
TOTAL INCOME: $100,000   FOR OVERSEAS MINISTRIES: $100,000
PERSONNEL:

NORTH AMERICANS OVERSEAS		NON-NORTH AMERICANS OVERSEAS:		NR
MARRIED:	NR	NORTH AMERICAN ADM. STAFF:		4
SINGLE MEN:	NR		SHORT TERM:	NR
SINGLE WOMEN:	NR		RETIRED:	NR
TOTAL ACTIVE:	NR			

NOTES: Income estimated by agency.
    Volunteer personnel are not included in figures.

Robert Forester Evangelistic Foundation, Inc. SEE: Forester Foundation, Inc.

Romanian Missionary Society

801 S Ocean Dr.
Hollywood FL 33019

Tel. (305) 920-5639
EXECUTIVE OFFICER: Peter Trutza
ORGANIZED: 1968
DESCRIPTION: A nondenominational specialized agency of Baptist
    tradition engaged in radio broadcasting, literature and
    Bible distribution. Also involved in evangelism, medicine
    and relief.
TOTAL INCOME: $20,000   FOR OVERSEAS MINISTRIES: NR
PERSONNEL:

NORTH AMERICANS OVERSEAS		NON-NORTH AMERICANS OVERSEAS:		0
MARRIED:	0	NORTH AMERICAN ADM. STAFF:		0
SINGLE MEN:	0		SHORT TERM:	0
SINGLE WOMEN:	0		RETIRED:	0
TOTAL ACTIVE:	0			

Rosell Evangelistic Foundation SEE: Global Concern, Inc.

Rural Gospel and Medical Missions of India, Inc.

1689 Homewood Dr.
Pasadena CA 91001
P.O. ADDRESS:
Box 4426
Pasadena CA 91106

Tel. (213) 282-9238
EXECUTIVE OFFICER: John Klotzler
ORGANIZED: 1938
DESCRIPTION: A nondenominational sending agency of independent
    tradition establishing churches and engaged in education,
    medical work, childcare, evangelism and the support of
    national workers.
TOTAL INCOME: NR   FOR OVERSEAS MINISTRIES: NR
PERSONNEL:

NORTH AMERICANS OVERSEAS		NON-NORTH AMERICANS OVERSEAS:		NR
MARRIED:	NR	NORTH AMERICAN ADM. STAFF:		NR
SINGLE MEN:	NR		SHORT TERM:	NR

TOTAL ACTIVE: NR
- -

FIELD OF SERVICE	YEAR BEGAN	PERSONNEL NOW NEW	RELATED CHURCHES	PEOPLE GROUPS	NOTES
India	1938				

Russia for Christ, Inc.

3009 A and B De La Vina
Santa Barbara CA 93105
P.O. ADDRESS:
Box 30,000
Santa Barbara CA 93105

Tel. (805) 687-7696
EXECUTIVE OFFICER: David Benson
ORGANIZED: 1958
DESCRIPTION: An interdenominational service agency of
    evangelical tradition evangelizing and ministering in and
    to communist-dominated nations. Involved in broadcasting
    and literature distribution. Minister exclusively to
    Russian immigrants in various countries.
TOTAL INCOME: $90,000   FOR OVERSEAS MINISTRIES: NR
PERSONNEL:
    NORTH AMERICANS OVERSEAS   NON-NORTH AMERICANS OVERSEAS: NR
               MARRIED: 0   NORTH AMERICAN ADM. STAFF: 5
           SINGLE MEN: 0   SHORT TERM: NR
         SINGLE WOMEN: 0   RETIRED: 0

         TOTAL ACTIVE: 0

Salvation Army, Canada and Bermuda

20 Altert Ave.
Toronto ON M8V 2L4
Canada
P.O. ADDRESS:
Box 4021, Postal Sta. A
Toronto ON M5W 2B1
Canada

Tel. (416) 598-2071
EXECUTIVE OFFICER: John D. Waldron
ORGANIZED: 1884
DESCRIPTION: A denominational sending and service agency of
    Wesleyan tradition engaged in evangelism, education and
    self-help and social welfare projects. Administrated
    from International Headquarters in a world-wide ministry.
TOTAL INCOME: $1,380,000   FOR OVERSEAS MINISTRIES: $1,276,000
PERSONNEL:
    NORTH AMERICANS OVERSEAS   NON-NORTH AMERICANS OVERSEAS: NA
               MARRIED: 34   NORTH AMERICAN ADM. STAFF: 1305
           SINGLE MEN: 0   SHORT TERM: 8
         SINGLE WOMEN: 24   RETIRED: NA

         TOTAL ACTIVE: 58
NOTES: Income estimated by MARC.
- -

FIELD OF SERVICE	YEAR BEGAN	PERSONNEL NOW NEW	RELATED CHURCHES	PEOPLE GROUPS	NOTES
Africa-general	1896	6			

FIELD OF SERVICE	YEAR BEGAN	PERSONNEL NOW	PERSONNEL NEW	RELATED CHURCHES	PEOPLE GROUPS	NOTES
Caribbean-general	1887	6				
Ghana	1922	1				
India	1892	2				
Indonesia	1894	3				
Latin America-gen.	1890	5				
Mexico	1904	1				
Pakistan	1883	5				
Singapore	1935	3				
South Africa	1883	5				
Sri Lanka	1883	3				
Zaire	1934	2				
Zambia	1891	4				
Zimbabwe	1891	2				

Salvation Army, The

120 W 14th St.
New York NY 10011

Tel. (212) 620-4910
EXECUTIVE OFFICER: Ernest W. Holz
ORGANIZED: 1865
DESCRIPTION: An international, denominational agency of
  Wesleyan tradition engaged in evangelism, education,
  literature production and distribution, medicine and
  support of national churches. Overseas assignments are
  handled through the international headquarters in London.
TOTAL INCOME: $4,917,954   FOR OVERSEAS MINISTRIES: $4,917,954
PERSONNEL:
```
     NORTH AMERICANS OVERSEAS    NON-NORTH AMERICANS OVERSEAS:    0
                 MARRIED:  65       NORTH AMERICAN ADM. STAFF:   NA
             SINGLE MEN:   0                    SHORT TERM:       2
           SINGLE WOMEN:  21                      RETIRED:       80
                       -----
          TOTAL ACTIVE:  86
```

FIELD OF SERVICE	YEAR BEGAN	PERSONNEL NOW	PERSONNEL NEW	RELATED CHURCHES	PEOPLE GROUPS	NOTES
Argentina	1890	6		89		1
Brazil	1922	3		47		
Caribbean-general	1895	15		42		2
Chile	1909	6		56		3
India	1882	7		4968		
Indonesia	1894	2		246		
Kenya	1896	3		717		5
Korea, Rep. of	1908	3		131		
Mexico		8				6
Philippines	1937	3		46		
South Africa	1883	3		220		
Sri Lanka	1883	2		172		
Taiwan Rep of China		2		21		4
Zaire	1934			444		
Zambia	1924	3		88		
Zimbabwe	1891			208		

1. Inc. Paraguay and Uruguay.
2. Inc. Jamaica, pts. of C.America.
3. Inc. Peru and Bolivia.
4. Inc. Hong-Kong.
5. Inc. Tanzania and Uganda.
6. Inc. pts. of C.America.

Samaritan's Purse

1717 N Highland
Hollywood CA 90028
P.O. ADDRESS:
Box 3000
Arcadia CA 91006

Tel. (213) 462-2341
EXECUTIVE OFFICER: William F. Graham, III
ORGANIZED: 1969
DESCRIPTION: A nondenominational relief agency of evangelical
    tradition engaged in meeting emergency needs through aid
    and relief, providing medical supplies and equipment, and
    serving other agencies.
TOTAL INCOME: $390,000   FOR OVERSEAS MINISTRIES: $360,000
PERSONNEL:

NORTH AMERICANS OVERSEAS		NON-NORTH AMERICANS OVERSEAS:		NR
MARRIED:	1	NORTH AMERICAN ADM. STAFF:		2
SINGLE MEN:	0	SHORT TERM:		NR
SINGLE WOMEN:	0	RETIRED:		0
TOTAL ACTIVE:	1			

FIELD OF SERVICE	YEAR BEGAN	PERSONNEL NOW	NEW	RELATED CHURCHES	PEOPLE GROUPS	NOTES
Thailand	1979	1			1	

Samuel Zwemer Institute

1539 E Howard St.
Pasadena CA 91104
P.O. ADDRESS:
Box 365
Altadena CA 91001

Tel. (213) 794-1121
EXECUTIVE OFFICER: Don M. McCurry, Jr.
ORGANIZED: 1979
DESCRIPTION: An interdenominational institute of evangelical
    tradition engaged in research and education specifically
    aimed at reaching Muslims. Serves as an information
    service involved in missionary education, orientation and
    training and also serves other agencies.
TOTAL INCOME: $39,718   FOR OVERSEAS MINISTRIES: $0
PERSONNEL:

NORTH AMERICANS OVERSEAS		NON-NORTH AMERICANS OVERSEAS:		0
MARRIED:	0	NORTH AMERICAN ADM. STAFF:		0
SINGLE MEN:	0	SHORT TERM:		0
SINGLE WOMEN:	0	RETIRED:		0
TOTAL ACTIVE:	0			

Schwenkfelder Church in the United
States of America Home and Foreign
Board of Missions

Main and Towamencin Ave.
Lansdale PA 19446

Tel. (215) 855-2863
EXECUTIVE OFFICER: Arlan M. Bond
ORGANIZED: 1895
DESCRIPTION: A denominational non-sending agency of Baptist
    and evangelical tradition partially supporting
    missionaries in India, Indonesia, South Africa, Honduras
    and Brazil.
TOTAL INCOME: $24,750   FOR OVERSEAS MINISTRIES: $8,800

PERSONNEL:
```
    NORTH AMERICANS OVERSEAS    NON-NORTH AMERICANS OVERSEAS:    0
              MARRIED:    0        NORTH AMERICAN ADM. STAFF:    0
           SINGLE MEN:    0                    SHORT TERM:       0
         SINGLE WOMEN:    0                      RETIRED:        0
                        -----
         TOTAL ACTIVE:    0
```

FIELD OF SERVICE	YEAR BEGAN	PERSONNEL NOW	PERSONNEL NEW	RELATED CHURCHES	PEOPLE GROUPS	NOTES
Brazil				4		
Honduras				4		
India				4		
Indonesia				4		
South Africa				4		

Scripture Gift Mission (Canada), Inc.

32-300 Steelcase Rd. W
Markham ON L3R 2W2
Canada

Tel. (416) 495-0521
EXECUTIVE OFFICER: W. E. Wright
ORGANIZED: 1888
DESCRIPTION: A nondenominational service agency of evangelical
    tradition providing grants of booklets and leaflets
    containing Scripture selections in 350-400 languages to
    missionaries and national workers for personal
    distribution (15-19 million copies), in most countries of
    the world. Agency is autonomous but cooperates with
    Scripture Gift Mission of London, which is the original
    founding body.
TOTAL INCOME: $37,840   FOR OVERSEAS MINISTRIES: $18,920
PERSONNEL:
```
    NORTH AMERICANS OVERSEAS    NON-NORTH AMERICANS OVERSEAS:    0
              MARRIED:    0        NORTH AMERICAN ADM. STAFF:    0
           SINGLE MEN:    0                    SHORT TERM:       0
         SINGLE WOMEN:    0                      RETIRED:        0
                        -----
         TOTAL ACTIVE:    0
```

Scripture Union, U.S.A.

1716 Spruce St.
Philadelphia PA 19103

Tel. (215) 732-2079
EXECUTIVE OFFICER: Clifford L. Swanson
ORGANIZED: 1959
DESCRIPTION: An interdenominational service agency of
    evangelical tradition encouraging Bible study, especially
    among children. Working in 85 countries.
TOTAL INCOME: $495,859   FOR OVERSEAS MINISTRIES: $80,123
PERSONNEL:
```
    NORTH AMERICANS OVERSEAS    NON-NORTH AMERICANS OVERSEAS:    0
              MARRIED:    2        NORTH AMERICAN ADM. STAFF:    1
           SINGLE MEN:    0                    SHORT TERM:       0
         SINGLE WOMEN:    0                      RETIRED:        0
                        -----
         TOTAL ACTIVE:    2
```

FIELD OF SERVICE	YEAR BEGAN	PERSONNEL NOW	PERSONNEL NEW	RELATED CHURCHES	PEOPLE GROUPS	NOTES
Mexico	1978	1	1			

```
----------------------------------------------------------------
                   YEAR    PERSONNEL   RELATED    PEOPLE
FIELD OF SERVICE   BEGAN   NOW   NEW   CHURCHES   GROUPS  NOTES
----------------------------------------------------------------
```
Peru   1940   1
    Note: Funds are also donated to
    support work in Argentina, Bolivia,
    Brazil, Chile and Panama.

Self Help Foundation

Highway 3 East
Waverly IA 50677
P.O. ADDRESS:
Box 88
Waverly IA 50677

Tel. (319) 352-4040
EXECUTIVE OFFICER: Ray C. Howland
ORGANIZED: 1959
DESCRIPTION: A nondenominational specialized service agency
    supplying small scale farm machinery to farmers in
    developing countries. Also involved in agricultural
    assistance, community development, education, self-help
    projects, training and development of human resources.
TOTAL INCOME: $403,400   FOR OVERSEAS MINISTRIES: $403,400
PERSONNEL:
  NORTH AMERICANS OVERSEAS   NON-NORTH AMERICANS OVERSEAS: 0
        MARRIED: 1   NORTH AMERICAN ADM. STAFF: 2
    SINGLE MEN: 0   SHORT TERM: 4
  SINGLE WOMEN: 0   RETIRED: 0

    TOTAL ACTIVE: 1

```
----------------------------------------------------------------
                   YEAR    PERSONNEL   RELATED    PEOPLE
FIELD OF SERVICE   BEGAN   NOW   NEW   CHURCHES   GROUPS  NOTES
----------------------------------------------------------------
```
Cameroon   1964   1
Honduras   1977   1   1   1

Self Help, Inc. SEE: Self Help Foundation

Seventh Day Baptist Missionary Society

401 Washington Tr. Bldg.
Westerly RI 02891

Tel. (401) 596-4326
EXECUTIVE OFFICER: Leon R. Lawton
ORGANIZED: 1818   AFFILIATION: DOM-NCCCUSA-Affil. Bd.
DESCRIPTION: A denominational sending agency of Baptist
    tradition establishing churches and supporting national
    churches through independent national Seventh Day Baptist
    Conferences. Also engaged in evangelism, education and
    home missions, as well as church extension for the
    denomination.
TOTAL INCOME: $163,000   FOR OVERSEAS MINISTRIES: $50,000
PERSONNEL:
  NORTH AMERICANS OVERSEAS   NON-NORTH AMERICANS OVERSEAS: 0
        MARRIED: 6   NORTH AMERICAN ADM. STAFF: 1
    SINGLE MEN: 0   SHORT TERM: 2
  SINGLE WOMEN: 0   RETIRED: 4

    TOTAL ACTIVE: 6

FIELD OF SERVICE	YEAR BEGAN	PERSONNEL NOW	NEW	RELATED CHURCHES	PEOPLE GROUPS	NOTES
Burma	1974			13		
Guyana	1920			7		
India	1974			301	3	
Jamaica	1927			29		
Malawi	1947	4	2	84		
Mexico	1976			32		
Philippines	1974	2	2	8		

Share the Care International

1561 Yosemite Dr.
Los Angeles CA 90041
P.O. ADDRESS:
Box 485
Pasadena CA 91102

Tel. (213) 258-3529
EXECUTIVE OFFICER: Kenneth J. Stroman
ORGANIZED: 1960
DESCRIPTION: Formerly Mexican Fellowship, name changed in
1975. An interdenominational service agency of evangelical
tradition engaged in literature distribution, childcare,
fund raising and missionary orientation and training. Also
serving other agencies and supporting nationals.
TOTAL INCOME: $40,338   FOR OVERSEAS MINISTRIES: $16,212
PERSONNEL:
```
    NORTH AMERICANS OVERSEAS      NON-NORTH AMERICANS OVERSEAS:     NR
              MARRIED:   NR           NORTH AMERICAN ADM. STAFF:     NR
           SINGLE MEN:   NR                       SHORT TERM:        NR
         SINGLE WOMEN:   NR                         RETIRED:          1
                      -----
          TOTAL ACTIVE:   4
```

FIELD OF SERVICE	YEAR BEGAN	PERSONNEL NOW	NEW	RELATED CHURCHES	PEOPLE GROUPS	NOTES
India	1976					
Mexico	1960	4		20		

Short Terms Abroad SEE: Intercristo

Slavic Gospel Association

139 N Washington St.
Wheaton IL 60187
P.O. ADDRESS:
Box 1122
Wheaton IL 60187

Tel. (312) 690-8900
EXECUTIVE OFFICER: Peter Deyneka, Jr.
ORGANIZED: 1934   AFFILIATION: IFMA
DESCRIPTION: An interdenominational sending agency of
evangelical tradition with a ministry focused on Slavic
people. Engaged in evangelism and establishing churches,
Russian literature production and Bible distribution,
Russian gospel radio programming and broadcasting,
sponsoring three Bible training institutes and a
correspondence school for Christian leaders, and the
support of missionaries and national workers.
TOTAL INCOME: $2,516,835   FOR OVERSEAS MINISTRIES: $1,934,924

```
PERSONNEL:
     NORTH AMERICANS OVERSEAS    NON-NORTH AMERICANS OVERSEAS:    0
                MARRIED:    66        NORTH AMERICAN ADM. STAFF:   16
             SINGLE MEN:     7                      SHORT TERM:    4
           SINGLE WOMEN:    16                         RETIRED:   36
                         -----
        TOTAL ACTIVE:    89
```

FIELD OF SERVICE	YEAR BEGAN	PERSONNEL NOW	NEW	RELATED CHURCHES	PEOPLE GROUPS	NOTES
Argentina	1940	3				
Australia	1952	2				
Austria	1976	7				
Bermuda	1975	1				
Ecuador	1940	6				
France	1961	1				
Germany, Fed. Rep.	1943	4				
Italy	1953	4				
Korea, Rep. of	1955	2				
Monaco	1955	2				
Spain	1975	2				

Society for Europe's Evangelization (S.E.E.)

2910 Oakwood Ave.
Michigan City IN 46360
P.O. ADDRESS:
Box 176
Michigan City IN 46360

Tel. (219) 874-4428
EXECUTIVE OFFICER: Arthur Sommerville
ORGANIZED: 1956
DESCRIPTION: An independent sending agency of fundamental
    Baptist tradition establishing churches and engaged in
    theological education and evangelism. Also has a camp
    ministry and supports on the field training for high
    school graduates called Intensive Missionary Training
    (I.M.T.).

```
TOTAL INCOME:    $100,000   FOR OVERSEAS MINISTRIES:    $100,000
PERSONNEL:
     NORTH AMERICANS OVERSEAS    NON-NORTH AMERICANS OVERSEAS:    0
                MARRIED:    12       NORTH AMERICAN ADM. STAFF:    5
             SINGLE MEN:    10                     SHORT TERM:    0
           SINGLE WOMEN:    14                        RETIRED:    0
                         -----
        TOTAL ACTIVE:    36
```

FIELD OF SERVICE	YEAR BEGAN	PERSONNEL NOW	NEW	RELATED CHURCHES	PEOPLE GROUPS	NOTES
France	1954	37	21	4	4	

    Note: Overseas personnel includes
    nationals.

Society of Central Asian News (SCAN)

30 Bucknell Ave.
Lancaster PA 17603

Tel. (717) 397-7759
EXECUTIVE OFFICER: Karl Kotanchik
ORGANIZED: 1974
DESCRIPTION: A nondenominational, international prayer
    fellowship of reformed tradition offering an information
    service and engaged in mission related research.
TOTAL INCOME: $500   FOR OVERSEAS MINISTRIES: $0

PERSONNEL:
```
    NORTH AMERICANS OVERSEAS   NON-NORTH AMERICANS OVERSEAS:    0
            MARRIED:    0       NORTH AMERICAN ADM. STAFF:      0
         SINGLE MEN:    0                      SHORT TERM:      0
       SINGLE WOMEN:    0                         RETIRED:      0
                       -----
       TOTAL ACTIVE:    0
```

Society of St. John the Evangelist

980 Memorial Dr.
Cambridge MA 02138

Tel. (617) 876-3037
EXECUTIVE OFFICER: Paul Wessinger
ORGANIZED: 1866
DESCRIPTION: A denominational sending agency of Episcopal
    tradition. Missionaries find support within the community
    they serve. Ministry involves teaching, conducting
    retreats and supplying ministerial staff in parishes when
    needed.

```
TOTAL INCOME:          NR          FOR OVERSEAS MINISTRIES:    NR
PERSONNEL:
    NORTH AMERICANS OVERSEAS   NON-NORTH AMERICANS OVERSEAS:   NR
            MARRIED:   NR       NORTH AMERICAN ADM. STAFF:     NR
         SINGLE MEN:   NR                      SHORT TERM:      1
       SINGLE WOMEN:   NR                         RETIRED:     NR
                      -----
       TOTAL ACTIVE:   NR
```

FIELD OF SERVICE	YEAR BEGAN	PERSONNEL NOW	NEW	RELATED CHURCHES	PEOPLE GROUPS	NOTES
Japan	1928					

Source of Light Ministries, International

Hwy 441 S. Eatonton Hwy
Madison GA 30650
P.O. ADDRESS:
Box 8
Madison GA 30650

Tel. (404) 342-0397
EXECUTIVE OFFICER: Glenn E. Dix
ORGANIZED: 1953
DESCRIPTION: A nondenominational sending and service agency of
    evangelical and fundamentalist tradition engaged in
    evangelism through literature distribution, literature
    production and providing correspondence courses in various
    languages.

```
TOTAL INCOME:     $494,000        FOR OVERSEAS MINISTRIES:    NR
PERSONNEL:
    NORTH AMERICANS OVERSEAS   NON-NORTH AMERICANS OVERSEAS:   NR
            MARRIED:   NR       NORTH AMERICAN ADM. STAFF:     64
         SINGLE MEN:   NR                      SHORT TERM:      0
       SINGLE WOMEN:   NR                         RETIRED:      0
                      -----
       TOTAL ACTIVE:   10
```

FIELD OF SERVICE	YEAR BEGAN	PERSONNEL NOW	NEW	RELATED CHURCHES	PEOPLE GROUPS	NOTES
Chile		1				

FIELD OF SERVICE	YEAR BEGAN	PERSONNEL NOW	NEW	RELATED CHURCHES	PEOPLE GROUPS	NOTES
Guyana		1				
India		4				
Liberia		1				
Nigeria		2				
Philippines		1				

Source of Light Mission, Inc. SEE: Source of Light Ministries, International

South America Mission, Inc.

5217 S Military Trail
Lake Worth FL 33463
P.O. ADDRESS:
Box 6560
Lake Worth FL 33461

Tel. (305) 965-1833
EXECUTIVE OFFICER: G. Hunter Norwood
ORGANIZED: 1914   AFFILIATION: IFMA
DESCRIPTION: An interdenominational sending agency of
    evangelical tradition establishing churches and engaged in
    evangelism, literature distribution, theological education
    and aviation.
TOTAL INCOME: $1,390,248   FOR OVERSEAS MINISTRIES: $1,163,635
PERSONNEL:

NORTH AMERICANS OVERSEAS		NON-NORTH AMERICANS OVERSEAS:	0
MARRIED:	82	NORTH AMERICAN ADM. STAFF:	13
SINGLE MEN:	3	SHORT TERM:	4
SINGLE WOMEN:	14	RETIRED:	11
TOTAL ACTIVE:	99		

South American Crusades, Inc.

6152 N Verde Trail
Boca Raton FL 33433
P.O. ADDRESS:
Box 2530
Boca Raton FL 33432

Tel. (305) 395-0880
EXECUTIVE OFFICER: Bruce Woodman
ORGANIZED: 1959   AFFILIATION: IFMA-Assoc. member
DESCRIPTION: An interdenominational sending agency of
    evangelical tradition serving the Spanish-speaking
    churches of the three Americas. Involved primarily with
    radio ministry. Also engaged in evangelism crusades, Bible
    studies, TV and literature distribution. Overseas work
    includes Mexico and Latin America except for Brazil and
    Nicaragua.
TOTAL INCOME: NR   FOR OVERSEAS MINISTRIES: NR
PERSONNEL:

NORTH AMERICANS OVERSEAS		NON-NORTH AMERICANS OVERSEAS:	NR
MARRIED:	NR	NORTH AMERICAN ADM. STAFF:	4
SINGLE MEN:	NR	SHORT TERM:	0
SINGLE WOMEN:	NR	RETIRED:	0
TOTAL ACTIVE:	NR		

South Pacific Evangelical Fellowship

NW 7-46-22 W 4th
Wetaskiwin AB T9A 2G3
Canada

Tel. (403) 352-3146
EXECUTIVE OFFICER: H. R. Jespersen
ORGANIZED: 1951
DESCRIPTION: An interdenominational sending agency of
    evangelical tradition establishing churches and engaged in
    evangelism, correspondence courses and the support and
    training of nationals.
TOTAL INCOME: $50,004   FOR OVERSEAS MINISTRIES: $50,004
PERSONNEL:

NORTH AMERICANS OVERSEAS	NON-NORTH AMERICANS OVERSEAS:	2
MARRIED: 4	NORTH AMERICAN ADM. STAFF:	NR
SINGLE MEN: 0	SHORT TERM:	0
SINGLE WOMEN: 1	RETIRED:	0
TOTAL ACTIVE: 5		

FIELD OF SERVICE	YEAR BEGAN	PERSONNEL NOW	NEW	RELATED CHURCHES	PEOPLE GROUPS	NOTES
Australia		1	1	1		
Fiji		6	4	2		
New Zealand		4		1		

Southern Baptist Convention, Foreign Mission Board

3806 Monument Ave.
Richmond VA 23230
P.O. ADDRESS:
Box 6597
Richmond VA 23230

Tel. (804) 353-0151
EXECUTIVE OFFICER: R. Keith Parks
ORGANIZED: 1845
DESCRIPTION: A denominational sending agency of Baptist
    tradition establishing churches and engaged in aid and/or
    relief, development of human resources, radio and TV
    broadcasting and medicine.
TOTAL INCOME: $70,926,000   FOR OVERSEAS MINISTRIES: $62,376,000
PERSONNEL:

NORTH AMERICANS OVERSEAS	NON-NORTH AMERICANS OVERSEAS:	0
MARRIED: 2504	NORTH AMERICAN ADM. STAFF:	46
SINGLE MEN: 69	SHORT TERM:	2866
SINGLE WOMEN: 333	RETIRED:	224
TOTAL ACTIVE: 2906		

FIELD OF SERVICE	YEAR BEGAN	PERSONNEL NOW	NEW	RELATED CHURCHES	PEOPLE GROUPS	NOTES
Angola	1968	2		37		
Antigua	1968	6	6	2		
Argentina	1903	72		328		
Austria	1965	12	3	7		
Bahamas	1951	18	3	213		
Bangladesh	1957	17		14		
Barbados	1972	8	3	4		

FIELD OF SERVICE	YEAR BEGAN	PERSONNEL NOW	NEW	RELATED CHURCHES	PEOPLE GROUPS	NOTES
Belgium	1967	9	2	12		
Belize	1977	2	2			
Benin	1970	14	6	19		
Bermuda	1966	2		1		
Bolivia	1979					
Bophuthatswana	1977	12	12			
Botswana	1968	13		3		
Brazil	1881	295	26	2739		
British Virgin Is.	1976	3	3	1		
Burundi	1978	2	2			
Cayman Islands	1977	4	4	1		
Chile	1917	72	14	164		
Colombia	1941	83	6	84		
Costa Rica	1949	20		26		
Dominica	1975	5	3	2		
Dominican Republic	1962	25	1	9		
Ecuador	1950	38	8	53		
El Salvador	1975	6	4	41		
Ethiopia	1967	8				
France	1960	15	1	52		
Germany, Fed. Rep.	1961	9	4	23		
Ghana	1947	54	3	88		
Greece	1972	2		1		
Grenada	1972	6	2	2		
Guadeloupe	1964	9		5		
Guam	1961	8		3		
Guatemala	1948	32		59		
Guyana	1962	2		15		
Haiti	1978	2	2	94		
Honduras	1954	31	13	31		
Hong-Kong	1949	69	3	41		
India	1962	12		19		
Indonesia	1951	109		103		
Iran	1968	6		1		
Israel	1921	76	24	7		
Italy	1870	14	4	108		
Ivory Coast	1966	24	2	35		
Jamaica	1963	4	1	274		
Japan	1889	165	9	195		
Jordan	1952	23		7		
Kenya	1956	127	3	373		
Korea, Rep. of	1950	83	7	590		
Lebanon	1948	23	1	10		
Liberia	1960	55		99		
Libya	1965	2		1		
Macao	1910			3		
Malawi	1959	34	5	172		
Malaysia	1951	22		40		
Martinique	1977	7	7			
Mauritius	1978	2	2			
Mexico	1880	83	4	373		
Morocco	1966	8	6			
Namibia	1968	4		3		
Netherlands Antilles	1979	2	2			
Nicaragua	1976	6	6	41		

FIELD OF SERVICE	YEAR BEGAN	PERSONNEL NOW	PERSONNEL NEW	RELATED CHURCHES	PEOPLE GROUPS	NOTES
Niger	1969	2				
Nigeria	1850	132		2500		
Panama	1975	18		54		
Paraguay	1945	38	2	25		
Peru	1950	34	6	39		
Philippines	1948	132	21	388		
Portugal	1959	16	8	54		
Rwanda	1977	8	8	1		
Senegal	1969	13	1			
Singapore	1956	19		14		
South Africa	1977	19	19			
Spain	1921	37		59		
Sri Lanka	1977	6	6			
St. Vincent	1977	5	2	2		
Surinam	1971	7		2		
Switzerland	1948	16				
Taiwan Rep of China	1948	107	10	67		
Tanzania	1956	79	7	330		
Thailand	1949	58	1	21		
Togo	1964	21		8		
Transkei	1979					
Trinidad and Tobago	1962	6		1		
Turkey	1966	2		1		
Uganda	1962	4				
United Kingdom	1977	4	4	1		
Upper Volta	1971	13	2	22		
Uruguay	1911	30	7	37		
Venezuela	1949	58	19	58		
Yemen Arab Republic	1964	24	1			
Zambia	1959	38	2	67		
Zimbabwe	1956	49		70		

Southern European Mission, Inc.

520 1/2 4th St.
Niagara Falls NY 14301

EXECUTIVE OFFICER: Frank Scorza
ORGANIZED: 1942
DESCRIPTION: No current information available. Information
    from 1976 directory. A nondenominational service agency
    of conservative evangelical tradition supporting
    nationals, planting and supporting national churches,
    and involved in evangelism, childcare and scripture
    distribution. Primary focus is upon Italy and expatriate
    Italians in the countries of southern Europe.

TOTAL INCOME: NR   FOR OVERSEAS MINISTRIES: NR
PERSONNEL:
    NORTH AMERICANS OVERSEAS   NON-NORTH AMERICANS OVERSEAS: NR
            MARRIED: 0   NORTH AMERICAN ADM. STAFF: NR
         SINGLE MEN: 0   SHORT TERM: NR
       SINGLE WOMEN: 0   RETIRED: NR

       TOTAL ACTIVE: 0

FIELD OF SERVICE	YEAR BEGAN	PERSONNEL NOW	PERSONNEL NEW	RELATED CHURCHES	PEOPLE GROUPS	NOTES
France						

```
--------------------------------------------------------------
                   YEAR     PERSONNEL    RELATED    PEOPLE
FIELD OF SERVICE   BEGAN    NOW   NEW    CHURCHES   GROUPS   NOTES
--------------------------------------------------------------
Italy              1942
Spain
Switzerland
    1. Italy has an orphanage and a camp.
```

Southern Methodist, General Conference Board of Missions

P.O. ADDRESS:
Box 668 Rt. 2
Orangeburg SC 29115

DESCRIPTION: No data is reported for this agency for one of the
    following reasons: it is currently inactive or no longer
    exists; it has terminated overseas ministries or has ceased
    to operate as a North American entity.

Spanish Evangelical Literature Fellowship, Inc.

5353 N Fed. Hwy, Ste.311
Fort Lauderdale FL 33308
P.O. ADDRESS:
Box 11918
Fort Lauderdale FL 33339

Tel. (305) 776-4743
EXECUTIVE OFFICER: David Vila
ORGANIZED: 1969
DESCRIPTION: Known in Spanish-speaking countries as Editorial
    Clie. An interdenominational service agency of independent
    and evangelical tradition producing and distributing
    Bibles and evangelical literature in Spain, Argentina and
    Peru. Also engaged in Bible translation, broadcasting and
    support of nationals.
TOTAL INCOME: $127,928   FOR OVERSEAS MINISTRIES: $98,339
PERSONNEL:
    NORTH AMERICANS OVERSEAS   NON-NORTH AMERICANS OVERSEAS: 4
             MARRIED: 0   NORTH AMERICAN ADM. STAFF: 2
          SINGLE MEN: 0   SHORT TERM: 0
        SINGLE WOMEN: 0   RETIRED: 0

        TOTAL ACTIVE: 0

Spanish-World Gospel Mission, Inc.

P.O. ADDRESS:
Box 542
Winona Lake IN 46590

Tel. (219) 267-8821
EXECUTIVE OFFICER: Florent D. Toirac
ORGANIZED: 1959
DESCRIPTION: An interdenominational agency of Baptist and
    evangelical tradition reaching Spanish-speaking people
    through radio broadcasting, Bible and literature
    distribution and correspondence courses. Also engaged in
    missionary education.
TOTAL INCOME: $175,000   FOR OVERSEAS MINISTRIES: $175,000
PERSONNEL:
    NORTH AMERICANS OVERSEAS   NON-NORTH AMERICANS OVERSEAS: NR
             MARRIED: 0   NORTH AMERICAN ADM. STAFF: 7
          SINGLE MEN: 0   SHORT TERM: 0
        SINGLE WOMEN: 2   RETIRED: NR

        TOTAL ACTIVE: 2
NOTES: Income estimated by agency.

FIELD OF SERVICE	YEAR BEGAN	PERSONNEL NOW	NEW	RELATED CHURCHES	PEOPLE GROUPS	NOTES
Mexico	1970	2				

Sports Ambassadors SEE: O.C. Ministries, Inc.

Steer, Inc.

120 E Turnpike
Bismarck ND 58501
P.O. ADDRESS:
Box 1236
Bismarck ND 58501

Tel. (701) 258-4911
EXECUTIVE OFFICER: LaRue Geotz
ORGANIZED: 1958
DESCRIPTION: An interdenominational agency of evangelical
    tradition serving other agencies through a stewardship
    program involving donors, farmers and approved mission
    societies.
TOTAL INCOME: $187,349   FOR OVERSEAS MINISTRIES: $121,943
PERSONNEL:

NORTH AMERICANS OVERSEAS		NON-NORTH AMERICANS OVERSEAS:	0
MARRIED:	0	NORTH AMERICAN ADM. STAFF:	0
SINGLE MEN:	0	SHORT TERM:	0
SINGLE WOMEN:	0	RETIRED:	0
TOTAL ACTIVE:	0		

Student Foreign Missions Fellowship SEE: Inter-Varsity Christian Fellowship

Sudan Interior Mission, Inc.

2 Woodstone Dr.
Cedar Grove NJ 07009

Tel. (201) 857-1100
EXECUTIVE OFFICER: Ian M. Hay
ORGANIZED: 1893   AFFILIATION: IFMA
DESCRIPTION: An international, interdenominational sending
    agency of evangelical tradition establishing churches,
    assisting national churches and engaged in evangelism,
    education, literature, medicine, linguistics, translation,
    literacy, broadcasting, agriculture and community
    development. Known in Ethiopia as Society of International
    Missionaries.
TOTAL INCOME: $13,071,000   FOR OVERSEAS MINISTRIES: $11,079,000
PERSONNEL:

NORTH AMERICANS OVERSEAS		NON-NORTH AMERICANS OVERSEAS:	168
MARRIED:	383	NORTH AMERICAN ADM. STAFF:	128
SINGLE MEN:	11	SHORT TERM:	28
SINGLE WOMEN:	196	RETIRED:	172
TOTAL ACTIVE:	590		

FIELD OF SERVICE	YEAR BEGAN	PERSONNEL NOW	NEW	RELATED CHURCHES	PEOPLE GROUPS	NOTES
Benin	1946	44	21	105	8	

FIELD OF SERVICE	YEAR BEGAN	PERSONNEL NOW	NEW	RELATED CHURCHES	PEOPLE GROUPS	NOTES
Ethiopia	1927	36	27	2400	10	
Ghana	1956	16	5		5	
Ivory Coast	1968	13	7		1	
Kenya	1977	22	22		3	
Liberia	1951	73	28		3	
Niger	1924	85	35	28	9	
Nigeria	1893	228	77	1400	16	
Sudan	1937	37	17	13	8	
Upper Volta	1930	22	4	64	4	

Summer Institute of Linguistics SEE: Wycliffe Bible Translators

Sundanese Missionary Fellowship

P.O. ADDRESS:
Box 3017
Lynchburg VA 24503

Tel. (804) 384-8541
EXECUTIVE OFFICER: J. Carlton Londeree
ORGANIZED: 1969
DESCRIPTION: A nondenominational sending agency of evangelical
    and Reformed tradition establishing churches and engaged
    in evangelism, literature distribution, education and
    correspondence courses. Also involved in broadcasting,
    Bible distribution and training.
TOTAL INCOME: $18,108   FOR OVERSEAS MINISTRIES: $18,108
PERSONNEL:
    NORTH AMERICANS OVERSEAS   NON-NORTH AMERICANS OVERSEAS: 0
            MARRIED: 2   NORTH AMERICAN ADM. STAFF: 0
         SINGLE MEN: 0   SHORT TERM: 0
       SINGLE WOMEN: 0   RETIRED: 0

       TOTAL ACTIVE: 2
NOTES: Administrative personnel are volunteer.

FIELD OF SERVICE	YEAR BEGAN	PERSONNEL NOW	NEW	RELATED CHURCHES	PEOPLE GROUPS	NOTES
Indonesia	1969	2		50	1	

Tainan Evangelical Mission

4606 Ave. H
Lubbock TX 79404

Tel. (806) 747-5417
EXECUTIVE OFFICER: Mrs. Frank Lin
ORGANIZED: 1972
DESCRIPTION: Formerly Kuang Ming Vocational Institute. An
    interdenominational service agency of independent and
    fundamentalist tradition. The USA office provides support
    to the institute which is a home for children with polio.
TOTAL INCOME: $3,444   FOR OVERSEAS MINISTRIES: NR
PERSONNEL:
    NORTH AMERICANS OVERSEAS   NON-NORTH AMERICANS OVERSEAS: 1
            MARRIED: 1   NORTH AMERICAN ADM. STAFF: 0
         SINGLE MEN: 0   SHORT TERM: 0
       SINGLE WOMEN: 0   RETIRED: 0

       TOTAL ACTIVE: 1

FIELD OF SERVICE	YEAR BEGAN	PERSONNEL NOW NEW	RELATED CHURCHES	PEOPLE GROUPS	NOTES
Taiwan Rep of China	1972	1			

TEAM SEE: Evangelical Alliance Mission, The

Team Ventures International

P.O. ADDRESS:
Box 7301 Station E
Calgary AB T3C 3M2
Canada

Tel. (403) 242-4179
EXECUTIVE OFFICER: Mel Slack
ORGANIZED: 1978
DESCRIPTION: A nondenominational agency of evangelical
    tradition sending short-term teams to intern in mission
    and evangelism.
TOTAL INCOME: $191,280   FOR OVERSEAS MINISTRIES: $67,448
PERSONNEL:
```
    NORTH AMERICANS OVERSEAS    NON-NORTH AMERICANS OVERSEAS:    0
            MARRIED:    0        NORTH AMERICAN ADM. STAFF:    7
        SINGLE MEN:    0                    SHORT TERM:    28
      SINGLE WOMEN:    0                      RETIRED:    0
                    -----
      TOTAL ACTIVE:    0
```

FIELD OF SERVICE	YEAR BEGAN	PERSONNEL NOW NEW	RELATED CHURCHES	PEOPLE GROUPS	NOTES
India				2	
Japan				2	
Philippines				2	

Technical Support Mission

7120 Gronby St.
Norfolk VA 23505

Tel. (804) 423-8266
EXECUTIVE OFFICER: James R. Herndon
ORGANIZED: 1979
DESCRIPTION: A nondenominational service agency assisting
    field missionaries through technical assitance,
    particularly in the area of mechanical maintenance.
TOTAL INCOME: $50,000   FOR OVERSEAS MINISTRIES: $37,500
PERSONNEL:
```
    NORTH AMERICANS OVERSEAS    NON-NORTH AMERICANS OVERSEAS:    NR
            MARRIED:    2        NORTH AMERICAN ADM. STAFF:    2
        SINGLE MEN:    0                    SHORT TERM:    1
      SINGLE WOMEN:    0                      RETIRED:    0
                    -----
      TOTAL ACTIVE:    2
NOTES:    Administrative personnel are
          volunteer.
```

FIELD OF SERVICE	YEAR BEGAN	PERSONNEL NOW NEW	RELATED CHURCHES	PEOPLE GROUPS	NOTES
Ecuador	1980	2 2			

Technoserve, Inc.

11 Belden Ave.
Norwalk CT 06852

Tel. (203) 655-7981
EXECUTIVE OFFICER: Edward P. Bullard
ORGANIZED: 1968
DESCRIPTION: No current information available. Information
    from 1976 directory. A nondenominational service agency
    providing on-site management and technical assistance to
    low income countries in order to help them become
    self-sufficient.
TOTAL INCOME: $1,137,500   FOR OVERSEAS MINISTRIES: NR
PERSONNEL:
    NORTH AMERICANS OVERSEAS   NON-NORTH AMERICANS OVERSEAS: 7
              MARRIED: 5   NORTH AMERICAN ADM. STAFF: 6
           SINGLE MEN: 2   SHORT TERM: 1
         SINGLE WOMEN: 0   RETIRED: 16

       TOTAL ACTIVE: 7
NOTES: Income estimated by MARC.
        Spouses not included in total overseas personnel.

FIELD OF SERVICE	YEAR BEGAN	PERSONNEL NOW	NEW	RELATED CHURCHES	PEOPLE GROUPS	NOTES
El Salvador	1975					
Ghana	1969					
Honduras	1969					
Kenya	1972					

Teen Missions International, Inc.

885 Hall Rd.
Merritt Island FL 32952
P.O. ADDRESS:
Box 1056
Merritt Island FL 32952

Tel. (305) 453-0350
EXECUTIVE OFFICER: Robert M. Bland
ORGANIZED: 1970
DESCRIPTION: An interdenominational sending agency of
    evangelical tradition with an emphasis on summmer work
    projects and evangelistic teams for teens 13 years and
    older. Also trains youth to assist existing missions in
    building programs, conducting school and youth camps and
    outreach evangelism. Also sponsors adult work and relief
    aid teams. Operates a training and placement program for
    secretaries and youth specialists and two youth centers
    and a European training camp in Scotland.
TOTAL INCOME: $1,614,621   FOR OVERSEAS MINISTRIES: $1,614,621
PERSONNEL:
    NORTH AMERICANS OVERSEAS   NON-NORTH AMERICANS OVERSEAS: 0
              MARRIED: 9   NORTH AMERICAN ADM. STAFF: 40
           SINGLE MEN: 3   SHORT TERM: 1800
         SINGLE WOMEN: 7   RETIRED: 0

       TOTAL ACTIVE: 19

FIELD OF SERVICE	YEAR BEGAN	PERSONNEL NOW	NEW	RELATED CHURCHES	PEOPLE GROUPS	NOTES
Colombia	1977	1				

FIELD OF SERVICE	YEAR BEGAN	PERSONNEL NOW	NEW	RELATED CHURCHES	PEOPLE GROUPS	NOTES
United Kingdom	1977	18				

Tele-Missions International, Inc.

653 Waters Edge
Valley Cottage NY 10989
P.O. ADDRESS:
Box 22
Nyack NY 10960

Tel. (914) 268-9222
EXECUTIVE OFFICER: Gordon S. Anderson
ORGANIZED: 1954
DESCRIPTION: A nondenominational service agency of evangelical
   tradition engaged in broadcasting, Bible distribution,
   education and evangelism. Also providing aid, relief and
   childcare.
TOTAL INCOME: $126,702   FOR OVERSEAS MINISTRIES: $9,146
PERSONNEL:
```
     NORTH AMERICANS OVERSEAS    NON-NORTH AMERICANS OVERSEAS:    0
            MARRIED:  NR           NORTH AMERICAN ADM. STAFF:    17
         SINGLE MEN:  NR                        SHORT TERM:      0
       SINGLE WOMEN:  NR                           RETIRED:      0
                      -----
         TOTAL ACTIVE:   5
```

FIELD OF SERVICE	YEAR BEGAN	PERSONNEL NOW	NEW	RELATED CHURCHES	PEOPLE GROUPS	NOTES
Ecuador	1978	2	2	25	65	
Israel	1977	1	1		30	
Kenya	1978	1	1	18	18	
Sierra Leone	1976	1	1	42	70	

The Associated Missions of the International Council of Christian Churches SEE: TAM-ICCC, Mission Association Section

Things to Come Mission, Inc.

Washington at Main
Cope CO 80812
P.O. ADDRESS:
Box 96
Cope CO 80812

Tel. (303) 357-4291
EXECUTIVE OFFICER: Eldred Sidebottom
ORGANIZED: 1955
DESCRIPTION: A nondenominational sending agency of evangelical
   and fundamentalist tradition establishing churches and
   engaged in theological education, support of nationals,
   broadcasting and Bible distribution.
TOTAL INCOME: $177,000   FOR OVERSEAS MINISTRIES: $155,000
PERSONNEL:
```
     NORTH AMERICANS OVERSEAS    NON-NORTH AMERICANS OVERSEAS:    1
            MARRIED:  12          NORTH AMERICAN ADM. STAFF:      3
         SINGLE MEN:   1                        SHORT TERM:       5
       SINGLE WOMEN:   0                           RETIRED:       0
                      -----
         TOTAL ACTIVE:   13
```

FIELD OF SERVICE	YEAR BEGAN	PERSONNEL NOW	PERSONNEL NEW	RELATED CHURCHES	PEOPLE GROUPS	NOTES
Brazil	1968	2		6		
India	1960			1		
Indonesia	1973	2	1	1		
Nigeria	1972			24		
Philippines	1958	7	1	150		
United Kingdom	1971	2				

Today's Mission Incorporated

924 Anacapa, Ste. 4B
Santa Barbara CA 93101

Tel. (805) 966-4524
EXECUTIVE OFFICER: G. Aeschliman/D. Dolan
ORGANIZED: 1980
DESCRIPTION: A non-profit organization serving missions by
    offering a magazine publication which seeks to stimulate
    interest in cross-cultural world mission service. Exists
    as an information and service agency to established
    organizations by directing Christians toward mission
    involvement.
TOTAL INCOME: $169,200   FOR OVERSEAS MINISTRIES: $0
PERSONNEL:
    NORTH AMERICANS OVERSEAS   NON-NORTH AMERICANS OVERSEAS: 0
                MARRIED: 0   NORTH AMERICAN ADM. STAFF: 0
             SINGLE MEN: 0   SHORT TERM: 0
           SINGLE WOMEN: 0   RETIRED: 0

        TOTAL ACTIVE: 0
NOTES: Income estimated by agency.

Tokyo Evangelistic Center

P.O. ADDRESS:
Box 11
Torrance CA 90507

EXECUTIVE OFFICER: William S. La Sor
ORGANIZED: 1958
DESCRIPTION: No current information available. Information
    from 1976 directory. A nondenominational agency of
    evangelical tradition establishing and serving churches,
    training university students for campus witness, and
    sponsoring a children's camp.
TOTAL INCOME: $69,000   FOR OVERSEAS MINISTRIES: NR
PERSONNEL:
    NORTH AMERICANS OVERSEAS   NON-NORTH AMERICANS OVERSEAS: 3
                MARRIED: 2   NORTH AMERICAN ADM. STAFF: NR
             SINGLE MEN: 1   SHORT TERM: 1
           SINGLE WOMEN: 0   RETIRED: 0

        TOTAL ACTIVE: 3
NOTES: Income estimated by MARC.

FIELD OF SERVICE	YEAR BEGAN	PERSONNEL NOW	PERSONNEL NEW	RELATED CHURCHES	PEOPLE GROUPS	NOTES
Japan						1

1. Dorm and children's camps.

Tokyo Gospel Mission, Inc.

1402 Magnolia
Norman OK 73069

Tel. (405) 329-5931
EXECUTIVE OFFICER: Hugh Moreton
ORGANIZED: 1951
DESCRIPTION: A nondenominational agency of conservative
    evangelical tradition related to a now totally indigenous
    Japanese mission. All money is raised in Japan and all
    staff are Japanese.

TOTAL INCOME:	$0	FOR OVERSEAS MINISTRIES:		$0

PERSONNEL:

NORTH AMERICANS OVERSEAS		NON-NORTH AMERICANS OVERSEAS:	0
MARRIED:	0	NORTH AMERICAN ADM. STAFF:	2
SINGLE MEN:	0	SHORT TERM:	0
SINGLE WOMEN:	0	RETIRED:	0
TOTAL ACTIVE:	0		

Toronto Christian Mission, Inc. SEE: Christian Churches/Churches of Christ

Toronto Institute of Linguistics

25 Ballyconnor Ct.
Willowdale ON M2M 4B3
Canada

Tel. (416) 226-6380
EXECUTIVE OFFICER: Donald A. Larson
ORGANIZED: 1950
DESCRIPTION: A nondenominational educational institute of
    evangelical tradition training missionary candidates for
    bilingual and cross-cultural ministry. Intensive 30-day
    courses include training in phonetics, foreign language
    techniques and mastery, and cross-cultural living. Has
    close relationship with Ontario Bible College and Ontario
    Theological Seminary.

TOTAL INCOME:	$50,596	FOR OVERSEAS MINISTRIES:		$0

PERSONNEL:

NORTH AMERICANS OVERSEAS		NON-NORTH AMERICANS OVERSEAS:	0
MARRIED:	0	NORTH AMERICAN ADM. STAFF:	1
SINGLE MEN:	0	SHORT TERM:	0
SINGLE WOMEN:	0	RETIRED:	0
TOTAL ACTIVE:	0		

Totonac Bible Center, Inc.

3423 E Chapman Ste. A
Orange CA 92669
P.O. ADDRESS:
Box 2050
Orange CA 92669

Tel. (714) 997-3920
EXECUTIVE OFFICER: Manuel Arenas
ORGANIZED: 1972
DESCRIPTION: A nondenominational fund raising and transmittal
    agency of evangelical tradition supporting the Totonac
    Bible Center (Centro Totonaco) in Mexico. The center
    trains leaders within the Totonac tribe, carries out radio
    evangelism and provides medical and development
    assistance. Donors can support individual students.

TOTAL INCOME:	$46,747	FOR OVERSEAS MINISTRIES:	$46,747

PERSONNEL:
```
    NORTH AMERICANS OVERSEAS    NON-NORTH AMERICANS OVERSEAS:    0
              MARRIED:    0        NORTH AMERICAN ADM. STAFF:    0
           SINGLE MEN:    0                      SHORT TERM:   19
         SINGLE WOMEN:    0                         RETIRED:    0
                        -----
         TOTAL ACTIVE:    0
```

FIELD OF SERVICE	YEAR BEGAN	PERSONNEL NOW	NEW	RELATED CHURCHES	PEOPLE GROUPS	NOTES
Mexico	1972			40		

Trans World Missions

4205 Santa Monica Blvd.
Los Angeles CA 90029
P.O. ADDRESS:
Box 10
Glendale CA 91209

Tel. (213) 663-1176
EXECUTIVE OFFICER: John G. Olson
ORGANIZED: 1949
DESCRIPTION: An interdenominational sending agency of
    evangelical tradition involved in the training of
    nationals, radio and TV broadcasting, literature
    distribution and correspondence courses. Also supports
    children's homes, youth camps, Christian centers and
    provides emergency relief.
TOTAL INCOME: NR   FOR OVERSEAS MINISTRIES: $154,000
PERSONNEL:
```
    NORTH AMERICANS OVERSEAS    NON-NORTH AMERICANS OVERSEAS:    NR
              MARRIED:    6        NORTH AMERICAN ADM. STAFF:    NR
           SINGLE MEN:    0                      SHORT TERM:     2
         SINGLE WOMEN:    1                         RETIRED:    NR
                        -----
         TOTAL ACTIVE:    7
```
NOTES: Financial data said to be available to any
    responsible party. Overseas income estimated
    by MARC.

FIELD OF SERVICE	YEAR BEGAN	PERSONNEL NOW	NEW	RELATED CHURCHES	PEOPLE GROUPS	NOTES
Brazil	1965	7				
Costa Rica	1968					
Guatemala	1976					
Mexico	1949	3				
Nicaragua	1966					
Trinidad and Tobago	1976	2				

Trans World Radio

560 Main St.
Chatham NJ 07928

Tel. (201) 635-5775
EXECUTIVE OFFICER: Paul E. Freed
ORGANIZED: 1952   AFFILIATION: EFMA
DESCRIPTION: An interdenominational, international service
    and sending agency of independent tradition engaged in
    broadcasting, literature distribution, recording and
    providing correspondence courses.
TOTAL INCOME: $10,000,000   FOR OVERSEAS MINISTRIES: NR

PERSONNEL:
```
     NORTH AMERICANS OVERSEAS    NON-NORTH AMERICANS OVERSEAS:   20
                MARRIED:  138       NORTH AMERICAN ADM. STAFF:   40
             SINGLE MEN:    3                      SHORT TERM:    7
           SINGLE WOMEN:   10                         RETIRED:    0
                         -----
           TOTAL ACTIVE:  151
```

FIELD OF SERVICE	YEAR BEGAN	PERSONNEL NOW	NEW	RELATED CHURCHES	PEOPLE GROUPS	NOTES
Cyprus	1974					
Guam	1975	28				
Monaco	1059	38	1			
Morocco	1954					
Netherlands Antilles	1964	66				
Sri Lanka	1975	17				
Swaziland	1974	50				

Trinitarian Bible Society, Canada

26 Gracey Blvd.
Weston ON M9R 1Z9
Canada

Tel. (416) 249-0718
EXECUTIVE OFFICER: G. D. Meelish
ORGANIZED: 1968
DESCRIPTION: A nondenominational international service agency
    of evangelical and fundamentalist tradition engaged in
    Bible translation, distribution and memorization. A branch
    of the international agency of the same name headquartered
    in London, England.
TOTAL INCOME: $72,604   FOR OVERSEAS MINISTRIES: $72,604
PERSONNEL:
```
     NORTH AMERICANS OVERSEAS    NON-NORTH AMERICANS OVERSEAS:    0
                MARRIED:    0       NORTH AMERICAN ADM. STAFF:    2
             SINGLE MEN:    0                      SHORT TERM:    0
           SINGLE WOMEN:    0                         RETIRED:    0
                         -----
           TOTAL ACTIVE:    0
```

Ukrainian Evangelical Alliance of North America

5610 Trowbridge Dr.
Dunwoody GA 30338

Tel. (404) 394-7795
EXECUTIVE OFFICER: Wladimir Borowsky
ORGANIZED: 1922
DESCRIPTION: A nondenominational coordination agency of
    Reformed tradition supporting nationals and national
    churches. Also engaged in Bible distribution and Christian
    literature.
TOTAL INCOME: NR   FOR OVERSEAS MINISTRIES: NR
PERSONNEL:
```
     NORTH AMERICANS OVERSEAS    NON-NORTH AMERICANS OVERSEAS:   NR
                MARRIED:   NR       NORTH AMERICAN ADM. STAFF:   NR
             SINGLE MEN:   NR                      SHORT TERM:   NR
           SINGLE WOMEN:   NR                         RETIRED:   NR
                         -----
           TOTAL ACTIVE:   NR
```

Undenominational Church of the Lord

1022 N Bradford Ave.
Placentia CA 92670

Tel. (714) 996-9720
EXECUTIVE OFFICER: Robert Wallace
ORGANIZED: 1930
DESCRIPTION: A nondenominational agency of Holiness tradition
    engaged in Bible distribution and literature production
    and distribution. Agency supports two nationals in South
    India.
TOTAL INCOME: $17,800   FOR OVERSEAS MINISTRIES: $17,800
PERSONNEL:
    NORTH AMERICANS OVERSEAS   NON-NORTH AMERICANS OVERSEAS: 0
        MARRIED: 0   NORTH AMERICAN ADM. STAFF: 0
        SINGLE MEN: 0   SHORT TERM: 0
        SINGLE WOMEN: 0   RETIRED: 0

        TOTAL ACTIVE: 0

Underground Christian Missions, Inc.

1819 N La Palmas
Hollywood CA 90028
P.O. ADDRESS:
Box 1076
Los Angeles CA 90028

Tel. (213) 466-3453
EXECUTIVE OFFICER: Jim Dimov
ORGANIZED: 1973
DESCRIPTION: A service agency of evangelical tradition
    involved in Bible and literature distribution, evangelism
    and aid and relief to people in communist countries.
TOTAL INCOME: NR   FOR OVERSEAS MINISTRIES: NR
PERSONNEL:
    NORTH AMERICANS OVERSEAS   NON-NORTH AMERICANS OVERSEAS: NR
        MARRIED: 0   NORTH AMERICAN ADM. STAFF: 4
        SINGLE MEN: 0   SHORT TERM: 0
        SINGLE WOMEN: 0   RETIRED: 0

        TOTAL ACTIVE: 0

Underground Evangelism SEE: Evangelism Center, Inc.

Unevangelized Fields Mission

306 Bala Ave.
Bala-Cynwyd PA 19004
P.O. ADDRESS:
Box 306
Bala-Cynwyd PA 19004

Tel. (215) 667-7660
EXECUTIVE OFFICER: Alfred Larson
ORGANIZED: 1931   AFFILIATION: IFMA
DESCRIPTION: A nondenominational sending agency of
    fundamentalist and evangelical tradition establishing
    national churches and emphasizing evangelism and training
    of national leadership. Also engaged in education,
    literature production and distribution, linguistics,
    translation, radio broadcasting and medicine.
TOTAL INCOME: $3,750,000   FOR OVERSEAS MINISTRIES: $3,750,000
PERSONNEL:
    NORTH AMERICANS OVERSEAS   NON-NORTH AMERICANS OVERSEAS: 0
        MARRIED: 242   NORTH AMERICAN ADM. STAFF: 25
        SINGLE MEN: 2   SHORT TERM: 4

462

```
SINGLE WOMEN:   68                          RETIRED:    22
                -----
    TOTAL ACTIVE:  312
-------------------------------------------------------------------
                    YEAR    PERSONNEL   RELATED   PEOPLE
FIELD OF SERVICE    BEGAN   NOW   NEW   CHURCHES  GROUPS  NOTES
-------------------------------------------------------------------
Brazil              1931    102    17
Dominican Republic  1943     17     4
France              1962     40    13
Germany, Fed. Rep.  1976      2     2
Guyana              1949      2     1
Haiti               1943     44    10
Indonesia           1957     42     7
Italy               1974      6     2
Mexico              1971     23    12
South Africa        1979      4     4
```

Unevangelized Tribes Mission, Inc.

Open Door Estates-F23
Ft. Washington PA 19034

Tel. (215) 646-4523
EXECUTIVE OFFICER: David W. Allen
ORGANIZED: 1929
DESCRIPTION: A nondenominational fund transmittal agency of
    Baptist tradition supporting approved personnel sent under
    other Baptist mission boards.
TOTAL INCOME: $22,730   FOR OVERSEAS MINISTRIES: NR
PERSONNEL:
    NORTH AMERICANS OVERSEAS   NON-NORTH AMERICANS OVERSEAS: NR
            MARRIED: 0   NORTH AMERICAN ADM. STAFF: 1
         SINGLE MEN: 0   SHORT TERM: 0
       SINGLE WOMEN: 0   RETIRED: 2

       TOTAL ACTIVE: 0

United Board for Christian Higher
Education in Asia

475 Riverside Dr Rm 1221
New York NY 10115

Tel. (212) 870-2608
EXECUTIVE OFFICER: Paul T. Lauby
ORGANIZED: 1932   AFFILIATION: DOM-NCCCUSA-Frat. Rel.
DESCRIPTION: An interdenominational specialized service agency
    supporting higher education. Gives basic support to and
    provides program assistance for a number of Christian
    universities in Asia.
TOTAL INCOME: $13,623,501   FOR OVERSEAS MINISTRIES: $3,361,857
PERSONNEL:
    NORTH AMERICANS OVERSEAS   NON-NORTH AMERICANS OVERSEAS: NR
            MARRIED: NR   NORTH AMERICAN ADM. STAFF: 8
         SINGLE MEN: NR   SHORT TERM: 4
       SINGLE WOMEN: NR   RETIRED: 1

       TOTAL ACTIVE: NR

                    YEAR   PERSONNEL   RELATED   PEOPLE
FIELD OF SERVICE   BEGAN   NOW   NEW   CHURCHES GROUPS NOTES

Hong-Kong   1950
```
```

FIELD OF SERVICE	YEAR BEGAN	PERSONNEL NOW	NEW	RELATED CHURCHES	PEOPLE GROUPS	NOTES
India						
Indonesia	1950					
Japan	1950					
Korea, Rep. of	1950					
Philippines	1950					
Taiwan Rep of China	1950					
Thailand						

United Brethren in Christ SEE: Church of the United Brethren in Christ

United Christian Missionary Society SEE: Christian Church, Disciples of Christ

United Church Board For World Ministries

475 Riverside Dr.
New York NY 10115

Tel. (212) 870-2637
EXECUTIVE OFFICER: David M. Stowe
ORGANIZED: 1810   AFFILIATION: DOM-NCCCUSA
DESCRIPTION: A denominational sending agency of Reformed and
    Congregational tradition nurturing national churches and
    involved in development of human resources, medicine, aid
    and all forms of education.
TOTAL INCOME: $9,495,679   FOR OVERSEAS MINISTRIES: $9,495,679
PERSONNEL:
    NORTH AMERICANS OVERSEAS   NON-NORTH AMERICANS OVERSEAS: 7
            MARRIED: 126   NORTH AMERICAN ADM. STAFF: 52
        SINGLE MEN: 6   SHORT TERM: 0
      SINGLE WOMEN: 28   RETIRED: NR

        TOTAL ACTIVE: 160
NOTES: Total appointed overseas staff is 250.
        Those not listed as North Americans overseas
        are either self-supporting or supported by
        field institutions.

FIELD OF SERVICE	YEAR BEGAN	PERSONNEL NOW	NEW	RELATED CHURCHES	PEOPLE GROUPS	NOTES
Angola	1880					
Argentina	1955					
Australia	1972					
Belgium	1977					
Belize	1975					
Botswana	1971	7	5			
Cameroon	1977					
Costa Rica	1974	4	2			
Cyprus	1974					
Ecuador	1945					
France	1946					
Germany, Fed. Rep.	1945					
Ghana	1946	5	3			
Honduras	1921	3				
Hong-Kong	1950					

FIELD OF SERVICE	YEAR BEGAN	PERSONNEL NOW	NEW	RELATED CHURCHES	PEOPLE GROUPS	NOTES
India	1813	29	2			
Indonesia	1956	4				
Iran	1973					
Jamaica	1978					
Japan	1869	34				
Kenya	1966	2	2			
Lebanon	1819	2				
Mexico	1872	2				
Nepal	1966	2	2			
Niger	1977					
Pacific Trust Terr.	1852	2	2			
Peru	1970					
Philippines	1902	8	2			
South Africa	1835	5	2			
Sri Lanka	1816	3	3			
Swaziland	1978	2	2			
Switzerland	1960					
Taiwan Rep of China	1957	4	2			
Tanzania	1962					
Thailand	1970					
Togo	1946	2				
Turkey	1819	31	6			
United Kingdom	1945					
Zaire	1973	1	1			
Zambia	1965	8	6			
Zimbabwe	1892					

United Church of Canada, Division of World Outreach

85 St. Clair Ave. E
Toronto ON M4T 1M8
Canada

Tel. (416) 925-5931
EXECUTIVE OFFICER: G. W. Legge
ORGANIZED: 1925
DESCRIPTION: A denominational sending agency of ecumenical
    tradition working in cooperation with partner churches and
    Christian agencies overseas by responding to their
    requests for personnel, financial support and solidarity
    action in Canada.
TOTAL INCOME: $5,092,912   FOR OVERSEAS MINISTRIES: $5,092,912
PERSONNEL:
    NORTH AMERICANS OVERSEAS   NON-NORTH AMERICANS OVERSEAS: 0
                MARRIED: 80   NORTH AMERICAN ADM. STAFF: 15
             SINGLE MEN: 9   SHORT TERM: 0
           SINGLE WOMEN: 26   RETIRED: NA

        TOTAL ACTIVE: 115

FIELD OF SERVICE	YEAR BEGAN	PERSONNEL NOW	NEW	RELATED CHURCHES	PEOPLE GROUPS	NOTES
Argentina		2		1		
Brazil		6		1		
Cayman Islands		2		1		
Haiti		2		1		

FIELD OF SERVICE	YEAR BEGAN	PERSONNEL NOW	NEW	RELATED CHURCHES	PEOPLE GROUPS	NOTES
Hong-Kong		2		1		
India		12		1		
Jamaica		2		1		
Japan		19		1		
Kenya		4		1		
Korea, Rep. of		13		1		
Lesotho		8		1		
Malawi		2		1		
Nepal		15				
Nicaragua				1		
Panama		2		1		
Papua New Guinea		1		1		
Philippines		1		1		
Zaire		3		1		
Zambia		18		1		

United Church of Christ United Church Bd. for Wld. Min. SEE: United Church Board for World Ministries

United Evangelical Churches

303 S Alta Vista
Monrovia CA 91016
P.O. ADDRESS:
Box 28
Monrovia CA 91016

Tel. (213) 357-2238
EXECUTIVE OFFICER: Charles J. Hardin
ORGANIZED: 1961
DESCRIPTION: A nondenominational service agency of charismatic
    and independent tradition, engaged in education,
    evangelism, literature distribution and training and
    financially assisting missionaries and ministers.
    Missionaries are supported through Christians United in
    Action, Inc.
TOTAL INCOME: NR   FOR OVERSEAS MINISTRIES: NR
PERSONNEL:
    NORTH AMERICANS OVERSEAS   NON-NORTH AMERICANS OVERSEAS: NR
            MARRIED: 0   NORTH AMERICAN ADM. STAFF: 5
         SINGLE MEN: 0   SHORT TERM: 0
       SINGLE WOMEN: 0   RETIRED: 0

       TOTAL ACTIVE: 0
NOTES: Personnel who are overseas are included
        in the report of Christians United in
        Action, Inc.

United Fellowship for Christian Service SEE: BMMF International (USA)

United Fundamentalist Church

3236 Larga Ave.
Los Angeles CA 90039
P.O. ADDRESS:
Box 28
Los Angeles CA 90053

Tel. (213) 661-1390
EXECUTIVE OFFICER: E. Paul Kopp
ORGANIZED: 1939
DESCRIPTION: A nondenominational sending agency of Pentecostal
    and Holiness tradition engaged in evangelism, broadcasting,
    fund transmittal and literature distribution.

```
TOTAL INCOME:        NR     FOR OVERSEAS MINISTRIES:     $132,000
PERSONNEL:
   NORTH AMERICANS OVERSEAS    NON-NORTH AMERICANS OVERSEAS:    0
             MARRIED:  NR          NORTH AMERICAN ADM. STAFF:   2
          SINGLE MEN:  NR                        SHORT TERM:    0
        SINGLE WOMEN:  NR                           RETIRED:    0
                       -----
      TOTAL ACTIVE:    6
NOTES:  Overseas income estimated by MARC.
-----------------------------------------------------------------
                     YEAR      PERSONNEL    RELATED    PEOPLE
FIELD OF SERVICE     BEGAN     NOW   NEW    CHURCHES   GROUPS  NOTES
-----------------------------------------------------------------
Israel               1954       6     2
```

United Indian Missions, Inc.

2920 N Third St.
Flagstaff AZ 86001
P.O. ADDRESS:
Box U
Flagstaff AZ 86001

```
Tel. (601) 774-0651
EXECUTIVE OFFICER: Donald G. Fredericks
ORGANIZED: 1956
DESCRIPTION:  No current information available.  Information
    from 1976 directory.  A nondenominational sending agency
    of independent and fundamentalist tradition establishing
    churches and engaged in evangelism and leadership
    training. Also ministers to American Indians in USA and
    Canada.
TOTAL INCOME:    $690,000   FOR OVERSEAS MINISTRIES:    $103,500
PERSONNEL:
   NORTH AMERICANS OVERSEAS    NON-NORTH AMERICANS OVERSEAS:   10
             MARRIED:  8            NORTH AMERICAN ADM. STAFF:   1
          SINGLE MEN:  0                        SHORT TERM:    0
        SINGLE WOMEN:  2                           RETIRED:    2
                       -----
      TOTAL ACTIVE:    10
NOTES:  Incomes estimated by MARC. Overseas approximate
        amount spent in Mexico based on
        previous estimate by agency.
-----------------------------------------------------------------
                     YEAR      PERSONNEL    RELATED    PEOPLE
FIELD OF SERVICE     BEGAN     NOW   NEW    CHURCHES   GROUPS  NOTES
-----------------------------------------------------------------
Mexico
    Note: By extension.
```

United Lutheran Church in America SEE: Lutheran Church in America

United Methodist Church United
Methodist Committee on Relief

475 Riverside Dr. Rm. 1470
New York NY 10115

```
Tel. (212) 678-6161
EXECUTIVE OFFICER: J. Harry Hanes
ORGANIZED: 1940    AFFILIATION: DOM-NCCCUSA
DESCRIPTION:  Formerly, U.M. Committee on Overseas Relief.
    Name changed in 1972. A denominational specialized service
    agency of Methodist tradition involved in relief,
    rehabilitation, refugee resettlement, community
    development, medicine, agriculture, childcare and
```

technical assistance. Also responsible for emergency
disaster relief in USA.
TOTAL INCOME: $12,800,000   FOR OVERSEAS MINISTRIES: $12,100,000
PERSONNEL:
```
    NORTH AMERICANS OVERSEAS    NON-NORTH AMERICANS OVERSEAS:    NR
            MARRIED:    NR          NORTH AMERICAN ADM. STAFF:     6
         SINGLE MEN:    NR                        SHORT TERM:   985
       SINGLE WOMEN:    NR                           RETIRED:     5
                        -----
       TOTAL ACTIVE:   650
```

United Methodist Church World
Division of the Board of Global
Ministries

475 Riverside Dr.
New York NY 10115

Tel. (212) 678-6098
EXECUTIVE OFFICER: Lois Miller
ORGANIZED: 1940   AFFILIATION: DOM-NCCCUSA
DESCRIPTION: Formerly, Board of Missions. Name changed in
    1971. A denominational sending agency of Methodist
    tradition supporting national churches and ecumenical
    agencies, engaged in church extension, medicine, Christian
    communication, education, agriculture, childcare and
    community development.
TOTAL INCOME: $19,377,430   FOR OVERSEAS MINISTRIES: $18,780,041
PERSONNEL:
```
    NORTH AMERICANS OVERSEAS    NON-NORTH AMERICANS OVERSEAS:    NR
            MARRIED:    NR          NORTH AMERICAN ADM. STAFF:    22
         SINGLE MEN:    NR                        SHORT TERM:   166
       SINGLE WOMEN:    NR                           RETIRED:    NR
                        -----
       TOTAL ACTIVE:   938
```

FIELD OF SERVICE	YEAR BEGAN	PERSONNEL NOW	NEW	RELATED CHURCHES	PEOPLE GROUPS	NOTES
Algeria	1908					
Argentina	1836					
Austria						
Belgium						
Bolivia	1878					
Botswana	1969					
Brazil	1880					
Caribbean-general						
Chile	1884					
Ecuador						
Fiji						
France						
Hong-Kong	1950					
India	1870					
Japan	1873					
Kenya	1962					
Korea, Rep. of	1884					
Liberia	1833					
Mexico	1873					
Mozambique	1881					
Nigeria	1926					
Pakistan	1924					

FIELD OF SERVICE	YEAR BEGAN	PERSONNEL NOW	NEW	RELATED CHURCHES	PEOPLE GROUPS	NOTES
Panama	1905					
Papua New Guinea						
Peru	1887					
Philippines	1899					
Samoa						
Sierra Leone	1855					
South Africa	1898					
Taiwan Rep of China	1952					
Tonga						
Tunisia	1839					
Uruguay	1839					
Zaire	1914					
Zambia	1966					
Zimbabwe	1898					

Note: Total overseas personnel includes nationals.

United Missionary Fellowship

3636 Auburn Blvd.
Sacramento CA 95821
P.O. ADDRESS:
Box 21-4095
Sacramento CA 95821

Tel. (916) 483-8917
EXECUTIVE OFFICER: Robert E. Jeffcott
ORGANIZED: 1948
DESCRIPTION: A nondenominational sending agency of independent and fundamentalist tradition establishing churches and engaged in education, ministry to servicemen, evangelism and ministry to the deaf and deaf/blind.
TOTAL INCOME: $687,961 FOR OVERSEAS MINISTRIES: $89,432
PERSONNEL:

NORTH AMERICANS OVERSEAS		NON-NORTH AMERICANS OVERSEAS:	0
MARRIED:	27	NORTH AMERICAN ADM. STAFF:	7
SINGLE MEN:	0	SHORT TERM:	7
SINGLE WOMEN:	3	RETIRED:	0
TOTAL ACTIVE:	30		

FIELD OF SERVICE	YEAR BEGAN	PERSONNEL NOW	NEW	RELATED CHURCHES	PEOPLE GROUPS	NOTES
Cyprus	1971	2		1		1
Haiti	1970	2		2		
Honduras	1954	2		4		
Mexico	1951	3	1	12		
New Zealand	1968	6		3		
Puerto Rico	1968	10	4	2		

Note: 1. Includes Lebanon.

United Pentecostal Church
International Foreign Missions
Division

8855 Dunn Rd.
Hazelwood MO 63042

Tel. (314) 837-7300
EXECUTIVE OFFICER: Harry E. Scism
ORGANIZED: 1924
DESCRIPTION: A denominational sending agency of Pentecostal tradition establishing churches and engaged in evangelism, literature, education and training.

```
TOTAL INCOME:  $5,747,516        FOR OVERSEAS MINISTRIES:   NR
PERSONNEL:
   NORTH AMERICANS OVERSEAS    NON-NORTH AMERICANS OVERSEAS:   NR
          MARRIED:   NR          NORTH AMERICAN ADM. STAFF:   14
       SINGLE MEN:   NR                        SHORT TERM:    5
     SINGLE WOMEN:   NR                           RETIRED:    7
                  -----
     TOTAL ACTIVE:  187
```

FIELD OF SERVICE	YEAR BEGAN	PERSONNEL NOW	NEW	RELATED CHURCHES	PEOPLE GROUPS	NOTES
Argentina	1967	6				
Australia	1956	6				
Austria	1971	2				
Bolivia	1974	4				
Botswana						
Brazil	1952	12				
Burma						
Chile	1964	2				
Colombia	1937	2				
Costa Rica	1975	2				
Dominican Republic	1962	2				
Ecuador	1959	5				
Egypt						
El Salvador	1975	2				
Ethiopia	1967					
Fiji		4				
France	1973	2				
Germany, Fed. Rep.	1966	8				
Ghana	1969	5				
Greece	1975	2				
Guatemala		2				
Guyana						
Haiti	1962	2				
Honduras		2				
Hong-Kong	1975	2				
India	1949					
Italy	1972	4				
Ivory Coast	1975	2				
Japan	1979	2				
Kenya	1972	4				
Korea, Rep. of	1965	6				
Liberia	1936	2				
Madagascar	1969	4				
Malawi	1979	2				
Malaysia						
Mexico	1979	2				
Netherlands		2				
New Zealand	1969	2				
Nicaragua	1970	2				
Nigeria	1972	2				
Norway		2				
Pakistan	1971	7				
Paraguay	1973	2				
Peru	1962	8				
Philippines	1957	12				
Portugal	1972	2				
Puerto Rico	1962	2				

FIELD OF SERVICE	YEAR BEGAN	PERSONNEL NOW	NEW	RELATED CHURCHES	PEOPLE GROUPS	NOTES
Senegal	1978	2				
Sierra Leone	1975	2				
South Africa	1948	8				
Spain	1979	4				
Sri Lanka						
Switzerland		2				
Taiwan Rep of China	1978	2				
Thailand	1962	1				
Tonga		2				
United Kingdom	1965	2				
Uruguay	1956	4				
Venezuela	1955	6				
Zimbabwe	1968	3				

United Presbyterian Center for Mission Studies

1605 E Elizabeth Ste.22
Pasadena CA 91104

Tel. (213) 798-7527
EXECUTIVE OFFICER: Franklin E. Satterberg
ORGANIZED: 1972
DESCRIPTION: A denominational specialized service agency of
    Presbyterian tradition providing an information service
    and doing research in support of cross-cultural mission.
    Also counseling prospective missionary candidates. Related
    to the United Presbyterian Church in the USA.
TOTAL INCOME: $15,000   FOR OVERSEAS MINISTRIES: $0
PERSONNEL:

NORTH AMERICANS OVERSEAS		NON-NORTH AMERICANS OVERSEAS:	0
MARRIED:	0	NORTH AMERICAN ADM. STAFF:	3
SINGLE MEN:	0	SHORT TERM:	0
SINGLE WOMEN:	0	RETIRED:	0
TOTAL ACTIVE:	0		

United Presbyterian Church in the USA Program Agency

475 Riverside Dr.
New York NY 10115

Tel. (212) 870-2687
EXECUTIVE OFFICER: J. Oscar McCloud
ORGANIZED: 1837   AFFILIATION: DOM-NCCCUSA
DESCRIPTION: A denominational sending agency of Presbyterian
    tradition establishing churches and engaged in evangelism,
    community development and education. Also supports
    national churches.
TOTAL INCOME: $12,008,328   FOR OVERSEAS MINISTRIES: $6,890,424
PERSONNEL:

NORTH AMERICANS OVERSEAS		NON-NORTH AMERICANS OVERSEAS:	3
MARRIED:	298	NORTH AMERICAN ADM. STAFF:	4
SINGLE MEN:	6	SHORT TERM:	20
SINGLE WOMEN:	55	RETIRED:	0
TOTAL ACTIVE:	359		

FIELD OF SERVICE	YEAR BEGAN	PERSONNEL NOW	NEW	RELATED CHURCHES	PEOPLE GROUPS	NOTES
Afghanistan		2				

FIELD OF SERVICE	YEAR BEGAN	PERSONNEL NOW	PERSONNEL NEW	RELATED CHURCHES	PEOPLE GROUPS	NOTES
Argentina		2				
Bangladesh		2	2			
Belgium		2				
Brazil	1859	12				
Cameroon	1879	8	2			
Chile	1845	6	4			
Colombia	1856	11	1			
Costa Rica		4	2			
Egypt	1954	9	4			
Ethiopia	1820	12				
Germany, Fed. Rep.		1	1			
Guatemala	1882	14	3			
Hong-Kong	1844	3	1			
India	1834	28	2			
Indonesia	1951	2	2			
Iran	1835	16	2			
Japan	1859	25	6			
Jordan		2	2			1
Kenya		12	4			
Korea, Rep. of	1884	30	5			
Lebanon	1823	10				
Malawi		1	6			
Malaysia		2	2			
Mexico	1872	4				
Middle East-general		2				
Mozambique		2				
Nepal		12	3			
Netherlands		1				
Nigeria		2				
Pacific Trust Terr.			2			
Pakistan	1834	31	2			
Papua New Guinea		2	2			
Peru		2				
Philippines	1899	7				
Portugal			1			
Singapore		2				
Sudan	1900	10	3			
Switzerland		2				
Taiwan Rep of China	1952	8	2			
Thailand	1840	21	5			
Togo		2	2			
United Kingdom			2			
Venezuela	1897	4	2			
Zaire		2				
Zambia		5	4			

Note: 1. Includes Syrian Arab Republic.

United Presbyterian Order for World Evangelization

1605 E Elizabeth St.
Pasadena CA 91104

Tel. (213) 794-7155
EXECUTIVE OFFICER: Mary Frances Redding
ORGANIZED: 1974
DESCRIPTION: A denominational agency of Presbyterian tradition
involved in support of mission projects. It functions
within the general governance of the United Presbyterian
Church providing an alternate channel for overseas project
activity. Also is a community with a "Rule of Order" based
on living with a disciplined level of personal consumption
and committing additional resources to mission endeavors.

```
TOTAL INCOME:      $17,860        FOR OVERSEAS MINISTRIES:    $0
PERSONNEL:
   NORTH AMERICANS OVERSEAS    NON-NORTH AMERICANS OVERSEAS:    0
           MARRIED:   0         NORTH AMERICAN ADM. STAFF:      0
        SINGLE MEN:   0                       SHORT TERM:       0
      SINGLE WOMEN:   0                          RETIRED:       0
                    -----
      TOTAL ACTIVE:   0
```

United States Center for World Mission

1605 E Elizabeth St.
Pasadena CA 91104
P.O. ADDRESS:
Box 9
Pasadena CA 91109

Tel. (213) 794-7155
EXECUTIVE OFFICER: Ralph D. Winter
ORGANIZED: 1976
DESCRIPTION: An interdenominational specialized service agency
   of evangelical tradition dedicated exclusively to the
   cause of frontier missions to unreached people groups in
   which there is no indigenous church. Provides research,
   information service and instructional programs.

```
TOTAL INCOME:     $850,000        FOR OVERSEAS MINISTRIES:    $0
PERSONNEL:
   NORTH AMERICANS OVERSEAS    NON-NORTH AMERICANS OVERSEAS:    0
           MARRIED:   0         NORTH AMERICAN ADM. STAFF:     40
        SINGLE MEN:   0                       SHORT TERM:       5
      SINGLE WOMEN:   0                          RETIRED:      NR
                    -----
      TOTAL ACTIVE:   0
```

United World Mission, Incorporated

10900 Navajo Dr.
St. Petersburg FL 33708
P.O. ADDRESS:
Box 8000
St. Petersburg FL 33738

Tel. (813) 391-0195
EXECUTIVE OFFICER: Gerald Boyer
ORGANIZED: 1946   AFFILIATION: IFMA/EFMA
DESCRIPTION: A nondenominational sending agency of evangelical
   tradition establishing churches and engaged in education,
   evangelism and medicine. Also supports national churches.

```
TOTAL INCOME:  $1,275,134  FOR OVERSEAS MINISTRIES:  $1,076,263
PERSONNEL:
   NORTH AMERICANS OVERSEAS    NON-NORTH AMERICANS OVERSEAS:    8
           MARRIED:  44         NORTH AMERICAN ADM. STAFF:     13
        SINGLE MEN:   0                       SHORT TERM:      10
      SINGLE WOMEN:   8                          RETIRED:       3
                    -----
      TOTAL ACTIVE:  52
NOTES:  Also two part-time administrative personnel.
```

FIELD OF SERVICE	YEAR BEGAN	PERSONNEL NOW	PERSONNEL NEW	RELATED CHURCHES	PEOPLE GROUPS	NOTES
Belgium	1970	2		3		

FIELD OF SERVICE	YEAR BEGAN	PERSONNEL NOW	PERSONNEL NEW	RELATED CHURCHES	PEOPLE GROUPS	NOTES
Bolivia	1946	6	3	6		
Brazil	1961	2		3		
Congo	1948	3	1	12	2	
Cuba	1946			10		
Guatemala	1953	6	2	14		
India	1958			1	1	
Korea, Rep. of	1955	4		4	1	
Mali	1953	13	3	10	2	
Nicaragua	1969			6		
Philippines	1946			15		
Senegal	1961	10		2	2	
Spain	1946	1		3		
United Kingdom	1956	2				
Venezuela	1946	8		35		

Upward, Inc. SEE: MAP International

Vacation Samaritans

4202 Genesee Ave. Ste300
San Diego CA 92117
P.O. ADDRESS:
Box 17008
San Diego CA 92117

Tel. (714) 279-6861
EXECUTIVE OFFICER: Darold H. Jones
ORGANIZED: 1967
DESCRIPTION: An interdenominational service agency of
    evangelical tradition conducting a youth ministry with
    emphasis on medical services.
TOTAL INCOME: $200,000   FOR OVERSEAS MINISTRIES: $200,000
PERSONNEL:
   NORTH AMERICANS OVERSEAS   NON-NORTH AMERICANS OVERSEAS: NR
        MARRIED: NR   NORTH AMERICAN ADM. STAFF: 5
      SINGLE MEN: NR   SHORT TERM: 325
    SINGLE WOMEN: NR   RETIRED: NR

     TOTAL ACTIVE: 20
NOTES: All personnel are volunteer full and part-time
    Overseas income estimated by MARC.

Vellore Christian Medical College
Board, (USA) Inc.

475 Riverside Dr. Rm.243
New York NY 10115

Tel. (212) 870-2640
EXECUTIVE OFFICER: Herbert O. Muenstermann
ORGANIZED: 1948
DESCRIPTION: A nondenominational service agency of ecumenical
    tradition engaged in fund raising and transmitting
    personnel, and purchasing services for the Vellore
    Christian Medical College and Hospital in India.
TOTAL INCOME: $846,958   FOR OVERSEAS MINISTRIES: $625,958
PERSONNEL:
   NORTH AMERICANS OVERSEAS   NON-NORTH AMERICANS OVERSEAS: 15
        MARRIED: 0   NORTH AMERICAN ADM. STAFF: 4
      SINGLE MEN: 0   SHORT TERM: 0

```
SINGLE WOMEN:        0                              RETIRED:      0
                   -----
     TOTAL ACTIVE:   0
NOTES:  Member boards and agencies sent 11
        American appointees in 1979.
```

Victory Mission of the Americas

4005 Emerald Oaks
Ft. Worth TX 76117
P.O. ADDRESS:
Box 14444
Ft. Worth TX 76117

```
Tel. (817) 838-6342
EXECUTIVE OFFICER: William L. McCall
ORGANIZED: 1964
DESCRIPTION:  A nondenominational sending agency of evangelical
    and fundamentalist tradition primarily involved in
    childcare and adoption programs in Colombia. Also involved
    in church planting, evangelism and missionary orientation
    for North American college students.
TOTAL INCOME:      $10,258   FOR OVERSEAS MINISTRIES:      $10,258
PERSONNEL:
    NORTH AMERICANS OVERSEAS    NON-NORTH AMERICANS OVERSEAS:      1
            MARRIED:    0           NORTH AMERICAN ADM. STAFF:     0
         SINGLE MEN:    0                      SHORT TERM:         0
       SINGLE WOMEN:    1                         RETIRED:         0
                      -----
       TOTAL ACTIVE:    1
------------------------------------------------------------------
                    YEAR      PERSONNEL    RELATED    PEOPLE
FIELD OF SERVICE    BEGAN    NOW    NEW    CHURCHES   GROUPS   NOTES
------------------------------------------------------------------
Colombia            1964      1                1        1
```

Virginia Mennonite Board of
Missions and Charities

1151 Greystone St.
Harrisonburg VA 22801

```
Tel. (703) 434-9727
EXECUTIVE OFFICER: Isaac M. Risser
ORGANIZED: 1919
DESCRIPTION:  A denominational sending agency of Mennonite
    tradition establishing churches and supporting nationals
    and missionaries. Also engaged in education, medicine,
    relief, literature and self-help projects.
TOTAL INCOME:     $285,614   FOR OVERSEAS MINISTRIES:     $150,000
PERSONNEL:
    NORTH AMERICANS OVERSEAS    NON-NORTH AMERICANS OVERSEAS:      0
            MARRIED:    8           NORTH AMERICAN ADM. STAFF:     1
         SINGLE MEN:    1                      SHORT TERM:         8
       SINGLE WOMEN:    0                         RETIRED:         7
                      -----
       TOTAL ACTIVE:    9
------------------------------------------------------------------
                    YEAR      PERSONNEL    RELATED    PEOPLE
FIELD OF SERVICE    BEGAN    NOW    NEW    CHURCHES   GROUPS   NOTES
------------------------------------------------------------------
Italy                 1949     4      2        2        1
Trinidad and Tobago   1971     4      2        1        1
```

Virginia Mennonite Conference SEE: Virginia Mennonite Board of
Missions and Charities

Voice of Calvary

1655 St. Charles Street
Jackson MS 39209
P.O. ADDRESS:
Box 10562
Jackson MS 39209

Tel. (601) 353-1635
EXECUTIVE OFFICER: Lemuel Tucker
ORGANIZED: 1960
DESCRIPTION: A service agency of evangelical tradition engaged
    in community development, evangelism, medicine, education
    and agriculture. Serving in Africa, Kenya, Ghana and
    Haiti.
TOTAL INCOME: $555,040   FOR OVERSEAS MINISTRIES: NR
PERSONNEL:
    NORTH AMERICANS OVERSEAS   NON-NORTH AMERICANS OVERSEAS: NR
        MARRIED: 0   NORTH AMERICAN ADM. STAFF: 15
        SINGLE MEN: 0   SHORT TERM: 0
        SINGLE WOMEN: 0   RETIRED: 0

        TOTAL ACTIVE: 0

Voice of China and Asia Missionary Society, Inc.

251 S Fair Oaks Ave.
Pasadena CA 91105
P.O. ADDRESS:
Box 15-M
Pasadena CA 91102

Tel. (213) 796-3117
EXECUTIVE OFFICER: Robert B. Hammond
ORGANIZED: 1946
DESCRIPTION: A nondenominational sending agency of evangelical
    and fundamentalist tradition supporting national churches
    and engaged in evangelism, radio and TV broadcasting,
    childcare and secular education.
TOTAL INCOME: NR   FOR OVERSEAS MINISTRIES: $44,000
PERSONNEL:
    NORTH AMERICANS OVERSEAS   NON-NORTH AMERICANS OVERSEAS: 0
        MARRIED: 2   NORTH AMERICAN ADM. STAFF: 3
        SINGLE MEN: 0   SHORT TERM: 0
        SINGLE WOMEN: 0   RETIRED: 10

        TOTAL ACTIVE: 2
NOTES: Overseas income estimated by MARC.

FIELD OF SERVICE	YEAR BEGAN	PERSONNEL NOW	NEW	RELATED CHURCHES	PEOPLE GROUPS	NOTES
Hong-Kong	1913	2		5		
India	1950			4		
Korea, Rep. of	1946			12		
Philippines	1948			2		
Taiwan Rep of China	1948			4		

W. Shabaz Associates, Inc.

16580 Eastland Ave.
Roseville MI 48066

Tel. (313) 774-2300
EXECUTIVE OFFICER: Wayne W. Shabaz
ORGANIZED: 1977
DESCRIPTION: An interdenominational service agency of
    evangelical tradition involved in serving other agencies
    and churches desirous of sharing the Gospel overseas
    through self-supported witnesses.

```
TOTAL INCOME:        NR          FOR OVERSEAS MINISTRIES:    NR
PERSONNEL:
   NORTH AMERICANS OVERSEAS    NON-NORTH AMERICANS OVERSEAS:   0
            MARRIED:    0       NORTH AMERICAN ADM. STAFF:      4
         SINGLE MEN:    0                    SHORT TERM:        0
       SINGLE WOMEN:    0                    RETIRED:           0
                      -----
      TOTAL ACTIVE:    0
```

We Go, Inc. (World Encounter Gospel Organization)

927 W Tenth
Dallas TX 75208

Tel. (214) 943-6365
EXECUTIVE OFFICER: Paul L. Morell
ORGANIZED: 1974
DESCRIPTION: An interdenominational sending agency of
   evangelical and Wesleyan tradition engaged in fund
   transmittal, nurture and support of nationals and
   national churches, and mass evangelism.

```
TOTAL INCOME:    $144,085   FOR OVERSEAS MINISTRIES:    $65,825
PERSONNEL:
   NORTH AMERICANS OVERSEAS    NON-NORTH AMERICANS OVERSEAS:   0
            MARRIED:    6       NORTH AMERICAN ADM. STAFF:      2
         SINGLE MEN:    3                    SHORT TERM:        1
       SINGLE WOMEN:    1                    RETIRED:           0
                      -----
      TOTAL ACTIVE:   10
```

FIELD OF SERVICE	YEAR BEGAN	PERSONNEL NOW	NEW	RELATED CHURCHES	PEOPLE GROUPS	NOTES
Belgium	1979	1	1			
Colombia	1974	1		15	6	
Ghana	1975	2				
India	1979	2	2			
Mexico	1979	2	2			
Sri Lanka	1974	1			3	

WEFMinistries of Ontario SEE: WEFMinistries, Inc.

WEFMinistries, Inc.

116 N Bellevue Ave.
Langhorne PA 19047
P.O. ADDRESS:
Box 307
Langhorne PA 19047

Tel. (215) 752-1818
EXECUTIVE OFFICER: Henry J. Heijermans
ORGANIZED: 1959   AFFILIATION: FOM
DESCRIPTION: Founded as Worldwide European Fellowship, Inc.
   Name changed in 1979. A nondenominational sending agency
   of fundamentalist and independent tradition engaged in
   church planting.

```
TOTAL INCOME:  $1,676,123   FOR OVERSEAS MINISTRIES:  $1,388,768
PERSONNEL:
   NORTH AMERICANS OVERSEAS    NON-NORTH AMERICANS OVERSEAS:   8
            MARRIED:  110       NORTH AMERICAN ADM. STAFF:     24
         SINGLE MEN:    3                    SHORT TERM:        0
       SINGLE WOMEN:   19                    RETIRED:           0
                      -----
      TOTAL ACTIVE:  132
NOTES:   Income figures include Canada.
```

FIELD OF SERVICE	YEAR BEGAN	PERSONNEL NOW	NEW	RELATED CHURCHES	PEOPLE GROUPS	NOTES
Andorra	1978	1				
Argentina	1979	2	2			
Austria	1963	5	1			
Belgium	1978	2	2			
Colombia	1979	2				
France	1959	4				
Germany, Fed. Rep.	1959	28	7			
Ireland	1975	10	1			
Italy	1959	16	4			
Korea, Rep. of	1975	2				
Luxembourg	1973	8	3			
Netherlands	1959	8				
Oceania-general	1970	2				
South Africa	1976	10	10			
Spain	1959	11	4			
United Kingdom	1970	10	6			
Uruguay	1965	8	1			

Welfare of the Blind, Inc., A Christian Agency for the Sightless

4813 Woodway Lane, NW
Washington DC 20016

Tel. (202) 363-9471
EXECUTIVE OFFICER: Elgin Groseclose
ORGANIZED: 1951
DESCRIPTION: A nondenominational fund transmittal agency of
    evangelical tradition working to create interest in and
    support for Christian missions caring for blind in
    non-Christian lands in which Christian evangelism is the
    principal object.
TOTAL INCOME: $15,000   FOR OVERSEAS MINISTRIES: $15,000
PERSONNEL:
    NORTH AMERICANS OVERSEAS   NON-NORTH AMERICANS OVERSEAS: 0
              MARRIED: 0   NORTH AMERICAN ADM. STAFF: 0
           SINGLE MEN: 0   SHORT TERM: 0
         SINGLE WOMEN: 0   RETIRED: 0

         TOTAL ACTIVE: 0

Wesleyan Church General Department of World Missions

1900 West 300 South
Marion IN 46952
P.O. ADDRESS:
Box 2000
Marion IN 36952

Tel. (317) 674-3301
EXECUTIVE OFFICER: Robert N. Lytle
ORGANIZED: 1968   AFFILIATION: EFMA
DESCRIPTION: A denominational sending agency of Wesleyan
    tradition establishing churches, serving national churches
    and engaged in evangelism, education, literature and
    medicine.
TOTAL INCOME: $2,255,521   FOR OVERSEAS MINISTRIES: $2,255,521
PERSONNEL:
    NORTH AMERICANS OVERSEAS   NON-NORTH AMERICANS OVERSEAS: 5
              MARRIED: 158   NORTH AMERICAN ADM. STAFF: 5
           SINGLE MEN: 3   SHORT TERM: 31

```
        SINGLE WOMEN:    40                          RETIRED:    8
                      -----
        TOTAL ACTIVE:   201
NOTES:  Supports 60 others under denominational pension plan.
-----------------------------------------------------------------
                    YEAR    PERSONNEL   RELATED    PEOPLE
FIELD OF SERVICE    BEGAN   NOW   NEW   CHURCHES   GROUPS   NOTES
-----------------------------------------------------------------
```

FIELD OF SERVICE	YEAR BEGAN	PERSONNEL NOW	PERSONNEL NEW	RELATED CHURCHES	PEOPLE GROUPS	NOTES
Australia	1945	9	7	24		
Brazil	1960	7	3	6		
Caribbean-general	1902			170		2
Colombia	1941	10	2	17		
Guyana	1924	7	2	28		
Haiti	1946	18	4	79		
Honduras	1957	4	2	5		
India	1910	2		16		
Indonesia	1975	3	1	13		
Japan	1919	2				
Korea, Rep. of	1977	2	2			
Liberia	1978	2	2	6		
Mexico	1922	1		132		
Nepal		1				
Papua New Guinea	1962	17	8	44		
Peru	1903	3		55		
Philippines	1932	7	3	154		
Puerto Rico	1952	31	10	12		
Sierra Leone	1889	30	14	57		
South Africa	1902	24	5	278		1
Surinam	1945	2		4		
Zambia	1900	31	7	70		

```
        Note: 1.Inc. Swaziland, Zimbabwe,
        Mozambique and Transkei.  2.Inc. Grand
        Cayman, Jamaica, V.I., Saba/Barbuda,
        Dominica, St. Lucia, Barbados, St. Vincent,
        Trinidad and Tobago, Curacao, Antigua,
        Montserrat, St. Kitts and Nevis.
```

Wesleyan Gospel Corps SEE: Wesleyan Church

West Indies Mission SEE: Worldteam

Western Tract Mission

401-33 St. West
Saskatoon SK S7L 0V5 CANADA

```
Tel. (306) 244-0446
EXECUTIVE OFFICER: Melvin Anhorn
ORGANIZED: 1941
DESCRIPTION:  A nondenominational agency of evangelical
     tradition whose primary function is to promote the
     Gospel by means of literature production and distribution.
TOTAL INCOME:     $158,693       FOR OVERSEAS MINISTRIES:    $0
PERSONNEL:
     NORTH AMERICANS OVERSEAS    NON-NORTH AMERICANS OVERSEAS:    NR
             MARRIED:    0           NORTH AMERICAN ADM. STAFF:    13
          SINGLE MEN:    0                        SHORT TERM:     0
        SINGLE WOMEN:    0                          RETIRED:     0
                      -----
        TOTAL ACTIVE:    0
NOTES:  Three employees in administration are part-time.
```

Westminister Biblical Missions, Inc.

203 S Lincoln Ave.
Tampa FL 33609
P.O. ADDRESS:
Box 18976
Tampa FL 33679

Tel. (813) 879-2209
EXECUTIVE OFFICER: Earl E. Pinckney
ORGANIZED: 1974
DESCRIPTION: A nondenominational sending agency of
    fundamentalist and Presbyterian tradition engaged in
    nurture and support of national churches, theological
    education, literacy programs and training.
TOTAL INCOME: $70,000   FOR OVERSEAS MINISTRIES: $55,700
PERSONNEL:
    NORTH AMERICANS OVERSEAS   NON-NORTH AMERICANS OVERSEAS: NR
              MARRIED: 0   NORTH AMERICAN ADM. STAFF: 2
           SINGLE MEN: 0   SHORT TERM: 0
         SINGLE WOMEN: 0   RETIRED: 0

       TOTAL ACTIVE: 0
NOTES: N. Amer. personnel travel to fields infrequently.

Wider Ministries Commission

101 Quaker Hill Dr.
Richmond IN 47374

Tel. (317) 962-7573
EXECUTIVE OFFICER: Harold V. Smuck
ORGANIZED: 1894   AFFILIATION: DOM-NCCCUSA
DESCRIPTION: A denominational sending agency of Friends
    tradition involved in secular education and theological
    education by extension (TEE), agriculture assistance,
    medicine and training of nationals.
TOTAL INCOME: NR   FOR OVERSEAS MINISTRIES: $424,000
PERSONNEL:
    NORTH AMERICANS OVERSEAS   NON-NORTH AMERICANS OVERSEAS: 2
              MARRIED: 10   NORTH AMERICAN ADM. STAFF: 3
           SINGLE MEN: 2   SHORT TERM: 2
         SINGLE WOMEN: 6   RETIRED: 1

       TOTAL ACTIVE: 18

FIELD OF SERVICE	YEAR BEGAN	PERSONNEL NOW	NEW	RELATED CHURCHES	PEOPLE GROUPS	NOTES
Cuba	1902			5		
Israel	1869	6		1		
Jamaica	1865	2		16		
Kenya	1902	6	3	600		
Mexico	1870			1		

Wings of Healing

110 S Garfield Ave.
Montebello CA 90640
P.O. ADDRESS:
Box 22290
Los Angeles CA 90022

Tel. (213) 724-3873
EXECUTIVE OFFICER: Dale Collins
ORGANIZED: 1942
DESCRIPTION: A nondenominational agency of Pentecostal
    tradition engaged in radio broadcasting, literature
    distribution, evangelism and childcare. Wings of Healing
    radio broadcasts are aired in USSR, China, Southeast Asia,

Philippines, Australia, New Zealand, India, Israel, Moslem
countries, Europe, Caribbean, Central America, Mexico and
Africa.
TOTAL INCOME: $165,000   FOR OVERSEAS MINISTRIES: $140,000
PERSONNEL:
    NORTH AMERICANS OVERSEAS   NON-NORTH AMERICANS OVERSEAS: NR
             MARRIED: NR   NORTH AMERICAN ADM. STAFF: NR
          SINGLE MEN: NR   SHORT TERM: NR
        SINGLE WOMEN: NR   RETIRED: NR

        TOTAL ACTIVE: NR

Wings of Mercy Missions Inc.

2108 N Main
Santa Ana CA 92706
P.O. ADDRESS:
835
Santa Ana CA 92706

Tel. (714) 558-7243
EXECUTIVE OFFICER: John Nichol
ORGANIZED: 1956
DESCRIPTION: No current information available. Information
    from 1976 directory. A nondenominational sending agency
    supporting nationals and engaged in relief, medicine,
    childcare and education.
TOTAL INCOME: $14,000   FOR OVERSEAS MINISTRIES: NA
PERSONNEL:
    NORTH AMERICANS OVERSEAS   NON-NORTH AMERICANS OVERSEAS: NR
             MARRIED: NR   NORTH AMERICAN ADM. STAFF: NR
          SINGLE MEN: NR   SHORT TERM: NR
        SINGLE WOMEN: NR   RETIRED: NR

        TOTAL ACTIVE: NR
NOTES: Income estimated by MARC.

Wisconsin Evangelical Lutheran
Synod, Board for World Missions

3512 W North Ave.
Milwaukee WI 53208

Tel. (414) 445-4030
EXECUTIVE OFFICER: R. H. Zimmermann
ORGANIZED: 1955
DESCRIPTION: A denominational sending agency of Lutheran
    tradition establishing churches and supporting national
    churches. Also engaged in evangelism, broadcasting,
    literature production, education and medicine.
TOTAL INCOME: $1,930,000   FOR OVERSEAS MINISTRIES: $1,514,000
PERSONNEL:
    NORTH AMERICANS OVERSEAS   NON-NORTH AMERICANS OVERSEAS: 0
             MARRIED: 38   NORTH AMERICAN ADM. STAFF: 12
          SINGLE MEN: 0   SHORT TERM: 1
        SINGLE WOMEN: 4   RETIRED: 0

        TOTAL ACTIVE: 42

| | YEAR | PERSONNEL | | RELATED | PEOPLE | |
FIELD OF SERVICE	BEGAN	NOW	NEW	CHURCHES	GROUPS	NOTES
Cameroon	1965			31		

FIELD OF SERVICE	YEAR BEGAN	PERSONNEL NOW	NEW	RELATED CHURCHES	PEOPLE GROUPS	NOTES
Colombia	1974	5		5		
Hong-Kong	1964	3		3		
Indonesia	1969	2	2	3		
Japan	1952	7		10		
Malawi	1962	4	1	35		
Mexico	1968			5		
Puerto Rico	1963	3	1	2		
Taiwan Rep of China	1968	2	2	3		
Zambia	1953	8		71		

WIVV Radio SEE: Calvary Evangelistic Mission, Inc.

Women's Christian College, Madras, Associate Board, Inc. SEE: Associate Boards for Women's Christian College, Madras, Inc. and St. Christopher's Training College

Word of Life Fellowship
Schroon Lake NY 12870

Tel. (518) 532-7111
EXECUTIVE OFFICER: Jack Wyrtzen/Harry Bollback
ORGANIZED: 1940
DESCRIPTION: A nondenominational sending agency of
    fundamentalist tradition engaged in personal and small
    group evangelism, support of national churches,
    theological and general Christian education, and radio
    and TV broadcasting.
TOTAL INCOME: $4,600,000   FOR OVERSEAS MINISTRIES: $1,800,000
PERSONNEL:
    NORTH AMERICANS OVERSEAS   NON-NORTH AMERICANS OVERSEAS: 39
                MARRIED: 59   NORTH AMERICAN ADM. STAFF: 2
             SINGLE MEN: 4   SHORT TERM: NA
           SINGLE WOMEN: 8   RETIRED: 25

        TOTAL ACTIVE: 71

FIELD OF SERVICE	YEAR BEGAN	PERSONNEL NOW	NEW	RELATED CHURCHES	PEOPLE GROUPS	NOTES
Argentina	1969	5	1			
Australia	1970	3	3			
Brazil	1957	20	8			
Chile	1977	2	2			
Colombia	1980	4	4			
Ecuador	1972	4	2			
France	1978	2	2			
Germany, Fed. Rep.	1970	10	2			
Israel	1972	4	2			
Japan	1975	3	3			
Kenya	1969	4	3			
Netherlands Antilles	1978	2	2			
Paraguay	1980	2	2			
Philippines	1973	7	5			
Portugal	1974	9	7			
Spain	1976	6	6			
Turkey	1978	1	1			
United Kingdom	1979	2	2			

FIELD OF SERVICE	YEAR BEGAN	PERSONNEL NOW	PERSONNEL NEW	RELATED CHURCHES	PEOPLE GROUPS	NOTES
Uruguay	1977	1	1			
Venezuela	1978	3	3			

World Baptist Fellowship Mission Agency International

3001 W Division
Arlington TX 76013
P.O. ADDRESS:
Box 13459
Arlington TX 76013

Tel. (817) 274-2742
EXECUTIVE OFFICER: Robert O. Schmidt
ORGANIZED: 1928   AFFILIATION: TAM-ICCC
DESCRIPTION: A denominational sending agency of Baptist and
    evangelical tradition establishing churches and engaged
    in evangelism, education and fund transmittal.
TOTAL INCOME: $1,862,858   FOR OVERSEAS MINISTRIES: $1,862,858
PERSONNEL:
```
    NORTH AMERICANS OVERSEAS     NON-NORTH AMERICANS OVERSEAS:    NR
           MARRIED:  146           NORTH AMERICAN ADM. STAFF:     4
        SINGLE MEN:  1                          SHORT TERM:       0
      SINGLE WOMEN:  7                             RETIRED:       0
                     -----
       TOTAL ACTIVE:  154
```

FIELD OF SERVICE	YEAR BEGAN	PERSONNEL NOW	PERSONNEL NEW	RELATED CHURCHES	PEOPLE GROUPS	NOTES
Bolivia	1979	2	2			
Brazil	1960	44	9	38		
Colombia	1968	8	2	3		
Costa Rica	1963	2		2		
Ecuador	1972	8		4		
France	1954	2		1		
Germany, Fed. Rep.	1961	4		2		
Ghana	1977	2		1		
Guatemala	1968	4		4		
Honduras	1969	7		3		
Indonesia	1969	9		10		
Japan	1966	1		1		
Mexico	1953	28	4	25		
Paraguay	1978	2				
Peru	1965	4	2	3		
Philippines	1972	2	2	2		
Spain	1955	4		4		
United Kingdom	1972	2		2		

World Concern SEE: World Concern/Crista International

World Concern/Crista International

19303 Fremont Ave.North
Seattle WA 98133
P.O. ADDRESS:
Box 33000
Seattle WA 98133

Tel. (206) 546-7201
EXECUTIVE OFFICER: Arthur L. Beals
ORGANIZED: 1973   AFFILIATION: EFMA-Assoc. Member
DESCRIPTION: An interdenominational sending agency of
    evangelical tradition specializing in relief,

rehabilitation and self-help projects in developing
countries. Also aids with furloughed missionary support
and medical supplies.
TOTAL INCOME: $2,592,083   FOR OVERSEAS MINISTRIES: $951,351
PERSONNEL:
   NORTH AMERICANS OVERSEAS   NON-NORTH AMERICANS OVERSEAS: 2
        MARRIED: 22   NORTH AMERICAN ADM. STAFF: 3
     SINGLE MEN: 1   SHORT TERM: 8
   SINGLE WOMEN: 10   RETIRED: 0

   TOTAL ACTIVE: 33
NOTES: Of the overseas personnel 21 are seconded to existing
mission agencies.

FIELD OF SERVICE	YEAR BEGAN	PERSONNEL NOW	NEW	RELATED CHURCHES	PEOPLE GROUPS	NOTES
Bangladesh	1975	5	5			
Bolivia	1974		1			
Bophuthatswana	1979	2	2			
Colombia	1978	1	1			
Costa Rica	1976		1			
Guatemala	1976		2			
Haiti	1976	3	3			
Honduras	1974	1	6			
Hong-Kong	1975	1	1			
India	1976	1	1			
Mexico	1975		2			
Philippines	1975	5	10			
Sudan	1979		1			
Thailand	1976	2	2			

World Encounter Gospel Organization, Inc. SEE: We Go, Inc. (World Encounter Gospel Organization)

World Evangelism Foundation

511 N Akard, Ste. 929
Dallas TX 75201

Tel. (214) 651-9777
EXECUTIVE OFFICER: W. H. Jackson, Jr.
ORGANIZED: 1970
DESCRIPTION: A denominational agency of Baptist tradition
coordinating short-term teams of pastors, laymen and
laywomen who go to various countries for approximately
10 days of concentrated evangelism. Teams work through
local churches in a person-to-person ministry.
TOTAL INCOME: NA   FOR OVERSEAS MINISTRIES: NA
PERSONNEL:
   NORTH AMERICANS OVERSEAS   NON-NORTH AMERICANS OVERSEAS: 0
        MARRIED: 0   NORTH AMERICAN ADM. STAFF: 0
     SINGLE MEN: 0   SHORT TERM: 605
   SINGLE WOMEN: 0   RETIRED: 0

   TOTAL ACTIVE: 0

World Evangelism, Inc. SEE: Morris Cerullo World Evangelism, Inc.

World for Christ Missions SEE: Christian Baptist Church of God Association World for Christ Missions

World Gospel Crusades

1294 W Seventh St.
Upland CA 91786
P.O. ADDRESS:
Box 3
Upland CA 91786

Tel. (714) 982-1564
EXECUTIVE OFFICER: Joe A. Rogers
ORGANIZED: 1949   AFFILIATION: EFMA-Assoc. member
DESCRIPTION: A nondenominational service and sending agency of
    evangelical tradition engaged in Bible distribution,
    correspondence courses, literature production and
    distribution. Also includes Mercy, Inc., a subsidiary,
    engaged in aid and relief work via airlifts to famine and
    disaster areas.
TOTAL INCOME: $306,153   FOR OVERSEAS MINISTRIES: $103,000
PERSONNEL:

NORTH AMERICANS OVERSEAS		NON-NORTH AMERICANS OVERSEAS:	2
MARRIED:	NR	NORTH AMERICAN ADM. STAFF:	2
SINGLE MEN:	NR	SHORT TERM:	4
SINGLE WOMEN:	NR	RETIRED:	2
TOTAL ACTIVE:	6		

FIELD OF SERVICE	YEAR BEGAN	PERSONNEL NOW	NEW	RELATED CHURCHES	PEOPLE GROUPS	NOTES
Uruguay	1979	2	2			

World Gospel Mission

3783 Rte. 18 East
Marion IN 46952
P.O. ADDRESS:
Box 948
Marion IN 46952

Tel. (317) 664-7331
EXECUTIVE OFFICER: Thomas H. Hermmiz
ORGANIZED: 1910   AFFILIATION: EFMA
DESCRIPTION: A nondenominational sending agency of Wesleyan
    tradition establishing churches, serving national churches
    and cooperating with other mission organizations. Involved
    in evangelism, education, literature, medicine, radio and
    TV.
TOTAL INCOME: $4,811,232   FOR OVERSEAS MINISTRIES: $3,541,055
PERSONNEL:

NORTH AMERICANS OVERSEAS		NON-NORTH AMERICANS OVERSEAS:	4
MARRIED:	108	NORTH AMERICAN ADM. STAFF:	75
SINGLE MEN:	0	SHORT TERM:	18
SINGLE WOMEN:	38	RETIRED:	36
TOTAL ACTIVE:	146		

FIELD OF SERVICE	YEAR BEGAN	PERSONNEL NOW	NEW	RELATED CHURCHES	PEOPLE GROUPS	NOTES
Argentina	1970	7	3	1		
Bangladesh	1974	3			1	
Bolivia	1944	29	6	56		
Brazil	1966	3		1		

FIELD OF SERVICE	YEAR BEGAN	PERSONNEL NOW	PERSONNEL NEW	RELATED CHURCHES	PEOPLE GROUPS	NOTES
Burundi	1943	25	7	203		
Egypt	1957	1	1			
Haiti	1962	13	8	79		
Honduras	1944	33	11	86		
India	1937	10	4	77		
Japan	1952	7	3	237	1	
Kenya	1932	56	27	319	1	
Mexico	1945	6		9		

Note: Overseas Personnel include missionaries under appointment and those serving as associates and short-termers.

World Home Bible League

16801 Van Dam Rd.
South Holland IL 60473

Tel. (312) 331-2094
EXECUTIVE OFFICER: William A. Ackerman
ORGANIZED: 1938
DESCRIPTION: An interdenominational service agency distributing Scriptures in more than 70 different countries. Also publishes translation material, Bible portions and other literature in dialects.
TOTAL INCOME: $4,750,000   FOR OVERSEAS MINISTRIES: $4,750,000
PERSONNEL:

NORTH AMERICANS OVERSEAS		NON-NORTH AMERICANS OVERSEAS:	0
MARRIED:	0	NORTH AMERICAN ADM. STAFF:	85
SINGLE MEN:	0	SHORT TERM:	0
SINGLE WOMEN:	0	RETIRED:	NR
TOTAL ACTIVE:	0		

World Hope Foundation

P.O. ADDRESS:
Box 9027
Austin TX 78766

Tel. (512) 327-3388
EXECUTIVE OFFICER: Harold Davies
ORGANIZED: 1976
DESCRIPTION: A sending agency of evangelical tradition engaged in radio broadcasts, literature distribution, mass evangelism through teams, support of national evangelists, childcare and relief work.
TOTAL INCOME: $150,000   FOR OVERSEAS MINISTRIES: $150,000
PERSONNEL:

NORTH AMERICANS OVERSEAS		NON-NORTH AMERICANS OVERSEAS:	NR
MARRIED:	NR	NORTH AMERICAN ADM. STAFF:	5
SINGLE MEN:	NR	SHORT TERM:	100
SINGLE WOMEN:	NR	RETIRED:	NR
TOTAL ACTIVE:	2		

FIELD OF SERVICE	YEAR BEGAN	PERSONNEL NOW	PERSONNEL NEW	RELATED CHURCHES	PEOPLE GROUPS	NOTES
Brazil	1979					

FIELD OF SERVICE	YEAR BEGAN	PERSONNEL NOW	NEW	RELATED CHURCHES	PEOPLE GROUPS	NOTES
India	1979					
Japan	1976					
Korea, Rep. of	1978					

World Literature Crusade

20232 Sunburst
Chatsworth CA 91311
P.O. ADDRESS:
Box 1313
Studio City CA 91604

Tel. (213) 341-7870
EXECUTIVE OFFICER: Jack McAlister
ORGANIZED: 1946
DESCRIPTION: An interdenominational specialized service agency
of evangelical tradition engaged in mass evangelism
through visitation and distribution of literature written
and produced by national leaders within their own
countries. Engaged in follow-up correspondence courses,
channeling new believers to local churches where available
and teaching in groups where not available. Also involved
in broadcasting and serving other agencies.
TOTAL INCOME: $14,753,960   FOR OVERSEAS MINISTRIES: $9,785,320
PERSONNEL:

NORTH AMERICANS OVERSEAS		NON-NORTH AMERICANS OVERSEAS:	0
MARRIED:	0	NORTH AMERICAN ADM. STAFF:	89
SINGLE MEN:	0	SHORT TERM:	0
SINGLE WOMEN:	0	RETIRED:	4
TOTAL ACTIVE:	0		

NOTES: Supports overseas staff of 1641 national
workers.

FIELD OF SERVICE	YEAR BEGAN	PERSONNEL NOW	NEW	RELATED CHURCHES	PEOPLE GROUPS	NOTES
Argentina	1962					
Austria	1966					
Bangladesh	1975					
Belgium	1970					
Bolivia	1969					
Botswana	1976					
Brazil	1962					
Chile	1962					
Colombia	1975					
Ecuador	1975					
France	1963					
Germany, Fed. Rep.	1963					
Ghana	1975					
Guatemala	1963					
Hong-Kong	1961					
India	1963					
Indonesia	1969					
Italy	1962					
Japan	1953					
Kenya	1962					

```
                       YEAR    PERSONNEL   RELATED   PEOPLE
FIELD OF SERVICE       BEGAN   NOW   NEW   CHURCHES  GROUPS  NOTES
```

FIELD OF SERVICE	YEAR BEGAN	PERSONNEL NOW	NEW	RELATED CHURCHES	PEOPLE GROUPS	NOTES
Korea, Rep. of	1958					
Malawi	1970					
Mexico	1963					
Nigeria	1975					
Norway	1968					
Paraguay	1975					
Peru	1963					
Philippines	1961					
Portugal	1963					
Singapore	1963					
Spain	1975					
Sri Lanka	1970					
Switzerland	1975					
Taiwan Rep of China	1961					
Tanzania	1963					
Thailand	1964					
Uruguay	1975					
Venezuela	1973					
Zambia	1970					
Zimbabwe	1963					

Note: All personnel are nationals
and involved in literature
distribution.

World Medical Mission

702 State Farm Rd.
Boone NC 28607

Tel. (704) 262-1980
EXECUTIVE OFFICER: Franklin Graham
ORGANIZED: 1977
DESCRIPTION: A specialized service agency offering short-term
    surgical assistance overseas. Associated with Samaritan's
    Purse. Serves in Nepal, India, Thailand, Kenya, Zaire,
    Guyana and Indonesia.
TOTAL INCOME: $116,000   FOR OVERSEAS MINISTRIES: $81,200
PERSONNEL:
    NORTH AMERICANS OVERSEAS   NON-NORTH AMERICANS OVERSEAS: 0
            MARRIED: 0   NORTH AMERICAN ADM. STAFF: 4
         SINGLE MEN: 0   SHORT TERM: 30
       SINGLE WOMEN: 0   RETIRED: 0

       TOTAL ACTIVE: 0
NOTES: Income estimated by agency.

World Ministries Commission

1451 Dundee Ave.
Elgin IL 60120

Tel. (312) 742-5100
EXECUTIVE OFFICER: Ruby Rhoades
ORGANIZED: 1884   AFFILIATION: DOM-NCCCUSA
DESCRIPTION: A denominational sending agency of Brethren
    tradition supporting national churches and engaged in
    self-help projects, community development, agricultural
    assistance and development of human resources.
TOTAL INCOME: $1,635,259   FOR OVERSEAS MINISTRIES: $962,399
PERSONNEL:
    NORTH AMERICANS OVERSEAS   NON-NORTH AMERICANS OVERSEAS: 0
            MARRIED: 24   NORTH AMERICAN ADM. STAFF: 9
         SINGLE MEN: 11   SHORT TERM: 21

```
   SINGLE WOMEN:    10                              RETIRED:    39
                   -----
   TOTAL ACTIVE:    45
-----------------------------------------------------------------------
                   YEAR     PERSONNEL    RELATED   PEOPLE
FIELD OF SERVICE   BEGAN    NOW   NEW    CHURCHES  GROUPS   NOTES
-----------------------------------------------------------------------
Germany, Fed. Rep.          2
Haiti                       1
Honduras                    2
India                       5
Ireland                     4
Israel                      7
Niger                       5
Poland                      9
Puerto Rico                 3
Switzerland                 1
```

World Mission in Church and Society

815 Second Ave.
New York NY 10017

Tel. (212) 867-8400
EXECUTIVE OFFICER: Samuel VanCulin
ORGANIZED: 1921
DESCRIPTION: A denominational sending agency of Episcopal
    tradition serving national churches. Involved in
    establishing churches, aid and relief, development of
    human resources and theological education.
TOTAL INCOME: $15,800,000   FOR OVERSEAS MINISTRIES: $5,585,000
PERSONNEL:
```
   NORTH AMERICANS OVERSEAS    NON-NORTH AMERICANS OVERSEAS:    0
          MARRIED:    NR         NORTH AMERICAN ADM. STAFF:    9
       SINGLE MEN:    NR                      SHORT TERM:    19
     SINGLE WOMEN:    NR                         RETIRED:    95
                    -----
   TOTAL ACTIVE:    69
```
NOTES: Overseas personnel are only partially
        supported.
        Number of retired personnel is estimated
        by agency.
        Income estimated by agency.
```
-----------------------------------------------------------------------
                     YEAR     PERSONNEL    RELATED   PEOPLE
FIELD OF SERVICE     BEGAN    NOW   NEW    CHURCHES  GROUPS   NOTES
-----------------------------------------------------------------------
Argentina            1965     1
Brazil               1907     4     2
Colombia             1963     1
Dominican Republic   1940     3     2
Ecuador              1963     1
El Salvador          1956     2     2
Guam                 1960     1
Guatemala            1956     2     1
Haiti                1861     2
Honduras             1956     6     2
Hong-Kong                     1
Israel                        2     1
Japan                1859     6     1
Kenya                         3     3
```

489

FIELD OF SERVICE	YEAR BEGAN	PERSONNEL NOW	NEW	RELATED CHURCHES	PEOPLE GROUPS	NOTES
Liberia	1850	3	1			
Malawi		1	1			
Malaysia	1976	1	1			
Mexico	1904	4	1			
Nicaragua	1956	2	1			
Panama	1919	2	1			
Philippines	1901	12	5			
Puerto Rico	1901	1				
South Africa	1966	1				
Taiwan Rep of China	1960	1				
Tanzania	1964	3	2			
U.S. Virgin Is.	1919	2				
Zaire	1978	1	1			

World Mission Information Bank

P.O. ADDRESS:
Box 344091
Dallas TX 75234

Tel. (214) 241-0800
EXECUTIVE OFFICER: Lynn D. Yocum
ORGANIZED: 1973
DESCRIPTION: A nondenominational service agency of Christian
   "Restoration Movement" tradition. WMIB provides churches
   of Christ and other mission organizations with mission
   data from 132 nations where works are currently being
   conducted by Churches of Christ.
TOTAL INCOME: NR   FOR OVERSEAS MINISTRIES: NR
PERSONNEL:
   NORTH AMERICANS OVERSEAS   NON-NORTH AMERICANS OVERSEAS: 0
          MARRIED: 0   NORTH AMERICAN ADM. STAFF: 0
       SINGLE MEN: 0   SHORT TERM: 0
     SINGLE WOMEN: 0   RETIRED: 0

     TOTAL ACTIVE: 0

World Mission Prayer League

232 Clifton Ave.
Minneapolis MN 55403

Tel. (612) 871-6843
EXECUTIVE OFFICER: Jonathan Lindell
ORGANIZED: 1937
DESCRIPTION: A denominational sending agency of independent
   Lutheran tradition establishing churches and engaged in
   education, evangelism and medicine.
TOTAL INCOME: $1,024,355   FOR OVERSEAS MINISTRIES: $893,718
PERSONNEL:
   NORTH AMERICANS OVERSEAS   NON-NORTH AMERICANS OVERSEAS: 0
          MARRIED: 94   NORTH AMERICAN ADM. STAFF: 16
       SINGLE MEN: 2   SHORT TERM: 0
     SINGLE WOMEN: 37   RETIRED: 20

     TOTAL ACTIVE: 133

FIELD OF SERVICE	YEAR BEGAN	PERSONNEL NOW	NEW	RELATED CHURCHES	PEOPLE GROUPS	NOTES
Bangladesh	1972	11	2			

FIELD OF SERVICE	YEAR BEGAN	PERSONNEL NOW	PERSONNEL NEW	RELATED CHURCHES	PEOPLE GROUPS	NOTES
Bolivia	1939	18	4			
Ecuador	1951	22	7			
Hong-Kong	1976	2				
India	1941	2				
Kenya	1968	13	5			
Mexico	1945	6	4			
Nepal	1956	14	8			
Pakistan	1946	17	8			

World Mission Prayer League Canada

5408 - 49 Ave.
Camrose AB T4V 0N7
Canada

Tel. (403) 672-0464
EXECUTIVE OFFICER: Arnold B. H. Hagen
ORGANIZED: 1969
DESCRIPTION: A denominational sending agency of Lutheran
    tradition involved in agricultural assistance, education,
    medicine, evangelism and aid and relief.
TOTAL INCOME: $61,245   FOR OVERSEAS MINISTRIES: $52,374
PERSONNEL:
    NORTH AMERICANS OVERSEAS   NON-NORTH AMERICANS OVERSEAS: 0
            MARRIED: 8   NORTH AMERICAN ADM. STAFF: 2
         SINGLE MEN: 2   SHORT TERM: 0
       SINGLE WOMEN: 2   RETIRED: 0

    TOTAL ACTIVE: 12
NOTES: Overseas personnel are not fully
         supported by Canadian office. Some support
         comes from office in USA.

FIELD OF SERVICE	YEAR BEGAN	PERSONNEL NOW	PERSONNEL NEW	RELATED CHURCHES	PEOPLE GROUPS	NOTES
Bolivia		2				
Ecuador		3	3			
Nepal		2	1			
Pakistan		4	2			
Zaire		1	1			

World Missionary Assistance Plan

900 N Glenoaks Blvd.
Burbank CA 91502

Tel. (213) 843-7233
EXECUTIVE OFFICER: Ralph Mahoney
ORGANIZED: 1960   AFFILIATION: EFMA
DESCRIPTION: An interdenominational service agency of
    evangelical and charismatic tradition serving
    missionaries and engaged in evangelism, literature
    production and leadership training. Conducts overseas
    Spiritual Renewal Seminars.
TOTAL INCOME: $940,300   FOR OVERSEAS MINISTRIES: $435,100
PERSONNEL:
    NORTH AMERICANS OVERSEAS   NON-NORTH AMERICANS OVERSEAS: 0
            MARRIED: 22   NORTH AMERICAN ADM. STAFF: 15
         SINGLE MEN: 1   SHORT TERM: 0

SINGLE WOMEN: 4   RETIRED: 0

     TOTAL ACTIVE: 27
NOTES: Income figures include Canadian office.

| | YEAR | PERSONNEL | | RELATED | PEOPLE | |
FIELD OF SERVICE	BEGAN	NOW	NEW		CHURCHES	GROUPS	NOTES
Argentina		3		1		
Belize		2				
Brazil		2		1		
Chile		2				
Costa Rica		2	2			
Guatemala		5	1	17		
Honduras		1	1			
Israel		4	1			
Japan		1				
Paraguay		1		1		
Philippines		2	2			
South Africa		2		6		

World Missionary Evangelism, Inc.

2216 S Vernon
Dallas TX 75224
P.O. ADDRESS:
Box 222813
Dallas TX 75222

Tel. (214) 942-1564
EXECUTIVE OFFICER: John E. Douglas, Sr.
ORGANIZED: 1954
DESCRIPTION: An interdenominational service agency supporting
   nationals, national churches and orphanages. Also involved
   in evangelism, medical work, Chrisitan education, radio
   broadcasting, training of nationals and hunger relief.
TOTAL INCOME: NA   FOR OVERSEAS MINISTRIES: $3,780,865
PERSONNEL:
   NORTH AMERICANS OVERSEAS   NON-NORTH AMERICANS OVERSEAS: NR
            MARRIED: NA   NORTH AMERICAN ADM. STAFF: NA
         SINGLE MEN: NA   SHORT TERM: NA
       SINGLE WOMEN: NA   RETIRED: NA

     TOTAL ACTIVE: NA
NOTES: Sponsors more than 30,000 children.

| | YEAR | PERSONNEL | | RELATED | PEOPLE | |
FIELD OF SERVICE	BEGAN	NOW	NEW		CHURCHES	GROUPS	NOTES
Bangladesh						
Bhutan						
Guatemala	1975					
Haiti						
Hong-Kong						
India						
Indonesia						
Japan						
Korea, Rep. of						
Mexico						
Philippines						
Sri Lanka						

World Missionary Press, Inc.

Marietta Dr.
New Paris IN 46553
P.O. ADDRESS:
Box 120
New Paris IN 46553

Tel. (219) 831-2111
EXECUTIVE OFFICER: Watson Goodman
ORGANIZED: 1961
DESCRIPTION: A nondenominational service agency of evangelical
    and fundamentalist tradition working interdenominationally
    printing Scripture booklets and literature in 144
    languages for free distribution in 170 countries.
TOTAL INCOME: $757,750   FOR OVERSEAS MINISTRIES: $697,131
PERSONNEL:
    NORTH AMERICANS OVERSEAS   NON-NORTH AMERICANS OVERSEAS: 0
            MARRIED: 0   NORTH AMERICAN ADM. STAFF: 24
        SINGLE MEN: 0   SHORT TERM: 5
      SINGLE WOMEN: 0   RETIRED: NR

    TOTAL ACTIVE: 0
NOTES: Administrative personnel incl. 10 part-time.

World Missions Fellowship

5961 New Hope Rd.
Grants Pass OR 97526
P.O. ADDRESS:
Box 1048
Grants Pass OR 97526

Tel. (503) 479-3731
EXECUTIVE OFFICER: Robert C. Minter
ORGANIZED: 1946   AFFILIATION: IFMA
DESCRIPTION: Previously known as World Missions to Children.
    Name changed in 1978. An interdenominational sending
    agency of evangelical and independent tradition
    establishing churches and engaged in evangelism, medical
    relief, childcare, leadership programs and literature.
    Particularly concerned with Bible school, secondary
    Christian education and ministry to fatherless children.
TOTAL INCOME: $188,457   FOR OVERSEAS MINISTRIES: $146,129
PERSONNEL:
    NORTH AMERICANS OVERSEAS   NON-NORTH AMERICANS OVERSEAS: 11
            MARRIED: 12   NORTH AMERICAN ADM. STAFF: 3
        SINGLE MEN: 0   SHORT TERM: 4
      SINGLE WOMEN: 0   RETIRED: 0

    TOTAL ACTIVE: 12

FIELD OF SERVICE	YEAR BEGAN	PERSONNEL NOW	NEW	RELATED CHURCHES	PEOPLE GROUPS	NOTES
Austria	1954	2				
Brazil	1957	2		1		
India	1953	2		2		
Ireland	1950	4				
Japan	1951	2		4		

World Missions to Children SEE: World Missions Fellowship

World Missions, Inc.   1938 Pacific Ave.
                                             Long Beach CA 90806
                                             P.O. ADDRESS:
                                             Box 2611
                                             Long Beach CA 90801

Tel. (213) 427-9885
EXECUTIVE OFFICER: J. Leonard Bell
ORGANIZED: 1958
DESCRIPTION: A nondenominational sending agency of evangelical
    tradition establishing churches and engaged in evangelism,
    literature production, childcare and Bible distribution.
    Also supports nationals.
TOTAL INCOME: NR   FOR OVERSEAS MINISTRIES: $836,000
PERSONNEL:
    NORTH AMERICANS OVERSEAS   NON-NORTH AMERICANS OVERSEAS: NR
             MARRIED: NR   NORTH AMERICAN ADM. STAFF: NR
         SINGLE MEN: NR   SHORT TERM: NR
       SINGLE WOMEN: NR   RETIRED: NR

       TOTAL ACTIVE: 38
NOTES: Overseas income estimated by MARC.

FIELD OF SERVICE	YEAR BEGAN	PERSONNEL NOW	PERSONNEL NEW	RELATED CHURCHES	PEOPLE GROUPS	NOTES
Bangladesh	1972	2		5		
Bolivia	1977	3	3			
Brazil	1964	2				
Germany, Fed. Rep.	1973	3				
India	1965			2000		1
Jamaica	1966	1				
Korea, Rep. of	1978	3	3			
Mexico	1959	11	2	25		
Peru	1963	1				
Philippines	1975	4	3			
Singapore	1979	2	2			
South Africa	1959	6				

    Note: 1. Supports 300-400 nationals.

World Neighbors, Inc.   5116 N Portland Ave.
                                             Oklahoma City OK 73112

Tel. (405) 946-3333
EXECUTIVE OFFICER: James O. Morgan
ORGANIZED: 1951
DESCRIPTION: A nondenominational sending agency of evangelical
    tradition supporting nationals and engaged in self-help
    projects, agriculture and training. Also has a short-term
    program overseas working with production of film strips
    for evangelization.
TOTAL INCOME: $2,000,000   FOR OVERSEAS MINISTRIES: $1,460,000
PERSONNEL:
    NORTH AMERICANS OVERSEAS   NON-NORTH AMERICANS OVERSEAS: NR
             MARRIED: NR   NORTH AMERICAN ADM. STAFF: 27
         SINGLE MEN: NR   SHORT TERM: 6
       SINGLE WOMEN: NR   RETIRED: NR

       TOTAL ACTIVE: 14

FIELD OF SERVICE	YEAR BEGAN	PERSONNEL NOW	PERSONNEL NEW	RELATED CHURCHES	PEOPLE GROUPS	NOTES
Benin						
Bolivia						
Brazil						
Ghana						
Guatemala						
Haiti						
India						
Indonesia						
Kenya						
Nepal						
Niger						
Paraguay						
Peru						
Philippines						
Tanzania						
Togo						
Uganda						
Upper Volta						

World Opportunities International

1415 Cahuenga Blvd.
Hollywood CA 90028

Tel. (213) 466-7187
EXECUTIVE OFFICER: Roy McKeown
ORGANIZED: 1961   AFFILIATION: EFMA-Assoc. member
DESCRIPTION: An interdenominational service and sending agency
  of evangelical tradition engaged in evangelism, church
  planting, aid and relief, literature distribution and
  youth guidance.
TOTAL INCOME: $3,600,000   FOR OVERSEAS MINISTRIES: $200,000
PERSONNEL:
```
    NORTH AMERICANS OVERSEAS    NON-NORTH AMERICANS OVERSEAS:    0
              MARRIED:   10       NORTH AMERICAN ADM. STAFF:    0
           SINGLE MEN:    4                    SHORT TERM:   20
         SINGLE WOMEN:   14                       RETIRED:    6
                     -----
        TOTAL ACTIVE:   28
```

FIELD OF SERVICE	YEAR BEGAN	PERSONNEL NOW	PERSONNEL NEW	RELATED CHURCHES	PEOPLE GROUPS	NOTES
Japan	1970	24	5	20		
Kenya	1971	2		50		
Korea, Rep. of	1978	2				
Philippines	1970	2				

World Outreach

2215 W Beltline
Garland TX 75042

Tel. (214) 495-3813
EXECUTIVE OFFICER: Mervyn Walker
ORGANIZED: 1932
DESCRIPTION: An international nondenominational sending agency
  of Pentecostal tradition engaged in broadcasting,
  literature production, childcare, correspondence courses
  and theological education.
TOTAL INCOME: $20,000   FOR OVERSEAS MINISTRIES: $20,000

```
PERSONNEL:
    NORTH AMERICANS OVERSEAS     NON-NORTH AMERICANS OVERSEAS:    0
              MARRIED:    4         NORTH AMERICAN ADM. STAFF:    1
           SINGLE MEN:    0                       SHORT TERM:    2
         SINGLE WOMEN:    2                          RETIRED:    0
                      -----
         TOTAL ACTIVE:    6
NOTES:  Administrative staff is part-time.
```

FIELD OF SERVICE	YEAR BEGAN	PERSONNEL NOW	NEW	RELATED CHURCHES	PEOPLE GROUPS	NOTES
Bangladesh						
India						
Indonesia						
Kenya						
Korea, Rep. of						
Malawi						
Philippines						
South Africa						
Thailand						
Zambia						
Zimbabwe						

World Presbyterian Missions, Inc.

901 N Broom St.
Wilmington DE 19806

```
Tel. (302) 652-3204
EXECUTIVE OFFICER: Nelson K. Malkus
ORGANIZED: 1957
DESCRIPTION:  A denominational sending agency of Reformed and
    Presbyterian tradition establishing churches and engaged
    in Bible translation, medicine, childcare and theological
    education.
TOTAL INCOME:  $1,400,000   FOR OVERSEAS MINISTRIES:  $1,400,000
PERSONNEL:
    NORTH AMERICANS OVERSEAS     NON-NORTH AMERICANS OVERSEAS:    0
              MARRIED:   56         NORTH AMERICAN ADM. STAFF:   12
           SINGLE MEN:    2                       SHORT TERM:    5
         SINGLE WOMEN:   12                          RETIRED:   NR
                      -----
         TOTAL ACTIVE:   70
```

FIELD OF SERVICE	YEAR BEGAN	PERSONNEL NOW	NEW	RELATED CHURCHES	PEOPLE GROUPS	NOTES
Australia	1966	4		4	1	
Chile	1957	13	4			
India	1957	12	2	5	1	
Japan	1961	7	4		1	
Jordan	1966	10	4		1	
Kenya	1961	9	4			
Korea, Rep. of	1957	4				
Peru	1957	9				
Spain	1978					

World Radio Missionary Fellowship, Inc.

20201 NW 37th Ave.
Opa-Locka FL 33055
P.O. ADDRESS:
Box 3000
Opa-Locka FL 33055

Tel. (305) 624-4252
EXECUTIVE OFFICER: Abe C. Van Der Puy
ORGANIZED: 1931   AFFILIATION: IFMA
DESCRIPTION: An interdenominational sending agency of
    evangelical tradition, specializing in radio, involved in
    medicine, television, literature, Bible correspondence
    courses and local evangelism. Operates Radio Station HCJB
    in Quito, Ecuador, utilizing 15 languages and reaching
    around the world by means of shortwave.
TOTAL INCOME: $4,037,000   FOR OVERSEAS MINISTRIES: $3,882,000
PERSONNEL:

NORTH AMERICANS OVERSEAS		NON-NORTH AMERICANS OVERSEAS:	23
MARRIED:	139	NORTH AMERICAN ADM. STAFF:	27
SINGLE MEN:	1	SHORT TERM:	43
SINGLE WOMEN:	21	RETIRED:	16
TOTAL ACTIVE:	161		

FIELD OF SERVICE	YEAR BEGAN	PERSONNEL NOW	NEW	RELATED CHURCHES	PEOPLE GROUPS	NOTES
Brazil	1975	4				
Ecuador	1931	280	80	15		
Italy	1979	2	2			
Panama	1954	2				
United Kingdom	1975	2				

World Relief Commission, Inc. SEE: World Relief Corporation

World Relief Corporation

450 Gundersen Dr.
Carol Stream IL 60187
P.O. ADDRESS:
Box WRC
Wheaton IL 60187

Tel. (312) 665-0235
EXECUTIVE OFFICER: Jerry Ballard
ORGANIZED: 1945
DESCRIPTION: An interdenominational service agency of
    evangelical tradition engaged in relief, rehabilitation,
    refugee resettlement and self-help development. WRC is the
    disaster relief and development arm of the National
    Association of Evangelicals.
TOTAL INCOME: $1,880,662   FOR OVERSEAS MINISTRIES: $1,880,662
PERSONNEL:

NORTH AMERICANS OVERSEAS		NON-NORTH AMERICANS OVERSEAS:	0
MARRIED:	2	NORTH AMERICAN ADM. STAFF:	43
SINGLE MEN:	1	SHORT TERM:	14
SINGLE WOMEN:	0	RETIRED:	16
TOTAL ACTIVE:	3		

FIELD OF SERVICE	YEAR BEGAN	PERSONNEL NOW	NEW	RELATED CHURCHES	PEOPLE GROUPS	NOTES
Bangladesh	1972					
Brazil	1977					
Haiti						

FIELD OF SERVICE	YEAR BEGAN	PERSONNEL NOW	PERSONNEL NEW	RELATED CHURCHES	PEOPLE GROUPS	NOTES
Hong-Kong	1978					
India						
Indonesia	1978					
Kenya						
Korea, Rep. of	1965					
Philippines		1	1			
Thailand	1972					
Upper Volta						

World Thrust Films, Inc.

P.O. ADDRESS:
Box 2000
Largo FL 33540

Tel. (813) 527-5205
EXECUTIVE OFFICER: Clair Dean Hutchins
ORGANIZED: 1973
DESCRIPTION: An interdenominational specialized service agency
    of evangelical tradition involved in translating Christian
    motion pictures into other languages and distributing them
    throughout the world.
TOTAL INCOME: NR   FOR OVERSEAS MINISTRIES: NR
PERSONNEL:
    NORTH AMERICANS OVERSEAS   NON-NORTH AMERICANS OVERSEAS: 0
               MARRIED: 0   NORTH AMERICAN ADM. STAFF: 0
            SINGLE MEN: 0   SHORT TERM: 0
          SINGLE WOMEN: 0   RETIRED: 0

        TOTAL ACTIVE: 0

World Vision International

919 W Huntington Dr.
Monrovia CA 91016

Tel. (213) 357-7979
EXECUTIVE OFFICER: W. Stanley Mooneyham
ORGANIZED: 1978
DESCRIPTION: Founded in 1950 as World Vision, Incorporated.
    Reorganized as World Vision International in 1978. An
    international, interdenominational specialized service
    agency of evangelical tradition engaged in childcare,
    community development, emergency relief, evangelism,
    leadership development and missions research and technical
    assistance. Programs and projects are carried out
    primarily through national churches. Income is derived
    wholly from other members of the World Vision
    International partnership, including World Vision, Inc.,
    World Vision of Canada and other World Vision entities.
TOTAL INCOME: $37,889,621   FOR OVERSEAS MINISTRIES: $34,814,569
PERSONNEL:
    NORTH AMERICANS OVERSEAS   NON-NORTH AMERICANS OVERSEAS: 16
               MARRIED: 31   NORTH AMERICAN ADM. STAFF: 92
            SINGLE MEN: 2   SHORT TERM: 30
          SINGLE WOMEN: 1   RETIRED: NR

        TOTAL ACTIVE: 34
NOTES: Income figures shown are funds administered
        for World Vision of Canada and World Vision, Inc.,
        as well as other World Vision entities throughout
        the world.

FIELD OF SERVICE	YEAR BEGAN	PERSONNEL NOW	NEW	RELATED CHURCHES	PEOPLE GROUPS	NOTES
Bangladesh	1970	1				
Brazil	1961	2				
Colombia	1960	2	1			
Ecuador		1	1			
El Salvador	1975					
Ethiopia	1975					
Germany, Fed. Rep.	1975	1				
Ghana	1975	1	1			
Guatemala	1975	6	5			
Haiti	1959	4	3			
Honduras	1973					
Hong-Kong	1953					
Kampuchea	1979	2	2			

World Vision of Canada

6630 Turner Valley Rd.
Mississauga ON L5N 2S4
Canada

Tel. (416) 881-3030
EXECUTIVE OFFICER: William J. Newell
ORGANIZED: 1954
DESCRIPTION: An interdenominational specialized service agency
  of evangelical tradition supporting nationals and involved
  in support of agriculture, education, medicine, self-help
  projects and relief assistance.
TOTAL INCOME: $8,858,620   FOR OVERSEAS MINISTRIES: $6,236,338
PERSONNEL:
```
      NORTH AMERICANS OVERSEAS    NON-NORTH AMERICANS OVERSEAS:     0
                MARRIED:   1          NORTH AMERICAN ADM. STAFF:  110
             SINGLE MEN:   0                        SHORT TERM:    4
           SINGLE WOMEN:   0                           RETIRED:    2
                         -----
          TOTAL ACTIVE:   1
```

FIELD OF SERVICE	YEAR BEGAN	PERSONNEL NOW	NEW	RELATED CHURCHES	PEOPLE GROUPS	NOTES
Guatemala	1970	1	1			

World Vision Relief Organization, Inc. SEE: World Vision, Inc.

World Vision, Incorporated

919 W Huntington Dr.
Monrovia CA 91016
P.O. ADDRESS:
Box O
Pasadena CA 91109

Tel. (213) 357-7979
EXECUTIVE OFFICER: Ted W. Engstrom
ORGANIZED: 1950   AFFILIATION: EFMA-Assoc. member
DESCRIPTION: An interdenominational service agency of
  evangelical tradition supporting the work of childcare,
  community development, emergency relief, evangelism,
  leadership development and calling on Christians to
  carry out the work of Jesus Christ wherever opportunity
  presents itself. Programs and projects outside of the
  United States are carried out through World Vision
  International.
TOTAL INCOME: $46,681,140   FOR OVERSEAS MINISTRIES: $28,966,600

PERSONNEL:

NORTH AMERICANS OVERSEAS		NON-NORTH AMERICANS OVERSEAS:	0
MARRIED:	0	NORTH AMERICAN ADM. STAFF:	466
SINGLE MEN:	0	SHORT TERM:	0
SINGLE WOMEN:	0	RETIRED:	12

TOTAL ACTIVE:	0		

NOTES: Income figures include cash and gifts-in-kind.

Worldwide Christian Education Ministries SEE: O.C. Ministries, Inc.

World Wide Evangelical Mission of Canada SEE: Christian World-Wide Evangelical Mission of Canada, The

World Wide Missionary Crusader, Inc.

4606 Ave. H
Lubbock TX 79404

Tel. (806) 747-5417
EXECUTIVE OFFICER: Homer Duncan
ORGANIZED: 1943
DESCRIPTION: An interdenominational service agency of
   evangelical, fundamentalist and independent tradition
   producing and distributing a series of 75 books and
   booklets on the Christian life, some published in foreign
   languages.
TOTAL INCOME: $160,000   FOR OVERSEAS MINISTRIES: $120,000
PERSONNEL:

NORTH AMERICANS OVERSEAS		NON-NORTH AMERICANS OVERSEAS:	0
MARRIED:	0	NORTH AMERICAN ADM. STAFF:	0
SINGLE MEN:	0	SHORT TERM:	0
SINGLE WOMEN:	0	RETIRED:	0

TOTAL ACTIVE:	0		

World Wide Prayer and Missionary Union

6821 N Ottawa Ave.
Chicago IL 60631

Tel. (312) 763-2553
EXECUTIVE OFFICER: Mrs. R. Husten
ORGANIZED: 1931
DESCRIPTION: An interdenominational fund transmittal agency of
   evangelical tradition serving other agencies and acting as
   an information service and nurturing nationals and
   national churches.
TOTAL INCOME: NR   FOR OVERSEAS MINISTRIES: NR
PERSONNEL:

NORTH AMERICANS OVERSEAS		NON-NORTH AMERICANS OVERSEAS:	0
MARRIED:	0	NORTH AMERICAN ADM. STAFF:	1
SINGLE MEN:	0	SHORT TERM:	0
SINGLE WOMEN:	0	RETIRED:	NR

TOTAL ACTIVE:	0		

World's Christian Endeavor Union

1221 E Broad St.
Columbus OH 43205
P.O. ADDRESS:
Box 1110
Columbus OH 43216

Tel. (614) 258-9545
EXECUTIVE OFFICER: Charles W. Barner
ORGANIZED: 1895
DESCRIPTION: An interdenominational specialized service agency

of evangelical tradition engaged in literature, evangelism
and training work as part of a world-wide movement with
emphasis on youth ministry. Most work is carried on by
volunteers. Each national Christian Endeavor Union
supplies its own personnel.

TOTAL INCOME: $25,000   FOR OVERSEAS MINISTRIES: NR
PERSONNEL:
   NORTH AMERICANS OVERSEAS   NON-NORTH AMERICANS OVERSEAS: 0
         MARRIED: 0   NORTH AMERICAN ADM. STAFF: 0
     SINGLE MEN: 0   SHORT TERM: 0
   SINGLE WOMEN: 0   RETIRED: 0

    TOTAL ACTIVE: 0

World-Wide Missions International

1593 E Colorado Blvd.
Pasadena CA 91106
P.O. ADDRESS:
Box G
Pasadena CA 91109

Tel. (213) 449-4313
EXECUTIVE OFFICER: Esther M. Howard
ORGANIZED: 1950
DESCRIPTION: An interdenominational sending agency of
evangelical tradition primarily concerned with supporting
national workers. Involved in establishing churches,
evangelism, education, literature production and
distribution, childcare and medicine.

TOTAL INCOME: $979,400   FOR OVERSEAS MINISTRIES: $793,600
PERSONNEL:
   NORTH AMERICANS OVERSEAS   NON-NORTH AMERICANS OVERSEAS: 2
         MARRIED: 17   NORTH AMERICAN ADM. STAFF: 26
     SINGLE MEN: 1   SHORT TERM: 2
   SINGLE WOMEN: 2   RETIRED: 0

    TOTAL ACTIVE: 20

FIELD OF SERVICE	YEAR BEGAN	PERSONNEL NOW	PERSONNEL NEW	RELATED CHURCHES	PEOPLE GROUPS	NOTES
Bolivia	1961	2		13		
Brazil	1963	2		1		
Cameroon	1961	2		15		
Chile	1970			15		
Colombia	1964			1		
Costa Rica	1965					
Egypt	1960			10		
El Salvador	1955			20		
Germany, Fed. Rep.	1960	2				
Guatemala	1962			7		
Haiti	1961			217		
Honduras	1975			1		
Hong-Kong	1962			1		
Hungary	1971			1		
India	1960			9		
Indonesia	1963			15		
Italy	1963			7		
Jamaica	1961			1		
Japan	1964			1		

FIELD OF SERVICE	YEAR BEGAN	PERSONNEL NOW	PERSONNEL NEW	RELATED CHURCHES	PEOPLE GROUPS	NOTES
Jordan	1963			1		
Kenya	1961			16		
Korea, Rep. of	1961			3		
Liberia	1961			34		
Malawi	1974			10		
Mexico	1960			16		
Nepal	1964	2		1		
Nigeria	1957			10		
Pakistan	1962			1		
Panama	1975					
Papua New Guinea	1971			12		
Paraguay	1971			1		
Philippines	1962			1		
Sierra Leone	1965			1		
Sri Lanka	1978			1		
Syria	1962			1		
Taiwan Rep of China	1961			2		
Turkey	1961			1		
Venezuela	1964	2				
Yugoslavia	1974			1		
Zaire	1963	3		1		

Worldteam

1607 Ponce de Leon Blvd.
Coral Gables FL 33134
P.O. ADDRESS:
Box 343038
Coral Gables FL 33134

Tel. (305) 446-0861
EXECUTIVE OFFICER: J. Allen Thompson
ORGANIZED: 1928   AFFILIATION: IFMA
DESCRIPTION: Previously known as West Indies Mission. Name
    changed in 1978. A nondenominational sending agency of
    independent and evangelical tradition establishing and
    nurturing national churches. Also engaged in community
    development, radio and TV broadcasting, education and
    medicine.
TOTAL INCOME: $2,319,310   FOR OVERSEAS MINISTRIES: $2,149,957
PERSONNEL:
    NORTH AMERICANS OVERSEAS   NON-NORTH AMERICANS OVERSEAS: 23
            MARRIED: 149   NORTH AMERICAN ADM. STAFF: 48
        SINGLE MEN: 2   SHORT TERM: 10
      SINGLE WOMEN: 22   RETIRED: 30

        TOTAL ACTIVE: 173
NOTES: Of the administrative staff 17 are representatives.

FIELD OF SERVICE	YEAR BEGAN	PERSONNEL NOW	PERSONNEL NEW	RELATED CHURCHES	PEOPLE GROUPS	NOTES
Bahamas	1967	2		3	1	
Brazil	1958	12		5	1	
Central African Rep.	1977	2				
Cuba	1928	2		61	1	
Dominican Republic	1939	9		34	2	

FIELD OF SERVICE	YEAR BEGAN	PERSONNEL NOW	NEW	RELATED CHURCHES	PEOPLE GROUPS	NOTES
France	1979	2		1	1	
Grenada	1957	4		6	1	
Guadeloupe	1947	9		24	1	
Haiti	1936	98		293		
Italy	1972	8		2	1	
Jamaica	1945	2				
Spain	1972	11		7	1	
St. Lucia	1949	3		9	1	
St. Vincent	1952	2		11		
Surinam	1956	20		9	6	
Trinidad and Tobago	1951	10		12	2	

Worldwide Discipleship Association, Inc.

1001 Virginia Ave Ste315
Atlanta GA 30354

Tel. (404) 762-9521
EXECUTIVE OFFICER: Carl W. Wilson
ORGANIZED: 1974
DESCRIPTION: An interdenominational service agency of
    evangelical tradition involved in church planting,
    education, evangelism and literature production. Will be
    sending people to other countries in 1982.
TOTAL INCOME: $640,000   FOR OVERSEAS MINISTRIES: $3,850
PERSONNEL:
    NORTH AMERICANS OVERSEAS   NON-NORTH AMERICANS OVERSEAS: 0
            MARRIED: 0   NORTH AMERICAN ADM. STAFF: NR
        SINGLE MEN: 0   SHORT TERM: 0
      SINGLE WOMEN: 0   RETIRED: NR

        TOTAL ACTIVE: 0

Worldwide European Fellowship, Inc. SEE: WEFMinistries, Inc.

Worldwide Evangelization Crusade

709 Pennsylvania Ave.
Ft. Washington PA 19034
P.O. ADDRESS:
Box A
Ft. Washington PA 19034

Tel. (215) 646-2322
EXECUTIVE OFFICER: Elwin D. Palmer
ORGANIZED: 1913   AFFILIATION: EFMA
DESCRIPTION: An international, interdenominational sending
    agency of evangelical tradition establishing churches and
    engaged in evangelism, Bible translation, medicine and
    theological education.
TOTAL INCOME: $980,698   FOR OVERSEAS MINISTRIES: $779,784
PERSONNEL:
    NORTH AMERICANS OVERSEAS   NON-NORTH AMERICANS OVERSEAS: 0
            MARRIED: 95   NORTH AMERICAN ADM. STAFF: 22
        SINGLE MEN: 5   SHORT TERM: 7
      SINGLE WOMEN: 34   RETIRED: 22

        TOTAL ACTIVE: 134
NOTES: All figures include Canadian office.

FIELD OF SERVICE	YEAR BEGAN	PERSONNEL NOW	PERSONNEL NEW	RELATED CHURCHES	PEOPLE GROUPS	NOTES
Brazil	1957	6		7	1	
Chad	1962			2		
Colombia	1933	8		31	3	
France	1950			3	1	
Gambia	1957	10	7	2	3	
Germany, Fed. Rep.	1953	1			1	
Ghana	1940			30	10	
Guinea-Bissau	1939	8	4	24	2	
Hong-Kong	1972					
India	1926	5		3		
Indonesia	1949	17	8	85	17	
Iran	1963	1		1	1	
Italy	1964	2		3	1	
Ivory Coast	1934	18	9	33	20	
Japan	1950	7		7	2	
Liberia	1938	12	2	50	3	
Middle East-general	1962	9	5		3	
Portugal	1979				1	
Senegal	1936	6	2	8	5	
Spain	1967			2	1	1
Taiwan Rep of China	1947	1	1	1	1	
Thailand	1947	13	5	50	2	
United Arab Emirates	1963				1	
United Kingdom	1966	11	2		3	
Upper Volta	1937			23	3	
Venezuela	1954	2	2	10	2	
Zaire	1913	4	2	800		

Note: 1. Includes Canary Islands.

Worldwide Fellowship with Jesus
Christ Mission

Terra Alta WV 26764

Tel. (304) 379-7332
EXECUTIVE OFFICER: Berlin Wilhelm
ORGANIZED: 1951
DESCRIPTION: No current information available. Information
    from 1976 directory. A nondenominational sending agency
    of Brethren tradition establishing churches and engaged
    in education, literature and medicine.

TOTAL INCOME: NR   FOR OVERSEAS MINISTRIES: NR
PERSONNEL:
    NORTH AMERICANS OVERSEAS   NON-NORTH AMERICANS OVERSEAS: NR
            MARRIED: NR   NORTH AMERICAN ADM. STAFF: NR
        SINGLE MEN: NR   SHORT TERM: NR
      SINGLE WOMEN: NR   RETIRED: NR

        TOTAL ACTIVE: NR

FIELD OF SERVICE	YEAR BEGAN	PERSONNEL NOW	PERSONNEL NEW	RELATED CHURCHES	PEOPLE GROUPS	NOTES

Japan

Wycliffe Associates, Inc.

202 S Prospect
Orange CA 92669
P.O. ADDRESS:
Box 2000
Orange CA 92669

Tel. (714) 639-9950
EXECUTIVE OFFICER: Roger Tompkins
ORGANIZED: 1967

DESCRIPTION: A nondenominational agency of evangelical
    tradition. Wycliffe Associates is the authorized lay
    division of Wycliffe Bible translators and serves as a
    fund-raising, support and service organization.
TOTAL INCOME: $1,200,000   FOR OVERSEAS MINISTRIES: $700,000
PERSONNEL:
    NORTH AMERICANS OVERSEAS   NON-NORTH AMERICANS OVERSEAS: 0
              MARRIED: 0   NORTH AMERICAN ADM. STAFF: 0
           SINGLE MEN: 0   SHORT TERM: 79
         SINGLE WOMEN: 0   RETIRED: 0

         TOTAL ACTIVE: 0

Wycliffe Bible Translators
International, Inc.

19891 Beach Blvd.
Huntington Beach CA 92648

Tel. (714) 536-9346
EXECUTIVE OFFICER: Frank E. Robbins
ORGANIZED: 1935
DESCRIPTION: A nondenominational, international parent
    organization for 18 national sending agencies. Involved in
    Bible translation, aviation, training, literacy and
    linguistics. Affiliated with Summer Institute of
    Linguistics, Jungle Aviation and Radio Service, and
    Wycliffe Associates. Agency has 466 short-term personnel
    in addition to its regular staff.
TOTAL INCOME: $19,866,000   FOR OVERSEAS MINISTRIES: $19,866,000
PERSONNEL:
    NORTH AMERICANS OVERSEAS   NON-NORTH AMERICANS OVERSEAS: 658
           MARRIED: 1400   NORTH AMERICAN ADM. STAFF: 200
        SINGLE MEN: 33   SHORT TERM: 466
      SINGLE WOMEN: 348   RETIRED: 15

      TOTAL ACTIVE: 1781

FIELD OF SERVICE	YEAR BEGAN	PERSONNEL NOW	NEW	RELATED CHURCHES	PEOPLE GROUPS	NOTES
Asia-general	1966	15			13	
Australia	1961	30			22	
Bolivia	1955	78			17	
Brazil	1956	158			44	
Cameroon	1968	51			21	
Chad	1978					
Colombia	1962	185			36	
Ecuador	1953	74			12	
France	1975	2			1	
Germany, Fed. Rep.	1977	4			2	
Ghana	1962	14			16	
Guatemala	1952	59			38	
Honduras	1960	2			1	
Indonesia	1971	75			18	
Ivory Coast	1970	25			17	
Kenya	1978	4			2	
Malaysia	1978	29			3	
Mali	1979	2			1	
Mexico	1936	288			112	
Panama	1970	16			5	
Papua New Guinea	1956	306			148	

FIELD OF SERVICE	YEAR BEGAN	PERSONNEL NOW	NEW	RELATED CHURCHES	PEOPLE GROUPS	NOTES
Peru	1946	207			43	
Philippines	1953	206			63	
Solomon Is.	1977	8			12	
Sudan	1977	39			9	
Surinam	1967	15			7	
Thailand	1978	4			4	
Togo	1967	7			6	
Upper Volta	1971	5			6	
Zaire	1977	3			3	

Young Life

720 W Monument
Colorado Spgs CO 80901
P.O. ADDRESS:
Box 520
Colorado Spgs CO 80901

Tel. (303) 598-5316
EXECUTIVE OFFICER: Bob Mitchell
ORGANIZED: 1939
DESCRIPTION: A nondenominational sending agency of evangelical
    tradition advising national Christian leaders in
    evangelism and training among youth 16-23 years of age.
TOTAL INCOME: $250,000   FOR OVERSEAS MINISTRIES: NR
PERSONNEL:
    NORTH AMERICANS OVERSEAS   NON-NORTH AMERICANS OVERSEAS: NR
              MARRIED: NR   NORTH AMERICAN ADM. STAFF: 4
           SINGLE MEN: NR   SHORT TERM: 14
         SINGLE WOMEN: NR   RETIRED: NR

         TOTAL ACTIVE: NR

FIELD OF SERVICE	YEAR BEGAN	PERSONNEL NOW	NEW	RELATED CHURCHES	PEOPLE GROUPS	NOTES
Algeria	1978					
Australia	1970					
Austria	1975					
Bermuda	1964					
Brazil	1963					
Costa Rica	1976					
France	1952					
Germany, Fed. Rep.	1975					
India	1980					
Japan	1974					
Korea, Rep. of	1972					
Peru	1973					
Philippines	1972					
Singapore	1980					

Young Life Campaign SEE: Young Life

Youth Enterprises, Inc.

1605 E Elizabeth
Pasadena CA 91104

P.O. ADDRESS:
Box 653
Sierra Madre CA 91024

Tel. (213) 797-5349
EXECUTIVE OFFICER: James Gordon
ORGANIZED: 1960
DESCRIPTION: An interdenominational agency of evangelical
    tradition engaged in outreach through sports evangelism
    team ministries. Also uses correspondence courses and
    literature distribution.
TOTAL INCOME: $164,653   FOR OVERSEAS MINISTRIES: $102,950
PERSONNEL:
    NORTH AMERICANS OVERSEAS   NON-NORTH AMERICANS OVERSEAS: 0
            MARRIED: 5   NORTH AMERICAN ADM. STAFF: 3
        SINGLE MEN: 0   SHORT TERM: 150
        SINGLE WOMEN: 1   RETIRED: NR

        TOTAL 'ACTIVE: 6

FIELD OF SERVICE	YEAR BEGAN	PERSONNEL NOW	NEW	RELATED CHURCHES	PEOPLE GROUPS	NOTES
Mexico	1960	5		15		

Youth for Christ (Canada)

1180 Martin Grove Rd.
Rexdale ON M9W 5M9
Canada
P.O. ADDRESS:
Box 214
Rexdale ON M9W 5L1
Canada

Tel. (416) 243-3420
EXECUTIVE OFFICER: Brian C. Stiller
ORGANIZED: 1971
DESCRIPTION: Originally Youth for Christ International. The
    international council is headquartered in Switzerland with
    56 autonomous countries in association. The overseas
    division of YFC (Canada) provides funds and services.
    Focus of ministry is on youth evangelism and training.
    Work overseas is mainly done in Kenya, Netherlands,
    Switzerland and Chile.
TOTAL INCOME: $7,000,000   FOR OVERSEAS MINISTRIES: $300,000
PERSONNEL:
    NORTH AMERICANS OVERSEAS   NON-NORTH AMERICANS OVERSEAS: NR
            MARRIED: NR   NORTH AMERICAN ADM. STAFF: 175
        SINGLE MEN: NR   SHORT TERM: 0
        SINGLE WOMEN: NR   RETIRED: 8

        TOTAL ACTIVE: 12

Youth For Christ Intl., U.S.A. SEE: Youth For Christ/U.S.A.

Youth For Christ/U.S.A.

360 S Main Place
Carol Stream IL 60187
P.O. ADDRESS:
Box 419
Wheaton IL 60187

Tel. (312) 668-6600
EXECUTIVE OFFICER: Jay Kesler
ORGANIZED: 1944   AFFILIATION: EFMA
DESCRIPTION: Originally called Youth For Christ International.
    Name changed in 1979. Related to national Youth For

507

Christ programs in 56 other countries through the offices
of Youth For Christ International in Switzerland. YFC
helps fund the international organization and also
develops local YFC chapters in the USA. Serves 165
existing autonomous YFC chapters in the United States.
Focus of ministry is on youth evangelism and training.
TOTAL INCOME: $5,762,781   FOR OVERSEAS MINISTRIES: $775,000
PERSONNEL:
   NORTH AMERICANS OVERSEAS   NON-NORTH AMERICANS OVERSEAS: 0
        MARRIED: 24   NORTH AMERICAN ADM. STAFF: 2
     SINGLE MEN: 2   SHORT TERM: 1
   SINGLE WOMEN: 2   RETIRED: 0

    TOTAL ACTIVE: 28

FIELD OF SERVICE	YEAR BEGAN	PERSONNEL NOW	NEW	RELATED CHURCHES	PEOPLE GROUPS	NOTES
Brazil	1950	2				
Costa Rica		4				
France	1949	1				
Kenya		2				
Lebanon	1960	2				
Liberia		2				
Netherlands	1948	4				
New Zealand		2				
Portugal	1966	2				
South Africa		2				
Switzerland	1964	5				

Youth With A Mission

Rte.2 Box 304 Dallas Hwy
Tyler TX 75710
P.O. ADDRESS:
Box YWAM
Tyler TX 75710

Tel. (214) 597-1171
EXECUTIVE OFFICER: Loren Cunningham
ORGANIZED: 1960
DESCRIPTION: An international interdenominational sending
   agency of evangelical tradition engaged in evangelism and
   training for evangelism with emphasis on short term
   service for youth. Also involved in education, Bible and
   literature distribution, and aid and relief.
TOTAL INCOME: NA   FOR OVERSEAS MINISTRIES: NA
PERSONNEL:
   NORTH AMERICANS OVERSEAS   NON-NORTH AMERICANS OVERSEAS: NR
        MARRIED: 380   NORTH AMERICAN ADM. STAFF: 200
     SINGLE MEN: 203   SHORT TERM: 5000
   SINGLE WOMEN: 304   RETIRED: NR

    TOTAL ACTIVE: 887
NOTES: Personnel figures estimated by agency.
     YWAM is comprised of approximately 90 centers
     established as separate corporations.

FIELD OF SERVICE	YEAR BEGAN	PERSONNEL NOW	NEW	RELATED CHURCHES	PEOPLE GROUPS	NOTES
American Samoa	1973					

FIELD OF SERVICE	YEAR BEGAN	PERSONNEL NOW	NEW	RELATED CHURCHES	PEOPLE GROUPS	NOTES
Argentina	1977					
Australia	1968					
Austria	1977					
Brazil	1975					
Chile	1978					
Colombia	1974					
Cyprus	1973					
Denmark	1970					
Fiji	1979					
Finland	1971					
France	1972					
Germany, Fed. Rep.	1971					
Guam	1975					
Iceland	1979					
India	1973					
Ivory Coast	1978					
Japan	1972					
Kenya	1979					
Namibia	1979					
Nepal	1972					
Netherlands	1970					
New Zealand	1967					
Norway	1970					
Pacific Trust Terr.	1978					
Pakistan	1972					
Philippines	1971					
Singapore	1980					
South Africa	1973					
Spain	1971					
Sweden	1976					
Switzerland	1968					
Thailand	1973					
United Kingdom	1969					

Indices to Agencies

The following pages contain various indices to the basic directory of agencies. These indices permit the reader to find agencies grouped within certain geographic and ecclesiastical categories. The specific indices list agencies by state or province in which the headquarters is located and by the church tradition which the agency claims. One additional listing shows international agencies with North American offices.

The index by headquarters location shows that many agencies are found in the four states of California, Illinois, New York and Pennsylvania, and the Canadian province of Ontario.

The index by church tradition is non-exclusive; that is, an agency may appear under more than one descriptor. The most frequently used term is "evangelical," claimed by almost 350 agencies. This was followed by 149 agencies listing themselves as "non-denominational." More than 100 agencies called themselves "fundamentalist," while 86 were listed as "independent." Among traditional ecclesiastical names, Baptist agencies far outnumbered those from other traditions such as Lutheran, Mennonite, Reformed, Presbyterian and Wesleyan.

AGENCIES LISTED BY STATE

ALABAMA

Anis Shorrosh Evangelistic
Association
Apostolic Overcoming Holy
Church of God
Baptist World Mission
Church of God, USA
Headquarters

ALBERTA

Japan Evangelical Mission
Christian INFO
Mission to Europe's
Millions, Inc.
Operation Eyesight
Universal
Team Ventures International
World Mission Prayer League
Canada
International Biblical
Baptist Fellowship, Inc.
Evangelical Tract
Distributors (Canada)
South Pacific Evangelical
Fellowship

ARIZONA

Food For The Hungry
International
Jewish Voice Broadcast
Korea Gospel Mission
United Indian Missions,
Inc.

ARKANSAS

Baptist Missionary
Association of America

BRITISH COLUMBIA

Bible Holiness Movement
Japan Evangelistic Band
(Canada)
Glad Tidings Missionary
Society, Inc.
Food for the Hungry/Canada
Christian World-Wide Evang.
Msn. of Canada
International Christian
Leprosy Mission, Inc.
(Canada)

CALIFORNIA

African Enterprise
AIM, Inc. (Assistance in
Missions)
Air Crusade, Inc.

Alberto Mottesi
Evangelistic Association,
Inc.
American European Bethel
Mission, Inc.
Back-Country Evangelism,
Inc.
Bethany Missionary
Association
Bethel Mission of China,
Inc.
Biblical Literature
Fellowship
Bookmates International,
Incorporated
Breakthrough Ministries
California Yearly Meeting
of Friends Church, Bd. of
Msns.
CAM International Practical
Missionary Training, Inc.
Campus Crusade for Christ,
International (Overseas
Dept.)
China Missionary and
Evangelistic Association
Chinese Christian Mission
Chinese for Christ, Inc.
Chinese World Mission
Center
Christian Nationals'
Evangelism Commission,
Inc. (CNEC)
Christian Pilots
Association, Inc.
Christian World Publishers,
Inc.
Christians In Action
Christians United in
Action, Inc.
Eastern European Mission
Episcopal Church Missionary
Community
Erhlin Christian Polio Home
Evangel Bible Translators
Evangelical Leadership
International
Evangelism Center, Inc.
Evangelism to Communist
Lands
Evangelize China
Fellowship, Inc.
Faith Center Global
Ministries
Far East Broadcasting
Company, Inc.
Fellowship of Artists For
Cultrual Evangelism
(FACE)
Fellowship of Christian
Assemblies Mission to
Liberia

Forester Foundation, Inc.
Foundation For His
  Ministry-Orphanage
  Committee
Friends of Indonesia
  Fellowship, Inc.
Friendship Ministry
  International
Fuller Evangelistic
  Association
Fundamental Evangelistic
  Association
Go-Ye Fellowship
Gospel Literature
  International
Gospel Outreach
Gospel Recordings
  Incorporated
Greater Mexican Missions
Haggai Community
Handclasp International
  Inc.
Harvest Fields Missionary
  and Evangelistic Assn.,
  Inc.
Harvesters International
  Mission, Inc.
Hermano Pablo, Inc.
Hindustan Bible Institute,
  Inc.
Independent Assemblies of
  God, International
India Evangelical Mission,
  Inc.
India National Inland
  Mission
Institute of Chinese
  Studies
International Bible
  Institute
International Evangelism
  Crusades, Inc.
International Films, Inc.
International Gospel League
International Missionary
  Advance
Intl. Church of the
  Foursquare Gospel--Dept.
  of Msns. Intl.
Japan Evangelistic Band
Japanese Evangelical
  Missionary Society
Jesus Evangelism
Jesus to the Communist
  World, Inc.
Jews For Jesus
Korea International
  Mission, Inc.
Language Institute For
  Evangelism (LIFE)
Latin America Assistance
Life For Latins, Inc.

Link Care Center
Lord's Way Inn Ministries,
  Inc.
Lutheran Bible Translators,
  Inc.
Lutheran Braille Workers
Lutheran Frontier Missions
Lutherans For World
  Evangelization
Message of Life, Inc.
Mexican Christian Mission,
  Inc.
Ministry of Mission
  Services
Mission Aides, Incorporated
Mission Aviation Fellowship
Mission Renewal Team, Inc.
Mission SOS
Mission to Japan, Inc.
Mission Training and
  Resource Center
Missionary Electronics,
  Inc.
Missionary Gospel
  Fellowship, Inc.
Missionary Service
  Organization, Inc.
Missionary Strategy Agency
Missions Advanced Research
  and Communication Center
  (MARC)
Missions of Baja
Moody Institute of Science
Morris Cerullo World
  Evangelism, Inc.
Mustard Seed, Inc., The
Narramore Christian
  Foundation
New Life International
Nora Lam Ministries
O.C. Ministries, Inc.
Open Doors With Brother
  Andrew
Oriental Missionary
  Crusade, Inc.
Pan American Missions, Inc.
Prison Mission Assn., Inc.
Providence Mission Homes,
  Inc.
R.E.A.P.
REACH, Incorporated
REAP International
Rural Gospel and Medical
  Missions of India, Inc.
Russia for Christ, Inc.
Samaritan's Purse
Samuel Zwemer Institute
Share the Care
  International
Today's Mission
  Incorporated
Tokyo Evangelistic Center

Totonac Bible Center, Inc.
Trans World Missions
Undenominational Church of the Lord
Underground Christian Missions, Inc.
United Evangelical Churches
United Fundamentalist Church
United Missionary Fellowship
United Presbyterian Center for Mission Studies
United Presbyterian Order for World Evangelization
United States Center for World Mission
Vacation Samaritans
Voice of China and Asia Missionary Society, Inc.
Wings of Healing
Wings of Mercy Missions Inc.
World Gospel Crusades
World Literature Crusade
World Missionary Assistance Plan
World Missions, Inc.
World Opportunities International
World Vision International
World Vision, Incorporated
World-Wide Missions International
Wycliffe Associates, Inc.
Wycliffe Bible Translators International, Inc.
Youth Enterprises, Inc.

COLORADO

Amateur Radio Missionary Service (ARMS)
Bible Missionary Church, World Missions Department
Christian Dental Society
Church of God (Seventh Day), Gen. Conf., Msns. Abroad
Compassion International, Inc.
Compassion Relief and Development, Inc.
Evangelical Friends Church, Eastern Region, Fr. For. Msny. S
Friends of Turkey
International Church Relief Fund, Inc.
International Students, Inc.
Navigators, The

Overseas Christian Servicemen's Centers
Things to Come Mission, Inc.
Young Life

CONNECTICUT

Refugee Children, Inc.
Technoserve, Inc.

DELAWARE

World Presbyterian Missions, Inc.

FLORIDA

Adib Eden Evangelistic Missionary Society, Inc.
Bible Alliance Mission, Inc.
Chinese Gospel Crusade, Inc.
Evangelical Bible Mission, Inc.
Globe Missionary Evangelism
Gospel Association for the Blind, Inc.
Gospel Baptist Missions
Gospel Crusade World Wide Mission Outreach
Gospel Mission of South America
Great Commission Crusades, Inc.
Latin America Mission, Inc.
Logoi, Inc.
Logos Translators
Macedonian Service Foundation, Inc.
Men in Action
Missionary Flights International
New Tribes Mission
Pan American Missionary Society, Inc.
Romanian Missionary Society
South America Mission, Inc.
South American Crusades, Inc.
Spanish Evangelical Literature Fellowship, Inc.
Teen Missions International, Inc.
United World Mission, Incorporated
Westminister Biblical Missions, Inc.
World Radio Missionary Fellowship, Inc.

World Thrust Films, Inc.
Worldteam

GEORGIA

Carver Foreign Missions, Inc.
Congregational Holiness Church Foreign Mission Dept.
Friends For Missions, Inc.
Haggai Institute for Advanced Leadership Training, Inc.
Helps International Ministries, Inc.
International Messianic Outreach
Intl Pentecostal Ch. of Christ, Global Msns. Dept.
Mailbox Club, The
Mission to the World
Presbyterian Church in the U.S.A., Div. of Intl. Msn.
Source of Light Ministries, Intl.
Ukrainian Evangelical Alliance of North America
Worldwide Discipleship Association, Inc.

HAWAII

Christian Translation Ministries
Missionary Evangelistic Fellowship, Inc.

ILLINOIS

American Association for Jewish Evangelism
American Committee for KEEP, Inc.
American Messianic Fellowship
Apostolic Christian Church (Nazarene), Apos. Chr. Ch. Found.
Apostolic Christian Mission Fund
Baptist General Conference Board of World Missions
Bibles For The World, Inc.
Brazil Gospel Fellowship Mission
Christian Blind Mission International (CBM Intl.)
Christian Catholic Church
Christian Information

Service, Inc.
Christian Life Missions
Church of God General Conference Mission Department
Committee To Assist Ministry Education Overseas (CAMEO)
Conservative Baptist Association of America
Conservative Baptist Foreign Mission Society
Conservative Congregational Christian Conference
David C. Cook Foundation
European Evangelistic Society
Evangelical Alliance Mission (TEAM)
Evangelical Christian Education Ministries Inc.
Evangelical Covenant Church of America, Brd. of Wrld. Msn.
Evangelical Literature Overseas (ELO)
Evangelical Missions Information Service, Inc.
General Association of Regular Baptist Churches
Gospel Outreach to India, Inc.
Grace and Truth, Inc.
Greater Europe Mission
Home Finders International
Home of Onesiphorus
Institute of Holy Land Studies
International Christian Fellowship
International Crusades, Inc.
International Institute, Inc.
Living Bibles International
Mahon Mission
MAP International (Medical Assistance Programs)
Middle East Media
Missionary Leasing Company
Missionary Services, Inc.
Moody Literature Ministries
New Life League
North American Baptist Gen. Msny. Soc., Inc.
Open Air Campaigners (USA)
Pacific Broadcasting Association, Inc.
Paul Carlson Medical Program, Inc.
Pillar of Fire Missions
Pioneer Bible Translators

Project Partner, Inc.
Slavic Gospel Association
World Home Bible League
World Ministries Commission
World Relief Corporation
World Wide Prayer and
Missionary Union
Youth For Christ/U.S.A.

INDIANA

Africa Inter-Mennonite
Mission, Inc.
Bethel Foreign Mission
Foundation
Central Yearly Meeting of
Friends Missionary
Committee
Christian Amateur Radio
Fellowship
Christian Church (Disciples
of Christ) Div. of Oseas.
Min.
Christian Missionary
Fellowship
Church of God (Anderson,
Indiana) Msny. Bd.
Church of the United
Brethren in Christ, Bd.
of Msns.
Evangelical Baptist
Missions, Inc.
Evangelical Mennonite
Church, Comm. on Oseas.
Msns.
Evangelistic Faith Mission,
Inc.
Fellowship of Grace
Brethren Churches, For.
Msny. Soc.
Free Methodist Church of N.
America Gen. Mssy. Brd.
Lester Sumrall Evangelistic
Association
Men For Missions
International
Mennonite Board of Missions
Mission Services
Association, Inc.
Missionary Church, Div. of
Overseas Ministries
OMS International, Inc.
Pentecostal Assemblies of
the World, Inc. For.
Msns. Dept.
Society for Europe's
Evangelization (S.E.E.)
Spanish-World Gospel
Mission, Inc.
Wesleyan Church Gen. Dept.
of Wld. Msns.
Wider Ministries Commission

World Gospel Mission
World Missionary Press,
Inc.

IOWA

Good Shepherd Agricultural
Mission, Inc.
Open Bible Standard
Missions, Inc.
Self Help Foundation

KANSAS

All Peoples Baptist Mission
Church of God (Holiness)
For. Msn. Bd.
Church of God in Christ,
Mennonite Gen. Msn. Bd.,
Inc.
Evangelical Methodist
Church World Missions
General Conference
Mennonite Church, Comm.
on Oseas. Msn.
Kansas Yearly Meeting of
Friends Africa Gospel
Mission
Mennonite Brethren
Missions/Services
Reformation Translation
Fellowship

KENTUCKY

Baptist Faith Missions
Evangelical Missions
Council of Good News
Evangelism Resources

MANITOBA

Janz Team
Evangelical Mennonite
Conference Board of
Missions
Christian Business Men's
Committee International
(Canada)

MARYLAND

Christian Missions, Inc.

MASSACHUSETTS

Protestant Episcopal Church
in the USA, Soc. of St.
Margaret
Society of St. John the
Evangelist

AGENCIES LISTED BY STATE

MICHIGAN

ACTS International
Anchor Bay Evangelistic
    Association
Baptist Haiti Mission, Inc.
Chiang Mai Mission Board,
    The
Christ For The Philippines,
    Inc.
Christian Mission for the
    Deaf
Christian Reformed Board
    For World Missions
Christian Reformed World
    Relief Committee
Christian Salvage Mission,
    Inc.
Evangelical Literature
    League (T.E.L.L.)
Far Eastern Gospel Crusade
Gospel Films, Inc.
Grace Mission, Inc.
International Fellowship of
    Christians
Missionary Information
    Exchange
Missionary Internship, Inc.
Outreach, Inc.
Overcomer Press, Inc.
Portable Recording
    Ministries, Inc.
Protestant Reformed
    Churches in America
W. Shabaz Associates, Inc.

MINNESOTA

American Lutheran Ch., Div.
    For Wld. Msn.
Association of Free
    Lutheran Congregations
Bethany Fellowship Msns.
    (Div. of Bethany
    Fellowship, Inc.)
Bethesda Mission, Inc.
Billy Graham Evangelistic
    Association
Christian Service
    Fellowship
Christian Services
    Fellowship, Inc.
Church of the Lutheran
    Brethren of America, Bd.
    of Wld. Msns
Church of the Nazarene,
    Gen. Bd. Dept. of Wld.
    Msns.
Evangelical Free Ch. of
    America, Bd. of Oseas.
    Msn.
Global Concern, Inc.

Hague Foreign Mission, Inc.
Lutheran Orient Mission
    Society
Minneapolis Friends of
    Israel
Minnesota Bible Fellowship,
    Inc.
N. American Committee for
    IME, Institut Medical
    Evangelique
World Mission Prayer League

MISSISSIPPI

African Bible Colleges,
    Inc.
Maranatha Baptist Mission,
    Inc.
Methodist Protestant
    Church, Board of Msns.
Voice of Calvary

MISSOURI

Appleman Campaigns, Inc.
Assemblies of God, Div. of
    For. Msns.
Baptist Bible Fellowship
    International
Berean Mission, Inc.
Bible Memory Association
    International
Child Evangelism
    Fellowship, Inc.
Church of God at Baden,
    I.H.P.
Concordia Tract Mission
Full Gospel Native
    Missionary Association
General Baptist Foreign
    Mission Society, Inc.
Gospel Missionary Union
Holy Land Christian Mission
International Lutheran
    Laymen's League
Lutheran Church-Missouri
    Synod
Missions Outreach, Inc.
Open Door Missionary
    Fellowship, Inc.
Pentecostal Church of God,
    World Missions Department
United Pentecostal Church
    Intl. For. Msns. Div.

NEBRASKA

Back to the Bible
    Missionary Agency
Evangelical Mennonite
    Brethren Commission on
    Mission

NEW HAMPSHIRE

H.O.P.E. Bible Mission,
Inc.

NEW JERSEY

Africa Evangelical
Fellowship
America's Keswick, Inc.
American Leprosy Missions,
Inc.
Andes Evangelical Mission
Armenian Missionary
Association of America,
Inc.
Association of Baptists For
World Evangelism, Inc.
Cedar Lane Missionary
Homes, Inc.
Christ's Mission
Christian Missions in Many
Lands, Inc.
Friends of Israel Gospel
Ministry, Inc.
High School Evangelism
Fellowship, Inc.
International Missions,
Inc.
Liberty Corner Mission
Liebenzell Mission of
U.S.A., Inc.
Messengers of the New
Covenant, Inc.
National Religious
Broadcasters
New York International
Bible Society
Operation Mobilization Send
the Light, Inc.
Overseas Ministries Study
Center
Pocket Testament League,
Inc.
Ramabai Mukti Mission
(American Council of)
Sudan Interior Mission,
Inc.
Trans World Radio

NEW YORK

Africa Inland Mission
African Methodist Episcopal
Church, Inc. Dept. of
Msns.
African Methodist Episcopal
Zion Ch., Dept. of Oseas.
Msns.
Agricultural Missions, Inc.
American Bible Society
American Board of Missions
to the Jews, Inc.
American European
Fellowship Chr. Oneness
Evang., Inc.
American Mc All Association
American Waldensian Aid
Society
Arthur Bradford
Evangelistic Association
Bethany Home, Inc.
Bread for the World
Christian and Missionary
Alliance
Church of our Lord Jesus
Christ of the Apostolic
Faith, Inc.
Church World Service
Division of DOM-NCCCUSA
CODEL (Coordination in
Development, Inc.)
Comm. on Children's
Literature For Women and
Children
Council for Cooperation
Dominican Evang. Ch.
Defenders of the Christian
Faith Movement, Inc.
Elim Fellowship, Inc.
FARMS International, Inc.
Global Outreach Mission
India Christian Mission,
Inc.
International Everlasting
Gospel Mission, Inc.
International Foundation
For EWHA Woman's
University
Japan International
Christian Univ. Found.,
Inc.
Japan-North American
Commission on Cooperative
Mission
John Milton Society for the
Blind
Ludhiana Christian Medical
College Board, U.S.A.,
Inc.
Lutheran Church in
America-Div. for Wld.
Msn. and Ecumenism
Lutheran World Federation,
U.S.A. National Committee
Lutheran World Relief,
Incorporated
Native Preacher Company,
Inc.
Protestant Episcopal Church
(Order of the Holy Cross)
Reformed Church in America
General Program Council
Salvation Army, The

Southern European Mission, Inc.
Tele-Missions International, Inc.
United Board for Christian Higher Education in Asia
United Church Board For World Ministries
United Methodist Ch. Wld. Div. of the Bd. of Global Min.
United Methodist Church Comm. on Relief
United Presbyterian Church in the USA Program Agency
Vellore Christian Medical College Board, (USA Inc.
Women's Chrn. Clg. Madras Inc./St. Christopher's Trng. Clg.
Word of Life Fellowship
World Mission in Church and Society

NORTH CAROLINA

Advent Christian Gen. Conf. of America
American Advent Mission Society
Anglican Orthodox Church
Correll Missionary Ministries
General Conference of the Evangelical Baptist Church, Inc.
Heritage Village Church and Missionary Fellowship, Inc.
Independent Faith Mission, Inc.
Jungle Aviation and Radio Service, Inc. (JAARS)
New Testament Missionary Union
Pentecostal Free Will Baptist Church, Inc.
World Medical Mission

NORTH DAKOTA

Steer, Inc.

NOVA SCOTIA

International Christian Mission

OHIO

Allegheny Wesleyan Methodist Missions

Baptist Mid-Missions
Bible Literature International
Brethren Church, Missionary Board of The Brethren Church
Christian Baptist Ch. of God Assn. Wld. for Christ Msns.
Christian Union General Mission Board
Churches of Christ in Christian Union: Foreign Msny. Dept.
Churches of God, General Conference Comm. on Wld. Msns.
Conservative Mennonite Board of Missions and Charities
Evangelical Friends Mission
OMI Brotherhood Foundation of America, Inc.
Project Partner with Christ, Inc.
World's Christian Endeavor Union

OKLAHOMA

Chr. Echoes Natl. Min., Inc. (Chr. Crusade)
Church of God of the Apostolic Faith, Inc.
Faith Christian Fellowship World Outreach
Full Gospel Grace Fellowship
Literacy and Evangelism, Inc.
Mission Mailbag, Inc.
Osborn Foundation
Pentecostal Holiness Church-World Missions Department
Tokyo Gospel Mission, Inc.
World Neighbors, Inc.

ONTARIO

Pentecostal Assemblies of Canada, Oseas. Msns. Dept.
Ling A. Juane Ministries, Inc.
Emmanuel International
Christian Canadian Mission to Overseas Students
Operation Mobilization - Canada
Navigators of Canada International, The

519

Scripture Gift Mission
(Canada), Inc.
World Vision of Canada
Bible Club Movement of
Canada
Africa Inland Mission
(Canada)
BMMF International/Canada
Africa Evangelical
Fellowship (Canada)
Regions Beyond Missionary
Union (Canada)
Missionary Health
Institute, Inc.
Toronto Institute of
Linguistics
Fellowship of Evangelical
Baptist Chs. in Canada
Liebenzell Mission of
Canada
Presbyterian Church in
Canada, Board of World
Mission
Everyday Publications
Apostolic Church in Canada,
The
Canadian Bible Society
Inter-Varsity Christian
Fellowship of Canada
United Church of Canada,
Division of World
Outreach
Christian Transportation
Fellowship of Faith For
Muslims
Leprosy Mission Canada
Christian Literature
Crusade (Ontario) Inc.
Overseas Missionary
Fellowship
Canadian Yearly Mtg. of the
Rel. Soc. of Frnds. Serv.
Comm.
Regular Baptists of Canada,
Women's Missionary
Society
Canadian Baptist Overseas
Mission Board
Salvation Army, Canada and
Bermuda
Gospel Recordings of
Canada, Inc.
Christian Nationals'
Evangelism Commission,
Inc. (Canada)
Trinitarian Bible Society,
Canada
Youth for Christ (Canada)
New Tribes Mission of
Canada
Mission Aviation Fellowship
of Canada

Bible Research
International
Bibles for the Nations
Crusade Evangelism
International
Compassion of Canada
Anglican Church of Canada,
Natl. and Wld. Program

OREGON

Apostolic Faith Mission of
Portland, Oregon
Christian Literature
International
Daystar Communications,
Inc.
Frontier Ministries
International
Holt International
Children's Services, Inc.
International Christian
Leprosy Mission, Inc.
(USA)
Luis Palau Evangelistic
Team, Inc.
Mennonite Mission Brd. of
Pacific Coast Conf.
(Mexico Brd.)
Northwest Yearly Meeting of
Friends Ch., Dept. of
Msns.
Outreach, Inc.
World Missions Fellowship

PENNSYLVANIA

Afghan Border Crusade
African Mission Services,
Inc.
Afro-American Missionary
Crusade, Inc.
Ambassadors For Christ,
Inc.
American Baptist Churches
in the U.S.A., Intl. Min.
American Board for the
Syrian Orphanage
American Board of
International Missions
American Friends Service
Committee
American Missionary
Fellowship
American Scripture Gift
Mission
Bible Christian Union, Inc.
Bible Club Movement, Inc.
Bible Presbyterian Church,
Ind. Bd. for Presb. For.
Msns.
BMMF/International (U.S.A.)

AGENCIES LISTED BY STATE

Brethren in Christ Missions
Christian Church of North
America, Msns. Dept.
Christian Literature
Crusade, Inc.
D.M. Stearns Missionary
Fund, Inc.
Eastern Mennonite Board of
Missions and Charities
Evangelical Congregational
Church Division of
Missions
Evangelization Society of
the Pittsburgh Bible
Institute
Faith Ministries
Fellowship of Independent
Missions
Franconia Mennonite
Conference Mission
Commission
Free Gospel Church, Inc.
Grand Old Gospel
Fellowship, Inc.
Independent Gospel Missions
Jubilee, Inc.
Mennonite Central Committee
Mennonite Economic
Development Associates
Million Testaments
Campaigns, Inc.
Missionary Auto-Truck
Service
Missions, Inc.
Moravian Church in America,
Brd. of Wrld. Msn.
National Baptist
Convention, U.S.A., Inc.
For. Msn. Bd.
North Africa Mission
North East India General
Mission, Inc.
Open Bible Ministries, Inc.
Orthodox Presbyterian
Church Committee on
Foreign Missions
Overseas Missionary
Fellowship
Pilgrim Fellowship, Inc.,
The
Primitive Methodist Church
in the USA, Intl. Msn.
Bd.
Progressive Natl. Bapt.
Conv. USA, Inc. Bapt.
For. Msn. Bur.
Reformed Episcopal Church
Bd. of For. Msns.
Reformed Presbyterian Ch.
of N. America, Bd. of
For. Msns.
Regions Beyond Missionary

Union (U.S.A.)
Schwenkfelder Church in the
USA and For. Bd. of Msns.
Scripture Union, U.S.A.
Society of Central Asian
News (SCAN)
Unevangelized Fields
Mission
Unevangelized Tribes
Mission, Inc.
WEFMinistries, Inc.
Worldwide Evangelization
Crusade

PROVINCE OF QUEBEC

Leprosy Relief, Canada,
Inc.
Chrn. Homes Children, Inc.
Harold Martin Evang.
Assn., Inc.

PUERTO RICO

Calvary Evangelistic
Mission, Inc./WIVV Msny.
Radio Station
Movimiento Misionero
Mundial, Inc.

RHODE ISLAND

Children of India
Foundation
Seventh Day Baptist
Missionary Society

SASKATCHEWAN

Evangelical Alliance
Mission of Canada, Inc.
Christian and Missionary
Alliance in Canada
Apostolic Church of
Pentecost of
Canada-Missionary Dept.
Evangelical Lutheran
Church, Division of World
Missions
Western Tract Mission

SOUTH CAROLINA

Associate Reformed Presb.
Ch., Wld. Witness
Evangelical Methodist
Church Bible Methodist
Missions
Org. of Continuing Educ.
for American Nurses
(OCEAN)

SOUTH DAKOTA

Middle East Christian
Outreach--USA Council

TENNESSEE

AMG International
(Advancing the Ministries
of the Gospel)
Baptist International
Missions, Inc.
Christian Business Men's
Committee of USA
Christian Literature and
Bible Center, Inc.
Church of God of Prophecy,
World Mission Committee
Church of God World
Missions
Cumberland Presbyterian
Church, Board of Missions
Gideons International
International Board of
Jewish Missions, Inc.
National Association of
Free Will Baptists, Brd.
of For. Msn

TEXAS

Amazing Grace Missions
American Baptist
Association, Missionary
Committee
American Tract Society
Bible Translations On Tape,
Inc.
Border Missions
CAM International
Children's Haven
International, Inc.
Christ For The Nations,
Inc.
Christian Medical Society
Evangelical Latin League,
Inc.
Full Gospel Evangelistic
Association
Houses of Refuge, Intl.
Orphanages Assn. Inc.
International Bible
Translators
International Prison
Ministry
Japan Evangelistic
Association, Inc.
Living Waters
Mexican Border Missions
Mexican Mission Ministries,
Inc.
Mexican Missions, Inc.

Mission Possible
Foundation, Inc.
Missionary Air Transport,
Inc.
Missionary Revival Crusade
Missionary TECH Team
Natl. Baptist Convention of
Amer., For. Msn. Bd.
Next Towns Crusade, Inc.
Outreach International
Petra International, Inc.
Red Sea Mission Team, Inc.,
U.S.A. Council
Release the World for
Christ
Tainan Evangelical Mission
Victory Mission of the
Americas
We Go, Inc. (World
Encounter Gospel
Organization)
World Baptist Fellowship
Mission Agency
International
World Evangelism Foundation
World Hope Foundation
World Mission Information
Bank
World Missionary
Evangelism, Inc.
World Outreach
World Wide Missionary
Crusader, Inc.
Youth With A Mission

VIRGINIA

Bible Protestant Missions,
Inc.
Chinese Overseas Christian
Mission, Inc.
Christian Aid Mission
Christian Broadcasting
Network
Media Ministries Division,
Mennonite Bd. of Msns.
Missionary Communications,
Inc.
Southern Baptist
Convention, Foreign
Mission Board
Sundanese Missionary
Fellowship
Technical Support Mission
Virginia Mennonite Board of
Missions and Charities

WASHINGTON

Action International
Ministries
Bethel Pentecostal Temple,

Inc.
Calcutta Mission of Mercy
Evangelical Scripture
   Mission
Intercristo
International Needs-USA
Life messengers, Inc.
Missionary Dentist, Inc.
Overseas Radio and
   Television, Inc.
World Concern/Crista
   International

(WASHINGTON) DISTRICT OF COLUMBIA

Christian Service Corps
General Conference of
   Seventh-day Adventists
Lott Carey Baptist Foreign
   Mission Convention
Laos, Inc.

WEST VIRGINIA

Worldwide Fellowship with
   Jesus Christ Mission

WISCONSIN

Evangelical Lutheran Synod
   Board For Missions
Inter-Varsity Christian
   Fellowship
International Fellowship of
   Evangelical Students -
   USA
Metropolitan Church
   Association
Natl. Assn. of
   Congregational Chr. Chs.
   of the U.S.A.
Wisconsin Evangelical
   Lutheran Synod, Bd. for
   Wld. Msns.

AGENCIES LISTED BY TRADITION

Adventist

American Advent Mission
  Society
Church of God (Seventh
  Day), Gen. Conf., Msns.
  Abroad
Church of God General
  Conference Mission
  Department
General Conference of
  Seventh-day Adventists

Anglican

Anglican Church of Canada,
  Natl. and Wld. Program
Anglican Orthodox Church
Episcopal Church Missionary
  Community
World Mission in Church and
  Society

Apostolic

Apostolic Christian Mission
  Fund
Apostolic Overcoming Holy
  Church of God

Baptist

ACTS International
Afghan Border Crusade
Africa Evangelical
  Fellowship
Africa Evangelical
  Fellowship (Canada)
Africa Inland Mission
  (Canada)
Alberto Mottesi
  Evangelistic Association,
  Inc.
All Peoples Baptist Mission
Amazing Grace Missions
American Association for
  Jewish Evangelism
American Baptist
  Association, Missionary
  Committee
American Baptist Churches
  in the U.S.A., Intl. Min.
American Board of Missions
  to the Jews, Inc.
AMG International
  (Advancing the Ministries
  of the Gospel)
Anis Shorrosh Evangelistic
  Association
Appleman Campaigns, Inc.
Association of Baptists For
  World Evangelism, Inc.
Baptist Bible Fellowship

International
Baptist Faith Missions
Baptist General Conference
  Board of World Missions
Baptist Haiti Mission, Inc.
Baptist International
  Missions, Inc.
Baptist Mid-Missions
Baptist Missionary
  Association of America
Baptist World Mission
Berean Mission, Inc.
Bethany Home, Inc.
Bible Alliance Mission,
  Inc.
Calvary Evangelistic
  Mission, Inc./WIVV Msny.
  Radio Station
CAM International Practical
  Missionary Training, Inc.
Canadian Baptist Overseas
  Mission Board
Carver Foreign Missions,
  Inc.
Child Evangelism
  Fellowship, Inc.
Children's Haven
  International, Inc.
Christ For The Philippines,
  Inc.
Christian Salvage Mission,
  Inc.
Christian Services
  Fellowship, Inc.
Church of God (Holiness)
  For. Msn. Bd.
Conservative Baptist
  Association of America
Conservative Baptist
  Foreign Mission Society
Defenders of the Christian
  Faith Movement, Inc.
Evangelical Baptist
  Missions, Inc.
Evangelical Latin League,
  Inc.
Faith Ministries
Far East Broadcasting
  Company, Inc.
Far Eastern Gospel Crusade
Fellowship of Evangelical
  Baptist Chs. in Canada
General Association of
  Regular Baptist Churches
General Baptist Foreign
  Mission Society, Inc.
General Conference of the
  Evangelical Baptist
  Church, Inc.
Good Shepherd Agricultural
  Mission, Inc.
Gospel Baptist Missions
Gospel Mission of South

America
Gospel Missionary Union
Greater Mexican Missions
Hindustan Bible Institute,
  Inc.
Independent Faith Mission,
  Inc.
Independent Gospel Missions
International Biblical
  Baptist Fellowship, Inc.
International Institute,
  Inc.
Japan Evangelistic
  Association, Inc.
Korea Gospel Mission
Lott Carey Baptist Foreign
  Mission Convention
Macedonian Service
  Foundation, Inc.
Maranatha Baptist Mission,
  Inc.
Messengers of the New
  Covenant, Inc.
Mexican Mission Ministries,
  Inc.
Middle East Christian
  Outreach--USA Council
Ministry of Mission
  Services
Mission Mailbag, Inc.
Missionary Evangelistic
  Fellowship, Inc.
Missionary Flights
  International
Missionary Leasing Company
National Association of
  Free Will Baptists, Brd.
  of For. Msn
National Baptist
  Convention, U.S.A., Inc.
  For. Msn. Bd.
Natl. Baptist Convention of
  Amer., For. Msn. Bd.
North American Baptist Gen.
  Msny. Soc., Inc.
Open Bible Ministries, Inc.
Outreach, Inc.
Pan American Missions, Inc.
Progressive Natl. Bapt.
  Conv. USA, Inc. Bapt.
  For. Msn. Bur.
Regions Beyond Missionary
  Union (Canada)
Regions Beyond Missionary
  Union (U.S.A.)
Regular Baptists of Canada,
  Women's Missionary
  Society
Romanian Missionary Society
Schwenkfelder Church in the
  USA and For. Bd. of Msns.
Seventh Day Baptist
  Missionary Society

Society for Europe's
  Evangelization (S.E.E.)
Southern Baptist
  Convention, Foreign
  Mission Board
Spanish Evangelical
  Literature Fellowship,
  Inc.
Spanish-World Gospel
  Mission, Inc.
World Baptist Fellowship
  Mission Agency
  International
World Evangelism Foundation

Brethren

Brethren Church, Missionary
  Board of The Brethren
  Church
Fellowship of Grace
  Brethren Churches, For.
  Msny. Soc.
World Ministries Commission
Worldwide Fellowship with
  Jesus Christ Mission

Charismatic

Asian Outreach
Bethany Fellowship Msns.
  (Div. of Bethany
  Fellowship, Inc.)
Christ For The Nations,
  Inc.
Evangel Bible Translators
Faith Christian
  Fellowship World Outreach
Forester Foundation, Inc.
Foundation For His
  Ministry-Orphanage
  Committee
Frontier Ministries
  International
Globe Missionary Evangelism
Gospel Crusade World Wide
  Mission Outreach
Gospel Outreach
Heritage Village Church and
  Missionary Fellowship,
  Inc.
Literacy and Evangelism,
  Inc.
Living Waters
Logos Translators
Missionary Information
  Exchange
Missionary Revival Crusade
Morris Cerullo World
  Evangelism, Inc.
Nora Lam Ministries
Oriental Missionary
  Crusade, Inc.

Petra International, Inc.
United Evangelical Churches
World Missionary Assistance
Plan

Christian
(Restoration Movement)

Christian Amateur Radio
Fellowship
Christian Missionary
Fellowship
European Evangelistic
Society
Mission Services
Association, Inc.
Outreach International
Pioneer Bible Translators
World Mission Information
Bank

Congregational

American Mc All Association
Andes Evangelical Mission
Armenian Missionary
Association of America,
Inc.
Christian Missionary
Fellowship
Conservative Congregational
Christian Conference
Missionary Church, Div. of
Overseas Ministries
Natl. Assn. of
Congregational Chr. Chs.
of the U.S.A.
Primitive Methodist Church
in the USA, Intl. Msn.
Bd.
Schwenkfelder Church in the
USA and For. Bd. of Msns.
United Church Board For
World Ministries

Congregational, Holiness

Church of God (Holiness)
For. Msn. Bd.

Ecumenical

African Mission Services,
Inc.
Agricultural Missions, Inc.
American Leprosy Missions,
Inc.
Bread for the World
Christian Church (Disciples
of Christ) Div. of Oseas.
Min.
Christian Life Missions
Christian Medical Society

Christian Service Corps
CODEL (Coordination in
Development, Inc.)
Japan-North American
Commission on Cooperative
Mission
John Milton Society for the
Blind
Link Care Center
Lutheran Church in
America-Div. for Wld.
Msn. and Ecumenism
Lutheran World Relief,
Incorporated
Mennonite Economic
Development Associates
OMI Brotherhood Foundation
of America, Inc.
Salvation Army, Canada
and Bermuda
United Church Board For
World Ministries
United Church of Canada,
Division of World
Outreach
Vellore Christian Medical
College Board, (USA Inc.

Episcopal

American Committee for
KEEP, Inc.
Episcopal Church Missionary
Community
Free Methodist Church of N.
America Gen. Mssy. Brd.
Protestant Episcopal Church
(Order of the Holy Cross)
Protestant Episcopal Church
in the USA, Soc. of St.
Margaret
Society of St. John the
Evangelist
World Mission in Church and
Society

Evangelical

Action International
Ministries
Africa Evangelical
Fellowship (Canada)
Africa Inland Mission
Africa Inland Mission
(Canada)
African Bible Colleges,
Inc.
African Enterprise
African Mission Services,
Inc.
Afro-American Missionary
Crusade, Inc.
AIM, Inc. (Assistance in

527

Missions)
Air Crusade, Inc.
Alberto Mottesi
  Evangelistic Association,
  Inc.
All Peoples Baptist Mission
Ambassadors For Christ,
  Inc.
American Leprosy Missions,
  Inc.
American Missionary
  Fellowship
American Scripture Gift
  Mission
AMG International
  (Advancing the Ministries
  of the Gospel)
Apostolic Christian Church
  (Nazarene), Apos. Chr.
  Ch. Found.
Armenian Missionary
  Association of America,
  Inc.
Arthur Bradford
  Evangelistic Association
Asian Outreach
Assemblies of God, Div. of
  For. Msns.
Associate Reformed Presb.
  Ch., Wld. Witness
Back to the Bible
  Missionary Agency
Baptist General Conference
  Board of World Missions
Baptist Haiti Mission, Inc.
Bethany Fellowship Msns.
  (Div. of Bethany
  Fellowship, Inc.)
Bethany Home, Inc.
Bethel Mission of China,
  Inc.
Bethesda Mission, Inc.
Bible Alliance Mission,
  Inc.
Bible Christian Union, Inc.
Bible Club Movement of
  Canada
Bible Club Movement, Inc.
Bible Translations On Tape,
  Inc.
Bibles for the Nations
Bibles For The World, Inc.
Biblical Literature
  Fellowship
Billy Graham Evangelistic
  Association
BMMF International/Canada
BMMF/International (U.S.A.)
Bookmates International,
  Incorporated
Border Missions
Breakthrough Ministries
California Yearly Meeting

of Friends Church, Bd. of
  Msns.
CAM International
CAM International Practical
  Missionary Training, Inc.
Campus Crusade for Christ,
  International (Overseas
  Dept.)
Canadian Baptist Overseas
  Mission Board
Carver Foreign Missions,
  Inc.
Child Evangelism
  Fellowship, Inc.
Children's Haven
  International, Inc.
Chinese Christian Mission
Chinese Gospel Crusade,
  Inc.
Chinese World Mission
  Center
Christ For The Nations,
  Inc.
Christ For The Philippines,
  Inc.
Christ's Mission
Christian Aid Mission
Christian and Missionary
  Alliance
Christian and Missionary
  Alliance in Canada
Christian Blind Mission
  International (CBM Intl.)
Christian Broadcasting
  Network
Christian Business Men's
  Committee International
  (Canada)
Christian Business Men's
  Committee of USA
Christian Canadian Mission
  to Overseas Students
Christian Catholic Church
Christian Church of North
  America, Msns. Dept.
Christian Information
  Service, Inc.
Christian Life Missions
Christian Literature
  Crusade (Ontario) Inc.
Christian Literature
  Crusade, Inc.
Christian Literature
  International
Christian Medical Society
Christian Missionary
  Fellowship
Christian Nationals'
  Evangelism Commission,
  Inc. (Canada)
Christian Nationals'
  Evangelism Commission,
  Inc. (CNEC)

Christian Pilots
Association, Inc.
Christian Service Corps
Christian Translation
Ministries
Christian Union General
Mission Board
Christian World Publishers,
Inc.
Christian World-Wide Evang.
Msn. of Canada
Christians In Action
Christians United in
Action, Inc.
Chrn. Homes Children, Inc.
Harold Martin Evang.
Assn., Inc.
Church of God (Anderson,
Indiana) Msny. Bd.
Church of God at Baden,
I.H.P.
Church of God of Prophecy,
World Mission Committee
Church of the Nazarene,
Gen. Bd. Dept. of Wld.
Msns.
Church of the United
Brethren in Christ, Bd.
of Msns.
Churches of God, General
Conference Comm. on Wld.
Msns.
Committee To Assist
Ministry Education
Overseas (CAMEO)
Compassion International,
Inc.
Compassion of Canada
Compassion Relief and
Development, Inc.
Conservative Baptist
Association of America
Conservative Baptist
Foreign Mission Society
Conservative Mennonite
Board of Missions and
Charities
Correll Missionary
Ministries
Crusade Evangelism
International
Cumberland Presbyterian
Church, Board of Missions
D.M. Stearns Missionary
Fund, Inc.
David C. Cook Foundation
Daystar Communications,
Inc.
Defenders of the Christian
Faith Movement, Inc.
Eastern European Mission
Emmanuel International
Episcopal Church Missionary

Community
Erhlin Christian Polio Home
Evangelical Alliance
Mission (TEAM)
Evangelical Alliance
Mission of Canada, Inc.
Evangelical Christian
Education Ministries Inc.
Evangelical Congregational
Church Division of
Missions
Evangelical Covenant Church
of America, Brd. of Wrld.
Msn.
Evangelical Free Ch. of
America, Bd. of Oseas.
Msn.
Evangelical Friends Church,
Eastern Region, Fr. For.
Msny. S
Evangelical Friends Mission
Evangelical Leadership
International
Evangelical Literature
League (T.E.L.L.)
Evangelical Literature
Overseas (ELO)
Evangelical Mennonite
Brethren Commission on
Mission
Evangelical Mennonite
Church, Comm. on Oseas.
Msns.
Evangelical Methodist
Church World Missions
Evangelical Missions
Council of Good News
Evangelical Missions
Information Service, Inc.
Evangelism Center, Inc.
Evangelism Resources
Evangelistic Faith Mission,
Inc.
Evangelize China
Fellowship, Inc.
Faith Ministries
Far East Broadcasting
Company, Inc.
Far Eastern Gospel Crusade
FARMS International, Inc.
Fellowship of Artists For
Cultrual Evangelism
(FACE)
Fellowship of Evangelical
Baptist Chs. in Canada
Fellowship of Faith For
Muslims
Fellowship of Grace
Brethren Churches, For.
Msny. Soc.
Food For The Hungry
International
Food for the Hungry/Canada

AGENCIES LISTED BY TRADITION

Foundation For His
  Ministry-Orphanage
  Committee
Free Methodist Church of N.
  America Gen. Mssy. Brd.
Friends of Turkey
Friendship Ministry
  International
Frontier Ministries
  International
Full Gospel Grace
  Fellowship
Fuller Evangelistic
  Association
General Conference
  Mennonite Church, Comm.
  on Oseas. Msn.
General Conference of
  Seventh-day Adventists
Global Concern, Inc.
Global Outreach Mission
Go-Ye Fellowship
Good Shepherd Agricultural
  Mission, Inc.
Gospel Association for the
  Blind, Inc.
Gospel Crusade World Wide
  Mission Outreach
Gospel Films, Inc.
Gospel Missionary Union
Gospel Outreach to India,
  Inc.
Gospel Recordings
  Incorporated
Grace Mission, Inc.
Great Commission Crusades,
  Inc.
H.O.P.E. Bible Mission,
  Inc.
Haggai Community
Haggai Institute for
  Advanced Leadership
  Training, Inc.
Heritage Village Church and
  Missionary Fellowship,
  Inc.
Holy Land Christian Mission
Home Finders International
  Home of Onesiphorus
India Christian Mission,
  Inc.
India Evangelical Mission,
  Inc.
India National Inland
  Mission
Institute of Chinese
  Studies
Institute of Holy Land
  Studies
Inter-Varsity Christian
  Fellowship
Inter-Varsity Christian
  Fellowship of Canada

Intercristo
International Bible
  Institute
International Bible
  Translators
International Board of
  Jewish Missions, Inc.
International Christian
  Fellowship
International Evangelism
  Crusades, Inc.
International Everlasting
  Gospel Mission, Inc.
International Fellowship of
  Christians
International Fellowship of
  Evangelical Students -
  USA
International Films, Inc.
International Gospel League
International Institute,
  Inc.
International Messianic
  Outreach
International Missionary
  Advance
International Needs-USA
International Students,
  Inc.
Intl. Church of the
  Foursquare Gospel--Dept.
  of Msns. Intl.
Janz Team
Japan Evangelical Mission
Japan Evangelistic
  Association, Inc.
Japanese Evangelical
  Missionary Society
Jesus Evangelism
Jesus to the Communist
  World, Inc.
Jewish Voice Broadcast
Jews For Jesus
Jubilee, Inc.
Latin America Assistance
Latin America Mission, Inc.
Leprosy Mission Canada
Liberty Corner Mission
Liebenzell Mission of
  Canada
Liebenzell Mission of
  U.S.A., Inc.
Life For Latins, Inc.
Life messengers, Inc.
Link Care Center
Literacy and Evangelism,
  Inc.
Living Bibles International
Logoi, Inc.
Lord's Way Inn Ministries,
  Inc.
Lott Carey Baptist Foreign
  Mission Convention

Luis Palau Evangelistic
Team, Inc.
Lutheran Church in
America-Div. for Wld.
Msn. and Ecumenism
Mahon Mission
MAP International (Medical
Assistance Programs)
Men For Missions
International
Mexican Border Missions
Mexican Christian Mission,
Inc.
Mexican Mission Ministries,
Inc.
Middle East Christian
Outreach--USA Council
Middle East Media
Minneapolis Friends of
Israel
Minnesota Bible Fellowship,
Inc.
Mission Aides, Incorporated
Mission Aviation
Fellowship
Mission Aviation Fellowship
of Canada
Mission Possible
Foundation, Inc.
Mission Renewal Team, Inc.
Mission to Japan, Inc.
Missionary Church, Div. of
Overseas Ministries
Missionary Dentist, Inc.
Missionary Electronics,
Inc.
Missionary Evangelistic
Fellowship, Inc.
Missionary Gospel
Fellowship, Inc.
Missionary Health
Institute, Inc.
Missionary Internship, Inc.
Missionary Services, Inc.
Missionary Strategy Agency
Missionary TECH Team
Missions Advanced Research
and Communication Center
(MARC)
Missions of Baja
Missions Outreach, Inc.
Moody Institute of Science
Moody Literature Ministries
Mustard Seed, Inc., The
N. American Committee for
IME, Institut Medical
Evangelique
Narramore Christian
Foundation
National Religious
Broadcasters
Navigators of Canada
International, The

Navigators, The
New Testament Missionary
Union
North Africa Mission
North East India General
Mission, Inc.
Northwest Yearly Meeting of
Friends Ch., Dept. of
Msns.
O.C. Ministries, Inc.
OMS International, Inc.
Open Bible Ministries, Inc.
Open Bible Standard
Missions, Inc.
Open Door Missionary
Fellowship, Inc.
Open Doors With Brother
Andrew
Operation Mobilization -
Canada
Operation Mobilization Send
the Light, Inc.
Org. of Continuing Educ.
for American Nurses
(OCEAN)
Oriental Missionary
Crusade, Inc.
Outreach, Inc.
Outreach, Inc.
Overseas Christian
Servicemen's Centers
Overseas Missionary
Fellowship
Overseas Missionary
Fellowship
Overseas Radio and
Television, Inc.
Pacific Broadcasting
Association, Inc.
Pan American Missionary
Society, Inc.
Paul Carlson Medical
Program, Inc.
Pentecostal Assemblies of
Canada, Oseas. Msns.
Dept.
Pentecostal Church of God,
World Missions Department
Pentecostal Holiness
Church-World Missions
Department
Petra International, Inc.
Pilgrim Fellowship, Inc.,
The
Pillar of Fire Missions
Pocket Testament League,
Inc.
Portable Recording
Ministries, Inc.
Primitive Methodist Church
in the USA, Intl. Msn.
Bd.
Project Partner with

Christ, Inc.
Project Partner, Inc.
Providence Mission Homes,
  Inc.
  Ramabai Mukti Mission
  (American Council of)
REAP International
Red Sea Mission Team, Inc.,
  U.S.A. Council
Regions Beyond Missionary
  Union (Canada)
Regions Beyond Missionary
  Union (U.S.A.)
Russia for Christ, Inc.
Salvation Army, Canada and
  Bermuda
Samaritan's Purse
Samuel Zwemer Institute
Schwenkfelder Church in the
  USA and For. Bd. of Msns.
Scripture Gift Mission
  (Canada), Inc.
Scripture Union, U.S.A.
Share the Care
  International
Slavic Gospel Association
Source of Light Ministries,
  Intl.
South America Mission, Inc.
South American Crusades,
  Inc.
South Pacific Evangelical
  Fellowship
Southern European Mission,
  Inc.
Spanish Evangelical
  Literature Fellowship,
  Inc.
Spanish-World Gospel
  Mission, Inc.
Steer, Inc.
Sudan Interior Mission,
  Inc.
Sundanese Missionary
  Fellowship
Team Ventures International
Teen Missions
  International, Inc.
Tele-Missions
  International, Inc.
Things to Come Mission,
  Inc.
Tokyo Evangelistic Center
Tokyo Gospel Mission, Inc.
Toronto Institute of
  Linguistics
Totonac Bible Center, Inc.
Trans World Missions
Trinitarian Bible Society,
  Canada
Underground Christian
  Missions, Inc.
Unevangelized Tribes

Mission, Inc.
United Fundamentalist
  Church
United States Center for
  World Mission
United World Mission,
  Incorporated
Vacation Samaritans
Victory Mission of the
  Americas
Voice of Calvary
Voice of China and Asia
  Missionary Society, Inc.
W. Shabaz Associates, Inc.
We Go, Inc. (World
  Encounter Gospel
  Organization)
Welfare of the Blind, Inc.
Wesleyan Church Gen. Dept.
  of Wld. Msns.
Western Tract Mission
World Baptist Fellowship
  Mission Agency
  International
World Concern/Crista
  International
World Gospel Crusades
World Gospel Mission
World Home Bible League
World Hope Foundation
World Missionary Assistance
  Plan
World Missionary
  Evangelism, Inc.
World Missionary Press,
  Inc.
World Missions Fellowship
World Missions, Inc.
World Neighbors, Inc.
World Opportunities
  International
  World Radio Missionary
  Fellowship, Inc.
World Relief Corporation
World Thrust Films, Inc.
World Vision International
World Vision of Canada
World Vision, Incorporated
World Wide Missionary
  Crusader, Inc.
World Wide Prayer and
  Missionary Union
World's Christian Endeavor
  Union
Worldteam
Worldwide Discipleship
  Association, Inc.
Worldwide Evangelization
  Crusade
Wycliffe Associates, Inc.
Wycliffe Bible Translators
  International, Inc.
Young Life

Youth Enterprises, Inc.
Youth For Christ/U.S.A.
Youth With A Mission

Friends

American Friends Service
  Committee
California Yearly Meeting
  of Friends Church, Bd. of
  Msns.
Central Yearly Meeting of
  Friends Missionary
  Committee
Evangelical Friends Church,
  Eastern Region, Fr. For.
  Msny. S
Evangelical Friends Mission
Kansas Yearly Meeting of
  Friends Africa Gospel
  Mission
Northwest Yearly Meeting of
  Friends Ch., Dept. of
  Msns.
Wider Ministries Commission

Fundamentalist

Afghan Border Crusade
Africa Evangelical
  Fellowship
Afro-American Missionary
  Crusade, Inc.
All Peoples Baptist Mission
America's Keswick, Inc.
American European
  Fellowship Chr. Oneness
  Evang., Inc.
American Messianic
  Fellowship
American Scripture Gift
  Mission
Andes Evangelical Mission
Apostolic Christian Church
  (Nazarene), Apos. Chr.
  Ch. Found.
Baptist Bible Fellowship
  International
Baptist Haiti Mission, Inc.
Baptist International
  Missions, Inc.
Baptist World Mission
Berean Mission, Inc.
Bethany Home, Inc.
Bethesda Mission, Inc.
Bible Alliance Mission,
  Inc.
Bible Club Movement of
  Canada
Bible Club Movement, Inc.
Bible Protestant Missions,
  Inc.
Biblical Literature

Fellowship
CAM International
CAM International Practical
  Missionary Training, Inc.
Carver Foreign Missions,
  Inc.
Cedar Lane Missionary
  Homes, Inc.
Chinese Gospel Crusade,
  Inc.
Chr. Echoes Natl. Min.,
  Inc. (Chr. Crusade)
Christ For The Philippines,
  Inc.
Christian Aid Mission
Christian Canadian Mission
  to Overseas Students
Christian Literature and
  Bible Center, Inc.
Christian Literature
  Crusade (Ontario) Inc.
Christian Union General
  Mission Board
Christians In Action
Church of God (Seventh
  Day), Gen. Conf., Msns.
  Abroad
Church of God General
  Conference Mission
  Department
Church of God World
  Missions
Evangelical Alliance
  Mission of Canada, Inc.
Evangelical Baptist
  Missions, Inc.
Evangelical Methodist
  Church Bible Methodist
  Missions
Evangelization Society of
  the Pittsburgh Bible
  Institute
Faith Ministries
Far Eastern Gospel Crusade
Fellowship of Evangelical
  Baptist Chs. in Canada
Fellowship of Grace
  Brethren Churches, For.
  Msny. Soc.
Fellowship of Independent
  Missions
Friends of Indonesia
  Fellowship, Inc.
Friends of Israel Gospel
  Ministry, Inc.
Fundamental Evangelistic
  Association
General Conference of
  Seventh-day Adventists
Global Outreach Mission
Gospel Mission of South
  America
Gospel Outreach to India,

Inc.
Grace Mission, Inc.
Greater Mexican Missions
Helps International
Ministries, Inc.
Independent Faith Mission,
Inc.
International Biblical
Baptist Fellowship, Inc.
International Board of
Jewish Missions, Inc.
International Institute,
Inc.
International Needs-USA
Intl. Church of the
Foursquare Gospel--Dept.
of Msns. Intl.
Jesus to the Communist
World, Inc.
Liberty Corner Mission
Life messengers, Inc.
Macedonian Service
Foundation, Inc.
Mailbox Club, The
Maranatha Baptist Mission,
Inc.
Methodist Protestant
Church, Board of Msns.
Minneapolis Friends of
Israel
Missionary Air Transport,
Inc.
Missionary Flights
International
Missionary TECH Team
Missions, Inc.
National Association of
Free Will Baptists, Brd.
of For. Msn
New Tribes Mission
New Tribes Mission of
Canada
Next Towns Crusade, Inc.
Open Air Campaigners (USA)
Open Bible Ministries, Inc.
Pacific Broadcasting
Association, Inc.
Pentecostal Assemblies of
Canada, Oseas. Msns.
Dept.
Pillar of Fire Missions
R.E.A.P.
Ramabai Mukti Mission
(American Council of)
Regions Beyond Missionary
Union (Canada)
Regions Beyond Missionary
Union (U.S.A.)
Salvation Army, Canada and
Bermuda
Society for Europe's
Evangelization (S.E.E.)
Source of Light Ministries,

Intl.
Tainan Evangelical Mission
Things to Come Mission,
Inc.
Trinitarian Bible Society,
Canada
Unevangelized Tribes
Mission, Inc.
United Indian Missions,
Inc.
United Missionary
Fellowship
Victory Mission of the
Americas
Voice of China and Asia
Missionary Society, Inc.
WEFMinistries, Inc.
Westminister Biblical
Missions, Inc.
Word of Life Fellowship
World Missionary Press,
Inc.
World Wide Missionary
Crusader, Inc.

Greek Orthodox

Release the World for
Christ

Holiness

Bethany Fellowship Msns.
(Div. of Bethany
Fellowship, Inc.)
Bible Holiness Movement
Bible Missionary Church,
World Missions Department
California Yearly Meeting
of Friends Church, Bd. of
Msns.
Christian Church of North
America, Msns. Dept.
Church of God (Anderson,
Indiana) Msny. Bd.
Church of God of Prophecy,
World Mission Committee
Church of God World
Missions
Church of the Nazarene,
Gen. Bd. Dept. of Wld.
Msns.
Evangelical Bible Mission,
Inc.
Evangelical Friends Church,
Eastern Region, Fr. For.
Msny. S
Evangelical Methodist
Church World Missions
Full Gospel Evangelistic
Association
Great Commission Crusades,
Inc.

AGENCIES LISTED BY TRADITION

Japan Evangelistic Band
Japan Evangelistic Band
(Canada)
Liberty Corner Mission
Men For Missions
International
Methodist Protestant
Church, Board of Msns.
Missionary Information
Exchange
Northwest Yearly Meeting of
Friends Ch., Dept. of
Msns.
OMS International, Inc.
Pentecostal Church of God,
World Missions Department
Pentecostal Holiness
Church-World Missions
Department
Pillar of Fire Missions
Undenominational Church of
the Lord
United Fundamentalist
Church
Wesleyan Church Gen. Dept.
of Wld. Msns.
World Gospel Mission

Independent

Air Crusade, Inc.
America's Keswick, Inc.
American Board of
International Missions
American Board of Missions
to the Jews, Inc.
American Messianic
Fellowship
American Missionary
Fellowship
Andes Evangelical Mission
Apostolic Christian Church
(Nazarene), Apos. Chr.
Ch. Found.
Back to the Bible
Missionary Agency
Back-Country Evangelism,
Inc.
Baptist Faith Missions
Baptist International
Missions, Inc.
Bethany Missionary
Association
Bible Memory Association
International
Biblical Literature
Fellowship
Calvary Evangelistic
Mission, Inc./WIVV Msny.
Radio Station
CAM International
Cedar Lane Missionary
Homes, Inc.

Child Evangelism
Fellowship, Inc.
Children of India
Foundation
Chinese Christian Mission
Chinese for Christ, Inc.
Christian Aid Mission
Christian Canadian Mission
to Overseas Students
Christian Salvage Mission,
Inc.
Christian Services
Fellowship, Inc.
Christian World-Wide Evang.
Msn. of Canada
Eastern European Mission
Evangelical Alliance
Mission (TEAM)
Evangelical Baptist
Missions, Inc.
Evangelical Scripture
Mission
Evangelism to Communist
Lands
Fellowship of Faith For
Muslims
Forester Foundation, Inc.
Foundation For His
Ministry-Orphanage
Committee
Friends of Turkey
Glad Tidings Missionary
Society, Inc.
Global Outreach Mission
Go-Ye Fellowship
Gospel Outreach to India,
Inc.
Hindustan Bible Institute,
Inc.
Home of Onesiphorus
Houses of Refuge, Intl.
Orphanages Assn. Inc.
Independent Faith Mission,
Inc.
India Evangelical Mission,
Inc.
International Board of
Jewish Missions, Inc.
International Church Relief
Fund, Inc.
International Evangelism
Crusades, Inc.
International Messianic
Outreach
International Missions,
Inc.
Japan Evangelical Mission
Jews For Jesus
Laos, Inc.
Lester Sumrall Evangelistic
Association
Lord's Way Inn Ministries,
Inc.

Macedonian Service
Foundation, Inc.
Mexican Border Missions
Missionary Air Transport,
Inc.
Missionary Communications,
Inc.
Missionary TECH Team
Missions, Inc.
Native Preacher Company,
Inc.
New Life League
Nora Lam Ministries
Overseas Ministries Study
Center
Pacific Broadcasting
Association, Inc.
Pan American Missionary
Society, Inc.
Ramabai Mukti Mission
(American Council of)
Regular Baptists of Canada,
Women's Missionary
Society
Release the World for
Christ
Rural Gospel and Medical
Missions of India, Inc.
Society for Europe's
Evangelization (S.E.E.)
Spanish Evangelical
Literature Fellowship,
Inc.
Spanish-World Gospel
Mission, Inc.
Tainan Evangelical
Mission
Trans World Radio
Trinitarian Bible Society,
Canada
United Evangelical Churches
United Indian Missions,
Inc.
United Missionary
Fellowship
WEFMinistries, Inc.
World Baptist Fellowship
Mission Agency
International
World Mission Prayer League
World Missions Fellowship
World Opportunities
International
World Wide Missionary
Crusader, Inc.
Worldteam
Youth Enterprises, Inc.

Interdenominational

Christian Service
Fellowship
Gospel Literature

International
International Evangelism
Crusades, Inc.
Japan International
Christian Univ. Found.,
Inc.
Luis Palau Evangelistic
Team, Inc.
MAP International (Medical
Assistance Programs)
Mission Aviation Fellowship
Mission to Europe's
Millions, Inc.
Osborn Foundation
Overseas Missionary
Fellowship
Refugee Children, Inc.
Steer, Inc.
Teen Missions
International, Inc.

Lutheran

American Board for the
Syrian Orphanage
American Lutheran Ch., Div.
For Wld. Msn.
Association of Free
Lutheran Congregations
Church of the Lutheran
Brethren of America, Bd.
of Wld. Msns
Concordia Tract Mission
Evangelical Lutheran
Church, Division of World
Missions
Evangelical Lutheran Synod
Board For Missions
Hague Foreign Mission, Inc.
International Lutheran
Laymen's League
Liebenzell Mission of
Canada
Lutheran Bible Translators,
Inc.
Lutheran Braille Workers
Lutheran Church in
America-Div. for Wld.
Msn. and Ecumenism
Lutheran Church-Missouri
Synod
Lutheran Frontier Missions
Lutheran Orient Mission
Society
Lutheran World Federation,
U.S.A. National Committee
Lutheran World Relief,
Incorporated
Lutherans For World
Evangelization
Wisconsin Evangelical
Lutheran Synod, Bd. for
Wld. Msns.

World Mission Prayer League
World Mission Prayer League
Canada

Mennonite

Africa Inter-Mennonite
Mission, Inc.
Brethren in Christ Missions
Children's Haven
International, Inc.
Church of God in Christ,
Mennonite Gen. Msn. Bd.,
Inc.
Conservative Mennonite
Board of Missions and
Charities
Eastern Mennonite Board of
Missions and Charities
Evangelical Mennonite
Brethren Commission on
Mission
Evangelical Mennonite
Conference Board of
Missions
Franconia Mennonite
Conference Mission
Commission
General Conference
Mennonite Church, Comm.
on Oseas. Msn.
Media Ministries Division,
Mennonite Bd. of Msns.
Mennonite Board of Missions
Mennonite Brethren
Missions/Services
Mennonite Central Committee
Mennonite Economic
Development Associates
Mennonite Mission Brd. of
Pacific Coast Conf.
(Mexico Brd.)
Mexican Mission Ministries,
Inc.
Virginia Mennonite Board of
Missions and Charities

Methodist

African Methodist Episcopal
Church, Inc. Dept. of
Msns.
African Methodist Episcopal
Zion Ch., Dept. of Oseas.
Msns.
Church of the United
Brethren in Christ, Bd.
of Msns.
Evangelical Missions
Council of Good News
Methodist Protestant
Church, Board of Msns.
Primitive Methodist Church

in the USA, Intl. Msn.
Bd.
United Methodist Ch. Wld.
Div. of the Bd. of Global
Min.
United Methodist Church
Comm. on Relief

Moravian

Moravian Church in America,
Brd. of Wrld. Msn.

Nondenominational

Adib Eden Evangelistic
Missionary Society, Inc.
Africa Evangelical
Fellowship
African Bible Colleges,
Inc.
African Mission Services,
Inc.
Afro-American Missionary
Crusade, Inc.
AIM, Inc. (Assistance in
Missions)
Air Crusade, Inc.
Alberto Mottesi
Evangelistic Association,
Inc.
Amateur Radio Missionary
Service (ARMS)
America's Keswick, Inc.
American Bible Society
American European Bethel
Mission, Inc.
American Leprosy Missions,
Inc.
American Messianic
Fellowship
American Missionary
Fellowship
AMG International
(Advancing the Ministries
of the Gospel)
Back to the Bible
Missionary Agency
Berean Mission, Inc.
Bible Literature
International
Bibles For The World, Inc.
Canadian Bible Society
Cedar Lane Missionary
Homes, Inc.
Children of India
Foundation
Chinese Christian Mission
Christ For The Nations,
Inc.
Christ's Mission
Christian INFO
Christian Life Missions

AGENCIES LISTED BY TRADITION

Christian Literature
Crusade (Ontario) Inc.
Christian Literature
International
Christian Medical Society
Christian Nationals'
Evangelism Commission,
Inc. (Canada)
Christian Nationals'
Evangelism Commission,
Inc. (CNEC)
Christian Salvage Mission,
Inc.
Christian Service Corps
Christian Services
Fellowship, Inc.
Christian Transportation
Christian World Publishers,
Inc.
Christians In Action
Daystar Communications,
Inc.
Eastern European Mission
Evangel Bible Translators
Evangelical Alliance
Mission (TEAM)
Evangelical Missions
Information Service, Inc.
Everyday Publications
Far East Broadcasting
Company, Inc.
Fellowship of Artists For
Cultrual Evangelism
(FACE)
Fellowship of Faith For
Muslims
Food for the Hungry/Canada
Friends of Turkey
Frontier Ministries
International
Go-Ye Fellowship
Good Shepherd Agricultural
Mission, Inc.
Gospel Association for the
Blind, Inc.
Gospel Crusade World Wide
Mission Outreach
Gospel Missionary Union
Gospel Outreach
Gospel Recordings
Incorporated
Gospel Recordings of
Canada, Inc.
Greater Europe Mission
H.O.P.E. Bible Mission,
Inc.
Handclasp International
Inc.
Helps International
Ministries, Inc.
Heritage Village Church and
Missionary Fellowship,
Inc.

High School Evangelism
Fellowship, Inc.
Hindustan Bible Institute,
Inc.
Holt International
Children's Services, Inc.
Home of Onesiphorus
Houses of Refuge, Intl.
Orphanages Assn. Inc.
India Christian Mission,
Inc.
India National Inland
Mission
Institute of Holy Land
Studies
International Bible
Institute
International Church Relief
Fund, Inc.
International Films, Inc.
Janz Team
Japan Evangelical Mission
John Milton Society for the
Blind
Jubilee, Inc.
Jungle Aviation and Radio
Service, Inc. (JAARS)
Korea International
Mission, Inc.
Language Institute For
Evangelism (LIFE)
Life For Latins, Inc.
Life messengers, Inc.
Ling A. Juane Ministries,
Inc.
Living Bibles International
Lord's Way Inn Ministries,
Inc.
Ludhiana Christian Medical
College Board, U.S.A.,
Inc.
Men For Missions
International
Message of Life, Inc.
Mexican Border Missions
Minneapolis Friends of
Israel
Mission Aides, Incorporated
Mission Aviation Fellowship
of Canada
Mission SOS
Mission to Europe's
Millions, Inc.
Mission Training and
Resource Center
Missionary Auto-Truck
Service
Missionary Dentist, Inc.
Missionary Health
Institute, Inc.
Missionary Strategy Agency
Missions Outreach, Inc.
Moody Institute of Science

Moody Literature Ministries
Narramore Christian
  Foundation
National Religious
  Broadcasters
Navigators of Canada
  International, The
Navigators, The
New Tribes Mission
North Africa Mission
OMI Brotherhood Foundation
  of America, Inc.
Open Doors With Brother
  Andrew
Overcomer Press, Inc.
Overseas Christian
  Servicemen's Centers
Pan American Missionary
  Society, Inc.
Paul Carlson Medical
  Program, Inc.
Portable Recording
  Ministries, Inc.
Prison Mission Assn., Inc.
Project Partner, Inc.
R.E.A.P.
REACH, Incorporated
Red Sea Mission Team, Inc.,
  U.S.A. Council
Samaritan's Purse
Scripture Gift Mission
  (Canada), Inc.
Self Help Foundation
Society of Central Asian
  News (SCAN)
Sundanese Missionary
  Fellowship
Team Ventures International
Technical Support Mission
Tele-Missions
  International, Inc.
Things to Come Mission,
  Inc.
Today's Mission
  Incorporated
Tokyo Gospel Mission, Inc.
Toronto Institute of
  Linguistics
Totonac Bible Center, Inc.
Undenominational Church of
  the Lord
Unevangelized Fields
  Mission
United Missionary
  Fellowship
Victory Mission of the
  Americas
Voice of China and Asia
  Missionary Society, Inc.
World Gospel Crusades
World Missionary Press,
  Inc.
World Missions, Inc.

World Outreach
World Radio Missionary
  Fellowship, Inc.
World Vision of Canada
Worldteam
Worldwide Discipleship
  Association, Inc.
Wycliffe Bible Translators
  International, Inc.
Youth Enterprises, Inc.
Youth For Christ/U.S.A.

Nonsectarian

Operation Eyesight
  Universal

Pentecostal

Anchor Bay Evangelistic
  Association
Apostolic Church in Canada,
  The
Apostolic Church of
  Pentecost of
  Canada-Missionary Dept.
Apostolic Faith Mission of
  Portland, Oregon
Apostolic Overcoming Holy
  Church of God
Arthur Bradford
  Evangelistic Association
Assemblies of God, Div. of
  For. Msns.
Bethel Foreign Mission
  Foundation
Bethel Pentecostal Temple,
  Inc.
Bible Way Chs. of Our Lord
  Jesus Christ Worldwide,
  Inc.
Calcutta Mission of Mercy
Christian Church of North
  America, Msns. Dept.
Church of God of Prophecy,
  World Mission Committee
Church of God of the
  Apostolic Faith, Inc.
Church of God World
  Missions
Church of God, USA
  Headquarters
Congregational Holiness
  Church Foreign Mission
  Dept.
Defenders of the Christian
  Faith Movement, Inc.
Elim Fellowship, Inc.
Evangel Bible Translators
Evangelization Society of
  the Pittsburgh Bible
  Institute
Faith Center Global

Ministries
Faith Christian Fellowship
  World Outreach
Fellowship of Christian
  Assemblies Mission to
  Liberia
Free Gospel Church, Inc.
Full Gospel Evangelistic
  Association
Full Gospel Native
  Missionary Association
Harvest Fields Missionary
  and Evangelistic Assn.,
  Inc.
Independent Assemblies of
  God, International
Intl Pentecostal Ch. of
  Christ, Global Msns.
  Dept.
Intl. Church of the
  Foursquare Gospel--Dept.
  of Msns. Intl.
Lester Sumrall Evangelistic
  Association
Mexican Missions, Inc.
Movimiento Misionero
  Mundial, Inc.
New Life International
Next Towns Crusade, Inc.
Open Bible Standard
  Missions, Inc.
Pentecostal Assemblies of
  Canada, Oseas. Msns.
  Dept.
Pentecostal Assemblies of
  the World, Inc. For.
  Msns. Dept.
Pentecostal Church of God,
  World Missions Department
Pentecostal Free Will
  Baptist Church, Inc.
Pentecostal Holiness
  Church-World Missions
  Department
United Fundamentalist
  Church
United Pentecostal Church
  Intl. For. Msns. Div.
Wings of Healing

Plymouth Brethren

Christian Mission for the
  Deaf
Christian Missions in Many
  Lands, Inc.
Grace and Truth, Inc.
Grand Old Gospel
  Fellowship, Inc.
India Evangelical Mission,
  Inc.
International Crusades,
  Inc.

Overcomer Press, Inc.

Presbyterian

American Mc All Association
Armenian Missionary
  Association of America,
  Inc.
Associate Reformed Presb.
  Ch., Wld. Witness
Bible Presbyterian Church,
  Ind. Bd. for Presb. For.
  Msns.
Chiang Mai Mission Board,
  The
Christian World-Wide
  Evang. Msn. of Canada
Cumberland Presbyterian
  Church, Board of Missions
Korea Gospel Mission
Literacy and Evangelism,
  Inc.
Mission to the World
Mustard Seed, Inc., The
Orthodox Presbyterian
  Church Committee on
  Foreign Missions
Presbyterian Church in
  Canada, Board of World
  Mission
Presbyterian Church in the
  U.S.A., Div. of Intl.
  Msn.
Reformation Translation
  Fellowship
Reformed Presbyterian Ch.
  of N. America, Bd. of
  For. Msns.
United Presbyterian Center
  for Mission Studies
United Presbyterian Church
  in the USA Program Agency
United Presbyterian Order
  for World Evangelization
Westminister Biblical
  Missions, Inc.
World Presbyterian
  Missions, Inc.

Reformed

Associate Reformed Presb.
  Ch., Wld. Witness
Christian Reformed Board
  For World Missions
Christian Reformed World
  Relief Committee
Evangelical Literature
  League (T.E.L.L.)
Logoi, Inc.
Men in Action
Mission to the World
Outreach, Inc.

AGENCIES LISTED BY TRADITION

Protestant Reformed
  Churches in America
Reformation Translation
  Fellowship
Reformed Church in America
  General Program Council
Reformed Episcopal Church
  Bd. of For. Msns.
Reformed Presbyterian Ch.
  of N. America, Bd. of
  For. Msns.
Society of Central Asian
  News (SCAN)
Sundanese Missionary
  Fellowship
Ukrainian Evangelical
  Alliance of North America
United Church Board For
  World Ministries
United Presbyterian Center
  for Mission Studies
World Presbyterian
  Missions, Inc.

Missionary Information
  Exchange
OMS International, Inc.
Salvation Army, The
We Go, Inc. (World
  Encounter Gospel
  Organization)
Wesleyan Church Gen. Dept.
  of Wld. Msns.
  World Gospel Mission

Wesleyan

Allegheny Wesleyan
  Methodist Missions
Bible Holiness Movement
Brethren in Christ Missions
Christian Baptist Ch. of
  God Assn. Wld. for Christ
  Msns.
Church of God (Anderson,
  Indiana) Msny. Bd.
Church of God (Holiness)
  For. Msn. Bd.
Church of the Nazarene,
  Gen. Bd. Dept. of Wld.
  Msns.
Churches of Christ in
  Christian Union: Foreign
  Msny. Dept.
Evangelical Bible Mission,
  Inc.
Evangelical Congregational
  Church Division of
  Missions
Evangelical Methodist
  Church Bible Methodist
  Missions
Evangelical Methodist
  Church World Missions
Evangelical Missions
  Council of Good News
Evangelistic Faith Mission,
  Inc.
Free Methodist Church of N.
  America Gen. Mssy. Brd.
Great Commission Crusades,
  Inc.
Metropolitan Church
  Association

INTERNATIONAL AGENCIES

International Organization	(City) Country	North American Affiliate (As Listed)
African Evangelical Fellowship International	(Reading) England	African Evangelical Fellowship, U.S. & Canada
African Evangelistic Enterprise International Council	(Nairobi) Kenya	African Enterprise
African Mission Services	(Cape Town) Rep. of S. Africa	African Mission Services
BMMF International	(London) England	BMMF International (U.S. & Canada)
Centro Pro-Totonaco	(Puebla) Mexico	Totonac Bible Center, Inc.
Christoffel-Blindenmission	(Bensheim) W. Germany	Christian Blind Mission Intl. (CBM Intl.)
Church of Christ in Zaire	(Kinshasa) Zaire	Paul Carlson Medical Program, Inc.
Council of International Needs	(Wellington) New Zealand	International Needs, U.S.A.
Daystar Communications	(Nairobi) Kenya	Daystar Communications
Defenders of the Christian Faith Movement	(Boyaca) Colombia	Defenders of the Christian Faith Movement
European Christian Mission	(Paris) France	Mission to Europe's Millions, Inc.
Institute of Holy Land Studies	(Jerusalem) Israel	Institute of Holy Land Studies
International Christian Fellowship	(Hounslow) England	International Christian Fellowship
International Federation of Anti-Leprosy Associations	(London) England	American Leprosy Missions, Inc.
International Fellowship of Evangelical Students (IFES)	(Middlesex) England	Inter-Varsity Christian Fellowship of U.S. & Canada
International Films	(London) England	International Films
International Headquarters of the Salvation Army	(London) England	Salvation Army (U.S., Canada, Bermuda)

International Organization	(City) Country	North American Affiliate (As Listed)
Japan Evangelistic Band	(Kohe) Japan	Japan Evangelistic Band (U.S. & Canada)
Leprosy Mission International	(London) England	Leprosy Mission, Canada
Liebenzeller Mission	W. Germany	Liebenzell Mission of U.S.A. Inc./Canada
Ludhiana Christian Medical College	Punjab, India	Ludhiana Christian Medical College Board, U.S.A.
Lutheran World Federation	(Geneva) Switzerland	Lutheran World Federation, U.S.A. National Committee
Marburger Mission	(Marburg) W. Germany	Liberty Corner Mission
Middle East Christian Outreach	(Limassol) Cyprus	Middle East Christian Outreach - U.S.A. Council
North Africa Mission	(Aix-en-Provence) France	North Africa Mission
Operation Mobilization	(Bromley, Kent) England	Operation Mobilization Canada
Pacific Broadcasting Association	(Tokyo) Japan	Pacific Broadcasting Association
Red Sea Mission Team	(Birmingham) England	Red Sea Mission Team
Scripture Gift Mission	(London) England	Scripture Gift Mission (U.S. & Canada)
Scripture Union International	(London) England	Scripture Union U.S.A.
Trinitarian Bible Society	(London) England	Trinitarian Bible Society
United Bible Societies	(Stuttgart) Germany	United Bible Societies
World Outreach International	(Wellington) New Zealand	World Outreach
Worldwide Evangelization Crusade	(Buckingham) England	Worldwide Evangelization Crusade
Youth For Christ International	(Geneva) Switzerland	Youth For Christ U.S.A./Canada

Countries of Service

Special Notes

There are several special situations in the geographic listing which should be noted:

ASIA - GENERAL: This designation applies to agency representatives not responsible for a particular nation within the larger continental region and/or to list representatives present in a nation which the agency feels is sensitive to their presence.
BENIN: formerly Dahomey.
BOPHUTHATSWANA: Designated by South Africa as an independent Black homeland.
CARIBBEAN - GENERAL: This designation includes agency representatives not responsible for a particular nation within the larger region and/or to list representatives present in a nation which the agency feels is sensitive to their presence.
CENTRAL AMERICA: This designation applies to agency representatives not responsible for a particular nation within the larger continental region and/or to list representatives present in a nation which the agency feels is sensitive to their presence.
DJIBOUTI: formerly French Afars and Issas.
EASTERN EUROPE - GENERAL: This designation applies to agency representatives not responsible for a particular nation within the larger continental region and/or to list representatives present in a nation which the agency feels is sensitive to their presence.
INDONESIA: Totals were sometimes reported for subdivisions of Indonesia such as Java, Kalimantan or West Irian. These totals have been included in the general total for Indonesia.
KAMPUCHEA: formerly Cambodia.
KIRIBATI: formerly Gilbert Island.
LATIN AMERICA - GENERAL: This designation applies to agency representatives not responsible for a particular nation within the larger continental region and/or to list representatives present in a nation which the agency feels is sensitive to their presence.
MARSHALL ISLANDS: now separate from Pacific Trust Territory.
MIDDLE EAST - GENERAL: This designation applies to agency representatives not responsible for a particular nation within the larger continental region and/or to list representatives present in a nation which the agency feels is sensitive to their presence.

NAMIBIA: Official U.N. designation for South-West Africa. This term, however, is not recognized by the Republic of South Africa.

OCEANIA - GENERAL: This designation applies to agency representatives not responsible for a particular nation within the larger region and/or to list representatives present in a nation which the agency feels is sensitive to their presence.

OKINAWA: Statistics are included in the general total for Japan.

PACIFIC TRUST TERRITORY: The Trust Territory of the Pacific Islands is the official designation for these island groups including the Marianas (except the Marshall Islands and Guam) and the Carolines.

SIKKIM: Statistics are included in the general total for India.

TAIWAN, REPUBLIC OF CHINA: This designation has been used to distinguish this country from **CHINA, PEOPLE'S REPUBLIC OF.**

TRANSKEI: Designated by South Africa as an independent Black homeland.

TUVALU: formerly Ellice Island.

UNITED ARAB EMIRATES: Formed from a union of the Persian Gulf sheikdoms of Abu Dhabi, Dubai, Sharjah, Fujairah, Ajman and Umm al Quaiwain.

U.S. VIRGIN ISLANDS: Includes St. Croix, St. John and St. Thomas.

VANUATU: formerly New Hebrides.

VENDA: Designated by South Africa as an independent Black homeland.

WESTERN SAHARA: formerly Spanish Sahara.

ZIMBABWE: formerly Rhodesia.

ORGANIZATION NAME	BEGAN	NOW	NEW	CHURCHES	GROUPS
Afghanistan					
Assemblies of God, Div. of For. Msns.	1972	0	0	0	0
BMMF International/Canada	1966	0	0	0	0
MAP International (Medical Assistance Programs)	1965	0	0	0	0
Mennonite Board of Missions	1975	1	0	0	0
Mennonite Brethren Missions/Services	1969	2	2	0	1
Presbyterian Church in Canada, Board of World Mission	1974	0	2	0	0
United Presbyterian Church in the USA Program Agency	0	0	2	0	0
TOTALS		3	4	0	1
Africa-general					
Maranatha Baptist Mission, Inc.	1896	0	0	1	0
Salvation Army, Canada and Bermuda		6	0	0	0
TOTALS		6	0	1	0
Albania					
Mission to Europe's Millions, Inc.	0	0	0	0	0
TOTALS		0	0	0	0
Algeria					
Mennonite Board of Missions	1957	1	0	0	0
North Africa Mission	1881	7	0	3	2
United Methodist Ch. Wld. Div. of the Bd. of Global Min.	1908	0	0	0	0
Young Life	1978	0	0	0	0
TOTALS		8	0	3	2
American Samoa					
Assemblies of God, Div. of For. Msns.	1928	2	0	12	0
Baptist Bible Fellowship International	1975	2	0	2	0
Maranatha Baptist Mission, Inc.	0	0	0	2	0

ORGANIZATION NAME	BEGAN	NOW	NEW	CHURCHES	GROUPS
American Samoa continued...					
Youth With A Mission	1973	0	0	0	0
TOTALS		4	0	14	0
Andorra					
WEFMinistries, Inc.	1978	1	0	0	0
TOTALS		1	0	0	0
Angola					
Africa Evangelical Fellowship	1914	10	1	300	5
Africa Evangelical Fellowship (Canada)	1912	2	2	0	0
American Leprosy Missions, Inc.	1944	8	0	0	0
Brethren Assemblies	0	0	0	0	0
Mahon Mission	0	0	0	8	0
MAP International (Medical Assistance Programs)	0	0	0	0	0
Southern Baptist Convention, Foreign Mission Board	1968	2	0	37	0
United Church Board For World Ministries	1880	0	0	0	0
TOTALS		22	3	345	5
Anguilla					
Church of God (Holiness) For. Msn. Brd.	1975	2	0	1	0
TOTALS		2	0	1	0
Antigua					
Christian Churches/Churches of Christ	0	2	0	0	0
Christian Literature Crusade, Inc.	1961	0	0	0	0
Church of God World Missions	1966	0	0	3	0
Churches of Christ in Christian Union: Foreign Msny. Dept.	1962	0	0	2	0
MAP International (Medical Assistance Programs)	0	0	0	0	0
Moravian Church in America, Bd. of Wld. Msn.	1732	0	0	0	0

ORGANIZATION NAME	BEGAN	NOW	NEW	CHURCHES	GROUPS
	1968	6	6	2	0
Antigua continued...					
Southern Baptist Convention, Foreign Mission Board				7	0
	TOTALS	8	6	7	0
Argentina					
American Board of Missions to the Jews, Inc.	1942	1	0	0	0
Apostolic Christian Church (Nazarene), Apos. Chr. Ch. Found.	1965	0	0	15	0
Assemblies of God, Div. of For. Msns.	1914	13	0	106	0
Baptist Bible Fellowship International	1959	12	4	0	0
Baptist General Conference Board of World Missions	1955	2	0	14	0
Baptist International Missions, Inc.	0	2	0	0	0
Baptist World Mission	0	0	0	0	0
Brethren Assemblies	0	22	0	0	0
Brethren Church, Missionary Board of The Brethren Church	1948	4	0	0	0
Campus Crusade for Christ, International	1963	32	0	0	0
Child Evangelism Fellowship, Inc. (Overseas Dept.)	1947	1	0	0	0
Christian Aid Mission	1977	0	0	200	8
Christian and Missionary Alliance	1897	13	9	47	0
Christian Church (Disciples of Christ) Div. of Oseas. Min.	1906	4	0	0	0
Christian Church of North America, Msns. Dept.	1975	0	2	80	0
Christian Literature Crusade, Inc.	1959	0	0	0	0
Christian Nationals' Evangelism Commission, Inc. (CNEC)	1979	0	0	0	0
Christian Nationals' Evangelism Commission, Inc. (Canada)	1979	0	0	0	0
Christian Reformed Board For World Missions	1930	15	3	0	0
Church of God (Anderson, Indiana) Msny. Bd.	1927	2	0	20	0
Church of God of Prophecy, World Mission Committee	1955	0	0	11	0
Church of God World Missions	1944	11	0	125	0
Church of the Nazarene, Gen. Bd. Dept. of Wld. Msns.	1919	40	5	44	0
Conservative Baptist Foreign Mission Society	1948	4	4	99	4
Elim Fellowship, Inc.	1956	6	0	20	0
Evangelical Baptist Missions, Inc.	1974	0	0	2	0
Evangelical Methodist Church Bible Methodist Missions	0	0	0	0	0
Fellowship of Grace Brethren Churches, For. Msny. Soc.	1909	11	9	17	0

Argentina continued...

ORGANIZATION NAME	BEGAN	NOW	NEW	CHURCHES	GROUPS
Fellowship of Independent Missions	1964	0	0	0	0
Full Gospel Grace Fellowship	0	0	0	0	0
General Conference of Seventh-day Adventists	1890	6	4	197	0
Go-Ye Fellowship	1969	3	0	0	0
Gospel Mission of South America	1971	10	3	4	1
Gospel Missionary Union	1956	22	0	13	0
Intl. Church of the Foursquare Gospel--Dept. of Msns. Intl.	1970	4	0	139	0
Jesus to the Communist World, Inc.	0	0	0	0	0
Jews For Jesus	1976	2	2	0	0
Latin America Mission, Inc.	1976	2	0	0	0
Logoi, Inc.	1978	6	2	0	0
Luis Palau Evangelistic Team, Inc.	1974	5	4	0	0
Lutheran Church in America-Div. for Wld. Msn. and Ecumenism	1948	0	0	0	0
Lutheran Church-Missouri Synod	1905	0	0	187	0
Maranatha Baptist Mission, Inc.		0	0	0	0
Media Ministries Division, Mennonite Bd. of Msns.	1950	12	0	28	0
Mennonite Board of Missions	1917	0	2	29	0
Mennonite Economic Development Associates	1974	2	2	0	0
Navigators, The	1973	6	0	0	0
Pentecostal Assemblies of Canada, Oseas. Msns. Dept.	1925	4	0	309	1
Pentecostal Holiness Church-World Missions Department	1965	3	0	72	0
Salvation Army, The	1890	72	0	89	0
Slavic Gospel Association	1940	0	0	0	0
Southern Baptist Convention, Foreign Mission Board	1903	2	0	328	0
United Church Board For World Ministries	1955	0	0	0	0
United Church of Canada, Division of World Outreach	0	6	0	1	0
United Methodist Ch. Wld. Div. of the Bd. of Global Min.	1836	0	0	0	0
United Pentecostal Church Intl. For. Msns. Div.	1967	0	0	0	0
United Presbyterian Church in the USA Program Agency	0	0	0	0	0
WEFMinistries, Inc.	1979	2	2	0	0
Word of Life Fellowship	1969	5	1	1	0
World Gospel Mission	1970	7	3	1	0
World Literature Crusade	1962	0	0	0	0

Argentina continued...

ORGANIZATION NAME	BEGAN	NOW	NEW	CHURCHES	GROUPS
World Mission in Church and Society	1965	1	0	0	0
World Missionary Assistance Plan	0	3	0	1	0
Youth With A Mission	1977	0	0	0	0
	TOTALS	398	61	2198	14

Asia-general

ORGANIZATION NAME	BEGAN	NOW	NEW	CHURCHES	GROUPS
BMMF/International (U.S.A.)	1976	0	0	0	0
Christian and Missionary Alliance	0	7	5	0	0
Christian Churches/Churches of Christ	0	17	0	0	0
Wycliffe Bible Translators International, Inc.	1966	15	0	0	13
	TOTALS	39	5	0	13

Australia

ORGANIZATION NAME	BEGAN	NOW	NEW	CHURCHES	GROUPS
ACTS International	1971	11	4	700	0
American Baptist Association, Missionary Committee	1968	1	0	2	0
American Lutheran Ch., Div. For Wld. Msn.	1974	7	3	1	0
Back to the Bible Missionary Agency	1957	0	0	0	0
Baptist Bible Fellowship International	1954	20	0	0	0
Baptist International Missions, Inc.	1970	14	0	0	0
Baptist Mid-Missions	1968	23	1	0	0
Baptist Missionary Association of America	1965	3	1	0	0
Baptist World Mission	0	1	0	0	0
Campus Crusade for Christ, International (Overseas Dept.)	1967	46	0	0	0
Child Evangelism Fellowship, Inc.	1949	3	1	0	0
Christian and Missionary Alliance	1969	14	4	23	0
Christian Broadcasting Network	0	0	0	0	0
Christian Catholic Church	1888	0	0	2	0
Christian Church of North America, Msns. Dept.	1967	10	0	4	0
Christian Literature Crusade, Inc.	1945	0	0	0	0
Christian Reformed Board For World Missions	1978	2	2	0	0
Christians United in Action, Inc.	0	2	0	0	0

ORGANIZATION NAME

ORGANIZATION NAME	BEGAN	NOW	NEW	CHURCHES	GROUPS
Australia continued...					
Church of God (Anderson, Indiana) Msny. Bd.	0	6	6	3	0
Church of God of Prophecy, World Mission Committee	1956	0	2	4	0
Church of God World Missions	1968	0	0	3	0
Church of the Nazarene, Gen. Bd. Dept. of Wld. Msns.	1946	0	0	24	0
Evangelical Baptist Missions, Inc.	1972	6	4	3	0
Faith Christian Fellowship World Outreach	1979	2	0	2	0
General Conference of Seventh-day Adventists	1885	5	4	422	0
Globe Missionary Evangelism	1978	2	2	0	0
Haggai Institute for Advanced Leadership Training, Inc.	1973	0	0	0	0
Heritage Village Church and Missionary Fellowship, Inc.	0	0	0	0	0
Intl. Church of the Foursquare Gospel--Dept. of Msns. Intl.	1953	2	0	24	0
Jesus to the Communist World, Inc.	0	0	0	0	0
Jews For Jesus	1977	0	0	0	0
Maranatha Baptist Mission, Inc.	0	0	0	1	0
Mission to Europe's Millions, Inc.	0	0	0	3	3
Navigators, The	1964	6	0	0	0
New Tribes Mission	1956	27	0	0	0
Slavic Gospel Association	1952	2	1	1	0
South Pacific Evangelical Fellowship	1972	0	1	0	0
United Church Board For World Ministries	1956	6	0	0	0
United Pentecostal Church Intl. For. Msns. Div.	1945	9	7	24	0
Wesleyan Church Gen. Dept. of Wld. Msns.	1970	3	3	0	0
Word of Life Fellowship	1966	4	0	4	1
World Presbyterian Missions, Inc.	1961	30	0	0	22
Wycliffe Bible Translators International, Inc.	1970	0	0	0	0
Young Life	1968	0	0	0	0
Youth With A Mission	1968	0	0	0	0
	TOTALS	268	44	1250	26

Austria

America's Keswick, Inc.	0	4	2	0	0
Assemblies of God, Div. of For. Msns.	1967	2	0	31	0

Austria continued...

ORGANIZATION NAME	BEGAN	NOW	NEW	CHURCHES	GROUPS
Baptist Mid-Missions, Inc.	1967	7	0	0	0
Bible Christian Union, Inc.	1962	4	0	0	2
Child Evangelism Fellowship, Inc.	1955	15	1	0	0
Christian Churches/Churches of Christ	1950	13	0	0	0
Christian Literature Crusade, Inc.	1957	0	0	0	0
Christians United in Action, Inc.		1	0	1	2
Conservative Baptist Foreign Mission Society	1970	10	2	1	1
Eastern European Mission	1962	2	2	3	2
Evangelical Alliance Mission (TEAM)	1965	21	2	4	1
Evangelical Alliance Mission of Canada, Inc.	1965	1	0	4	2
Fellowship of Independent Missions	1971	0	0	0	0
Gospel Missionary Union	1966	9	6	4	0
Greater Europe Mission	1965	10	0	1	0
International Crusades, Inc.	1973	17	15	0	0
Jesus to the Communist World, Inc.		0	0	0	0
Mennonite Brethren Missions/Services	1953	8	9	6	0
Mission to Europe's Millions, Inc.		6	6	9	1
Navigators, The		0	0	0	0
Operation Mobilization - Canada	1973	12	0	0	0
Operation Mobilization Send the Light, Inc.	1962	40	0	50	0
Slavic Gospel Association	1961	10	0	0	0
Southern Baptist Convention, Foreign Mission Board	1976	7	3	7	0
United Methodist Ch. Wld. Div. of the Bd. of Global Min.	1965	12	0	0	0
United Pentecostal Church Intl. For. Msns. Div.	1971	0	0	0	0
WEFMinistries, Inc.	1963	2	1	0	0
World Literature Crusade	1966	5	0	0	0
World Missions Fellowship	1954	0	0	0	0
Young Life	1975	2	0	0	0
Youth With A Mission	1977	0	0	0	0
TOTALS		220	55	116	8

ORGANIZATION NAME	BEGAN	NOW	NEW	CHURCHES	GROUPS

Bahamas

ORGANIZATION NAME	BEGAN	NOW	NEW	CHURCHES	GROUPS
African Methodist Episcopal Church, Inc. Dept. of Msns.	1877	0	0	0	0
African Methodist Episcopal Zion Ch., Dept. of Oseas. Msns.	1877	2	0	0	0
Assemblies of God, Div. of For. Msns.	1953	47	0	17	0
Baptist International Missions, Inc.	1968	2	0	0	0
Bethany Fellowship Msns. (Div. of Bethany Fellowship, Inc.)	1968	2	0	0	0
Christian and Missionary Alliance	1971	2	0	1	0
Christian Churches/Churches of Christ	1960	0	0	1	0
Church of God of Prophecy, World Mission Committee	1923	0	0	55	0
Church of God World Missions	1944	0	0	57	0
Church of the Nazarene, Gen. Bd. Dept. of Wld. Msns.	1971	2	0	5	0
Global Outreach Mission	1974	0	0	0	0
Gospel Missionary Union	1956	18	3	0	0
National Baptist Convention, U.S.A., Inc. For. Msn. Bd.	1942	0	0	172	0
Pentecostal Assemblies of the World, Inc. For. Msns. Dept.	0	1	0	0	0
Southern Baptist Convention, Foreign Mission Board	1951	18	3	213	0
Worldteam	1967	2	0	3	1
TOTALS		96	6	524	1

Bahrain

ORGANIZATION NAME	BEGAN	NOW	NEW	CHURCHES	GROUPS
MAP International (Medical Assistance Programs)	0	0	0	0	0
Reformed Church in America General Program Council	1889	8	4	0	0
TOTALS		8	4	0	0

Bangladesh

ORGANIZATION NAME	BEGAN	NOW	NEW	CHURCHES	GROUPS
AMG International (Advancing the Ministries of the Gospel)	1978	2	0	2	0
Assemblies of God, Div. of For. Msns.	1956	13	0	12	0
Baptist Mid-Missions	1979	6	0	0	0
BMMF International/Canada	1972	2	4	0	0
BMMF International (U.S.A.)	1971	4	4	0	0
Campus Crusade for Christ, International (Overseas Dept.)	1975	48	0	0	0
Chr. Echoes Natl. Min., Inc. (Chr. Crusade)	0	0	0	0	0

Bangladesh continued...

ORGANIZATION NAME	BEGAN	NOW	NEW	CHURCHES	GROUPS
Christian Information Service, Inc.	1970	0	0	0	11
Christian Nationals' Evangelism Commission, Inc. (CNEC)	1975	0	0	7	0
Christian Nationals' Evangelism Commission, Inc. (Canada)	1975	5	0	0	14
Christian Reformed World Relief Committee	1973	0	5	0	0
Church of God (Anderson, Indiana) Msny. Bd.	1925	1	2	35	0
Church World Service Division of DOM-NCCUSA	0	0	0	0	0
Churches of God, General Conference Comm. on Wld. Msns.	1898	5	1	26	0
Food For The Hungry International	1972	1	1	0	0
General Conference of Seventh-day Adventists	1906	10	6	24	0
Global Outreach Mission	1975	2	0	0	0
International Christian Fellowship	1958	11	0	2	2
International Needs-USA	1974	0	0	2	0
Leprosy Mission Canada	1913	0	0	0	0
Liebenzell Mission of Canada	1973	3	0	0	0
Literacy & Evangelism, Inc.	0	0	0	8	0
Living Bibles International	1974	1	0	0	1
Lutheran World Relief, Incorporated	1972	0	0	0	0
MAP International (Medical Assistance Programs)	0	0	0	0	0
Mennonite Brethren Missions/Services	1974	1	0	0	1
Mennonite Central Committee	1970	35	0	0	0
Missionary Church, Div. of Overseas Ministries	0	2	0	0	0
Operation Eyesight Universal	1972	0	0	0	0
Operation Mobilization - Canada	1972	30	0	10	0
Presbyterian Church in the U.S.A., Div. of Intl. Msn.	1974	17	15	0	0
Southern Baptist Convention, Foreign Mission Board	1957	17	0	14	0
United Presbyterian Church in the USA Program Agency	1975	2	2	0	0
World Concern/Crista International	1975	5	5	0	0
World Gospel Mission	1974	3	0	0	1
World Literature Crusade	1975	0	0	0	0
World Mission Prayer League	1972	11	2	0	0
World Missionary Evangelism, Inc.	0	0	0	0	0
World Missions, Inc.	1972	2	0	5	0
World Outreach	0	0	0	0	0

ORGANIZATION NAME	BEGAN	NOW	NEW	CHURCHES	GROUPS
Bangladesh continued...					
World Relief Corporation	1972	0	0	0	0
World Vision International	1970	1	0	0	0
TOTALS		240	42	145	30
Barbados					
African Methodist Episcopal Church, Inc. Dept. of Msns.	1971	0	0	0	0
African Methodist Episcopal Zion Ch., Dept. of Oseas. Msns.	1977	0	0	0	0
Baptist Bible Fellowship International	1957	2	0	2	0
Berean Mission, Inc.	1958	3	0	4	1
Bible Missionary Church, World Missions Department	1979	2	2	0	0
Campus Crusade for Christ, International (Overseas Dept.)		0	0	0	0
Child Evangelism Fellowship, Inc.	0	0	0	0	0
Christian Church of North America, Msns. Dept.	0	2	0	0	0
Christian Churches/Churches of Christ	1965	0	0	0	0
Christian Literature Crusade, Inc.	1957	0	0	0	0
Church of God World Missions	1944	0	0	48	0
Church of the Nazarene, Gen. Bd. Dept. of Wld. Msns.	1926	0	0	32	0
Churches of Christ in Christian Union: Foreign Msny. Dept.	1961	2	0	7	0
Moravian Church in America, Bd. of Wld. Msn.	1732	0	0	0	0
National Baptist Convention, U.S.A., Inc. For. Msn. Bd.	1978	1	0	0	0
Pentecostal Assemblies of the World, Inc. For. Msns. Dept.	0	2	0	3	0
Southern Baptist Convention, Foreign Mission Board	1972	8	3	4	0
TOTALS		22	5	100	1
Belgium					
AMG International (Advancing the Ministries of the Gospel)	1978	0	0	1	0
Assemblies of God, Div. of For. Msns.	1951	29	0	31	0
Baptist Bible Fellowship International	1962	8	0	0	0
Biblical Literature Fellowship	1959	0	0	0	0
Brethren Assemblies		8	0	0	0
Child Evangelism Fellowship, Inc.	1955	0	0	0	0

Belgium continued...

ORGANIZATION NAME	BEGAN	NOW	NEW	CHURCHES	GROUPS
Christian Church of North America, Msns. Dept.	0	0	0	0	0
Christian Churches/Churches of Christ	1948	4	0	0	0
Church of God World Missions	1974	2	2	1	0
Fellowship of Evangelical Baptist Chs. in Canada	1977	2	0	5	0
Global Outreach Mission	1946	7	0	0	0
Gospel Missionary Union	1966	8	2	4	0
Greater Europe Mission	1972	12	4	0	0
International Crusades, Inc.	1979	1	1	1	0
Jesus to the Communist World, Inc.	1970	0	0	0	0
Leprosy Relief, Canada, Inc.	1976	1	1	0	0
Lutheran Church in America-Div. for Wld. Msn. and Ecumenism	1962	0	1	0	0
Media Ministries Division, Mennonite Bd. of Msns.	1950	2	0	6	0
Mennonite Board of Missions	1965	2	0	0	0
Mennonite Central Committee	1962	92	0	50	0
Operation Mobilization - Canada	1961	30	0	0	0
Operation Mobilization Send the Light, Inc.	1973	2	0	0	0
Presbyterian Church in the U.S.A., Div. of Intl. Msn.	1967	9	2	12	0
Southern Baptist Convention, Foreign Mission Board	1977	0	0	0	0
United Church Board For World Ministries	0	0	0	0	0
United Methodist Ch. Wld. Div. of the Bd. of Global Min.	0	2	0	0	0
United Presbyterian Church in the USA Program Agency	1970	2	0	3	0
United World Mission, Incorporated	1979	1	1	0	0
We Go, Inc. (World Encounter Gospel Organization)	1978	2	2	0	0
WEFMinistries, Inc.	1970	0	0	0	0
World Literature Crusade	1970	0	0	0	0
TOTALS		226	15	114	0

Belize

ORGANIZATION NAME	BEGAN	NOW	NEW	CHURCHES	GROUPS
Anchor Bay Evangelistic Association	0	2	0	0	0
Assemblies of God, Div. of For. Msns.	1946	4	0	6	0
Baptist Bible Fellowship International	1978	2	0	0	0
Campus Crusade for Christ, International (Overseas Dept.)	1979	0	0	0	0

ORGANIZATION NAME	BEGAN	NOW	NEW	CHURCHES	GROUPS
Belize continued...					
Church of God in Christ, Mennonite Gen. Msn. Bd., Inc.	0	0	0	0	0
Church of God World Missions	1944	0	0	5	0
Church of the Nazarene, Gen. Bd. Dept. of Wld. Msns.	1934	4	0	21	0
Compassion International, Inc.	1979	0	0	0	0
Conservative Baptist Association of America	1960	2	0	6	0
Eastern Mennonite Board of Missions and Charities	1960	12	8	5	0
Full Gospel Grace Fellowship	0	0	0	0	0
General Conference of Seventh-day Adventists	1929	2	0	23	0
Gospel Missionary Union	1955	13	3	9	0
MAP International (Medical Assistance Programs)	1972	0	0	4	0
Media Ministries Division, Mennonite Bd. of Msns.	1972	1	0	0	0
Mennonite Economic Development Associates	0	2	0	5	0
Methodist Protestant Church, Board of Msns.	1956	2	0	10	0
Pentecostal Church of God, World Missions Department	1977	2	2	0	0
Southern Baptist Convention, Foreign Mission Board	1975	2	2	0	0
United Church Board For World Ministries	0	0	0	0	0
World Missionary Assistance Plan	0	2	0	0	0
TOTALS		50	13	94	0

Benin

ORGANIZATION NAME	BEGAN	NOW	NEW	CHURCHES	GROUPS
Assemblies of God, Div. of For. Msns.	1921	6	0	35	0
Christian Mission for the Deaf	1976	0	0	0	0
Evangelical Baptist Missions, Inc.	1966	3	0	7	1
MAP International (Medical Assistance Programs)	1970	0	0	0	0
Southern Baptist Convention, Foreign Mission Board	1970	14	6	19	0
Sudan Interior Mission, Inc.	1946	44	21	105	8
World Neighbors, Inc.	0	0	0	0	0
TOTALS		67	27	166	9

Bermuda

ORGANIZATION NAME	BEGAN	NOW	NEW	CHURCHES	GROUPS
African Methodist Episcopal Church, Inc. Dept. of Msns.	0	0	0	0	0

ORGANIZATION NAME	BEGAN	NOW	NEW	CHURCHES	GROUPS
Bermuda continued...					
Child Evangelism Fellowship, Inc.	1974	1	1	0	0
Christian Broadcasting Network	0	0	0	0	0
Church of God (Anderson, Indiana) Msny. Bd.	1905	2	0	2	0
Church of God of Prophecy, World Mission Committee	1955	1	0	1	0
Church of God World Missions	1944	0	0	4	0
Slavic Gospel Association	1975	1	0	0	0
Southern Baptist Convention, Foreign Mission Board	1966	2	0	1	0
Young Life	1964	0	0	0	0
TOTALS		7	1	8	0

Bhutan

ORGANIZATION NAME	BEGAN	NOW	NEW	CHURCHES	GROUPS
BMMF International/Canada	1974	0	0	0	0
Leprosy Mission Canada	1966	0	0	0	0
MAP International (Medical Assistance Programs)	0	0	0	0	0
New Life League	0	0	0	0	0
World Missionary Evangelism, Inc.	0	0	0	0	0
TOTALS		0	0	0	0

Bolivia

ORGANIZATION NAME	BEGAN	NOW	NEW	CHURCHES	GROUPS
Andes Evangelical Mission	1907	42	18	370	0
Assemblies of God, Div. of For. Msns.	1948	14	0	509	0
Baptist Bible Fellowship International	1977	4	0	0	0
Baptist International Missions, Inc.	1969	8	0	0	0
Baptist Missionary Association of America	1965	3	3	0	0
Bethesda Mission, Inc.	1951	9	3	20	0
Brethren Assemblies		14	0	0	0
Campus Crusade for Christ, International (Overseas Dept.)	1965	21	0	0	0
Canadian Baptist Overseas Mission Board	1898	35	15	200	1
Central Yearly Meeting of Friends Missionary Committee	0	0	0	0	0
Child Evangelism Fellowship, Inc.	1974	0	0	0	0
Christian Nationals' Evangelism Commission, Inc. (CNEC)	1977	0	0	0	0

Bolivia continued...

ORGANIZATION NAME	BEGAN	NOW	NEW	CHURCHES	GROUPS
Christian Nationals' Evangelism Commission, Inc. (Canada)	1977	0	0	0	0
Christian Service Corps	1974	4	0	0	0
Church of God (Anderson, Indiana) Msny. Bd.	1974	2	0	96	0
Church of God (Holiness) For. Msn. Brd.	1945	2	0	105	0
Church of God of Prophecy, World Mission Committee	1974	0	0	20	0
Church of God World Missions	1960	1	1	14	0
Church of the Nazarene, Gen. Bd. Dept. of Wld. Msns.	1945	8	0	0	0
Compassion International, Inc.	1975	1	1	0	0
Evangelical Methodist Church World Missions	1975	6	6	6	3
Evangelistic Faith Mission, Inc.	0	3	0	0	0
Food For The Hungry International	1978	4	4	0	0
General Conference Mennonite Church, Comm. on Oseas. Msn.	1974	4	2	6	0
General Conference of Seventh-day Adventists	1907	6	2	59	2
Gospel Missionary Union	1937	32	1	23	2
Intl. Church of the Foursquare Gospel--Dept. of Msns. Intl.	1928	2	0	38	0
International Crusades, Inc.	1977	13	13	4	0
Jesus to the Communist World, Inc.	0	0	0	0	0
Lutheran World Relief, Incorporated	1977	0	0	0	0
MAP International (Medical Assistance Programs)	0	0	0	0	0
Maranatha Baptist Mission, Inc.	14	0	0	14	0
Mennonite Board of Missions	1959	6	6	5	0
Mennonite Central Committee	1959	51	6	0	0
Mennonite Economic Development Associates	1973	1	0	0	0
Mission to the World	1976	2	6	0	0
New Tribes Mission	1942	113	0	0	0
Northwest Yearly Meeting of Friends Ch., Dept. of Msns.	1931	8	2	160	0
South American Mission, Inc.	1922	34	12	18	1
Southern Baptist Convention, Foreign Mission Board	1979	0	0	0	0
United Methodist Ch. Wld. Div. of the Bd. of Global Min.	1878	0	0	0	0
United Pentecostal Church Intl. For. Msns. Div.	1974	4	0	0	0
United World Mission, Incorporated	1946	6	3	6	0
World Baptist Fellowship Mission Agency International	1979	2	2	0	0
World Concern/Crista International	1974	0	1	0	0

Bolivia continued...

ORGANIZATION NAME	BEGAN	NOW	NEW	CHURCHES	GROUPS
World Gospel Mission	1944	29	6	56	0
World Literature Crusade	1969	0	0	0	0
World Mission Prayer League	1939	18	4	0	0
World Mission Prayer League Canada	0	2	0	0	0
World Missions, Inc.	1977	3	3	0	0
World Neighbors, Inc.	0	0	0	0	0
World-Wide Missions International	1961	2	0	13	0
Wycliffe Bible Translators International, Inc.	1955	78	0	0	17
TOTALS		597	111	1742	24

Bophuthatswana

ORGANIZATION NAME	BEGAN	NOW	NEW	CHURCHES	GROUPS
Campus Crusade for Christ, International (Overseas Dept.)	1978	14	0	0	0
Church of God World Missions	1978	2	0	19	0
Church of the Nazarene, Gen. Bd. Dept. of Wld. Msns.	0	46	0	95	0
Open Bible Ministries, Inc.	1974	0	0	0	0
Southern Baptist Convention, Foreign Mission Board	1977	12	12	0	0
World Concern/Crista International	1979	2	2	0	0
TOTALS		76	14	114	0

Botswana

ORGANIZATION NAME	BEGAN	NOW	NEW	CHURCHES	GROUPS
Africa Evangelical Fellowship	1972	7	3	3	2
Africa Evangelical Fellowship (Canada)	1974	2	2	6	0
Africa Inter-Mennonite Mission, Inc.	1975	9	2	3	0
African Methodist Episcopal Church, Inc. Dept. of Msns.	0	0	0	0	0
Assemblies of God, Div. of For. Msns.	1963	2	0	17	0
Christian Aid Mission	1953	0	0	200	8
Church of God of Prophecy, World Mission Committee	1965	0	0	10	0
Church of God World Missions	1966	0	0	2	0
General Conference Mennonite Church, Comm. on Oseas. Msn.	1974	7	5	0	0
General Conference of Seventh-day Adventists	1921	3	3	21	0
Jesus to the Communist World, Inc.	0	0	0	0	0

ORGANIZATION NAME	BEGAN	NOW	NEW	CHURCHES	GROUPS
Botswana continued...					
Leprosy Relief, Canada, Inc.	1979	0	0	0	0
Lutheran World Relief, Incorporated	1974	0	0	0	0
MAP International (Medical Assistance Programs)	0	4	4	0	0
Mennonite Brethren Missions/Services	1976	32	2	0	0
Mennonite Central Committee	1968	2	2	0	0
Mission Aviation Fellowship	1979	2	2	18	0
Pentecostal Holiness Church-World Missions Department	1972	13	0	3	0
Southern Baptist Convention, Foreign Mission Board	1968	7	5	0	0
United Church Board For World Ministries	1971	0	0	0	0
United Methodist Ch. Wld. Div. of the Bd. of Global Min.	1969	0	0	0	0
United Pentecostal Church Intl. For. Msns. Div.	0	0	0	0	0
World Literature Crusade	1976	0	0	0	0
	TOTALS	90	28	283	10

Brazil

ORGANIZATION NAME	BEGAN	NOW	NEW	CHURCHES	GROUPS
American Leprosy Missions, Inc.	1968	4	0	0	0
American Lutheran Ch., Div. For Wld. Msn.	1958	19	9	1	0
AMG International (Advancing the Ministries of the Gospel)	1975	0	0	4	0
Anchor Bay Evangelistic Association	0	2	2	20	0
Apostolic Christian Church (Nazarene), Apos. Chr. Ch. Found.	1959	13	4	7	0
Apostolic Church in Canada, The	1970	4	2	0	0
Apostolic Church of Pentecost of Canada-Missionary Dept.	1972	4	0	0	0
Assemblies of God, Div. of For. Msns.	1911	25	0	0	0
Association of Free Lutheran Congregations	0	9	0	0	0
Baptist Bible Fellowship International	1952	8	2	36	0
Baptist Faith Missions	1923	9	0	0	0
Baptist General Conference Board of World Missions	1955	12	0	0	0
Baptist International Missions, Inc.	1967	51	0	0	0
Baptist Mid-Missions	1946	140	0	0	0
Baptist Missionary Association of America	1953	1	0	0	0
Baptist World Mission	0	0	0	0	0
Berean Mission, Inc.	1967	3	0	1	0

Brazil continued...

ORGANIZATION NAME	BEGAN	NOW	NEW	CHURCHES	GROUPS
Bethany Fellowship Msns. (Div. of Bethany Fellowship, Inc.)	1963	48	7	16	0
Bethany Missionary Association	1954	2	0	3	0
Bethesda Mission, Inc.	1957	8	1	5	0
Bible Memory Association International	1966	3	3	0	0
Bible Presbyterian Church, Ind. Bd. for Presb. For. Msns.	1948	5	0	4	0
Brethren Assemblies	0	15	0	0	0
Campus Crusade for Christ, International (Overseas Dept.)	1968	27	0	0	0
Canadian Baptist Overseas Mission Board	1974	10	8	125	0
Child Evangelism Fellowship, Inc.	1941	6	6	0	0
Christian and Missionary Alliance	1962	16	6	14	0
Christian Broadcasting Network	0	0	0	0	0
Christian Church (Disciples of Christ) Div. of Oseas. Min.	1968	2	0	0	0
Christian Churches/Churches of Christ	1956	54	0	0	0
Chr. Echoes Natl. Min., Inc. (Chr. Crusade)	0	0	0	0	0
Christian Literature Crusade, Inc.	1958	10	0	0	0
Christian Missionary Fellowship	1957	2	6	12	0
Christian Nationals' Evangelism Commission, Inc. (CNEC)	1969	2	0	9	0
Christian Nationals' Evangelism Commission, Inc. (Canada)	1969	2	0	0	0
Christian Reformed Board For World Missions	1934	6	6	0	0
Christian World Publishers, Inc.	1964	2	0	0	0
Christians In Action	1957	7	2	2	1
Church of God (Anderson, Indiana) Msny. Bd.	1923	6	2	34	0
Church of God of Prophecy, World Mission Committee	1965	0	0	0	0
Church of God World Missions	1954	0	0	73	0
Church of the Nazarene, Gen. Bd. Dept. of Wld. Msns.	1958	16	0	23	0
Compassion International, Inc.	1975	0	0	0	0
Congregational Holiness Church Foreign Mission Dept.	1972	0	0	15	0
Conservative Baptist Foreign Mission Society	1946	56	8	38	6
Eastern Mennonite Board of Missions and Charities	1975	2	0	0	0
Faith Center Global Ministries	0	1	0	0	0
Fellowship of Grace Brethren Churches, For. Msny. Soc.	1949	13	2	15	0
Fellowship of Independent Missions	1964	0	0	0	0
Free Methodist Church of N. America Gen. Msny. Bd.	1928	8	0	24	0

Brazil continued...

ORGANIZATION NAME	BEGAN	NOW	NEW	CHURCHES	GROUPS
General Conference Mennonite Church, Comm. on Oseas. Msn.	1975	4	2	24	0
General Conference of Seventh-day Adventists	1894	36	12	772	0
Global Outreach Mission	1973	2	0	0	0
Go-Ye Fellowship	1956	6	1	1	0
Gospel Missionary Union	1911	31	2	19	0
Gospel Recordings Incorporated	1977	5	0	0	0
Haggai Institute for Advanced Leadership Training, Inc.	1979	0	0	0	0
Intl. Church of the Foursquare Gospel--Dept. of Msns. Intl.	1946	6	0	1685	0
Internatl Fellowship of Evangelical Students - USA	0	1	0	0	0
Intl Pentecostal Ch. of Christ, Global Msns. Dept.	1938	0	0	200	0
Janz Team	1975	9	0	0	1
Japan Evangelical Mission	1972	10	5	1	1
Japanese Evangelical Missionary Society	1966	2	0	0	0
Jesus to the Communist World, Inc.	0	0	0	0	0
Jews For Jesus	1976	1	1	0	0
Latin America Mission, Inc.	1973	0	0	0	0
Leprosy Relief, Canada, Inc.	1975	2	0	0	0
Lester Sumrall Evangelistic Association	1966	2	0	0	1
Living Bibles International	1972	2	0	0	0
Lutheran Church-Missouri Synod	1901	2	0	998	0
Lutheran World Relief, Incorporated	1961	1	0	0	0
MAP International (Medical Assistance Programs)	0	0	0	0	0
Maranatha Baptist Mission, Inc.	0	0	0	3	0
Mennonite Board of Missions	1954	17	0	24	0
Mennonite Brethren Missions/Services	1944	14	4	25	0
Mennonite Central Committee	1968	27	0	0	0
Mission Aviation Fellowship	1956	30	4	0	35
Mission Aviation Fellowship of Canada	1972	4	2	0	0
Mission to the World	1973	3	2	0	0
Missionary Church, Div. of Overseas Ministries	1955	17	0	30	1
National Association of Free Will Baptists, Bd. of For. Msns	1958	24	4	12	0
Navigators, The	1963	8	2	0	0
New Life League	0	2	0	0	0

Brazil continued...

ORGANIZATION NAME	BEGAN	NOW	NEW	CHURCHES	GROUPS
New Tribes Mission	1945	206	0	0	0
North American Baptist Gen. Msny. Soc., Inc.	1966	8	2	41	5
O.C. Ministries, Inc.	1963	20	8	0	0
OMS International, Inc.	1950	23	10	50	3
Open Doors With Brother Andrew	0	0	0	0	0
Pentecostal Assemblies of Canada, Oseas. Msns. Dept.	1963	12	2	112	1
Pentecostal Church of God, World Missions Department	1956	2	0	52	0
Pilgrim Fellowship, Inc., The	1948	6	0	0	0
Pocket Testament League, Inc.	1964	4	0	0	0
Presbyterian Church in the U.S.A., Div. of Intl. Msn.	1869	92	10	0	0
Salvation Army, The	1922	3	0	47	0
Schwenkfelder Church in the USA and For. Bd. of Msns.	0	0	0	4	0
South American Mission, Inc.	1913	16	3	18	1
Southern Baptist Convention, Foreign Mission Board	1881	295	26	2739	0
Things to Come Mission, Inc.	1968	2	0	6	0
Trans World Missions	1965	7	0	0	0
Unevangelized Fields Mission	1931	102	17	0	0
United Church of Canada, Division of World Outreach	0	6	0	1	0
United Methodist Ch. Wld. Div. of the Bd. of Global Min.	1880	0	0	0	0
United Pentecostal Church Intl. For. Msns. Div.	1952	12	0	0	0
United Presbyterian Church in the USA Program Agency	1859	12	0	0	0
United World Mission, Incorporated	1961	2	0	3	0
Wesleyan Church Gen. Dept. of Wld. Msns.	1960	7	3	6	0
Word of Life Fellowship	1957	20	8	0	0
World Baptist Fellowship Mission Agency International	1960	44	9	38	0
World Gospel Mission	1966	3	0	1	0
World Hope Foundation	1979	0	0	0	0
World Literature Crusade	1962	0	0	0	0
World Mission in Church and Society	1907	4	2	0	0
World Missionary Assistance Plan	0	2	0	1	0
World Missions Fellowship	1957	2	0	1	0
World Missions, Inc.	1964	2	0	0	0
World Neighbors, Inc.	0	0	0	0	0

ORGANIZATION NAME	BEGAN	NOW	NEW	CHURCHES	GROUPS
Brazil continued...					
World Radio Missionary Fellowship, Inc.	1975	4	0	0	0
World Relief Corporation	1977	0	0	0	0
World Vision International	1961	2	0	1	0
World-Wide Missions International	1963	2	0	5	1
Worldteam	1958	12	0	7	1
Worldwide Evangelization Crusade	1957	6	0	0	44
Wycliffe Bible Translators International, Inc.	1956	158	0	0	0
Young Life	1963	0	0	0	0
Youth For Christ/U.S.A.	1950	2	0	0	0
Youth With A Mission	1975	0	0	0	0
TOTALS	1995	211	7408	101

British Virgin Is.					
Campus Crusade for Christ, International (Overseas Dept.)	1979	0	0	0	0
Church of God (Holiness) For. Msn. Brd.	1947	2	0	5	0
Church of God of Prophecy, World Mission Committee	1951	0	0	24	0
Church of God World Missions	1968	0	0	1	0
Southern Baptist Convention, Foreign Mission Board	1976	3	3	1	0
TOTALS	5	3	31	0

Bulgaria					
Assemblies of God, Div. of For. Msns.	1968	0	0	217	0
Mission to Europe's Millions, Inc.	0	0	0	0	0
TOTALS	217	0

Burma					
American Baptist Churches in the U.S.A., Intl. Min.	1814	0	0	2786	0
American Leprosy Missions, Inc.	1923	0	0	0	0
AMG International (Advancing the Ministries of the Gospel)	1974	6	4	20	0
Assemblies of God, Div. of For. Msns.	1931	0	0	400	0

Burma continued...

ORGANIZATION NAME	BEGAN	NOW	NEW	CHURCHES	GROUPS
Christian Aid Mission	1977	0	0	300	19
Christian Nationals' Evangelism Commission, Inc. (CNEC)	1978	0	0	17	0
Christian Nationals' Evangelism Commission, Inc. (Canada)	1978	0	0	0	0
Compassion International, Inc.	1972	6	4	0	0
Far East Broadcasting Company, Inc.	1973	0	0	0	0
Leprosy Mission Canada	1899	0	0	0	0
Living Bibles International	1971	1	0	0	1
MAP International (Medical Assistance Programs)	1972	0	0	0	0
Seventh Day Baptist Missionary Society	1974	0	0	13	0
United Pentecostal Church Intl. For. Msns. Div.	0	0	0	0	0
TOTALS		13	8	3536	20

Burundi

ORGANIZATION NAME	BEGAN	NOW	NEW	CHURCHES	GROUPS
Brethren Assemblies	0	9	0	0	0
Child Evangelism Fellowship, Inc.	1956	2	0	0	0
Church of God World Missions	1978	0	0	7	0
Churches of Christ in Christian Union: Foreign Msny. Dept.	0	1	1	0	0
Compassion International, Inc.	1979	1	1	0	0
Elim Fellowship, Inc.	1968	4	4	50	0
Free Methodist Church of N. America Gen. Msny. Bd.	1935	24	0	9	49
General Conference of Seventh-day Adventists	1925	10	2	109	0
Kansas Yearly Meeting of Friends Africa Gospel Mission	1932	0	0	6	0
MAP International (Medical Assistance Programs)	0	0	0	0	0
Southern Baptist Convention, Foreign Mission Board	1978	2	2	0	0
World Gospel Mission	1943	25	7	203	0
TOTALS		78	17	384	49

C. America-general

ORGANIZATION NAME	BEGAN	NOW	NEW	CHURCHES	GROUPS
Maranatha Baptist Mission, Inc.	0	0	0	0	0
TOTALS		0	0	0	0

ORGANIZATION NAME	BEGAN	NOW	NEW	CHURCHES	GROUPS
Cameroon					
American Leprosy Missions, Inc.	1935	0	0	0	0
American Lutheran Ch., Div. For Wld. Msn.	1923	36	16	1	0
Assemblies of God, Div. of For. Msns.	1974	4	0	1	0
Baptist General Conference Board of World Missions	1979	2	2	0	0
Christian Literature Crusade, Inc.	1972	0	0	0	0
Christian Mission for the Deaf	1977	1	0	0	0
Christian Service Corps	0	0	0	0	0
Church of God World Missions	1970	0	0	40	0
Church of the Lutheran Brethren of America, Bd. of Wld. Msns	1920	19	4	402	12
Evangelical Lutheran Church, Division of World Missions	1979	3	1	1	0
General Conference of Seventh-day Adventists	1928	4	2	69	0
Leprosy Relief, Canada, Inc.	1975	0	0	0	0
Lutheran World Relief, Incorporated	1971	0	0	0	0
MAP International (Medical Assistance Programs)	0	0	0	0	0
Mission Aviation Fellowship	1974	2	0	0	0
Natl. Baptist Convention of Amer., For. Msn. Bd.	1977	2	3	42	0
North American Baptist Gen. Msny. Soc., Inc.	1936	49	18	572	40
Prison Mission Assoc., Inc.	1971	1	0	0	0
Self Help Foundation	1964	0	0	1	0
United Church Board For World Ministries	1977	0	0	0	0
United Presbyterian Church in the USA Program Agency	1879	8	2	0	0
Wisconsin Evangelical Lutheran Synod, Bd. for Wld. Msns.	1965	0	0	31	0
World-Wide Missions International	1961	2	0	15	0
Wycliffe Bible Translators International, Inc.	1968	51	0	0	21
TOTALS	0	184	48	1175	73

ORGANIZATION NAME	BEGAN	NOW	NEW	CHURCHES	GROUPS
Canary Islands					
Assemblies of God, Div. of For. Msns.	0	7	0	4	0
TOTALS	0	7	0	4	0

ORGANIZATION NAME	BEGAN	NOW	NEW	CHURCHES	GROUPS

Cape Verde

ORGANIZATION NAME	BEGAN	NOW	NEW	CHURCHES	GROUPS
Baptist Missionary Association of America	1956	0	0	0	0
Church of the Nazarene, Gen. Bd. Dept. of Wld. Msns.	1903	4	0	17	0
TOTALS		4	0	17	0

Caribbean-general

ORGANIZATION NAME	BEGAN	NOW	NEW	CHURCHES	GROUPS
Baptist International Missions, Inc.	0	32	0	0	0
Brethren Assemblies	0	16	0	0	0
Church of the Nazarene, Gen. Bd. Dept. of Wld. Msns.	0	5	0	0	0
MAP International (Medical Assistance Programs)	0	0	0	0	0
Operation Eyesight Universal	1977	0	0	0	0
Pentecostal Assemblies of Canada, Oseas. Msns. Dept.	1918	8	2	167	1
Salvation Army, Canada and Bermuda	1887	6	0	0	0
Salvation Army, The	1895	15	0	42	0
United Methodist Ch. Wld. Div. of the Bd. of Global Min.		0	0	0	0
Wesleyan Church Gen. Dept. of Wld. Msns.	1902	0	0	170	0
TOTALS		82	2	379	1

Cayman Islands

ORGANIZATION NAME	BEGAN	NOW	NEW	CHURCHES	GROUPS
Christian Service Corps	0	2	0	0	0
Church of God (Holiness) For. Msn. Brd.	1933	2	0	3	0
Church of God of Prophecy, World Mission Committee	1978	0	0	1	0
Church of God World Missions	1972	0	0	3	0
Men in Action	1973	0	0	0	0
Southern Baptist Convention, Foreign Mission Board	1977	4	4	1	0
United Church of Canada, Division of World Outreach	0	2	0	1	0
TOTALS		10	4	9	0

Central African Rep.

ORGANIZATION NAME	BEGAN	NOW	NEW	CHURCHES	GROUPS
Africa Inland Mission	1924	17	8	70	0
Africa Inland Mission (Canada)	0	3	1	0	0

ORGANIZATION NAME	BEGAN	NOW	NEW	CHURCHES	GROUPS
Central African Rep. continued...					
American Lutheran Ch., Div. For Wld. Msn.	1974	16	7	1	0
Baptist Mid-Missions	1920	72	0	0	0
Bible Alliance Mission, Inc.		0	0	0	0
Christian Mission for the Deaf	1977	0	0	0	0
Fellowship of Grace Brethren Churches, For. Msny. Soc.	1921	51	10	450	2
Leprosy Relief, Canada, Inc.	1974	0	0	0	0
MAP International (Medical Assistance Programs)	0	0	0	0	0
Mission Aviation Fellowship	1977	4	2	0	0
Mission to the World	1979	2	2	0	0
Worldteam	1977	2	0	0	0
	TOTALS	167	30	521	2
Chad					
Baptist Mid-Missions	1925	17	0	0	0
Brethren Assemblies	0	3	0	0	0
Christian Mission for the Deaf	1976	0	0	0	0
Church of God World Missions	1968	0	0	3	0
Church of the Lutheran Brethren of America, Bd. of Wld. Msns	1920	8	2	420	11
Evangelical Alliance Mission (TEAM)	1969	29	7	537	8
Evangelical Alliance Mission of Canada, Inc.	1969	20	4	600	0
Fellowship of Grace Brethren Churches, For. Msny. Soc.	0	1	1	38	0
General Conference of Seventh-day Adventists	1977	2	2	3	0
MAP International (Medical Assistance Programs)	0	0	0	0	0
Mennonite Central Committee	1973	2	0	0	0
Worldwide Evangelization Crusade	1962	0	0	2	0
Wycliffe Bible Translators International, Inc.	1978	0	0	0	0
	TOTALS	82	16	1603	19
Chile					
Assemblies of God, Div. of For. Msns.	1941	18	0	69	0
Baptist Bible Fellowship International	1954	8	0	0	0

Chile continued...

ORGANIZATION NAME	BEGAN	NOW	NEW	CHURCHES	GROUPS
Baptist International Missions, Inc.	1945	4	0	0	0
Bible Presbyterian Church, Ind. Bd. for Presb. For. Msns.		3	0	22	0
Brethren Assemblies		19	0	0	0
Campus Crusade for Christ, International (Overseas Dept.)	1963	40	0	0	0
Child Evangelism Fellowship, Inc.	1952	3	2	0	0
Christian and Missionary Alliance	1897	21	4	209	0
Christian Broadcasting Network		0	0	0	0
Christian Churches/Churches of Christ	1958	26	0	0	0
Christian Literature Crusade, Inc.	1958	0	0	0	0
Christian Nationals' Evangelism Commission, Inc. (CNEC)	1977	0	0	0	0
Christian Nationals' Evangelism Commission, Inc. (Canada)	1977	0	0	0	0
Christians In Action	1978	7	8	1	0
Church of God of Prophecy, World Mission Committee	1975	0	0	7	0
Church of God World Missions	1956	0	0	117	0
Church of the Nazarene, Gen. Bd. Dept. of Wld. Msns.	1962	12	0	13	0
Evangelical Methodist Church Bible Methodist Missions		0	0	3	0
General Conference of Seventh-day Adventists	1895	6	6	133	0
Gospel Mission of South America	1923	38	2	57	3
Holy Land Christian Mission		0	0	0	0
Intl. Church of the Foursquare Gospel--Dept. of Msns. Intl.	1949	3	1	79	0
Jesus to the Communist World, Inc.		0	0	0	0
Logoi, Inc.	1977	3	0	0	0
Lutheran Church in America-Div. for Wld. Msn. and Ecumenism	1962	3	3	0	0
Lutheran Church-Missouri Synod	1954	0	0	2	0
Lutheran World Relief, Incorporated	1961	0	0	0	0
Maranatha Baptist Mission, Inc.		0	0	2	0
Salvation Army, The	1909	6	0	56	0
Source of Light Ministries, Intl.		1	0	0	0
Southern Baptist Convention, Foreign Mission Board	1917	72	14	164	0
United Methodist Ch. Wld. Div. of the Bd. of Global Min.	1884	2	0	0	0
United Pentecostal Church Intl. For. Msns. Div.	1964	2	0	0	0
United Presbyterian Church in the USA Program Agency	1845	6	4	0	0
Word of Life Fellowship	1977	2	2	0	0

Chile continued...

ORGANIZATION NAME	BEGAN	NOW	NEW	CHURCHES	GROUPS
World Literature Crusade	1962	0	0	0	0
World Missionary Assistance Plan	0	2	0	0	0
World Presbyterian Missions, Inc.	1957	13	4	0	0
World-Wide Missions International	1970	0	0	15	0
Youth With A Mission	1978	0	0	0	3
TOTALS		318	50	949	3

China, People's Rep.

ORGANIZATION NAME	BEGAN	NOW	NEW	CHURCHES	GROUPS
Asian Outreach	1968	0	0	0	0
Christian Nationals' Evangelism Commission, Inc. (CNEC)	1943	0	0	0	0
Christian Nationals' Evangelism Commission, Inc. (Canada)	1943	0	0	0	0
TOTALS		0	0	0	0

Colombia

ORGANIZATION NAME	BEGAN	NOW	NEW	CHURCHES	GROUPS
American Baptist Association, Missionary Committee	1971	2	0	4	0
American Lutheran Ch., Div. For Wld. Msn.	1944	10	6	1	0
AMG International (Advancing the Ministries of the Gospel)	1973	2	0	10	0
Anglican Orthodox Church	1972	0	0	0	0
Assemblies of God, Div. of For. Msns.	1932	11	0	81	0
Baptist Bible Fellowship International	1972	10	0	0	0
Baptist International Missions, Inc.	0	4	0	0	0
Brethren Assemblies	0	31	0	0	0
Campus Crusade for Christ, International (Overseas Dept.)	1963	291	1	0	0
Child Evangelism Fellowship, Inc.	1970	3	0	0	0
Christian Aid Mission	1953	0	0	75	9
Christian and Missionary Alliance	1923	36	8	193	0
Christian Broadcasting Network	0	2	0	0	0
Christian Churches/Churches of Christ	1967	10	0	0	0
Christian Literature Crusade, Inc.	1973	2	0	0	0
Christian Union General Mission Board	1978	2	2	0	0
Christians In Action	1969	2	0	2	0

Colombia continued...

ORGANIZATION NAME	BEGAN	NOW	NEW	CHURCHES	GROUPS
Church of God (Seventh Day), Gen. Conf., Msns. Abroad	1976	1	0	1	0
Church of God of Prophecy, World Mission Committee	1973	0	0	5	0
Church of God World Missions	1960	2	0	31	0
Church of the Nazarene, Gen. Bd. Dept. of Wld. Msns.	1975	8	0	2	0
Compassion International, Inc.	1973	4	0	0	0
Cumberland Presbyterian Chruch, Board of Missions	1925	4	1	18	0
Defenders of the Christian Faith Movement, Inc.	1978	0	0	4	0
Elim Fellowship, Inc.	1964	5	0	10	0
Evangelical Alliance Mission (TEAM)	1923	30	6	130	1
Evangelical Alliance Mission of Canada, Inc.	1918	1	1	119	0
Evangelical Covenant Church of America, Bd. of Wld. Msn.	1968	8	6	1	0
Evangelical Lutheran Church, Division of World Missions	1979	2	0	1	0
Evangelical Scripture Mission	1967	0	0	15	0
Fellowship of Evangelical Baptist Chs. in Canada	1969	21	8	20	0
General Conference Mennonite Church, Comm. on Oseas. Msn.	1945	7	4	10	0
General Conference of Seventh-day Adventists	1921	6	4	199	0
Gospel Missionary Union	1908	25	4	80	1
Holy Land Christian Mission	0	5	0	0	0
Intl. Church of the Foursquare Gospel--Dept. of Msns. Intl.	1943	5	0	578	0
Jesus to the Communist World, Inc.	0	0	0	0	0
Latin America Mission, Inc.	1937	24	7	0	0
Literacy & Evangelism, Inc.	0	2	0	10	0
Lutheran Frontier Missions	1972	3	0	4	4
MAP International (Medical Assistance Programs)	0	0	0	0	0
Mennonite Brethren Missions/Services	1945	22	27	23	0
Mennonite Economic Development Associates	1971	0	0	0	0
Mission Aviation Fellowship	1971	4	2	0	0
Mission to the World	1976	4	4	0	0
Missionary Revival Crusade	0	0	0	0	0
New Life League	0	3	0	0	0
New Tribes Mission	1945	54	0	0	0
O.C. Ministries, Inc.	1963	8	8	0	0
OMS International, Inc.	1943	29	19	49	3

Colombia continued...

ORGANIZATION NAME	BEGAN	NOW	NEW	CHURCHES	GROUPS
Pan American Missionary Society, Inc.	1974	0	0	0	0
Regular Baptists of Canada, Women's Missionary Society	1962	4	0	1	0
South American Mission, Inc.	1934	14	4	24	4
Southern Baptist Convention, Foreign Mission Board	1941	83	6	84	0
Teen Missions International, Inc.	1977	1	0	0	0
United Pentecostal Church Intl. For. Msns. Div.	1937	2	0	0	0
United Presbyterian Church in the USA Program Agency	1856	11	1	0	0
Victory Mission of the Americas	1964	1	1	1	1
We Go, Inc. (World Encounter Gospel Organization)	1974	1	0	15	6
WEFMinistries, Inc.	1979	2	0	0	0
Wesleyan Church Gen. Dept. of Wld. Msns.	1941	10	2	17	0
Wisconsin Evangelical Lutheran Synod, Bd. for Wld. Msns.	1974	5	4	5	0
Word of Life Fellowship	1980	4	4	0	0
World Baptist Fellowship Mission Agency International	1968	8	2	3	0
World Concern/Crista International	1978	1	1	0	0
World Literature Crusade	1975	0	0	0	0
World Mission in Church and Society	1963	1	0	0	0
World Vision International	1960	2	1	0	0
World-Wide Missions International	1964	0	0	1	0
Worldwide Evangelization Crusade	1933	8	0	31	3
Wycliffe Bible Translators International, Inc.	1962	185	0	0	36
Youth With A Mission	1974	0	0	0	0
	TOTALS	1043	139	1857	68

Comoro

ORGANIZATION NAME	BEGAN	NOW	NEW	CHURCHES	GROUPS
Africa Inland Mission (Canada)	1975	9	6	0	0
Africa Inland Mission	1975	0	0	0	0
American Leprosy Missions, Inc.	1978	0	0	0	0
	TOTALS	9	6	0	0

ORGANIZATION NAME	BEGAN	NOW	NEW	CHURCHES	GROUPS
Congo					
Global Outreach Mission	1974	2	0	0	0
Leprosy Relief, Canada, Inc.	1976	0	0	0	0
United World Mission, Incorporated	1948	3	1	12	2
TOTALS		5	1	12	2
Costa Rica					
American Baptist Association, Missionary Committee	1940	7	2	12	0
Assemblies of God, Div. of For. Msns.	1942	12	0	100	0
Baptist Bible Fellowship International	1968	13	0	0	0
Baptist International Missions, Inc.	1968	14	0	0	0
Baptist Missionary Association of America	1961	2	0	0	0
Baptist World Mission	0	1	0	0	0
Brethren Assemblies	0	6	0	0	0
Campus Crusade for Christ, International (Overseas Dept.)	1976	10	0	0	0
Child Evangelism Fellowship, Inc.	1957	2	0	0	0
Christian and Missionary Alliance	1975	0	0	4	0
Christian Broadcasting Network	0	3	0	0	0
Christian Churches/Churches of Christ	1967	2	0	0	0
Christian Reformed World Relief Committee	1975	0	0	0	0
Church of God (Anderson, Indiana) Msny. Bd.	1920	0	2	5	0
Church of God of Prophecy, World Mission Committee	1932	2	0	7	0
Church of God World Missions	1950	2	0	50	0
Church of the Nazarene, Gen. Bd. Dept. of Wld. Msns.	1948	14	0	10	0
Congregational Holiness Church Foreign Mission Dept.	1966	0	0	10	0
Conservative Baptist Association of America	1967	2	2	6	0
Conservative Mennonite Board of Missions and Charities	1962	11	7	12	1
Elim Fellowship, Inc.	1966	8	4	20	0
FARMS International, Inc.	1967	2	1	0	0
General Conference Mennonite Church, Comm. on Oseas. Msn.	1977	2	0	0	0
General Conference of Seventh-day Adventists	1903	2	0	49	0
Intl. Church of the Foursquare Gospel--Dept. of Msns. Intl.	1954	4	1	73	0
International Students, Inc.	0	0	0	0	0

Costa Rica continued...

ORGANIZATION NAME	BEGAN	NOW	NEW	CHURCHES	GROUPS
Latin America Mission, Inc.	1921	92	10	0	0
Lutheran Church-Missouri Synod	1964	0	0	0	0
MAP International (Medical Assistance Programs)	0	0	0	0	0
Media Ministries Division, Mennonite Bd. of Msns.	1950	0	0	7	0
Mennonite Economic Development Associates	1970	0	0	0	0
Mission Aviation Fellowship	1978	4	0	0	0
Navigators, The	1957	0	0	0	0
Pan American Missionary Society, Inc.	1961	2	0	0	0
Pentecostal Free Will Baptist Church, Inc.	1978	1	1	0	0
Pentecostal Holiness Church-World Missions Department	1930	2	2	26	0
Southern Baptist Convention, Foreign Mission Board	1949	20	0	26	0
Trans World Missions	1968	0	0	0	0
United Church Board For World Ministries	1974	4	2	0	0
United Pentecostal Church Intl. For. Msns. Div.	1975	2	0	0	0
United Presbyterian Church in the USA Program Agency	0	4	2	2	0
World Baptist Fellowship Mission Agency International	1963	2	0	0	0
World Concern/Crista International	1976	0	1	0	0
World Missionary Assistance Plan	0	2	2	0	0
World-Wide Missions International	1965	0	0	0	0
Young Life	1976	0	0	0	0
Youth For Christ/U.S.A.	0	4	0	0	0
TOTALS		260	39	419	1

Cuba

ORGANIZATION NAME	BEGAN	NOW	NEW	CHURCHES	GROUPS
Assemblies of God, Div. of For. Msns.	1920	0	0	115	0
Bible Club Movement, Inc.	1947	0	0	0	0
Church of God of Prophecy, World Mission Committee	1935	0	0	4	0
Church of God World Missions	1944	0	0	9	0
Church of the Nazarene, Gen. Bd. Dept. of Wld. Msns.	1902	0	0	10	0
Congregational Holiness, Church Foreign Mission Dept.	1955	0	0	7	0
Lutheran Church-Missouri Synod	1947	0	0	1	0
Open Bible Standard Missions, Inc.	0	0	0	11	0

ORGANIZATION NAME	BEGAN	NOW	NEW	CHURCHES	GROUPS
Cuba continued...					
Pentecostal Church of God, World Missions Department	1957	0	0	7	0
Pentecostal Holiness Church-World Missions Department	1952	0	0	13	0
United World Mission, Incorporated	1946	0	0	10	0
Wider Ministries Commission	1902	0	0	5	0
Worldteam	1928	2	0	61	1
	TOTALS	2	0	253	1

Cyprus

ORGANIZATION NAME	BEGAN	NOW	NEW	CHURCHES	GROUPS
AMG International (Advancing the Ministries of the Gospel)	1965	4	0	5	0
Campus Crusade for Christ, International (Overseas Dept.)	1978	20	0	0	0
Church of God of Prophecy, World Mission Committee	1935	0	0	1	0
General Conference of Seventh-day Adventists	1932	14	5	0	0
Middle East Christian Outreach--USA Council	0	0	0	0	0
Missionary Church, Div. of Overseas Ministries	0	2	0	0	0
Open Doors With Brother Andrew	0	0	0	0	0
Operation Mobilization - Canada	0	0	0	0	0
Trans World Radio	1974	0	0	0	0
United Church Board For World Ministries	1974	0	0	0	0
United Missionary Fellowship	1971	2	0	1	0
Youth With A Mission	1973	0	0	0	0
	TOTALS	42	5	7	0

Czechoslovakia

ORGANIZATION NAME	BEGAN	NOW	NEW	CHURCHES	GROUPS
Assemblies of God, Div. of For. Msns.	1968	0	0	92	0
Living Bibles International	1972	2	0	0	1
Mission to Europe's Millions, Inc.	0	0	0	0	0
	TOTALS	2	0	92	1

Denmark

ORGANIZATION NAME	BEGAN	NOW	NEW	CHURCHES	GROUPS
Bethany Missionary Association	1965	2	0	1	0

ORGANIZATION NAME	BEGAN	NOW	NEW	CHURCHES	GROUPS
Denmark continued...					
Campus Crusade for Christ, International (Overseas Dept.)	1973	3	0	0	0
Child Evangelism Fellowship, Inc.	1947	1	0	0	0
Church of the Nazarene, Gen. Bd. Dept. of Wld. Msns.	1959	0	2	2	0
Greater Europe Mission	1976	2	2	0	0
Jesus to the Communist World, Inc.	0	0	0	0	0
Living Bibles International	1975	2	0	0	1
Mission to Europe's Millions, Inc.	0	0	0	0	0
Navigators, The	1957	0	0	0	0
Youth With A Mission	1970	0	0	0	0
TOTALS		10	2	3	1
Djibouti					
Red Sea Mission Team, Inc., U.S.A. Council	1975	0	0	0	3
TOTALS		0	0	0	3
Dominica					
Berean Mission, Inc.	1971	4	0	2	0
Christian Literature Crusade, Inc.	1947	0	0	0	0
Churches of Christ in Christian Union: Foreign Msny. Dept.	1943	4	2	16	0
Emmanuel International	1979	2	0	0	0
Maranatha Baptist Mission, Inc.	0	0	0	2	0
Southern Baptist Convention, Foreign Mission Board	1975	5	3	2	0
TOTALS		15	5	22	0
Dominican Republic					
African Methodist Episcopal Church, Inc. Dept. of Msns.	0	0	0	0	0
Assemblies of God, Div. of For. Msns.	1933	6	0	238	0
Baptist International Missions, Inc.	1969	2	0	0	0
Baptist Mid-Missions	1950	14	0	0	0
Bethany Fellowship Msns. (Div. of Bethany Fellowship, Inc.)	1978	2	2	0	0

Dominican Republic continued...

ORGANIZATION NAME	BEGAN	NOW	NEW	CHURCHES	GROUPS
Brethren Assemblies	0	18	0	0	0
Campus Crusade for Christ, International (Overseas Dept.)	1977	15	0	0	0
Child Evangelism Fellowship, Inc.	1958	6	4	0	0
Christian and Missionary Alliance	1969	0	0	31	1
Christian Broadcasting Network	0	0	0	0	0
Christian Churches/Churches of Christ	0	9	0	0	0
Christian Medical Society	1960	2	1	0	0
Church of God in Christ, Mennonite Gen. Msn. Bd., Inc.	1976	4	0	0	0
Church of God of Prophecy, World Mission Committee	1940	0	0	79	0
Church of God World Missions	1944	0	0	136	0
Church of the Nazarene, Gen. Bd. Dept. of Wld. Msns.	1975	8	0	23	0
Church World Service Division of DOM-NCCUSA	0	3	0	0	0
Compassion International, Inc.	1970	4	3	0	0
Evangelical Mennonite Church, Comm. on Oseas. Msns.	1946	10	5	30	0
Free Methodist Church of N. America Gen. Msny. Bd.	1889	3	0	55	0
Leprosy Relief, Canada, Inc.	1979	0	0	0	0
Lutheran World Relief, Incorporated	1979	0	0	0	0
MAP International (Medical Assistance Programs)	0	0	0	0	0
Media Ministries Division, Mennonite Bd. of Msns.	1950	0	0	25	0
Missionary Church, Div. of Overseas Ministries	1945	16	6	87	0
Moravian Church in America, Bd. of Wld. Msn.	1907	0	0	25	0
Southern Baptist Convention, Foreign Mission Board	1962	25	1	9	0
Unevangelized Fields Mission	1943	17	4	0	0
United Pentecostal Church Intl. For. Msns. Div.	1962	2	0	0	0
World Mission in Church and Society	1940	3	2	0	0
Worldteam	1939	9	0	34	2
TOTALS		178	28	772	3

Ecuador

ORGANIZATION NAME	BEGAN	NOW	NEW	CHURCHES	GROUPS
Anglican Church of Canada, Natl. and Wld. Program	1979	2	0	0	0
Assemblies of God, Div. of For. Msns.	1962	17	0	27	0
Back to the Bible Missionary Agency	1970	0	0	0	0

Ecuador   continued...

ORGANIZATION NAME	BEGAN	NOW	NEW	NEW CHURCHES	GROUPS
Baptist Bible Fellowship International	1975	8	0	0	0
Berean Mission, Inc.	1959	13	7	39	0
Bible Memory Association International	1974	2	0	0	0
Brethren Assemblies	0	21	0	0	0
Campus Crusade for Christ, International (Overseas Dept.)	1965	17	0	0	0
Child Evangelism Fellowship, Inc.	1952	2	0	0	0
Christian and Missionary Alliance	1897	76	29	162	0
Christian Churches/Churches of Christ	1962	5	0	0	0
Christian Service Corps	1973	1	0	0	0
Christians In Action	1976	5	5	2	0
Church of God World Missions	1972	0	0	10	0
Church of the Nazarene, Gen. Bd. Dept. of Wld. Msns.	1972	9	0	6	0
Church World Service Division of DOM-NCCCUSA	0	1	0	0	0
Compassion International, Inc.	1975	0	0	0	0
Evangelical Covenant Church of America, Bd. of Wld. Msn.	1947	11	0	0	0
Fellowship of Independent Missions	1967	0	0	0	0
General Conference of Seventh-day Adventists	1905	2	0	20	0
Gospel Missionary Union	1896	72	8	177	2
Intl. Church of the Foursquare Gospel--Dept. of Msns. Intl.	1956	4	0	73	0
International Students, Inc.	0	0	0	0	0
Jesus to the Communist World, Inc.	1975	2	0	0	0
Latin America Mission, Inc.	1965	1	0	0	0
Luis Palau Evangelistic Team, Inc.	1978	2	2	1	1
Lutheran Frontier Missions	0	0	0	0	0
MAP International (Medical Assistance Programs)	1953	5	1	0	0
Mennonite Brethren Missions/Services	1948	10	6	0	2
Mission Aviation Fellowship	1975	14	14	0	0
Mission to the World	1945	21	12	25	2
Missionary Church, Div. of Overseas Ministries	1959	1	1	0	11
Missionary Dentist, Inc.	1952	40	26	10	2
OMS International, Inc.	1946	6	2	0	0
Presbyterian Church in the U.S.A., Div. of Intl. Msn.	1940	6	0	0	0
Slavic Gospel Association					

Ecuador continued...

ORGANIZATION NAME	BEGAN	NOW	NEW	CHURCHES	GROUPS
Southern Baptist Convention, Foreign Mission Board	1950	38	8	53	0
Technical Support Mission	1980	2	2	0	0
Tele-Missions International, Inc.	1978	2	2	25	65
United Church Board For World Ministries	1945	0	0	0	0
United Methodist Ch. Wld. Div. of the Bd. of Global Min.		0	0	0	0
United Pentecostal Church Intl. For. Msns. Div.	1959	5	0	0	0
Word of Life Fellowship	1972	4	2	0	0
World Baptist Fellowship Mission Agency International	1972	8	0	4	0
World Literature Crusade	1975	0	0	0	0
World Mission in Church and Society	1963	1	0	0	0
World Mission Prayer League	1951	22	7	0	0
World Mission Prayer League Canada	0	3	3	0	0
World Radio Missionary Fellowship, Inc.	1931	280	80	15	0
World Vision International	0	1	1	0	0
Wycliffe Bible Translators International, Inc.	1953	74	0	0	12
TOTALS		816	218	649	97

Egypt

ORGANIZATION NAME	BEGAN	NOW	NEW	CHURCHES	GROUPS
American Lutheran Ch., Div. For Wld. Msn.	1979	1	0	0	0
AMG International (Advancing the Ministries of the Gospel)	1978	0	0	1	0
Assemblies of God, Div. of For. Msns.	1910	4	0	144	0
Baptist Bible Fellowship International	1974	2	0	0	0
Campus Crusade for Christ, International (Overseas Dept.)	1971	9	0	0	0
Child Evangelism Fellowship, Inc.	1971	0	0	0	0
Church of God (Anderson, Indiana) Msny. Bd.	1908	2	2	12	0
Church of God of Prophecy, World Mission Committee	1935	0	0	11	0
Church of God World Missions	1946	0	0	23	0
Evangelistic Faith Mission, Inc.	1905	0	0	0	0
Free Methodist Church of N. America Gen. Msny. Bd.	1899	3	0	120	0
General Conference of Seventh-day Adventists	1879	2	0	14	0
Global Outreach Mission	1974	8	0	0	0
Harvest Fields Missionary and Evangelistic Assn., Inc.	0	2	0	1	1

Egypt continued...

ORGANIZATION NAME	BEGAN	NOW	NEW	CHURCHES	GROUPS
International Students, Inc.	1979	0	0	0	0
Leprosy Relief, Canada, Inc.		0	0	0	0
Lutheran Orient Mission Society		2	0	0	0
MAP International (Medical Assistance Programs)	1968	11	0	0	0
Mennonite Central Committee		4	0	0	0
Middle East Christian Outreach--USA Council	1976	4	4	0	0
Middle East Media	1975	3	0	0	0
Navigators, The		0	0	0	0
Operation Mobilization - Canada		4	4	0	0
Orthodox Presbyterian Church Committee on Foreign Missions	1975	1	0	1	1
Pentecostal Assemblies of the World, Inc. For. Msns. Dept.		2	0	0	0
Reformed Church in America General Program Council	1972	0	0	0	0
United Pentecostal Church Intl. For. Msns. Div.	1954	9	4	0	0
United Presbyterian Church in the USA Program Agency	1957	1	1	0	0
World Gospel Mission	1960	0	0	10	0
World-Wide Missions International		0	0	0	0
TOTALS		70	15	337	2

El Salvador

ORGANIZATION NAME	BEGAN	NOW	NEW	CHURCHES	GROUPS
All Peoples Baptist Mission	1911	6	4	1	0
American Baptist Churches in the U.S.A., Intl. Min.	1979	5	2	44	0
Apostolic Church of Pentecost of Canada-Missionary Dept.	1929	2	2	0	0
Assemblies of God, Div. of For. Msns.		8	0	535	0
Baptist Bible Fellowship International	1976	6	0	0	0
Baptist International Missions, Inc.	1970	4	0	0	0
Brethren Assemblies		7	0	0	0
California Yearly Meeting of Friends Church, Bd. of Msns.	1902	4	2	6	0
CAM International	1896	20	0	116	1
Campus Crusade for Christ, International (Overseas Dept.)	1966	6	6	0	0
Christian Reformed Board For World Missions	1978	6	0	0	0
Church of God of Prophecy, World Mission Committee	1954	0	0	38	0
Church of God World Missions	1944	4	0	200	0

El Salvador continued...

ORGANIZATION NAME	BEGAN	NOW	NEW	CHURCHES	GROUPS
Church of the Nazarene, Gen. Bd. Dept. of Wld. Msns.	1964	2	0	7	0
Compassion International, Inc.	1976	2	2	0	0
Evangelistic Faith Mission, Inc.	1964	0	0	0	0
Food For The Hungry International	1979	2	0	0	0
Intl. Church of the Foursquare Gospel--Dept. of Msns. Intl.	1973	2	0	5	0
Lutheran Church-Missouri Synod	1952	0	0	14	0
Lutheran World Relief, Incorporated	1975	2	2	0	0
Mission to the World	1978	2	2	0	0
Open Bible Standard Missions, Inc.	1975	2	2	7	0
Southern Baptist Convention, Foreign Mission Board	1975	6	4	41	0
Technoserve, Inc.	1975	0	0	0	0
United Pentecostal Church Intl. For. Msns. Div.	1975	2	0	0	0
World Mission in Church and Society	1956	2	2	0	0
World Vision International	1975	0	0	0	0
World-Wide Missions International	1955	0	0	20	0
TOTALS		92	28	1034	1

Ethiopia

ORGANIZATION NAME	BEGAN	NOW	NEW	CHURCHES	GROUPS
American Leprosy Missions, Inc.	1965	2	0	0	0
American Lutheran Ch., Div. For Wld. Msn.	1957	2	0	1	0
Assemblies of God, Div. of For. Msns.	1975	0	0	0	0
Baptist Bible Fellowship International	1960	26	0	0	0
Baptist General Conference Board of World Missions	1950	13	0	29	0
Eastern Mennonite Board of Missions and Charities	1948	7	3	14	0
Emmanuel International	1975	0	0	0	0
Evangelistic Faith Mission, Inc.	1950	0	0	0	0
General Conference of Seventh-day Adventists	1907	13	11	87	0
Leprosy Relief, Canada, Inc.	1979	0	0	0	0
Lutheran World Relief, Incorporated	1963	0	0	0	0
Mennonite Central Committee	1962	2	0	0	0
Mennonite Economic Development Associates	1969	0	0	0	0
Middle East Christian Outreach--USA Council	1956	0	0	0	0

ORGANIZATION NAME	BEGAN	NOW	NEW	CHURCHES	GROUPS
Ethiopia continued...					
Reformed Church in America General Program Council	1963	2	0	0	0
Southern Baptist Convention, Foreign Mission Board	1967	8	0	0	0
Sudan Interior Mission, Inc.	1927	36	27	2400	10
United Pentecostal Church Intl. For. Msns. Div.	1967	0	0	0	0
United Presbyterian Church in the USA Program Agency	1820	12	0	0	0
World Vision International	1975	0	0	0	0
TOTALS		123	41	2531	10

Europe-general

ORGANIZATION NAME	BEGAN	NOW	NEW	CHURCHES	GROUPS
American Baptist Churches in the U.S.A., Intl. Min.	1832	8	0	0	0
Evangelical Alliance Mission (TEAM)	1960	4	0	1	1
Greater Europe Mission	1973	4	2	0	0
New Life International	1979	0	0	0	0
Pentecostal Assemblies of Canada, Oseas. Msns. Dept.	1976	1	0	0	0
TOTALS		17	2	1	1

Fiji

ORGANIZATION NAME	BEGAN	NOW	NEW	CHURCHES	GROUPS
Anglican Church of Canada, Natl. and Wld. Program	1964	0	0	0	0
Anglican Orthodox Church	1974	0	0	0	0
Assemblies of God, Div. of For. Msns.	1926	6	0	105	0
Campus Crusade for Christ, International (Overseas Dept.)	1974	12	0	0	0
Christian Nationals' Evangelism Commission, Inc. (CNEC)	1974	0	0	0	0
Christian Nationals' Evangelism Commission, Inc. (Canada)	1974	0	0	0	0
Jesus to the Communist World, Inc.	0	0	0	0	0
Presbyterian Church in the U.S.A., Div. of Intl. Msn.	1974	2	4	0	0
South Pacific Evangelical Fellowship	0	6	4	2	0
United Methodist Ch. Wld. Div. of the Bd. of Global Min.	0	0	0	0	0
United Pentecostal Church Intl. For. Msns. Div.	0	4	0	0	0
Youth With A Mission	1979	0	0	0	0
TOTALS		30	4	107	0

Finland

ORGANIZATION NAME	BEGAN	NOW	NEW	CHURCHES	GROUPS
Baptist Mid-Missions	0	2	0	0	0
Campus Crusade for Christ, International (Overseas Dept.)	1967	28	0	0	0
Child Evangelism Fellowship, Inc.	1966	4	2	0	0
Jesus to the Communist World, Inc.	0	0	0	0	0
Living Bibles International	1973	2	0	0	1
Lutheran Church in America-Div. for Wld. Msn. and Ecumenism	1978	1	1	0	0
Navigators, The	1970	2	0	0	0
Operation Mobilization - Canada	1970	4	0	30	0
Operation Mobilization Send the Light, Inc.	0	0	0	0	0
Youth With A Mission	1971	0	0	0	0
TOTALS		43	3	30	1

France

ORGANIZATION NAME	BEGAN	NOW	NEW	CHURCHES	GROUPS
America's Keswick, Inc.	1973	2	0	0	0
American Baptist Association, Missionary Committee	1935	1	0	1	0
American Board of Missions to the Jews, Inc.	1883	1	0	0	0
American Mc All Association	0	0	0	12	0
Assemblies of God, Div. of For. Msns.	1964	8	0	999	0
Baptist Bible Fellowship International	1970	12	0	0	0
Baptist International Missions, Inc.	1969	12	0	0	0
Baptist Mid-Missions	1948	32	0	0	0
Baptist World Mission	1969	0	0	0	0
Berean Mission, Inc.	1969	2	0	0	0
Bible Christian Union, Inc.	1979	28	0	0	1
Brethren Assemblies	1938	21	10	7	0
Campus Crusade for Christ, International (Overseas Dept.)	1970	24	0	0	0
Child Evangelism Fellowship, Inc.	1949	12	4	0	0
Christian and Missionary Alliance	0	9	4	8	0
Christian Church of North America, Msns. Dept.	0	0	0	8	0
Christian Literature Crusade, Inc.	1952	0	0	0	0
Christian Nationals' Evangelism Commission, Inc. (CNEC)	1980	2	2	0	0
Christian Nationals' Evangelism Commission, Inc. (Canada)	1980	0	0	0	0

France continued...

ORGANIZATION NAME	BEGAN	NOW	NEW	CHURCHES	GROUPS
Christians United in Action, Inc.	1960	2	0	0	0
Church of God World Missions	0	0	0	7	0
Church of the Nazarene, Gen. Bd. Dept. of Wld. Msns.	1962	4	2	5	3
Conservative Baptist Foreign Mission Society	1955	12	2	2	0
Eastern Mennonite Board of Missions and Charities	1978	2	0	0	0
Evangel Bible Translators	1953	2	9	1	2
Evangelical Alliance Mission (TEAM)	1952	37	4	15	1
Evangelical Alliance Mission of Canada, Inc.	1956	4	8	7	0
Evangelical Baptist Missions, Inc.	1971	22	2	7	1
Evangelical Christian Education Ministries Inc.	1978	2	2	1	0
Fellowship of Evangelical Baptist Chs. in Canada	1951	2	7	2	2
Fellowship of Grace Brethren Churches, For. Msny. Soc.	1970	11	0	0	0
Fellowship of Independent Missions	1946	10	0	0	0
Global Outreach Mission	1978	47	0	0	0
Globe Missionary Evangelism	1960	2	2	0	0
Gospel Missionary Union	1965	13	4	7	0
Gospel Recordings Incorporated	1949	0	0	0	0
Greater Europe Mission	0	47	15	4	0
H.O.P.E. Bible Mission, Inc.	0	0	0	0	0
Heritage Village Church and Missionary Fellowship, Inc.	1969	0	0	1	0
Independent Faith Mission, Inc.	0	4	8	0	1
International Crusades, Inc.	1973	8	0	7	0
Jesus to the Communist World, Inc.	1953	0	0	0	0
Living Bibles International	1946	2	2	3	0
Mennonite Board of Missions	1973	6	0	0	1
Mennonite Central Committee	1979	1	0	0	1
Mission to Europe's Millions, Inc.	1966	2	0	7	1
Mission to the World	1972	11	9	0	0
Missionary Church, Div. of Overseas Ministries	1963	2	2	0	1
National Association of Free Will Baptists, Bd. of For. Msns	1979	12	3	3	0
Navigators, The		3	1	0	0
North Africa Mission		45	19	0	2
O.C. Ministries, Inc.		2	2	0	0

France continued...

ORGANIZATION NAME	BEGAN	NOW	NEW	CHURCHES	GROUPS
Operation Mobilization - Canada	1962	39	0	0	0
Operation Mobilization Send the Light, Inc.	1961	25	0	0	0
Overseas Missionary Fellowship	1979	2	2	0	0
Reformed Episcopal Church Bd. of For. Msns.	1964	4	0	0	0
Slavic Gospel Association	1961	1	0	0	0
Society for Europe's Evangelization (S.E.E.)	1954	37	21	4	4
Southern Baptist Convention, Foreign Mission Board	1960	15	1	52	0
Southern European Mission, Inc.	0	0	0	0	0
The Navigators of Canada International	1972	1	1	0	0
Unevangelized Fields Mission	1962	40	13	0	0
United Church Board For World Ministries	1946	0	0	0	0
United Methodist Ch. Wld. Div. of the Bd. of Global Min.	0	0	0	0	0
United Pentecostal Church Intl. For. Msns. Div.	1973	2	0	0	0
WEFMinistries, Inc.	1959	4	0	0	0
Word of Life Fellowship	1978	2	2	0	0
World Baptist Fellowship Mission Agency International	1954	2	0	1	0
World Literature Crusade	1963	0	0	0	0
Worldteam	1979	2	0	1	1
Worldwide Evangelization Crusade	1950	0	0	3	1
Wycliffe Bible Translators International, Inc.	1975	2	0	0	1
Young Life	1952	0	0	0	0
Youth For Christ/U.S.A.	1949	1	0	0	0
Youth With A Mission	1972	0	0	0	0
TOTALS		652	157	1150	19

French Guiana

ORGANIZATION NAME	BEGAN	NOW	NEW	CHURCHES	GROUPS
Brethren Assemblies	1972	2	0	0	0
Christian Literature Crusade, Inc.		0	0	0	0
TOTALS		2	0	0	0

ORGANIZATION NAME	BEGAN	NOW	NEW	CHURCHES	GROUPS
French Polynesia					
Assemblies of God, Div. of For. Msns.	1977	4	0	0	0
Baptist Bible Fellowship International		2	0	0	0
TOTALS		6	0	0	0
Gabon					
Christian and Missionary Alliance	1934	42	10	124	0
Christian Mission for the Deaf	1980	0	0	0	0
TOTALS		42	10	124	0
Gambia					
Anglican Church of Canada, Natl. and Wld. Program	1976	1	0	0	0
Christian Service Corps	0	1	0	0	0
General Conference of Seventh-day Adventists	1978	4	4	1	0
Worldwide Evangelization Crusade	1957	10	7	2	3
TOTALS		16	11	3	3
Germany, Dem. Rep.					
Jews For Jesus	1979	0	0	0	0
Mission to Europe's Millions, Inc.	0	0	0	0	0
TOTALS		0	0	0	0
Germany, Fed. Rep.					
All Peoples Baptist Mission	0	0	0	0	0
America's Keswick, Inc.	0	4	0	0	0
American Baptist Association, Missionary Committee	1957	1	0	2	0
American Lutheran Ch., Div. For Wld. Msn.	1972	15	6	0	0
Assemblies of God, Div. of For. Msns.	1948	27	0	146	0
Baptist Bible Fellowship International	1970	16	0	0	0
Baptist International Missions, Inc.	1969	16	0	0	0

Gilbert Islands

ORGANIZATION NAME	BEGAN	NOW	NEW	CHURCHES	GROUPS
Campus Crusade for Christ, International (Overseas Dept.)	1974	0	0	0	0
Church of God World Missions	1956	2	2	18	0
TOTALS		2	2	18	0

Greece

ORGANIZATION NAME	BEGAN	NOW	NEW	CHURCHES	GROUPS
American Board of Missions to the Jews, Inc.	1969	1	0	0	0
American European Bethel Mission, Inc.	1963	1	0	0	0
AMG International (Advancing the Ministries of the Gospel)	1946	2	0	30	0
Assemblies of God, Div. of For. Msns.	1931	5	0	11	0
Baptist International Missions, Inc.	0	1	0	0	0
Bible Christian Union, Inc.	1968	3	0	2	0
Campus Crusade for Christ, International (Overseas Dept.)	1978	5	0	0	1
Child Evangelism Fellowship, Inc.	1967	1	1	0	0
Church of God of Prophecy, World Mission Committee	1931	0	0	1	0
Church of God World Missions	1964	2	2	2	0
Eastern European Mission	1953	5	0	1	0
General Conference of Seventh-day Adventists	1907	7	3	10	0
Global Outreach Mission	1960	3	0	0	0
Gospel Missionary Union	1959	3	0	13	0
Greater Europe Mission	1966	8	2	0	0
Intl. Church of the Foursquare Gospel--Dept. of Msns. Intl.	0	2	0	7	0
International Gospel League	1975	0	0	0	0
Jesus to the Communist World, Inc.	0	2	0	0	0
Living Bibles International	1977	1	0	0	1
Mission to Europe's Millions, Inc.	0	2	1	2	0
Mission to the World	1978	0	2	0	0
Natl. Assn. of Congregational Chr. Chs. of the U.S.A.	1961	3	1	0	0
O.C. Ministries, Inc.	1966	4	2	3	0
OMS International, Inc.	1947	2	0	1	0
Southern Baptist Convention, Foreign Mission Board	1972	2	0	0	0
United Pentecostal Church Intl. For. Msns. Div.	1975	0	0	0	0
TOTALS		65	14	83	2

Germany, Fed. Rep. continued...

ORGANIZATION NAME	BEGAN	NOW	NEW	CHURCHES	GROUPS
Baptist Mid-Missions	1959	17	0	0	0
Baptist World Mission	1969	0	0	0	0
Bible Christian Union, Inc.	1910	11	1	0	5
Bible Club Movement, Inc.	1952	0	0	0	0
Bible Memory Association International	1971	2	0	0	0
Brethren Assemblies	0	12	0	0	0
Campus Crusade for Christ, International (Overseas Dept.)	1966	99	0	0	0
Child Evangelism Fellowship, Inc.	1948	5	4	0	0
Christian and Missionary Alliance	1970	4	4	2	0
Christian Church of North America, Msns. Dept.	0	0	0	0	0
Christian Churches/Churches of Christ	0	14	0	0	0
Christian Literature Crusade, Inc.	1948	0	0	0	0
Christians In Action	1976	6	4	2	1
Church of God (Seventh Day), Gen. Conf., Msns. Abroad	1961	0	0	0	0
Church of God of Prophecy, World Mission Committee	1959	2	0	2	0
Church of God World Missions	1944	4	0	54	0
Church of the Nazarene, Gen. Bd. Dept. of Wld. Msns.	1958	0	0	14	0
Church World Service Division of DOM-NCCUSA	0	1	0	0	0
Conservative Mennonite Board of Missions and Charities	1952	6	3	0	0
Eastern European Mission	1951	2	1	0	1
Eastern Mennonite Board of Missions and Charities	1957	3	2	8	0
Elim Fellowship, Inc.	1973	2	0	0	0
European Evangelistic Society	1949	2	0	1	0
Evangelical Baptist Missions, Inc.	1977	2	2	0	0
Evangelical Mennonite Conference Board of Missions	1975	4	2	1	2
Fellowship of Grace Brethren Churches, For. Msny. Soc.	1969	7	5	0	0
General Conference of Seventh-day Adventists	1875	2	0	392	0
Global Outreach Mission	1946	8	0	0	0
Go-Ye Fellowship	1976	2	0	0	0
Gospel Missionary Union	1961	6	2	1	0
Gospel Outreach	1973	14	20	1	0
Gospel Recordings Incorporated	1965	2	0	0	0
Greater Europe Mission	1954	41	8	0	0

Germany, Fed. Rep. continued...

ORGANIZATION NAME	BEGAN	NOW	NEW	CHURCHES	GROUPS
H.O.P.E. Bible Mission, Inc.	0	0	0	0	0
International Fellowship of Evangelical Students - USA	1972	1	0	0	0
International Films, Inc.	1954	73	0	0	0
Janz Team	0	0	0	0	0
Jesus to the Communist World, Inc.	1979	0	0	0	0
Jews For Jesus	1977	2	0	1	1
Korea International Mission, Inc.	1970	2	0	0	1
Living Bibles International	1975	5	4	0	0
Lutheran Church in America-Div. for Wld. Msn. and Ecumenism	1953	8	11	5	0
Mennonite Brethren Missions/Services	1946	14	0	0	0
Mennonite Central Committee	1977	2	2	0	0
Mission SOS		2	2	0	0
Mission to Europe's Millions, Inc.	1958	0	0	0	0
Natl. Assn. of Congregational Chr. Chs. of the U.S.A.	1951	10	2	0	0
Navigators, The	1979	0	1	30	1
New Life International	1963	4	0	0	1
Open Air Campaigners (USA)	1962	27	0	100	0
Operation Mobilization - Canada	0	0	0	0	0
Operation Mobilization Send the Light, Inc.	1972	19	14	0	0
Overseas Christian Servicemen's Centers	1960	4	0	0	0
Pocket Testament League, Inc.	1953	5	0	0	0
Reformed Episcopal Church Bd. of For. Msns.	1953	0	0	0	0
Refugee Children, Inc.	1943	4	0	0	0
Slavic Gospel Association	1961	9	4	23	0
Southern Baptist Convention, Foreign Mission Board	1976	2	2	0	0
Unevangelized Fields Mission	1945	0	0	0	0
United Church Board For World Ministries	1966	8	0	0	0
United Pentecostal Church Intl For. Msns. Div.	0	1	1	0	0
United Presbyterian Church in the USA Program Agency	1959	28	7	0	0
WEFMinistries, Inc.	1970	10	2	0	0
Word of Life Fellowship	1961	4	0	2	0
World Baptist Fellowship Mission Agency International	1963	0	0	2	0
World Literature Crusade		0	0	0	0

ORGANIZATION NAME	BEGAN	NOW	NEW	CHURCHES	GROUPS
Germany, Fed. Rep. continued...					
World Ministries Commission	1973	2	0	0	0
World Missions, Inc.	1975	3	0	0	0
World Vision International	1960	1	0	0	0
World-Wide Missions International	1953	2	0	0	0
Worldwide Evangelization Crusade	1977	1	0	0	1
Wycliffe Bible Translators International, Inc.	1975	4	0	0	2
Young Life	1975	0	0	0	0
Youth With A Mission	1971	0	0	0	0
TOTALS		616	110	788	14
Ghana					
African Methodist Episcopal Church, Inc. Dept. of Msns.	1896	0	0	0	0
African Methodist Episcopal Zion Ch., Dept. of Oseas. Msns.	1967	1	0	0	0
Anglican Church of Canada, Natl. and Wld. Program	1972	1	1	0	0
Apostolic Christian Church (Nazarene), Apos. Chr. Ch. Found.	1979	0	1	5	0
Apostolic Church of Pentecost of Canada-Missionary Dept.	1979	2	2	0	0
Assemblies of God, Div. of For. Msns.	1931	30	0	230	0
Baptist International Missions, Inc.	1974	12	0	0	0
Baptist Mid-Missions	1946	23	0	0	0
Bible Holiness Movement	1952	2	0	2	0
Bible Translations On Tape, Inc.	1979	2	2	0	0
Campus Crusade for Christ, International (Overseas Dept.)	1966	4	0	0	0
Child Evangelism Fellowship, Inc.	1970	1	0	0	0
Christian Aid Mission	1953	0	0	100	14
Christian Church of North America, Msns. Dept.	0	0	0	0	0
Christian Churches/Churches of Christ	0	3	0	0	0
Christian Mission for the Deaf	1957	0	0	0	0
Christian Nationals' Evangelism Commission, Inc. (CNEC)	1973	0	0	0	0
Christian Nationals' Evangelism Commission, Inc. (Canada)	1973	0	0	0	0
Church of God General Conference Mission Department	1970	1	0	4	0
Church of God World Missions	1966	2	0	16	0
General Conference of Seventh-day Adventists	1894	8	6	216	0

Ghana continued...

ORGANIZATION NAME	BEGAN	NOW	NEW	CHURCHES	GROUPS
Global Outreach Mission	1974	2	0	0	0
International Gospel League	1968	0	0	0	0
Jesus to the Communist World, Inc.	0	0	0	0	7
Living Bibles International	1973	17	1	0	1
Lutheran Church-Missouri Synod	1961	5	1	19	0
MAP International (Medical Assistance Programs)	0	0	0	0	0
Mennonite Board of Missions	1957	6	2	16	0
Mennonite Economic Development Associates	1974	0	0	0	0
Natl. Baptist Convention of Amer., For. Msn. Bd.	1980	1	1	15	0
National Baptist Convention, U.S.A., Inc. For. Msn. Bd.	1950	0	0	3	0
Navigators, The	1974	7	1	0	0
Open Bible Standard Missions, Inc.	1971	1	0	7	0
Pentecostal Assemblies of the World, Inc. For. Msns. Dept.	0	1	0	0	0
Salvation Army, Canada and Bermuda	1922	1	0	0	0
Southern Baptist Convention, Foreign Mission Board	1947	54	3	88	5
Sudan Interior Mission, Inc.	1956	16	5	0	5
Technoserve, Inc.	1969	0	0	0	0
United Church Board For World Ministries	1946	5	3	0	0
United Pentecostal Church Intl. For. Msns. Div.	1969	5	0	0	0
We Go, Inc. (World Encounter Gospel Organization)	1975	2	0	0	0
World Baptist Fellowship Mission Agency International	1977	2	0	1	0
World Literature Crusade	1975	0	0	0	0
World Neighbors, Inc.	0	0	0	0	0
World Vision International	1975	1	1	0	0
Worldwide Evangelization Crusade	1940	0	0	30	10
Wycliffe Bible Translators International, Inc.	1962	14	0	0	16
TOTALS	1974	230	28	752	53

Gibraltar

ORGANIZATION NAME	BEGAN	NOW	NEW	CHURCHES	GROUPS
Christian Literature Crusade, Inc.	1974	0	0	0	0
TOTALS		0	0	0	0

ORGANIZATION NAME	BEGAN	NOW	NEW	CHURCHES	GROUPS
Grenada					
Baptist International Missions, Inc.	0	2	0	0	0
Berean Mission, Inc.	1957	13	3	7	0
Church of God World Missions	1964	0	0	6	0
Mennonite Central Committee	1976	8	0	0	0
Southern Baptist Convention, Foreign Mission Board	1972	6	2	2	0
Worldteam	1957	4	0	6	1
TOTALS		33	5	21	1
Guadeloupe					
Church of God World Missions	1968	0	0	1	0
Southern Baptist Convention, Foreign Mission Board	1964	9	0	5	0
Worldteam	1947	9	0	24	1
TOTALS		18	0	30	1
Guam					
Assemblies of God, Div. of For. Msns.	1960	2	0	3	0
Baptist Bible Fellowship International	1975	2	0	0	0
Campus Crusade for Christ, International (Overseas Dept.)	1976	16	0	0	0
Child Evangelism Fellowship, Inc.	1962	1	0	0	0
Christian Reformed Board For World Missions	1962	4	4	0	0
Christians In Action	1979	2	2	1	0
Church of God (Anderson, Indiana) Msny. Bd.	1958	2	2	1	0
Conservative Baptist Association of America	1957	2	2	2	0
General Conference of Seventh-day Adventists	1948	38	18	8	0
Liebenzell Mission of U.S.A., Inc.	1952	2	0	1	1
Southern Baptist Convention, Foreign Mission Board	1961	8	0	3	0
Trans World Radio	1975	28	0	0	0
World Mission in Church and Society	1960	1	0	0	0
Youth With A Mission	1975	0	0	0	0
TOTALS		108	28	19	1

Guatemala

ORGANIZATION NAME	BEGAN	NOW	NEW	CHURCHES	GROUPS
Air Crusade, Inc.	1959	0	0	10	0
AMG International (Advancing the Ministries of the Gospel)	1974	4	0	10	0
Apostolic Church of Pentecost of Canada-Missionary Dept.	1975	4	2	0	0
Assemblies of God, Div. of For. Msns.	1937	9	0	644	0
Baptist Bible Fellowship International	1975	6	0	0	0
Baptist International Missions, Inc.	1971	2	0	0	0
Baptist Missionary Association of America	1978	1	1	2	0
Bethel Foreign Mission Foundation	1969	7	0	0	0
Bible Club Movement, Inc.	0	0	0	0	0
Bible Presbyterian Church, Ind. Bd. for Presb. For. Msns.	0	2	0	1	0
Brethren Assemblies	0	4	0	0	0
California Yearly Meeting of Friends Church, Bd. of Msns.	1902	11	5	122	1
CAM International	1899	97	12	806	1
Campus Crusade for Christ, International (Overseas Dept.)	1963	49	0	0	0
Child Evangelism Fellowship, Inc.	1945	2	0	0	0
Christian and Missionary Alliance	1970	2	0	39	2
Christian Broadcasting Network	0	0	0	0	0
Christian Churches/Churches of Christ	1959	2	0	0	0
Christian Nationals' Evangelism Commission, Inc. (CNEC)	1964	2	0	0	0
Christian Nationals' Evangelism Commission, Inc. (Canada)	1964	0	0	0	0
Christian Reformed Board For World Missions	1978	4	4	0	0
Christian Reformed World Relief Committee	1976	1	1	12	3
Christian Service Corps	1974	3	0	0	0
Christians In Action	1970	8	2	6	0
Church of God in Christ, Mennonite Gen. Msn. Bd., Inc.	1976	4	0	0	0
Church of God of Prophecy, World Mission Committee	1951	2	0	94	0
Church of God World Missions	1944	8	2	529	0
Church of the Nazarene, Gen. Bd. Dept. of Wld. Msns.	1976	10	0	75	0
Church World Service Division of DOM-NCCCUSA	0	1	0	0	0
Congregational Holiness Church Foreign Mission Dept.	1974	0	0	7	0
Defenders of the Christian Faith Movement, Inc.	1958	0	0	20	0
Eastern Mennonite Board of Missions and Charities	1968	17	2	29	0
Elim Fellowship, Inc.	1974	6	4	0	0

ORGANIZATION NAME	BEGAN	NOW	NEW	CHURCHES	GROUPS
Guatemala continued...					
Emmanuel International	1977	6	0	0	0
Evangelistic Faith Mission, Inc.	1960	0	0	0	0
Food For The Hungry International	1976	2	2	0	0
General Conference of Seventh-day Adventists	1908	4	0	68	0
Globe Missionary Evangelism	1971	4	0	1	0
Gospel Outreach	1974	14	21	0	0
Holy Land Christian Mission	0	0	0	0	0
Intl. Church of the Foursquare Gospel--Dept. of Msns. Intl.	1955	3	0	67	0
Jesus to the Communist World, Inc.	0	0	0	0	0
Lester Sumrall Evangelistic Association	0	0	0	0	0
Luis Palau Evangelistic Team, Inc.	1970	2	0	0	0
Lutheran Church-Missouri Synod	1947	4	0	15	0
Lutheran Frontier Missions	1974	2	2	1	0
Lutheran World Relief, Incorporated	1965	0	0	0	3
MAP International (Medical Assistance Programs)	0	0	0	0	0
Mennonite Central Committee	1976	6	0	0	0
Mennonite Economic Development Associates	1973	0	0	0	0
Mission Aviation Fellowship	1976	8	2	0	3
Mission to the World	1975	2	4	0	0
Missionary Air Transport, Inc.	1975	0	2	0	0
Missionary TECH Team	1978	2	2	0	0
Natl. Assn. of Congregational Chr. Chs. of the U.S.A.	1976	0	0	0	0
New Life League	1976	0	0	0	0
O.C. Ministries, Inc.	1979	2	2	0	0
Open Bible Standard Missions, Inc.	1975	0	0	6	0
Pentecostal Church of God, World Missions Department	1965	2	0	65	0
Presbyterian Church in the U.S.A., Div. of Intl. Msn.	1972	1	1	0	0
Primitive Methodist Church in the USA, Intl. Msn. Bd.	1921	15	2	80	1
Southern Baptist Convention, Foreign Mission Board	1948	32	0	59	0
Trans World Missions	1976	0	0	0	0
United Pentecostal Church Intl. For. Msns. Div.	0	2	0	0	0
United Presbyterian Church in the USA Program Agency	1882	14	3	0	0
United World Mission, Incorporated	1953	6	2	14	0

ORGANIZATION NAME	BEGAN	NOW	NEW	CHURCHES	GROUPS
Guatemala continued...					
World Baptist Fellowship Mission Agency International	1968	4	0	4	0
World Concern/Crista International	1976	0	2	0	0
World Literature Crusade	1963	0	0	0	0
World Mission in Church and Society	1956	2	1	0	0
World Missionary Assistance Plan	0	5	1	17	0
World Missionary Evangelism, Inc.	1975	0	0	0	0
World Neighbors, Inc.	0	0	0	0	0
World Vision International	1975	6	5	0	0
World Vision of Canada	1970	1	1	0	0
World-Wide Missions International	1962	0	0	7	0
Wycliffe Bible Translators International, Inc.	1952	59	0	0	38
	TOTALS	478	88	2810	51

Guinea

ORGANIZATION NAME	BEGAN	NOW	NEW	CHURCHES	GROUPS
Christian and Missionary Alliance	1918	11	0	295	0
	TOTALS	11	0	295	0

Guinea-Bissau

ORGANIZATION NAME	BEGAN	NOW	NEW	CHURCHES	GROUPS
Christian Literature Crusade, Inc.	1964	0	0	0	0
Worldwide Evangelization Crusade	1939	8	4	24	2
	TOTALS	8	4	24	2

Guyana

ORGANIZATION NAME	BEGAN	NOW	NEW	CHURCHES	GROUPS
African Methodist Episcopal Church, Inc. Dept. of Msns.	1911	0	0	0	0
African Methodist Episcopal Zion Ch., Dept. of Oseas. Msns.	1978	0	0	0	0
American Leprosy Missions, Inc.	1957	2	0	0	0
Assemblies of God, Div. of For. Msns.	1958	2	0	35	2
Bible Missionary Church, World Missions Department	1945	0	0	9	0
Christian Catholic Church	1956	0	0	6	0
Church of God of Prophecy, World Mission Committee		0	0	5	0

ORGANIZATION NAME	BEGAN	NOW	NEW	CHURCHES	GROUPS
Guyana continued...					
Church of God World Missions	1966	0	0	16	0
Church of the Nazarene, Gen. Bd. Dept. of Wld. Msns.	1946	2	0	38	0
Evangelical Methodist Church Bible Methodist Missions	0	0	0	2	0
Lott Carey Baptist Foreign Mission Convention	0	2	0	0	0
Lutheran Church in America-Div. for Wld. Msn. and Ecumenism	1943	4	1	0	0
Moravian Church in America, Bd. of Wld. Msn.	1878	0	0	8	0
Presbyterian Church in Canada, Board of World Mission	0	0	0	0	0
Seventh Day Baptist Missionary Society	1920	0	0	7	0
Source of Light Ministries, Intl.	0	1	0	0	0
Southern Baptist Convention, Foreign Mission Board	1962	2	0	15	0
Unevangelized Fields Mission	1949	2	1	0	0
United Pentecostal Church Intl. For. Msns. Div.	0	0	0	0	0
Wesleyan Church Gen. Dept. of Wld. Msns.	1924	7	2	28	0
TOTALS		24	4	169	2

Haiti

ORGANIZATION NAME	BEGAN	NOW	NEW	CHURCHES	GROUPS
African Methodist Episcopal Church, Inc. Dept. of Msns.	1968	0	0	0	0
Allegheny Wesleyan Methodist Missions	1968	6	1	4	0
American Baptist Churches in the U.S.A., Intl. Min.	1923	14	2	86	0
AMG International (Advancing the Ministries of the Gospel)	1976	3	0	20	0
Apostolic Overcoming Holy Church of God	1975	2	0	0	0
Assemblies of God, Div. of For. Msns.	1957	6	0	78	0
Baptist Haiti Mission, Inc.	1943	17	0	161	1
Baptist International Missions, Inc.		4	0	0	0
Baptist Mid-Missions	1949	13	0	0	0
Bethany Fellowship Msns. (Div. of Bethany Fellowship, Inc.)	1975	1	1	6	0
Bethel Foreign Mission Foundation	1960	4	0	0	0
Bible Holiness Movement	1979	0	0	3	0
Campus Crusade for Christ, International (Overseas Dept.)	1977	0	0	0	0
Child Evangelism Fellowship, Inc.	0	0	0	0	0
Christian Aid Mission	1975	8	0	10	3
Christian Churches/Churches of Christ	0	0	0	0	0

Haiti continued...

ORGANIZATION NAME	BEGAN	NOW	NEW	CHURCHES	GROUPS
Christian Reformed World Relief Committee	1975	5	5	54	0
Christian Service Corps	1975	4	0	0	0
Church of God (Holiness) For. Msn. Brd.	1966	1	0	4	0
Church of God in Christ, Mennonite Gen. Msn. Bd., Inc.	1966	15	0	0	0
Church of God of Prophecy, World Mission Committee	1931	0	0	185	0
Church of God World Missions	1944	5	2	284	0
Church of the Nazarene, Gen. Bd. Dept. of Wld. Msns.	1950	8	0	117	0
Church World Service Division of DOM-NCCUSA	0	2	0	0	0
Churches of God, General Conference Comm. on Wld. Msns.	1967	13	2	10	0
Compassion International, Inc.	1968	5	5	0	0
Eastern Mennonite Board of Missions and Charities	1968	2	0	0	0
Elim Fellowship, Inc.	1969	2	0	0	0
Emmanuel International	1978	12	0	0	0
Evangel Bible Translators	1978	2	0	0	0
Evangelical Bible Mission, Inc.	1943	4	0	5	0
Evangelical Scripture Mission	1975	0	0	200	0
FARMS International, Inc.	1975	1	1	0	0
Food For The Hungry International	1971	1	1	0	0
Free Methodist Church of N. America Gen. Msny. Bd.	1964	4	3	24	0
Friends For Missions, Inc.	1969	0	0	0	0
Full Gospel Native Missionary Association	0	0	0	70	0
General Conference of Seventh-day Adventists	1905	12	10	154	0
Gospel Crusade World Wide Mission Outreach	1953	2	0	115	0
Great Commission Crusades, Inc.	1946	4	2	0	1
International Gospel League	1970	0	0	0	0
Lester Sumrall Evangelistic Association	0	0	0	0	0
MAP International (Medical Assistance Programs)	0	0	0	0	0
Maranatha Baptist Mission, Inc.	0	0	0	2	0
Men in Action	1969	0	0	0	0
Mennonite Central Committee	1959	10	0	0	0
Mission to the World	1975	3	5	0	0
Missionary Church, Div. of Overseas Ministries	1952	18	9	71	0
Missionary Dentist, Inc.	1958	1	0	0	3

ORGANIZATION NAME	BEGAN	NOW	NEW	CHURCHES	GROUPS
Haiti continued...					
Natl. Baptist Convention of Amer., For. Msn. Bd.	0	0	0	8	0
New Life League	0	2	0	0	0
OMS International, Inc.	1958	39	21	44	0
Open Bible Standard Missions, Inc.	1976	2	2	0	0
Operation Eyesight Universal	1977	0	0	0	0
Pentecostal Assemblies of the World, Inc. For. Msns. Dept.	0	4	0	0	0
Pentecostal Church of God, World Missions Department	1952	4	2	150	0
Pentecostal Holiness Church-World Missions Department	1978	2	2	17	0
Presbyterian Church in the U.S.A., Div. of Intl. Msn.	1974	5	2	0	0
Protestant Episcopal Church in the USA, Soc. of St. Margaret	0	4	0	0	0
Southern Baptist Convention, Foreign Mission Board	1978	2	2	94	0
Unevangelized Fields Mission	1943	44	10	0	0
United Church of Canada, Division of World Outreach	0	2	0	1	0
United Missionary Fellowship	1970	2	0	2	0
United Pentecostal Church Intl. For. Msns. Div.	1962	2	0	0	0
Wesleyan Church Gen. Dept. of Wld. Msns.	1946	18	4	79	0
World Concern/Crista International	1976	3	3	0	0
World Gospel Mission	1962	13	8	79	0
World Ministries Commission	0	1	0	0	0
World Mission in Church and Society	1861	2	0	0	0
World Missionary Evangelism, Inc.	0	0	0	0	0
World Neighbors, Inc.	0	0	0	0	0
World Relief Corporation	0	0	0	0	0
World Vision International	1959	4	3	0	0
World-Wide Missions International	1961	0	0	217	0
Worldteam	1936	98	0	293	0
TOTALS		467	105	2647	8

Honduras

ORGANIZATION NAME	BEGAN	NOW	NEW	CHURCHES	GROUPS
Air Crusade, Inc.	1973	0	0	0	0
Assemblies of God, Div. of For. Msns.	1937	13	0	165	0
Baptist Bible Fellowship International	1974	6	0	0	0

Honduras continued...

ORGANIZATION NAME	BEGAN	NOW	NEW	CHURCHES	GROUPS
Baptist Faith Missions	1972	0	0	3	0
Baptist International Missions, Inc.	1970	10	0	0	0
Baptist Mid-Missions	1954	6	2	0	0
Baptist Missionary Association of America	1976	2	2	0	0
Bethany Fellowship Msns. (Div. of Bethany Fellowship, Inc.)	1979	6	6	0	0
Brethren Assemblies	0	6	0	0	0
California Yearly Meeting of Friends Church, Bd. of Msns.	1902	1	0	29	1
CAM International	1896	45	5	146	1
Campus Crusade for Christ, International (Overseas Dept.)	1966	50	0	0	0
Christian Broadcasting Network	0	0	0	0	0
Christian Churches/Churches of Christ	0	4	0	0	0
Christian Medical Society	1960	1	0	0	0
Christian Reformed Board For World Missions	1971	10	10	40	0
Christian Reformed World Relief Committee	1973	3	3	40	0
Christians In Action	1978	2	2	1	0
Church of God of Prophecy, World Mission Committee	1942	0	0	47	0
Church of God World Missions	1946	6	4	140	0
Church of the Nazarene, Gen. Bd. Dept. of Wld. Msns.	1971	4	0	3	0
Church of the United Brethren in Christ, Bd. of Msns.	1945	4	0	29	0
Churches of Christ in Christian Union: Foreign Msny. Dept.	0	4	0	0	0
Compassion International, Inc.	1974	0	0	0	0
Congregational Holiness Church Foreign Mission Dept.	1967	0	0	47	0
Conservative Baptist Association of America	1951	10	4	78	0
Eastern Mennonite Board of Missions and Charities	1950	17	7	35	0
Evangelistic Faith Mission, Inc.	1968	0	0	0	0
Food For The Hungry International	1974	0	0	0	0
General Conference of Seventh-day Adventists	1891	13	5	399	0
Globe Missionary Evangelism	1976	9	9	0	0
Gospel Crusade World Wide Mission Outreach	1965	3	2	14	2
Intl. Church of the Foursquare Gospel--Dept. of Msns. Intl.	1952	4	0	70	0
Jesus to the Communist World, Inc.	1976	0	0	0	0
Latin America Mission, Inc.	1976	2	2	0	0
Lutheran Church-Missouri Synod	1964	1	1	3	0

Honduras continued...

ORGANIZATION NAME	BEGAN	NOW	NEW	CHURCHES	GROUPS
Lutheran World Relief, Incorporated	1978	0	0	0	0
MAP International (Medical Assistance Programs)	0	0	0	0	0
Media Ministries Division, Mennonite Bd. of Msns.	1950	0	0	0	0
Mennonite Economic Development Associates	1970	0	0	35	0
Mission Aviation Fellowship	1949	13	9	0	0
Mission Aviation Fellowship of Canada	1978	2	2	0	0
Missionary Air Transport, Inc.	1974	0	0	0	0
Moravian Church in America, Bd. of Wld. Msn.	1930	8	0	34	0
Natl. Assn. of Congregational Chr. Chs. of the U.S.A.	1975	0	0	0	0
Presbyterian Church in the U.S.A., Div. of Intl. Msn.	1973	2	0	0	0
Refugee Children, Inc.	1974	0	0	0	0
Schwenkfelder Church in the USA and For. Bd. of Msns.	0	0	0	4	0
Self Help Foundation	1977	1	1	1	0
Southern Baptist Convention, Foreign Mission Board	1954	31	13	31	0
Technoserve, Inc.	1969	0	0	0	0
United Church Board For World Ministries	1921	3	0	0	0
United Missionary Fellowship	1954	2	0	4	0
United Pentecostal Church Intl. For. Msns. Div.	0	2	0	0	0
Wesleyan Church Gen. Dept. of Wld. Msns.	1957	4	2	5	0
World Baptist Fellowship Mission Agency International	1969	7	0	3	0
World Concern/Crista International	1974	1	6	0	0
World Gospel Mission	1944	33	11	86	0
World Ministries Commission	0	2	2	0	0
World Mission in Church and Society	1956	6	2	0	0
World Missionary Assistance Plan	0	1	1	0	0
World Vision International	1973	0	0	0	0
World-Wide Missions International	1975	0	0	1	0
Wycliffe Bible Translators International, Inc.	1960	2	0	0	1
TOTALS		362	109	1453	4

Hong Kong

	BEGAN	NOW	NEW	CHURCHES	GROUPS
American Baptist Churches in the U.S.A., Intl. Min.	1842	11	2	8	0

Hong Kong   continued...

ORGANIZATION NAME	BEGAN	NOW	NEW	CHURCHES	GROUPS
American Lutheran Ch., Div. For Wld. Msn.	1890	10	12	1	0
AMG International (Advancing the Ministries of the Gospel)	1978	2	0	1	0
Asian Outreach	1955	4	2	0	0
Assemblies of God, Div. of For. Msns.	1928	17	0	12	0
Baptist Bible Fellowship International	1950	2	0	0	0
Baptist Mid-Missions	1958	2	0	0	0
Bethel Mission of China, Inc.	1940	0	0	1	0
Brethren Assemblies	0	7	0	0	0
Campus Crusade for Christ, International (Overseas Dept.)	1972	18	0	0	0
Child Evangelism Fellowship, Inc.	1963	2	0	0	0
Chinese Christian Mission	1965	2	0	150	1
Christian Aid Mission	1953	0	0	7	2
Christian and Missionary Alliance	1933	27	10	38	0
Christian Church (Disciples of Christ) Div. of Oseas. Min.	1963	3	0	0	0
Christian Churches/Churches of Christ	1925	11	0	0	0
Chr. Echoes Natl. Min., Inc. (Chr. Crusade)	0	0	0	0	11
Christian Information Service, Inc.	1970	0	0	0	0
Christian Literature Crusade, Inc.	1974	5	0	0	0
Christian Nationals' Evangelism Commission, Inc. (CNEC)	1950	4	2	16	0
Christian Nationals' Evangelism Commission, Inc. (Canada)	1950	0	0	0	0
Christian World-Wide Evang. Msn. of Canada	1950	3	4	0	0
Church of God (Anderson, Indiana) Msny. Bd.	1953	3	0	0	0
Church of the Nazarene, Gen. Bd. of Wld. Msns.	1971	2	0	1	0
Church of the United Brethren in Christ, Bd. of Msns.	1949	0	0	5	0
Compassion International, Inc.	1974	0	0	0	0
Conservative Baptist Foreign Mission Society	1963	10	4	5	3
Cumberland Presbyterian Church, Board of Missions	1949	1	0	4	0
Eastern Mennonite Board of Missions and Charities	1965	2	0	1	0
Evangelical Friends Church, Eastern Region, Fr. For. Msny.	1975	2	0	0	0
Evangelical Literature Overseas (ELO)	0	1	0	0	0
Evangelize China Fellowship, Inc.	1949	0	0	7	0
Far East Broadcasting Company, Inc.	1959	1	0	0	0
Food For The Hungry International	1979	0	0	0	0

Hong Kong continued...

ORGANIZATION NAME	BEGAN	NOW	NEW	CHURCHES	GROUPS
Free Methodist Church of N. America Gen. Msny. Bd.	1951	2	2	8	0
General Conference Mennonite Church, Comm. on Oseas. Msn.	1980	2	2	1	0
General Conference of Seventh-day Adventists	1888	37	18	14	0
Glad Tidings Missionary Society, Inc.	1959	0	0	0	0
Home of Onesiphorus	1949	2	0	1	1
Intl. Church of the Foursquare Gospel--Dept. of Msns. Intl.	1936	4	2	4	2
International Gospel League	1975	0	0	0	0
International Missions, Inc.	1950	7	3	8	1
Intl Pentecostal Ch. of Christ, Global Msns. Dept.	1930	1	0	1	0
Jesus to the Communist World, Inc.	0	0	0	0	0
Korea International Mission, Inc.	1979	0	0	2	1
Leprosy Relief, Canada, Inc.	1979	0	0	2	0
Lester Sumrall Evangelistic Association	1959	0	0	0	0
Living Bibles International	1972	0	0	0	1
Lutheran Church in America-Div. for Wld. Msn. and Ecumenism	1948	4	2	0	0
Lutheran Church-Missouri Synod	1950	23	9	28	0
Lutheran Frontier Missions	1978	2	2	1	1
Lutheran World Relief, Incorporated	1954	0	0	0	0
MAP International (Medical Assistance Programs)	0	0	0	0	0
Missionary Evangelistic Fellowship, Inc.	1979	2	2	0	0
Natl. Assn. of Congregational Chr. Chs. of the U.S.A.	0	0	0	0	0
New Life League	0	0	0	0	0
OMS International, Inc.	1954	6	2	8	1
Overseas Missionary Fellowship	1954	14	4	0	0
Pentecostal Assemblies of Canada, Oseas. Msns. Dept.	1948	6	0	19	0
Pentecostal Holiness Church-World Missions Department	1910	11	5	14	2
Reformed Church in America General Program Council	1951	2	0	0	0
Southern Baptist Convention, Foreign Mission Board	1949	69	3	41	0
United Board for Christian Higher Education in Asia	1950	0	0	0	0
United Church Board For World Ministries	1950	0	0	0	0
United Church of Canada, Division of World Outreach	0	0	0	1	0
United Methodist Ch. Wld. Div. of the Bd. of Global Min.	1950	2	0	0	0
United Pentecostal Church Intl. For. Msns. Div.	1975	2	0	0	0

Hong Kong   continued...

ORGANIZATION NAME	BEGAN	NOW	NEW	CHURCHES	GROUPS
United Presbyterian Church in the USA Program Agency	1844	3	1	0	0
Voice of China and Asia Missionary Society, Inc.	1913	2	0	5	0
Wisconsin Evangelical Lutheran Synod, Bd. for Wld. Msns.	1964	3	0	3	0
World Concern/Crista International	1975	1	1	0	0
World Literature Crusade	1961	0	0	0	0
World Mission in Church and Society	0	1	0	0	0
World Mission Prayer League	1976	2	0	0	0
World Missionary Evangelism, Inc.	0	0	0	0	0
World Relief Corporation	1978	0	0	0	0
World Vision International	1953	0	0	0	0
World-Wide Missions International	1962	0	0	1	0
Worldwide Evangelization Crusade	1972	0	0	0	0
TOTALS		362	94	417	27

Hungary

ORGANIZATION NAME	BEGAN	NOW	NEW	CHURCHES	GROUPS
Assemblies of God, Div. of For. Msns.	1968	0	0	191	0
Living Bibles International	1977	1	0	0	1
Mennonite Central Committee	1947	1	0	0	0
Mission to Europe's Millions, Inc.	0	0	0	0	0
World-Wide Missions International	1971	0	0	1	0
TOTALS		2	0	192	1

Iceland

ORGANIZATION NAME	BEGAN	NOW	NEW	CHURCHES	GROUPS
Jesus to the Communist World, Inc.	0	0	0	0	0
Living Bibles International	1973	1	0	0	1
Youth With A Mission	1979	0	0	0	0
TOTALS		1	0	0	1

India

ORGANIZATION NAME	BEGAN	NOW	NEW	CHURCHES	GROUPS
Advent Christian Gen. Conf. of America	0	4	0	0	0

India continued...

ORGANIZATION NAME	BEGAN	NOW	NEW	CHURCHES	GROUPS
American Baptist Association, Missionary Committee	1973	4	0	11	0
American Baptist Churches in the U.S.A., Intl. Min.	1836	25	2	3916	0
American Leprosy Missions, Inc.	1906	2	0	0	0
American Lutheran Ch., Div. For Wld. Msn.	1865	4	0	2	0
AMG International (Advancing the Ministries of the Gospel)	1968	2	0	2000	0
Anglican Church of Canada, Natl. and Wld. Program	1912	0	0	0	0
Anglican Orthodox Church	1965	0	0	0	0
Apostolic Church of Pentecost of Canada-Missionary Dept.	1946	4	0	0	0
Assemblies of God, Div. of For. Msns.	1906	35	0	331	0
Association of Free Lutheran Congregations	0	0	0	0	0
Back to the Bible Missionary Agency	1970	0	0	0	0
Baptist Bible Fellowship International	1955	4	0	0	0
Baptist General Conference Board of World Missions	1946	1	0	300	0
Baptist International Missions, Inc.	0	4	0	0	0
Baptist Mid-Missions	1935	20	0	0	0
Baptist Missionary Association of America	1975	0	0	0	0
BMMF International/Canada	1852	10	8	0	0
BMMF/International (U.S.A.)	1852	16	5	0	0
Brethren Assemblies	0	10	0	0	0
Brethren in Christ Missions	1904	6	0	28	0
Calcutta Mission of Mercy	1954	1	0	0	0
Campus Crusade for Christ, International (Overseas Dept.)	1963	136	0	0	0
Canadian Baptist Overseas Mission Board	1874	23	6	200	2
Child Evangelism Fellowship, Inc.	1947	3	0	0	0
Children of India Foundation	0	0	0	0	0
Christian Aid Mission	1953	0	0	4500	84
Christian and Missionary Alliance	1887	33	4	76	0
Christian Broadcasting Network	0	0	0	0	0
Christian Church (Disciples of Christ) Div. of Oseas. Min.	1882	11	0	0	0
Christian Church of North America, Msns. Dept.	0	0	0	0	0
Christian Churches/Churches of Christ	1963	24	0	0	0
Chr. Echoes Natl. Min., Inc. (Chr. Crusade)	0	0	0	0	0
Christian Information Service, Inc.	1966	2	2	0	11

ORGANIZATION NAME	BEGAN	NOW	NEW	CHURCHES	GROUPS
Christian Literature Crusade, Inc.	1946	0	0	0	0
Christian Nationals' Evangelism Commission, Inc. (CNEC)	1969	2	2	38	0
Christian Nationals' Evangelism Commission, Inc. (Canada)	1969	2	2	0	0
Church of God (Seventh Day), Gen. Conf., Msns. Abroad	1936	0	0	15	0
Church of God General Conference Mission Department	1964	5	0	8	0
Church of God in Christ, Mennonite Gen. Msn. Bd., Inc.	0	0	0	0	0
Church of God of Prophecy, World Mission Committee	1957	0	0	206	0
Church of God World Missions	1944	0	0	409	0
Church of the Nazarene, Gen. Bd. Dept. of Wld. Msns.	1902	12	0	28	0
Church of the United Brethren in Christ, Bd. of Msns.	1974	1	0	0	0
Church World Service Division of DOM-NCCUSA	0	2	0	0	0
Churches of God, General Conference Comm. on Wld. Msns.	1898	1	0	1	0
Compassion International, Inc.	1968	7	3	0	4
Conservative Baptist Foreign Mission Society	1945	13	1	177	4
Evangel Bible Translators	1978	1	0	0	0
Evangelical Alliance Mission (TEAM)	1892	53	3	83	4
Evangelical Alliance Mission of Canada, Inc.	1903	18	0	58	0
Evangelical Friends Church, Eastern Region, Fr. For. Msny.	1896	2	0	3	0
Evangelical Lutheran Church, Division of World Missions	1979	2	0	1	0
Evangelical Scripture Mission	1952	0	0	350	11
Faith Christian Fellowship World Outreach	1979	0	0	40	0
FARMS International, Inc.	1977	2	2	0	0
Food For The Hungry International	1973	0	0	0	0
Free Gospel Church, Inc.	1940	2	0	3	0
Free Methodist Church of N. America Gen. Msny. Bd.	1885	2	0	18	0
Full Gospel Native Missionary Association	0	7	0	100	0
General Conference Mennonite Church, Comm. on Oseas. Msn.	1900	39	5	10	0
General Conference of Seventh-day Adventists	1895	0	4	589	0
General Conference of the Evangelical Baptist Church, Inc.	1937	0	0	0	0
Glad Tidings Missionary Society, Inc.	1965	18	0	0	0
Global Outreach Mission	1974	2	0	0	0
Go-Ye Fellowship	1951	0	0	0	0
Good Shepherd Agricultural Mission, Inc.	1948	3	0	4	5

India continued...

ORGANIZATION NAME	BEGAN	NOW	NEW	CHURCHES	GROUPS
Haggai Institute for Advanced Leadership Training, Inc.	1979	0	0	0	0
Heritage Village Church and Missionary Fellowship, Inc.	0	0	0	0	0
Holt International Children's Services, Inc.	1979	1	0	0	0
Holy Land Christian Mission	0	0	0	0	0
India Christian Mission, Inc.	1897	0	0	0	0
India Evangelical Mission, Inc.	1970	45	0	15	0
India National Inland Mission	1964	80	25	28	28
International Biblical Baptist Fellowship, Inc.	1962	0	0	0	0
International Christian Fellowship	1893	10	0	38	4
International Films, Inc.	1977	1	0	0	0
International Gospel League	1906	0	0	0	0
International Missions, Inc.	1930	16	0	100	3
International Needs-USA	1974	0	0	0	0
Intl Pentecostal Ch. of Christ, Global Msns. Dept.	1943	2	1	2	0
Jesus to the Communist World, Inc.	0	0	0	0	0
Leprosy Mission Canada	1874	1	0	0	0
Leprosy Relief, Canada, Inc.	1961	0	0	0	0
Lester Sumrall Evangelistic Association	0	0	0	0	0
Living Bibles International	1971	35	0	0	13
Lott Carey Baptist Foreign Mission Convention	0	1	0	0	0
Ludhiana Christian Medical College Board, U.S.A., Inc.	1894	20	0	0	0
Lutheran Church in America-Div. for Wld. Msn. and Ecumenism	1842	19	6	0	0
Lutheran Church-Missouri Synod	1895	11	2	664	2
Lutheran World Relief, Incorporated	1951	0	0	0	0
MAP International (Medical Assistance Programs)	0	0	0	0	0
Mennonite Board of Missions	1899	10	0	37	0
Mennonite Brethren Missions/Services	1899	6	17	700	4
Mennonite Central Committee	1942	9	0	0	0
Mennonite Economic Development Associates	1972	0	0	0	0
Metropolitan Church Association	1910	4	0	0	0
Missionary Church, Div. of Overseas Ministries	1908	0	0	29	2
Missionary Dentist, Inc.	1950	2	0	0	16
Missionary Evangelistic Fellowship, Inc.	1970	6	2	0	0

India continued...

ORGANIZATION NAME	BEGAN	NOW	NEW	CHURCHES	GROUPS
Natl. Assn. of Congregational Chr. Chs. of the U.S.A.	0	0	0	0	0
National Association of Free Will Baptists, Bd. of For. Msns	1935	2	0	14	0
New Life League	0	0	0	0	0
New Tribes Mission	1945	3	0	0	0
OMS International, Inc.	1941	11	4	128	7
Operation Eyesight Universal	1963	0	0	0	0
Operation Mobilization - Canada	1963	332	0	100	10
Operation Mobilization Send the Light, Inc.	1964	50	0	0	0
Pentecostal Assemblies of the World, Inc. For. Msns. Dept.	1976	1	0	0	0
Pentecostal Free Will Baptist Church, Inc.	1962	1	0	0	0
Pentecostal Holiness Church-World Missions Department	1920	10	2	67	3
Pocket Testament League, Inc.	1979	0	0	0	0
Presbyterian Church in Canada, Board of World Mission	1898	8	0	0	0
Presbyterian Church in the U.S.A., Div. of Intl. Msn.	1976	2	2	0	0
R.E.A.P.	1964	0	0	0	0
Ramabai Mukti Mission (American Council of)	1929	4	0	4	3
Reformed Church in America General Program Council	1853	8	2	0	0
Reformed Episcopal Church Bd. of For. Msns.	1890	2	0	0	0
Regions Beyond Missionary Union (U.S.A.)	1899	4	0	0	0
Rural Gospel and Medical Missions of India, Inc.	1938	0	0	0	0
Salvation Army, Canada and Bermuda	1892	2	0	0	0
Salvation Army, The	1882	7	0	4968	0
Schwenkfelder Church in the USA and For. Bd. of Msns.	0	0	0	4	0
Seventh Day Baptist Missionary Society	1974	0	0	301	3
Share the Care International	1976	0	0	0	0
Source of Light Ministries, Intl.	0	4	0	0	0
Southern Baptist Convention, Foreign Mission Board	1962	12	0	19	0
Team Ventures International	0	0	0	0	2
Things to Come Mission, Inc.	1960	0	0	1	0
United Board For Christian Higher Education in Asia	0	0	0	0	0
United Church Board For World Ministries	1813	29	2	0	0
United Church of Canada, Division of World Outreach	0	12	0	1	0
United Methodist Ch. Wld. Div. of the Bd. of Global Min.	1870	0	0	0	0

India continued...

ORGANIZATION NAME	BEGAN	NOW	NEW	CHURCHES	GROUPS
United Pentecostal Church Intl. For. Msns. Div.	1949	0	0	0	0
United Presbyterian Church in the USA Program Agency	1834	28	2	0	0
United World Mission, Incorporated	1958	0	0	1	1
Voice of China and Asia Missionary Society, Inc.	1950	0	2	4	0
We Go, Inc. (World Encounter Gospel Organization)	1979	2	2	0	0
Wesleyan Church Gen. Dept. of Wld. Msns.	1910	2	0	16	0
World Concern/Crista International	1976	1	1	0	0
World Gospel Mission	1937	10	4	77	0
World Hope Foundation	1979	0	0	0	0
World Literature Crusade	1963	0	0	0	0
World Ministries Commission	0	5	0	0	0
World Mission Prayer League	1941	2	0	0	0
World Missionary Evangelism, Inc.	0	2	0	0	0
World Missions Fellowship	1953	2	0	2	0
World Missions, Inc.	1965	0	0	2000	0
World Neighbors, Inc.	0	0	0	0	0
World Outreach	0	0	0	0	0
World Presbyterian Missions, Inc.	1957	12	2	5	1
World Relief Corporation	0	0	0	0	0
World-Wide Missions International	1960	0	0	9	0
Worldwide Evangelization Crusade	1926	5	0	3	0
Young Life	1980	0	0	0	0
Youth With A Mission	1973	0	0	0	0
TOTALS		1433	125	22842	223

Indonesia

ORGANIZATION NAME	BEGAN	NOW	NEW	CHURCHES	GROUPS
AMG International (Advancing the Ministries of the Gospel)	0	2	0	300	0
Anchor Bay Evangelistic Association	0	2	0	0	0
Asian Outreach	1979	0	0	0	0
Assemblies of God, Div. of For. Msns.	1945	31	0	205	0
Baptist Bible Fellowship International	1972	12	0	0	0
Baptist International Missions, Inc.	1971	4	0	0	0

Indonesia continued...

ORGANIZATION NAME	BEGAN	NOW	NEW	CHURCHES	GROUPS
Bethany Fellowship Msns. (Div. of Bethany Fellowship, Inc.)	1971	11	7	0	0
Bethel Mission of China, Inc.	1940	0	0	12	0
Bethel Pentecostal Temple, Inc.		0	0	0	0
Brethren Assemblies		0	0	0	0
Campus Crusade for Christ, International (Overseas Dept.)	1968	134	0	0	0
Canadian Baptist Overseas Mission Board	1972	4	0	100	1
Child Evangelism Fellowship, Inc.	1963	0	0	0	0
Christian Aid Mission	1968	0	0	120	16
Christian and Missionary Alliance	1929	151	9	1407	0
Christian Church (Disciples of Christ) Div. of Oseas. Min.	1964	4	0	0	0
Christian Churches/Churches of Christ	1967	21	0	0	0
Chr. Echoes Natl. Min., Inc. (Chr. Crusade)		0	0	0	0
Christian Information Service, Inc.	1970	0	0	0	0
Christian Literature Crusade, Inc.	1954	3	0	0	0
Christian Missionary Fellowship	1978	4	4	0	1
Christian Nationals' Evangelism Commission, Inc. (CNEC)	1971	0	0	43	0
Christian Nationals' Evangelism Commission, Inc. (Canada)	1971	0	0	0	0
Christian Union General Mission Board	1975	2	0	0	1
Christian World-Wide Evang. Msn. of Canada	1949	5	7	0	0
Church of God of Prophecy, World Mission Committee	1971	0	0	108	0
Church of God World Missions	1968	2	0	564	0
Church of the Nazarene, Gen. Bd. Dept. of Wld. Msns.	1974	8	0	7	0
Church World Service Division of DOM-NCCUSA		1	0	0	0
Compassion International, Inc.	1968	17	3	0	0
Conservative Baptist Foreign Mission Society	1961	40	9	61	4
Eastern Mennonite Board of Missions and Charities	1974	2	0	5	0
Elim Fellowship, Inc.	1972	2	2	0	0
Evangelical Alliance Mission (TEAM)	1952	63	21	300	9
Evangelical Scripture Mission	1923	0	0	655	9
Evangelize China Fellowship, Inc.	1951	0	0	20	0
Far East Broadcasting Company, Inc.	1962	0	0	0	0
Free Methodist Church of N. America Gen. Msny. Bd.	1974	4	4	9	0
Friends of Indonesia Fellowship, Inc.	1926	0	0	0	0

Indonesia continued...

ORGANIZATION NAME	BEGAN	NOW	NEW	CHURCHES	GROUPS
Full Gospel Native Missionary Association	0	0	0	0	0
General Conference of Seventh-day Adventists	1900	26	10	662	0
Go-Ye Fellowship	1938	5	0	100	0
Gospel Crusade World Wide Mission Outreach	1962	0	0	0	1
Harvest Fields Missionary and Evangelistic Assn., Inc.	0	2	0	1	1
International Christian Fellowship	1973	0	0	0	1
Korea International Mission, Inc.	1974	2	0	10	1
Leprosy Mission Canada	1969	0	0	0	0
Leprosy Relief, Canada, Inc.	1979	0	0	0	0
Lester Sumrall Evangelistic Association	0	0	0	0	0
Living Bibles International	1972	2	0	0	1
Lutheran Church in America-Div. for Wld. Msn. and Ecumenism	1970	5	3	0	0
MAP International (Medical Assistance Programs)	0	4	0	0	2
Mennonite Brethren Missions/Services	1975	5	0	0	0
Mennonite Central Committee	1948	0	0	0	0
Mennonite Economic Development Associates	1970	98	27	0	82
Mission Aviation Fellowship	1954	2	7	0	0
Mission Aviation Fellowship of Canada	1972	7	7	0	0
Mission to the World	1976	18	6	0	0
Missionary Evangelistic Fellowship, Inc.	1970	12	2	0	0
Navigators, The	1967	115	0	0	0
New Tribes Mission	1970	8	4	0	0
O.C. Ministries, Inc.	1968	20	11	17	2
OMS International, Inc.	1970	89	24	0	0
Overseas Missionary Fellowship	1954	2	0	75	0
Pentecostal Church of God, World Missions Department	1950	6	2	0	0
Pocket Testament League, Inc.	1965	0	0	56	0
Presbyterian Church in the U.S.A., Div. of Intl. Msn.	1968	31	14	100	1
R.E.A.P.	1964	100	44	246	15
Regions Beyond Missionary Union (Canada)	1948	3	0	0	0
Regions Beyond Missionary Union (U.S.A.)	1948	2	0	246	0
Salvation Army, Canada and Bermuda	1894		0		0
Salvation Army, The	1894		0		0

ORGANIZATION NAME	BEGAN	NOW	NEW	CHURCHES	GROUPS
Indonesia continued...					
Schwenkfelder Church in the USA and For. Bd. of Msns.	0	0	0	4	0
Southern Baptist Convention, Foreign Mission Board	1951	109	0	103	0
Sundanese Missionary Fellowship	1969	2	2	50	1
The Mustard Seed, Inc.	1973	2	1	0	0
Things to Come Mission, Inc.	1973	2	7	1	0
Unevangelized Fields Mission	1957	42	0	0	0
United Board for Christian Higher Education in Asia	1950	0	0	0	0
United Church Board For World Ministries	1956	4	2	0	0
United Presbyterian Church in the USA Program Agency	1951	2	2	0	0
Wesleyan Church Gen. Dept. of Wld. Msns.	1975	3	1	13	0
Wisconsin Evangelical Lutheran Synod, Bd. for Wld. Msns.	1969	2	2	3	0
World Baptist Fellowship Mission Agency International	1969	9	0	10	0
World Literature Crusade	1969	0	0	0	0
World Missionary Evangelism, Inc.	0	0	0	0	0
World Neighbors, Inc.	0	0	0	0	0
World Outreach	0	0	0	0	0
World Relief Corporation	1978	0	0	0	0
World-Wide Missions International	1963	0	0	15	0
Worldwide Evangelization Crusade	1949	17	8	85	17
Wycliffe Bible Translators International, Inc.	1971	75	0	0	18
TOTALS		1362	243	5713	194

Iran

ORGANIZATION NAME	BEGAN	NOW	NEW	CHURCHES	GROUPS
American Messianic Fellowship	1977	0	4	1	1
Assemblies of God, Div. of For. Msns.	1965	4	0	11	0
Baptist Bible Fellowship International	1966	2	0	0	0
BMF International/Canada	1972	1	2	0	0
BMMF/International (U.S.A.)	1970	0	0	0	0
Brethren Assemblies	0	2	0	0	0
Campus Crusade for Christ, International (Overseas Dept.)	1967	4	0	0	0
Child Evangelism Fellowship, Inc.	1974	3	1	0	0
Chr. Echoes Natl. Min., Inc. (Chr. Crusade)	0	0	0	0	0

ORGANIZATION NAME	BEGAN	NOW	NEW	CHURCHES	GROUPS
Iran continued...					
General Conference of Seventh-day Adventists	1911	6	2	6	0
International Christian Fellowship	1969	0	0	0	0
International Missions, Inc.	1955	2	0	1	3
MAP International (Medical Assistance Programs)	0	0	0	0	0
Operation Mobilization Send the Light, Inc.	1964	10	0	0	0
Southern Baptist Convention, Foreign Mission Board	1968	6	0	1	0
United Church Board For World Ministries	1973	0	0	0	0
United Presbyterian Church in the USA Program Agency	1835	16	2	0	0
Worldwide Evangelization Crusade	1963	1	0	1	1
TOTALS		57	11	21	5

Ireland

ORGANIZATION NAME	BEGAN	NOW	NEW	CHURCHES	GROUPS
Assemblies of God, Div. of For. Msns.	0	0	0	0	0
Baptist International Missions, Inc.	0	6	0	0	0
Bible Christian Union, Inc.	1979	12	12	0	0
Bible Club Movement, Inc.	1964	0	0	0	0
Brethren Assemblies	0	6	0	0	0
Campus Crusade for Christ, International (Overseas Dept.)	1972	28	0	0	0
Child Evangelism Fellowship, Inc.	1954	1	0	0	0
Christian Service Corps	1974	8	0	0	0
Global Outreach Mission	1965	6	5	0	0
Greater Europe Mission	1974	0	0	0	0
Haggai Institute for Advanced Leadership Training, Inc.	1979	0	0	0	0
Jesus to the Communist World, Inc.	0	0	0	0	0
Jews For Jesus	1976	2	2	0	0
Mennonite Board of Missions	1979	2	2	0	0
Mennonite Central Committee	1978	2	0	0	0
Mission to Europe's Millions, Inc.	0	0	0	1	0
WEFMinistries, Inc.	1975	10	1	0	0
World Ministries Commission	0	4	0	0	0
World Missions Fellowship	1950	4	0	0	0
TOTALS		89	20	1	0

Israel

ORGANIZATION NAME	BEGAN	NOW	NEW	CHURCHES	GROUPS
American Association for Jewish Evangelism	0	1	0	0	0
American Baptist Association, Missionary Committee	1967	1	1	1	0
American Board of Missions to the Jews, Inc.	1964	4	1	0	0
American European Bethel Mission, Inc.	1950	8	4	0	0
American Messianic Fellowship	1957	5	5	2	1
AMG International (Advancing the Ministries of the Gospel)	1975	0	0	1	0
Apostolic Church of Pentecost of Canada-Missionary Dept.	0	1	0	0	0
Assemblies of God, Div. of For. Msns.	1908	0	0	0	0
Baptist Bible Fellowship International	1979	2	0	0	0
Baptist World Mission	0	0	0	0	0
Bible Presbyterian Church, Ind. Bd. for Presb. For. Msns.	1945	8	2	1	0
Brethren Assemblies	0	0	0	0	0
Child Evangelism Fellowship, Inc.	1951	2	0	0	0
Christian and Missionary Alliance	1890	6	0	2	0
Christian Catholic Church	1929	0	0	3	0
Church of God of Prophecy, World Mission Committee	1965	0	2	3	0
Church of God World Missions	1968	4	0	1	0
Church of the Nazarene, Gen. Bd. Dept. of Wld. Msns.	1952	4	0	1	0
Elim Fellowship, Inc.	1977	2	2	0	0
Glad Tidings Missionary Society, Inc.	1976	0	2	0	0
Gospel Crusade World Wide Mission Outreach	1975	4	2	0	0
Harvest Fields Missionary and Evangelistic Assn., Inc.	0	2	0	1	1
Holy Land Christian Mission	0	0	0	0	0
Home of Onesiphorus	1951	2	2	0	1
Institute of Holy Land Studies	1959	19	9	50	0
Jews For Jesus	1975	0	0	0	0
Leprosy Relief, Canada, Inc.	1977	0	0	0	0
Lester Sumrall Evangelistic Association	0	0	0	0	0
MAP International (Medical Assistance Programs)	0	0	0	0	0
Mennonite Board of Missions	1953	8	2	1	0
Messengers of the New Covenant, Inc.	1965	0	0	0	0
Operation Mobilization - Canada	1966	17	0	10	0
Pentecostal Holiness Church-World Missions Department	1979	1	1	0	1

ORGANIZATION NAME	BEGAN	NOW	NEW	CHURCHES	GROUPS
Israel continued...					
Southern Baptist Convention, Foreign Mission Board	1921	76	24	7	0
Tele-Missions International, Inc.	1977	1	1	0	30
United Fundamentalist Church	1954	6	2	0	0
Wider Ministries Commission	1869	6	0	1	0
Word of Life Fellowship	1972	4	2	0	0
World Ministries Commission		7	0	0	0
World Mission in Church and Society	0	2	1	0	0
World Missionary Assistance Plan	0	4	1	0	0
TOTALS		207	63	85	34

Italy

ORGANIZATION NAME	BEGAN	NOW	NEW	CHURCHES	GROUPS
AMG International (Advancing the Ministries of the Gospel)	1973	2	0	1	0
Assemblies of God, Div. of For. Msns.	1908	12	2	755	0
Back to the Bible Missionary Agency	1961	2	2	0	0
Baptist Bible Fellowship International	1978	2	0	0	0
Baptist International Missions, Inc.	0	5	0	0	0
Baptist Mid-Missions	1951	14	0	0	0
Baptist Missionary Association of America	1953	0	0	0	0
Bible Christian Union, Inc.	1950	19	8	4	1
Bible Club Movement, Inc.	1963	0	0	0	0
Brethren Assemblies	0	11	0	0	0
Campus Crusade for Christ, International (Overseas Dept.)	1969	18	0	0	0
Child Evangelism Fellowship, Inc.	1956	1	0	0	0
Christ's Mission	1980	27	0	0	0
Christian Church of North America, Msns. Dept.	1949	2	0	700	0
Christian Churches/Churches of Christ	1949	13	0	0	0
Christian Literature Crusade, Inc.	1956	0	0	0	0
Church of God World Missions	1960	2	0	8	0
Church of the Nazarene, Gen. Bd. Dept. of Wld. Msns.	1948	5	5	14	0
Conservative Baptist Foreign Mission Society	1947	19	3	10	2
Gospel Missionary Union	1950	8	3	3	0
Greater Europe Mission	1954	14	8	0	0

Italy continued...

ORGANIZATION NAME	BEGAN	NOW	NEW	CHURCHES	GROUPS
Independent Faith Mission, Inc.	0	6	0	0	0
International Fellowship of Evangelical Students - USA	1952	1	0	0	0
Intl Pentecostal Ch. of Christ, Global Msns. Dept.	0	0	0	1	0
Jesus to the Communist World, Inc.	0	0	0	0	0
Lester Sumrall Evangelistic Association	1975	2	0	0	1
Living Bibles International	1957	0	0	0	0
Media Ministries Division, Mennonite Bd. of Msns.	1976	1	0	1	0
Mennonite Central Committee	0	0	0	0	0
Mission to Europe's Millions, Inc.	0	0	0	5	0
Mission to the World	1979	1	1	0	0
Natl. Assn. of Congregational Chr. Chs. of the U.S.A.	0	0	0	0	0
Open Air Campaigners (USA)	1969	1	0	0	0
Slavic Gospel Association	1953	4	0	0	0
Southern Baptist Convention, Foreign Mission Board	1870	14	4	108	0
Southern European Mission, Inc.	1942	0	0	0	0
Unevangelized Fields Mission	1974	6	2	0	0
United Pentecostal Church Intl. For. Msns. Div.	1972	4	0	2	0
Virginia Mennonite Board of Missions and Charities	1949	4	2	2	1
WEFMinistries, Inc.	1959	16	4	0	0
World Literature Crusade	1962	0	0	0	0
World Radio Missionary Fellowship, Inc.	1979	2	2	2	0
World-Wide Missions International	1963	0	0	7	0
Worldteam	1972	8	0	2	1
Worldwide Evangelization Crusade	1964	2	0	3	1
TOTALS		248	41	1624	7

Ivory Coast

ORGANIZATION NAME	BEGAN	NOW	NEW	CHURCHES	GROUPS
Apostolic Church of Pentecost of Canada-Missionary Dept.	0	1	0	0	0
Assemblies of God, Div. of For. Msns.	1927	12	0	93	0
Baptist General Conference Board of World Missions	1977	4	4	0	0
Baptist International Missions, Inc.	1970	10	0	0	0
Baptist Mid-Missions	1974	9	0	0	0

ORGANIZATION NAME	BEGAN	NOW	NEW	CHURCHES	GROUPS
Ivory Coast continued...					
Campus Crusade for Christ, International (Overseas Dept.)	1975	3	0	0	0
Child Evangelism Fellowship, Inc.	1976	2	2	0	0
Christian and Missionary Alliance	1930	28	7	716	0
Christian Literature Crusade, Inc.	1962	0	0	0	0
Christian Mission for the Deaf	1974	0	0	0	0
Christian Nationals' Evangelism Commission, Inc. (CNEC)	1972	0	0	0	0
Christian Nationals' Evangelism Commission, Inc. (Canada)	1972	0	0	0	0
Church of God of Prophecy, World Mission Committee	1978	0	0	4	0
Church of God World Missions	1978	0	0	1	0
Conservative Baptist Foreign Mission Society	1947	75	12	133	5
Evangelical Baptist Missions, Inc.	1979	2	2	0	0
Jesus to the Communist World, Inc.	0	0	0	0	0
MAP International (Medical Assistance Programs)	0	0	0	0	0
Mennonite Board of Missions	1978	4	4	0	0
Mission to the World	1976	2	2	0	0
National Association of Free Will Baptists, Bd. of For. Msns	1957	31	9	35	5
Southern Baptist Convention, Foreign Mission Board	1966	24	2	35	0
Sudan Interior Mission, Inc.	1968	13	7	0	1
United Pentecostal Church Intl. For. Msns. Div.	1975	2	0	0	0
Worldwide Evangelization Crusade	1934	18	9	33	20
Wycliffe Bible Translators International, Inc.	1970	25	0	0	17
Youth With A Mission	1978	0	0	0	0
TOTALS		265	60	1050	48

Jamaica

ORGANIZATION NAME	BEGAN	NOW	NEW	CHURCHES	GROUPS
African Methodist Episcopal Church, Inc. Dept. of Msns.	1966	0	0	0	0
African Methodist Episcopal Zion Ch.; Dept. of Oseas. Msns.	1978	0	0	0	0
AMG International (Advancing the Ministries of the Gospel)	1978	2	0	1	0
Anglican Church of Canada, Natl. and Wld. Program	1972	0	0	0	0
Assemblies of God, Div. of For. Msns.	1937	5	0	35	0
Back to the Bible Missionary Agency	1958	0	0	0	0
Baptist Bible Fellowship International	1972	4	0	0	0

Jamaica   continued...

ORGANIZATION NAME	BEGAN	NOW	NEW	CHURCHES	GROUPS
Baptist International Missions, Inc.	1939	4	0	0	0
Baptist Mid-Missions	1979	8	0	0	0
Bible Holiness Movement	1958	0	0	1	0
Bible Way Chs. of Our Lord Jesus Christ Worldwide, Inc.	1977	0	0	0	0
Campus Crusade for Christ, International (Overseas Dept.)	1916	0	0	0	0
Christian Catholic Church	1885	6	0	0	0
Christian Church (Disciples of Christ) Div. of Oseas. Min.	1965	3	0	0	0
Christian Churches/Churches of Christ	1951	0	0	0	0
Christian Literature Crusade, Inc.	1977	0	0	0	0
Christian Nationals' Evangelism Commission, Inc. (CNEC)	1977	0	0	0	0
Christian Nationals' Evangelism Commission, Inc. (Canada)	1974	3	0	0	0
Christian Service Corps	1933	4	0	38	0
Church of God (Holiness) For. Msn. Brd.	1931	0	0	50	0
Church of God (Seventh Day), Gen. Conf., Msns. Abroad	1923	0	0	260	0
Church of God of Prophecy, World Mission Committee	1944	0	0	272	0
Church of God World Missions	1966	22	0	0	0
Church of the Nazarene, Gen. Bd. Dept. of Wld. Msns.	1945	0	0	19	0
Church of the United Brethren in Christ, Bd. of Msns.	1970	0	0	0	0
Compassion International, Inc.	0	0	0	0	0
Evangelical Methodist Church Bible Methodist Missions	1975	0	0	4	0
Evangelical Scripture Mission	1979	1	0	11	0
Faith Christian Fellowship World Outreach	1979	1	0	1	0
General Baptist Foreign Mission Society, Inc.	1965	2	0	8	0
General Conference of Seventh-day Adventists	1893	10	6	235	0
Glad Tidings Missionary Society, Inc.	1970	0	0	0	0
Gospel Crusade World Wide Mission Outreach	1968	0	0	7	0
Intl. Church of the Foursquare Gospel--Dept. of Msns. Intl.	1962	2	0	40	0
International Evangelism Crusades, Inc.	1960	10	0	60	0
Maranatha Baptist Mission, Inc.	0	0	0	0	0
Media Ministries Division, Mennonite Bd. of Msns.	1957	0	0	9	0
Men in Action	1969	0	0	0	0
Mennonite Central Committee	1970	17	0	0	0
Mennonite Economic Development Associates	1979	0	0	0	0

Jamaica continued...

ORGANIZATION NAME	BEGAN	NOW	NEW	CHURCHES	GROUPS
Methodist Protestant Church, Board of Msns.	0	0	0	5	0
Missionary Church, Div. of Overseas Ministries	1949	4	0	38	0
Moravian Church in America, Bd. of Wld. Msn.	1732	1	0	0	0
Natl. Baptist Convention of Amer., For. Msn. Bd.	0	0	0	25	0
National Baptist Convention, U.S.A., Inc. For. Msn. Bd.	1972	0	0	21	0
Open Bible Standard Missions, Inc.	1948	0	0	23	0
Pentecostal Church of God, World Missions Department	1954	2	0	50	0
Protestant Reformed Churches in America	1980	0	0	0	0
Seventh Day Baptist Missionary Society	1927	0	0	29	0
Southern Baptist Convention, Foreign Mission Board	1963	4	1	274	0
United Church Board For World Ministries	1978	0	0	0	0
United Church of Canada, Division of World Outreach	0	2	0	1	0
Wider Ministries Commission	1865	2	0	16	0
World Missions, Inc.	1966	1	0	0	0
World-Wide Missions International	1961	0	0	1	0
Worldteam	1945	2	0	0	0
	TOTALS	121	7	1534	0

Japan

ORGANIZATION NAME	BEGAN	NOW	NEW	CHURCHES	GROUPS
Advent Christian Gen. Conf. of America	0	7	0	0	0
American Baptist Association, Missionary Committee	1952	6	3	11	0
American Baptist Churches in the U.S.A., Intl. Min.	1872	15	2	65	0
American Lutheran Ch., Div. For Wld. Msn.	1898	61	14	1	0
AMG International (Advancing the Ministries of the Gospel)	1978	0	0	0	0
Anglican Church of Canada, Natl. and Wld. Program	1910	0	0	0	0
Apostolic Christian Mission Fund	1952	2	0	0	0
Apostolic Church of Pentecost of Canada-Missionary Dept.	1951	2	0	0	0
Asian Outreach	1975	0	0	0	0
Assemblies of God, Div. of For. Msns.	1913	30	0	93	0
Baptist Bible Fellowship International	1950	27	0	0	0
Baptist General Conference Board of World Missions	1948	13	2	26	0
Baptist International Missions, Inc.	1965	40	0	0	0

Japan   continued...

ORGANIZATION NAME	BEGAN	NOW	NEW	CHURCHES	GROUPS
Baptist Mid-Missions	1949	27	0	0	0
Baptist Missionary Association of America	1953	1	0	0	0
Baptist World Mission		6	0	0	0
Bethany Missionary Association	1959	4	1	5	0
Bethel Foreign Mission Foundation	1958	11	0	4	0
Bethel Pentecostal Temple, Inc.		0	0	0	0
Bible Club Movement, Inc.		0	0	0	0
Bible Missionary Church, World Missions Department	1965	8	0	6	2
Bible Protestant Missions, Inc.		2	0	0	0
Brethren Assemblies		31	0	0	0
Brethren in Christ Missions	1953	4	0	7	0
Campus Crusade for Christ, International (Overseas Dept.)	1962	15	0	0	0
Child Evangelism Fellowship, Inc.	1948	6	0	0	0
Christian and Missionary Alliance	1891	16	7	42	0
Christian Broadcasting Network		0	0	0	0
Christian Catholic Church	1951	2	0	2	0
Christian Church (Disciples of Christ) Div. of Oseas. Min.	1883	10	0	0	0
Christian Churches/Churches of Christ	1890	62	0	0	0
Chr. Echoes Natl. Min., Inc. (Chr. Crusade)		0	0	0	0
Christian Literature Crusade, Inc.	1950	0	0	0	0
Christian Nationals' Evangelism Commission, Inc. (CNEC)	1977	0	0	0	0
Christian Nationals' Evangelism Commission, Inc. (Canada)	1977	0	0	0	0
Christian Reformed Board For World Missions	1951	24	2	0	0
Christian Union General Mission Board	1962	2	0	1	1
Christians In Action	1957	13	6	11	3
Church of God (Anderson, Indiana) Msny. Bd.	1906	8	0	18	0
Church of God at Baden, I.H.P.	1951	2	0	0	0
Church of God World Missions	1954	0	0	6	0
Church of the Lutheran Brethren of America, Bd. of Wld. Msns	1950	8	6	15	0
Church of the Nazarene, Gen. Bd. Dept. of Wld. Msns.	1905	17	6	77	0
Conservative Baptist Foreign Mission Society	1947	39	13	42	3
Cumberland Presbyterian Church, Board of Missions	1950	0	0	7	0
Elim Fellowship, Inc.	1975	4	2	0	0

Japan continued...

ORGANIZATION NAME	BEGAN	NOW	NEW	CHURCHES	GROUPS
Evangelical Alliance Mission (TEAM)	1891	149	35	227	1
Evangelical Alliance Mission of Canada, Inc.	1891	10	0	125	0
Evangelical Congregational Church Division of Missions	1963	1	1	0	0
Evangelical Covenant Church of America, Bd. of Wld. Msn.	1949	15	3	10	0
Evangelical Scripture Mission	1947	0	0	10	0
Far Eastern Broadcasting Company, Inc.	1959	0	0	0	0
Far Eastern Gospel Crusade	1947	68	17	33	2
Fellowship of Evangelical Baptist Chs. in Canada	1950	9	2	8	1
Free Methodist Church of N. America Gen. Msny. Bd.	1895	4	2	31	0
General Conference Mennonite Church, Comm. on Oseas. Msn.	1950	19	9	16	0
General Conference of Seventh-day Adventists	1896	37	15	90	0
Glad Tidings Missionary Society, Inc.	1965	0	0	0	0
Go-Ye Fellowship	1957	4	2	0	0
Heritage Village Church and Missionary Fellowship, Inc.	1950	0	0	0	0
High School Evangelism Fellowship, Inc.	1950	10	2	0	0
Intl. Church of the Foursquare Gospel--Dept. of Msns. Intl.	1951	1	1	18	0
International Crusades, Inc.	1979	5	5	12	0
International Films, Inc.	1974	0	0	0	0
International Gospel League	1949	0	0	0	0
International Missionary Advance	1975	0	0	75	0
Intl Pentecostal Ch. of Christ, Global Msns. Dept.	1950	10	4	3	1
International Students, Inc.	0	1	0	0	0
Japan Evangelical Mission	1951	40	8	18	1
Japan Evangelistic Association, Inc.	1950	4	0	18	0
Japan Evangelistic Band	1903	3	0	0	0
Japan Evangelistic Band (Canada)	1903	3	0	0	0
Japan International Christian Univ. Found., Inc.	1949	11	0	0	0
Japan-North American Commission on Cooperative Mission	1859	235	30	1715	0
Jesus to the Communist World, Inc.	0	0	0	0	0
Language Institute For Evangelism (LIFE)	1967	20	10	4	1
Liberty Corner Mission	1951	8	2	4	0
Liebenzell Mission of Canada	1923	0	0	0	0

Japan continued...

ORGANIZATION NAME	BEGAN	NOW	NEW	CHURCHES	GROUPS
Living Bibles International	1972	6	0	0	1
Lutheran Church in America-Div. for Wld. Msn. and Ecumenism	1892	26	11	0	0
Lutheran Church-Missouri Synod	1948	29	28	32	0
MAP International (Medical Assistance Programs)	0	0	0	0	0
Maranatha Baptist Mission, Inc.	1956	0	0	2	0
Media Ministries Division, Mennonite Bd. of Msns.	1949	15	0	16	0
Mennonite Board of Missions	1950	17	18	16	0
Mennonite Brethren Missions/Services				23	1
Missionary Church, Div. of Overseas Ministries	1951	1	0	0	0
Missionary Evangelistic Fellowship, Inc.	0	6	2	0	0
Natl. Assn. of Congregational Chr. Chs. of the U.S.A.		0	0	0	0
National Association of Free Will Baptists, Bd. of For. Msns	1954	9	0	10	1
Navigators, The	1951	12	4	0	0
New Life League	1954	0	0	0	0
New Tribes Mission	1949	5	0	15	0
Next Towns Crusade, Inc.	1957	2	0	6	5
North American Baptist Gen. Msny. Soc., Inc.	1951	20	7	135	1
OMS International, Inc.	1901	20	2	8	0
Open Bible Standard Missions, Inc.	0	0	0	50	1
Orthodox Presbyterian Church Committee on Foreign Missions	1951	6	2	0	0
Overseas Christian Servicemen's Centers	1962	13	5	0	0
Overseas Missionary Fellowship	1951	82	19	0	0
Pacific Broadcasting Association, Inc.	1951	4	0	0	0
Pentecostal Church of God, World Missions Department	1953	2	0	5	0
Pilgrim Fellowship, Inc., The	1948	8	0	0	0
Presbyterian Church in Canada, Board of World Mission	1927	7	2	0	0
Presbyterian Church in the U.S.A., Div. of Intl. Msn.	1885	33	4	0	0
R.E.A.P.	1951	3	0	2	0
Reformed Church in America General Program Council	1860	18	2	0	0
Reformed Presbyterian Ch. of N. America, Bd. of For. Msns.	1950	6	2	69	0
Society of St. John the Evangelist	1928	0	0	0	0
Southern Baptist Convention, Foreign Mission Board	1889	165	9	195	0
Team Ventures International	0	0	0	0	2

Japan continued...

ORGANIZATION NAME	BEGAN	NOW	NEW	CHURCHES	GROUPS
Tokyo Evangelistic Center	1950	0	0	0	0
United Board for Christian Higher Education in Asia	1869	34	0	0	0
United Church Board For World Ministries	0	19	0	0	0
United Church of Canada, Division of World Outreach	1873	1	0	1	0
United Methodist Ch. Wld. Div. of the Bd. of Global Min.	1979	2	0	0	0
United Pentecostal Church Intl. For. Msns. Div.	1859	25	6	0	0
United Presbyterian Church in the USA Program Agency	1919	2	0	0	0
Wesleyan Church Gen. Dept. of Wld. Msns.	1952	7	0	10	0
Wisconsin Evangelical Lutheran Synod, Bd. for Wld. Msns.	1975	3	3	0	0
Word of Life Fellowship	1966	1	3	1	0
World Baptist Fellowship Mission Agency International	1952	7	3	237	1
World Gospel Mission	1976	0	0	0	0
World Hope Foundation	1953	6	1	0	0
World Literature Crusade	1859	1	0	0	0
World Mission in Church and Society	0	0	0	0	0
World Missionary Assistance Plan	1951	2	0	4	0
World Missionary Evangelism, Inc.	1970	24	5	20	0
World Missions Fellowship	1961	7	4	0	1
World Opportunities International	1964	0	0	1	0
World Presbyterian Missions, Inc.	1950	7	0	7	2
World-Wide Missions International					
Worldwide Evangelization Crusade					
Worldwide Fellowship with Jesus Christ Mission	0	0	0	0	0
Young Life	1974	0	0	0	0
Youth With A Mission	1972	0	0	0	0
TOTALS		1855	345	3711	32

Jordan

ORGANIZATION NAME	BEGAN	NOW	NEW	CHURCHES	GROUPS
American Board for the Syrian Orphanage	1960	0	0	0	0
Assemblies of God, Div. of For. Msns.	1908	6	0	4	0
Baptist Mid-Missions	1970	2	0	0	0
Christian and Missionary Alliance	1890	8	5	3	0

ORGANIZATION NAME	BEGAN	NOW	NEW	CHURCHES	GROUPS
Jordan continued...					
Christian Reformed Board For World Missions	1979	2	2	0	0
Church of God of Prophecy, World Mission Committee	1976	0	2	1	0
Church of the Nazarene, Gen. Bd. Dept. of Wld. Msns.	1948	8	0	4	2
Conservative Baptist Foreign Mission Society	1956	8	4	5	2
Global Outreach Mission	0	4	0	0	0
Lutheran World Relief, Incorporated	1948	0	0	0	0
MAP International (Medical Assistance Programs)	0	0	0	0	0
Mennonite Central Committee	1950	11	0	0	0
Middle East Christian Outreach--USA Council	0	1	1	0	0
Mission to the World	1977	1	1	0	0
Navigators, The	1976	2	2	0	0
Operation Mobilization Send the Light, Inc.	0	0	0	0	0
Southern Baptist Convention, Foreign Mission Board	1952	23	0	7	0
United Presbyterian Church in the USA Program Agency	0	2	2	0	0
World Presbyterian Missions, Inc.	1966	10	4	0	1
World-Wide Missions International	1963	0	0	1	0
TOTALS		87	20	25	3

Kampuchea

ORGANIZATION NAME	BEGAN	NOW	NEW	CHURCHES	GROUPS
Christian and Missionary Alliance	1923	0	0	0	0
Christian Information Service, Inc.	1968	0	0	0	11
Christian Pilots Association, Inc.	0	0	0	0	0
Church World Service Division of DOM-NCCCUSA	0	3	0	0	0
Lutheran World Relief, Incorporated	1974	0	0	0	0
World Vision International	1979	2	2	0	0
TOTALS		5	2	0	11

Kenya

ORGANIZATION NAME	BEGAN	NOW	NEW	CHURCHES	GROUPS
Africa Inland Mission	1895	430	144	3000	0
Africa Inland Mission (Canada)	1895	61	16	3000	0
African Enterprise	1975	1	1	0	0

Kenya continued...

ORGANIZATION NAME	BEGAN	NOW	NEW	CHURCHES	GROUPS
Assemblies of God, Div. of For. Msns.	1972	26	0	215	0
Baptist Bible Fellowship International	1962	28	0	0	0
Baptist General Conference Board of World Missions	1978	2	2	0	0
Berean Mission, Inc.	1965	5	0	0	0
Bible Alliance Mission, Inc.	1978	0	0	0	0
Bible Club Movement, Inc.	1948	0	0	0	0
Bible Presbyterian Church, Ind. Bd. for Presb. For. Msns.	1943	7	0	90	0
Bible Translations On Tape, Inc.	1979	1	1	0	0
Brethren Assemblies	0	5	0	0	0
Campus Crusade for Christ, International (Overseas Dept.)	1972	80	0	0	0
Canadian Baptist Overseas Mission Board	1970	12	7	0	1
Child Evangelism Fellowship, Inc.	1966	5	2	0	0
Christian Aid Mission	1953	0	0	300	12
Christian Churches/Churches of Christ	1965	26	0	0	0
Chr. Echoes Natl. Min., Inc. (Chr. Crusade)	0	0	0	0	0
Christian Missionary Fellowship	1977	20	10	0	2
Christian Nationals' Evangelism Commission, Inc. (CNEC)	1972	1	1	0	0
Christian Nationals' Evangelism Commission, Inc. (Canada)	1972	0	0	0	0
Christian Service Corps	0	5	0	0	0
Christians United in Action, Inc.	0	2	0	0	0
Church of God (Anderson, Indiana) Msny. Bd.	1905	9	3	400	0
Church of God of Prophecy, World Mission Committee	1978	0	0	6	0
Church of God World Missions	1978	2	2	4	0
Church World Service Division of DOM-NCCCUSA	0	1	0	0	0
Churches of Christ in Christian Union: Foreign Msny. Dept.	0	4	0	0	0
Conservative Baptist Foreign Mission Society	1975	6	0	6	3
Daystar Communications, Inc.	1974	22	11	0	15
Eastern Mennonite Board of Missions and Charities	1964	33	17	48	0
Elim Fellowship, Inc.	1940	34	11	600	0
Evangelical Literature Overseas (ELO)	0	2	0	0	0
Evangelical Scripture Mission	1970	0	0	225	3
Food For The Hungry International	1976	3	3	0	0
Frontier Ministries International	1979	2	2	0	1

Kenya continued...

ORGANIZATION NAME	BEGAN	NOW	NEW	CHURCHES	GROUPS
General Conference of Seventh-day Adventists	1906	50	34	491	0
Globe Missionary Evangelism	1974	2	2	0	0
Gospel Recordings of Canada, Inc.	1977	2	2	0	0
Independent Faith Mission, Inc.	0	10	0	0	0
International Fellowship of Evangelical Students - USA	0	1	0	0	0
International Gospel League	1978	0	0	0	0
International Missions, Inc.	1956	19	13	2	2
Intl Pentecostal Ch. of Christ, Global Msns. Dept.	1938	14	3	300	0
Leprosy Relief, Canada, Inc.	1979	0	0	0	0
Literacy & Evangelism, Inc.		2	0	15	0
Living Bibles International	1973	18	0	0	5
Lutheran Church in America-Div. for Wld. Msn. and Ecumenism	1969	1	1	0	0
Lutheran Church-Missouri Synod	1970	1	1	0	0
Lutheran World Relief, Incorporated	1976	1	1	0	0
MAP International (Medical Assistance Programs)	1962	0	0	0	0
Mennonite Central Committee	1971	6	0	0	0
Mennonite Economic Development Associates	1959	1	0	0	0
Mission Aviation Fellowship	1979	2	0	0	0
Mission to the World	1968	2	2	0	0
Navigators, The	1973	4	4	0	0
Operation Eyesight Universal	1979	0	0	0	1
Orthodox Presbyterian Church Committee on Foreign Missions	1979	2	2	22	1
Pentecostal Assemblies of Canada, Oseas. Msns. Dept.	1921	48	20	1618	5
Pentecostal Holiness Church-World Missions Department	1973	6	6	78	1
Petra International, Inc.	1977	0	0	6	0
Reformed Church in America General Program Council	1977	4	2	0	0
Reformed Episcopal Church Bd. of For. Msns.	1956	2	0	0	0
Salvation Army, The	1896	3	0	717	0
Southern Baptist Convention, Foreign Mission Board	1956	127	3	373	3
Sudan Interior Mission, Inc.	1977	22	22	0	0
Technoserve, Inc.	1972	0	0	0	3
Tele-Missions International, Inc.	1978	1	1	18	18
United Church Board For World Ministries	1966	2	2	0	0

Kenya continued...

ORGANIZATION NAME	BEGAN	NOW	NEW	CHURCHES	GROUPS
United Church of Canada, Division of World Outreach	0	4	0	1	0
United Methodist Ch. Wld. Div. of the Bd. of Global Min.	1962	0	0	0	0
United Pentecostal Church Intl. For. Msns. Div.	1972	4	0	0	0
United Presbyterian Church in the USA Program Agency	0	12	4	0	0
Wider Ministries Commission	1902	6	3	600	0
World of Life Fellowship	1969	4	3	0	0
World Gospel Mission	1932	56	27	319	1
World Literature Crusade	1962	0	0	0	0
World Mission in Church and Society	0	3	3	0	0
World Mission Prayer League	1968	13	5	0	0
World Neighbors, Inc.	0	0	0	0	0
World Opportunities International	1971	2	0	50	0
World Outreach	0	0	0	0	0
World Presbyterian Missions, Inc.	1961	9	4	0	0
World Relief Corporation	0	0	0	0	0
World-Wide Missions International	1961	0	0	16	0
Wycliffe Bible Translators International, Inc.	1978	4	0	0	2
Youth For Christ/U.S.A.	0	2	0	0	2
Youth With A Mission	1979	0	0	0	0
	TOTALS	1307	400	12520	75

Korea, Dem. P. Rep.

ORGANIZATION NAME	BEGAN	NOW	NEW	CHURCHES	GROUPS
Evangelistic Faith Mission, Inc.	1971	0	0	0	0
R.E.A.P.	1959	0	0	0	0
	TOTALS	0	0	0	0

Korea, Rep. of

ORGANIZATION NAME	BEGAN	NOW	NEW	CHURCHES	GROUPS
American Baptist Association, Missionary Committee	1972	7	1	15	0
American Leprosy Missions, Inc.	1909	0	0	0	0
AMG International (Advancing the Ministries of the Gospel)	1977	0	0	1	0
Asian Outreach	1971	0	0	0	0

Korea, Rep. of continued...

ORGANIZATION NAME	BEGAN	NOW	NEW	CHURCHES	GROUPS
Assemblies of God, Div. of For. Msns.	1952	13	0	310	0
Baptist Bible Fellowship International	1950	28	0	0	0
Baptist Faith Missions	1971	1	0	4	0
Baptist International Missions, Inc.	0	4	0	0	0
Baptist Mid-Missions	1966	0	0	0	0
Baptist Missionary Association of America	1978	2	0	0	0
Baptist World Mission					
Bethel Foreign Mission Foundation	1961	8	0	16	0
Bible Presbyterian Church, Ind. Bd. for Presb. For. Msns.	1936	3	0	30	0
Brethren Assemblies	0	10	0	0	0
Campus Crusade for Christ, International (Overseas Dept.)	1958	115	0	0	0
Child Evangelism Fellowship, Inc.	1957	2	0	0	0
Christian Aid Mission	1953	0	0	600	1
Christian Churches/Churches of Christ	1930	9	0	0	0
Chr. Echoes Natl. Min., Inc. (Chr. Crusade)	1974	0	0	0	0
Christian Literature Crusade, Inc.	1976	0	0	35	0
Christian Nationals' Evangelism Commission, Inc. (CNEC)	1976	0	0	0	0
Christian Nationals' Evangelism Commission, Inc. (Canada)					
Christian Service Corps	0	3	7	0	0
Christians In Action	1957	7	7	2	0
Church of God (Anderson, Indiana) Msny. Bd.	1936	4	4	27	0
Church of God of Prophecy, World Mission Committee	1969	0	0	29	0
Church of God World Missions	1966	0	0	38	0
Church of the Nazarene, Gen. Bd. Dept. of Wld. Msns.	1948	4	2	46	0
Churches of Christ in Christian Union: Foreign Msny. Dept.	1975	2	2	0	0
Compassion International, Inc.	1952	10	7	0	0
Elim Fellowship, Inc.	1942	3	4	0	0
Evangelical Alliance Mission (TEAM)	1953	22	2	0	1
Far East Broadcasting Company, Inc.	1972	6	2	0	0
Full Gospel Native Missionary Association	0	0	0	310	0
General Conference of Seventh-day Adventists	1904	17	7	1	0
Global Orphanages, Inc.	1951	0	0	0	0
Global Outreach Mission	1974	2	0	0	0

Korea, Rep. of continued...

ORGANIZATION NAME	BEGAN	NOW	NEW	CHURCHES	GROUPS
Haggai Institute for Advanced Leadership Training, Inc.	1978	0	0	0	0
Holt International Children's Services, Inc.	1956	0	0	0	0
Intl. Church of the Foursquare Gospel--Dept. of Msns. Intl.	1969	2	0	12	0
International Evangelism Crusades, Inc.	1975	10	0	36	0
International Gospel League	1954	0	0	0	0
International Missionary Advance	1973	1	0	3000	0
International Needs-USA	1975	0	0	0	0
Jesus to the Communist World, Inc.	0	0	0	0	0
Korea Gospel Mission	1952	0	0	0	0
Korea International Mission, Inc.	1968	8	0	100	0
Leprosy Mission Canada	0	0	0	0	0
Leprosy Relief, Canada, Inc.	1977	0	0	0	0
Living Bibles International	1972	2	0	0	1
Lutheran Church-Missouri Synod	1958	4	1	9	0
MAP International (Medical Assistance Programs)	0	0	0	0	0
Maranatha Baptist Mission, Inc.	0	2	0	2	0
Methodist Protestant Church, Board of Msns.	0	2	0	75	0
Mission to the World	1974	11	11	0	0
Missionary Evangelistic Fellowship, Inc.	1970	2	0	0	0
Natl. Assn. of Congregational Chr. Chs. of the U.S.A.	0	0	0	0	0
Navigators, The	1966	4	4	0	0
OMS International, Inc.	1907	12	7	956	2
Orthodox Presbyterian Church Committee on Foreign Missions	1937	6	3	4000	1
Overseas Christian Servicemen's Centers	1975	3	1	0	0
Overseas Missionary Fellowship	1968	5	2	0	0
Pentecostal Holiness Church-World Missions Department	1979	2	2	142	0
Pocket Testament League, Inc.	1975	0	0	0	0
Presbyterian Church in the U.S.A., Div. of Intl. Msn.	1892	62	17	0	0
Salvation Army, The	1908	3	0	131	0
Slavic Gospel Association	1955	2	0	0	0
Southern Baptist Convention, Foreign Mission Board	1950	83	7	590	0
United Board for Christian Higher Education in Asia	1950	0	0	0	0
United Church of Canada, Division of World Outreach	0	13	0	1	0

Korea, Rep. of continued...

ORGANIZATION NAME	BEGAN	NOW	NEW	CHURCHES	GROUPS
United Methodist Ch. Wld. Div. of the Bd. of Global Min.	1884	0	0	0	0
United Pentecostal Church Intl. For. Msns. Div.	1965	6	0	0	0
United Presbyterian Church in the USA Program Agency	1884	30	5	0	0
United World Mission, Incorporated	1955	4	0	4	1
Voice of China and Asia Missionary Society, Inc.	1946	0	0	12	0
WEFMinistries, Inc.	1975	2	0	0	0
Wesleyan Church Gen. Dept. of Wld. Msns.	1977	2	2	0	0
World Hope Foundation	1978	0	0	0	0
World Literature Crusade	1958	0	0	0	0
World Missionary Evangelism, Inc.	0	0	0	0	0
World Missions, Inc.	1978	3	3	0	0
World Opportunities International	1978	2	0	0	0
World Outreach	0	0	0	0	0
World Presbyterian Missions, Inc.	1957	4	0	0	0
World Relief Corporation	1965	0	0	0	0
World-Wide Missions International	1961	0	0	3	0
Young Life	1972	0	0	0	0
TOTALS	1900	572	99	10537	7

Kuwait

ORGANIZATION NAME	BEGAN	NOW	NEW	CHURCHES	GROUPS
Reformed Church in America General Program Council	1900	5	4	0	0
TOTALS		5	4	0	0

Lao, People's Dem. R.

ORGANIZATION NAME	BEGAN	NOW	NEW	CHURCHES	GROUPS
Christian and Missionary Alliance	1929	0	0	0	0
Christian Information Service, Inc.	1968	0	0	0	11
MAP International (Medical Assistance Programs)	0	0	0	0	0
Mennonite Central Committee	1975	4	0	0	0
TOTALS		4	0	0	11

Latin America-gen.

ORGANIZATION NAME	BEGAN	NOW	NEW	CHURCHES	GROUPS
Free Methodist Church of N. America Gen. Msny. Bd.	0	2	0	0	0
Heritage Village Church and Missionary Fellowship, Inc.	0	0	0	0	0
Salvation Army, Canada and Bermuda	1890	5	0	0	0
TOTALS		7	0	0	0

Lebanon

ORGANIZATION NAME	BEGAN	NOW	NEW	CHURCHES	GROUPS
American Board for the Syrian Orphanage	1960	0	0	0	0
AMG International (Advancing the Ministries of the Gospel)	1973	0	0	1	0
Assemblies of God, Div. of For. Msns.	1920	2	0	3	0
Baptist Bible Fellowship International	1956	2	0	0	0
BMMF International/Canada	1966	0	0	0	0
Brethren Assemblies	0	4	0	0	0
Campus Crusade for Christ, International (Overseas Dept.)	1968	3	0	0	0
Christian and Missionary Alliance	1890	0	0	5	0
Church of the Nazarene, Gen. Bd. Dept. of Wld. Msns.	1954	0	0	7	0
Fellowship of Independent Missions	1965	0	0	0	0
General Conference of Seventh-day Adventists	1908	6	2	10	0
Home of Onesiphorus	1950	2	0	0	0
Living Bibles International	1973	2	0	0	1
MAP International (Medical Assistance Programs)	0	2	0	0	0
Mennonite Central Committee	1976	2	0	0	0
Middle East Christian Outreach-USA Council	1860	0	0	0	0
Middle East Media	1976	2	0	0	0
Navigators, The	1960	2	0	0	0
Operation Mobilization Send the Light, Inc.	1965	20	0	0	0
Orthodox Presbyterian Church Committee on Foreign Missions	1974	0	3	1	2
Presbyterian Church in the U.S.A., Div. of Intl. Msn.	1971	2	0	0	0
Reformed Church in America General Program Council	1967	2	0	0	0
Southern Baptist Convention, Foreign Mission Board	1948	23	1	10	0
United Church Board For World Ministries	1819	2	0	0	0
United Presbyterian Church in the USA Program Agency	1823	10	0	0	0
Youth For Christ/U.S.A.	1960	2	0	0	0
TOTALS		88	6	37	3

Lesotho

ORGANIZATION NAME	BEGAN	NOW	NEW	CHURCHES	GROUPS
Africa Inter-Mennonite Mission, Inc.	1973	6	2	4	0
African Methodist Episcopal Church, Inc. Dept. of Msns.	0	0	0	0	0
Anglican Church of Canada, Natl. and Wld. Program	1977	1	0	0	0
Assemblies of God, Div. of For. Msns.	1950	2	0	27	0
Campus Crusade for Christ, International (Overseas Dept.)	1979	6	0	0	0
Christian Aid Mission	1953	0	0	60	7
Church of God World Missions	1968	4	0	26	0
Evangelical Mennonite Church, Comm. on Oseas. Msns.	1972	0	0	0	0
General Conference Mennonite Church, Comm. on Oseas. Msn.	1973	4	4	0	0
General Conference of Seventh-day Adventists	1960	5	2	14	0
Jesus to the Communist World, Inc.	0	0	0	0	0
Leprosy Mission Canada	1976	0	0	0	0
Leprosy Relief, Canada, Inc.	1979	0	0	0	0
MAP International (Medical Assistance Programs)					
Mennonite Central Committee	1973	13	0	0	0
National Baptist Convention, U.S.A., Inc. For. Msn. Bd.	1961	0	0	19	0
Presbyterian Church in the U.S.A., Div. of Intl. Msn.	1977	2	2	0	0
United Church of Canada, Division of World Outreach	0	8	0	1	0
TOTALS		51	10	151	7

Liberia

ORGANIZATION NAME	BEGAN	NOW	NEW	CHURCHES	GROUPS
African Bible Colleges, Inc.	1977	6	6	0	0
African Methodist Episcopal Church, Inc. Dept. of Msns.	0	0	0	0	0
African Methodist Episcopal Zion Ch., Dept. of Oseas. Msns.	1876	0	0	0	2
Afro-American Missionary Crusade, Inc.	1948	3	0	16	0
American Leprosy Missions, Inc.	1928	0	0	0	0
Assemblies of God, Div. of For. Msns.	1908	11	0	248	0
Baptist Mid-Missions	1938	44	0	0	0
Bible Holiness Movement	1979	0	0	2	0
Bible Way Chs. of Our Lord Jesus Christ Worldwide, Inc.	1958	2	0	2	0
Campus Crusade for Christ, International (Overseas Dept.)	1979	5	0	0	0
Carver Foreign Missions, Inc.	1956	9	0	1	1

Liberia continued...

ORGANIZATION NAME	BEGAN	NOW	NEW	CHURCHES	GROUPS
Child Evangelism Fellowship, Inc.	1955	1	0	0	0
Christian Churches/Churches of Christ	0	5	0	0	0
Christian Literature Crusade, Inc.	1946	2	0	0	0
Christian Nationals' Evangelism Commission, Inc. (CNEC)	1964	2	0	108	0
Christian Nationals' Evangelism Commission, Inc. (Canada)	1964	0	0	0	0
Christian Reformed Board For World Missions	1975	7	5	0	0
Christian Service Corps	0	1	0	0	0
Christian Union General Mission Board	1964	3	0	0	11
Church of God General Conference Mission Department	1967	2	0	2	0
Church of God World Missions	1968	4	2	20	0
Compassion International, Inc.	1975	0	0	0	0
Evangelical Congregational Church	1971	1	1	0	0
Fellowship of Christian Assemblies Mission to Liberia	1920	0	0	0	0
General Conference of Seventh-day Adventists	1927	8	8	28	0
International Gospel League	1947	0	0	0	0
Lott Carey Baptist Foreign Mission Convention	1900	4	0	0	0
Lutheran Bible Translators, Inc.	1969	25	10	0	9
Lutheran Church in America-Div. for Wld. Msn. and Ecumenism	1862	21	10	0	9
Lutheran Church-Missouri Synod	1978	1	1	0	2
Lutheran World Relief, Incorporated	1960	0	0	0	0
MAP International (Medical Assistance Programs)	0	0	0	0	23
Missionary Dentist, Inc.	1973	2	1	0	0
Natl. Baptist Convention of Amer., For. Msn. Bd.	1959	2	0	2	0
National Baptist Convention, U.S.A., Inc. For. Msn. Bd.	1880	11	0	19	0
Open Bible Standard Missions, Inc.	1935	9	1	18	0
Operation Eyesight Universal	1979	0	0	0	0
Pentecostal Assemblies of Canada, Oseas. Msns. Dept.	1915	18	7	313	2
Pentecostal Assemblies of the World, Inc. For. Msns. Dept.	0	4	0	0	0
Pillar of Fire Missions	1960	3	2	16	0
Source of Light Ministries, Intl.	0	1	0	0	0
Southern Baptist Convention, Foreign Mission Board	1960	55	0	99	0
Sudan Interior Mission, Inc.	1951	73	28	0	3
United Methodist Ch. Wld. Div. of the Bd. of Global Min.	1833	0	0	0	0

ORGANIZATION NAME	BEGAN	NOW	NEW	CHURCHES	GROUPS
Liberia continued...					
United Pentecostal Church Intl. For. Msns. Div.	1936	2	0	0	0
Wesleyan Church Gen. Dept. of Wld. Msns.	1978	2	2	6	0
World Mission in Church and Society	1850	3	1	0	0
World-Wide Missions International	1961	0	0	34	0
Worldwide Evangelization Crusade	1938	12	2	50	3
Youth For Christ/U.S.A.	0	2	0	0	0
TOTALS		366	87	982	56

Libya

ORGANIZATION NAME	BEGAN	NOW	NEW	CHURCHES	GROUPS
All Peoples Baptist Mission	1965	0	2	0	0
Southern Baptist Convention, Foreign Mission Board		2	0	1	0
TOTALS		2	2	1	0

Luxembourg

ORGANIZATION NAME	BEGAN	NOW	NEW	CHURCHES	GROUPS
Christian Church of North America, Msns. Dept.	1954	4	0	80	0
WEFMinistries, Inc.	1973	8	3	0	0
TOTALS		12	3	80	0

Macao

ORGANIZATION NAME	BEGAN	NOW	NEW	CHURCHES	GROUPS
Campus Crusade for Christ, International (Overseas Dept.)	1975	7	0	0	0
Christian Nationals' Evangelism Commission, Inc. (CNEC)	1962	0	0	1	0
Christian Nationals' Evangelism Commission, Inc. (Canada)	1962	0	0	0	0
Christians In Action	1973	3	3	1	1
Evangelize China Fellowship, Inc.	1949	0	0	0	0
Pentecostal Assemblies of Canada, Oseas. Msns. Dept.	1961	0	0	1	0
Southern Baptist Convention, Foreign Mission Board	1910	0	0	3	0
TOTALS		10	3	6	1

ORGANIZATION NAME	BEGAN	NOW	NEW	CHURCHES	GROUPS

Madagascar

ORGANIZATION NAME	BEGAN	NOW	NEW	CHURCHES	GROUPS
American Lutheran Ch., Div. For Wld. Msn.	1888	35	13	1	0
Anglican Orthodox Church	1969	2	0	0	0
Campus Crusade for Christ, International (Overseas Dept.)	1979	1	0	0	0
Church World Service Division of DOM-NCCUSA	0	0	0	0	3
Conservative Baptist Foreign Mission Society	1965	8	0	7	0
Lutheran World Relief, Incorporated	1959	0	0	0	0
MAP International (Medical Assistance Programs)	0	0	0	0	0
United Pentecostal Church Intl. For. Msns. Div.	1969	4	0	0	0
TOTALS		50	13	8	3

Malawi

ORGANIZATION NAME	BEGAN	NOW	NEW	CHURCHES	GROUPS
Africa Evangelical Fellowship	1900	15	1	70	1
Africa Evangelical Fellowship (Canada)	1901	3	0	0	0
African Methodist Episcopal Church, Inc. Dept. of Msns.		0	0	0	0
American Leprosy Missions, Inc.	1974	0	0	0	0
Apostolic Church of Pentecost of Canada-Missionary Dept.	1947	4	0	0	0
Assemblies of God, Div. of For. Msns.	1930	16	0	83	0
Campus Crusade for Christ, International (Overseas Dept.)	1975	1	0	0	0
Christian Churches/Churches of Christ	1908	0	0	0	0
Chr. Echoes Natl. Min., Inc. (Chr. Crusade)		0	0	0	0
Church of God of Prophecy, World Mission Committee	1977	0	0	16	0
Church of God World Missions	1966	2	0	15	0
Church of the Nazarene, Gen. Bd. Dept. of Wld. Msns.	1957	10	0	47	0
Free Methodist Church of N. America Gen. Msny. Bd.	1973	2	2	13	0
General Conference of Seventh-day Adventists	1902	26	13	202	0
Glad Tidings Missionary Society, Inc.	1976	0	0	0	0
Leprosy Relief, Canada, Inc.	1979	0	0	0	0
MAP International (Medical Assistance Programs)		0	0	0	0
Mennonite Central Committee	1963	5	0	0	0
National Baptist Convention, U.S.A., Inc. For. Msn. Bd.	1900	0	0	472	0
Pentecostal Assemblies of Canada, Oseas. Msns. Dept.	1978	2	0	25	0
Pentecostal Holiness Church-World Missions Department	1950	4	2	24	0

ORGANIZATION NAME	BEGAN	NOW	NEW	CHURCHES	GROUPS
Malawi continued...					
Presbyterian Church in Canada, Board of World Mission	0	2	0	0	0
Seventh Day Baptist Missionary Society	1947	4	2	84	0
Southern Baptist Convention, Foreign Mission Board	1959	34	5	172	0
United Church of Canada, Division of World Outreach		2	0	1	0
United Pentecostal Church Intl. For. Msns. Div.	1979	2	0	0	0
United Presbyterian Church in the USA Program Agency	0	1	6	0	0
Wisconsin Evangelical Lutheran Synod, Bd. for Wld. Msns.	1962	4	1	35	0
World Literature Crusade	1970	0	0	0	0
World Mission in Church and Society	0	1	1	0	0
World Outreach	0	0	0	0	0
World-Wide Missions International	1974	0	0	10	0
TOTALS		140	33	1269	1
Malaysia					
Advent Christian Gen. Conf. of America	0	0	0	0	0
Anglican Church of Canada, Natl. and Wld. Program	1973	1	0	0	0
Asian Outreach	1971	0	0	0	0
Assemblies of God, Div. of For. Msns.	1957	16	0	43	0
Campus Crusade for Christ, International (Overseas Dept.)	1968	24	0	0	0
Christian and Missionary Alliance	1965	29	14	0	0
Christian Nationals' Evangelism Commission, Inc. (CNEC)	1954	0	0	7	0
Christian Nationals' Evangelism Commission, Inc. (Canada)	1954	0	0	0	0
Church World Service Division of DOM-NCCCUSA		13	0	0	0
Compassion International, Inc.	1973	0	0	0	0
Evangelize China Fellowship, Inc.	1951	0	0	2	0
General Conference of Seventh-day Adventists	1961	10	4	138	0
Jesus to the Communist World, Inc.		0	0	0	0
Lutheran Church in America-Div. for Wld. Msn. and Ecumenism	1949	4	1	0	0
Navigators, The	1966	2	0	0	0
Overseas Missionary Fellowship	1928	62	17	0	0
Southern Baptist Convention, Foreign Mission Board	1951	22	0	40	0
The Mustard Seed, Inc.	1968	8	0	0	0

ORGANIZATION NAME	BEGAN	NOW	NEW	CHURCHES	GROUPS
Malaysia continued...					
United Pentecostal Church Intl. For. Msns. Div.		0	0	0	0
United Presbyterian Church in the USA Program Agency		2	2	0	0
World Mission in Church and Society	1976	1	1	0	0
Wycliffe Bible Translators International, Inc.	1978	29	0	0	3
TOTALS		223	39	230	3
Mali					
Campus Crusade for Christ, International (Overseas Dept.)	1972	2	0	0	0
Christian and Missionary Alliance	1923	39	13	342	0
Christian Service Corps	0	0	0	0	0
Evangelical Baptist Missions, Inc.	1951	12	4	4	2
Gospel Missionary Union	1919	37	3	37	1
MAP International (Medical Assistance Programs)	0	0	0	0	0
United World Mission, Incorporated	1953	13	3	10	2
Wycliffe Bible Translators International, Inc.	1979	2	0	0	1
TOTALS		105	23	393	6
Malta					
Jesus to the Communist World, Inc.	0	0	0	0	0
TOTALS		0	0	0	0
Marshall Is. .					
Assemblies of God, Div. of For. Msns.	0	4	0	3	0
TOTALS		4	0	3	0
Martinique					
Christian Literature Crusade, Inc.	1979	0	0	0	0
Evangelical Baptist Missions, Inc.	1946	8	0	7	0
Southern Baptist Convention, Foreign Mission Board	1977	7	7	0	0
TOTALS		15	7	7	0

ORGANIZATION NAME	BEGAN	NOW	NEW	CHURCHES	GROUPS

Mauritania

ORGANIZATION NAME	BEGAN	NOW	NEW	CHURCHES	GROUPS
Lutheran World Relief, Incorporated	1974	0	0	0	0
	TOTALS	0	0	0	0

Mauritius

ORGANIZATION NAME	BEGAN	NOW	NEW	CHURCHES	GROUPS
Africa Evangelical Fellowship	1969	4	0	2	3
Africa Evangelical Fellowship (Canada)	1966	2	0	3	0
Southern Baptist Convention, Foreign Mission Board	1978	2	2	0	0
	TOTALS	8	2	5	3

Mexico

ORGANIZATION NAME	BEGAN	NOW	NEW	CHURCHES	GROUPS
Air Crusade, Inc.	1954	0	0	22	0
America's Keswick, Inc.	0	4	2	0	0
American Association for Jewish Evangelism	1955	21	6	32	0
American Baptist Association, Missionary Committee	1870	2	0	10	0
American Baptist Churches in the U.S.A., Intl. Min.	1979	2	2	3	1
American Messianic Fellowship	1976	4	4	12	0
American Missionary Fellowship	1975	2	0	1	0
AMG International (Advancing the Ministries of the Gospel)		6	0	0	0
Anchor Bay Evangelistic Association	1963	8	2	0	0
Apostolic Church of Pentecost of Canada-Missionary Dept.	1915	27	0	811	0
Assemblies of God, Div. of For. Msns.	1878	11	3	100	4
Associate Reformed Presb. Ch., Wld. Witness	0	1	0	0	0
Association of Free Lutheran Congregations	1953	0	0	0	0
Back-Country Evangelism, Inc.	1950	58	8	0	0
Baptist Bible Fellowship International	1951	15	8	12	0
Baptist General Conference Board of World Missions	1965	28	0	0	0
Baptist International Missions, Inc.	1960	17	0	0	0
Baptist Mid-Missions	1953	4	2	0	0
Baptist Missionary Association of America	1965	4	0	0	0
Baptist World Mission	1971	14	2	1	0
Bethany Fellowship Msns. (Div. of Bethany Fellowship, Inc.)					

Mexico continued...

ORGANIZATION NAME	BEGAN	NOW	NEW	CHURCHES	GROUPS
Bethany Missionary Association	1959	2	3	3	0
Bethel Foreign Mission Foundation	1956	27	0	50	0
Bible Club Movement, Inc.	1960	2	0	0	0
Bible Memory Association International	1974	2	2	0	0
Bible Missionary Church, World Missions Department	1965	8	3	15	2
Bible Translations On Tape, Inc.	1977	2	2	0	0
Breakthrough Ministries	1966	0	0	0	0
Brethren Assemblies	0	14	0	0	0
CAM International	1959	46	7	15	1
Campus Crusade for Christ, International (Overseas Dept.)	1962	153	0	0	0
Child Evangelism Fellowship, Inc.	1943	6	0	0	0
Children's Haven International, Inc.	1972	11	71	0	1
Christian and Missionary Alliance	1954	2	0	19	1
Christian Church (Disciples of Christ) Div. of Oseas. Min.	1895	5	0	0	0
Christian Churches/Churches of Christ	1933	100	0	0	0
Chr. Echoes Natl. Min., Inc. (Chr. Crusade)	0	0	0	0	0
Christian Nationals' Evangelism Commission, Inc. (CNEC)	1968	2	0	0	0
Christian Nationals' Evangelism Commission, Inc. (Canada)	1968	0	0	0	0
Christian Reformed Board For World Missions	1962	23	5	0	0
Christian Reformed World Relief Committee	1969	4	3	35	12
Christians In Action	1957	7	7	5	0
Church of God (Anderson, Indiana) Msny. Bd.	1946	5	4	31	0
Church of God (Holiness) For. Msn. Brd.	1967	4	0	8	0
Church of God General Conference Mission Department	1963	1	0	1	0
Church of God in Christ, Mennonite Gen. Msn. Bd., Inc.	1933	45	0	126	0
Church of God of Prophecy, World Mission Committee	1944	0	0	0	0
Church of God of the Apostolic Faith, Inc.	0	0	0	0	0
Church of God World Missions	1944	4	2	712	0
Church of the Nazarene, Gen. Bd. Dept. of Wld. Msns.	1903	0	0	219	0
Churches of Christ in Christian Union: Foreign Msny. Dept.	1944	6	0	8	0
Compassion International, Inc.	1979	0	0	0	0
Congregational Holiness Church Foreign Mission Dept.	1963	5	1	75	0
Conservative Baptist Association of America	1952	9	0	34	0

Mexico continued...

ORGANIZATION NAME	BEGAN	NOW	NEW	CHURCHES	GROUPS
Elim Fellowship, Inc.	1962	10	4	0	0
Evangelical Congregational Church	1965	1	1	0	0
Evangelical Covenant Church of America, Bd. of Wld. Msn.	1946	10	4	0	0
Evangelical Friends Mission	1967	4	4	3	0
Evangelical Latin League, Inc.	0	0	0	0	0
Evangelical Mennonite Conference Board of Missions	1954	19	6	10	40
Evangelical Methodist Church World Missions	1946	6	6	35	3
Faith Christian Fellowship World Outreach	1979	3	0	50	0
FARMS International, Inc.	1977	2	2	0	0
Fellowship of Grace Brethren Churches, For. Msny. Soc.	1951	6	0	7	0
Fellowship of Independent Missions	1971	0	0	0	0
Food For The Hungry International	1978	0	0	0	0
Foundation For His Ministry-Orphanage Committee	1967	26	17	0	0
Franconia Mennonite Conference Mission Commission	1958	6	0	8	1
Free Methodist Church of N. America Gen. Msny. Bd.	1917	6	2	11	0
Full Gospel Grace Fellowship	0	0	0	0	0
Full Gospel Native Missionary Association	0	0	0	0	0
General Conference Mennonite Church, Comm. on Oseas. Msn.	1950	13	16	3	0
General Conference of Seventh-day Adventists	1893	31	16	378	0
General Conference of the Evangelical Baptist Church, Inc.	1965	0	0	0	0
Glad Tidings Missionary Society, Inc.	1972	0	0	0	0
Globe Missionary Evangelism	1971	14	4	0	0
Gospel Crusade World Wide Mission Outreach	1972	2	0	0	0
Gospel Missionary Union	1956	19	4	5	0
Gospel Recordings Incorporated	1961	2	0	0	0
Houses of Refuge, Intl. Orphanages Assn. Inc.	1977	12	12	5	1
International Bible Institute	1976	1	0	1	0
Intl. Church of the Foursquare Gospel--Dept. of Msns. Intl.	1943	3	0	110	1
International Fellowship of Evangelical Students - USA	0	2	0	0	0
Intl Pentecostal Ch. of Christ, Global Msns. Dept.	1952	2	2	6	0
Latin America Mission, Inc.	1970	10	0	0	0
Lester Sumrall Evangelistic Association	0	0	0	0	0
Life For Latins, Inc.	1978	2	2	0	0

Mexico continued...

ORGANIZATION NAME	BEGAN	NOW	NEW	CHURCHES	GROUPS
Logoi, Inc.	1980	2	0	0	0
Luis Palau Evangelistic Team, Inc.	1967	11	2	0	0
Lutheran Church-Missouri Synod	1940	3	0	15	0
MAP International (Medical Assistance Programs)	0	0	0	0	0
Maranatha Baptist Mission, Inc.	0	0	0	10	0
Media Ministries Division, Mennonite Bd. of Msns.	1950	0	0	12	0
Mennonite Board of Missions	1976	2	2	0	0
Mennonite Brethren Missions/Services	1950	11	15	1	0
Mennonite Mission Bd. of Pacific Coast Conf. (Mexico Bd.)	1950	2	0	7	0
Metropolitan Church Association	1930	1	0	0	0
Mexican Border Missions	1961	4	2	500	0
Mexican Christian Mission, Inc.	1956	3	0	55	0
Mexican Mission Ministries, Inc.	1954	5	0	35	0
Mexican Missions, Inc.	1960	1	0	0	0
Ministry of Mission Services	1968	5	2	3	1
Mission Aides, Incorporated	1978	4	4	0	0
Mission Aviation Fellowship	1946	6	8	0	25
Mission SOS	1976	2	0	0	0
Mission to the World	1973	16	9	0	0
Missionary Revival Crusade	0	0	0	0	0
Missions of Baja	1967	5	0	0	0
Navigators, The	1966	12	4	0	0
New Life League	0	1	0	0	0
New Tribes Mission	1943	27	0	0	0
Next Towns Crusade, Inc.	1957	6	0	14	0
O.C. Ministries, Inc.	1979	2	2	0	0
Open Bible Standard Missions, Inc.	1965	2	2	3	0
Operation Mobilization Send the Light, Inc.	1958	20	0	0	0
Pan American Missionary Society, Inc.	1958	1	1	3	1
Pan American Missions, Inc.	1959	2	0	0	0
Pentecostal Church of God, World Missions Department	1949	2	0	55	0
Pentecostal Free Will Baptist Church, Inc.	1963	2	0	0	0
Pentecostal Holiness Church-World Missions Department	1931	2	0	112	0

Mexico continued...

ORGANIZATION NAME	BEGAN	NOW	NEW	CHURCHES	GROUPS
Petra International, Inc.	1977	5	0	2	0
Presbyterian Church in the U.S.A., Div. of Intl. Msn.	1874	8	3	0	0
Reformed Church in America General Program Council	1925	16	2	0	0
Salvation Army, Canada and Bermuda	1904	1	0	0	0
Salvation Army, The	0	8	0	0	0
Scripture Union, U.S.A.	1978	1	1	0	0
Seventh Day Baptist Missionary Society	1976	0	0	32	0
Share the Care International	1960	4	0	20	0
Southern Baptist Convention, Foreign Mission Board	1880	83	4	373	0
Spanish-World Gospel Mission, Inc.	1970	2	0	0	0
Totonac Bible Center, Inc.	1972	0	0	40	0
Trans World Missions	1949	3	0	0	0
Unevangelized Fields Mission	1971	23	12	0	0
United Church Board For World Ministries	1872	2	0	0	0
United Indian Missions, Inc.	0	0	0	0	0
United Methodist Ch. Wld. Div. of the Bd. of Global Min.	1873	0	0	0	0
United Missionary Fellowship	1951	3	1	12	0
United Pentecostal Church Intl. For. Msns. Div.	1979	2	0	0	0
United Presbyterian Church in the USA Program Agency	1872	4	0	0	0
We Go, Inc. (World Encounter Gospel Organization)	1979	2	2	0	0
Wesleyan Church Gen. Dept. of Wld. Msns.	1922	1	0	132	0
Wider Ministries Commission	1870	0	0	1	0
Wisconsin Evangelical Lutheran Synod, Bd. for Wld. Msns.	1968	0	0	5	0
World Baptist Fellowship Mission Agency International	1953	28	4	25	0
World Concern/Crista International	1975	0	2	0	0
World Gospel Mission	1945	6	0	9	0
World Literature Crusade	1963	0	0	0	0
World Mission in Church and Society	1904	4	1	0	0
World Mission Prayer League	1945	6	4	0	0
World Missionary Evangelism, Inc.	0	0	0	0	0
World Missions, Inc.	1959	11	2	25	0
World-Wide Missions International	1960	0	0	16	0
Wycliffe Bible Translators International, Inc.	1936	288	0	0	112

Mexico continued...

ORGANIZATION NAME	BEGAN	NOW	NEW	CHURCHES	GROUPS
Youth Enterprises, Inc.	1960	5	0	15	0
TOTALS		1611	334	4523	207

Micronesia

ORGANIZATION NAME	BEGAN	NOW	NEW	CHURCHES	GROUPS
Campus Crusade for Christ, International (Overseas Dept.)	1973	2	0	0	0
TOTALS		2	0	0	0

Middle East-general

ORGANIZATION NAME	BEGAN	NOW	NEW	CHURCHES	GROUPS
BMMF/International (U.S.A.)	1979	2	2	0	0
Christian Literature Crusade, Inc.	1976	2	0	0	0
Conservative Baptist Foreign Mission Society	1977	2	2	0	1
Lutheran Church in America-Div. for Wld. Msn. and Ecumenism	1967	6	5	0	0
Lutheran Church-Missouri Synod	1960	2	0	0	0
Operation Mobilization - Canada	1963	63	0	20	0
United Presbyterian Church in the USA Program Agency	0	2	0	0	0
Worldwide Evangelization Crusade	1962	9	5	0	3
TOTALS		88	14	20	4

Monaco

ORGANIZATION NAME	BEGAN	NOW	NEW	CHURCHES	GROUPS
Slavic Gospel Association	1955	2	0	0	0
Trans World Radio	1059	38	1	0	0
TOTALS		40	1	0	0

Montserrat

ORGANIZATION NAME	BEGAN	NOW	NEW	CHURCHES	GROUPS
Pentecostal Assemblies of the World, Inc. For. Msns. Dept.	1976	2	0	0	0
TOTALS		2	0	0	0

ORGANIZATION NAME	BEGAN	NOW	NEW	CHURCHES	GROUPS

Morocco

ORGANIZATION NAME	BEGAN	NOW	NEW	CHURCHES	GROUPS
Fellowship of Independent Missions	1950	0	0	0	0
Gospel Missionary Union	1894	23	3	4	1
MAP International (Medical Assistance Programs)	0	0	0	0	0
Natl. Assn. of Congregational Chr. Chs. of the U.S.A.	0	0	0	0	0
North Africa Mission	1884	9	2	7	2
Refugee Children, Inc.	1967	1	0	0	0
Southern Baptist Convention, Foreign Mission Board	1966	8	6	0	0
Trans World Radio	1954	0	0	0	0
TOTALS		41	11	11	3

Mozambique

ORGANIZATION NAME	BEGAN	NOW	NEW	CHURCHES	GROUPS
Africa Evangelical Fellowship	1936	0	0	400	1
Africa Evangelical Fellowship (Canada)	1936	0	0	0	0
African Methodist Episcopal Church, Inc. Dept. of Msns.	0	0	0	0	0
Assemblies of God, Div. of For. Msns.	1974	0	0	50	0
Church of God of Prophecy, World Mission Committee	1979	0	0	9	0
Church of God World Missions	1966	0	0	150	0
Church of the Nazarene, Gen. Bd. Dept. of Wld. Msns.	1922	8	0	203	0
Free Methodist Church of N. America Gen. Msny. Bd.	1885	0	0	80	0
Lutheran World Relief, Incorporated	1975	0	0	0	0
MAP International (Medical Assistance Programs)	0	0	0	0	0
Pentecostal Assemblies of Canada, Oseas. Msns. Dept.	1938	1	0	370	0
United Methodist Ch. Wld. Div. of the Bd. of Global Min.	1881	0	0	0	0
United Presbyterian Church in the USA Program Agency	0	2	0	0	0
TOTALS		11	0	1262	1

Namibia

ORGANIZATION NAME	BEGAN	NOW	NEW	CHURCHES	GROUPS
Africa Evangelical Fellowship	1971	3	0	0	2
Africa Evangelical Fellowship (Canada)	1972	0	0	0	0
African Methodist Episcopal Church, Inc. Dept. of Msns.	0	2	0	0	0
Church of God World Missions	0		0	23	0

ORGANIZATION NAME	BEGAN	NOW	NEW	CHURCHES	GROUPS
Namibia continued...					
Church of the Nazarene, Gen. Bd. Dept. of Wld. Msns.	0	4	0	1	0
Global Outreach Mission	0	2	0	0	0
Southern Baptist Convention, Foreign Mission Board	1968	4	0	3	0
Youth With A Mission	1979	0	0	0	0
TOTALS		15	0	27	2

Nepal

ORGANIZATION NAME	BEGAN	NOW	NEW	CHURCHES	GROUPS
American Lutheran Ch., Div. For Wld. Msn.	1978	0	0	0	0
AMG International (Advancing the Ministries of the Gospel)	1978	0	0	1	0
Assemblies of God, Div. of For. Msns.	1973	2	0	0	0
BMMF International/Canada	1954	6	5	0	0
BMMF/International (U.S.A.)	1954	5	2	0	0
Christian Aid Mission	1953	0	0	29	12
Christian Church (Disciples of Christ) Div. of Oseas. Min.	1955	2	0	0	0
General Conference of Seventh-day Adventists	1960	2	2	1	0
International Christian Fellowship	1969	1	0	0	1
International Needs-USA	1974	0	0	0	0
Leprosy Mission Canada	1963	0	0	0	0
Living Bibles International	1973	6	0	0	1
Lutheran Church in America-Div. for Wld. Msn. and Ecumenism	1974	2	1	0	0
MAP International (Medical Assistance Programs)	0	0	0	0	0
Mennonite Board of Missions	1957	3	0	0	0
Mennonite Brethren Missions/Services	1969	2	0	0	1
Mennonite Central Committee	1957	18	0	0	0
New Life League	0	0	0	0	0
Operation Eyesight Universal	1977	0	0	0	0
Operation Mobilization - Canada	1964	2	0	5	0
Operation Mobilization Send the Light, Inc.	0	0	0	0	0
Presbyterian Church in Canada, Board of World Mission	1973	3	1	0	0
Regions Beyond Missionary Union (U.S.A.)	1954	11	4	0	0
United Church Board For World Ministries	1966	2	2	0	0
United Church of Canada, Division of World Outreach	0	15	0	0	0

ORGANIZATION NAME	BEGAN	NOW	NEW	CHURCHES	GROUPS
Nepal continued...					
United Presbyterian Church in the USA Program Agency	0	12	3	0	0
Wesleyan Church Gen. Dept. of Wld. Msns.	0	1	0	0	0
World Mission Prayer League	1956	14	8	0	0
World Mission Prayer League Canada	0	2	1	0	0
World Neighbors, Inc.	0	0	0	0	0
World-Wide Missions International	1964	2	0	1	0
Youth With A Mission	1972	0	0	0	0
	TOTALS	113	29	37	15
Netherlands					
Assemblies of God, Div. of For. Msns.	1965	6	0	55	0
Baptist Bible Fellowship International	1978	4	0	0	0
Baptist Mid-Missions	1954	6	0	0	0
Bible Christian Union, Inc.	1946	17	6	3	2
Bible Club Movement, Inc.	1948	0	0	0	0
Brethren Assemblies	0	2	0	0	0
Campus Crusade for Christ, International (Overseas Dept.)	1968	42	0	0	0
Child Evangelism Fellowship, Inc.	1949	2	0	0	0
Christian and Missionary Alliance	0	4	0	3	0
Christian Literature Crusade, Inc.	1962	0	0	0	0
Church of God World Missions	1966	0	0	1	0
Church of the Nazarene, Gen. Bd. Dept. of Wld. Msns.	1967	0	0	3	0
Eastern European Mission	1955	2	1	1	0
Global Outreach Mission	0	8	0	0	0
Gospel Recordings Incorporated	1965	0	0	0	0
International Crusades, Inc.	1979	6	6	1	0
International Missions, Inc.	1976	2	0	1	3
Jesus to the Communist World, Inc.	0	0	0	0	0
Living Bibles International	1973	2	0	0	0
Lutheran Church in America-Div. for Wld. Msn. and Ecumenism	1977	1	1	0	1
Maranatha Baptist Mission, Inc.	0	0	0	0	0
Mission to Europe's Millions, Inc.	0	0	0	2	0

ORGANIZATION NAME	BEGAN	NOW	NEW	CHURCHES	GROUPS
Netherlands continued...					
Navigators, The	1950	0	0	0	0
Open Doors With Brother Andrew	0	0	0	0	0
Operation Mobilization - Canada	1962	5	0	100	0
United Pentecostal Church Intl. For. Msns. Div.	0	2	0	0	0
United Presbyterian Church in the USA Program Agency	0	1	0	0	0
WEFMinistries, Inc.	1959	8	0	0	0
Youth For Christ/U.S.A.	1948	4	0	0	0
Youth With A Mission	1970	0	0	0	0
TOTALS		124	14	170	6

Netherlands Antilles

ORGANIZATION NAME	BEGAN	NOW	NEW	CHURCHES	GROUPS
Baptist International Missions, Inc.	0	4	0	0	0
Bethesda Mission, Inc.	1953	6	0	1	0
Calvary Evangelistic Mission, Inc./WIVV Msny. Radio Station	1955	2	0	0	0
Church of God of Prophecy, World Mission Committee	1935	2	0	21	0
Church of God World Missions	1948	0	0	3	0
Evangelical Alliance Mission (TEAM)	1931	23	5	10	1
Evangelical Alliance Mission of Canada, Inc.	1931	1	0	12	0
General Conference of Seventh-day Adventists	1934	2	2	5	0
Global Outreach Mission	1946	4	0	0	0
Southern Baptist Convention, Foreign Mission Board	1979	2	2	0	0
Trans World Radio	1964	66	0	0	0
Word of Life Fellowship	1978	2	2	0	0
TOTALS		112	11	52	1

New Caledonia

ORGANIZATION NAME	BEGAN	NOW	NEW	CHURCHES	GROUPS
Assemblies of God, Div. of For. Msns.	1969	4	0	4	0
TOTALS		4	0	4	0

ORGANIZATION NAME	BEGAN	NOW	NEW	CHURCHES	GROUPS
New Zealand					
ACTS International	1974	2	0	50	0
Baptist Bible Fellowship International	1971	6	0	0	0
Baptist International Missions, Inc.	1973	4	0	0	0
Baptist Mid-Missions	1973	9	0	0	0
Campus Crusade for Christ, International (Overseas Dept.)	1972	17	0	0	0
Child Evangelism Fellowship, Inc.	1951	1	0	0	0
Christian and Missionary Alliance	1972	8	6	4	0
Christian Literature Crusade, Inc.	1961	0	0	0	0
Church of the Nazarene, Gen. Bd. Dept. of Wld. Msns.	1952	0	0	13	0
Jews For Jesus	0	0	0	0	0
Navigators, The	1978	0	0	0	0
Protestant Reformed Churches in America	1953	6	0	0	0
South Pacific Evangelical Fellowship	0	0	0	1	0
United Missionary Fellowship	1968	6	0	3	0
United Pentecostal Church Intl. For. Msns. Div.	1969	2	0	0	0
Youth For Christ/U.S.A.	0	2	0	0	0
Youth With A Mission	1967	0	0	0	0
	TOTALS	67	6	71	0
Nicaragua					
American Baptist Association, Missionary Committee	1963	1	0	1	0
American Baptist Churches in the U.S.A., Intl. Min.	1917	9	2	42	0
AMG International (Advancing the Ministries of the Gospel)	1978	0	0	30	0
Assemblies of God, Div. of For. Msns.	1926	6	0	122	0
Baptist Bible Fellowship International	1969	4	0	0	0
Baptist Missionary Association of America	1965	0	0	0	0

ORGANIZATION NAME	BEGAN	NOW	NEW	CHURCHES	GROUPS
Nicaragua continued..					
Brethren Assemblies	0	2	0	0	0
Brethren in Christ Missions	1965	4	0	31	0
CAM International	1900	8	0	68	1
Campus Crusade for Christ, International (Overseas Dept.)	1976	4	0	0	0
Chr. Echoes Natl. Min., Inc. (Chr. Crusade)	0	0	0	0	0
Christian Reformed Board For World Missions	1973	5	1	0	0
Christian Reformed World Relief Committee	1972	0	0	0	0
Church of God of Prophecy, World Mission Committee	1962	0	0	30	0
Church of God World Missions	1952	2	0	48	0
Church of the Nazarene, Gen. Bd. Dept. of Wld. Msns.	1943	5	0	52	0
Church of the United Brethren in Christ, Bd. of Msns.	1966	0	0	5	0
Compassion International, Inc.	1974	0	0	0	0
Conservative Mennonite Board of Missions and Charities	1968	26	19	9	0
Evangelical Mennonite Conference Board of Missions	1966	9	2	4	3
Gospel Outreach	1980	0	0	0	0
Holt International Children's Services, Inc.	1978	0	0	0	0
Intl. Church of the Foursquare Gospel-Dept. of Msns. Intl.	1955	2	0	22	0
Lutheran World Relief, Incorporated	1973	0	0	0	0
MAP International (Medical Assistance Programs)	0	0	0	0	0
Mennonite Central Committee	1978	2	0	0	0
Mennonite Economic Development Associates	1972	0	0	0	0
Missionary Air Transport, Inc.	1975	0	0	0	0
Moravian Church in America, Bd. of Wld. Msn.	1849	2	3	118	0
National Baptist Convention, U.S.A., Inc. For. Msn. Bd.	1958	1	0	3	0
Pentecostal Free Will Baptist Church, Inc.	1971	0	0	0	0
Southern Baptist Convention, Foreign Mission Board	1976	6	6	41	0
Trans World Missions	1966	0	0	0	0
United Church of Canada, Division of World Outreach	0	0	0	1	0
United Pentecostal Church Intl.For. Msns. Div.	1970	2	0	0	0
United World Mission, Incorporated	1969	0	0	6	0
World Mission in Church and Society	1956	2	1	0	0
TOTALS		102	34	633	4

ORGANIZATION NAME	BEGAN	NOW	NEW	CHURCHES	GROUPS
Niger					
Baptist International Missions, Inc.	1966	4	0	0	0
Christian Reformed World Relief Committee	1975	2	1	0	0
Church World Service Division of DOM-NCCCUSA	0	2	0	0	0
Evangelical Baptist Missions, Inc.	1929	19	4	6	1
Fellowship of Independent Missions	1971	0	0	0	0
Lutheran World Relief, Incorporated	1974	4	2	0	0
MAP International (Medical Assistance Programs)	0	0	0	0	0
Southern Baptist Convention, Foreign Mission Board	1969	2	0	0	0
Sudan Interior Mission, Inc.	1924	85	35	28	9
United Church Board For World Ministries	1977	0	0	0	0
World Ministries Commission	0	5	0	0	0
World Neighbors, Inc.	0	0	0	0	0
TOTALS		123	42	34	10
Nigeria					
Advent Christian Gen. Conf. of America	0	0	0	0	0
African Methodist Episcopal Church, Inc. Dept. of Msns.	1930	0	0	0	0
African Methodist Episcopal Zion Ch., Dept. of Oseas. Msns.	1976	1	0	0	0
American Baptist Association, Missionary Committee	1913	15	5	2	0
American Lutheran Ch., Div. For Wld. Msn.	1980	2	0	1	0
AMG International (Advancing the Ministries of the Gospel)	1970	0	0	0	0
Anglican Orthodox Church	1939	30	0	1759	0
Assemblies of God, Div. of For. Msns.	1952	0	0	15	0
Bible Holiness Movement	1969	0	0	25	1
Bible Missionary Church, World Missions Department	0	0	0	0	0
Bible Way Chs. of Our Lord Jesus Christ Worldwide, Inc.	1969	12	0	0	0
Brethren Assemblies	0	38	0	0	0
Campus Crusade for Christ, International (Overseas Dept.)	1969	0	0	0	0
Child Evangelism Fellowship, Inc.	1974	0	0	0	0
Christian Aid Mission	1953	6	0	350	28
Christian Churches/Churches of Christ	1950	0	0	0	0
Christian Mission for the Deaf	1959	0	0	0	0

Nigeria continued...

ORGANIZATION NAME	BEGAN	NOW	NEW	CHURCHES	GROUPS
Christian Nationals' Evangelism Commission, Inc. (CNEC)	1963	0	0	0	0
Christian Nationals' Evangelism Commission, Inc. (Canada)	1963	0	0	0	0
Christian Reformed Board For World Missions	1940	97	41	0	0
Christian Reformed World Relief Committee	1970	2	1	150	0
Christian Service Corps	0	1	0	0	2
Christian Union General Mission Board	1943	1	0	0	0
Church of God (Seventh Day), Gen. Conf., Msns. Abroad	1939	0	0	50	0
Church of God General Conference Mission Department	1967	6	0	8	0
Church of God in Christ, Mennonite Gen. Msn. Bd., Inc.	1963	8	0	0	0
Church of God of Prophecy, World Mission Committee	1971	0	0	17	0
Church of God World Missions	1952	2	0	58	0
Church of God, USA Headquarters	0	0	0	0	0
Church of the Nazarene, Gen. Bd. Dept. of Wld. Msns.	1976	0	0	20	0
Elim Fellowship, Inc.	1975	4	3	0	0
Emmanuel International	1979	6	0	0	0
Evangelical Bible Mission, Inc.	1970	0	0	10	0
Evangelical Scripture Mission	1970	0	0	3	3
Evangelism Resources	1980	2	2	0	0
Fellowship of Evangelical Baptist Chs. in Canada	1979	2	2	830	3
General Conference of Seventh-day Adventists	1914	14	10	270	0
Haggai Institute for Advanced Leadership Training, Inc.	1979	0	0	0	0
Intl. Church of the Foursquare Gospel--Dept. of Msns. Intl.	1954	2	0	69	0
International Gospel League	1958	0	0	0	0
Jesus to the Communist World, Inc.	0	0	0	0	0
Living Bibles International	1973	18	0	0	7
Lott Carey Baptist Foreign Mission Convention	0	3	0	0	0
Lutheran Church-Missouri Synod	1936	17	6	250	4
Lutheran World Relief, Incorporated	1968	0	0	0	0
MAP International (Medical Assistance Programs)	0	0	0	0	0
Mennonite Board of Missions	1959	2	2	53	0
Mennonite Brethren Missions/Services	1944	1	0	0	0
Mennonite Central Committee	1963	15	0	0	0
Mennonite Economic Development Associates	1970	0	0	0	0

ORGANIZATION NAME	BEGAN	NOW	NEW	CHURCHES	GROUPS
Nigeria continued...					
Mission to the World	1975	4	2	0	0
Missionary Church, Div. of Overseas Ministries	1905	12	0	235	0
Natl. Assn. of Congregational Chr. Chs. of the U.S.A.	0	0	0	0	0
Navigators, The	1976	0	0	0	0
North American Baptist Gen. Msny. Soc., Inc.	1961	16	3	115	20
Pentecostal Assemblies of the World, Inc. For. Msns. Dept.	0	2	0	0	0
Pentecostal Holiness Church-World Missions Department	1955	2	0	30	0
Pillar of Fire Missions	1979	2	0	4	0
Presbyterian Church in Canada, Board of World Mission	1956	4	4	0	0
Presbyterian Church in the U.S.A., Div. of Intl. Msn.	1974	2	2	0	0
Source of Light Ministries, Intl.	0	2	0	0	0
Southern Baptist Convention, Foreign Mission Board	1850	132	0	2500	0
Sudan Interior Mission, Inc.	1893	228	77	1400	16
Things to Come Mission, Inc.	1972	0	0	24	0
United Methodist Ch. Wld. Div. of the Bd. of Global Min.	1926	0	0	0	0
United Pentecostal Church Intl. For. Msns. Div.	1972	2	0	0	0
United Presbyterian Church in the USA Program Agency	0	2	0	0	0
World Literature Crusade	1975	0	0	0	0
World-Wide Missions International	1957	0	0	10	0
TOTALS		715	160	8258	84

Norway

ORGANIZATION NAME	BEGAN	NOW	NEW	CHURCHES	GROUPS
Baptist Bible Fellowship International	1971	8	0	0	0
Baptist International Missions, Inc.	1973	6	0	0	0
Bible Club Movement, Inc.	0	0	0	0	0
Campus Crusade for Christ, International (Overseas Dept.)	1974	2	0	0	0
Child Evangelism Fellowship, Inc.	1950	3	0	0	0
Jesus to the Communist World, Inc.	0	0	0	0	0
Living Bibles International	1973	2	0	0	1
Navigators, The	1957	0	0	0	0
United Pentecostal Church Intl. For. Msns. Div.	0	2	0	0	0
World Literature Crusade	1968	0	0	0	0

ORGANIZATION NAME	BEGAN	NOW	NEW	CHURCHES	GROUPS
Norway continued...					
Youth With A Mission	1970	0	0	0	0
	TOTALS	23	0	0	1
Oceania-general					
Anglican Church of Canada, Natl. and Wld. Program	1976	1	0	0	0
General Baptist Foreign Mission Society, Inc.	1947	2	0	1	0
Liebenzell Mission of Canada	1920	0	0	0	0
WEFMinistries, Inc.	1970	2	0	0	0
	TOTALS	5	0	1	0
Oman					
Reformed Church in America General Program Council	1892	12	3	0	0
	TOTALS	12	3	0	0
Pacific Trust Terr.					
Assemblies of God, Div. of For. Msns.	0	4	0	2	0
Baptist Bible Fellowship International	1973	2	0	0	0
Baptist International Missions, Inc.	0	4	0	0	0
Bible Club Movement, Inc.	0	0	0	0	0
Christian Service Corps	0	4	0	0	0
Far East Broadcasting Company, Inc.	1976	8	10	0	0
General Conference of Seventh-day Adventists	1930	7	7	0	0
Liebenzell Mission of U.S.A., Inc.	1906	13	3	29	3
United Church Board For World Ministries	1852	2	2	0	0
United Presbyterian Church in the USA Program Agency		0	2	0	0
Youth With A Mission	1978	0	0	0	0
	TOTALS	44	24	31	3

Pakistan

ORGANIZATION NAME	BEGAN	NOW	NEW	CHURCHES	GROUPS
Afghan Border Crusade	1944	7	0	5	0
AMG International (Advancing the Ministries of the Gospel)	1976	2	0	2	0
Anglican Orthodox Church	1969	0	0	0	0
Assemblies of God, Div. of For. Msns.		2	0	0	0
Associate Reformed Presb. Ch., Wld. Witness	1907	17	7	120	5
Baptist Bible Fellowship International	1952	2	2	0	0
BMMF International/Canada	1852	7	5	0	1
BMMF International (U.S.A.)	1852	4	2	0	0
Brethren Assemblies		1	0	0	0
Campus Crusade for Christ, International (Overseas Dept.)	1960	19	0	0	0
Christian Literature Crusade, Inc.	1960	2	0	0	0
Christian Nationals' Evangelism Commission, Inc. (CNEC)	1975	0	0	0	0
Christian Nationals' Evangelism Commission, Inc. (Canada)	1975	0	0	0	0
Church of God World Missions	1978	0	0	2	0
Church World Service Division of DOM-NCCCUSA		2	0	0	0
Conservative Baptist Foreign Mission Society	1954	15	0	8	6
Evangelical Alliance Mission (TEAM)	1946	49	7	19	1
Evangelical Alliance Mission of Canada, Inc.	1947	6	2	6	0
Evangelical Methodist Church Bible Methodist Missions		0	0	100	0
Evangelism Center, Inc.	1980	0	0	0	0
Fellowship of Evangelical Baptist Chs. in Canada	1971	4	2	15	3
General Conference of Seventh-day Adventists	1914	39	13	36	0
International Christian Fellowship	1953	9	0	0	3
International Missions, Inc.	1954	14	4	5	2
MAP International (Medical Assistance Programs)		0	0	0	0
Operation Eyesight Universal	1976	0	0	0	0
Operation Mobilization - Canada	1978	49	0	10	0
Red Sea Mission Team, Inc., U.S.A. Council	1977	0	0	0	1
Salvation Army, Canada and Bermuda	1883	5	0	0	0
United Methodist Ch. Wld. Div. of the Bd. of Global Min.	1924	0	0	0	0
United Pentecostal Church Intl. For. Msns. Div.	1971	7	2	0	0
United Presbyterian Church in the USA Program Agency	1834	31	8	0	0
World Mission Prayer League	1946	17	8	0	0

ORGANIZATION NAME	BEGAN	NOW	NEW	CHURCHES	GROUPS
Pakistan continued...					
World Mission Prayer League Canada	0	4	2	0	0
World-Wide Missions International	1962	0	0	1	0
Youth With A Mission	1972	0	0	0	0
	TOTALS	314	54	329	22

Panama

ORGANIZATION NAME	BEGAN	NOW	NEW	CHURCHES	GROUPS
Assemblies of God, Div. of For. Msns.	1967	12	0	16	0
Baptist Bible Fellowship International	1977	2	0	0	0
Baptist International Missions, Inc.	0	2	0	0	0
CAM International	1944	9	2	17	1
Campus Crusade for Christ, International (Overseas Dept.)	1965	29	0	0	0
Chinese Christian Mission	1979	2	2	2	1
Christian Literature Crusade, Inc.	1976	0	0	0	0
Church of God (Anderson, Indiana) Msny. Bd.	1910	2	2	22	0
Church of God of Prophecy, World Mission Committee	1946	0	0	16	0
Church of God World Missions	1944	9	2	37	0
Church of God, USA Headquarters	0	0	0	0	0
Church of the Nazarene, Gen. Bd. Dept. of Wld. Msns.	1953	2	0	11	0
Food For The Hungry International	1975	0	0	0	0
General Conference of Seventh-day Adventists	1906	2	2	70	1
Gospel Missionary Union	1953	15	4	0	0
Intl. Church of the Foursquare Gospel--Dept. of Msns. Intl.	1928	4	2	361	0
International Gospel League	1972	0	0	0	0
Latin America Mission, Inc.	1955	2	2	0	0
Lutheran Church-Missouri Synod	1942	0	0	0	0
Maranatha Baptist Mission, Inc.	0	0	0	2	0
Mennonite Brethren Missions/Services	1958	4	5	10	2
National Association of Free Will Baptists, Bd. of For. Msns	1962	5	0	10	0
Natl. Baptist Convention of Amer., For. Msn. Bd.	0	1	0	4	0
New Tribes Mission	1953	60	0	0	0
Overseas Christian Servicemen's Centers	1958	2	2	0	0
Pan American Missionary Society, Inc.	1958	0	0	7	4

ORGANIZATION NAME	BEGAN	NOW	NEW	CHURCHES	GROUPS
Panama continued...					
Southern Baptist Convention, Foreign Mission Board	1975	18	0	54	0
United Church of Canada, Division of World Outreach	0	2	0	1	0
United Methodist Ch. Wld. Div. of the Bd. of Global Min.	1905	0	0	0	0
World Mission in Church and Society	1919	2	1	0	0
World Radio Missionary Fellowship, Inc.	1954	2	0	0	0
World-Wide Missions International	1975	0	0	0	0
Wycliffe Bible Translators International, Inc.	1970	16	0	0	5
TOTALS		204	26	640	14

Papua New Guinea

ORGANIZATION NAME	BEGAN	NOW	NEW	CHURCHES	GROUPS
American Lutheran Ch., Div. For Wld. Msn.	1886	67	17	1	0
Apostolic Christian Church (Nazarene), Apos. Chr. Ch. Found.	1959	9	3	32	0
Baptist Bible Fellowship International	1961	12	0	0	0
Baptist International Missions, Inc.	1968	6	0	0	0
Baptist World Mission	0	6	0	0	0
Bethel Foreign Mission Foundation	1959	6	0	0	0
Bible Missionary Church, World Missions Department	1960	11	2	65	1
Brethren Assemblies	0	4	0	0	0
Campus Crusade for Christ, International (Overseas Dept.)	1978	0	0	0	0
Christian Literature Crusade, Inc.	1959	2	0	0	0
Christian Service Corps	0	2	0	0	0
Church of the Nazarene, Gen. Bd. Dept. of Wld. Msns.	1955	46	0	30	0
Churches of Christ in Christian Union: Foreign Msny. Dept.	1963	21	5	75	0
Compassion International, Inc.	1978	0	0	0	0
Evangelical Bible Mission, Inc.	1948	32	12	100	3
Evangelical Lutheran Church, Division of World Missions	1979	3	1	1	0
General Conference of Seventh-day Adventists	1949	2	2	382	0
Intl. Church of the Foursquare Gospel--Dept. of Msns. Intl.	1956	5	3	213	0
Leprosy Mission Canada	1965	0	0	0	0
Liebenzell Mission of Canada	1914	0	0	0	0
Liebenzell Mission of U.S.A., Inc.	1914	3	0	16	2
Lutheran Church-Missouri Synod	1948	25	5	335	5

ORGANIZATION NAME	BEGAN	NOW	NEW	CHURCHES	GROUPS
Papua New Guinea continued...					
Lutheran World Relief, Incorporated	1960	0	0	0	0
MAP International (Medical Assistance Programs)	0	0	0	0	0
Maranatha Baptist Mission, Inc.	0	0	0	0	0
Mission to the World	1975	3	7	0	0
New Life League	0	2	0	0	0
New Tribes Mission	1950	175	0	0	0
Open Bible Standard Missions, Inc.	1973	2	0	6	0
Pioneer Bible Translators	1977	17	4	0	5
The Mustard Seed, Inc.	1971	7	0	0	0
United Church of Canada, Division of World Outreach	0	1	0	1	0
United Methodist Ch. Wld. Div. of the Bd. of Global Min.	0	0	0	0	0
United Presbyterian Church in the USA Program Agency	0	2	2	0	0
Wesleyan Church Gen. Dept. of Wld. Msns.	1962	17	8	44	0
Worl-Wide Missions International	1971	0	0	12	0
Wycliffe Bible Translators International, Inc.	1956	306	0	0	148
TOTALS		790	70	1313	164

Paraguay

ORGANIZATION NAME	BEGAN	NOW	NEW	CHURCHES	GROUPS
American Leprosy Missions, Inc.	1951	2	2	0	0
Assemblies of God, Div. of For. Msns.	1945	9	0	19	0
Brethren Assemblies	0	10	0	0	0
Campus Crusade for Christ, International (Overseas Dept.)	1966	7	0	0	0
Child Evangelism Fellowship, Inc.	1973	2	0	0	0
Christian Church (Disciples of Christ) Div. of Oseas. Min.	1917	6	0	0	0
Church of God of Prophecy, World Mission Committee	1977	0	0	2	0
Church of God World Missions	1954	2	0	30	0
Compassion International, Inc.	1975	0	0	0	0
Elim Fellowship, Inc.	1974	3	2	0	0
Evangelical Mennonite Conference Board of Missions	1959	25	8	7	3
Evangelical Methodist Church Bible Methodist Missions	0	0	0	7	0
Free Methodist Church of N. America Gen. Msny. Bd.	1946	3	0	6	0
Full Gospel Grace Fellowship	0	0	0	0	0

Paraguay continued...

ORGANIZATION NAME	BEGAN	NOW	NEW	CHURCHES	GROUPS
General Conference Mennonite Church, Comm. on Oseas. Msn.	1948	3	3	0	0
Leprosy Relief, Canada, Inc.	1979	0	0	0	0
Logoi, Inc.	1978	0	0	0	0
Luis Palau Evangelistic Team, Inc.	1979	0	0	5	0
Lutheran Church-Missouri Synod	1935	0	0	5	0
MAP International (Medical Assistance Programs)	0	8	5	19	0
Mennonite Brethren Missions/Services	1935	5	0	0	0
Mennonite Central Committee	1930	0	0	0	0
Mennonite Economic Development Associates	1954	0	0	0	0
New Tribes Mission	1946	76	0	0	0
Southern Baptist Convention, Foreign Mission Board	1945	38	2	25	0
United Pentecostal Church Intl. For. Msns. Div.	1973	2	2	0	0
Word of Life Fellowship	1980	2	2	0	0
World Baptist Fellowship Mission Agency International	1978	2	0	0	0
World Literature Crusade	1975	0	0	0	0
World Missionary Assistance Plan	0	1	0	1	0
World Neighbors, Inc.	0	0	0	0	0
World-Wide Missions International	1971	0	0	1	0
TOTALS		206	24	122	3

Peru

ORGANIZATION NAME	BEGAN	NOW	NEW	CHURCHES	GROUPS
Allegheny Wesleyan Methodist Missions	1972	5	2	7	0
American Baptist Association, Missionary Committee	1960	2	0	10	0
AMG International (Advancing the Ministries of the Gospel)	1973	0	0	1	0
Andes Evangelical Mission	1968	1	1	0	0
Assemblies of God, Div. of For. Msns.	1919	7	0	575	0
Baptist Bible Fellowship International	1958	17	0	0	0
Baptist Faith Missions	1935	1	0	17	0
Baptist International Missions, Inc.	1969	9	0	0	0
Baptist Mid-Missions	1937	17	0	0	0
Brethren Assemblies	0	13	0	0	0
Campus Crusade for Christ, International (Overseas Dept.)	1961	9	0	0	0

Peru continued...

ORGANIZATION NAME	BEGAN	NOW	NEW	CHURCHES	GROUPS
Christian Aid Mission	1977	0	0	20	5
Christian and Missionary Alliance	1925	31	6	135	0
Christian Broadcasting Network	0	2	0	0	0
Christian Churches/Churches of Christ	0	2	2	1	0
Christians In Action	1979	2	2	0	0
Church of God (Anderson, Indiana) Msny. Bd.	1962	1	0	25	0
Church of God of Prophecy, World Mission Committee	1955	0	0	57	0
Church of God World Missions	1950	2	0	86	0
Church of the Nazarene, Gen. Bd. Dept. of Wld. Msns.	1917	13	0	107	0
Compassion International, Inc.	1979	0	0	0	0
Elim Fellowship, Inc.	1964	5	1	40	0
Evangel Bible Translators	1979	2	0	0	0
Evangelical Alliance Mission (TEAM)	1962	9	1	1	1
Evangelical Alliance Mission of Canada, Inc.	1961	1	0	0	0
Evangelical Lutheran Synod Board For Missions	1968	8	0	0	0
Fellowship of Independent Missions	1962	0	0	0	0
Food For The Hungry International	1979	2	2	0	0
General Conference of Seventh-day Adventists	1898	16	10	151	0
Global Outreach Mission	1975	2	0	0	0
Jesus to the Communist World, Inc.	0	0	0	0	0
Latin America Mission, Inc.	1975	2	0	0	0
Leprosy Relief, Canada, Inc.	1974	0	0	0	0
Luis Palau Evangelistic Team, Inc.	1971	1	0	0	0
Lutheran Church in America-Div. for Wld. Msn. and Ecumenism	1966	6	2	0	0
Lutheran World Relief, Incorporated	1970	1	1	0	0
MAP International (Medical Assistance Programs)	0	0	0	0	0
Maranatha Baptist Mission, Inc.	0	0	0	3	0
Mennonite Board of Missions	1965	2	0	0	0
Mennonite Brethren Missions/Services	1946	5	4	0	1
Northwest Yearly Meeting of Friends Ch., Dept. of Msns.	1961	8	4	27	0
Operation Eyesight Universal	1978	0	0	0	0
Regions Beyond Missionary Union (Canada)	0	7	5	70	3
Regions Beyond Missionary Union (U.S.A.)	1922	34	15	75	2

ORGANIZATION NAME	BEGAN	NOW	NEW	CHURCHES	GROUPS

Peru continued...

ORGANIZATION NAME	BEGAN	NOW	NEW	CHURCHES	GROUPS
Scripture Union, U.S.A.	1940	1	0	0	0
South American Mission, Inc.	1921	36	6	44	2
Southern Baptist Convention, Foreign Mission Board	1950	34	6	39	0
United Church Board For World Ministries	1970	0	0	0	0
United Methodist Ch. Wld. Div. of the Bd. of Global Min.	1887	8	0	0	0
United Pentecostal Church Intl. For. Msns. Div.	1962	2	0	0	0
United Presbyterian Church in the USA Program Agency	0	2	0	0	0
Wesleyan Church Gen. Dept. of Wld. Msns.	1903	3	0	55	0
World Baptist Fellowship Mission Agency International	1965	4	2	3	0
World Literature Crusade	1963	0	0	0	0
World Missions, Inc.	1963	1	0	0	0
World Neighbors, Inc.	0	0	0	0	0
World Presbyterian Missions, Inc.	1957	9	0	0	0
Wycliffe Bible Translators International, Inc.	1946	207	0	0	43
Young Life	1973	0	0	0	0
	TOTALS	548	70	1549	57

Philippines

ORGANIZATION NAME	BEGAN	NOW	NEW	CHURCHES	GROUPS
Action International Ministries	1974	28	24	0	4
Advent Christian Gen. Conf. of America	0	8	0	0	0
American Baptist Association, Missionary Committee	1961	5	4	25	0
American Baptist Churches in the U.S.A., Intl. Min.	1900	9	2	387	0
American Leprosy Missions, Inc.	1906	0	0	0	0
AMG International (Advancing the Ministries of the Gospel)	1970	5	0	0	0
Anchor Bay Evangelistic Association	0	8	0	0	0
Anglican Orthodox Church	1978	0	0	0	0
Assemblies of God, Div. of For. Msns.	1930	57	0	520	0
Association of Baptists For World Evangelism, Inc.	1927	68	19	400	0
Back to the Bible Missionary Agency	1957	0	0	0	0
Baptist Bible Fellowship International	1950	62	0	0	0
Baptist General Conference Board of World Missions	1950	26	4	33	0
Baptist International Missions, Inc.	1970	37	0	0	0

Philippines continued...

ORGANIZATION NAME	BEGAN	NOW	NEW	CHURCHES	GROUPS
Baptist Missionary Association of America	1974	6	5	0	0
Berean Mission, Inc.	1953	3	0	9	0
Bethany Fellowship Msns. (Div. of Bethany Fellowship, Inc.)	1971	6	6	2	0
Bethany Home, Inc.	1946	9	7	1	0
Bible Holiness Movement	1963	0	0	30	0
Bible Missionary Church, World Missions Department	1978	2	0	2	1
Brethren Assemblies	0	25	0	0	0
Campus Crusade for Christ, International (Overseas Dept.)	1965	207	0	0	0
Child Evangelism Fellowship, Inc.	1952	4	0	0	0
Chinese Christian Mission	1970	1	0	45	1
Christ For The Philippines, Inc.	1975	0	0	0	0
Christian Aid Mission	1953	0	0	390	42
Christian and Missionary Alliance	1902	69	20	987	0
Christian Broadcasting Network	0	2	0	0	0
Christian Catholic Church	1945	0	0	35	0
Christian Church (Disciples of Christ) Div. of Oseas. Min.	1901	6	0	0	0
Christian Church of North America, Msns. Dept.	0	0	0	0	0
Christian Churches/Churches of Christ	1925	23	0	0	0
Chr. Echoes Natl. Min., Inc. (Chr. Crusade)	0	0	0	0	0
Christian Information Service, Inc.	1970	1	1	0	11
Christian Literature Crusade, Inc.	1957	0	0	0	0
Christian Nationals' Evangelism Commission, Inc. (CNEC)	1968	0	0	0	0
Christian Nationals' Evangelism Commission, Inc. (Canada)	1968	0	0	0	0
Christian Reformed Board For World Missions	1961	18	10	0	0
Christian Reformed World Relief Committee	1970	4	3	15	0
Christian Service Corps	0	5	0	0	0
Christian Union General Mission Board	1969	2	0	0	0
Christians In Action	1977	4	4	1	0
Christians United in Action, Inc.	0	1	0	0	0
Church of God (Seventh Day), Gen. Conf., Msns. Abroad	1935	0	0	12	0
Church of God General Conference Mission Department	1961	9	0	8	0
Church of God in Christ, Mennonite Gen. Msn. Bd., Inc.	1974	10	0	0	0
Church of God of Prophecy, World Mission Committee	1952	0	0	17	0

ORGANIZATION NAME	BEGAN	NOW	NEW	CHURCHES	GROUPS
Philippines continued...					
Church of God World Missions	1948	6	2	189	0
Church of the Nazarene, Gen. Bd. Dept. of Wld. Msns.	1948	17	0	89	0
Compassion International, Inc.	1974	0	6	0	9
Conservative Baptist Foreign Mission Society	1952	47	6	82	0
Eastern Mennonite Board of Missions and Charities	1971	4	2	22	0
Elim Fellowship, Inc.	1966	8	0	30	0
Emmanuel International	1980	11	0	0	0
Evangelical Friends Church, Eastern Region, Fr. For. Msny.	1978	0	0	1	0
Faith Christian Fellowship World Outreach	1979	6	0	1	0
Far East Broadcasting Company, Inc.	1947	22	6	0	0
Far Eastern Gospel Crusade	1947	69	32	23	7
Free Gospel Church, Inc.	1925	2	2	8	0
Free Methodist Church of N. America Gen. Msny. Bd.	1949	6	0	38	0
Full Gospel Native Missionary Association		0	0	0	0
General Baptist Foreign Mission Society, Inc.	1961	7	5	75	1
General Conference of Seventh-day Adventists	1906	25	8	1600	0
Gospel Crusade World Wide Mission Outreach	1962	0	0	244	5
Harvest Fields Missionary and Evangelistic Assn., Inc.	1976	2	1	2	2
Holt International Children's Services, Inc.	1979	0	0	0	0
International Bible Institute	1926	1	1	18	0
Intl. Church of the Foursquare Gospel--Dept. of Msns. Intl.	1960	9	6	988	13
International Gospel League	1951	0	0	0	3
International Missions, Inc.	1975	14	5	36	3
International Needs-USA	1976	0	0	0	0
Leprosy Relief, Canada, Inc.	1952	0	0	0	0
Lester Sumrall Evangelistic Association	1970	2	0	0	0
Liebenzell Mission of U.S.A., Inc.	1975	2	2	0	0
Ling A. Juane Ministries, Inc.	1972	2	0	0	2
Living Bibles International	1946	0	0	0	0
Lutheran Church-Missouri Synod	1967	17	16	81	5
MAP International (Medical Assistance Programs)	0	0	0	0	0
Maranatha Baptist Mission, Inc.	0	0	0	0	0

Philippines continued...

ORGANIZATION NAME	BEGAN	NOW	NEW	CHURCHES	GROUPS
Mennonite Central Committee	1977	3	0	0	0
Mennonite Economic Development Associates	1972	0	0	0	0
Mission SOS	1979	4	0	0	0
Mission to the World	1975	4	6	0	0
Missionary Church, Div. of Overseas Ministries	0	2	0	0	0
Missionary Evangelistic Fellowship, Inc.	1970	6	4	0	0
Natl. Assn. of Congregational Chr. Chs. of the U.S.A.	0	0	0	0	0
Navigators, The	1961	5	0	0	0
New Tribes Mission	1951	127	0	0	0
O.C. Ministries, Inc.	1952	18	6	0	0
Open Bible Standard Missions, Inc.	1978	4	4	0	0
Open Doors With Brother Andrew	0	0	0	0	0
Oriental Missionary Crusade, Inc.	1958	12	2	300	0
Overseas Christian Servicemen's Centers	1955	4	2	0	0
Overseas Missionary Fellowship	1951	131	60	0	0
Pentecostal Assemblies of the World, Inc. For. Msns. Dept.	1980	2	0	0	0
Pentecostal Church of God, World Missions Department	1950	10	0	250	0
Pentecostal Free Will Baptist Church, Inc.	1969	2	0	0	0
Pentecostal Holiness Church-World Missions Department	1975	6	6	126	1
Pocket Testament League, Inc.	1974	0	0	0	0
REACH, Incorporated	0	3	0	0	0
Reformed Church in America General Program Council	1950	2	2	0	0
Salvation Army, The	1937	3	0	46	0
Seventh Day Baptist Missionary Society	1974	2	2	8	0
Source of Light Ministries, Intl.	0	1	0	0	0
Southern Baptist Convention, Foreign Mission Board	1948	132	21	388	0
Team Ventures International	0	0	0	0	2
Things to Come Mission, Inc.	1958	7	1	150	0
United Board For Christian Higher Education in Asia	1950	0	0	0	0
United Church Board For World Ministries	1902	8	2	0	0
United Church of Canada, Division of World Outreach	0	1	0	0	0
United Methodist Ch. Wld. Div. of the Bd. of Global Min.	1899	0	0	1	0
United Pentecostal Church Intl. For. Msns. Div.	1957	12	0	0	0

ORGANIZATION NAME	BEGAN	NOW	NEW	CHURCHES	GROUPS
Philippines continued...					
United Presbyterian Church in the USA Program Agency	1899	7	0	0	0
United World Mission, Incorporated	1946	0	0	15	0
Voice of China and Asia Missionary Society, Inc.	1948	0	0	2	0
Wesleyan Church Gen. Dept. of Wld. Msns.	1932	7	3	154	0
Word of Life Fellowship	1973	7	5	0	0
World Baptist Fellowship Mission Agency International	1972	2	2	2	0
World Concern/Crista International	1975	5	10	0	0
World Literature Crusade	1961	0	0	0	0
World Mission in Church and Society	1901	12	5	0	0
World Missionary Assistance Plan	0	2	2	0	0
World Missionary Evangelism, Inc.	0	0	0	0	0
World Missions, Inc.	1975	4	3	0	0
World Neighbors, Inc.	0	0	0	0	0
World Opportunities International	1970	2	0	0	0
World Outreach	0	0	1	0	0
World Relief Corporation	0	1	0	0	0
World-Wide Missions International	1962	0	0	1	0
Wycliffe Bible Translators International, Inc.	1953	206	0	0	63
Young Life	1972	0	0	0	0
Youth With A Mission	1971	0	0	0	0
TOTALS	1775	350	7889	172

Pitcairn Islands

	BEGAN	NOW	NEW	CHURCHES	GROUPS
General Conference of Seventh-day Adventists	1895	2	2	1	0
TOTALS	2	2	1	0

Poland

	BEGAN	NOW	NEW	CHURCHES	GROUPS
Assemblies of God, Div. of For. Msns.	1968	0	0	201	0
Eastern European Mission	1927	7	4	0	1
Eastern Mennonite Board of Missions and Charities	0	2	2	0	0
Living Bibles International	1977	1	0	0	1

ORGANIZATION NAME	BEGAN	NOW	NEW	CHURCHES	GROUPS
Poland continued...					
Mennonite Central Committee	1971	1	0	0	0
Mission to Europe's Millions, Inc.	0	0	0	0	0
World Ministries Commission	0	9	0	0	0
TOTALS		20	6	201	2
Portugal					
Africa Evangelical Fellowship	1979	1	0	0	0
Africa Evangelical Fellowship (Canada)	1980	1	1	0	0
Assemblies of God, Div. of For. Msns.	1973	8	0	325	0
Association of Baptists For World Evangelism, Inc.	1979	8	4	0	0
Baptist Missionary Association of America	1962	0	0	0	0
Bible Christian Union, Inc.	1966	2	1	0	1
Brethren Assemblies	0	6	0	0	0
Campus Crusade for Christ, International (Overseas Dept.)	1975	11	0	0	0
Child Evangelism Fellowship, Inc.	1949	1	0	0	0
Christian Churches/Churches of Christ	0	2	0	0	0
Church of God of Prophecy, World Mission Committee	1976	0	0	1	0
Church of God World Missions	1966	0	0	3	0
Church of the Nazarene, Gen. Bd. Dept. of Wld. Msns.	1974	4	0	2	0
Conservative Baptist Foreign Mission Society	1949	4	0	4	1
Evangelical Alliance Mission (TEAM)	1936	9	0	9	1
Evangelism Center, Inc.	1978	0	0	0	0
General Conference of Seventh-day Adventists	1904	2	2	43	0
Global Outreach Mission	1952	3	0	0	0
Greater Europe Mission	1971	9	3	0	0
Jesus to the Communist World, Inc.	0	0	0	0	0
Living Bibles International	1972	2	0	0	1
Mission to the World	1979	5	5	0	0
Pentecostal Church of God, World Missions Department	1960	2	0	2	0
Pocket Testament League, Inc.	1979	0	0	0	0
Southern Baptist Convention, Foreign Mission Board	1959	16	8	54	0
United Pentecostal Church Intl. For. Msns. Div.	1972	2	0	0	0

Portugal continued...

ORGANIZATION NAME	BEGAN	NOW	NEW	CHURCHES	GROUPS
United Presbyterian Church in the USA Program Agency	1974	0	1	0	0
Word of Life Fellowship	1963	9	7	0	0
World Literature Crusade	1979	0	0	0	1
Worldwide Evangelization Crusade	1966	2	0	0	0
Youth For Christ/U.S.A.					
TOTALS		109	32	443	5

Puerto Rico

ORGANIZATION NAME	BEGAN	NOW	NEW	CHURCHES	GROUPS
Baptist Bible Fellowship International	1955	10	0	0	0
Baptist International Missions, Inc.	0	12	0	0	0
Baptist Mid-Missions	1959	14	0	0	0
Bethany Fellowship Msns. (Div. of Bethany Fellowship, Inc.)	1965	15	10	0	0
Brethren Assemblies	0	5	0	0	0
Calvary Evangelistic Mission, Inc./WIVV Msny. Radio Station	1955	17	20	0	0
Campus Crusade for Christ, International (Overseas Dept.)	1971	15	0	0	0
Christian Broadcasting Network	0	2	0	0	0
Christian Church (Disciples of Christ) Div. of Oseas. Min.	1889	2	0	0	0
Christian Churches/Churches of Christ	1953	32	0	0	0
Christian Reformed Board For World Missions	1967	10	2	0	0
Christian Service Corps	0	3	0	0	0
Church of God (Anderson, Indiana) Msny. Bd.	1966	4	4	3	0
Church of God of Prophecy, World Mission Committee	1940	0	0	20	0
Church of God World Missions	1944	0	0	131	0
Church of the Nazarene, Gen. Bd. Dept. of Wld. Msns.	1944	4	0	25	0
Conservative Baptist Association of America	2	0	0	4	0
Fellowship of Grace Brethren Churches, For. Msny. Soc.	1958	2	2	2	0
General Conference of Seventh-day Adventists	1901	67	37	219	0
International Gospel League	1949	0	0	0	0
Intl Pentecostal Ch. of Christ, Global Msns. Dept.	1962	0	0	2	0
MAP International (Medical Assistance Programs)	0	0	0	0	0
Media Ministries Division, Mennonite Bd. of Msns.	1953	0	0	15	0
Mennonite Board of Missions	1945	5	0	16	0

ORGANIZATION NAME	BEGAN	NOW	NEW	CHURCHES	GROUPS
Puerto Rico continued...					
Open Bible Standard Missions, Inc.	1958	4	2	1	0
Pentecostal Free Will Baptist Church, Inc.	1963	1	0	0	0
United Missionary Fellowship	1968	10	4	2	0
United Pentecostal Church Intl. For. Msns. Div.	1962	2	0	0	0
Wesleyan Church Gen. Dept. of Wld. Msns.	1952	31	10	12	0
Wisconsin Evangelical Lutheran Synod, Bd. for Wld. Msns.	1963	3	1	2	0
World Ministries Commission	0	3	0	0	0
World Mission in Church and Society	1901	1	0	0	0
TOTALS		274	92	454	0

Reunion

ORGANIZATION NAME	BEGAN	NOW	NEW	CHURCHES	GROUPS
Africa Evangelical Fellowship	1971	0	2	4	3
Africa Evangelical Fellowship (Canada)	1970	0	0	6	0
Africa Inland Mission	1977	2	0	2	0
Child Evangelism Fellowship, Inc.	0	2	2	0	0
TOTALS		4	4	12	3

Romania

ORGANIZATION NAME	BEGAN	NOW	NEW	CHURCHES	GROUPS
Assemblies of God, Div. of For. Msns.	1968	0	0	835	0
Living Bibles International	1975	1	0	0	1
Mission to Europe's Millions, Inc.	0	0	0	0	0
TOTALS		1	0	835	1

Rwanda

ORGANIZATION NAME	BEGAN	NOW	NEW	CHURCHES	GROUPS
Brethren Assemblies	0	3	0	0	0
Compassion International, Inc.	1979	0	0	0	0
Conservative Baptist Foreign Mission Society	1972	8	2	93	2
Free Methodist Church of N. America Gen. Msny. Bd.	1942	17	9	97	0
General Conference of Seventh-day Adventists	1920	6	2	366	0
MAP International (Medical Assistance Programs)	0	0	0	0	0

ORGANIZATION NAME	BEGAN	NOW	NEW	CHURCHES	GROUPS
Rwanda continued...					
Presbyterian Church in the U.S.A., Div. of Intl. Msn.	1975	2	2	0	0
Southern Baptist Convention, Foreign Mission Board	1977	8	8	1	0
	TOTALS	44	23	557	2

Samoa

ORGANIZATION NAME	BEGAN	NOW	NEW	CHURCHES	GROUPS
Assemblies of God, Div. of For. Msns.	1928	2	0	26	0
Church of the Nazarene, Gen. Bd. Dept. of Wld. Msns.	1960	6	0	8	0
Leprosy Relief, Canada, Inc.	1977	0	0	0	0
United Methodist Ch. Wld. Div. of the Bd. of Global Min.	0	0	0	0	0
	TOTALS	8	0	34	0

Saudi Arabia

ORGANIZATION NAME	BEGAN	NOW	NEW	CHURCHES	GROUPS
Bible Presbyterian Church, Ind. Bd. for Presb. For. Msns.	1940	3	0	0	0
	TOTALS	3	0	0	0

Senegal

ORGANIZATION NAME	BEGAN	NOW	NEW	CHURCHES	GROUPS
American Lutheran Ch., Div. For Wld. Msn.	1976	7	7	0	0
Assemblies of God, Div. of For. Msns.	1956	15	0	26	0
Baptist International Missions, Inc.	0	8	0	0	0
Brethren Assemblies	0	2	0	0	0
Christian Mission for the Deaf	1977	0	0	0	0
Christian Service Corps	1973	1	0	0	0
Church World Service Division of DOM-NCCCUSA	0	1	0	0	0
Conservative Baptist Foreign Mission Society	1962	14	0	2	2
Leprosy Relief, Canada, Inc.	1975	0	0	0	0
New Tribes Mission	1954	64	0	0	0
Southern Baptist Convention, Foreign Mission Board	1969	13	1	0	0
United Pentecostal Church Intl. For. Msns. Div.	1978	2	0	0	0
United World Mission, Incorporated	1961	10	0	2	2
Worldwide Evangelization Crusade	1936	6	2	8	5
	TOTALS	143	10	38	9

ORGANIZATION NAME	BEGAN	NOW	NEW	CHURCHES	GROUPS

Seychelles

ORGANIZATION NAME	BEGAN	NOW	NEW	CHURCHES	GROUPS
Africa Inland Mission	1977	6	0	0	0
TOTALS		6	0	0	0

Sierra Leone

ORGANIZATION NAME	BEGAN	NOW	NEW	CHURCHES	GROUPS
African Methodist Episcopal Church, Inc. Dept. of Msns.	1916	0	0	0	0
Assemblies of God, Div. of For. Msns.	1967	8	0	32	0
Christian Literature Crusade, Inc.	1978	0	0	0	0
Christian Mission for the Deaf	1969	7	7	3	1
Christians In Action	1934	0	0	24	0
Church of God of Prophecy, World Mission Committee	1855	0	5	52	0
Church of the United Brethren in Christ, Bd. of Msns.	1855	22	2	12	0
Free Gospel Church, Inc.	1925	4	5	19	0
General Conference of Seventh-day Adventists	1905	8	0	0	0
International Gospel League	1960	0	0	0	9
Lutheran Bible Translators, Inc.	1974	23	21	0	0
MAP International (Medical Assistance Programs)	0	0	0	0	0
Mennonite Brethren Missions/Services	1979	2	2	0	3
Missionary Church, Div. of Overseas Ministries	1945	30	12	45	0
National Baptist Convention, U.S.A., Inc. For. Msn. Bd.	1951	0	0	1	70
Tele-Missions International, Inc.	1976	1	1	42	0
United Methodist Ch. Wld. Div. of the Bd. of Global Min.	1855	0	0	0	0
United Pentecostal Church Intl. For. Msns. Div.	1975	2	0	0	0
Wesleyan Church Gen. Dept. of Wld. Msns.	1889	30	14	57	0
World-Wide Missions International	1965	0	0	1	0
TOTALS		137	69	288	83

Singapore

ORGANIZATION NAME	BEGAN	NOW	NEW	CHURCHES	GROUPS
Asian Outreach	1965	0	0	0	0
Assemblies of God, Div. of For. Msns.	1957	5	0	13	0
Baptist Bible Fellowship International	1967	2	0	0	0
Baptist International Missions, Inc.	0	2	0	0	0

Singapore continued...

ORGANIZATION NAME	BEGAN	NOW	NEW	CHURCHES	GROUPS
Bible Presbyterian Church, Ind. Bd. for Presb. For. Msns.	1964	2	0	28	0
Campus Crusade for Christ, International (Overseas Dept.)	1969	38	0	0	0
Chinese Christian Mission	1977	0	1	30	1
Christian Nationals' Evangelism Commission, Inc. (CNEC)	1952	3	2	30	0
Christian Nationals' Evangelism Commission, Inc. (Canada)	1952	0	0	0	0
Compassion International, Inc.	1969	0	0	0	0
Evangelize China Fellowship, Inc.	1951	0	0	1	0
Far East Broadcasting Company, Inc.	1962	2	4	0	0
General Conference of Seventh-day Adventists	1904	63	31	6	0
Glad Tidings Missionary Society, Inc.	1965	1	0	0	0
Haggai Institute for Advanced Leadership Training, Inc.	1970	1	0	0	0
Jesus to the Communist World, Inc.	0	0	0	0	0
Lutheran Church in America-Div. for Wld. Msn. and Ecumenism	1966	3	0	0	0
Navigators, The	1962	7	2	0	0
Operation Mobilization - Canada	1971	5	0	50	0
Operation Mobilization Send the Light, Inc.	0	0	0	0	0
Overseas Missionary Fellowship	1951	19	2	0	0
Protestant Reformed Churches in America	1979	1	0	0	0
Salvation Army, Canada and Bermuda	1935	3	0	0	0
Southern Baptist Convention, Foreign Mission Board	1956	19	0	14	0
United Presbyterian Church in the USA Program Agency	0	2	0	0	0
World Literature Crusade	1963	0	0	0	0
World Missions, Inc.	1979	2	2	0	0
Young Life	1980	0	0	0	0
Youth With A Mission	1980	0	0	0	0
TOTALS		179	44	172	1

Solomon Is.

ORGANIZATION NAME	BEGAN	NOW	NEW	CHURCHES	GROUPS
American Baptist Association, Missionary Committee	1969	2	1	12	0
Assemblies of God, Div. of For. Msns.	0	4	0	16	0
Campus Crusade for Christ, International (Overseas Dept.)	1974	4	0	0	0
Child Evangelism Fellowship, Inc.	1975	0	0	0	0

ORGANIZATION NAME	BEGAN	NOW	NEW	CHURCHES	GROUPS
Solomon Is. continued...					
Wycliffe Bible Translators International, Inc.	1977	8	0	0	12
TOTALS		18	1	28	12

Somalia

ORGANIZATION NAME	BEGAN	NOW	NEW	CHURCHES	GROUPS
MAP International (Medical Assistance Programs)	0	0	0	0	0
TOTALS		0	0	0	0

South Africa

ORGANIZATION NAME	BEGAN	NOW	NEW	CHURCHES	GROUPS
Africa Evangelical Fellowship	1889	36	7	144	3
Africa Evangelical Fellowship (Canada)	1894	20	3	40	0
African Enterprise	1962	4	4	0	0
African Methodist Episcopal Church, Inc. Dept. of Msns.	0	0	0	0	0
African Methodist Episcopal Zion Ch., Dept. of Oseas. Msns.	1969	10	0	0	0
American Lutheran Ch., Div. For Wld. Msn.	1844	0	0	1	0
AMG International (Advancing the Ministries of the Gospel)	1979	2	0	1	0
Apostolic Church of Pentecost of Canada-Missionary Dept.	0	0	0	0	0
Assemblies of God, Div. of For. Msns.	1910	34	0	137	0
Baptist International Missions, Inc.	1968	10	0	0	0
Baptist Missionary Association of America	1974	2	0	1	0
Bethany Missionary Association	1970	2	2	0	0
Bible Memory Association International	1966	3	2	0	0
Brethren Assemblies	0	20	0	0	0
Campus Crusade for Christ, International (Overseas Dept.)	1971	120	0	0	0
Child Evangelism Fellowship, Inc.	1944	0	0	0	0
Christian Aid Mission	1953	0	0	750	14
Christian Churches/Churches of Christ	1950	31	0	0	0
Chr. Echoes Natl. Min., Inc. (Chr. Crusade)	0	0	0	0	0
Christian Literature and Bible Center, Inc.	1938	0	0	0	0
Christian Nationals' Evangelism Commission, Inc. (CNEC)	1975	0	0	0	0
Christian Nationals' Evangelism Commission, Inc. (Canada)	1975	0	0	0	0
Church of God of Prophecy, World Mission Committee	1967	0	0	8	0

South Africa continued...

ORGANIZATION NAME	BEGAN	NOW	NEW	CHURCHES	GROUPS
Church of God World Missions	1951	2	0	660	0
Church of the Nazarene, Gen. Bd. Dept. of Wld. Msns.	1919	29	0	147	0
Evangelical Alliance Mission (TEAM)	1892	96	7	309	7
Evangelical Alliance Mission of Canada, Inc.	1892	5	0	150	0
Fellowship of Independent Missions	1968	0	0	0	0
Free Methodist Church of N. America Gen. Msny. Bd.	1885	20	0	90	0
General Conference of Seventh-day Adventists	1887	4	4	167	0
Go-Ye Fellowship	1953	1	0	0	0
Independent Faith Mission, Inc.	0	2	0	0	0
International Fellowship of Evangelical Students - USA	0	2	0	0	0
Jesus to the Communist World, Inc.	0	0	0	0	0
Living Bibles International	1972	11	0	0	3
Mahon Mission	1904	0	0	0	0
MAP International (Medical Assistance Programs)	0	0	0	0	0
Metropolitan Church Association	0	1	0	0	0
Mission Aviation Fellowship	0	2	0	0	0
National Baptist Convention, U.S.A., Inc. For. Msn. Bd.	1898	0	0	154	0
Open Bible Ministries, Inc.	1971	2	0	0	0
Open Doors With Brother Andrew	0	0	0	0	0
Outreach International	1979	2	2	1	2
Pentecostal Assemblies of Canada, Oseas. Msns. Dept.	1915	12	1	1400	1
Pentecostal Holiness Church-World Missions Department	1913	14	20	300	0
Petra International, Inc.	1977	0	0	1	0
Pilgrim Fellowship, Inc., The	1949	2	2	0	0
Salvation Army, Canada and Bermuda	1883	5	0	0	0
Salvation Army, The	1883	3	0	220	0
Schwenkfelder Church in the USA and For. Bd. of Msns.	0	0	0	4	0
Southern Baptist Convention, Foreign Mission Board	1977	19	19	0	0
Unevangelized Fields Mission	1979	4	4	0	0
United Church Board For World Ministries	1835	5	2	0	0
United Methodist Ch. Wld. Div. of the Bd. of Global Min.	1898	0	0	0	0
United Pentecostal Church Intl. For. Msns. Div.	1948	8	0	0	0
WEFMinistries, Inc.	1976	10	10	0	0

ORGANIZATION NAME	BEGAN	NOW	NEW	CHURCHES	GROUPS
South Africa continued...					
Wesleyan Church Gen. Dept. of Wld. Msns.	1902	24	5	278	0
World Mission in Church and Society	1966	1	0	0	0
World Missionary Assistance Plan	0	2	0	6	0
World Missions, Inc.	1959	6	0	0	0
World Outreach	0	0	0	0	0
Youth For Christ/U.S.A.	0	2	0	0	0
Youth With A Mission	1973	0	0	0	0
TOTALS		588	92	4969	30

Spain

ORGANIZATION NAME	BEGAN	NOW	NEW	CHURCHES	GROUPS
AMG International (Advancing the Ministries of the Gospel)	1975	0	0	1	0
Assemblies of God, Div. of For. Msns.	1947	23	0	25	0
Association of Baptists For World Evangelism, Inc.	1968	20	6	2	0
Baptist Bible Fellowship International	1970	8	0	0	0
Baptist International Missions, Inc.	1965	15	0	0	0
Baptist Mid-Missions	1979	4	0	0	0
Baptist World Mission	0	0	1	0	0
Bible Christian Union, Inc.	1934	6	1	3	1
Bible Club Movement, Inc.	1947	0	0	0	0
Brethren Assemblies	0	13	0	0	0
CAM International	1971	14	4	6	1
Campus Crusade for Christ, International (Overseas Dept.)	1970	28	0	0	0
Child Evangelism Fellowship, Inc.	1967	2	8	0	0
Christian and Missionary Alliance	1978	6	8	2	0
Christian Churches/Churches of Christ		4	0	0	0
Christian Information Service, Inc.	1965	0	0	0	11
Christian Literature Crusade, Inc.	1966	0	0	0	0
Church of God World Missions	1960	2	0	4	2
Compassion International, Inc.	1973	0	0	0	0
Elim Fellowship, Inc.	1966	4	2	0	0
Evangelical Alliance Mission (TEAM)	1953	17	3	11	1
Global Outreach Mission	1946	9	0	0	0

ORGANIZATION NAME	BEGAN	NOW	NEW	CHURCHES	GROUPS
Spain continued...					
Gospel Missionary Union	1967	4	2	2	0
Greater Europe Mission	1960	14	11	0	0
H.O.P.E. Bible Mission, Inc.		4	0	0	0
Intl. Church of the Foursquare Gospel--Dept. of Msns. Intl.	1974	4	2	4	0
Jesus to the Communist World, Inc.	0	0	0	0	1
Living Bibles International	1973	2	0	0	0
Mennonite Board of Missions	1975	6	2	1	0
Mennonite Brethren Missions/Services		8	18	0	0
Mission SOS	1977	4	0	0	0
Mission to Europe's Millions, Inc.	0	6	2	2	0
National Association of Free Will Baptists, Bd. of For. Msns	1974	4	2	1	0
Navigators, The	1970	25	0	0	0
OMS International, Inc.	1972	2	17	1	1
Open Bible Standard Missions, Inc.	1969	4	0	3	0
Overseas Christian Servicemen's Centers	1974	2	0	0	0
Pilgrim Fellowship, Inc., The	1976	5	2	2	0
Pillar of Fire Missions	1978	1	5	0	0
Pocket Testament League, Inc.	1968	2	0	2	0
Primitive Methodist Church in the USA, Intl. Msn. Bd.	1977	2	2	80	0
Slavic Gospel Association	1975	2	0	0	0
Southern Baptist Convention, Foreign Mission Board	1921	37	0	59	0
Southern European Mission, Inc.	0	0	0	0	0
United Pentecostal Church, Intl. For. Msns. Div.	1979	4	0	0	0
United World Mission, Incorporated	1946	1	0	3	0
WEFMinistries, Inc.	1959	11	4	0	0
Word of Life Fellowship	1976	6	6	0	0
World Baptist Fellowship Mission Agency International	1955	4	6	4	0
World Literature Crusade	1975	0	0	0	0
World Presbyterian Missions, Inc.	1978	0	0	0	1
Worldteam	1972	11	0	7	1
Worldwide Evangelization Crusade	1967	0	0	2	1
Youth With A Mission	1971	0	0	0	0
TOTALS		346	99	225	20

Sri Lanka

ORGANIZATION NAME	BEGAN	NOW	NEW	CHURCHES	GROUPS
AMG International (Advancing the Ministries of the Gospel)	1970	0	0	50	0
Assemblies of God, Div. of For. Msns.	1925	2	0	22	0
Back to the Bible Missionary Agency	1955	1	0	0	0
Campus Crusade for Christ, International (Overseas Dept.)	1968	9	0	0	0
Child Evangelism Fellowship, Inc.	1973	0	0	0	2
Christian Aid Mission	1953	0	0	10	2
Chr. Echoes Natl. Min., Inc. (Chr. Crusade)	0	0	0	0	0
Christian Literature Crusade, Inc.	1975	0	0	0	0
Christian Nationals' Evangelism Commission, Inc. (CNEC)	1972	0	0	1	0
Christian Nationals' Evangelism Commission, Inc. (Canada)	1972	0	0	0	0
Evangelical Alliance Mission (TEAM)	1955	2	2	1	1
FARMS International, Inc.	1972	1	0	1	1
Full Gospel Native Missionary Association		0	0	0	0
General Conference of Seventh-day Adventists	1922	8	2	23	0
India Christian Mission, Inc.	1924	2	2	0	0
Intl. Church of the Foursquare Gospel--Dept. of Msns. Intl.	1979	2	2	0	2
Jesus to the Communist World, Inc.	1979	0	0	0	0
Leprosy Relief, Canada, Inc.	1979	0	0	0	0
Living Bibles International	1971	2	2	0	1
Lutheran Church-Missouri Synod	1927	2	2	6	1
O.C. Ministries, Inc.	1979	6	6	0	0
Salvation Army, Canada and Bermuda	1883	3	0	0	0
Salvation Army, The	1883	2	0	172	0
Southern Baptist Convention, Foreign Mission Board	1977	6	6	0	0
Trans World Radio	1975	17	6	0	0
United Church Board For World Ministries	1975	3	3	0	0
United Pentecostal Church Intl. For. Msns. Div.	1816	3	0	0	0
We Go, Inc. (World Encounter Gospel Organization)	0	0	0	0	0
World Literature Crusade	1974	1	0	0	3
World Missionary Evangelism, Inc.	1970	0	0	0	0
World-Wide Missions International	1978	0	0	1	0
TOTALS		67	23	286	10

ORGANIZATION NAME	BEGAN	NOW	NEW	CHURCHES	GROUPS
St. Kitts-Nevis					
Church of God (Anderson, Indiana) Msny. Bd.	1946	2	2	7	0
Church of God World Missions	1944	0	0	8	0
Moravian Church in America, Bd. of Wld. Msn.	1732	0	0	0	0
	TOTALS	2	2	15	0
St. Lucia					
Baptist Mid-Missions	1946	8	0	0	0
Christian Literature Crusade, Inc.	1960	0	0	0	0
International Crusades, Inc.	1978	18	18	2	0
Worldteam	1949	3	0	9	1
	TOTALS	29	18	11	1
St. Vincent					
Baptist Mid-Missions	1947	4	0	0	0
Bible Missionary Church, World Missions Department	1958	2	0	4	1
Christian Churches/Churches of Christ	0	2	0	0	0
Christian Literature Crusade, Inc.	1977	0	0	0	0
Church of God World Missions	1944	0	0	14	0
International Crusades, Inc.	1978	4	4	4	0
Southern Baptist Convention, Foreign Mission Board	1977	5	2	2	0
Worldteam	1952	2	0	11	0
	TOTALS	19	6	35	1
Sudan					
Africa Inland Mission	1949	18	4	15	0
Africa Inland Mission (Canada)	0	0	0	0	0
Anglican Church of Canada, Natl. and Wld. Program	1974	2	0	0	0
Bible Alliance Mission, Inc.	0	0	0	0	0
Campus Crusade for Christ, International (Overseas Dept.)	1975	14	0	0	0
Christian Nationals' Evangelism Commission, Inc. (CNEC)	1973	0	0	0	0

ORGANIZATION NAME | BEGAN | NOW | NEW | CHURCHES | GROUPS

Sudan continued...

ORGANIZATION NAME	BEGAN	NOW	NEW	CHURCHES	GROUPS
Christian Nationals' Evangelism Commission, Inc. (Canada)	1973	0	0	0	0
Church World Service Division of DOM-NCCUSA	0	1	0	0	0
Eastern Mennonite Board of Missions and Charities	1972	1	0	0	0
Evangelistic Faith Mission, Inc.	0	1	1	0	0
Gospel Recordings of Canada, Inc.	1978	0	1	0	0
Leprosy Relief, Canada, Inc.	1976	1	1	0	0
Lutheran World Relief, Incorporated	1972	1	1	0	0
MAP International (Medical Assistance Programs)	1974	4	0	0	0
Mennonite Central Committee	1972	0	0	0	0
Middle East Christian Outreach--USA Council	1973	2	0	0	0
Mission Aviation Fellowship	1977	2	0	0	2
Mission Aviation Fellowship of Canada	0	2	0	0	0
Operation Mobilization - Canada	1978	2	2	0	2
Red Sea Mission Team, Inc., U.S.A. Council	1949	2	0	0	0
Reformed Church in America General Program Council	1937	2	2	0	0
Sudan Interior Mission, Inc.	1900	37	17	13	8
United Presbyterian Church in the USA Program Agency	1979	10	3	0	0
World Concern/Crista International	1979	0	1	0	0
Wycliffe Bible Translators International, Inc.	1977	39	0	0	9
TOTALS		136	29	28	19

Surinam

ORGANIZATION NAME	BEGAN	NOW	NEW	CHURCHES	GROUPS
African Methodist Episcopal Church, Inc. Dept. of Msns.	0	0	0	0	0
Assemblies of God, Div. of For. Msns.	1958	2	0	4	0
Bible Club Movement, Inc.	1968	2	0	0	0
Campus Crusade for Christ, International (Overseas Dept.)	1979	0	0	0	0
Child Evangelism Fellowship, Inc.	1974	2	2	1	0
Christian and Missionary Alliance	1978	2	2	0	0
Chr. Echoes Natl. Min., Inc. (Chr. Crusade)	0	0	0	0	0
Evangelical Methodist Church Bible Methodist Missions	0	0	0	4	0
Full Gospel Grace Fellowship	0	0	0	0	0
General Conference of Seventh-day Adventists	1945	2	2	9	0

ORGANIZATION NAME	BEGAN	NOW	NEW	CHURCHES	GROUPS
Surinam continued...					
Independent Faith Mission, Inc.	0	12	0	0	0
International Missions, Inc.	1961	6	2	2	3
Mission Aviation Fellowship	1963	10	3	0	7
Mission to the World	1976	1	1	0	0
Southern Baptist Convention, Foreign Mission Board	1971	7	0	2	0
Wesleyan Church Gen. Dept. of Wld. Msns.	1945	2	0	4	0
Worldteam	1956	20	0	9	6
Wycliffe Bible Translators International, Inc.	1967	15	0	0	7
TOTALS		79	10	35	23
Swaziland					
Africa Evangelical Fellowship	1891	6	2	20	0
Africa Evangelical Fellowship (Canada)	1894	6	6	23	0
African Methodist Episcopal Church, Inc. Dept. of Msns.	0	0	0	0	0
Campus Crusade for Christ, International (Overseas Dept.)	1973	60	0	0	0
Christian Aid Mission	1953	0	0	30	6
Church of God of Prophecy, World Mission Committee	1977	0	0	7	0
Church of God World Missions	1966	2	0	4	0
Church of the Nazarene, Gen. Bd. Dept. of Wld. Msns.	1910	59	0	77	0
Eastern Mennonite Board of Missions and Charities	1971	5	3	0	0
General Conference of Seventh-day Adventists	1968	2	0	7	0
Jesus to the Communist World, Inc.	0	0	0	0	0
MAP International (Medical Assistance Programs)	0	0	0	0	0
Mennonite Central Committee	1971	23	0	0	0
National Baptist Convention, U.S.A., Inc. For. Msn. Bd.	1971	2	2	9	0
Trans World Radio	1974	50	0	0	0
United Church Board For World Ministries	1978	2	2	0	0
TOTALS		217	15	177	6
Sweden					
Baptist World Mission	0	1	0	0	0

ORGANIZATION NAME	BEGAN	NOW	NEW	CHURCHES	GROUPS

Sweden continued...

ORGANIZATION NAME	BEGAN	NOW	NEW	CHURCHES	GROUPS
Campus Crusade for Christ, International (Overseas Dept.)	1972	8	0	0	0
Evangelical Baptist Missions, Inc.	1975	2	0	1	0
Fellowship of Independent Missions	1972	0	0	0	0
Global Outreach Mission	1975	2	0	0	0
Gospel Crusade World Wide Mission Outreach	1974	2	0	0	0
Greater Europe Mission	1956	15	4	0	0
Jesus to the Communist World, Inc.	0	0	0	0	1
Living Bibles International	1972	5	1	0	0
Lutheran Church in America-Div. for Wld. Msn. and Ecumenism	1974	1	1	0	0
Mission SOS	1976	2	0	0	0
Mission to Europe's Millions, Inc.	0	0	0	0	0
Navigators, The	1955	2	0	0	0
New Life International	1979	0	1	600	0
Operation Mobilization - Canada	1964	10	0	50	0
Operation Mobilization Send the Light, Inc.	0	0	0	0	0
Pocket Testament League, Inc.	1973	5	0	0	0
Youth With A Mission	1976	0	0	0	0
TOTALS		55	6	651	1

Switzerland

ORGANIZATION NAME	BEGAN	NOW	NEW	CHURCHES	GROUPS
Assemblies of God, Div. of For. Msns.	1967	2	0	255	0
Baptist Bible Fellowship International	1973	2	0	0	0
Bible Christian Union, Inc.	1954	2	0	0	2
Campus Crusade for Christ, International (Overseas Dept.)	1969	9	0	0	0
Child Evangelism Fellowship, Inc.	1950	10	1	0	0
Christian Church of North America, Msns. Dept.	0	0	0	0	0
Christian Churches/Churches of Christ	1955	2	0	0	0
Christian Service Corps	0	1	0	0	0
Christians In Action	1957	2	0	2	0
Church of the Nazarene, Gen. Bd. Dept. of Wld. Msns.	1958	0	0	14	0
General Conference of Seventh-day Adventists	1870	2	2	59	0
Gospel Recordings Incorporated	1965	0	0	0	0

Switzerland continued...

ORGANIZATION NAME	BEGAN	NOW	NEW	CHURCHES	GROUPS
Independent Faith Mission, Inc.	0	2	0	0	0
Jesus to the Communist World, Inc.	0	0	0	0	0
Jews For Jesus	1975	0	1	0	0
Lutheran Church in America-Div. for Wld. Msn. and Ecumenism	1979	1	1	0	0
Mennonite Central Committee	1950	2	0	0	0
Mission to Europe's Millions, Inc.	0	0	0	1	0
Operation Mobilization - Canada	1963	7	0	30	0
Operation Mobilization Send the Light, Inc.	0	0	0	0	0
Southern Baptist Convention, Foreign Mission Board	1948	16	0	0	0
Southern European Mission, Inc.	0	0	0	0	0
United Church Board For World Ministries	1960	0	0	0	0
United Pentecostal Church Intl. For. Msns. Div.	0	2	0	0	0
United Presbyterian Church in the USA Program Agency	0	2	0	0	0
World Literature Crusade	1975	1	0	0	0
World Ministries Commission	0	5	0	0	0
Youth For Christ/U.S.A.	1964	0	0	0	0
Youth With A Mission	1968	0	0	0	0
TOTALS		70	4	361	2

Syria

ORGANIZATION NAME	BEGAN	NOW	NEW	CHURCHES	GROUPS
Christian and Missionary Alliance	1890	0	0	13	0
Church of the Nazarene, Gen. Bd. Dept. of Wld. Msns.	1920	0	0	7	0
Middle East Christian Outreach--USA Council	0	0	0	0	0
World-Wide Missions International	1962	0	0	1	0
TOTALS		0	0	21	0

Taiwan Rep. of China

ORGANIZATION NAME	BEGAN	NOW	NEW	CHURCHES	GROUPS
American Leprosy Missions, Inc.	1955	0	0	0	0
American Lutheran Ch., Div. For Wld. Msn.	1952	12	1	1	0
AMG International (Advancing the Ministries of the Gospel)	1974	0	0	0	0
Apostolic Church of Pentecost of Canada-Missionary Dept.	0	4	0	0	0

Taiwan Rep of China continued...

ORGANIZATION NAME	BEGAN	NOW	NEW	CHURCHES	GROUPS
Asian Outreach	1975	0	0	0	0
Assemblies of God, Div. of For. Msns.	1948	16	0	47	0
Baptist Bible Fellowship International	1950	17	0	0	0
Baptist International Missions, Inc.	0	8	0	0	0
Baptist Mid-Missions	1972	2	0	0	0
Baptist Missionary Association of America	1953	1	0	0	0
Bethel Mission of China, Inc.	1940	0	0	1	0
Bible Presbyterian Church, Ind. Bd. for Presb. For. Msns.	1935	2	0	5	0
Brethren Assemblies	0	4	0	0	0
Campus Crusade for Christ, International (Overseas Dept.)	1964	32	0	0	0
Child Evangelism Fellowship, Inc.	1954	2	0	0	0
Chinese Christian Mission	1961	23	3	200	1
Chinese for Christ, Inc.	1970	1	0	0	0
Christian Aid Mission	1953	0	0	20	6
Christian and Missionary Alliance	1952	18	8	15	0
Christian Churches/Churches of Christ	1950	14	0	0	0
Chr. Echoes Natl. Min., Inc. (Chr. Crusade)	0	0	0	0	0
Christian Nationals' Evangelism Commission, Inc. (CNEC)	1959	0	0	3	0
Christian Nationals' Evangelism Commission, Inc. (Canada)	1959	0	0	0	0
Christian Reformed Board For World Missions	1953	7	0	0	0
Christian World-Wide Evang. Msn. of Canada	1965	2	2	0	0
Church of the Lutheran Brethren of America, Bd. of Wld. Msns	1951	6	2	15	2
Church of the Nazarene, Gen. Bd. of Wld. Msns.	1956	8	0	28	2
Conservative Baptist Foreign Mission Society	1952	27	5	20	4
Erhlin Christian Polio Home	1964	1	0	10	1
Evangelical Alliance Mission (TEAM)	1951	74	19	27	1
Evangelical Alliance Mission of Canada, Inc.	1951	5	2	20	0
Evangelical Covenant Church of America, Bd. of Wld. Msn.	1952	4	2	0	0
Evangelical Friends Church, Eastern Region, Fr. For. Msny.	1953	10	3	30	0
Evangelical Scripture Mission	1947	0	0	25	0
Evangelization Society of the Pittsburgh Bible Institute	1951	4	0	9	0
Evangelize China Fellowship, Inc.	1948	0	0	0	0
Far Eastern Gospel Crusade	1967	11	7	3	3

Taiwan Rep of China continued...

ORGANIZATION NAME	BEGAN	NOW	NEW	CHURCHES	GROUPS
Free Methodist Church of N. America Gen. Msny. Bd.	1952	7	1	28	0
General Conference Mennonite Church, Comm. on Oseas. Msn.	1954	21	29	17	0
General Conference of Seventh-day Adventists	1909	31	8	29	0
Glad Tidings Missionary Society, Inc.	1952	0	0	0	0
Globe Missionary Evangelism	1975	2	0	0	0
Go-Ye Fellowship	1951	1	0	1	0
Harvest Fields Missionary and Evangelistic Assn., Inc.	0	1	0	1	1
Home of Onesiphorus	1971	3	0	0	1
International Gospel League	1955	0	0	0	0
International Missionary Advance	1978	0	0	1000	0
Leprosy Relief, Canada, Inc.	1976	0	0	0	0
Liberty Corner Mission	1952	10	3	9	0
Liebenzell Mission of Canada	1955	0	0	0	0
Living Bibles International	1972	0	0	0	0
Lutheran Church in America-Div. for Wld. Msn. and Ecumenism	1951	2	0	0	0
Lutheran Church-Missouri Synod	1952	4	3	27	0
Lutheran World Relief, Incorporated	1959	0	0	0	0
MAP International (Medical Assistance Programs)	0	0	0	0	0
Mission to the World	1974	18	15	0	0
Missionary Evangelistic Fellowship, Inc.	1979	3	3	0	0
Natl. Assn. of Congregational Chr. Chs. of the U.S.A.	0	0	0	0	0
Navigators, The	1971	2	0	0	0
New Life League	0	0	0	0	0
O.C. Ministries, Inc.	1950	4	2	0	0
OMS International, Inc.	1951	21	24	59	1
Orthodox Presbyterian Church Committee on Foreign Missions	1950	6	4	20	0
Overseas Missionary Fellowship	1952	56	20	0	1
Overseas Radio and Television, Inc.	1960	4	1	0	3
Pentecostal Assemblies of Canada, Oseas. Msns. Dept.	1963	8	2	14	0
Pilgrim Fellowship, Inc., The	1978	1	1	0	0
Pocket Testament League, Inc.	1940	1	0	0	0
Presbyterian Church in Canada, Board of World Mission	1872	11	2	0	0
Presbyterian Church in the U.S.A., Div. of Intl. Msn.	1953	18	4	0	0

Taiwan Rep of China continued...

ORGANIZATION NAME	BEGAN	NOW	NEW	CHURCHES	GROUPS
R.E.A.P.	1959	0	0	0	0
Reformation Translation Fellowship	1965	0	0	0	0
Reformed Church in America General Program Council	1952	8	4	0	0
Salvation Army, The	0	2	0	21	0
Southern Baptist Convention, Foreign Mission Board	1948	107	10	67	0
Tainan Evangelical Mission	1972	1	0	0	0
The Mustard Seed, Inc.	1954	2	0	0	0
The Navigators of Canada International	1971	3	0	0	0
United Board for Christian Higher Education in Asia	1950	0	0	0	0
United Church Board For World Ministries	1957	4	2	0	0
United Methodist Ch. Wld. Div. of the Bd. of Global Min.	1952	0	0	0	0
United Pentecostal Church Intl. For. Msns. Div.	1978	2	0	0	0
United Presbyterian Church in the USA Program Agency	1952	8	2	0	0
Voice of China and Asia Missionary Society, Inc.	1948	0	0	4	0
Wisconsin Evangelical Lutheran Synod, Bd. for Wld. Msns.	1968	2	2	3	0
World Literature Crusade	1961	0	0	0	0
World Mission in Church and Society	1960	1	0	0	0
World-Wide Missions International	1961	0	0	2	0
Worldwide Evangelization Crusade	1947	1	1	1	1
TOTALS		691	195	1782	26

Tanzania

ORGANIZATION NAME	BEGAN	NOW	NEW	CHURCHES	GROUPS
Africa Inland Mission	1908	45	4	650	0
Africa Inland Mission (Canada)	1909	3	0	300	0
African Enterprise	1974	0	0	0	0
African Methodist Episcopal Church, Inc. Dept. of Msns.	0	0	0	0	0
American Leprosy Missions, Inc.	1941	2	0	0	0
American Lutheran Ch., Div. For Wld. Msn.	1948	7	4	1	0
Assemblies of God, Div. of For. Msns.	1930	21	0	190	0
Bible Alliance Mission, Inc.	0	0	0	0	0
Bible Club Movement, Inc.	1948	0	0	0	0
Brethren Assemblies	0	2	0	0	0

Tanzania continued...

ORGANIZATION NAME	BEGAN	NOW	NEW	CHURCHES	GROUPS
Campus Crusade for Christ, International (Overseas Dept.)	1977	0	0	0	0
Church of God (Anderson, Indiana) Msny. Bd.	1968	8	4	54	0
Church of God of Prophecy, World Mission Committee	1978	0	0	1	0
Church of God World Missions	1972	1	0	40	0
Church World Service Division of DOM-NCCCUSA		1	0	0	0
Eastern Mennonite Board of Missions and Charities	1934	31	14	650	0
Elim Fellowship, Inc.	1955	4	0	100	0
General Conference of Seventh-day Adventists	1903	15	8	236	0
Leprosy Relief, Canada, Inc.	1979	0	0	0	0
Lutheran Church in America-Div. for Wld. Msn. and Ecumenism	1924	20	5	0	0
Lutheran World Relief, Incorporated	1961	1	1	0	0
MAP International (Medical Assistance Programs)	0	0	0	0	0
Mennonite Central Committee	1962	3	0	0	0
Mennonite Economic Development Associates	1965	1	0	0	0
Moravian Church in America, Bd. of Wld. Msn.	1892	2	0	200	0
Operation Eyesight Universal	1979	0	0	0	0
Pentecostal Assemblies of Canada, Oseas. Msns. Dept.	1921	14	4	372	4
Southern Baptist Convention, Foreign Mission Board	1956	79	7	330	0
United Church Board For World Ministries	1962	0	0	0	0
World Literature Crusade	1963	0	0	0	0
World Mission in Church and Society	1964	3	2	0	0
World Neighbors, Inc.	0	0	0	0	0
TOTALS		263	53	3124	4

Thailand

ORGANIZATION NAME	BEGAN	NOW	NEW	CHURCHES	GROUPS
American Baptist Churches in the U.S.A., Intl. Min.	1952	33	2	96	0
American Leprosy Missions, Inc.	1908	0	0	0	0
AMG International (Advancing the Ministries of the Gospel)	1974	1	0	5	0
Assemblies of God, Div. of For. Msns.	1969	8	0	11	0
Baptist International Missions, Inc.	0	6	0	0	0
Baptist World Mission	0	1	0	0	0
Campus Crusade for Christ, International (Overseas Dept.)	1971	15	0	0	0

Thailand continued...

ORGANIZATION NAME	BEGAN	NOW	NEW	CHURCHES	GROUPS
Chiang Mai Mission Board, The	1974	0	0	0	0
Child Evangelism Fellowship, Inc.	1957	1	0	0	0
Christian Aid Mission	1974	0	0	8	2
Christian and Missionary Alliance	1929	55	11	121	0
Christian Church (Disciples of Christ) Div. of Oseas. Min.	1951	11	0	0	0
Christian Churches/Churches of Christ	1957	27	0	0	0
Chr. Echoes Natl. Min., Inc. (Chr. Crusade)	0	0	0	0	0
Christian Information Service, Inc.	1966	0	0	0	11
Christian Literature Crusade, Inc.	1958	2	0	0	0
Christian Nationals' Evangelism Commission, Inc. (CNEC)	1955	0	0	7	0
Christian Nationals' Evangelism Commission, Inc. (Canada)	1955	0	0	5	0
Church of God (Anderson, Indiana) Msny. Bd.	1975	4	2	6	0
Church of God of Prophecy, World Mission Committee	1968	0	2	2	0
Church of God World Missions	1972	2	2	2	0
Church World Service Division of DOM-NCCUSA	0	2	0	0	0
Compassion International, Inc.	1970	1	1	0	0
Evangelical Covenant Church of America, Bd. of Wld. Msn.	1971	4	2	0	0
Evangelism Center, Inc.	1979	0	0	0	0
Evangelize China Fellowship, Inc.	1958	0	0	1	0
Far East Broadcasting Company, Inc.	1960	0	0	0	0
Food For The Hungry International	1975	5	2	0	0
Full Gospel Native Missionary Association	0	0	0	0	0
General Conference of Seventh-day Adventists	1919	19	12	13	0
Heritage Village Church and Missionary Fellowship, Inc.	0	0	0	0	0
Holt International Children's Services, Inc.	1976	0	0	0	0
Korea International Mission, Inc.	1956	6	0	0	2
Leprosy Mission Canada	1960	0	0	0	0
Leprosy Relief, Canada, Inc.	1979	0	0	0	0
Living Bibles International	1973	2	0	0	1
Lutheran Church in America-Div. for Wld. Msn. and Ecumenism	1975	3	1	0	0
MAP International (Medical Assistance Programs)	0	0	0	0	0
Maranatha Baptist Mission, Inc.	0	0	0	0	0
Mennonite Central Committee	1975	3	0	0	0

Thailand continued...

ORGANIZATION NAME	BEGAN	NOW	NEW	CHURCHES	GROUPS
New Tribes Mission	1951	48	0	0	0
Overseas Missionary Fellowship	1952	263	46	0	0
Pentecostal Assemblies of Canada, Oseas. Msns. Dept.	1961	15	2	29	1
Samaritan's Purse	1979	0	1	0	1
Southern Baptist Convention, Foreign Mission Board	1949	58	1	21	0
United Board for Christian Higher Education in Asia	0	0	0	0	0
United Church Board For World Ministries	1970	0	0	0	0
United Pentecostal Church Intl. For. Msns. Div.	1962	1	0	0	0
United Presbyterian Church in the USA Program Agency	1840	21	5	0	0
World Concern/Crista International	1976	2	2	0	0
World Literature Crusade	1964	0	0	0	0
World Outreach	0	0	0	0	0
World Relief Corporation	1972	0	0	0	0
Worldwide Evangelization Crusade	1947	13	5	50	2
Wycliffe Bible Translators International, Inc.	1978	4	0	0	4
Youth With A Mission	1973	0	0	0	0
	TOTALS	637	98	375	24

Togo

ORGANIZATION NAME	BEGAN	NOW	NEW	CHURCHES	GROUPS
Assemblies of God, Div. of For. Msns.	1921	18	0	40	0
Association of Baptists For World Evangelism, Inc.	1973	25	15	4	0
Baptist International Missions, Inc.	0	2	0	0	0
Campus Crusade for Christ, International (Overseas Dept.)	1979	0	0	0	0
Christian Mission for the Deaf	1976	0	0	0	0
Church of God World Missions	1976	0	0	3	0
Lutheran Church-Missouri Synod	1979	1	1	0	1
Lutheran World Relief, Incorporated	1975	1	1	0	0
Southern Baptist Convention, Foreign Mission Board	1964	21	0	8	0
United Church Board For World Ministries	1946	2	0	0	0
United Presbyterian Church in the USA Program Agency	0	2	2	0	0
World Neighbors, Inc.	0	0	0	0	0
Wycliffe Bible Translators International, Inc.	1967	7	0	0	6
	TOTALS	79	19	55	7

ORGANIZATION NAME	BEGAN	NOW	NEW	CHURCHES	GROUPS
Tonga					
Anglican Orthodox Church	1976	0	0	0	0
Assemblies of God, Div. of For. Msns.	1972	2	0	16	0
Campus Crusade for Christ, International (Overseas Dept.)	1974	1	0	0	0
United Methodist Ch. Wld. Div. of the Bd. of Global Min.	0	0	0	0	0
United Pentecostal Church Intl. For. Msns. Div.	0	2	0	0	0
	TOTALS	5	0	16	0
Transkei					
Christian Aid Mission	1953	0	0	100	4
Christian Churches/Churches of Christ	0	1	0	0	0
Church of God World Missions	1966	4	0	17	0
Intl. Church of the Foursquare Gospel-Dept. of Msns. Intl.	1929	3	0	105	2
Jesus to the Communist World, Inc.	0	0	0	0	0
Mennonite Central Committee	1978	2	0	0	0
Open Bible Ministries, Inc.	1976	2	0	0	0
Southern Baptist Convention, Foreign Mission Board	1979	0	0	0	0
	TOTALS	12	0	222	6
Trinidad and Tobago					
African Methodist Episcopal Church, Inc. Dept. of Msns.	0	0	0	0	0
Anglican Church of Canada, Natl. and Wld. Program	1974	0	0	0	0
Baptist International Missions, Inc.	1974	2	0	0	0
Bible Way Chs. of Our Lord Jesus Christ Worldwide, Inc.	1958	0	0	0	0
Campus Crusade for Christ, International (Overseas Dept.)	1977	2	2	0	0
Child Evangelism Fellowship, Inc.	1964	2	2	0	0
Christian Literature Crusade, Inc.	1950	2	0	0	0
Church of God (Seventh Day), Gen. Conf., Msns. Abroad	1931	0	0	4	0
Church of God of Prophecy, World Mission Committee	1961	2	2	11	0
Church of God World Missions	1956	2	0	35	0
Church of the Nazarene, Gen. Bd. Dept. of Wld. Msns.	1926	7	0	20	0
Church World Service Division of DOM-NCCUSA	0	1	0	0	0

Trinidad and Tobago continued...

ORGANIZATION NAME	BEGAN	NOW	NEW	CHURCHES	GROUPS
Evangelical Alliance Mission (TEAM)	1964	14	6	10	1
General Conference of Seventh-day Adventists	1893	11	5	117	0
Lutheran Church in America-Div. for Wld. Msn. and Ecumenism	1966	0	1	0	0
Media Ministries Division, Mennonite Bd. of Msns.	1969	0	0	3	0
Moravian Church in America, Bd. of Wld. Msn.	1732	0	0	0	0
Open Bible Standard Missions, Inc.	1953	0	0	65	0
Pentecostal Church of God, World Missions Department	1969	0	0	5	0
Southern Baptist Convention, Foreign Mission Board	1962	6	0	1	0
Trans World Missions	1976	2	2	0	0
Virginia Mennonite Board of Missions and Charities	1971	4	2	1	1
Worldteam	1951	10	0	12	2
TOTALS		66	18	284	4

Tunisia

ORGANIZATION NAME	BEGAN	NOW	NEW	CHURCHES	GROUPS
Assemblies of God, Div. of For. Msns.	0	2	0	0	0
North Africa Mission	1885	11	2	2	1
United Methodist Ch. Wld. Div. of the Bd. of Global Min.	1839	0	0	0	0
TOTALS		13	2	2	1

Turkey

ORGANIZATION NAME	BEGAN	NOW	NEW	CHURCHES	GROUPS
AMG International (Advancing the Ministries of the Gospel)	1979	2	0	0	0
Friends of Turkey	1970	3	1	0	4
International Missions, Inc.	1975	0	0	0	0
Living Bibles International	1977	1	0	0	1
Mission to Europe's Millions, Inc.	0	0	0	1	0
Operation Mobilization - Canada	1963	26	0	5	0
Southern Baptist Convention, Foreign Mission Board	1966	2	0	1	0
United Church Board For World Ministries	1819	31	6	0	0
Word of Life Fellowship	1978	1	1	0	0
World-Wide Missions International	1961	0	0	1	0
TOTALS		66	8	8	5

ORGANIZATION NAME	BEGAN	NOW	NEW	CHURCHES	GROUPS
Turks and Caicos Is.					
Church of God of Prophecy, World Mission Committee	1932	0	0	6	0
Church of God World Missions	1944	0	0	1	0
	TOTALS	0	0	7	0
U.S. Virgin Is.					
African Methodist Episcopal Zion Ch., Dept. of Oseas. Msns.	1917	0	0	0	0
Baptist Bible Fellowship International	1972	2	0	0	0
Baptist International Missions, Inc.	0	14	0	0	0
Bethany Fellowship Msns. (Div. of Bethany Fellowship, Inc.)	1966	6	2	0	0
Campus Crusade for Christ, International (Overseas Dept.)	1978	4	2	0	0
Church of God (Holiness) For. Msn. Brd.	1963	6	0	2	0
Church of God of Prophecy, World Mission Committee	1926	0	2	12	0
Church of God World Missions	1966	2	0	3	0
Maranatha Baptist Mission, Inc.	0	0	0	0	0
Moravian Church in America, Bd. of Wld. Msn.	1732	10	2	38	0
Natl. Baptist Convention of Amer., For. Msn. Bd.	0	0	0	11	0
World Mission in Church and Society	1919	2	0	0	0
	TOTALS	46	6	66	0
Uganda					
Africa Inland Mission	1918	15	2	650	0
Africa Inland Mission (Canada)	0	0	0	0	0
African Enterprise	1971	0	0	0	0
Anglican Church of Canada, Natl. and Wld. Program	1964	0	0	0	0
Campus Crusade for Christ, International (Overseas Dept.)	1971	17	0	300	0
Elim Fellowship, Inc.	1962	3	0	0	0
Glad Tidings Missionary Society, Inc.	1960	0	0	0	0
International Gospel League	1979	0	0	0	0
Lutheran World Relief, Incorporated	1979	0	0	0	0
MAP International (Medical Assistance Programs)	0	0	0	0	0
Mennonite Central Committee	1979	3	0	0	0

ORGANIZATION NAME	BEGAN	NOW	NEW	CHURCHES	GROUPS
Uganda continued...					
Pentecostal Assemblies of Canada, Oseas. Msns. Dept.	1956	0	0	265	1
Reformed Episcopal Church Bd. of For. Msns.	1956	2	0	0	0
Southern Baptist Convention, Foreign Mission Board	1962	4	0	0	0
World Neighbors, Inc.	0	0	0	0	0
TOTALS		44	2	1215	1

United Arab Emirates

ORGANIZATION NAME	BEGAN	NOW	NEW	CHURCHES	GROUPS
Evangelical Alliance Mission (TEAM)	1960	37	15	8	3
Evangelical Alliance Mission of Canada, Inc.	1961	5	1	3	0
MAP International (Medical Assistance Programs)	0	0	0	0	0
Middle East Christian Outreach--USA Council	1979	0	0	0	0
Worldwide Evangelization Crusade	1963	0	0	0	1
TOTALS		42	16	11	4

United Kingdom

ORGANIZATION NAME	BEGAN	NOW	NEW	CHURCHES	GROUPS
African Methodist Episcopal Zion Ch., Dept. of Oseas. Msns.	1971	0	0	0	0
Back to the Bible Missionary Agency	1954	0	0	0	0
Baptist Bible Fellowship International	1972	18	0	0	0
Baptist International Missions, Inc.	1972	17	0	0	0
Baptist Mid-Missions	1972	29	0	0	0
Baptist World Mission		2	0	0	0
Bible Christian Union, Inc.	1927	2	0	1	0
Bible Club Movement, Inc.	1946	0	0	0	0
Bible Presbyterian Church, Ind. Bd. for Presb. For. Msns.	1956	1	0	1	0
Campus Crusade for Christ, International (Overseas Dept.)	1967	80	1	0	0
Child Evangelism Fellowship, Inc.	1943	5	1	5	0
Christian and Missionary Alliance	1976	0	0	0	0
Christian Church of North America, Msns. Dept.	0	0	0	0	0
Christian Churches/Churches of Christ		18	0	0	0
Christian Literature Crusade, Inc.	1941	1	1	0	1
Christians In Action	1965	4	2	3	1

United Kingdom continued...

ORGANIZATION NAME	BEGAN	NOW	NEW	CHURCHES	GROUPS
Church of God of Prophecy, World Mission Committee	1952	2	0	97	0
Church of God World Missions	1972	0	0	87	0
Church of God, USA Headquarters	0	5	0	0	0
Evangelical Baptist Missions, Inc.	1976	5	5	1	0
Faith Christian Fellowship World Outreach	1978	4	0	1	0
Far East Broadcasting Company, Inc.	1960	2	2	0	0
General Conference of Seventh-day Adventists	1898	14	6	157	0
Global Outreach Mission	0	2	7	0	0
Globe Missionary Evangelism	1978	7	7	0	0
Gospel Outreach	1979	2	2	1	0
Greater Europe Mission	1971	4	2	0	0
Intl. Church of the Foursquare Gospel--Dept. of Msns. Intl.	1979	2	2	0	0
International Fellowship of Evangelical Students - USA	0	1	0	0	0
International Films, Inc.	1972	0	0	0	0
International Missions, Inc.	1966	6	2	2	2
Intl Pentecostal Ch. of Christ, Global Msns. Dept.	1975	0	0	0	2
Jesus to the Communist World, Inc.	0	0	0	0	0
Jews For Jesus	1976	0	0	0	0
Luis Palau Evangelistic Team, Inc.	1976	3	2	0	0
Lutheran Church in America-Div. for Wld. Msn. and Ecumenism	1973	2	1	0	0
Mennonite Board of Missions	1952	7	5	1	0
Mennonite Central Committee	1973	1	0	0	0
Mission to Europe's Millions, Inc.	0	0	0	0	0
Natl. Assn. of Congregational Chr. Chs. of the U.S.A.	1975	0	0	0	0
Navigators, The	1950	9	2	0	0
New Life International	1980	0	1	925	1
New Tribes Mission	1970	10	0	0	0
Operation Mobilization - Canada	1962	168	0	0	0
Operation Mobilization Send the Light, Inc.	0	0	0	0	0
Pentecostal Assemblies of the World, Inc. For. Msns. Dept.	1978	1	0	0	0
Pentecostal Holiness Church-World Missions Department	1977	4	4	8	3
Petra International, Inc.	1977	0	0	0	0
Pillar of Fire Missions	1930	15	3	2	0

ORGANIZATION NAME

ORGANIZATION NAME	BEGAN	NOW	NEW	CHURCHES	GROUPS
United Kingdom continued...					
Prison Mission Assoc., Inc.	1965	1	0	0	0
Red Sea Mission Team, Inc., U.S.A. Council	1977	0	0	0	1
Southern Baptist Convention, Foreign Mission Board	1977	4	4	1	0
Teen Missions International, Inc.	1977	18	0	0	0
Things to Come Mission, Inc.	1971	2	0	0	0
United Church Board For World Ministries	1945	0	0	0	0
United Pentecostal Church Intl. For. Msns. Div.	1965	2	0	0	0
United Presbyterian Church in the USA Program Agency	0	0	2	0	0
United World Mission, Incorporated	1956	2	0	0	0
WEFMinistries, Inc.	1970	10	6	0	0
Word of Life Fellowship	1979	2	2	0	0
World Baptist Fellowship Mission Agency International	1972	2	0	2	0
World Radio Missionary Fellowship, Inc.	1975	2	0	2	0
Worldwide Evangelization Crusade	1966	11	2	0	3
Youth With A Mission	1969	0	0	0	0
TOTALS		504	66	1295	11

Upper Volta

ORGANIZATION NAME	BEGAN	NOW	NEW	CHURCHES	GROUPS
Africa Inter-Mennonite Mission, Inc.	1978	4	4	2	0
Apostolic Church of Pentecost of Canada-Missionary Dept.	0	14	0	0	0
Assemblies of God, Div. of For. Msns.	1921	19	0	500	0
Christian and Missionary Alliance	1923	32	10	204	0
Christian Mission for the Deaf	1979	0	0	0	0
Emmanuel International	1980	1	0	0	0
General Conference Mennonite Church, Comm. on Oseas. Msn.	1977	4	4	0	0
General Conference of Seventh-day Adventists	1972	2	0	1	0
Jesus to the Communist World, Inc.	0	0	0	0	0
Leprosy Relief, Canada, Inc.	1979	0	0	0	0
MAP International (Medical Assistance Programs)	0	0	0	0	0
Mennonite Central Committee	1975	16	0	0	0
Operation Eyesight Universal	1980	0	0	0	0
Southern Baptist Convention, Foreign Mission Board	1971	13	2	22	0

Upper Volta continued...

ORGANIZATION NAME	BEGAN	NOW	NEW	CHURCHES	GROUPS
Sudan Interior Mission, Inc.	1930	22	4	64	4
World Neighbors, Inc.	0	0	0	0	0
World Relief Corporation	0	0	0	0	0
Worldwide Evangelization Crusade	1937	0	0	23	3
Wycliffe Bible Translators International, Inc.	1971	5	0	0	6
TOTALS		132	24	816	13

Uruguay

ORGANIZATION NAME	BEGAN	NOW	NEW	CHURCHES	GROUPS
Assemblies of God, Div. of For. Msns.	1944	6	0	50	0
Baptist Bible Fellowship International	1959	8	0	0	0
Baptist Missionary Association of America		0	0	0	0
Baptist World Mission	1964	5	0	0	0
Brethren Assemblies		6	0	0	0
Campus Crusade for Christ, International (Overseas Dept.)	1966	2	0	0	0
Christian and Missionary Alliance	1960	0	0	8	0
Christian Church of North America, Msns. Dept.		0	0	8	0
Christian Literature Crusade, Inc.	1951	4	0	0	0
Christians In Action	1979	2	4	1	1
Church of God of Prophecy, World Mission Committee	1957	4	0	8	0
Church of God World Missions	1946	4	0	20	0
Church of the Nazarene, Gen. Bd. Dept. of Wld. Msns.	1949	4	0	12	0
General Conference Mennonite Church, Comm. on Oseas. Msn.	1956	2	0	4	0
Gospel Mission of South America	1971	10	0	5	1
Logoi, Inc.	1978	2	0	0	0
Lutheran Church-Missouri Synod	1936	0	0	1	0
Media Ministries Division, Mennonite Bd. of Msns.	1950	0	0	4	0
Mennonite Board of Missions	1954	3	1	7	0
Mennonite Brethren Missions/Services	1966	8	5	6	0
Mennonite Economic Development Associates	1963	0	0	6	0
National Association of Free Will Baptists, Bd. of For. Msns	1962	5	0	6	0
Southern Baptist Convention, Foreign Mission Board	1911	30	7	37	0
United Methodist Ch. Wld. Div. of the Bd. of Global Min.	1839	0	0	0	0

ORGANIZATION NAME	BEGAN	NOW	NEW	CHURCHES	GROUPS
Uruguay continued...					
United Pentecostal Church Intl. For. Msns. Div.	1956	4	0	0	0
WEFMinistries, Inc.	1965	8	1	0	0
Word of Life Fellowship	1977	1	1	0	0
World Gospel Crusades	1979	2	2	0	0
World Literature Crusade	1975	0	0	0	0
TOTALS		116	21	169	2
U.S.S.R.					
Assemblies of God, Div. of For. Msns.	1958	2	0	0	0
Christian Broadcasting Network	0	0	0	0	0
Lutheran Church in America-Div. for Wld. Msn. and Ecumenism	1978	1	1	0	0
Mission to Europe's Millions, Inc.	0	0	0	0	0
TOTALS		3	1	0	0
Vanuatu					
Assemblies of God, Div. of For. Msns.	1973	4	0	21	0
TOTALS		4	0	21	0
Venezuela					
Assemblies of God, Div. of For. Msns.	1919	13	0	115	0
Baptist Bible Fellowship International	1958	4	0	0	0
Baptist International Missions, Inc.	0	6	0	0	0
Baptist Mid-Missions	1924	13	0	0	0
Brethren Assemblies	0	11	0	0	0
Campus Crusade for Christ, International (Overseas Dept.)	1972	190	0	0	0
Child Evangelism Fellowship, Inc.	1949	4	2	0	0
Christian and Missionary Alliance	1972	2	2	3	0
Christian Church (Disciples of Christ) Div. of Oseas. Min.	1963	1	0	0	0
Christian Church of North America, Msns. Dept.	1963	2	0	5	0
Christian Literature Crusade, Inc.	1970	0	0	0	0

Venezuela continued...

ORGANIZATION NAME	BEGAN	NOW	NEW	CHURCHES	GROUPS
Church of God (Anderson, Indiana) Msny. Bd.	1980	2	2	0	0
Church of God of Prophecy, World Mission Committee	1968	0	0	16	0
Church of God World Missions	1966	2	0	5	0
Churches of God, General Conference Comm. on Wld. Msns.	1979	0	0	0	0
Compassion International, Inc.	1973	0	0	0	0
Eastern Mennonite Board of Missions and Charities	1978	2	2	1	0
Evangelical Alliance Mission (TEAM)	1906	117	25	136	1
Evangelical Alliance Mission of Canada, Inc.	1906	12	3	133	0
Fellowship of Independent Missions	1968	0	0	0	0
General Conference of Seventh-day Adventists	1910	4	4	42	0
Intl. Church of the Foursquare Gospel--Dept. of Msns. Intl.	1955	2	0	44	0
Logos Translators	0	1	0	0	0
Lutheran Church-Missouri Synod	1951	7	5	11	0
Mission Aviation Fellowship	1965	6	2	0	0
Navigators, The	1975	6	2	0	0
New Tribes Mission	1946	99	0	0	0
Pentecostal Free Will Baptist Church, Inc.	1974	3	0	0	0
Pentecostal Holiness Church-World Missions Department	1979	3	3	1	0
Reformed Church in America General Program Council	1977	2	2	0	0
Southern Baptist Convention, Foreign Mission Board	1949	58	19	58	0
United Pentecostal Church Intl. For. Msns. Div.	1955	6	0	0	0
United Presbyterian Church in the USA Program Agency	1897	4	2	0	0
United World Mission, Incorporated	1946	8	0	35	0
Word of Life Fellowship	1978	3	3	0	0
World Literature Crusade	1973	0	0	0	0
World-Wide Missions International	1964	2	0	0	0
Worldwide Evangelization Crusade	1954	2	2	10	2
TOTALS		596	80	615	3

Viet Nam, Soc. Rep.

ORGANIZATION NAME	BEGAN	NOW	NEW	CHURCHES	GROUPS
Assemblies of God, Div. of For. Msns.	1972	0	0	0	0
Christian and Missionary Alliance	1911	0	0	0	0

ORGANIZATION NAME	BEGAN	NOW	NEW	CHURCHES	GROUPS
Viet Nam, Soc. Rep. continued...					
Christian Information Service, Inc.	1968	0	0	0	11
Church World Service Division of DOM-NCCUSA	0	1	0	0	0
Lutheran World Relief, Incorporated	1965	0	0	0	0
	TOTALS	1	0	0	11

Yemen Arab Republic

ORGANIZATION NAME	BEGAN	NOW	NEW	CHURCHES	GROUPS
MAP International (Medical Assistance Programs)	0	0	0	0	0
Red Sea Mission Team, Inc., U.S.A. Council	1969	1	1	0	1
Southern Baptist Convention, Foreign Mission Board	1964	24	1	0	0
	TOTALS	25	2	0	1

Yugoslavia

ORGANIZATION NAME	BEGAN	NOW	NEW	CHURCHES	GROUPS
AMG International (Advancing the Ministries of the Gospel)	1975	0	0	1	0
Assemblies of God, Div. of For. Msns.	1968	3	0	65	0
Church of God World Missions	1968	0	0	10	0
Eastern European Mission	1946	6	0	2	0
Eastern Mennonite Board of Missions and Charities	1971	3	2	0	0
Global Outreach Mission	0	2	0	0	0
Gospel Crusade World Wide Mission Outreach	1977	0	0	4	0
Living Bibles International	1973	9	0	0	2
Mission to Europe's Millions, Inc.	0	0	0	0	0
Pocket Testament League, Inc.	1966	3	0	0	0
World-Wide Missions International	1974	0	0	1	0
	TOTALS	26	2	83	2

Zaire

ORGANIZATION NAME	BEGAN	NOW	NEW	CHURCHES	GROUPS
Africa Inland Mission	1912	111	13	1800	0
Africa Inland Mission (Canada)	0	20	2	500	0
Africa Inter-Mennonite Mission, Inc.	1911	39	1	20	0
African Methodist Episcopal Church, Inc. Dept. of Msns.	0	0	0	0	0

Zaire continued...

ORGANIZATION NAME	BEGAN	NOW	NEW	CHURCHES	GROUPS
American Baptist Churches in the U.S.A., Intl. Min.	1884	52	2	283	0
American Leprosy Missions, Inc.	1935	0	0	40	0
AMG International (Advancing the Ministries of the Gospel)	1978	4	0	0	0
Anglican Church of Canada, Natl. and Wld. Program	1979	1	0	0	0
Assemblies of God, Div. of For. Msns.	1921	15	0	216	0
Baptist Bible Fellowship International	1957	2	0	0	0
Berean Mission, Inc.	1938	13	2	138	0
Bible Alliance Mission, Inc.	0	0	0	0	0
Bible Club Movement, Inc.	1970	0	0	0	0
Brethren Assemblies	0	27	0	0	0
Canadian Baptist Overseas Mission Board	1962	9	2	400	0
Child Evangelism Fellowship, Inc.	1959	0	0	0	0
Christian and Missionary Alliance	1884	31	11	2494	0
Christian Church (Disciples of Christ) Div. of Oseas. Min.	1899	17	0	0	0
Christian Churches/Churches of Christ	0	13	0	0	0
Christian Mission for the Deaf	1978	0	0	0	0
Christian Nationals' Evangelism Commission, Inc. (CNEC)	1969	0	0	0	0
Christian Nationals' Evangelism Commission, Inc. (Canada)	1969	1	0	0	0
Christian Service Corps	0	0	0	0	0
Church of God of Prophecy, World Mission Committee	1979	0	0	13	0
Church of God World Missions	1970	1	0	62	0
Church World Service Division of DOM-NCCCUSA	0	0	0	0	0
Conservative Baptist Foreign Mission Society	1946	45	10	557	6
Elim Fellowship, Inc.	1962	2	0	600	0
Evangelical Covenant Church of America, Bd. of Wld. Msn.	1937	48	7	0	0
Evangelical Mennonite Church, Comm. on Oseas. Msns.	1912	0	0	0	0
Evangelization Society of the Pittsburgh Bible Institute	1922	0	0	200	3
Free Methodist Church of N. America Gen. Msny. Bd.	1963	14	2	176	0
General Conference Mennonite Church, Comm. on Oseas. Msn.	1912	28	16	50	0
General Conference of Seventh-day Adventists	1921	24	10	283	0
Jesus to the Communist World, Inc.	0	0	0	0	0
Leprosy Mission Canada	1931	0	0	0	0
Leprosy Relief, Canada, Inc.	1975	0	0	0	0

ORGANIZATION NAME	BEGAN	NOW	NEW	CHURCHES	GROUPS
Zaire continued...					
MAP International (Medical Assistance Programs)	1975	0	0	0	0
Mennonite Board of Missions	1912	2	0	0	0
Mennonite Brethren Missions/Services	1960	28	21	74	2
Mennonite Central Committee	1968	37	0	0	0
Mennonite Economic Development Associates	1961	1	0	0	0
Mission Aviation Fellowship	1973	35	12	0	10
Mission Aviation Fellowship of Canada	1968	2	0	0	0
Paul Carlson Medical Program, Inc.	1980	13	7	1	1
Pioneer Bible Translators		2	0	0	0
Presbyterian Church in the U.S.A., Div. of Intl. Msn.	1891	44	19	0	1
Reformed Episcopal Church Bd. of For. Msns.	1951	1	0	0	0
Regions Beyond Missionary Union (Canada)	0	3	0	0	0
Regions Beyond Missionary Union (U.S.A.)	1878	10	1	400	0
Salvation Army, Canada and Bermuda	1934	2	0	0	0
Salvation Army, The	1934	0	0	444	0
United Church Board For World Ministries	1973	1	1	0	0
United Church of Canada, Division of World Outreach	0	3	0	1	0
United Methodist Ch. Wld. Div. of the Bd. of Global Min.	1914	0	0	0	0
United Presbyterian Church in the USA Program Agency	0	2	0	0	0
World Mission in Church and Society	1978	1	1	0	0
World Mission Prayer League Canada	0	1	1	0	0
World-Wide Missions International	1963	3	0	1	0
Worldwide Evangelization Crusade	1913	4	2	800	0
Wycliffe Bible Translators International, Inc.	1977	3	0	0	3
TOTALS		715	143	9553	25

Zambia

ORGANIZATION NAME	BEGAN	NOW	NEW	CHURCHES	GROUPS
Africa Evangelical Fellowship	1910	65	10	340	2
Africa Evangelical Fellowship (Canada)	1910	40	13	360	0
African Methodist Episcopal Church, Inc. Dept. of Msns.	0	0	0	0	0
Brethren Assemblies	0	38	0	0	0
Brethren in Christ Missions	1906	17	2	75	0

Zambia   continued...

ORGANIZATION NAME	BEGAN	NOW	NEW	CHURCHES	GROUPS
Campus Crusade for Christ, International (Overseas Dept.)	1975	2	0	0	0
Child Evangelism Fellowship, Inc.	1970	1	0	0	0
Christian Churches/Churches of Christ	0	24	0	0	0
Christian Nationals' Evangelism Commission, Inc. (CNEC)	1972	0	0	0	0
Christian Nationals' Evangelism Commission, Inc. (Canada)	1972	0	0	0	0
Church of God of Prophecy, World Mission Committee	1977	0	0	24	0
Church of God World Missions	1966	0	0	222	0
Church of the Nazarene, Gen. Bd. Dept. of Wld. Msns.	1964	6	0	7	0
Evangelical Baptist Missions, Inc.	1979	2	2	1	0
General Conference of Seventh-day Adventists	1905	33	19	190	0
Leprosy Mission Canada	1942	0	0	0	0
Leprosy Relief, Canada, Inc.	1979	0	0	0	0
Lutheran World Relief, Incorporated	1967	0	0	0	0
MAP International (Medical Assistance Programs)	0	0	0	0	0
Mennonite Central Committee	1962	18	0	0	0
Pentecostal Assemblies of Canada, Oseas. Msns. Dept.	1955	14	6	28	1
Pentecostal Holiness Church-World Missions Department	1950	6	4	24	0
Reformed Church in America General Program Council	1978	1	0	0	0
Salvation Army, Canada and Bermuda	1891	4	0	0	0
Salvation Army, The	1924	3	0	88	0
Southern Baptist Convention, Foreign Mission Board	1959	38	2	67	0
United Church Board For World Ministries	1965	8	6	0	0
United Church of Canada, Division of World Outreach	0	18	0	1	0
United Methodist Ch. Wld. Div. of the Bd. of Global Min.	1966	0	0	0	0
United Presbyterian Church in the USA Program Agency	0	5	4	0	0
Wesleyan Church Gen. Dept. of Wld. Msns.	1900	31	7	70	0
Wisconsin Evangelical Lutheran Synod, Bd. for Wld. Msns.	1953	8	0	71	0
World Literature Crusade	1970	0	0	0	0
World Outreach	0	0	0	0	0
TOTALS		382	75	1568	3

Zimbabwe

ORGANIZATION NAME	BEGAN	NOW	NEW	CHURCHES	GROUPS
Africa Evangelical Fellowship	1900	14	2	45	2
Africa Evangelical Fellowship (Canada)	1900	5	1	0	0
African Enterprise	1976	0	0	0	0
African Methodist Episcopal Church, Inc. Dept. of Msns.	1970	0	0	0	0
Anglican Orthodox Church	1951	6	0	7	0
Apostolic Church of Pentecost of Canada-Missionary Dept.	0	2	0	0	0
Assemblies of God, Div. of For. Msns.	1973	0	1	0	0
Bible Club Movement, Inc.	1966	1	1	0	0
Bible Memory Association International	0	6	0	0	0
Brethren Assemblies	1898	3	0	0	0
Brethren in Christ Missions	1978	4	0	0	0
Campus Crusade for Christ, International (Overseas Dept.)	1951	1	0	0	0
Child Evangelism Fellowship, Inc.	1953	0	0	150	17
Christian Aid Mission	1896	40	0	0	0
Christian Churches/Churches of Christ	1976	0	0	13	0
Church of God of Prophecy, World Mission Committee	1966	2	2	52	0
Church of God World Missions	1963	8	0	18	1
Church of the Nazarene, Gen. Bd. Dept. of Wld. Msns.	1963	1	0	0	1
Daystar Communications, Inc.	0	56	10	0	2
Evangelical Alliance Mission (TEAM)	1942	10	2	65	2
Evangelical Alliance Mission of Canada, Inc.	1939	3	0	100	0
Free Methodist Church of N. America Gen. Msny. Bd.	1938	43	16	18	0
General Conference of Seventh-day Adventists	1894	4	0	267	0
Independent Faith Mission, Inc.	0	1	0	0	0
International Fellowship of Evangelical Students - USA	0	0	0	0	0
Jesus to the Communist World, Inc.	0	3	0	0	0
Living Bibles International	1972	2	0	0	1
Mission Aviation Fellowship	1964	2	0	0	6
Pentecostal Assemblies of Canada, Oseas. Msns. Dept.	1948	2	0	63	1
Pentecostal Holiness Church-World Missions Department	1950	4	4	39	0
Petra International, Inc.	1977	1	0	4	0
Salvation Army, Canada and Bermuda	1891	2	0	0	0
Salvation Army, The	1891	0	0	208	0

ORGANIZATION NAME	BEGAN	NOW	NEW	CHURCHES	GROUPS
Zimbabwe continued...					
Southern Baptist Convention, Foreign Mission Board	1956	49	0	70	0
United Church Board For World Ministries	1892	0	0	0	0
United Methodist Ch. Wld. Div. of the Bd. of Global Min.	1898	0	0	0	0
United Pentecostal Church Intl. For. Msns. Div.	1968	3	0	0	0
World Literature Crusade	1963	0	0	0	0
World Outreach	0				
TOTALS		276	38	1119	30

Appendices

Questionnaire

The questionnaire on which the directory portion of this **Handbook** was based is included among these appendices and consists of two parts, covering the agency description, the missionary staff, fields of service, financial information and unreached peoples. Agencies which had been listed in the Eleventh Edition were also sent a copy of their previous listing for reference and correction.

Most respondents were able to complete the forms without difficulty. There was some uncertainty over the use of the terms referring to financial income. These questions of terminology do not seem to have significantly affected the overall totals reported. For certain church associations, "Total Income" was reported as the total income to the association rather than the total income to the mission board. "Short-Term Personnel" totals were sometimes not consistent with the other numbers given in the questionnaire, thereby requiring some assumptions on the short-term analysis.

Data Processing

The returned questionnaires were reviewed for consistency and then input to the computer data processing system. This edition was produced in entirety through the facilities of World Vision Inc.

Bibliography

A bibliography of general reference books and periodicals on Protestant missions is provided for those desiring further information on this broad topic.

MISSION HANDBOOK: NORTH AMERICAN PROTESTANT MINISTRIES OVERSEAS DIRECTORY

QUESTIONNAIRE PART ONE

TWELFTH EDITION

This is your official organizational questionnaire for the 1979 survey of North American Protestant organizations that have overseas ministries.

Please return before December 15, 1979

Send to: MARC
919 West Huntington Drive
Monrovia, CA 91016

Agencies listed in the *Mission Handbook* are those with a major concern for the work of the Church outside the United States and Canada, generally known as "overseas." It is recognized that there are some agencies that have major ministries within the United States or Canada that also have overseas ministries. Such agencies are also asked to report if the amount of money expended for overseas ministries exceeds $50,000.

NAME AND LOCATION OF YOUR ORGANIZATION

1. What is your agency's official name as you would like it listed in the *Directory*?

_____

2. Is your agency part of a larger organization?   [ ] Yes   [ ] No   If yes,

_____
           Name of larger organization

3. Of what major denomination (if any) do you consider yourself a part (e.g., UPCUSA, SBC, etc.)?

_____ [ ] None
           Name

4. Agency street address:

_____
     Street

_____
     City   State/Province   Zip/Postal Area

5. Agency telephone:_____(___)_____
                 Area Code   Number

6. Agency headquarters postal address (if different from street):

_____

_____

7. Name and title of the chief executive officer of your agency:

_____   _____
     Name   Title

8. Date of founding:_____

9. Name of original organization if changed since founding and date of last change:

_____ _____
     Original Name   Date of Current Name

RELATED ORGANIZATIONS AND ASSOCIATIONS

10. Is your agency considered part of an international agency with headquarters in this or a different country?   [ ] Yes   [ ] No

    If yes, please give details

_____
     Chief Executive Officer

_____
     Name of Organization

_____
     Street

_____
     City   State/Province   Zip/Postal Area

11. Is your agency the international headquarters for sister sending agencies in other countries? [ ] Yes [ ] No

12. Does your organization have any major operating divisions or ministries which are known by another name, e.g., MARC is a division of World Vision International, Men for Mission is a ministry of OMS. [ ] Yes [ ] No

    If the answer to the above was yes, please give name, address, telephone number and executive officer of each division or ministry.

    _____

    _____

DESCRIPTION OF YOUR ORGANIZATION

13. Which of the following terms best describe your organization?

    [ ] Denominational   [ ] Interdenominational   [ ] Nondenominational

    [ ] Other_____ _____

14. Select up to five descriptors from the following list which are primary officially adopted functions of your organization to which it has made major commitments of resources:

☐ Adoption programs	☐ Evangelism, mass	☐ Orphanage/childcare
☐ Agricultural assistance	☐ Evangelism, personal & small group	☐ Nuture or support of
☐ Aid and/or relief	☐ Evangelism, saturation	national churches
☐ Aviation	☐ Evangelism, student	☐ Psychological counseling
☐ Bible distribution	☐ Fund raising	☐ Purchasing service
☐ Bible memorization	☐ Fund transmittal	☐ Recording
☐ Broadcasting, radio and TV	☐ Furloughed missionary support	☐ Recruiting
☐ Church construction or financing	☐ Information service	☐ Reference board
☐ Church planting/establishing	☐ Linguistics	☐ Research (mission related)
☐ Community development	☐ Literacy	☐ Self-help projects
☐ Computer data proc. services	☐ Literature distribution	☐ Serving other agencies
☐ Correspondence courses	☐ Literature production	☐ Supplying equipment
☐ Development of human resources	☐ Management consulting	☐ Support of nationals
☐ Education, extension	☐ Medical supplies	☐ Technical assistance
☐ Education, general Christian	☐ Medicine, incl. dental & public	☐ Training
☐ Education, missionary	health	☐ Translation, Bible
☐ Education, secular	☐ Ministry to servicemen	☐ Translation, other
☐ Education, theological	☐ Missionary orientation & training	☐ Other (describe)
☐ Education, theological by extension	☐ Motion pictures	

_____

15. Which of the following terms most clearly describes the general doctrinal and/or
    ecclesiastical stance of your organization? (Check as many as apply.)

☐ Adventist   ☐ Evangelical   ☐ Nondenominational
☐ Anglican   ☐ Friends   ☐ Pentecostal
☐ Baptist   ☐ Fundamentalist   ☐ "Plymouth Brethren"
☐ Brethren   ☐ Holiness   ☐ Presbyterian
☐ Christian ("Restoration Movement")   ☐ Independent   ☐ Reformed
☐ Charismatic   ☐ Lutheran   ☐ Wesleyan
☐ Congregational   ☐ Mennonite   ☐ Other (Please specify):
☐ Ecumenical   ☐ Methodist
☐ Episcopal   ☐ Moravian   _____

16. Is your agency related to an association of missions? [ ] Yes [ ] No
    If yes,

    _____   _____
    Association   Relationship

17. In fifty words or less, please give any additional description you feel necessary
    to understand the character of your organization.

    _____
    _____
    _____
    _____

INCOME

18. What was your agency's total income for ministry of   Canadian $_____
    any kind inside or outside North America, for 1979
    or latest fiscal year?   or US $_____

19. What was your agency's total income (excluding gifts   Canadian $_____
    in kind) for overseas ministry for 1979 or latest
    fiscal year? (Denominational boards should report   or US $_____
    their board budget only.)
                                                 Fiscal Year 197_____

19A. Was the source of your income the result of your own fund raising efforts or did it come from parent or sister organizations?

      [ ] own efforts   [ ] parent   [ ] sister

20. Of the income for overseas work, what amount of dollars was spent for fund raising and administration in North America?

       Canadian $_____

       or US $_____

OVERSEAS PERSONNEL

21. During the fiscal year noted above, how many North American overseas personnel were in active service and fully supported under your agency, including those on furlough? (Note: North American branches of international organizations are asked to report only North American personnel.) Do not list personnel on loan from or supported by another agency, but do include your own personnel on loan to another agency. Please do not include short-termers in this total!

Married Men_____   Single Men_____

                                                               TOTAL_____

Married Women_____   Single Women_____

22. Did you count spouses of overseas staff as overseas personnel in answering Question 21?

      [ ] Yes   [ ] No

23. How many personnel included in Question 21 do you send through other agencies?

      [ ] None   _____Number

24. Number of personnel and/or employees assigned to administrative duties in USA or Canada?

      _____Number

25. Number of personnel supported under a retirement program:_____

26. How many newly appointed overseas personnel were sent out during the calendar years:

       1976_____   1977_____

       1978_____   1979_____

27. How many new personnel do you have under appointment who have not yet gone to the field? _____

28. Does your agency operate its own training program for overseas personnel before their departure for the field?   [ ] Yes   [ ] No

    What is its length?_____

29. How many non-North Americans are fully supported by your agency as overseas person- nel serving outside the country of their citizenship?_____

30. We realize that it may be difficult to answer the following question precisely, therefore only an approximation is needed.

    Of your overseas personnel, list the number and percentage in each of the categories:

	Number	Percent
Establishing new churches	_____	_____ %
Assisting existing churches	_____	_____ %
Other ministries	_____	_____ %
		100%

31. Does your agency have a short-term program?   [ ] Yes   [ ] No

    If no, proceed to Question 37.

32. What length of service do you consider short-term?   (Minimum)_____

    (Maximum)_____

33. What was the total number of short-termers active under your agency during the most recent calendar or fiscal year for which you have data?

    Women_____   Men_____   TOTAL_____   Year_____

34. What approximate percentage of short-termers returns to a full-time career?

    In your agency?_____

    With other agencies?_____

    Not known   [ ]

35. How many of your current personnel were short-termers under other agencies?

     _____Number   [ ] Not known

36. What is the purpose of your short-term program? (Please check any that are applicable.)

     [ ] Replacement of furloughed personnel

     [ ] Apprenticeship

     [ ] Stimulation of interest in overseas service

     [ ] Specific project assignments

     [ ] Other_____

37. Do you have a summer overseas program for students?   [ ] Yes   [ ] No

38. During the next two years do you expect the total number of short-termers to:

     [ ] Increase greatly   [ ] Increase some   [ ] Remain same

     [ ] Decrease some   [ ] Decrease greatly

CHANGES

39. What major changes, if any, have characterized your organization during the last three years (include such changes as growth, reduction, reorganization, new ministries, etc.)? If attaching a separate sheet, please check here. [   ]

     _____

     _____

     _____

FUNDING POLICIES

40. Are your overseas personnel primarily responsible for raising their own personal support funds?   [ ] Yes   [ ] No

41. Are your salaries or allowances related to another North American graduated salary or allowance scale? (E.g., high school teachers, bank staff, etc.)

     [ ] Yes   [ ] No   Kind of scale_____

42. How long has your present general support policy been in effect? _____
   Years

YOUR COMMENTS

43. Do you have any additional comments about your organization, the data supplied,
   this questionnaire or anything else you would care to share with us? Is there
   a significant question that should have been asked? (If attaching a separate
   sheet for comments, please check here [   ].)

   _____

   _____

   _____

   _____

   _____

   _____

   _____

DOCUMENTS

44. Do you make an annual fiscal report publicly available?   [   ] Yes   [   ] No

45. Do you make an annual narrative report publicly available?   [   ] Yes   [   ] No

   Please attach copies of what you have.   [   ]

Questionnaire completed by:

_____
   Name

_____
   Title

_____
   Date

PART TWO

For the Twelfth Edition of the *Mission Handbook* we are making a major attempt to relate mission agencies to the people groups they are attempting to reach. The assumption is that by being more specific than indicating we are working in a particular country, we can better assess the effectiveness and outreach of North American agencies.

Part Two requests that you supply information on the number of people groups you are attempting to reach within each country. We have limited this to people groups who, as far as you know, are less than three percent Christian.

To help us understand your answer in the last column, please answer the following questions:

46. Does the strategy being used by your agency attempt to focus primarily on countries as the primary description, or do you attempt to divide the work in a country by sub-groups?

      [ ] Country only   [ ] Sub-groups

47. If you attempt to look at a country in terms of sub-groups, do you usually consider only ethnolinguistic or tribal groups, or do you go further?

      [ ] Primarily ethnolinguistic or tribal groups

      [ ] Further

48. If you go further than ethnolinguistic or tribal groups, what categories do you use to describe such groups? (For example, occupation, class, location, etc.)?

_____

_____

Please complete both sides and return with Part One to: MARC
919 West Huntington Drive
Monrovia, California 91016

PART TWO

FIELDS AND PEOPLES SERVED

Please list all countries where you have overseas personnel or institutions regularly supported by your agency.
Be as specific as possible in specifying country, e.g. Kenya, not "Africa," West Germany, not "Germany," etc.

COUNTRY	Year Work Began in This Country	OVERSEAS PERSONNEL.		CHURCHES	Number of People Groups less than 3% Christian you are trying to reach
		Present	New 76-79	Approx. # of churches (congregations) relating to your agency	

Bibliography

These documents have been selected for general usefulness and availability to those persons interested in the recent work of North American Protestant missions. The emphasis is on those documents containing empirical or reasonably objective data, and with world or regional coverage.

Beach, Harlan P., and Charles H. Fahs, **World Missionary Atlas.** New York: Institute of Social and Religious Research, 1925.

Barrett, David, et al. (eds.), **World Christian Encyclopedia,** 1981 (projected). Oxford Press. Six editions, 1949-1981, under various editors and publishers.

Dayton, Edward R., and C. Peter Wagner (eds.), **Unreached Peoples Annual.** Elgin: David C. Cook, three editions, 1979.

Goddard, Burton L. (ed.), **The Encyclopedia of Modern Christian Missions.** Camden: Thomas Nelson & Sons, 1967.

Jacquet, Constant H., Jr. (ed.), **Yearbook of American and Canadian Churches.** Nashville: Abingdon Press, 48th ed., 1980.

Kane, J. Herbert, **A Global View of Christian Missions.** Grand Rapids: Baker Book House, 1971.

Latourette, Kenneth Scott, **The History of the Expansion of Christianity.** New York: Harper and Row, 1944.

Latourette, Kenneth Scott, **Christianity in a Revoluntionary Age,** Vols. IV, V. New York: Harper and Row, 1962.

Mead, Frank S., **Handbook of Denominations in the United States.** New York: Abingdon Press, 5th ed., 1980.

Missionary Research Library/Missions Advanced Research and Communications Center, **North American Protestant Ministries Overseas Directory.** Eleven editions, 1953-1975.

Missions Advanced Research and Communications Center, **World Christianity Series.** Four volumes, 1979.

Neill, Stephen, **A History of Christian Missions.** Penguin Books, 1964.

Neill, Stephen, Gerald Anderson and John Goodwin, **Concise Dictionary of the Christian World Mission.** New York: Abingdon Press, 1971.

Parker, J. K., (ed.), **Interpretative Statistical Survey of the World Mission of the Christian Church.** New York: International Missionary Council, 1938.

Basic English-language journals on mission include: **Evangelical Missions Quarterly,** published by Evangelical Missions Information Service, Box 794, Wheaton, IL 60187. **International Review of Mission,** quarterly, published by the Commission on World Mission and Evangelism, World Council of Churches, 150 route de Ferney, 1211 Geneva 20, Switzerland. **Missiology, An International Review,** published by the American Society of Missiology, 135 N. Oakland Ave., Pasadena, CA 91101. Includes **Practical Anthropology.**